Birds and Habitat

The successful conservation of bird species relies upon our understanding of their habitat use and requirements. In the coming decades the importance of such knowledge will only grow as climate change and the needs of human populations intensify the already significant pressures on the habitats that birds depend on. Drawing on valuable recent advances in our understanding of bird–habitat relationships, this book provides the first major review of avian habitat selection in over 20 years. It offers a synthesis of concepts, patterns and issues that will interest students, researchers and conservation practitioners. Spatial scales ranging from landscape to habitat patch are covered, and examples of responses to habitat change are examined. European landscapes are the main focus, but the book has far wider significance to similar habitats worldwide, with examples and relevant material also drawn from North America and Australia.

ROBERT J. FULLER is Director of Science at the British Trust for Ornithology, where he leads the Ecological Change Group. He has studied habitat relationships of birds throughout Britain and many parts of Europe for 30 years. Much of his recent work focuses on the effects of different forest management systems and increasing deer populations on biodiversity.

Ecological Reviews

Ecological Reviews publishes books at the cutting edge of modern ecology, providing a forum for volumes that discuss topics that are focal points of current activity and likely long-term importance to the progress of the field. The series is an invaluable source of ideas and inspiration for ecologists at all levels from graduate students to more-established researchers and professionals. The series has been developed jointly by the British Ecological Society and Cambridge University Press and encompasses the Society's Symposia as appropriate.

Birds and Habitat

Relationships in Changing Landscapes

Edited by

ROBERT J. FULLER
British Trust for Ornithology, UK

CAMBRIDGE
UNIVERSITY PRESS

CAMBRIDGE UNIVERSITY PRESS
Cambridge, New York, Melbourne, Madrid, Cape Town,
Singapore, São Paulo, Delhi, Mexico City

Cambridge University Press
The Edinburgh Building, Cambridge CB2 8RU, UK

Published in the United States of America by Cambridge University Press, New York

www.cambridge.org
Information on this title: www.cambridge.org/9780521897563

First published 2012

Printed and bound in the United Kingdom by the MPG Books Group

A catalogue record for this publication is available from the British Library

Library of Congress Cataloguing in Publication data
Birds and habitat : relationships in changing landscapes / edited by Robert J. Fuller.
    p.   cm. – (Ecological reviews)
ISBN 978-0-521-89756-3 (hardback)
1. Birds – Habitat.   2. Birds – Ecology.   3. Birds – Effect of habitat modification on.
I. Fuller, Robert J.
QL698.95.B579   2012
598–dc23

                                                                2012013425

ISBN 978-0-521-89756-3 Hardback
ISBN 978-0-521-72233-9 Paperback

Additional resources for this publication at www.cambridge.org/9780521897563

Contents

Contributors

RAPHAËL ARLETTAZ
Division of Conservation Biology,
Institute of Ecology and Evolution,
University of Bern,
Baltzerstrasse 6,
CH-3012 Bern,
Switzerland
and
Swiss Ornithological Institute,
Valais Field Station,
Rue du Rhône 11,
CH-1950 Sion,
Switzerland
raphael.arlettaz@iee.unibe.ch

MALCOLM AUSDEN
Royal Society for the Protection of Birds,
The Lodge, Sandy,
Bedfordshire SG19 2DL, UK
malcolm.ausden@rspb.org.uk

MARK BOLTON
Royal Society for the Protection of Birds,
The Lodge, Sandy,
Bedfordshire SG19 2DL, UK
mark.bolton@rspb.org.uk

CHRISTIAAN BOTH
Animal Ecology Group,
Centre for Ecological and Evolutionary
Studies (CEES),

University of Groningen
PO Box 11103,
9700 CC Groningen,
The Netherlands
c.both@rug.nl

NIALL H. K. BURTON
British Trust for Ornithology,
The Nunnery, Thetford,
Norfolk IP24 2PU, UK
niall.burton@bto.org

INGVAR BYRKJEDAL
University Museum of Bergen,
Allegaten 41,
N-5007, Bergen, Norway
ingvar.byrkjedal@zmb.uib.no

CARLA P. CATTERALL
School of Environment,
Griffith University,
Nathan, Queensland 4111,
Australia
c.catterall@griffith.edu.au

PAUL M. DOLMAN
School of Environmental
Sciences,
University of East Anglia,
Norwich NR4 7TJ, UK
p.dolman@uea.ac.uk

PIERRE DRAPEAU
Département des Sciences
Biologiques,
Université du Québec à Montréal,
Succ. Centre-ville, Montréal,
Québec H3C 3P8, Canada
drapeau.pierre@uqam.ca

LENORE FAHRIG
Geomatics and Landscape Ecology
Research Lab.,
Department of Biology,
Carleton University,
1125 Colonel By Drive,
Ottawa,
Ontario K1S 5B6, Canada
lenore_fahrig@carleton.ca

KATHRYN FREEMARK LINDSAY
National Wildlife Research Centre,
Environment Canada,
Ottawa,
Ontario KIA 0H3, Canada
kathryn.lindsay@ec.gc.ca

ROBERT J. FULLER
British Trust for Ornithology,
The Nunnery, Thetford,
Norfolk IP24 2PU, UK
rob.fuller@bto.org

GILLIAN GILBERT
Royal Society for the Protection of Birds
Scotland,
10 Park Quadrant,
Glasgow G3 6BS, UK
gillian.gilbert@rspb.org.uk

JENNIFER A. GILL
School of Biological Sciences,
University of East Anglia,
Norwich NR4 7TJ, UK
j.gill@uea.ac.uk

SIMON GILLINGS
British Trust for Ornithology,
The Nunnery, Thetford,
Norfolk IP24 2PU, UK
simon.gillings@bto.org

MURRAY C. GRANT
Royal Society for the Protection of Birds
Scotland,
2 Lochside View, Edinburgh Park,
Edinburgh EH12 9DH, UK
current address:
RPS Planning & Development,
Ocean Point One,
4th Floor, 94 Ocean Drive,
Edinburgh EH6 6JH, UK
Murray.Grant@rpsgroup.com

SHELLEY A. HINSLEY
Centre for Ecology and Hydrology,
Maclean Building,
Crowmarsh Gifford,
Wallingford,
Oxfordshire OX10 8BB, UK
sahi@ceh.ac.uk

JOHN ATLE KÅLÅS
Norwegian Institute for Nature
Research (NINA),
PO BOX 5685,
Sluppen No-7485,
Norway
john.a.kalas@nina.no

DAVID ANTHONY KIRK
Aquila Conservation &
Environment Consulting,
75 Albert Street, Suite 300,
Ottawa,
Ontario K1P 5E7, Canada
David.Kirk1@sympatico.ca

ADRIAN D. MANNING
The Fenner School of
Environment and Society,
The Australian National University,
Canberra,
0200 Australian Capital Territory,
Australia
adrian.manning@anu.edu.au

JEAN-LOUIS MARTIN
CEFE/CNRS UMR 5175,
1919 Route de Mende,
34293 Montpellier Cedex, France,
jean-louis.martin@cefe.cnrs.fr

TARA G. MARTIN
CSIRO Ecosystem Sciences,
GPO Box 2583,
Brisbane, Queensland 4001,
Australia
Tara.Martin@csiro.au

BEAT NAEF-DAENZER
Swiss Ornithological Institute,
CH-6204 Sempach, Switzerland
beat.naef@vogelwarte.ch

JAMES W. PEARCE-HIGGINS
Royal Society for the Protection of Birds
Scotland,
2 Lochside View, Edinburgh Park,
Edinburgh EH12 9DH, UK
james.pearce-higgins@bto.org
current address:
British Trust for Ornithology,
The Nunnery, Thetford,
Norfolk IP24 2PU, UK

THEUNIS PIERSMA
Animal Ecology Group,
Centre for Ecological and
Evolutionary Studies (CEES),

University of Groningen,
PO Box 11103,
9700 CC Groningen,
The Netherlands
and
Department of Marine Ecology,
Royal Netherlands Institute
for Sea Research (NIOZ),
PO Box 59,
1790 AB Den Burg,
Texel, The Netherlands
Theunis.Piersma@nioz.nl

ADAM C. SMITH
Geomatics and Landscape
Ecology Research Lab.,
Department of Biology,
Carleton University,
1125 Colonel By Drive,
Ottawa,
Ontario K1S 5B6, Canada
adam.smith@ec.gc.ca

KEN W. SMITH
24 Mandeville Rise,
Welwyn Garden City,
Hertfordshire AL8 7JU, UK
ken.smith910@ntlworld.com

JUDIT K. SZABO
The Ecology Centre,
School of Biological Sciences,
University of Queensland,
4072 Queensland, Australia
j.szabo@uq.edu.au

DES B. A. THOMPSON
Scottish Natural Heritage,
Silvan House,
231 Corstorphine Road,
Edinburgh EH12 7AT, UK
Des.Thompson@snh.gov.uk

JULIET VICKERY
Royal Society for the Protection of Birds,
The Lodge, Sandy,
Bedfordshire SG19 2DL, UK
and
British Trust for Ornithology,
The Nunnery, Thetford,
Norfolk IP24 2PU, UK
juliet.vickery@rspb.org.uk

MARC-ANDRÉ VILLARD
Département de biologie,
Université de Moncton,
Moncton,
New Brunswick E1A 3E9,
Canada
marc-andre.villard@umoncton.ca

TOMASZ WESOŁOWSKI
Laboratory of Forest Biology,
Wrocław University,
Sienkiewicza 21,
50 335 Wrocław,
Poland
tomwes@biol.uni.wroc.pl

Preface

Relationships between organisms and their habitats are central to many themes in ecology and evolutionary biology. Studies of birds have made large contributions to the understanding of how habitat can interact with population dynamics, community structure and behaviour. The adaptive value of habitat choices is also especially well illustrated by research on birds. In the last three decades there have been large advances in knowledge about the mechanisms affecting habitat selection, especially concerning the role of behavioural and landscape-scale processes. As the complexity of interactions between birds and their environments has become more fully appreciated, the difficulties of achieving a synthesis have escalated.

This book examines bird–habitat relationships mainly in the context of temperate cultural landscapes. The emphasis is on western Europe, but many chapters draw heavily on research emanating from other continents, notably North America. This approach has the advantage of making the subject more manageable, but it also stresses the multi-layered influences of human activities on habitat suitability for birds. Although the book is not overtly concerned with conservation, much of the material summarised in these pages has been accumulated through a strong desire on the part of researchers that a rich biodiversity should thrive alongside humans in the cultural landscapes of the future.

Part I contains seven chapters examining general patterns and processes in the habitat relationships of birds. Concepts of selection, use, occupancy and quality of habitats are reviewed in Chapters 1 and 2. Habitat associations of many bird species show striking variation in different parts of their ranges and this is explored in Chapter 3. The fact that patterns of habitat selection and habitat use vary spatially has serious implications for the generality of conservation strategies. Chapter 4 examines the evidence supporting the wide range of landscape-scale processes that have been proposed to affect birds. Chapter 5 offers a more specific review of how birds respond to the ecological transitions that are prominent in many cultural landscapes. Chapter 6 outlines the land-use processes, historical and contemporary, that have produced the complex and diverse cultural landscapes we see today. This chapter asks whether such landscapes tend to favour generalist species. Habitat heterogeneity is an important concept underlying biodiversity patterns within patchy cultural landscapes. This is examined in Chapter 7 in the context of European farmland birds which have been the subject of intense investigation since the early 1990s.

Part II presents seven 'case-study reviews' of bird–habitat relationships in different environments. These illustrate the variety of factors that can limit habitat occupancy and determine habitat suitability for birds in different contexts. The focus is Britain, where there has been a wealth of work on the selected environments, but the chapters are relevant in wider geographical contexts. These chapters do not provide comprehensive coverage of western European habitat types; they are presented as examples of the diverse nature of bird–habitat relationships. Two deal with moorland and mountain, two with freshwater wetlands, two with coastal wetlands and one considers woodland.

Part III presents broader perspectives on birds and habitat. Few species have been examined in greater depth worldwide than the red knot *Calidris canutus*. The insights into what constitutes habitat quality for this species, gained through a powerful blend of ecological, behavioural and physiological approaches, are summarised in Chapter 15. Habitat-based processes operating at the level of the individual bird are critically important in the dynamics of populations; this theme is explored in Chapter 16. Implications of changing climate for habitat quality, especially from the viewpoint of phenological mismatching, are discussed in Chapter 17. Perspectives are then provided from Australia and North America, the continents that have generated the greatest recent advances in understanding the multi-scaled nature of bird–habitat relationships. There are interesting questions about how relevant the findings are from these continents to European landscapes. Chapter 18 reviews how landscape change since European colonisation has affected Australian birds while Chapter 19 contrasts research approaches and findings between North America and Europe in the context of four different landscape types. Chapter 20 concludes the book with some general themes and emerging questions, taking a particular focus on conservation strategies.

I am grateful to the authors for the precious time they have devoted to producing their chapters. I also thank the reviewers of the chapters. My employer, the British Trust for Ornithology, generously allowed a sabbatical during which I laid the foundations of this book. Dominic Lewis and his colleagues at CUP have been patient sources of advice and encouragement. Carole Showell tracked down various elusive publications. Nicki Read gave great support with many aspects of the preparation of this book.

PART I

The complexity of patterns and processes

CHAPTER ONE

The bird and its habitat: an overview of concepts

ROBERT J. FULLER

British Trust for Ornithology

People have been describing habitat associations and asking deeper questions about how birds select their habitat, and the factors that determine their fine-scale distribution, for a long time (e.g. Brock, 1914; Grinnell, 1917a, b). This chapter outlines where concepts relating to habitat selection stand in the early twenty-first century. These concepts embrace a bewildering array of behavioural, ecological and evolutionary ideas. The processes involved in habitat selection have evolved to maximise fitness by ensuring that individuals can recognise and use suitable habitat. The notion of habitat quality (i.e. what constitutes 'good' or 'best' habitat) is therefore a central concept to which I have devoted a large part of the following chapter. Neither of these introductory chapters reviews the topics comprehensively, but the examples and references will, I hope, serve as useful background to the multi-faceted subject of habitat selection. I acknowledge the existence of some bias in the examples chosen because they lean towards terrestrial birds, especially those of forest and shrubland, reflecting my personal interests.

Not surprisingly, there has been a gradual shift towards more quantitative research and theoretical models. But description remains important, both to document how birds continue to respond to the ever-changing world and to provide crucial information upon which conservation policies can be founded. The literature is voluminous. The review of habitat selection in birds by Olavi Hildén (1965) covers much of the early work and continues to be a highly relevant source of ideas and examples. More recent reviews and discussions of aspects of habitat selection include Partridge (1978), Morse (1980), Cody (1985), Wiens (1989a), Block and Brennan (1993), Jones (2001), Johnson (2007) and Boulinier *et al.* (2008).

Habitat differences within and between species

At the simplest level, relationships between birds and habitat are biologically trivial, though they are a source of considerable human pleasure and cultural significance. Landscapes and vegetation types have their typical species. Each species can be readily identified with a set of habitat features such that an

Birds and Habitat: Relationships in Changing Landscapes, ed. Robert J. Fuller. Published by Cambridge University Press. © Cambridge University Press 2012.

experienced naturalist carries with them a view of what constitutes suitable and unsuitable habitat. This has long been appreciated, as shown in John Clare's poetry, rooted in the English countryside of the early nineteenth century. Habitat relationships become profoundly interesting at the finer scales – the adaptive value of microhabitat selection, for example, is of abiding interest. The spatial and temporal dynamics of habitat use by the individuals that constitute populations are of great importance in the context of population dynamics, lifetime reproductive success, range dynamics, behavioural flexibility and identifying critical habitat needs. Much research centres on elucidating the factors that influence the choices made by birds in their use of space and other resources.

In the 1970s ecologists started to develop quantitative methods of describing how species differ in their fine-scale relationships with vegetation (James, 1971). Detailed studies of particular groups of species have repeatedly demonstrated that sympatric species tend to select different habitats, though frequently the differences are fine-scale ones of microhabitat use (e.g. Kendeigh, 1941, 1945; Snow, 1954; Bond, 1957; Lack, 1971; Collins, 1981; Collins et al., 1982; Glück, 1983; Bairlein, 1983; Martin and Thibault, 1996). Clear separations between closely related species are not universal (Wiens, 1989a; Fig. 1.1). Nonetheless, such observations have underpinned a large amount of theory revolving around 'ecological segregation' and 'niche partitioning'.

Some important points need to be made about habitat differences. Variation in habitat occupancy and use is strongly evident within species, as well as between species. Within species, there can be variation in habitat use between sexes (Marquiss and Newton, 1981; Ebenman and Nilsson, 1982; Lynch et al., 1985; Winkler and Leisler, 1985; Steele, 1993; Parrish and Sherry, 1994; Sunde and Redpath, 2006) and ages of individuals (Marquiss and Newton, 1981; Morse, 1985; Reijnen and Foppen, 1994). Migrant and resident individuals of the same species may differ in habitat use (Adriaensen and Dhondt, 1990; Pérez-Tris and Tellería, 2002). Habitat use may also vary with weather (Petit, 1989), season and phase of the life cycle (Rice, 1980; Alatalo, 1981; Bilcke, 1984a; Moskát et al., 1993; Mills, 2005; Akresh et al., 2009), and time of day (McCaffery, 1998; Gillings et al., 2005). Patterns of habitat occupancy and use may also change spatially and temporally (Chapter 3).

An important and relatively neglected source of variation in habitat use may derive from individual niche specialisation arising from phenotypic differences within populations (Bolnick et al., 2003). Even within apparent habitat specialists there may be considerable variation in habitat use by individuals. The reed warbler Acrocephalus scirpaceus is widely regarded in Europe as an extreme habitat specialist, dependent on beds of the reed Phragmites australis for breeding. One study found that only 54% of nests were in Phragmites and that breeding success was lower there than in other

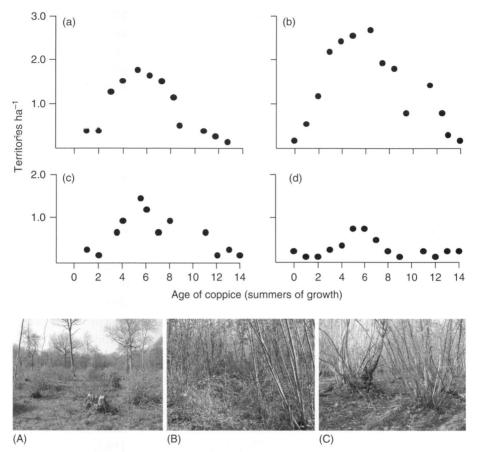

Figure 1.1 An example of overlap in breeding habitat use within closely related species. The territory density (territories ha^{-1}) of four foliage-feeding insectivorous warbler species in English coppiced woodland is shown in relation to the number of years of coppice regrowth since cutting: (a) garden warbler *Sylvia borin*, (b) willow warbler *Phylloscopus trochilus*, (c) blackcap *Sylvia atricapilla*, (d) chiffchaff *Phylloscopus collybita*. The three photographs show coppice structure at different stages of growth: (A) 1 year of growth, (B) 6 years growth, (C) 10 years growth. Each species reaches maximum density in coppice of about 3 to 7 years of growth when the complexity of low woody vegetation is high (photograph B). Redrawn from Fuller and Henderson (1992).

vegetation types (Catchpole, 1974). Although the species is undoubtedly specialised to use reeds in the way it constructs its nest, it seems to have retained flexibility of habitat use probably because reedbeds can be unstable habitats.

The factors determining how birds use habitat change considerably with time of year; this is especially the case for migratory species and for sedentary birds living in highly seasonal environments. Species may generally show tighter patterns of habitat association during the breeding season than at other times (Mills, 2005). Breeding can place constraints on habitat selection and use of space that apply more rigidly than at other seasons (Whitaker and Warkentin, 2010). Outside the breeding season, however, individuals only have to be concerned about survival and an entirely different suite of factors may come into play (Chapter 15).

Definitions and perceptions

The literature contains many studies of species that variously claim to identify habitat use, preferences, selection or choice. Clarity about the meaning of these and other habitat-related terms is essential (Hall *et al.*, 1997; Jones, 2001) so a series of definitions are offered in Box 1.1. Importantly, 'habitat selection' and 'habitat use' are not interchangeable terms, the former encompassing the processes involved in habitat choice, the latter is the way that birds use their habitat. Concepts of 'habitat' are various, but make most sense in terms of the environment in which an individual, rather than a population or a species, lives. The habitat of an individual bird will consist of a complex of biotic and abiotic elements embracing climate and microclimate, soil type, topography, plant species and vegetation structure. Some definitions exclude the social component of the environment (Danchin *et al.*, 2008), but I prefer to include both conspecifics and other species as integral to the habitat, as these can have strong effects on realised habitat quality and habitat use (Chapter 2).

The widespread use of 'habitat' as a distinct form of environment is an entirely different but familiar notion based on perceived differences in past and present land use, vegetation, hydrology and even landscape character. Hence, we divide landscapes into units or 'cover types' such as woodland, heathland and grassland, often with complex subdivisions based on phyto-sociology or structural attributes (e.g. Ratcliffe, 1977; Rodwell, 1991; Crick, 1992). Though useful for many purposes, these classifications have limitations. They tend not to describe transitional zones well and typically tell us little, if anything, about the critical resource needs of individuals that are so important in determining where animals live or the cues involved in habitat recognition.

There is a more fundamental limitation to our attempts to delineate the environment of an animal. Humans inevitably sense and perceive the environment in different ways to animals. The variables we choose to measure when attempting to define the habitat of an organism will almost certainly not exactly reflect the perceptions that the animal has of its environment. The concept that animals exist in their individual world (*Umwelt*) was developed by Von Uexküll (1926, cited in Manning *et al.*, 2004). Different organisms in the same location may have entirely differing perceptions (*Umwelten*) of the world about them, depending on their sensory apparatus, their body size, their

Box 1.1 Some definitions concerning habitat and landscape
(sources include Johnson, 1980; Dunning *et al.*, 1992; Koford *et al.*, 1994; Jones, 2001; Danchin *et al.*, 2008)

Habitat: The environment of the individual bird, including all biotic and abiotic elements. Note that 'habitat' is frequently and unhelpfully conflated with 'land use' (i.e. human activity) in habitat classifications and definitions.

Habitat association: The extent to which an individual or population depends upon, or shows disproportionate use or avoidance of, a defined habitat type. Can be positive, neutral or negative.

Habitat availability: The accessibility of a defined habitat type or habitat feature to an individual.

Habitat occupancy: The frequency or relative occurrence of individuals in a population within a defined habitat type or patch. See also *habitat use*.

Habitat patch: A homogeneous area distinctive from its surroundings due to environmental discontinuities. Habitat patches defined by humans and birds are likely to differ.

Habitat preference: A positive association (usually of individuals in a population) with a defined habitat type, i.e. non-random distribution resulting in a disproportionately high number of individuals in certain habitat types relative to their availability. Note that Johnson (1980) defined preference as the likelihood of a habitat being chosen when it is equally available to other habitats.

Habitat quality (or habitat suitability): The fitness potential or value of a defined habitat type. *Intrinsic habitat quality* is the fundamental fitness in the habitat taking no account of conspecific individuals and other species. *Realised habitat quality* combines intrinsic habitat quality with Allee effects, competition, predation risk etc. Some authors regard habitat suitability as effectively realised quality.

Habitat selection (or habitat choice): The processes by which individuals recognise and choose habitat for different functions resulting in observed patterns of *habitat association*, *habitat use* and *habitat occupancy*. Widely regarded as a hierarchical process.

Habitat structure (or physiognomy): A combination of the topography and physical architecture of vegetation constituting a defined patch or habitat type. Where it relates solely to the physical structure or complexity of vegetation (e.g. foliage density and cover), *vegetation structure* is more appropriate.

Habitat type: Any defined habitat in terms of vegetation composition and structure, hydrology, topography etc.

Box 1.1 (cont.)

Habitat use: The way that an individual or population uses habitat. Similar to *habitat occupancy*, but implies a need to specify the type of activity, e.g. nesting, roosting, foraging. Note that Johnson (1980) defined 'habitat usage' as the quantity of a habitat component used in a fixed period of time.

Landscape: Mosaic of habitat types covering an extensive area larger than the home-range of the study organism, typically for territorial songbirds extending over a scale of several square kilometres.

Landscape complementation: Situations where local abundance is affected by availability of different habitat patches providing non-substitutable resources, e.g. for nesting and feeding.

Landscape composition: Relative amounts of different habitat types in a landscape.

Landscape structure: Landscape pattern defined by a combination of *landscape composition* and the spatial arrangement of habitat types in a landscape.

Landscape supplementation: Situations where local abundance is affected by individuals being able to derive additional substitutable resources from different habitat patches.

Macrohabitat: Broad-scale attributes of occupied habitat, usually relating to a particular type of vegetation, wetland or landform, e.g. mature conifer forest, saltmarsh.

Microhabitat: Fine-scale attributes of used habitat, often relating to specific plants, vegetation structures or soil types. Nest site selection usually occurs at a microhabitat level.

predators, their feeding and mating behaviour and so on. The human ability to capture the essential attributes or characteristics of the *Umwelt* is limited. Not surprisingly, few studies of avian habitats take a deeply considered 'bird's eye view' of the environment as a starting point. We usually attempt to measure features that we perceive as potentially important to the bird in terms of cues, resources and physical structures, without considering how the individual bird might perceive the features around them. This may seem academic, especially in conservation applications, where the usual aim is to identify those habitat elements that require restoration before an endangered species can thrive – provided that the model works, then all is well. However, our inability to view the environment with the same perspective as the focal animal means that our predictors of what constitutes 'the best habitat' will always be surrogates or imperfect assessments.

Habitat recognition and cues

Basic ideas underlying modern habitat selection theory are evident in several far-sighted papers from the first half of the last century (Hildén, 1965). The 1930s and 1940s was a period when important advances were made by ecologists undertaking increasingly detailed observations in Fennoscandia, Britain and America. Palmgren's (1930) work in Finnish forests is one such example, soon to be followed by David Lack's influential work on the responses of birds to the creation of extensive conifer plantations in eastern England, supplemented with work on bird–habitat associations in Iceland. Lack (1933, 1937) pointed out that the distribution of birds was determined to some extent by a combination of what he termed 'direct' factors including climate, natural enemies, food and nest sites. However, his work in the plantations led him to state firmly that the distribution of birds was also strongly affected by species-specific habitat selection, such that each species had an innate ability to identify its ancestral habitat. The ability of a species to identify its habitat was vividly described by Svärdson (1949) for migrant warblers prospecting for territories soon after their spring arrival. The process determining where birds settled was anything but passive or random. In Lack's opinion it involved a strong psychological element whereby certain features were critical to how a species recognised suitable habitat. Examples of these features, especially the presence of song posts, are given in Lack (1937, 1939).

Ultimate factors and proximate cues

These early ideas may seem unremarkable now, but they represented a breakthrough in understanding how birds determined their habitat. Moreover, Lack's work pre-figured several important habitat concepts. First, the recognition that multiple factors determine distribution is closely linked with notions of hierarchical habitat selection, discussed below. Second, appreciating that species used recognition markers, such as song posts, was important in developing the idea that stimuli or cues were involved in triggering a settling reaction. Lack realised that these cues were not in themselves of importance to survival or success, but others developed the framework of proximate and ultimate factors in habitat selection (e.g. Klomp, 1954; Hildén, 1965; Morse, 1980; Box 1.2). This distinguishes the underlying factors determining the choice of habitat through its fitness potential (ultimate factors) from the immediate stimuli or cues used in habitat selection, but which in themselves are not necessarily of fitness value (proximate factors). The evolutionary and ecological processes shaping current patterns of habitat use broadly correspond to ultimate and proximate factors, respectively (Wiens, 1989a). To some extent, ultimate factors also equate with critical resource needs, defined as those components of the environment that potentially limit individual fitness or population dynamics (Wiens, 1989a).

Box 1.2 Ultimate and proximate factors in avian habitat selection
(This list broadly follows Hildén (1965). See text for further details.)

Ultimate factors

1. **Food:** Food-supply can limit bird numbers (Wiens, 1989a; Newton, 1998) so large reliable food supplies will characterise strongly preferred habitats in many species. Food availability may have a relatively strong role in habitat selection outside the breeding season.
2. **Shelter:** This includes factors that reduce the likelihood of predation (or assist early detection of predators by prey). Microhabitat attributes can maintain suitable microclimate at nests and roosts (Walsberg, 1985) and avoid flooding (Wesołowski et al., 2002).
3. **Space:** Species vary in minimum area needs for territory establishment and the acquisition of food, so that spatial pattern and structure of habitat may limit their occurrence.
4. **Structural and functional characteristics:** Through morphology and behaviour birds are adapted to life in particular macrohabitats and microhabitats in obvious and more subtle ways that affect habitat occupancy (Snow, 1954; Winkler and Leisler, 1985).
5. **Other species:** Avoiding habitats where predation risk is high or numbers of major competitors are high may be crucial to survival.

Proximate factors or cues

1. **Landscape and macrohabitat features:** Landscapes may be selected with particular general characteristics in terms of topography and composition/pattern of macrohabitats resulting in associations with certain levels of landscape openness, forest cover etc.
2. **Habitat structure:** Occupancy of habitat patches may depend on particular vegetation structures in terms of density or height, or soil properties, e.g. dampness, rockiness.
3. **Microhabitat – functional sites:** Presence of features offering suitable nest sites may be critical; examples include some cavity-nesters and ground-nesting colonial birds. Song posts and watch/foraging perches appear important cues for some birds, e.g. pipits, shrikes.
4. **Other animals (positive effects):** The presence or performance of conspecifics may be used as indicators of suitable habitat – conspecific attraction. Settling close to other aggressive species may confer protection from predators.
5. **Other animals (negative effects):** Presence of predators or competitors (or at least identifying their habitats) may be a cue for habitat

---

Box 1.2 (cont.)

avoidance. High densities of conspecifics may discourage further settlement in a habitat patch.

6. **Other animals (indirect cues):** Potentially competing species may
   be used as cues in habitat selection – heterospecific attraction.
7. **Food:** Species with specialised diets may use food as a cue in habitat
   recognition, e.g. some fruit and seed-eaters (waxwings *Bombycilla garrulus* and crossbills *Loxia* spp.) and arctic/boreal skuas, owls and raptors
   feeding on small mammals. Brambling *Fringilla montifringilla* may use
   insect abundance as a settling cue (Enemar *et al.*, 2004).

Those features or attributes identified by human observers as characteristic
of the habitat of a species are, of course, not necessarily the same as the cues
used by birds. Nonetheless, it is convenient to think of the 'important explanatory variables' that are derived from species-level habitat-association models
as proximate factors. Hildén (1965) reminds us that there must be an element of
speculation in identifying the factor or combination of factors used by a species
in habitat recognition. Experiments on the cues used by birds are difficult to
conduct because of the problems encountered in controlling for habitat quality
at the scale of territory or home range (Muller *et al.*, 1997), but increasing
numbers of examples exist (Mönkkönen *et al.*, 1990; Doligez *et al.*, 2002).

Proximate factors need to correlate with, or somehow indicate, the ultimate
factors. This is especially important where the quality of habitat cannot be
determined at the time of settling. This may apply in the case of insectivorous
species establishing territory in early spring when spatial variation in insect
abundance may not correspond with that during the critical chick-rearing
period (Morse, 1980). This was the case in a study of red-eyed vireos *Vireo
olivaceous*, where foliage density appeared to provide a fairly reliable cue,
being correlated with caterpillar abundance in the nestling period (Marshall
and Cooper, 2004). Another example is the selection of nesting habitat by
ground-nesting waders, where habitats that are suitable in early spring may
be entirely unsuitable later in the breeding season due to vegetation growth
(Klomp, 1954; Chapter 11).

Social information

Selection of breeding habitat is critical because it is closely linked with
reproductive success and will be subject to strong selection pressure.
Various strategies or mixtures of strategies can be adopted in which 'personal
information' or 'public information' is used in different ways to assess
habitat/patch quality (Doligez *et al.*, 2003; Boulinier *et al.*, 2008). Individuals

may merely select their natal patch or even settle at random. Alternatively they may use their own success as a measure of patch quality. Prospecting breeders may rely on environmental cues such as vegetation structure or the presence of predators. An especially important development is recognition of the importance of strategies involving 'social information' about habitat/patch quality gained through interactions with conspecifics or heterospecifics (Stamps and Krishnan, 2005; Seppänen *et al.*, 2007).

A complex of potential social information strategies exists accompanied by a plethora of hypotheses. It has long been appreciated that territorial animals may be attracted to one another resulting in clusters of territories which cannot be explained by spatial variation in habitat (references in Stamps, 1988; Danchin and Wagner, 1997). In its simplest form this may merely involve using the presence of conspecifics to identify potential habitat (conspecific attraction). The importance of this process is increasingly recognised in managing vulnerable populations. Availability of suitable habitat in the absence of conspecifics may not provide sufficient cues and small populations may have weak persistence due to their inability to provide a sufficiently strong cue to attract recruits (Ahlering and Faaborg, 2006; Laiolo and Tella, 2008). An inability to account for conspecific attraction and other social interactions may cause traditional resource-based models of habitat use to perform poorly (Harrison *et al.*, 2009; Folmer *et al.*, 2010; Nocera and Forbes, 2010). On the other hand, some studies have found that the presence of preferred habitat features is more important in determining site occupancy than presence of conspecifics (Cornell and Donovan, 2010).

Some species can assess habitat quality through the reproductive success of other individuals and use this information in subsequent habitat choice. This is termed 'habitat copying' and has been demonstrated in such diverse species as seabirds, tits, swallows, flycatchers and kingbirds (Doligez *et al.*,1999; Brown *et al.*, 2000; Wagner and Danchin, 2003; Parejo *et al.*, 2007; Boulinier *et al.*, 2008; Redmond *et al.*, 2009). Pre-requisites for habitat copying are that the environment should be patchy in quality and that it should be predictable, so that evidence obtained in one year will apply in the next year. Habitat copying may even occur between potentially competing species (Parejo *et al.*, 2005). Heterospecific attraction is discussed further in Chapter 2.

Flexible and inflexible behaviour

An implication of habitat copying is that individuals have some flexibility in their choices of habitat for different breeding attempts. An opposite situation might occur where natal experience has such an overwhelming influence on habitat choice that subsequent use of the natal habitat is strongly fixed. Where natal experience does play a role, the effect is to increase preference for the habitat in which the individual is reared (Davis, 2008). Site fidelity could have much the same effect and is difficult to distinguish from habitat imprinting (Hildén, 1965). Species vary considerably in the extent to which early experience affects later habitat use (Davis, 2008) and it is also likely that within populations there may be much individual variation in the response to the natal habitat. Furthermore, natal-type habitat may not always be available. There would seem to be much scope, therefore, for individuals of many species to show flexible behaviours in habitat selection.

The extent to which plasticity exists in individual habitat selection and its effect on how birds might respond to environmental change is an important topic. Some species have shown remarkable range shifts involving occupancy of new habitats (see examples in Chapter 3). One of the best documented examples is the rapid expansion of the mistle thrush *Turdus viscivorus* out of conifer forest into 'parkland' habitats in Germany in the 1920s (Peitzmeier, references in Hildén, 1965). This happened so rapidly that it was most probably initiated by some individuals colonising habitats that appeared to be entirely different to their natal habitats, perhaps triggered by some dramatic change in their forest habitat. Habitat copying (unless of a heterospecific kind which seems unlikely in this case) cannot have been the mechanism that caused the habitat change, and clearly it was not a gradual evolutionary process. Initial colonisation could not have occurred without latent behavioural plasticity in some individuals. Subsequent expansion in the new habitat may have been aided by site fidelity (low dispersal) and/or imprinting on natal habitat.

Issues of scale: landscape to microhabitat

Spatial scale is an essential consideration in habitat selection research, but this is a relatively recent development in thinking (Box 1.3). Organism–habitat associations frequently appear different depending on the scale on which they are observed. Identifying the appropriate scale on which to examine habitat relationships depends partly on the exact questions being asked and the ecology of the species. Habitat selection is frequently hierarchical with processes operating at a variety of scales, with selection at one scale contingent on another scale. The greatest insights about how habitat-related factors determine species distributions are generally derived from studies conducted at multiple scales, ideally with the choice of scales informed by knowledge of how the bird samples its habitat (Vaughan and Ormerod, 2003; Kristan, 2006). Examples of hierarchical analysis of habitat association now cover diverse bird species and environments (e.g. Steele, 1992; Saab, 1999; Rolstad *et al.*, 2000; Luck, 2002; Weakland and Bohall Wood, 2005; Bailey and Thompson, 2007; Buler *et al.*, 2007; Chalfoun and Martin, 2007; Burton, 2009; Mateo-Tomás and Olea, 2009; Mueller *et al.*, 2009; Zimmerman *et al.*, 2009; Webb *et al.*, 2010).

Box 1.3 Why spatial scale is a critical issue in habitat selection

1. Species vary hugely in the physical space they use. Birds are amongst the most mobile of organisms, having far larger space requirements than plants, most invertebrates and even many terrestrial mammals. Yet within birds there is great variation in territory and home-range size that needs to be accounted for in attempting to understand critical habitat needs.

2. Variation in habitat occurs at a range of scales, and habitat features are often spatially nested in a hierarchical form (Kristan, 2006). For example, climate, altitude, soils and human land uses place strong constraints on the exact type of vegetation that exists at any particular location. Vegetation types in turn influence the fine-scale vegetation structures that are important for providing nesting and roosting sites.

3. Mechanisms and cues used by birds in recognising and selecting their habitats may be spatially hierarchical, involving some kind of a behavioural filter. Species may initially identify potential habitat at relatively coarse scales, perhaps using cues concerning landscape character that can be assessed in flight. Choosing exact locations for nesting, foraging or roosting may depend on finer-scale cues that must be assessed by closer ground-level sampling. Alternatively, initial selection may be based on fine-grain features, such as preferred foliage structures, but the final choice could depend on attributes of the surrounding area. These contrasting behaviours are similar to 'top-down' and 'bottom-up' habitat selection processes (Kristan, 2006).

4. Birds may require different resources (e.g. food and nest sites) from different types of habitat patch. Availability of the scarcest resource will always determine the spatial pattern of settlement (Orians and Wittenberger, 1991; Dunning et al., 1992). Under these circumstances, habitat choice may involve a hierarchical process whereby initial selection depends on availability of the commoner resource, but precise settlement is determined by the location of the more limited resource.

5. Until the last two decades of the twentieth century it was generally assumed that the occurrence of species and structure of communities was mainly determined by processes operating at microhabitat or habitat-patch scales. These are certainly important influences on habitat quality, especially through provision of critical resources. However, the importance of processes affecting habitat selection at landscape or regional scales has gradually become appreciated (Chapter 4).

6. Two scale components influence the conclusions drawn from any study: *grain* is the size of study units or study plots, while *extent* is the total area over which observations are made (Wiens, 1989b).

The focus here is on spatial scale, but at least three other aspects of scale are relevant to understanding patterns of habitat selection and habitat use in birds. The first is temporal scale. For several reasons, one may draw rather different conclusions from short-term and long-term studies. This may arise because certain habitats may only be used under exceptional circumstances. Such a situation may arise with wintering waterbirds which undertake migration to escape occasional extreme winter weather events (Hulscher et al., 1996). Seasonality is also relevant – studies confined to just part of the year may overlook critical habitat dependencies in other seasons. Another factor causing temporal variation in habitat occupancy is population level. An expanding population may spread into new habitats due to overcrowding in the previously occupied habitats (Chapter 3). Changes in numbers of predators and competitors could also alter patterns of habitat use over time (Chapter 2). Second, an entirely different dimension of temporal scale in habitat selection was emphasised by Orians and Wittenberger (1991), that being the amount of time available to an individual when making a decision about where to settle. Some circumstances demand rapid decisions, such as where the breeding season is short, or the competition from conspecifics is high. This means that habitat choices are potentially based on incomplete information, which leads to questions about the irrevocability of habitat choices and the methods that birds may have evolved to maximise the gathering of information about habitat quality.

The third non-spatial component of scale concerns the range of environmental variation over which habitat associations are examined. This can be thought of as the 'habitat grain' of an investigation (Fuller, 1994). A complete picture of the habitat associations of a species requires sampling to be conducted over the full environmental gradients occupied by the species (Vaughan and Ormerod, 2003). Restricting sampling to part of any environmental gradient can give an incomplete representation of habitat association. Nonetheless, a focus on one part of the habitat spectrum of a species, such as one particular successional stage, may provide greater insights to those habitat elements limiting distribution than would be evident from a coarser-grained study (Fig. 1.2). It is important to appropriately match the habitat grain to the question of interest, to be explicit about the context of any investigation and not to extrapolate conclusions or derived models beyond the realm in which they were established.

In spatial ecology there has been a recent tendency to emphasise the importance of large-scale factors. This is exemplified by the vast quantity of literature on the sensitivity of bird species to landscape composition, especially in relation to forest fragmentation (Chapters 4 and 19). However, the fine-grain distribution of many species is limited by processes operating at much smaller scales (e.g. selection of particular vegetation microstructures)

Variations in microhabitat features and floristics

Gross differences in structural complexity

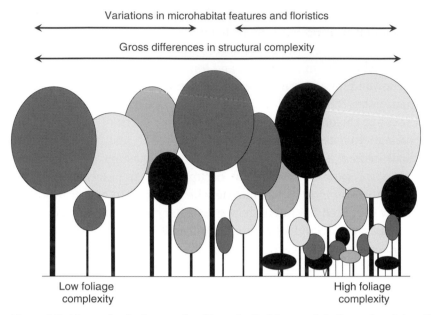

Low foliage
complexity

High foliage
complexity

Figure 1.2 A hypothetical example of how the 'habitat grain' of a study might affect the apparent relationships between birds and habitat in mature forest where there is spatial variation in foliage complexity. When measured across the full gradient in foliage complexity structure (coarse grain) it is to be expected that the distribution of many species and patterns in bird diversity will be best explained by gross variations in foliage structure. However, when bird–habitat relationships are examined in particular parts of the foliage complexity gradient (fine grain) more subtle relationships may be detected, such as ones with plant composition and microhabitat structure. Similarly, studies that pool observations from several successional stages will draw very different conclusions about habitat relationships than ones focusing on just one part of the successional gradient. Note that Wiens (1989b) uses 'grain' to mean the size of individual sample units in a study. Based on Fuller (1994).

and this requires an understanding of minimum habitat requirements (Haila *et al.*, 1996). In some species, density-dependent distributions across habitats may be most evident at fine scales of habitat variation (Chamberlain and Fuller, 1999). Habitat patches will not be used if they do not provide critical resources; these could include food abundance, suitable foraging sites, nesting sites or roosting sites. Microhabitat selection is closely linked with the provision of these resources and may simultaneously serve to minimise interspecific competition. In reality, both fine-scale and large-scale processes are important determinants of habitat quality for many species. To maintain populations it is essential to consider habitat availability and quality at all scales. To illustrate the complementarity of processes at different scales, I will first discuss how predation processes can interact with habitat quality in terrestrial environments and then summarise several specific case studies of multi-scale habitat influences.

Predation and scale

The nature of the predator assemblage is frequently linked with characteristics of the wider landscape (Chapters 4 and 5), whereas the ability of a species to reduce the risk of predation is more typically determined by fine-scale habitat quality. Diverse predator species prey on ground- and foliage-nesting birds in forests, shrublands and grassland. These predators include snakes, raptors, corvids and mammals of various sizes. Studies conducted mainly in North America and Scandinavia provide evidence that landscape context affects the numbers and types of predators. Predator impacts in forest can become more prevalent in fragmented landscapes, especially where agriculture is increasingly dominant, and the types of predators are different to more intact landscapes (Andrén, 1992; Donovan, *et al.*, 1997; Chalfoun *et al.*, 2002). Predator assemblages can also change with increasing urbanisation. Close to Seattle, Marzluff *et al.* (2007), for example, found that American crows *Corvus brachyrhynchos* were more abundant in areas where there was less forest cover, whereas Douglas squirrels *Tamiasciurus douglasii* showed the opposite response. This is not to say, of course, that predators do not respond to fine-scale habitat features. For instance, Klug *et al.* (2009) reported that abundances of nest predators of grassland birds in Nebraska and Iowa were associated with habitat features at a variety of scales. An important point is that different suites of predators will occur in different types of landscape and this will likely result in different types of predation pressure (see also Chapters 4 and 5).

At the territory level, species tend to select characteristic vegetation profiles (the 'niche gestalt' of James, 1971). At still finer scales, bird species are often highly selective of nesting and foraging microhabitats in terms of features such as height above ground, vegetation density and plant species (Morse, 1980; Holmes, 1990; Kouki *et al.*, 1992; Martin, 1998). Microhabitats used for these two activities may differ (Martin, 1992; Steele, 1993) and the choices are generally assumed to have fitness consequences. Predation can be an important process influencing microhabitat selection, as shown by the following examples for forest songbirds.

Winter feeding site selection by small, mainly insectivorous, species such as tits can be strongly influenced by the risk of predation (Suhonen, 1993; Carascal and Alonso, 2006). Of course predation is not the only factor determining exactly where the birds feed and Suhonen (1993) concluded that trade-offs between food availability, competition between species and predation risk are involved. Most of the detailed studies of microhabitat selection in nesting forest birds have been undertaken in North America. There are relatively few studies in Europe with the notable exception of work in Białowieża Forest, Poland (e.g. Tomiałojć, 1993; Wesołowski, 2002; Wesołowski and Rowiński, 2004; Mitrus and Soćko, 2008). The importance of minimising nest predation by using relatively safe nest sites has been stressed by the Białowieża studies and by Martin (1988a, b, 1992, 1998). The great majority of nest losses (>95%) occur through predation, so this is likely to be a strong selection pressure in the evolution of nest site selection (Martin, 1992). Working in forests on valley slopes in Arizona, he minutely examined nest site use in seven passerine species (Martin, 1998). The main predators of nesting birds were squirrels and chipmunks. With respect to vegetation structure and plant composition around the nest sites, these species differed in the types of nest sites they used and in each case they used sites that were non-random, indicating individual selection of nest site characteristics. For each species, nest survival was higher in preferred microhabitats, defined as those most frequently used, than in non-preferred microhabitats. This finding strongly suggests that choices of nest site in these seven species were adaptive.

Vegetation density is commonly thought to be a key factor in impeding the efficiency of predators, but the number of potential nest sites that a predator has to search could also be relevant. Chalfoun and Martin (2009) explored these two possibilities in sagebrush vegetation in Montana for the Brewer's sparrow *Spizella breweri*. They found that although birds chose to nest in patches with higher vegetation density and higher densities of potential nest sites, only the latter affected predation risk. This is another example of adaptive nest site selection. Exactly which features of vegetation are likely to reduce predation risk may depend on the focal species, on the local predator assemblage and on the type of habitat.

Some diverse examples of multi-scale habitat effects

For wide-ranging species, a particular combination of elements at the landscape scale may be important for different functions. A good example is provided by a study of the raven *Corvus corax* in Białowieża Forest, which forages over large areas for carrion (Mueller *et al.*, 2009). The bird nests only in tall pines within areas of conifer forest, but this type of forest is poor foraging habitat. Extensive areas of conifer forest around nest sites were associated with low breeding success. However, better breeding performance occurred where large areas of deciduous forest or open areas were accessible from the nest site. This is an example of resource or landscape complementation (Dunning *et al.*, 1992), in which different resource needs must be met by different landscape elements. In this case, one of the resources is provided at a very small scale (nest sites) and the other (food) at a far larger scale.

The green woodpecker *Picus viridis* in Scandinavia is at the northern limit of its breeding range and it only just penetrates into the boreal forest. Initially it is surprising that this species does not live in these northern forests because ants, its staple food, appear to be sufficiently available there. The ancestral habitat is probably broadleaved woodland with open areas of grassland or heath which provide the ants. Thus a mosaic of wooded and open areas may be preferred and Rolstad *et al.* (2000) suggested that large tracts of conifer forests may not provide settlement cues. Young dispersing woodpeckers may use patches of open farmland in forested landscapes as cues for habitat recognition. Home ranges at the southern edge of the boreal forest occur only in areas that have at least some small areas of farmland. Despite this requirement for open areas at the landscape scale, the birds feed heavily on ants within the conifer forest, choosing the younger stands in summer and older stands in winter (Rolstad *et al.*, 2000).

Multi-scale factors may operate in the selection of stopover habitat by migrant birds, just as they do in selection of breeding habitat. Efficient refuelling during migration is a critical survival factor and may affect timing of arrival and condition on the breeding grounds. Most studies of habitat use by migrant birds have been small scale (see Chapter 5), but an exception is the work on migrating landbirds in southern Mississippi by Buler *et al.* (2007). They suggested that migrating birds used the extent of hardwood cover at the landscape scale as a cue in making decisions about where to land. Rapidly homing in on potential feeding areas may be especially important for migrating birds which are under pressure to refuel. The amount of hardwood cover within 5.0 km was most strongly correlated with the densities of migrants at particular locations. At the scale of the habitat patch, food availability also appeared to influence migrant density. Invertebrate abundance and, in autumn, the quantity of fruit-bearing trees were important determinants of patch usage.

Distribution across habitats: models and theoretical perspectives

Several strands of theoretical thinking about habitat selection and its interaction with population dynamics and community structure have been exceedingly influential. A workable framework for the diverse concepts can be established through several broad groupings: (i) interaction-related processes that have underpinned much work on community structure, (ii) density-dependent processes acting through variation in habitat quality and their implications for population regulation, (iii) maladaptive habitat preference and (iv) landscape-scale processes. As already indicated, research effort at landscape scales has proliferated in recent decades, leading to conceptual developments in source–sink dynamics, landscape complementation and metapopulation dynamics (Dunning *et al.*, 1992; Newton, 1998). Landscape processes are the subject of Chapter 4 so are not considered further here.

Species interactions

Competition between species has long been held to be a mechanism by which species have evolved differences in habitat use (Svärdson, 1949; Lack, 1971). In the 1950s and 1960s a large body of theory revolving around competition and the niche was developed as a general basis for understanding how communities are structured. The flavour of the work conducted at this time is captured in Cody and Diamond (1975).

Many ecologists came to regard interspecific competition as the major force structuring bird communities and shaping habitat selection of species. Observed patterns were typically explained with reference to competition theory, as exemplified by Cody (1974). Not all community ecologists working on birds at that time felt it necessary to invoke competition and preferred to focus on relationships with environmental variation such as vegetation structure (James, 1971; Collins *et al.*, 1982; James and Wamer, 1982), a theme that has gathered strength to the present day. Some also recognised that predation could affect habitat selection and community structure (see chapters by Patrick and Connell in Cody and Diamond, 1975), a theme subsequently pursued vigorously by Martin (1988a, b, 1992, 1998). During the 1980s, John Wiens, in particular, became an increasingly severe critic, iconoclastic even, of the work founded on niche and competition theory, culminating in a monumental review (Wiens, 1989a). Competition-based modelling of bird communities may have fallen out of favour, but interspecific competition is undoubtedly an important mechanism in habitat selection (see below).

Habitat selection models and population processes

Svärdson (1949) pointed out that interspecific and intraspecific competition result in contrasting effects on habitat occupancy. While an increase in interspecific competition generally appears to result in species retreating to their optimal niche, the one to which they are most adapted, intraspecific competition is more likely to cause species to occupy a wider range of niches or habitats (Fig. 1.3). Competition between conspecifics for limiting resources is intrinsic to a set of similar models of how mobile animals, such as many birds, use patchy environments where patches differ in habitat quality. These models have foundations in optimal foraging theory and are concerned with how habitat choice by individuals is connected with their fitness. In all these cases there are consequences for population regulation, with habitat selection showing density-dependent properties.

The buffer model of Brown (1969) was one of the earliest models. It envisages a hierarchy of habitat preferences and occupancy whereby a species initially occupies the most preferred (highest quality) habitat up to the point at which it is saturated, when it starts to settle in the next preferred habitat

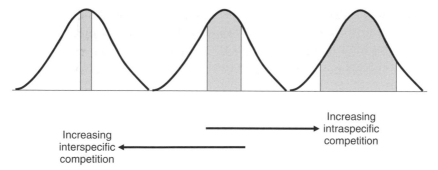

Figure 1.3 Svärdson's (1949) model of the contrasting effects of inter- and intraspecific competition. A species can potentially occupy a range of habitat types represented by a curve in which the peak represents the optimal or most suitable habitat. The extent of shading indicates breadth of habitat use. Under intense interspecific competition a species is expected to 'retreat' to its optimum habitat, but under intense intraspecific competition a relatively wide range of habitats is expected to be occupied.

and the process may continue into a third and subsequent habitat. Buffer effects have been demonstrated for black-tailed godwits *Limosa limosa* during a period of population increase. On the Icelandic breeding grounds, the birds colonised poorer-quality habitats as the numbers rose (Gunnarsson *et al.*, 2005), while in winter numbers increased most on those British coastal sites with initially low numbers, low food intake rates and low survival (Gill *et al.*, 2001). Other examples are given by Newton (1998).

The ideal free distribution model (Fretwell and Lucas, 1969) also assumes that habitats differ in their intrinsic quality, but the realised quality (fitness value) of habitats decreases with density. Individuals are free to settle in any habitat and can choose the most suitable habitat available. A habitat with relatively low intrinsic quality, but a low density of individuals may therefore be selected rather than one with higher intrinsic quality with a high density. The ideal free model is somewhat unrealistic in that individuals typically vary in competitive ability and will rarely have full knowledge of the quality of alternative patches. A variant is the despotic distribution, in which individuals are excluded from the highest quality habitats by the occupants, as might be the case for many territorial species. This results in fitness being maximised in the habitats of highest intrinsic quality that are settled first, but the density is not necessarily highest in these habitats. For reviews of these and other models, some of which incorporate the effects of interspecific competition, see Bernstein *et al.* (1991), Rosenzweig (1991) and Danchin *et al.* (2008).

Much evidence exists for the operation of various forms of density-dependent habitat distribution in birds (Newton, 1998). In some cases, however, no density-dependent distributions have been detected (Chamberlain and Fuller, 1999; Pöysä, 2001). There may even be apparent mismatches between habitat preference and fitness, which may be a consequence of researchers not identifying the habitat scale on which fitness is maximised (Chalfoun and Martin, 2007). Most studies assess density-dependence with respect to area rather than resource availability, but arguably the latter is more appropriate (G. Siriwardena pers. comm.).

The implication of density-dependent habitat selection is that habitat heterogeneity can have a regulatory effect on populations over large areas (Newton, 1998). Expressed at its simplest, as population size grows, and sequentially poorer-quality habitats are occupied or become the only ones available, the average individual breeding output or survival decreases. This comes about because resources are disproportionately concentrated into higher-quality habitats and intraspecific competition limits the numbers of individuals that benefit from these. Hence, spatial variation in habitat quality can potentially place a check on continued population growth, as is the case in the following three examples.

First, territory occupancy and breeding success of sparrowhawks *Accipiter nisus* in a Scottish forestry plantation were both highest in young dense stands of trees, but declined as the trees aged (Newton, 1991). The high-quality sites produced a surplus of individuals, but low-quality sites did not, and were only occupied through immigration. Population stability was maintained as a result of rotational forestry maintaining a patchwork of high- and low-quality sites. Second, Andrén (1990) found that jays *Garrulus glandarius* in Sweden conformed to a despotic model. Individuals in dense spruce forest had the highest breeding success and apparently excluded other individuals from using this habitat. This created a situation where density-dependent reproduction may have been regulating the population. Third, also in Sweden, breeding success of Siberian jays *Perisoreus infaustus* was highest away from human settlements and in patches with dense low spruce (Ekman *et al.*, 2001). Some birds dispersed in their first year and occupied low-quality territories, others delayed dispersal and waited for high-quality territories to become available. Both dispersers and non-dispersers preferred the high-quality territories, but when population density was high the latter were more likely to acquire one of these territories. Subsequently, the high-quality territories were demonstrated generally to act as population sources (Nystrand *et al.*, 2010).

In each of these examples it was suggested that there was an interaction between the quality of territories and the quality (often expressed as age) of the bird occupying it. In practice it is difficult to separate effects of habitat quality from those of individual quality (Balbontin and Ferrer, 2008). Each of these examples also involves birds showing a strong preference for high-quality habitat, but sometimes birds make bad choices.

Maladaptive or non-ideal habitat selection

Models of habitat selection usually assume that individuals are able to assess relative quality of habitat patches. However, there may be circumstances where an individual has incomplete information on the suitability of a habitat for survival or breeding such that its attractiveness becomes decoupled from its quality. The theme of maladaptive habitat selection is explored further in Chapter 2. At its most extreme, an ecological trap may occur where the cues evolved to select habitat are no longer reliable and actually result in low fitness outcomes for the individual, potentially leading to local extinction (Schlaepfer *et al.*, 2002; Battin, 2004; Robertson and Hutto, 2006).

It is thought that ecological traps are most likely to develop when habitat modification leads to reduction in suitability yet the habitat still provides strong settlement cues. Changes within agricultural systems provide several examples (Gilroy and Sutherland, 2007). Similarly, an increase in invasive predators or competitors may reduce habitat suitability, but cues may remain unchanged. There is uncertainty about the frequency with which ecological traps occur (Robertson and Hutto, 2006). Some species may cope with traps, through behavioural flexibility or by evolving new cues for habitat recognition – indeed it seems likely that most traps will be ephemeral because there will be strong selection pressure against them. Nonetheless, ecological traps could be symptomatic of a world in which human influence is increasingly disruptive of long-established ecosystems.

Not all cases of apparently maladaptive habitat selection can be explained as ecological traps. Some high-quality habitat may not be recognised because it does not provide cues for settlement (Gilroy and Sutherland, 2007; Shustack and Rodewald, 2010). This idea has been termed a 'perceptual trap' by Patten and Kelly (2010) who argue that such traps are potentially more persistant than ecological traps due to Allee effects (Chapter 2). Factors other than short-term measures of fitness may be relevant. In a study of breeding wheatears *Oenanthe oenanthe*, Arlt and Pärt (2007) found that territories located in patches with permanently short field vegetation had highest breeding success. However, birds did not show a preference for these patches; they preferred to settle in close proximity to other males, thus creating clusters of territories. The authors discuss several possible explanations of the preference for territory clustering. Individuals may be non-selective because the landscape may have been dominated by rather poor-quality habitat. Alternatively, some longer-term advantage might be gained from conspecific attraction, for example the future procurement of a higher-quality territory.

Evolutionary and life-history aspects of habitat choice

Species evolved physical structures and behaviour patterns that fit them for particular habitat types and niches. Habitat selection ensures that these adaptations match the environment and enable individuals to identify high-quality habitat. Although environmental variation in space and time underlies the evolution of particular traits that maximise fitness, clearly the evolution of habitat selection requires some level of predictability in environmental conditions.

The potential role of habitat as an isolating mechanism in speciation has been much debated and generally rejected or disregarded (Mayr, 1942; Lack, 1971; Newton, 2003). However, habitat could have a role at a microevolutionary level. The close association of different individuals with certain niches, through, for example, natal experience rigidly influencing later choice, could result in increasing local adaptation and reduced gene flow (Thorpe, 1945; Partridge, 1978; Davis and Stamps, 2004). Another mechanism may be non-random dispersal interacting with variation in habitat quality to reinforce small-scale spatial genetic differences (Garant et al., 2005). The purpose here is to consider some evolutionary processes in which habitat may have influenced patterns in the lives of birds today.

Ecological separation and competition

The classic view of how and why habitat differences arise among closely related sympatric species was developed by Lack (1971). Ecological isolation is widely held to be a general principle whereby two species cannot occupy exactly the same niche because interspecific competition would cause one to eventually exclude the other. Past interspecific competition has acted through natural selection to produce the species-specific differences in habitat and niche, and their accompanying physical and behavioural adaptations, that we observe today. Wiens (1989a) points out that variation between species in the way they use resources is actually more complex than envisaged by Lack. He also stresses that in many instances there are considerable similarities between closely related species. Nonetheless, the broad principle of ecological segregation has stood the test of time and it is clear that rather small differences in habitat can facilitate coexistence (Veen et al., 2010).

Although the effects of competition are extremely difficult to study, there is the famous evidence from the Galápagos finches (Grant and Grant, 2008). Here, previously isolated similar species that come into sympatry will show shifts in beak morphology as a result of natural selection acting through competition. In this case, natural selection acts on a trait closely involved in exploitation of critical resources, leading to reduced competition. A very different kind of evidence comes from Fennoscandian forest where the niches of foraging tits (Paridae) have been examined in various locations and combinations of species (Alatalo, 1982; Alatalo et al., 1986). Within mixed-species flocks there are divergent shifts in foraging sites between pairs of putative competing species when both are present that cannot be readily accounted for by habitat or other environmental variation. There are also geographical niche shifts that occur when one species is absent from part of the range of its competitor species. Foraging sites only change in species that are morphologically very similar to the species that are absent in allopatry.

Ecological and life-history strategies

The characteristics of habitats will be strongly influential in the evolutionary processes that match the ecology and behaviour of species to their environment. Theory has stressed relationships between habitat stability and ecological strategies reflected in, for example, the r–K continuum (Southwood et al., 1974). Habitat stability incorporates notions of permanence, predictability and ephemerality of the resources provided by a defined habitat type. Theoretically, one might expect bird species of early successional habitats to show higher reproductive rates and higher breeding dispersal (r-selected traits), than species of the later, relatively stable, stages of succession, where species may be expected to be K-selected. I am unaware of any general attempt to relate the ecology or life-history traits of birds to habitat stability, but these theoretical expectations are not clearly supported by the available evidence. In a study of dispersal in British birds, Paradis et al. (1998) found no evidence of dispersal differences between species of 'open' and 'closed' habitats. However, they did find that breeding dispersal, but not natal dispersal, was higher in species associated with wet rather than dry habitats. They suggested that species of wet habitats needed to disperse further than dry-habitat species because their habitats tended to be patchier in space and less persistent. Schlossberg (2009) found no evidence that dispersal rates of migratory North American shrubland birds were higher than those of forest birds. The pattern of reproductive output across successional stages was examined by Mönkkönen and Helle (1987) for European forests and compared with published data from North America, which showed the expected pattern. In Europe, however, the pattern did not conform to theory because average clutch size and egg production increased with successional stage. These continental differences were probably driven by divergent patterns of habitat selection of long-distance migrants (see below), which tend to show lower reproductive rates than residents.

Evolution of habitat selection patterns in migratory species

Due to their extreme mobility, birds can potentially exploit a great variety of habitats over huge geographical areas. Habitat choices made by migratory individuals in one season may have consequences for subsequent performance in another season (Chapter 2). Migration raises specific questions about the relative importance of selection pressures operating at different times of year. Migrants may be very time-limited in their selection of habitat, both on migration and when they arrive in their breeding areas (Chapter 17). This is likely to be an important factor in the evolution of mechanisms such as heterospecific attraction that assist rapid identification of suitable habitat. Three examples are given here of how evolution of migrancy, habitat selection and life-history patterns may have interacted.

It has been proposed that the balance of breeding and non-breeding habitats ('survival habitats' that are unsuitable for breeding) may have a profound effect on the strategies of migratory species (Alerstam and Högstedt, 1982). An example would be the tundra breeding grounds and overwintering intertidal feeding areas used by many migrant waders (shorebirds). These authors propose that B-species have extensive breeding habitat and are primarily limited by availability or extent of survival habitat, and vice versa for S-species, which have extensive survival habitat but are more limited by breeding habitat. Realistically, species are likely to occupy a continuum between extremes of habitat limitation operating in breeding or non-breeding areas. They suggested that B-species may include dabbling ducks, freshwater/grassland waders and small landbirds that exploit overabundant insect food supplies in summer. S-species may include seabirds and diving birds dependent on shallow water. Alerstam and Högstedt suggested that intertidal waders would be S-species, but this seems unlikely in many cases due to the specialisations shown by many species in selecting their winter foraging habitat and the localised distribution of many intertidal habitat types (Chapter 12). The proposed B–S spectrum complements the r–K spectrum by stressing the importance of mobility and seasonal habitat-use patterns rather than emphasising habitat stability.

The second example concerns Piersma's idea (1997, 2003) that the risk of parasitic infection in certain habitats has been an important factor connected with evolution of habitat selection in waders. These species roughly divide between ones that breed in the high arctic and winter in intertidal habitats, and ones that breed in the low arctic or boreal and winter in freshwater or grassland habitats. Global population sizes of the former species tend to be smaller than the latter. The idea is that these two suites of habitats differ in parasite burdens and infection risk, being relatively low in the former. Subsequently Mendes *et al.* (2005) confirmed that prevalence of malaria in freshwater species was higher than in coastal species, but mainly in the tropics. Piersma (1997) suggested that the habitat selection dichotomy may be driven by 'trade-offs between investments in immunofunctioning on the one hand and growth and sustained exercise on the other . . .'. The argument was made that a high-arctic/intertidal strategy requires little need to resist parasitic infection and allows much greater investment in rapid chick growth, and also the ability to sustain high levels of energy expenditure on long migrations and in exposed winter habitats. By contrast, it was argued that chick development in freshwater waders is relatively slow because a much greater nutritional investment has to be made in developing immune defences in these parasite-rich habitats. The hypothesis was later extended (Piersma, 2003) to the possibility that the relatively small populations of high-arctic breeding species may have experienced severe population bottlenecks as a result of historical climate change causing rapid contraction of habitat. A loss of genetic variability could have ensued, reducing that part of the genome determining adaptive immunity. It appears that there are evolutionary linkages amongst a complex of life-history elements, but the exact relationships have yet to be fully elucidated.

Third, a very different example is provided by the temperate–tropical migration systems of forest birds in North America and Europe. Migrant forest species on both sides of the Atlantic display a variety of lifestyles and occur in diverse habitat types in both summer and winter. Whilst one should be cautious about over-generalising, it is clear that differences exist in patterns of habitat use between the migration systems (Mönkkönen and Helle, 1989; Mönkkönen et al., 1992; Rappole, 1995; Böhning-Gaese and Oberrath, 2003; Fig. 1.4). In Europe, breeding migrants are more strongly represented in relatively early successional stages, whereas in eastern North America they are more strongly associated with later successional stages. Within North America, migrant species in the east tend to occupy a narrower range of successional stages than in the west, where the association with mature forest is not so marked as in the east. Though knowledge of habitat use by Palaearctic migrants wintering in Africa is far from complete, it is clear that many species heavily use open savannah and bushy habitats, with rather few wintering in closed evergreen tropical forest (Salewski and Jones, 2006). Within Africa many of these species are migratory, moving over large distances, tracking seasonal change in vegetation and food availability (Moreau, 1972; Pearson and Lack, 1992). By contrast, North American migrants depend to a much greater extent on tropical forest where many species are relatively site faithful through the winter (Rappole, 1995).

Several explanations for these differences have been suggested, but Mönkkönen et al. (1992) favour that made by Bilcke (1984b) whose idea was that habitat use by migrants on the breeding grounds is largely determined by habitat availability in the wintering areas. Species will tend to use similar habitat structures in different seasons as a result of evolved behaviours and physical adaptations to these particular structures. The relative availability of habitat types across migration systems differs markedly, with a far greater extent of shrubby vegetation and relatively little tropical forest in sub-Saharan Africa compared with the neotropics. Migrants in western North America appear to winter mainly in western Mexico where the range of desert, riparian, woodland and forest habitat types is very similar to that found further

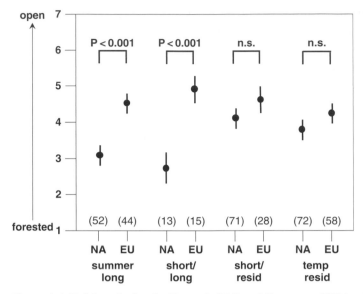

Figure 1.4 Habitat choice for Nearctic (NA) and European (EU) land birds on their breeding grounds. Habitats were classified with respect to a seven-stage structural gradient ranging from closed forest to open land without trees and bushes. Habitat scores were averaged within genera and for each group are shown as means ± SE. Numbers of genera are given in parentheses. The groups are: long-distance migrants (*summer long*), short-distance migrants in genera with long-distance migrants (*short/long*), short-distance migrants in genera without long-distance migrants (*short/resid*) and temperate residents (*temp resid*). Long-distance migrants, and short-distance migrants in genera with long-distance migrants, breed in significantly more open habitats in Europe than in North America. Redrawn from Böhning-Gaese and Oberrath (2003).

north in the west (Hutto, 1985). It appears, therefore, that geographical patterns in breeding habitat selection broadly match relative habitat availability in winter on both continents. The existence of the Sahara desert, the huge expanse of savannah vegetation, and the scarcity of tropical forest in west Africa relative to the neotropics have probably been major influences on which types of species evolved migratory behaviour in the two continents.

Concluding remarks

To understand habitat ecology fully, we need to understand how habitats are selected, what determines habitat quality, how selection and quality interact, and over what time frame this interaction occurs

(Kristan *et al.*, 2007).

The multi-scaled nature of bird–habitat relationships is now widely appreciated, but other unifying concepts of habitat selection have been difficult to pin down. Satisfactory field tests of almost any aspect of habitat selection theory are exceedingly difficult. Furthermore, where a species is shown to behave consistently with a particular model, it is impossible to know how far that result can be generalised. Clarity about habitat definition and context is crucial. The extent to which a species conforms to the expectations of any model will be affected by spatial scale, extent of habitat variation examined, population size, resource function etc. In the real, immensely diverse, world it is probable that many different concepts will apply to some species, at some places, some of the time. Indeed many of the concepts concerning how, why and when habitat selection occurs are not alternatives, but essentially complementary. One of the great challenges is to identify the circumstances under which the various elements of theory are likely to be relevant. However, for species of particular conservation concern there really is little option but to understand the processes as they apply to the focal species in clearly defined contexts; the cues and strategies that species have evolved are highly varied. Within certain limits set by morphology and resource needs, habitat requirements of individual species can vary in space and change in time. This intraspecific variation deserves far more attention. Multiple factors operating at different scales affect where birds actually settle – this is taken further in the next chapter.

Acknowledgements

The chapter was improved by comments from Chris Hewson, Theunis Piersma, Gavin Siriwardena and Tomasz Wesołowski.

References

Adriaensen, F. and Dhondt, A. A. (1990). Population dynamics and partial migration of the European robin (*Erithacus rubecula*) in different habitats. *J. Anim. Ecol.*, **59**, 1077–1090.

Ahlering, M. A. and Faaborg, J. (2006). Avian habitat management meets conspecific attraction: if you build it, will they come? *Auk*, **123**, 301–312.

Akresh, M. E., Dinse, K., Foufopoulos, J., Schubel, S. C. and Kowalczyk, T. (2009). Passerine breeding and post-fledging habitat use in riparian and upland temperate forests of the American Midwest. *Condor*, **111**, 756–762.

Alatalo, R. V. (1981). Habitat selection of forest birds in the seasonal environments of Finland. *Ann. Zool. Fenn.*, **18**, 103–114.

Alatalo, R. V. (1982). Evidence for interspecific competition among European tits *Parus* spp.: a review. *Ann. Zool. Fenn.*, **19**, 309–317.

Alatalo, R. V., Gustafsson, L. and Lundberg, A. (1986). Interspecific competition and niche changes in tits (*Parus* spp.): evaluation of nonexperimental data. *Am. Nat.*, **127**, 819–834.

Alerstam, T. and Högstedt, G. (1982). Bird migration and reproduction in relation to habitats for survival and breeding. *Ornis Scand.*, **13**, 25–37.

Andrén, H. (1990). Despotic distribution, unequal reproductive success, and population regulation in the jay *Garrulus glandarius* L. *Ecology*, **71**, 1796–1803.

Andrén, H. (1992). Corvid density and nest predation in relation to forest fragmentation: a landscape perspective. *Ecology*, **73**, 794–804.

Arlt, D. and Pärt, T. (2007). Nonideal breeding habitat selection: a mismatch between preference and fitness. *Ecology*, **88**, 792–801.

Bailey, J. W. and Thompson, F. R., III (2007). Multiscale nest-site selection by black-capped vireos. *J. Wildlife Manage.*, **71**, 828–836.

Bairlein, F. (1983). Habitat selection and associations of species in European passerine birds during southward, post-breeding migrations. *Ornis Scand.*, **14**, 239–245.

Balbontin, J. and Ferrer, M. (2008). Density dependence by habitat heterogeneity: individual quality versus territory quality. *Oikos*, **117**, 1111–1114.

Battin, J. (2004). When good animals love bad habitats: ecological traps and the conservation of animal populations. *Conserv. Biol.*, **18**, 1482–1491.

Bernstein, C. M., Krebs, J. R. and Kacelnik, A. (1991). Distribution of birds amongst habitats: theory and relevance to conservation. In *Bird Population Studies: Relevance to Conservation and Management*, ed. C. M. Perrins, J. D. Lebreton and G. J. M. Hirons, pp. 317–345. Oxford: Oxford University Press.

Bilcke, G. (1984a). Seasonal changes in habitat use of resident passerines. *Ardea*, **72**, 95–99.

Bilcke, G. (1984b). Residence and non-residence in passerines: dependence on the vegetation structure. *Ardea*, **72**, 223–227.

Block, W. M. and Brennan, L. A. (1993). The habitat concept in ornithology: theory and applications. *Curr. Ornithol.*, **11**, 35–91.

Böhning-Gaese, K. and Oberrath, R. (2003). Macroecology of habitat choice in long-distance migratory birds. *Oecologia*, **137**, 296–303.

Bolnick, D. I., Svanbäck, R., Fordyce, J. A. *et al.* (2003). The ecology of individuals: incidence and implications of individual specialization. *Am. Nat.*, **161**, 1–28.

Bond, R. R. (1957). Ecological distribution of breeding birds in the upland forests of Southern Wisconsin. *Ecol. Monogr.*, **27**, 351–384.

Boulinier, T., Mariette, M., Doligez, B. and Danchin, E. (2008). Choosing where to breed: breeding habitat choice. In *Behavioural Ecology*, ed. E. Danchin, L.-E. Giraldeau and F. Cézilly, pp. 285–320. Oxford: Oxford University Press.

Brock, S. E. (1914). Ecological relations of bird-distribution. *Brit. Birds*, **8**, 30–44.

Brown, C. R., Bomberger Brown, M. and Danchin, E. (2000). Breeding habitat selection in cliff swallows: the effect of conspecific reproductive success on colony choice. *J. Anim. Ecol.*, **69**, 133–142.

Brown, J. L. (1969). The buffer effect and productivity in tit populations. *Am. Nat.*, **103**, 347–354.

Buler, J. J., Moore, F. R. and Woltmann, S. (2007). A multi-scale examination of stopover habitat use by birds. *Ecology*, **88**, 1789–1802.

Burton, N. H. K. (2009). Reproductive success of Tree Pipits *Anthus trivialis* in relation to habitat selection in conifer plantations. *Ibis*, **151**, 361–372.

Carrascal, L. M. and Alonso, C. L. (2006). Habitat use under latent predation risk. A case study with wintering forest birds. *Oikos*, **112**, 51–62.

Catchpole, C. K. (1974). Habitat selection and breeding success in the reed warbler (*Acrocephalus scirpaceus*). *J. Anim. Ecol.*, **43**, 363–380.

Chalfoun, A. D. and Martin, T. E. (2007). Assessments of habitat preferences and quality depend on spatial scale and metrics of fitness. *J. Appl. Ecol.*, **44**, 983–992.

Chalfoun, A. D. and Martin, T. E. (2009). Habitat structure mediates predation risk for sedentary prey: experimental tests of alternative hypotheses. *J. Anim. Ecol.*, **78**, 497–503.

Chalfoun, A. D., Thompson, F. R., III and Ratnaswamy, M. J. (2002). Nest predators and fragmentation: a review and meta-analysis. *Conserv. Biol.*, **16**, 306–318.

Chamberlain, D. E. and Fuller, R. J. (1999). Density-dependent habitat distribution in birds: issues of scale, habitat definition and habitat availability. *J. Avian Biol.*, **30**, 427–436.

Cody, M. L. (1974). *Competition and the Structure of Bird Communities*. Princeton: Princeton University Press.

Cody, M. L. ed. (1985). *Habitat Selection in Birds*. London: Academic Press.

Cody, M. L. and Diamond, J. M. eds. (1975). *Ecology and the Evolution of Communities*. Cambridge, Mass.: Harvard University Press.

Collins, S. L. (1981). A comparison of nest-site and perch-site vegetation structure for seven species of warblers. *Wilson Bull.*, **93**, 542–547.

Collins, S. L., James, F. C. and Risser, P. G. (1982). Habitat relationships of wood warblers (Parulidae) in northern central Minnesota. *Oikos*, **39**, 50–58.

Cornell, K. L. and Donovan, T. M. (2010). Scale-dependent mechanisms of habitat selection for a migratory passerine: an experimental approach. *Auk*, **127**, 899–908.

Crick, H. Q. P. (1992). A bird-habitat coding system for use in Britain and Ireland incorporating aspects of land management and human activity. *Bird Study*, **39**, 1–12.

Danchin, E., Giraldeau, L.-A. and Cézilly, F. (ed.) (2008). *Behavioural Ecology*. Oxford: Oxford University Press.

Danchin, E. and Wagner, R. H. (1997). The evolution of coloniality: the emergence of new perspectives. *Trends Ecol. Evol.*, **12**, 342–347.

Davis, J. M. (2008). Patterns of variation in the influence of natal experience on habitat choice. *Q. Rev. Biol.*, **83**, 363–377.

Davis, J. M. and Stamps, J. A. (2004). The effect of natal experience on habitat preferences. *Trends Ecol. Evol.*, **19**, 411–416.

Doligez, B., Cadet, C., Danchin, E. and Boulinier, T. (2003). When to use public information for breeding habitat selection? The role of environmental predictability and density dependence. *Anim. Behav.*, **66**, 973–988.

Doligez, B., Danchin, E. and Clobert, J. (2002). Public information and breeding habitat selection in a wild bird population. *Science*, **297**, 1168–1170.

Doligez, B., Danchin, E., Clobert, J. and Gustafsson, L. (1999). The use of conspecific reproductive success for breeding habitat selection in a non-colonial, hole-nesting species, the collared flycatcher. *J. Anim. Ecol.*, **68**, 1193–1206.

Donovan, T. M., Jones, P. W., Annand, E. M. and Thompson, F. R., III. (1997). Variation in local scale edge effects: mechanisms and landscape context. *Ecology*, **78**, 2064–2075.

Dunning, J. B., Danielson, B. J. and Pulliam, H. R. (1992). Ecological processes that affect populations in complex landscapes. *Oikos*, **65**, 169–175.

Ebenman, B. and Nilsson, S. G. (1982). Components of niche width in a territorial bird species: habitat utilization in males and females of the chaffinch (*Fringilla coelebs*) on islands and mainland. *Am. Nat.*, **119**, 331–344.

Ekman, J., Eggers, S., Griesser, M. and Tegelstrom, H. (2001). Queuing for preferred territories: delayed dispersal of Siberian Jays. *J. Anim. Ecol.*, **70**, 317–324.

Enemar, A., Sjöstrand, B., Andersson, G. and von Proschwitz, T. (2004). The 37-year dynamics of a subalpine passerine bird community, with special emphasis on the influence of environmental temperature and *Epirrita autumnata* cycles. *Ornis Svecica*, **14**, 63–106.

Folmer, E. O., Olff, H. and Piersma, T. (2010). How well do food distributions predict spatial distributions of shorebirds with different degrees of self-organization? *J. Anim. Ecol.*, **79**, 747–756.

Fretwell, S. D. and Lucas, H. L. (1969). On territorial behavior and other factors influencing habitat distribution in birds. I. Theoretical development. *Acta Biotheor.*, **19**, 16–36.

Fuller, R. J. (1994). Relating birds to vegetation: influences of scale, floristics and habitat structure. In *Bird Numbers 1992: Distribution, Monitoring and Ecological Aspects*, pp.19–28. Beek-Ubbergen: Statistics Netherlands, Voorburg/Heerlen and SOVON.

Fuller, R. J. and Henderson, A. C. B. (1992). Distribution of breeding songbirds in Bradfield Woods, Suffolk, in relation to vegetation and coppice management. *Bird Study*, **39**, 73–88.

Garant, D., Kruuk, L. E. B., Wilkin, T. A., McCleery, R. H. and Sheldon, B. C. (2005). Evolution driven by differential dispersal within a wild bird population. *Nature*, **433**, 60–65.

Gill, J. A., Norris, K., Potts, P. M. *et al.* (2001). The buffer effect and large-scale population regulation in migratory birds. *Nature*, **412**, 436–438.

Gillings, S., Fuller, R. J. and Sutherland, W. J. (2005). Diurnal studies do not predict nocturnal habitat choice and site selection of European golden-plovers (*Pluvialis apricaria*) and northern lapwings (*Vanellus vanellus*). *Auk*, **122**, 1249–1260.

Gilroy, J. J. and Sutherland, W. J. (2007). Beyond ecological traps: perceptual errors and undervalued resources. *Trends Ecol. Evol.*, **22**, 351–356.

Glück, E. (1983). Nest-habitat separation of six European finch species in orchards (English title). *J. Ornithol.*, **124**, 369–392.

Grant, P. R. and Grant, R. (2008). *How and why Species Multiply: the Radiation of Darwin's Finches.* Princeton: Princeton University Press.

Grinnell, J. (1917a). Field tests of theories concerning distributional control. *Am. Nat.*, **51**, 115–128.

Grinnell, J. (1917b). The niche relationships of the California thrasher. *Auk*, **34**, 427–433.

Gunnarsson, T. G., Gill, J. A., Petersen, A., Appleton, G. F. and Sutherland, W. J. (2005). A double buffer effect in a migratory shorebird population. *J. Anim. Ecol.*, **74**, 965–971.

Haila, Y., Nicholls, A. O., Hanski, I. K. and Raivio, S. (1996). Stochasticity in bird habitat selection: year-to-year changes in territory locations in a boreal forest bird assemblage. *Oikos*, **76**, 536–552.

Hall, L. S., Krausman, P. R. and Morrison, M. L. (1997). The habitat concept and a plea for standard terminology. *Wildlife Soc. Bull.*, **25**, 173–182.

Harrison, M. L., Green, D. J. and Krannitz, P. G. (2009). Conspecifics influence the

settlement decisions of male Brewer's sparrows at the northern edge of their range. *Condor*, **111**, 722–729.

Hildén, O. (1965). Habitat selection in birds – a review. *Ann. Zool. Fenn.*, **2**, 53–75.

Holmes, R. T. (1990) The structure of a temperate deciduous forest bird community: variability in time and space. In *Biogeography and Ecology of Forest Bird Communities*, ed. A. Keast, pp. 121–139. The Hague: SPB Academic Publishing.

Hulscher, J. B., Exo, K. M. and Clark, N. A. (1996). Why do Oystercatchers migrate? In *The Oystercatcher: from Individuals to Populations*, ed. J. D. Goss-Custard, pp. 155–185. Oxford: Oxford University Press.

Hutto, R. L. (1985). Habitat selection by nonbreeding, migratory land birds. In *Habitat Selection in Birds*, ed. M. L. Cody, pp. 455–476. London: Academic Press.

James, F. C. (1971). Ordinations of habitat relationships among breeding birds. *Wilson Bull.*, **83**, 215–236.

James, F. C. and Wamer, N. O. (1982). Relationships between temperate forest bird communities and vegetation structure. *Ecology*, **63**, 159–171.

Johnson, D. H. (1980). The comparison of usage and availability measurements for evaluating resource preference. *Ecology*, **61**, 65–71.

Johnson, M. D. (2007). Measuring habitat quality: a review. *Condor*, **109**, 489–504.

Jones, J. (2001). Habitat selection studies in avian ecology: a critical review. *Auk*, **118**, 557–562.

Kendeigh, S. C. (1941). Birds of a prairie community. *Condor*, **43**, 165–174.

Kendeigh, S. C. (1945). Community selection by birds on the Helderberg plateau of New York. *Auk*, **62**, 418–436.

Klomp, H. (1954). De terreinkeus van de Kievit, *Vanellus vanellus* (L.). *Ardea*, **42**, 1–139.

Klug, P., Wolfenbarger, L. L. and McCarty, J. P. (2009). The nest predator community of grassland birds responds to agroecosystem habitat at multiple scales. *Ecography*, **32**, 973–982.

Koford, R. R., Dunning, J. B, Ribic, C. A. and Finch, D. M. (1994). A glossary for avian conservation biology. *Wilson Bull.*, **106**, 121–137.

Kouki, J., Niemi, G. J. and Rajasärkkä, A. (1992). Habitat associations of breeding peatland passerine species in eastern Finland. *Ornis Fennica*, **69**, 126–140.

Kristan, W. B. (2006). Sources and expectations for hierarchical structure in bird-habitat associations. *Condor*, **108**, 5–12.

Kristan, W. B., Johnson, M. D. and Rotenberry, J. T. (2007). Choices and consequences of habitat selection for birds. *Condor*, **109**, 485–488.

Lack, D. (1933). Habitat selection in birds with special reference to the effects of afforestation on the Breckland avifauna. *J. Anim. Ecol.*, **2**, 239–262.

Lack, D. (1937). The psychological factor in bird distribution. *Brit. Birds*, **31**, 130–136.

Lack, D. (1939). Further changes in the Beckland avifauna caused by afforestation. *J. Anim. Ecol.*, **8**, 277–285.

Lack, D. (1971). *Ecological Isolation in Birds*. Oxford: Blackwell Scientific Publications.

Laiolo, P. and Tella, J. L. (2008). Social determinants of songbird vocal activity and implications for the persistence of small populations. *Anim. Conserv.*, **11**, 433–441.

Luck, G. W. (2002). The habitat requirements of the rufous treecreeper (*Climacteris rufa*). 1. Preferential habitat use demonstrated at multiple spatial scales *Biol. Conserv.*, **105**, 383–394.

Lynch, J. F., Morton, E. S. and Van der Voort, M. E. (1985). Habitat segregation between the sexes of wintering Hooded Warblers (*Wilsonia citrina*). *Auk*, **102**, 714–721.

Manning, A. D., Lindenmayer, D. B. and Nix, H. A. (2004). Continua and Umwelt: novel perspectives on viewing landscapes. *Oikos*, **104**, 621–628.

Marquiss, M. and Newton, I. (1981). A radio-tracking study of the ranging behaviour and dispersion of European sparrowhawks *Accipiter nisus*. *J. Anim. Ecol.*, **51**, 111–133.

Marshall, M. R. and Cooper, R. J. (2004). Territory size of a migratory songbird in response to caterpillar density and foliage structure. *Ecology*, **82**, 432–445.

Martin, J-L. and Thibault, J. C. (1996). Coexistence in Mediterranean warblers: ecological differences or interspecific territoriality? *J. Biogeogr.*, **23**, 169–178.

Martin, T. E. (1988a). Habitat and area effects on forest bird assemblages: is nest predation an influence? *Ecology*, **69**, 74–84.

Martin, T. E. (1988b). Processes organizing open-nesting bird assemblages: competition or nest predation? *Evol. Ecol.*, **2**, 37–50.

Martin, T. E. (1992). Breeding productivity considerations: what are the appropriate habitat features for management? In *Ecology and Conservation of Neotropical Migrant Landbirds*, ed. J. M. Hagan and D. W. Johnston, pp. 455–473. Washington: Smithsonian Institution Press.

Martin, T. E. (1998). Are microhabitat preferences of coexisting species under selection and adaptive? *Ecology*, **79**, 656–670.

Marzluff, J. M., Withey, J. C., Whittaker, K. A. *et al.* (2007). Consequences of habitat utilization by nest predators and breeding songbirds across multiple scales in an urbanizing landscape. *Condor*, **109**, 516–534.

Mateo-Tomás, P. and Olea, P. P. (2009). Combining scales in habitat models to improve conservation planning in an endangered vulture. *Acta Oecol.*, **35**, 489–498.

Mayr, E. (1942). *Systematics and the Origin of Species*. New York: Columbia University Press.

McCaffery, B. J. (1998). Implications of freqent habitat switches in foraging bar-tailed godwits. *Auk*, **115**, 494–497.

Mendes, L., Piersma, T., Lecoq, M., Spaans, B. and Ricklefs, R. E. (2005). Disease-limited distributions? Contrasts in the prevalence of avian malaria in shorebird species using marine and freshwater habitats. *Oikos*, **109**, 396–404.

Mills, A. M. (2005). Can breeding habitat be sexually selected? *Auk*, **122**, 689–700.

Mitrus, C. and Soćko, B. (2008). Breeding success and nest-site characteristics of red-breasted flycatchers *Ficedula parva* in a primeval forest. *Bird Study*, **55**, 203–208.

Mönkkönen, M. and Helle, P. (1987). Avian reproductive output in European forest successions. *Oikos*, **50**, 239–246.

Mönkkönen, M. and Helle, P. (1989). Migratory habits of birds breeding in different stages of forest succession: a comparison between the Palaearctic and the Nearctic. *Ann. Zool. Fenn.*, **26**, 323–330.

Mönkkönen, M., Helle, P. and Soppela, K. (1990). Numerical and behavioural responses of migrant passerines to experimental manipulation of resident tits (*Parus* spp.): heterospecific attraction in northern breeding bird communites? *Oecologia*, **85**, 218–225.

Mönkkönen, M., Helle, P. and Welsh, D. (1992). Perspectives in Palaearctic and Nearctic bird migration; comparisons and overview of life-history and ecology of migrant passerines. *Ibis*, **134** (suppl. 1), 7–13.

Moreau, R. E. (1972). *The Palaearctic-African Bird Migration Systems*. London: Academic Press.

Morse, D. H. (1980). *Behavioral Mechanisms in Ecology* (Chapter 4). Cambridge, Mass.: Harvard University Press.

Morse, D. H. (1985). Habitat selection in North American Parulid warblers. In *Habitat Selection in Birds*, ed. M. L. Cody, pp. 131–157. London: Academic Press.

Moskát, C., Báldi, A. and Waliczky, Z. (1993). Habitat selection of breeding and migrating icterine warblers *Hippolais icterina*: a multivariate study. *Ecography*, **16**, 137–142.

Mueller, T., Selva, N., Pugacewicz, E. and Prins, E. (2009). Scale-sensitive landscape complementation determines habitat suitability for a territorial generalist. *Ecography*, **32**, 345–353.

Muller, K. L., Stamps, J. A., Krishnan, V. V. and Willits, N. H. (1997). The effects of conspecific attraction and habitat quality on habitat selection in territorial birds (*Troglodytes aedon*). *Am. Nat.*, **150**, 650–661.

Newton, I. (1991). Habitat variation and population regulation in sparrowhawks. *Ibis*, **133** (suppl.), 76–88.

Newton, I. (1998). *Population Limitation in Birds*. London: Academic Press.

Newton, I. (2003). *The Speciation and Biogeography of Birds*. London: Academic Press.

Nocera, J. J. and Forbes, G. J. (2010). Incorporating social information to improve the precision of models of avian habitat use. *Condor*, **112**, 235–244.

Nystrand, M., Griesser, M., Eggers, S. and Ekman, J. (2010). Habitat-specific demography and source-sink dynamics in a population of Siberian jays. *J. Anim. Ecol.*, **79**, 266–274.

Orians, G. H. and Wittenberger, J. F. (1991). Spatial and temporal scales in habitat selection. *Am. Nat.*, **137** (suppl.), S29–S49.

Palmgren, P. (1930). Quantitative Untersuchungen über die Vogelfauna in den Wäldern Südfinnlands. *Acta Zool. Fenn.*, **7**, 1–218.

Paradis, E., Baillie, S. R., Sutherland, W. J. and Gregory, R. D. (1998). Patterns of natal and breeding dispersal in birds. *J. Anim. Ecol.*, **67**, 518–536.

Parejo, D., Danchin, E. and Aviles, J. M. (2005). The heterospecific habitat copying hypothesis: can competitors indicate habitat quality? *Behav. Ecol.*, **16**, 96–105.

Parejo, D., White, J., Clobert, J., Dreiss, A. and Danchin, E. (2007). Blue tits use fledgling quantity and quality as public information in breeding site choice. *Ecology*, **88**, 2373–2382.

Parrish, J. D. and Sherry, T. W. (1994). Sexual habitat segregation by American redstarts wintering in Jamaica: importance of resource seasonality. *Auk*, **111**, 38–49.

Partridge, L. (1978). Habitat selection. In *Behavioural Ecology: An Evolutionary Approach*, ed. J. R. Krebs, and N. B. Davies, pp. 351–376. Oxford: Blackwell Scientific Publications.

Patten, M. A. and Kelly, J. F. (2010). Habitat selection and the perceptual trap. *Ecol. Appl.*, **20**, 2148–2156.

Pearson, D. J. and Lack, P. C. (1992). Migration patterns and habitat use by passerine and near-passerine migrant birds in eastern Africa. *Ibis*, **134** (suppl.1), 89–98.

Pérez-Tris, J. and Tellería, J. L. (2002). Migratory and sedentary blackcaps in sympatric non-breeding grounds: implications for the evolution of avian migration. *J. Anim. Ecol.*, **71**, 211–224.

Petit, D. R. (1989). Weather-dependent use of habitat patches by wintering woodland birds. *J. Field Ornithol.*, **60**, 241–247.

Piersma, T. (1997). Do global patterns of habitat use and migration strategies co-evolve with relative investments on immunocompetence due to spatial variation in parasite pressure? *Oikos*, **80**, 623–631.

Piersma, T. (2003). 'Coastal' versus 'inland' shorebird species; interlinked fundamental dichotomies between their life- and demographic histories? *Wader Study Group Bull.*, **100**, 5–9.

Pöysä, H. (2001). Dynamics of habitat distribution in breeding mallards: assessing the applicability of current habitat selection models. *Oikos*, **94**, 365–373.

Rappole, J. H. (1995). *The Ecology of Migrant Birds: a Neotropical Perspective*. Washington: Smithsonian Institution Press.

Ratcliffe, D. A. ed. (1977). *A Nature Conservation Review* (two volumes). Cambridge: Cambridge University Press.

Redmond, L. J., Murphy, M. T., Dolan, A. C. and Sexton, K. (2009). Public information facilitates habitat selection of a territorial species: the eastern kingbird. *Anim. Behav.*, **77**, 457–463.

Reijnen, R. and Foppen, R. (1994). The effects of car traffic on breeding bird populations in woodland. I. Evidence of reduced habitat quality for willow warblers (*Phylloscopus trochilus*) breeding close to a highway. *J. Appl. Ecol.*, **31**, 85–94.

Rice, J., Anderson, B. W. and Ohmart, R. D. (1980). Seasonal habitat selection by birds in the lower Colorado River Valley. *Ecology*, **61**, 1402–1411.

Robertson, B. A. and Hutto, R. L. (2006). A framework for understanding ecological traps and an evaluation of existing evidence. *Ecology*, **87**, 1075–1085.

Rodwell, J. S. (1991). *British Plant Communities Volume 1 – Woodlands and scrub*. Cambridge: Cambridge University Press.

Rolstad, J., Loken, B. and Rolstad, E. (2000). Habitat selection as a hierarchical spatial process: the green woodpecker at the northern edge of its distribution range. *Oecologia*, **124**, 116–129.

Rosenzweig, M. L. (1991). Habitat selection and population interactions: the search for mechanism. *Am. Nat.*, **137** (suppl.), S5–S28.

Saab, V. (1999). Importance of spatial scale to habitat use by breeding birds in riparian forests: a hierarchical analysis. *Ecol. Appl.*, **9**, 135–151.

Salewski, V. and Jones, P. (2006). Palearctic passerines in Afrotropical environments: a review. *J. Ornithol.*, **147**, 192–201.

Schlaepfer, M. A., Runge, M. C. and Sherman, P. W. (2002). Ecological and evolutionary traps. *Trends Ecol. Evol.*, **17**, 474–480.

Schlossberg, S. (2009). Site fidelity of shrubland and forest birds. *Condor*, **111**, 238–246.

Seppänen, J.-T., Forsman, J. T., Mönkkönen, M. and Thomson, R. L. (2007). Social information use is a process across time, space, and ecology, reaching heterospecifics. *Ecology*, **88**, 1622–1633.

Shustack, D. P. and Rodewald, A. D. (2010). A method for detecting undervalued resources with application to breeding birds. *Ecol. Appl.*, **20**, 2047–2057.

Snow, D. W. (1954). The habitats of Eurasian tits (Parus spp.). *Ibis*, **96**, 565–585.

Southwood, T. R. E., May, R. M., Hassell, M. P. and Conway, G. R. (1974). Ecological strategies and population parameters. *Am. Nat.*, **108**, 791–804.

Stamps, J. A. (1988). Conspecific attraction and aggregation in territorial species. *Am. Nat.*, **131**, 329–347.

Stamps, J. and Krishnan, V. V. (2005). Nonintuitive cue use in habitat selection. *Ecology*, **86**, 2860–2867.

Steele, B. B. (1992). Habitat selection by breeding Black-throated Blue Warblers at two spatial scales. *Ornis Scand.*, **23**, 33–42.

Steele, B. B. (1993). Selection of foraging and nesting sites by Black-Throated Blue Warblers: their relative influence on habitat choice. *Condor*, **95**, 568–579.

Suhonen, J. (1993). Predation risk influences the use of foraging sites by tits. *Ecology*, **74**, 1197–1203.

Sunde, P. and Redpath, S. M. (2006). Combining information from range use and habitat selection: sex-specific spatial responses to habitat fragmentation in tawny owls *Strix aluco*. *Ecography*, **29**, 152–158.

Svärdson, G. (1949). Competition and habitat selection in birds. *Oikos*, **1**, 157–174.

Thorpe, W. H. (1945). The evolutionary significance of habitat selection. *J. Anim. Ecol.*, **14**, 67–70.

Tomiałojć, L. (1993). Breeding ecology of the Blackbird *Turdus merula* studied in the primaeval forest of Bialowieza (Poland). Part 1. Breeding numbers, distribution and nest sites. *Acta Ornithol.*, **27**, 131–157.

Vaughan, I. P. and Ormerod, S. J. (2003). Improving the quality of distribution models for conservation by addressing shortcomings in the field collection of training data *Conserv. Biol.*, **17**, 1601–1611.

Veen, T., Sheldon, B. C., Weissing, F. J. *et al.* (2010). Temporal differences in food abundance promote coexistence between two congeneric passerines. *Oecologia*, **162**, 873–884.

Von Uexküll, J. (1926). *Theoretical Biology*. London: K. Paul, Trench, Trubner and Co.

Wagner, R. H. and Danchin, E. (2003). Conspecific copying: a general mechanism of social aggregation. *Anim. Behav.*, **65**, 405–408.

Walsberg, G. E. (1985). Physiological consequences of microhabitat selection. In *Habitat Selection in Birds*, ed. M. L. Cody, pp. 389–413. London: Academic Press.

Weakland, C. A. and Bohall Wood, P. B. (2005). Cerulean Warbler (*Dendroica cerulea*) microhabitat and landscape-level habitat characteristics in southern West Virginia. *Auk*, **122**, 497–508.

Webb, E. B., Smith, L. M., Vrtiska, M. P. and Lagrange, T. G. (2010). Effects of local and landscape variables on wetland bird habitat use during migration through the Rainwater Basin. *J. Wildlife Manage.*, **74**, 109–119.

Wesołowski, T. (2002). Anti-predator adaptations in nesting Marsh Tits *Parus palustris*: the role of nest-site security. *Ibis*, **144**, 593–601.

Wesołowski, T., Czeszczewik, D., Rowinski, P. and Walankiewicz, W. (2002). Nest soaking in natural holes – a serious cause of breeding failure? *Ornis Fennica*, **79**, 132–138.

Wesołowski, T. and Rowiński, P. (2004). Breeding behaviour of nuthatch *Sitta europaea* in relation to natural hole attributes in a primeval forest. *Bird Study*, **51**, 143–155.

Whitaker, D. M. and Warkentin, I. G. (2010). Spatial ecology of migratory passerines on temperate and boreal forest breeding grounds. *Auk*, **127**, 471–484.

Wiens, J. A. (1989a). *The Ecology of Bird Communities* (two volumes). Cambridge: Cambridge University Press.

Wiens, J. A. (1989b). Spatial scaling in ecology. *Funct. Ecol.*, **3**, 385–397.

Winkler, H. and Leisler, B. (1985). Morphological aspects of habitat selection in birds. In *Habitat Selection in Birds* ed. M. L. Cody, pp. 415–434. London: Academic Press.

Zimmerman, G. S., Gutiérrez, R. J., Thogmorton, W. E. and Banerjee, S. (2009). Multiscale habitat selection by ruffed grouse at low population densities. *Condor*, **111**, 294–304.

CHAPTER TWO

Habitat quality and habitat occupancy by birds in variable environments

ROBERT J. FULLER
British Trust for Ornithology

It is unwise to be dogmatic about the habitat associations of any bird species. Even the classification of species as habitat generalists or specialists requires careful consideration. Perceptions of specialisation depend on how niche breadth is measured and on locational, spatial and temporal context (Devictor *et al.*, 2010; Barnagaud *et al.*, 2011). Close examination of most species reveals variation across individuals in their occupancy and use of habitats. This chapter focuses on the diverse processes affecting habitat choices made by individual birds that determine which patches and habitat types are actually occupied at any particular place and time. Ecologists have given much attention to concepts of habitat quality – these are fundamental to any discussion about the processes of habitat choice. Many of the mechanisms discussed here were initially proposed many years ago (see Hildén, 1965) but, for brevity, I generally cite the recent evidence.

The broad limits of what constitutes potential habitat are set by a combination of the individual's functional needs and the mechanisms by which it recognises its habitat (Chapter 1). In reality most species, most of the time, do not occupy all potentially suitable habitat. Moreover, for various reasons, individuals may occupy, even select, poor-quality habitats. Habitat occupancy can, very broadly, be thought of as the outcome of an interaction between: (i) habitat quality, (ii) constraints that preclude settlement in part of the potential habitat spectrum, (iii) other factors that may stimulate settlement in certain parts of the potential habitat spectrum and (iv) phenotypic flexibility. This balance of diverse factors determines the observed distribution of birds across habitats. Habitat quality forms a logical starting point.

Habitat quality: fundamental but hard to measure

Habitat loss and deterioration is probably the most important cause of species declines worldwide. Consequently, distinguishing good and poor habitats for declining and scarce species is an abiding interest of conservation scientists. By identifying the essential ingredients of high-quality

Birds and Habitat: Relationships in Changing Landscapes, ed. Robert J. Fuller. Published by Cambridge University Press. © Cambridge University Press 2012.

Box 2.1 Potential surrogate measures for assessing habitat quality
See review by Johnson (2007) for examples and a discussion of limitations
of some of these approaches.

1. **Density:** Widely used and appears to correlate with reproductive
    output in a high proportion of cases (Bock and Jones, 2004) but
    there are many reasons why birds may occupy, or even apparently
    prefer, low-quality habitats, so density can be misleading.
2. **Frequency of occupancy:** Used especially at the patch or territory
    scale; the assumption is that the number of years a territory is occu-
    pied is correlated with its quality. This approach is useful in species
    where not all territories are occupied each year or where nests are
    difficult to find (see review in Sergio and Newton (2003), also Mermod
    et al., (2009)).
3. **Timing of territory or habitat occupancy:** It is normally assumed
    that the order of settlement correlates with quality, with the best
    territories occupied first. In the non-breeding season, the timing of
    arrival or departure of migrants from different habitats may indicate
    quality (e.g. Marra *et al.*, 1998).
4. **Population stability:** Expected to be greatest in optimal habitats
    (Wiens, 1989).
5. **Population age structure:** In species where adults are dominant
    over young birds, for example ones reared in the previous year, adult:
    young ratios are expected to be lower in poor-quality habitats. Note
    that the opposite is expected in the case of adult:juvenile ratios in the
    immediate post-breeding period.
6. **Territory size:** Often inversely related to food supply (Newton, 1998)
    and has been used as a measure of habitat quality (e.g. Brown *et al.*,
    2002).
7. **Pairing success:** May be greater in relatively high-quality habitat
    (Probst and Hayes, 1987; Bayne and Hobson, 2001).
8. **Polygyny:** May be more likely on higher-quality territories (Verner
    and Willson, 1966).
9. **Clutch size:** May be smaller on poor-quality territories or habitats
    (Dhondt *et al.*, 1992).
10. **Intake rate:** Higher intake rates are often assumed to indicate better-
    quality feeding habitat (e.g. Gill *et al.*, 2001).
11. **Body condition of individual birds:** A range of morphological or
    physiological attributes has been suggested, but these measures can
    be difficult to interpret in terms of habitat quality.

habitat, it is assumed that a positive contribution can be made to species conservation through the development of better habitat management plans. There are many successful examples, but the challenges of defining and measuring habitat quality are considerable. High-quality, or rich, habitats are conventionally regarded as ones where individual fitness or performance (reproductive output or survival) are highest. Direct measurement of fitness can be difficult to achieve. Consequently, indirect, or surrogate, measures are widely used (Box 2.1).

For any species, environments vary spatially in quality across gradients consisting of rich habitats at one extreme, through poor habitats, to non-habitat at the other extreme. The availability of limiting resources underlies this continuum. Hence, a habitat quality continuum can be envisaged such that temporal deterioration, or spatial variation, in habitat quality becomes equivalent at some point to habitat loss because it provides insufficient resources (Fig. 2.1). Resource availability is determined by a combination of quality and quantity of resources. For instance, very small patches of otherwise high-quality habitat may essentially be non-habitat because they do not meet minimum resource requirements. In practice, there may be trade-offs between the quality and quantity of resources available across different habitat types with potential consequences for habitat quality. This

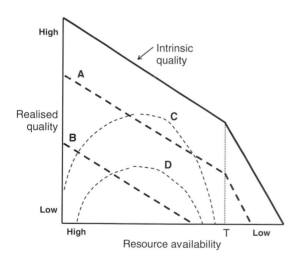

Figure 2.1 A conceptual model of a habitat quality–resource availability continuum that could apply in both spatial and temporal contexts. With declining availability of critical limiting resources, intrinsic habitat quality steadily declines until some threshold point (T) beyond which it rapidly collapses. Realised habitat quality under the same resource conditions can potentially take many different forms, depending on the constraints introduced by predators, competitors etc. Four hypothetical cases are shown. In A and B, realised habitat quality is progressively reduced by a constant amount across the resource availability gradient. In C and D, realised habitat quality peaks at some intermediate level of intrinsic quality. Resource availability will be determined by a combination of abundance and quality of resources.

possibility was explored by Johnson (2007), who defined habitat quality in terms of the per capita contribution that a habitat makes to population growth. Johnson showed that a habitat containing relatively few, but high-quality, resources (habitat A) may support a higher intrinsic rate of population growth, but have a lower long-term carrying capacity, than a habitat offering a relatively high abundance of lower-quality resources (habitat B). In evolutionary terms, the appropriate perspective on habitat quality is at the level of the individual, as animals will have evolved the capacity to assess the quality of different habitat patches and types. So from the perspective of the individual, habitat A would be the highest quality, at least for strongly competitive individuals. From a conservation perspective it is more appropriate to ask which habitat can support the largest population, which would lead to the conclusion that habitat B was of higher quality. Clearly, better still for conservation, would be a habitat that had both high quality and high quantity of resources.

The *intrinsic* or *fundamental quality* of a habitat is essentially influenced by the abundance and quality of resources that it offers individuals. The habitat quality actually experienced by individuals, *realised habitat quality*, is mainly a result of interactions with other organisms, including conspecifics. Across the gradient of resource availability it is theoretically possible for realised habitat quality to have many different types of relationship with intrinsic quality (Fig. 2.1). Under ideal free distributions (Chapter 1), individuals distribute themselves across habitats differing in intrinsic quality in such a way that they experience the same realised habitat quality. This comes about where habitat quality shows a density-dependent decline in fitness. When individuals vary in competitive ability, a despotic distribution may be evident, where dominant individuals command resources in the highest-quality habitat. Less competitive individuals experience lower fitness in poorer-quality habitat so that realised habitat quality varies across individuals. An implication of despotic models is that density does not necessarily reflect habitat quality.

Density and habitat quality

Most assessments of habitat quality relate to the breeding season and commonly rely on density. Density is probably a reasonable indicator of habitat quality in many instances. This was the conclusion of Bock and Jones (2004) who analysed 109 North American and European studies providing data on density and reproductive success of birds. In 72% of the studies, density was positively associated with per capita reproductive output, rising to 85% when the comparison was based on reproductive output per unit area of land. Consistent with the notion of ecological traps (Chapter 1), there was some evidence that density–reproduction relationships were more likely to be negative in areas subject to human disturbance. Two important points need to be made about this meta-analysis. First, by no means all the studies examined revealed higher reproductive success in higher-density areas. Second, there were insufficient studies to draw any conclusions about density–survival relationships.

A convincing demonstration that density can indicate breeding habitat quality was a study of ovenbirds *Seiurus aurocapilla* in New Brunswick forests by Pérot and Villard (2009). Across 23 plots, each of 25 hectares, breeding density was strongly positively correlated with the number of young fledged, but not with the proportion of territories producing at least one fledged young. Density was also found to be an effective measure of habitat quality for American redstarts *Setophaga ruticilla* wintering in Jamaica (Johnson *et al.*, 2006). Studies of several species in Białowieża Forest, Poland, also show that habitats occupied at highest density tend to produce more young per pair than low-density habitats (T. Wesołowski, pers. comm.).

Even though density often does reflect habitat quality, there are situations where it does not, and where habitat selection appears 'maladaptive or non-ideal' (Chapter 1). One of the earliest papers to question the density–quality assumption was by Van Horne (1983) who predicted that decoupling of density and quality was most likely under two types of environmental conditions. First, in highly seasonal environments where populations are limited by overwinter survival, winter densities, but not summer densities may reflect habitat quality. Second, in unpredictable and patchy environments, *r*-selected species may show large temporal variation in density within low-quality habitats as a result of their capacity for rapidly colonising such habitats from nearby population sources when conditions are favourable. A further mechanism was suggested by Zanette (2001), whereby numbers of breeding territories may be enhanced in isolated patches of poor-quality habitat as a result of impeded emigration. Local extinction risk for such populations would be high, so one might expect this phenomenon to be most characteristic of recently fragmented landscapes (see also Chapter 4). There may be many reasons, discussed below, as to why a species might be inhibited in its use of good habitat.

Two contrasting examples of mismatches between density and habitat quality are as follows. Vickery *et al.* (1992) compared the breeding success of three emberizine sparrows in high-, medium- and low-density patches in Maine grassland. Only one species achieved highest reproductive success in high-density patches. One species actually showed lowest success in the highest-density patches. The second example concerns breeding shelduck *Tadorna tadorna* in eastern Scotland (Pienkowski and Evans, 1982). The birds bred either in aggregations centred on small estuaries (high density) or were more dispersed, generally along open coasts (low density). Numbers of young produced per adult were consistently higher in low-density than high-density areas. This was a consequence of far higher predation of ducklings by gulls, which took advantage of fighting between adult shelducks when in close proximity. It was argued that this difference in breeding output was unlikely to be offset by higher post-fledging or adult survival. Predation pressure, apparently mediated by the birds' behaviour when occurring at high density, caused a reduction in the fitness value of the habitat.

Measuring habitat quality: beyond breeding density

It is often argued that breeding habitats are especially important because many species depend on particular features for nest sites and chick-rearing, though one suspects that the relative ease of counting and observing many species at this period is relevant. A reproduction-centred outlook also risks overlooking key influences of habitat quality that operate at other seasons. Habitat quality may be critical to individual survival during particular stages and conditions (Van Horne, 1983; Evans, 2004). These include: (i) moult periods when birds may be especially vulnerable to predators, (ii) at migration stopover sites when birds need to build energy reserves rapidly, (iii) in periods of severe weather, (iv) at the end of winter when food supplies have become depleted and (v) in the pre-breeding period when females are establishing reserves for egg formation.

Many birds are moulting and some are undergoing physiological change in advance of migration in the period immediately following breeding. Habitat use at this time can differ from breeding habitat use and be critical for juvenile and adult survival. For this reason, increasing attention is being given to post-breeding habitat use, mainly in North American songbirds, with the aim of developing more effective habitat management plans (e.g. Anders et al., 1998; Vega-Rivera et al., 1999; Rush and Stutchbury, 2008; Akresh et al., 2009; Whittaker and Marzluff, 2009).

An example of the importance of overwinter survival comes from Britain, where winter habitat quality is recognised as a major limiting factor for populations of several resident farmland bird species that declined in the 1970s and 1980s. Demographic analyses demonstrated that changes in survival were more frequently associated with declines of these species than changes in success of individual breeding attempts (Siriwardena et al., 1998, 2000). Reduction of winter food supplies has occurred as a result of more efficient crop harvesting, increasing homogenisation of crops, herbicide use and shifts in the timing of cultivation. Food availability appears to be especially limited at the end of the winter (Siriwardena et al., 2008).

Survival is not the only mechanism by which non-breeding habitat quality can affect population processes. For migrant birds, effects of habitat quality may 'carry-over' from one season to another (Norris, 2005; Norris and Marra,

2007; Harrison *et al.*, 2011). The condition of birds in the breeding season may be influenced by events in the previous season, including the quality of occupied habitats. One of the most striking findings is that overwinter habitat quality can be linked with individual fitness in the breeding season. The evidence comes from work on American redstarts (Marra *et al.*, 1998; Norris *et al.*, 2004). Birds wintering in high-quality moist forest habitats maintain or increase body mass over winter, unlike birds using lower-quality dry scrub habitats which tend to lose body mass. This does not appear to affect survival, but causes delayed departure of birds using the poor habitats. Females that overwinter in poor habitats, and that arrive late on the breeding grounds, produce fewer fledged young.

Appropriate scales for measuring habitat quality

The literature is replete with papers reporting on habitat quality in birds. In his review of habitat quality measurements, Johnson (2007) identified 173 empirical studies undertaken between 1984 and 2005. Features associated with good-quality habitat in birds are, of course, enormously varied, even within species occupying similar macrohabitats. Habitat quality can potentially be measured on different scales ranging from the habitat patch and territory, through macrohabitat or broad habitat type, up to the landscape level. In practice, habitat quality is most meaningful when it relates to the spatial scale on which the individual bird obtains its critical resources.

Wide-ranging species are frequently responsive to large-scale habitat mosaics because they may obtain different resources from different parts of the landscape (Chapter 1). The juxtaposition of different landscape elements is an important attribute of high-quality landscapes for some corvids and birds of prey. This is illustrated by Korpimäki's work (1988) on Tengmalm's owl *Aegolius funereus* in Finland. This forest species feeds on small mammals, mainly voles, and to a lesser extent on small birds. Pine forest is poorer-quality habitat than spruce because it carries lower and less-stable densities of small mammals, lower densities of small birds and possibly offers less-safe nest sites. Most interestingly, however, the highest-quality territories contain not just spruce but also agricultural land where, unlike the forest, *Microtus* voles are available, sometimes at high abundance. In years of high vole abundance, farmland offers especially rich feeding, but in poor vole years the birds are still able to exploit alternative prey (*Clethrionomys* voles, shrews and birds) in spruce forest. Habitat quality for this owl is thus related to both spatial and temporal variation in prey availability and individual owls show tenacity to the best territories over several consecutive years.

Assessment of habitat quality across broad habitat types such as 'woodland', 'farmland' and 'urban' may give insights into population processes in the most generalist species. An example is that of the carrion crow *Corvus corone* in Switzerland, where Richner (1989) demonstrated that farmland was a better-quality environment than urban areas. Growth of chicks was faster in farmland habitats and pairs reared more chicks there. Furthermore, Richner estimated that, based on relationships between body size and social dominance, 79% of chicks reared in urban areas would subsequently be excluded from obtaining breeding territories compared with just 24% of chicks fledged in farmland.

For territorial species with small home ranges, the most informative approaches tend to examine habitat quality in terms of microhabitat variation at the patch scale. Availability of safe and suitable nest sites (Martin, 1998), foraging sites (Walter and Gosler, 2001) and roost sites (Bijleveld *et al.*, 2010) will most likely determine habitat quality. In grassland habitats, the height, density and structural heterogeneity of vegetation affect both nest site availability and foraging efficiency (Chapters 7 and 11). Some insectivorous forest birds show innate preferences for foraging microhabitats in terms of the microstructure of bark and foliage offered by different tree species (Partridge, 1974; Parrish, 1995a, b; Whelan, 2001). Small-scale variations in food availability, for example in terms of caterpillar abundance on individual trees, may have consequences for patch quality and the performance of individual birds both within and between territories (Seki and Takano, 1998; Naef-Daenzer, 2000).

Requirements for specific foraging and nesting sites, coupled with food abundance, probably underpin the associations that many insectivorous birds show with particular types of forest stands. For instance, areas of high shrub density in New Hampshire forests constitute the highest-quality breeding habitat for black-throated blue warblers *Dendroica caerulescens* (Holmes *et al.*, 1996). Areas of high shrub density support large proportions of older birds and are characterised by a greater frequency of double broods, leading to higher reproductive output than in areas with few shrubs. A dense shrub layer appeared to result in good habitat for this species mainly by increasing food availability, which allowed more double broods. Other studies have emphasised the importance of particular tree species for habitat quality in small insectivores (Matthysen, 1990; Lambrechts *et al.*, 2004) and other species (Korpimäki, 1988; Ekman *et al.*, 2001).

Whilst patch level attributes will generally determine intrinsic habitat quality for birds with small territories or home ranges, landscape context may modify patch quality. Rodewald and Shustack (2008) found that breeding habitat quality for Acadian flycatchers *Empidonax virescens* using forest in Ohio was influenced by the proximity of urban development. Although annual survival of birds and nest survival were not affected by urbanisation, overall productivity was lower, nest initiation was later and turnover in territory occupancy was higher in urban landscapes.

Concluding thoughts about measuring habitat quality

Ideally, habitat quality should be measured through the demographic metrics of reproduction and year-round survival, combined with an appreciation of any consequences for fitness in other seasons. Knowledge of emigration and immigration can give additional insights by indicating whether habitats act as population sources and sinks. Of course, such comprehensive understanding is exceptionally rare and will only be achieved for a tiny proportion of species. Inevitably, incomplete information or surrogate measures of habitat quality will have to be relied on as a basis for conservation management of most populations (Box 2.1). There is considerable justification for using density as a short cut to assess habitat quality, but wherever possible it is advisable to test relationships between density and breeding productivity. Alternatively, adopting an independent surrogate measure alongside density would increase confidence that habitats of highest quality were being correctly identified (e.g. Brown *et al.*, 2002).

Habitat occupancy: the outcome of multiple selection processes

Birds sometimes avoid patches of apparently high-quality habitat and even select habitat of low intrinsic quality. As mentioned earlier, habitat occupancy – defined as the relative occurrence in a defined habitat type or patch – is the product of many different factors acting to constrain or stimulate the use of different parts of the potential habitat spectrum. The rest of this chapter outlines the diverse processes that may be involved in modifying habitat choices by birds in different places and at different times. To some extent these can be thought of as potential constraints that determine differences between intrinsic and realised habitat quality. This, however, risks too narrow an outlook, as realised habitat quality is often taken to reflect fitness constraints from competitors and predators. In reality, habitat occupancy can be the product of interactions between a much wider range of behavioural and ecological processes involved in habitat selection (Fig. 2.2). Here I emphasise processes mainly at patch scales (i.e. within the same habitat type in the same region); for a discussion of regional-scale variation in habitat occupancy and its causes see Chapter 3.

This account does not cover an exhaustive list of possibilities. For example, one habitat patch may be less suitable than a similar patch simply because it is more exposed to, or more resilient to, disturbance or pollution (Gill, 1996; Thiel *et al.*, 2008, 2011). Phenotypic variation expressed as local adaptation to environmental conditions (Blondel *et al.*, 1999) or individual specialisation or preference in habitat use (Stamps, 2001; Bolnick *et al.*, 2003) can also contribute to variation in habitat occupancy. There may even be apparent stochasticity in the settlement of individuals within apparently suitable habitat, although this is most likely at fine scales of habitat (Haila *et al.*, 1996; Campbell *et al.*, 2010).

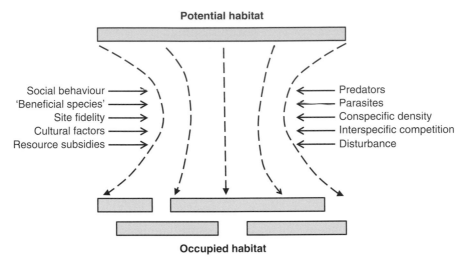

Figure 2.2 Processes acting to limit the distribution of individuals within certain parts of the potential habitat spectrum (wide bar at the top). Variation in factors operating at particular locations or times may constrain individuals to particular parts of the habitat spectrum, with the result that not all potential habitat is actually occupied (represented by shorter bars at the bottom). For a more complete list of the processes involved see text. Wiens (1989) shows a similar conceptual model. Note that some factors may, under some circumstances, cause expansion of occupancy beyond the previously known limits of the potential habitat spectrum (see Chapter 3). This can be true of cultural factors and conspecific density.

It is important to stress two things about the mechanisms outlined below. First they represent something of a continuum of overlapping and interacting processes relating to behavioural variation in individuals and the behavioural and ecological traits of species. Second, many of these processes can influence distribution across habitats in ways that have little to do with the underlying habitat quality in terms of resource availability. Ornithologists are frequently puzzled as to why a species does not occur in apparently suitable habitat – the possible reasons are numerous.

Interactions with other species
Heterospecific attraction
Patch choice by some birds may be positively influenced by the presence of other species in several ways. One species may use the presence of another species with similar ecological needs as a cue in recognition of breeding sites. It may be more beneficial for late-arriving species to use established species as a short cut to habitat, rather than directly sampling the habitat. Experimental work on northern territorial forest birds, involving manipulation of densities of breeding residents, demonstrates that migrant species do show such

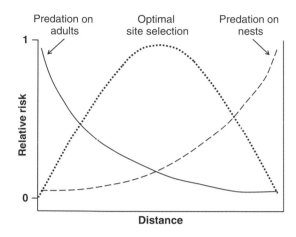

Figure 2.3 Relative risk for pied flycatchers *Ficedula hypoleuca* nesting at different distances from sparrowhawk *Accipiter nisus* nests. Selection of intermediate distances from hawk nests may represent a trade-off between the risk of adults being predated close to hawk nests and some level of protection conferred by hawks against nest predators such as woodpeckers and squirrels. From Thomson *et al.* (2006). Note that similar effects have been observed for goshawks *Accipiter gentilis* and their prey (Mönkkönen *et al.*, 2007).

responses (Mönkkönen and Forsman, 2002; Thomson *et al.*, 2003; Forsman *et al.*, 2009). Similar mechanisms may also occur in selection of feeding sites. For example, golden plovers *Pluvialis apricaria* and gulls in winter may use flocks of feeding lapwings *Vanellus vanellus* as markers of rich feeding areas (Barnard and Thompson, 1985).

The other main heterospecific attraction process is the behaviour of nesting in close association with other species that apparently offer protection from predators or some other benefit. Many such associations are the result of choice rather than merely similar patterns of habitat use (see review by Quinn and Ueta (2008), also Fig. 2.3). Especially in the tropics it has long been known that some nesting birds associate with aggressive social insects – most typically wasps, bees or ants (e.g. Myers, 1935; Hindwood, 1955). There are many examples of birds positioning their nests close to predatory birds or other birds that actively attack predators. Apparent 'beneficiaries of protection' include various ducks, geese, grebes, shorebirds and passerines. Amongst the species that offer such 'protection' are birds of prey (Quinn and Ueta, 2008) and species that show strong anti-predator defence, including terns and gulls (Koskimies, 1957), lapwings *Vanellus vanellus* and black-tailed godwits *Limosa limosa* (Dyrcz *et al.*, 1981; Eriksson and Götmark, 1982) and fieldfares *Turdus pilaris* (Slagsvold, 1980). Information transfer between species may underpin spatial structure in many mixed-species groups (Goodale *et al.*, 2010).

Avoiding predators and parasites
Risk of predation widely affects the selection of habitat patches by birds (Cresswell, 2008). This can occur in the absence of mortality from predation, with consequences for population dynamics that may be just as severe as

those of direct predation (Creel and Christianson, 2008). Alongside resource availability, predation risk is arguably the main factor determining how animals use space (Willems and Hill, 2009). The examples given in Box 2.2 illustrate diverse circumstances under which the avoidance of predation can influence how birds use space. Similar effects may occur with nest parasites (Forsman and Martin, 2009).

Box 2.2 Diverse examples of how avoidance of predation risk can affect occupancy of habitat patches and microhabitat use by birds

Nesting farmland birds in Finland (Suhonen *et al.*, 1994)
Kestrels *Falco tinnunculus* predate small birds such as skylark *Alauda arvensis* on open farmland. The distribution of kestrels was manipulated using nest-boxes. The abundance of small birds (but not of larger birds) was lower near kestrel nests and on plots with nesting kestrels.

Nesting meadow birds in the Netherlands (Van der Vliet *et al.*, 2008)
Nesting distributions of four wader species and two songbird species were examined in relation to nest sites of three predators – buzzard *Buteo buteo*, magpie *Pica pica* and crow *Corvus corone*. Densities were lower close to predator nests. Open landscapes appeared to enhance detection of predators.

Nesting pied flycatchers in Finland (Thomson *et al.*, 2006, 2010; Morosinotto *et al.*, 2010)
Nest-boxes positioned at different distances from sparrowhawk *Accipiter nisus* nests revealed complex responses of flycatchers to predator proximity (Fig. 2.3). Physiological measures of stress in flycatchers were higher close to hawk nests. Flycatchers also avoided pygmy owl *Glaucidium passerinum*, but not Tengmalm's owl *Aegolius funereus* – the former is a higher threat.

Nesting wood warblers in Poland (Wesołowski *et al.*, 2009)
Over a 30 year period, numbers of wood warbler *Phylloscopus sibilatrix* territories in sample plots of Białowieża Forest were inversely correlated with small mammal densities, but showed no relationship with spring temperature and were only weakly correlated with caterpillar abundance. Warbler numbers crashed to their lowest in rodent outbreak years. Wood warblers are nomadic, which may result from their ability to assess predation risk before settling. Predation risk probably arises directly from rodents and from predators attracted by high rodent numbers.

Nesting red-backed shrikes in Sweden (Roos and Pärt, 2004)
Distribution of shrike *Lanius collurio* nests was affected by the distribution of crow and magpie nests, both being nest predators of the shrikes. Occupancy of shrike territories increased with increasing distance to magpie nests.

Box 2.2 (cont.)

Changes in nest locations of both corvids resulted in changes in shrike nest location between years, consistent with the avoidance of corvids.

Intertidal habitat use by shorebirds in Alaska (Piersma *et al.*, 2006)

In autumn, several species used feeding and roosting sites close to shore during the day, but not at night, when they used offshore intertidal flats. This pattern of habitat use appeared to be linked with the nocturnal foraging of short-eared owls *Asio flammeus* close to the beach.

Foraging sites used by tits in Finland (Suhonen, 1993)

Willow tit *Poecile montanus* and crested tit *Lophophanes cristatus* are eaten by pygmy owls, especially in years when voles are scarce. When voles were unavailable, the tits shifted their foraging to the inner parts of conifer trees, and willow tit made greater use of the upper parts of trees. These changes in foraging sites were considered to be a response to elevated predation risk.

Foraging bullfinches in Scotland (Marquiss, 2007)

Bullfinches *Pyrrhula pyrrhula* in summer and autumn fed on a range of plant foods, all obtained close to or within scrub and woodland. As seed supplies became depleted, the birds increasingly depended on heather *Calluna vulgaris* seeds on moorland edges. This necessitated feeding in open habitats making them vulnerable to sparrowhawk predation. When feeding far from cover they formed large groups, probably an anti-predator tactic. Distribution across habitats was affected by an interaction between food, cover and predation risk.

Interspecific territoriality and competition

Some species may exclude others from some areas of otherwise suitable habitat. Explanations for this behaviour, which usually occurs between certain pairs of morphologically and ecologically similar species, have been much debated (Orians and Willson, 1964; Murray, 1971). Old world warblers provide several examples: *Sylvia* (Garcia, 1983), *Acrocephalus* (Catchpole, 1978) and *Phylloscopus* (Bourski and Forstmeier, 2000). There can be striking local variation in interspecific territoriality, as reported by Reed (1982), who studied chaffinch *Fringilla coelebs* and great tit *Parus major* on an island and the adjacent mainland in western Scotland. Territories of these two species overlapped on the mainland, but were mutually exclusive on the island, which may have been related to competition for food in the relatively poor island environment. An especially striking example of aggressive interspecific competition concerns *Manorina* honeyeaters in Australian woodland, which have a very strong negative effect on populations of small woodland passerines (Maron *et al.*, 2011; Chapter 18).

Competition between similar species may cause habitat shifts at different scales. Choice of fine-scale foraging niches by European tits is strongly influenced by exactly which combinations of species are present (Alatalo, 1982; Chapter 1). At the territory scale, breeding habitat use by American redstarts in north-west USA can be restricted by least flycatchers *Empidonax minimus*, which are dominant over redstarts (Sherry and Holmes, 1988). Adult redstarts avoid areas of forest occupied by flycatchers but will colonise such areas when flycatchers decline or are removed. In this study, the presence of flycatchers appeared to limit adult redstart distribution more than habitat attributes. Madsen (1985) suggested that autumn habitat use by feeding greylag geese *Anser anser* in Denmark is restricted by competition with pink-footed geese *Anser brachyrhynchus*. In early autumn, before arrival of the pinkfeet, greylags selected both stubbles and undersown stubbles. After the more numerous pinkfeet arrived, the greylags avoided the undersown stubbles and selected stubbles, whereas the pinkfeet used both habitats. When feeding in the same area, they tended to use different fields.

Mechanisms producing aggregations

Bird species demonstrate many different types of spatial pattern ranging from tight coloniality, where only the immediate vicinity of the nest is defended, as in many breeding seabirds, to highly dispersed territories, as in many raptors and owls. Between these extremes a few species live in extremely dense concentrations of territories (Fig. 2.4), whereas others exhibit looser aggregations of territories with areas of apparently suitable habitat left unoccupied. Close examination sometimes reveals that such clustering of territories is in fact a response to subtle variation in habitat (Dias *et al.*, 2009). However, aggregations of various kinds can occur in the absence of any clear variation in habitat, for reasons outlined below. The focus here is not on colonies, but on less pronounced forms of aggregation; for reviews of underlying behavioural processes see Danchin and Wagner (1997) and Danchin *et al.* (2008).

Conspecific attraction and habitat copying in patchy environments
The presence of conspecifics can be an important cue in habitat recognition and potentially leads to individuals accumulating in some patches of suitable habitat, but not others (Chapter 1). This may occur where it is difficult for individuals to sample the quality of habitat directly, or possibly where suitable habitat is somewhat ephemeral or patchy in distribution. Such attraction may allow exchange of information about patch quality, in both foraging and breeding contexts.

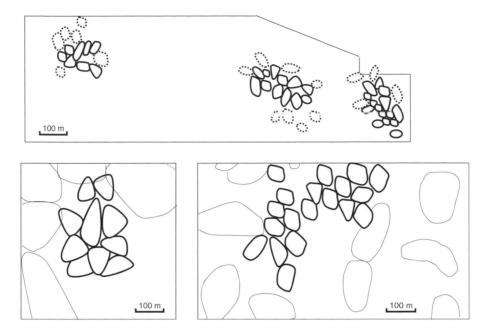

Figure 2.4 Territory aggregation in two forest songbirds. Upper – least flycatcher *Empidonax minimus* in New Hampshire (after Sherry and Holmes, 1985; broken lines indicate imprecisely mapped territories). Lower left and right – yellow-browed warbler *Phylloscopus inornatus* in Siberian taiga and floodplain habitat respectively (after Bourski and Forstmeier, 2000). The fine lines in the lower figures also show non-aggregated territories of *P. proregulus* (left) and *P. collybita* (right).

Hidden leks

The 'hidden lek' hypothesis offers a potential explanation for territory aggregations in socially monogamous species (Wagner, 1997). With the discovery that extra-pair copulation (EPC) is common in many species where one male pairs with one female, it was recognised that sexual selection could act to generate clusters of territories in these species. Hidden leks may occur in any species where females are receptive to EPC though there are several models of how hidden leks might operate (Fletcher and Miller, 2006). EPCs have a role in the evolution of coloniality (Danchin and Wagner, 1997) but the hidden lek idea extends this idea to aggregations of conventionally territorial species.

Predation-related aggregations

It is well known that benefits from coloniality can include reduced predation, but could this be the case for other aggregations? This appears to be so for the least flycatcher, which exhibits remarkable clustering of territories (Fig. 2.4). Working in Minnesota, Perry *et al.* (2008), found that within clusters, nests in territories at the edge had higher predation rates and lower success than interior nests. In another example, predation on lapwing *Vanellus vanellus* nests in loose colonies was found to be lower than on isolated nests (Berg, 1996). This was probably due to more effective nest defence in colonies, but it is possible that aggregation was a consequence of choosing safe nest sites.

Allee effects

Social species may have a threshold of abundance below which populations cease to be viable for a variety of behavioural reasons. This is a form of inverse density dependence in which individuals gain some benefit above a critical level of numbers. Møller and Danchin (2008) give three examples of mechanisms that could generate an Allee effect where at low population density: (i) predation may be higher, (ii) individuals may have difficulty finding a mate, (iii) foraging efficiency may be reduced where individuals depend on public information for locating good feeding sites.

Resource subsidies

Within homogeneous habitat there may be spatial variations in resources, especially invertebrate abundance, that do not reflect variations in habitat structure or habitat type. In particular, emergent aquatic invertebrates may provide an additional food resource for terrestrial insectivorous birds. The shores of Lake Huron, Michigan, provide rich feeding areas for migrant birds in spring (Smith *et al.*, 2007). The abundance of emergent aquatic chironomid midges is relatively high close to the shore, as is the abundance of spiders for which midges are prey. Consequently, migrant American redstarts and black-throated green warblers *Dendroica virens* are more abundant close to the shore (< 0.4 km) than in similar habitats further away. In riparian Japanese forest, flycatchers and foliage gleaners, but not bark probers, concentrated their foraging close to streams and were more numerous in areas with many stream meanders (Iwata *et al.*, 2003). Emergent insects declined with distance from the stream and were especially abundant in meander areas (Fig. 2.5). Further evidence of the dependence of insectivorous birds on Japanese forest streams was given by Iwata *et al.* (2010). One of the most striking examples of a resource subsidy is that derived from the nutrient influx from the death of Pacific salmon on their freshwater spawning sites (Christie and Reimchen, 2008). Salmon-derived nutrients enhance plant productivity and insect biomass with the consequence that forests adjacent to these areas carry higher densities of several songbirds than forests not adjacent to spawning areas.

Interactions between behavioural and population processes

Behavioural processes involved in habitat selection are closely linked with the dynamics and spatial structuring of populations. Some of these processes promote aggregation (see above), but other aspects of behaviour also lead to spatial variation in habitat occupancy.

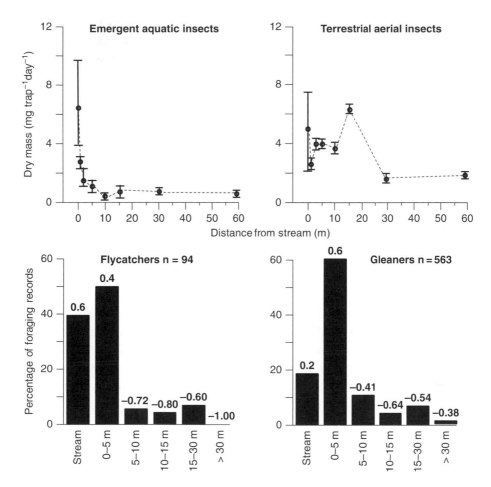

Figure 2.5 An example of a resource subsidy affecting fine-scale distribution of foraging insectivorous birds in spring within otherwise similar habitat in Japanese forest. The upper graphs show change in insect abundance with distance from streams. Emergent aquatic insects are totally confined to the immediate vicinity of streams (top left), unlike flying terrestrial insects (top right), though the latter are still at their most abundant within 25 m of the stream. Foraging flycatchers and foliage gleaning songbirds show strong selection for habitat within 5 m of the streams due to the food subsidy provided by aquatic insects – numbers above the bars show Jacobs preference indices at different distances from the streams. Redrawn from Iwata *et al.* (2003).

Intraspecific competition and habitat saturation

Spatial and temporal differences in habitat occupancy can arise through competition for space and resources arising from variation in population size. As outlined in Chapter 1, this can occur either through individuals being forced to occupy suboptimal habitats (despotic distributions) or choosing to do so (ideal free types). Broadly one would expect intraspecific competition to result in a wider range of habitat types being occupied when population density is high than when it is low (Svärdson, 1949). Patches of suitable habitat may, therefore, not be fully saturated.

Site fidelity and dispersal limitation

Many species will shift breeding location between successive years either based on conspecific information about patch quality, gathered through prospecting behaviour in the previous year, or based on decisions made at the start of the breeding season (Doligez *et al.*, 2004; Arlt and Pärt, 2008). There is clearly a balance of costs and benefits to shifting territory (Boulinier *et al.*, 2008) and species differ in their propensity to move. Many animals, especially males, show strong fidelity to sites, even when higher-quality patches are available and accessible presumably because there are long-term benefits from familiarity with the site (references in Piper *et al.*, 2008). Site fidelity can potentially result in a species continuing to occupy a deteriorating habitat patch or habitat type and therefore is one of the mechanisms that can cause the occupancy of low-quality habitat (Hildén, 1965; Wiens *et al.*, 1986; see also the example of *Larus canus* in Chapter 3). Site fidelity may differ between populations of the same species living in different landscape types. Individuals in isolated habitat patches may be less likely to show breeding dispersal than ones living in landscapes with greater availability of breeding habitat (Tryjanowski *et al.*, 2007; see also Zanette, 2001).

Previous experience versus flexibility in habitat choice

Previous experience of a particular habitat may influence subsequent habitat choice. Hildén (1965) discussed the possibility of young birds becoming imprinted onto a particular habitat. Stamps (2001) introduced the idea of 'habitat training', whereby experience of a particular habitat type confers some fitness advantage to using that habitat in future. Individuals are therefore expected to disperse into the same habitat type. Habitat choice of ortolan buntings *Emberiza hortulana* breeding on peat bogs or forest clear-cuts in Norway was studied by Dale and Christiansen (2010). They found little evidence that habitat choice following natal or breeding dispersal was affected by earlier habitat experience. The great majority of males (86%) changed habitats at least once during their lifetimes. Habitat choice appeared to be a random process for most males. Whilst these findings should obviously not be extrapolated to other species, they indicate that some species can show flexibility in habitat use.

Cultural factors

Learned behaviours can be transmitted across generations with evolutionary consequences. In their review of cultural evolution, Danchin and Wagner (2008) do not explicitly discuss how this might affect variation in habitat use. But there would seem to be no reason why species should not learn how to exploit new habitats or resources and pass this knowledge to subsequent generations through social interaction (see also Chapter 3). This could lead to spatial variation in habitat usage and to possible population increase and range expansion. For example, in the late twentieth century, wintering pink-footed geese in England started to feed on the remains of sugar beet crops. This appears to be a learned behaviour that enabled the birds to exploit a new agricultural habitat and to establish large numbers in Norfolk in the 1980s where much of the English sugar beet is grown (Gill *et al.*, 1997). Other examples are given in Chapter 3.

Functional and non-linear responses to habitat availability
Theoretically, a species can vary strikingly in its occupancy rate of identical habitat patches in different landscape contexts. Where a species obtains resources, such as food and shelter, from more than one habitat, the relative availability of the different habitat components within the landscape can influence the behaviour of individuals and the relative use made of each habitat (Mysterud and Ims, 1998). This may occur where, for example, the resource provided by one of the habitats is limiting and individuals adjust their habitat selection to ensure that a minimum quantity of that habitat is included within their home range or territory. As far as I am aware, such functional responses in habitat use have not been clearly demonstrated for birds, though they have for several mammals (references in Godvik *et al.*, 2009). Where one of the habitat components is missing, then use or occupancy of the other habitat(s) is expected to be zero.

Thresholds occur when there is some critical level of a resource within a patch, or of habitat extent within a landscape, below which individuals rapidly reduce their use or occupancy of patches or landscapes. Thresholds have been examined mainly at landscape scales in the context of habitat fragmentation. It is assumed that increasing loss of habitat will eventually reach a point at which disruption of the processes that underpin population persistence become so severe that occupancy of patches dramatically declines (Andrén, 1994; With and Crist, 1995). Empirical evidence for the existence of such thresholds in terrestrial birds is growing (Radford and Bennett, 2004; Betts *et al.*, 2007; Zuckerberg and Porter, 2010).

Conclusions

Habitat quality and habitat occupancy are complementary and related concepts, both of high relevance for species conservation. Identifying key habitats for conservation requires some assessment of habitat quality. But good habitats are not always occupied and conversely poor-quality habitats can sometimes be occupied. Understanding the processes that result in habitat occupancy is, therefore, an important part of developing conservation plans at the species level. Several points deserve particular emphasis:

1. Species respond to a complex of factors in selecting their habitat, making habitat occupancy difficult to predict. What constitutes acceptable habitat is strongly context dependent. Caution is needed in extrapolating from individual studies to other areas and time periods.
2. Species differ greatly in their habitat selection strategies and in the factors that influence occupancy. Studies of single species can give insights into the mechanisms involved, but extrapolating these to other species, even closely related ones, is risky.
3. Do not assume that all 'good' habitat is occupied – even the best habitat is not always saturated. To really understand why a bird occurs where it does, it is necessary to consider its 'total environment'. Sometimes it may be more informative to ask why it does not occur in certain places (Haila *et al.*, 1996).
4. Social information is a central factor in habitat selection. These behaviours probably produce aggregated distributions more often than is generally appreciated.
5. Modelling distributions in relation to human perceptions of habitat can sometimes work well, but frequently it does not. Inevitably our models miss many of the complexities involved in habitat selection, especially social factors and subtle variations in resource availability. Developing better understanding of the cues that birds use in assessing habitat quality could lead to better models.
6. Even low-quality habitat may be of value for supporting a reservoir of individuals, some of which may eventually colonise higher-quality patches.
7. The notion of habitat as a fixed species-specific trait does not withstand critical examination. Plasticity and flexibility are evident in the way that many species respond to and exploit their environments.

Acknowledgements

I am most grateful to Chris Hewson, Theunis Piersma, Gavin Siriwardena and Tomasz Wesołowski for their thoughtful comments.

References

Akresh, M. E., Dinse, K., Foufopoulos, J., Schubel, S. C. and Kowalczyk, T. (2009). Passerine breeding and post-fledgling habitat use in riparian and upland temperate forests of the American midwest. *Condor*, **111**, 756–762.

Alatalo, R. V. (1982). Evidence for interspecific competition among European tits *Parus* spp.: a review. *Ann. Zool. Fenn.*, **19**, 309–317.

Anders, A. D., Faaborg, J. and Thompson, F. R., III. (1998). Postfledging dispersal, habitat use, and home-range size of juvenile wood thrushes. *Auk*, **115**, 349–358.

Andrén, H. (1994). Effects of habitat fragmentation on birds and mammals in landscapes with different proportions of suitable habitat: a review. *Oikos*, **71**, 355–366.

Arlt, D. and Pärt, T. (2008). Post-breeding information gathering and breeding territory shifts in northern wheatears. *J. Anim. Ecol.*, **77**, 211–219.

Barnagaud, J. Y., Devictor, V., Jiguet, F. and Archaux, F. (2011). When species become generalists: on-going large-scale changes in bird habitat specialization. *Global Ecol. Biogeogr.*, **20**, 630–640.

Barnard, C. J. and Thompson, D. B. A. (1985). *Gulls and Plovers: The Ecology and Behaviour of Mixed-species Feeding Groups*. Beckenham: Croom Helm.

Bayne, E. M. and Hobson, K. A. (2001). Effects of habitat fragmentation on pairing success of ovenbirds: importance of male age and floater behaviour. *Auk*, **118**, 380–388.

Berg (1996). Predation on artificial, solitary and aggregated wader nests on farmland. *Oecologia*, **107**, 343–346.

Betts, M. G., Forbes, G. J. and Diamond, A. W. (2007). Thresholds in songbird occurrence in relation to landscape structure. *Conserv. Biol.*, **21**, 1046–1058.

Bijleveld, A. I., Egas, M., van Gils, J. A. and Piersma, T. (2010). Beyond the information centre hypothesis: communal roosting for information on food, predators, travel companions and mates? *Oikos*, **119**, 277–285.

Blondel, J., Dias, P. C., Perret, P., Maistre, M. and Lambrechts, M. M. (1999). Selection-based biodiversity at a small spatial scale in a low-dispersing insular bird. *Science*, **285**, 1399–1402.

Bock, C. E. and Jones, Z. F. (2004). Avian habitat evaluation: should counting birds count? *Front. Ecol. Environ.*, **2**, 403–410.

Bolnick, D. I., Svanbäck, R., Fordyce, J. A. *et al.* (2003). The ecology of individuals: incidence and implications of individual specialization. *Am. Nat.*, **161**, 1–28.

Boulinier, T., Mariette, M., Doligez, B. and Danchin, E. (2008). Choosing where to breed: breeding habitat choice. In *Behavioural Ecology*, ed. E. Danchin, L.-E. Giraldeau and F. Cézilly, pp. 285–320. Oxford: Oxford University Press.

Bourski, O. V. and Forstmeier, W. (2000). Does interspecific competition affect territorial distribution of birds? A long-term study on Siberian *Phylloscopus* warblers. *Oikos*, **88**, 341–350.

Brown, D. R., Strong, C. M. and Stouffer, P. C. (2002). Demographic effects of habitat selection by hermit thrushes wintering in a pine plantation landscape. *J. Wildlife Manage.*, **66**, 407–416.

Campbell, S. P., Witham, J. W. and Hunter, M. L. (2010). Stochasticity as an alternative to deterministic explanations for patterns of habitat use by birds. *Ecol. Monogr.*, **80**, 287–302.

Catchpole, C. K. (1978). Interspecific territorialism and competition in *Acrocephalus* warblers as revealed by playback experiments in areas of sympatry and allopatry. *Anim. Behav.*, **26**, 1072–1080.

Christie, K. S. and Reimchen, T. E. (2008). Presence of salmon increases passerine density on Pacific northwest streams. *Auk*, **125**, 51–59.

Creel, S. and Christianson, D. (2008). Relationships between direct predation and risk effects. *Trends Ecol. Evol.*, **23**, 194–201.

Cresswell, W. (2008). Non-lethal effects of predation in birds. *Ibis*, **150**, 3–17.

Dale, S. and Christiansen, P. (2010). Individual flexibility in habitat selection in the ortolan bunting *Emberiza hortulana*. *J. Avian Biol.*, **41**, 266–272.

Danchin, E., Giraldeau, L.-E. and Wagner, R. H. (2008). Animal aggregations: hypotheses and controversies. In *Behavioural Ecology*, ed. E. Danchin, L.-E. Giraldeau and F. Cézilly, pp. 503–545. Oxford: Oxford University Press.

Danchin, E. and Wagner, R. H. (1997). The evolution of coloniality: the emergence of new perspectives. *Trends Ecol. Evol.*, **12**, 342–347.

Danchin, E. and Wagner, R. H. (2008). Cultural evolution. In *Behavioural Ecology*, ed. E. Danchin, L.-E. Giraldeau and F. Cézilly, pp. 693–726. Oxford: Oxford University Press.

Devictor, V., Clavel, J., Julliard, R. *et al.* (2010). Defining and measuring ecological specialization. *J. Appl. Ecol.*, **47**, 15–25.

Dhondt, A. A., Kempenaers, B. and Adriaensen, F. (1992). Density-dependent clutch size caused by habitat heterogeneity. *J. Anim. Ecol.*, **61**, 643–648.

Dias, R. I., Kuhlmann, M., Lourenço, L. R. and Macedo, R. H. (2009). Territorial clustering in the blue-black grassquit: reproductive strategy in response to habitat and food requirements? *Condor*, **111**, 706–714.

Doligez, B., Pärt, T. and Danchin, E. (2004). Prospecting in the collared flycatcher: gathering public information for future breeding habitat selection? *Anim. Behav.*, **67**, 457–466.

Dyrcz, A., Witkowski, J. and Okulewicz, J. (1981). Nesting of 'timid' waders in the vicinity of 'bold' ones as an antipredator adaptation. *Ibis*, **123**, 542–545.

Ekman, J., Eggers, S., Griesser, M. and Tegelstrom, H. (2001). Queuing for preferred territories: delayed dispersal of Siberian Jays. *J. Anim. Ecol.*, **70**, 317–324.

Eriksson, M. O. G. and Götmark, F. (1982). Habitat selection: do passerines nest in association with Lapwings *Vanellus vanellus* as defence against predators? *Ornis Scand.*, **13**, 189–192.

Evans, K. L. (2004). The potential for interactions between predation and habitat change to cause population declines of farmland birds. *Ibis*, **146**, 1–13.

Fletcher, R. J. and Miller, C. W. (2006). On the evolution of hidden leks and the implications for reproductive and habitat selection behaviours. *Anim. Behav.*, **71**, 1247–1251.

Forsman, J. T., Hjernquist, M. B. and Gustafsson, L. (2009). Experimental evidence for the use of density based interspecific social information in forest birds. *Ecography*, **32**, 539–545.

Forsman, J. T. and Martin, T. E. (2009). Habitat selection for parasite-free space by hosts of parasitic cowbirds. *Oikos*, **118**, 464–470.

Garcia, E. F. J. (1983). An experimental test of competition for space between blackcaps *Sylvia atricapilla* and garden warblers *Sylvia borin* in the breeding season. *J. Anim. Ecol.*, **52**, 795–805.

Gill, J. A. (1996). Habitat choice in pink-footed geese: quantifying the constraints determining winter site use. *J. Appl. Ecol.*, **33**, 884–892.

Gill, J. A., Norris, K., Potts, P. M., *et al.* (2001). The buffer effect and large-scale population regulation in migratory birds. *Nature*, **412**, 436–438.

Gill, J. A., Watkinson, A. R. and Sutherland, W. J. (1997). Causes of the redistribution of pink-footed geese *Anser brachyrhynchus* in Britain. *Ibis*, **139**, 497–503.

Godvik, I. M. R., Loe, L. E., Vik, J. O. *et al.* (2009). Temporal scales, trade-offs, and functional responses in red deer habitat selection. *Ecology*, **90**, 699–710.

Goodale, E., Beauchamp, G., Magrath, R. D., Nieh, J. C. and Ruxton, G. D. (2010). Interspecific information transfer influences animal community structure. *Trends Ecol. Evol.*, **25**, 354–361.

Haila, Y., Nicholls, A. O., Hanski, I. K. and Raivio, S. (1996). Stochasticity in bird habitat selection: year-to-year changes in territory locations in a boreal forest bird assemblage. *Oikos*, **76**, 536–552.

Harrison, X. A., Blount, J. D., Inger, R., Norris, D. R. and Bearhop, S. (2011). Carry-over effects as drivers of fitness differences in animals. *J. Anim. Ecol.*, **80**, 4–18.

Hildén, O. (1965). Habitat selection in birds – a review. *Ann. Zool. Fenn.*, **2**, 53–75.

Hindwood, K. A. (1955). Bird / wasp nesting associations. *Emu*, **55**, 263–274.

Holmes, R. T., Marra, P. P. and Sherry, T. W. (1996). Habitat-specific demography of breeding black-throated blue warblers (*Dendroica caerulescens*): implications for population dynamics. *J. Anim. Ecol.*, **65**, 183–195.

Iwata, T., Nakano, S. and Murakami, M. (2003). Stream meanders increase insectivorous bird abundance in riparian deciduous forests. *Ecography*, **26**, 325–337.

Iwata, T., Urabe, J. and Mitsuhashi, H. (2010). Effects of drainage-basin geomorphology on insectivorous bird abundance in temperate forests. *Conserv. Biol.*, **24**, 1278–1289.

Johnson, M. D. (2007). Measuring habitat quality: a review. *Condor*, **109**, 489–504.

Johnson, M. D., Sherry, T. W., Holmes, R. T. and Marra, P. P. (2006). Assessing habitat quality for a migratory songbird wintering in natural and agricultural habitats. *Conserv. Biol.*, **20**, 1433–1444.

Korpimäki, E. (1988). Effects of territory quality on occupancy, breeding performance and breeding dispersal in Tengmalm's owl. *J. Anim. Ecol.*, **57**, 97–108.

Koskimies, J. (1957). Terns and gulls as features of habitat recognition for birds nesting in their colonies. *Ornis Fennica*, **34**, 1–6.

Lambrechts, M. M., Caro, S., Charmantier, A. *et al.* (2004). Habitat quality as a predictor of spatial variation in blue tit reproductive performance: a multi-plot analysis in a heterogeneous landscape. *Oecologia*, **141**, 555–561.

Madsen, J. (1985). Habitat selection of farmland feeding geese in West Jutland, Denmark: an example of a niche shift. *Ornis Scand.*, **16**, 140–144.

Maron, M., Main, A., Bowen, M. *et al.* (2011). Relative influence of habitat modification and interspecific competition on woodland bird assemblages in eastern Australia. *Emu*, **111**, 40–51.

Marquiss, M. (2007). Seasonal pattern in hawk predation on Common Bullfinches *Pyrrhula pyrrhula*: evidence of an interaction with habitat affecting food availability. *Bird Study*, **54**, 1–11.

Marra, P. P., Hobson, K. A. and Holmes, R. T. (1998). Linking winter and summer events in a migratory bird by using stable-carbon isotopes. *Science*, **282**, 1884–1886.

Martin, T. E. (1998). Are microhabitat preferences of coexisting species under selection and adaptive? *Ecology*, **79**, 656–670.

Matthysen, E. (1990). Behavioural and ecological correlates of territory quality in the Eurasian Nuthatch (*Sitta europaea*). *Auk*, **107**, 86–95.

Mermod, M., Reichlin, T. S., Arlettaz, R. and Schaub, M. (2009). The importance of ant-rich habitats for the persistence of the Wryneck *Jynx torquilla* on farmland. *Ibis*, **151**, 731–742.

Møller, A. P. and Danchin, E. (2008). Behavioural ecology and conservation. In *Behavioural Ecology*, ed. E. Danchin, L.-E. Giraldeau and F. Cézilly, pp. 647–664. Oxford: Oxford University Press.

Mönkkönen, M. and Forsman, J. T. (2002). Heterospecific attraction among forest birds: a review. *Ornithol. Science*, **1**, 41–51.

Mönkkönen, M., Husby, M., Tornberg, R., Helle, P. and Thomson, R. L. (2007). Predation as a landscape effect: the trading off by prey species between predation risks and protection benefits. *J. Anim. Ecol.*, **76**, 619–629.

Morosinotto, C., Thomson, R. L. and Korpimäki, E. (2010). Habitat selection as an antipredator behaviour in a multi-predator landscape: all enemies are not equal. *J. Anim. Ecol.*, **79**, 327–333.

Murray, B. G. (1971). The ecological consequences of interspecific territorial behavior in birds. *Ecology*, **52**, 414–423.

Myers, J. G. (1935). Nesting associations of birds with social insects. *T. Roy. Ent. Soc. Lond.*, **83**, 11–22.

Mysterud, A. and Ims, R. A. (1998). Functional responses in habitat use: availability influences relative use in trade-off situations. *Ecology*, **79**, 1435–1441.

Naef-Daenzer, B. (2000). Patch time allocation and patch sampling by foraging great and blue tits. *Anim. Behav.*, **59**, 989–999.

Newton, I. (1998). *Population Limitation in Birds.* London: Academic Press.

Norris, D. R. (2005). Carry-over effects and habitat quality in migratory populations. *Oikos*, **109**, 178–186.

Norris, D. R. and Marra, P. P. (2007). Seasonal interactions, habitat quality, and population dynamics in migratory birds. *Condor*, **109**, 535–547.

Norris, D. R., Marra, P. P., Kyser, T. K., Sherry, T. W. and Ratcliffe, L. M. (2004). Tropical winter habitat limits reproductive success on the temperate breeding grounds in a migratory bird. *Proc. R. Soc. B*, **271**, 59–64.

Orians, G. H. and Willson, M. F. (1964). Interspecific territories of birds. *Ecology*, **45**, 736–745.

Parrish, J. D. (1995a). Effects of needle architecture on warbler habitat selection in a coastal spruce forest. *Ecology*, **76**, 1813–1820.

Parrish, J. D. (1995b). Experimental evidence for intrinsic microhabitat preferences in the Black-throated Green Warbler. *Condor*, **97**, 935–943.

Partridge, L. (1974). Habitat selection in titmice. *Nature*, **247**, 573–574.

Pérot, A. and Villard, M.-A. (2009). Putting density back into the habitat-quality equation: case study of an open-nesting forest bird. *Conserv. Biol.*, **23**, 1550–1557.

Perry, E. F., Manolis, J. C. and Andersen, D. E. (2008). Reduced predation at interior nests in clustered all-purpose territories of least flycatchers *(Empidonax minimus)*. *Auk*, **125**, 643–650.

Pienkowski, M. W. and Evans, P. R. (1982). Breeding behaviour, productivity and survival of colonial and non-colonial Shelducks *Tadorna tadorna*. *Ornis Scand.*, **13**, 101–116.

Piersma, T., Gill, R. E., de Goeij, P. *et al.* (2006). Shorebird avoidance of nearshore feeding and roosting areas at night correlates with presence of a nocturnal avian predator. *Wader Study Group Bull.*, **109**, 73–76.

Piper, W. H., Walcott, C., Mager, J. N. and Spilker, F. J. (2008). Nestsite selection by male loons leads to sex-biased site familiarity. *J. Anim. Ecol.*, **77**, 205–210.

Probst, J. R. and Hayes, J. P. (1987). Pairing success of Kirtland's Warblers in marginal vs. suitable habitat. *Auk*, **104**, 234–241.

Quinn, J. L. and Ueta, M. (2008). Protective nesting associations in birds. *Ibis*, **150** (suppl.1), 146–167.

Radford, J. Q. and Bennett, A. F. (2004). Thresholds in landscape parameters: occurrence of the white-browed treecreeper *Climacteris affinis* in Victoria, Australia. *Biol. Conserv.*, **117**, 375–391.

Reed, T. M. (1982). Interspecific territoriality in the chaffinch and great tit on islands and the mainland of Scotland: playback and removal experiments. *Anim. Behav.*, **30**, 171–181.

Richner, H. (1989). Habitat-specific growth and fitness in Carrion Crows (*Corvus corone corone*). *J. Anim. Ecol.*, **58**, 427–440.

Rodewald, A. D. and Shustack, D. P. (2008). Urban flight: understanding individual and population-level responses of Nearctic-Neotropical migratory birds to urbanization. *J. Anim. Ecol.*, **77**, 83–91.

Roos, S. and Pärt, T. (2004). Nest predators affect spatial dynamics of breeding red-backed shrikes (*Lanius collurio*). *J. Anim. Ecol.*, **73**, 117–127.

Rush, S. A. and Stutchbury, B. J. M. (2008). Survival of fledgling hooded warblers (*Wilsonia citrina*) in small and large forest fragments. *Auk*, **125**, 183–191.

Seki, S. I. and Takano, H. (1998). Caterpillar abundance in the territory affects the breeding performance of great tit *Parus major minor*. *Oecologia*, **114**, 514–521.

Sergio, F. and Newton, I. (2003). Occupancy as a measure of habitat quality. *J. Anim. Ecol.*, **72**, 857–865.

Sherry, T. W. and Holmes, R. T. (1985). Dispersion patterns and habitat responses of birds in northern hardwoods forests. In *Habitat Selection in Birds*, ed. M. L. Cody, pp. 283–309. London: Academic Press.

Sherry, T. W. and Holmes, R. T. (1988). Habitat selection by breeding American redstarts in response to a dominant competitor, the least flycatcher. *Auk*, **105**, 350–364.

Siriwardena, G. M., Baillie, S. R., Crick, H. Q. P. and Wilson, J. D. (2000). The importance of variation in the breeding performance of seed-eating birds in determining their population trends on farmland. *J. Appl. Ecol.*, **37**, 128–148.

Siriwardena, G. M., Baillie, S. R. and Wilson, J. D. (1998). Variation in the survival rates of some British passerines with respect to their population trends on farmland. *Bird Study*, **45**, 276–292.

Siriwardena, G. M., Calbrade, N. A. and Vickery, J. A. (2008). Farmland birds and late winter food: does seed supply fail to meet demand? *Ibis*, **150**, 585–595.

Slagsvold, T. (1980). Habitat selection in birds: on the presence of other bird species with special regard to *Turdus pilaris*. *J. Anim. Ecol.*, **49**, 523–536.

Smith, R. J., Moore, F. R. and May, C. A. (2007). Stopover habitat along the shoreline of northern Lake Huron, Michigan: emergent aquatic insects as a food resource for spring migrating landbirds. *Auk*, **124**, 107–121.

Stamps, J. A. (2001). Habitat selection by dispersers: integrating proximate and ultimate approaches. In *Dispersal*, ed. J. Clobert, E. Danchin, A. A. Dhondt and J. D. Nichols, pp. 230–242. Oxford: Oxford University Press.

Suhonen, J. (1993). Predation risk influences the use of foraging sites by tits. *Ecology*, **74**, 1197–1203.

Suhonen, J., Norrdahl, K. and Korpimäki, E. (1994). Avian predation risk modifies breeding bird community on a farmland area. *Ecology*, **75**, 1626–1634.

Svärdson, G. (1949). Competition and habitat selection in birds. *Oikos*, **1**, 157–174.

Thiel, D., Jenni-Eiermann, S., Braunisch, V., Palme, R. and Jenni, L. (2008). Ski tourism affects habitat use and evokes a physiological stress response in capercaillie *Tetrao urogallus*: a new methodological approach. *J. Appl. Ecol.*, **45**, 845–853.

Thiel, D., Jenni-Eiermann, S., Palme, R. and Jenni, L. (2011). Winter tourism increases stress hormone levels in the capercaillie *Tetrao urogallus*. *Ibis*, **153**, 122–133.

Thomson, R. L., Forsman, J. T. and Mönkkönen, M. (2003). Positive interactions between migrant and resident birds: testing the heterospecific attraction hypothesis. *Oecologia*, **134**, 431–438.

Thomson, R. L., Forsman, J. T., Sardà-Palomera, F. and Mönkkönen, M. (2006). Fear factor: prey habitat selection and its consequences in a predation risk landscape. *Ecography*, **29**, 507–514.

Thomson, R. L., Tomás, G., Forsman, J. T., Broggi, J. and Mönkkönen, M. (2010). Predator proximity as a stressor in breeding flycatchers: mass loss, stress protein induction, and elevated provisioning. *Ecology*, **91**, 1832–1840.

Tryjanowski, P., Goławski, A., Kuźniak, S., Mokwa, T. and Antczak, M. (2007). Disperse or stay? Exceptionally high breeding-site infidelity in the Red-backed Shrike *Lanius collurio*. *Ardea*, **95**, 316–320.

van der Vliet, R. E., Schuller, E. and Wassen, M. J. (2008). Avian predators in a meadow landscape: consequences of their occurrence for breeding open-area birds. *J. Avian Biol.*, **39**, 523–529.

Van Horne, B. (1983). Density as a misleading indicator of habitat quality. *J. Wildlife Manage.*, **47**, 893–901.

Vega Rivera, J. H., McShea, W. J., Rappole, J. H. and Haas, C. A. (1999). Postbreeding movements and habitat use of adult wood thrushes in northern Virginia. *Auk*, **116**, 458–466.

Verner, J. and Willson, M. F. (1966). The influence of habitats on mating systems of North American passerine birds. *Ecology*, **47**, 143–147.

Vickery, P. D., Hunter, M. L. and Wells, J. V. (1992). Is density an indicator of breeding success? *Auk*, **109**, 706–710.

Wagner, R. H. (1997). Hidden leks: sexual selection and the clustering of avian territories. *Ornithol. Monogr.*, **49**, 123–145.

Walther, B. A. and Gosler, A. G. (2001). The effects of food availability and distance to protective cover on the winter foraging behaviour of tits (Aves:*Parus*). *Oecologia*, **129**, 312–320.

Wesołowski, T., Rowiński, P. and Maziarz, M. (2009). Wood Warbler *Phylloscopus sibilatrix*: a nomadic insectivore in search of safe breeding grounds? *Bird Study*, **56**, 26–33.

Whelan, C. J. (2001). Foliage structure influences foraging of insectivorous forest birds: an experimental study. *Ecology*, **82**, 219–231.

Wiens, J. A. (1989). *The Ecology of Bird Communities* (2 volumes). Cambridge: Cambridge University Press.

Whittaker, K. A. and Marzluff, J. M. (2009). Species-specific survival and relative habitat use in an urban landscape during the post-fledging period. *Auk*, **126**, 288–299.

Wiens, J. A., Rotenberry, J. T. and Van Horne, B. (1986). A lesson in the limitations of field experiments: shrubsteppe birds and habitat alteration. *Ecology*, **67**, 365–376.

Willems, E. P. and Hill, R. A. (2009). Predator-specific landscapes of fear and resource distribution: effects on spatial range use. *Ecology*, **90**, 546–555.

With, K. A. and Crist, T. O. (1995). Critical thresholds in species' responses to landscape structure. *Ecology*, **76**, 2446–2459.

Zanette, L. (2001). Indicators of habitat quality and the reproductive output of a forest songbird in small and large fragments. *J. Avian Biol.*, **32**, 38–46.

Zuckerberg, B. and Porter, W. F. (2010). Thresholds in the long-term responses of breeding birds to forest cover and fragmentation. *Biol. Conserv.*, **143**, 952–962.

CHAPTER THREE

Spatial variation and temporal shifts in habitat use by birds at the European scale

TOMASZ WESOŁOWSKI

Wrocław University

and

ROBERT J. FULLER

British Trust for Ornithology

Relationships between birds and habitat can be very tight. Without prior local knowledge, experienced birdwatchers often correctly predict occurrence of individual bird species in a given place, just on seeing the physiognomy of the landscape. The strong coupling of habitats and birds is widely used in different applications. These include mapping bird distribution in areas with no bird records using habitat features as proxies (Franco *et al.*, 2009), developing habitat management plans aimed at species conservation (e.g. Gilbert *et al.*, 2005; Wilson *et al.*, 2005), predicting future changes in distribution following climate change (von dem Bussche *et al.*, 2008), as well as in the reconstruction of prehistoric environmental conditions and ancient bird distributions (Tomek *et al.*, 2003; Yalden and Albarella, 2008). Bird–habitat relationships measured in one area, region or time period are frequently taken as representative for a given species, something of an invariable species-specific trait. Taking this for granted is rather puzzling, as we should rather expect the opposite to be true, namely that bird–habitat links have evolved, i.e. they changed through time and will continue to do so. Similarly, one might expect that, to adjust to contrasting conditions in different parts of their range, species would develop spatially varying habitat associations. This idea is not new (Svärdson, 1949; Mayr, 1963; Hildén, 1965), but until recently it has remained largely neglected. A growing number of quantitative studies, both in Europe and North America, indicate that spatial variation in avian habitat associations is widespread. However, with the exception of Fuller's (2002) preliminary analysis for forest birds, we are unaware of any recent overview of geographical variation in habitat use by birds at either the European or North American scales.

This chapter documents the extent of the phenomenon across Europe. We do not attempt a comprehensive review, but have selected examples that illustrate

Birds and Habitat: Relationships in Changing Landscapes, ed. Robert J. Fuller. Published by Cambridge University Press. © Cambridge University Press 2012.

its pervasive nature, drawing especially heavily on examples that contrast eastern and western Europe. For brevity, we refer often to the secondary sources. Therefore many references should be read as 'the paper and references therein'. We use 'habitat' in the broad sense (the environment of the individual bird, including all biotic and abiotic elements, Chapter 1). The focus is on the reproductive period; if not indicated otherwise, 'habitat' stands for the 'breeding season habitat'. Our emphasis is on spatial variation in habitat use, but many of the points made here apply equally to temporal variation, of which we provide examples. Clearly spatial and temporal variations are closely linked, especially where species expand the range of habitats used in particular parts of their range. Our main aims are to draw attention to a little-studied aspect of habitat occupancy, to discuss the scientific and conservation implications and to outline some underlying likely mechanisms. The evidence indicates that geographical variation in patterns of habitat occupancy is widespread and occurs across different scales of spatial resolution. These differences have to be accounted for in any attempt to extrapolate locally collected data on current bird–habitat relationships to situations far removed in space or time.

European examples of variation in habitat use

The examples that follow under six broad headings illustrate that regional differences in habitat use are common in Europe, that they are found in all taxonomic groups of birds from geese to small passerines, and in all major habitat types. They also show that habitat associations can sometimes change quite rapidly, challenging any assumptions of constancy of bird–habitat relationships within a region. The examples embrace a range of spatial scales, but we have tried to distinguish between variation in use of broad habitat types (macrohabitats) and use of particular structures within these habitats (microhabitats). Whilst the emphasis is on macrohabitat, spatial variation may also occur in use of nest sites. For instance, in the Białowieża Forest, eastern Poland, robin *Erithacus rubecula* and blackbird *Turdus merula* make more frequent use of holes for nesting than in forests further west (Tomiałojć *et al.*, 1984; Tomiałojć, 1993), while marsh tit *Poecile palustris* and nuthatch *Sitta europaea* use nest sites higher than those recorded in other areas (Wesołowski, 1996; Wesołowski and Rowiński, 2004). There may even be substantial variation in nest site distribution over small spatial scales, for example Wesołowski (1989) shows that sets of tree species used by hole-nesters, as well as heights of holes above the ground, differ among riverine and oak-hornbeam habitats in the Białowieża Forest.

Habitat shifts on islands relative to mainland

On islands birds often use habitats strikingly different from those used on the mainland. In mainland Sweden, blue tit *Cyanistes caeruleus* breeds only in

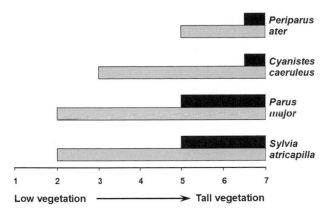

Figure 3.1 Habitat distribution of four forest bird species along a Mediterranean vegetation complexity gradient on the French mainland (Provence – dark) and in Corsica (light). Drawn from data in Blondel (1985). Stages are ordered along an increasing vegetation complexity gradient, from simplest (stage one, mean height 0.3 m, single layer), to most complex (stage seven, mean height 20–25 m, eight layers).

deciduous and coal tit *Periparus ater* in coniferous woods, whereas on the Baltic island of Gotland they abundantly use both types of forests (Svärdson, 1949). Wren *Troglodytes troglodytes*, a woodland bird across most of its range, inhabits completely treeless moorland habitats in Britain, Ireland and Iceland, as well as bare vertical cliffs at the sea coast (Armstrong, 1955; Wesołowski, 1983).

Studies in the Mediterranean provide quantitative data on habitat shifts between islands and the mainland. Birds restricted to high forest on the mainland (Provence) also use scrub habitats in Corsica (Fig. 3.1). Simultaneously, they breed in much higher densities there than on the mainland. Birds breeding in more open habitats (e.g. several *Sylvia* warblers) do not show similar habitat expansion and higher densities in Corsica (Blondel, 1985). These data illustrate a more general pattern: if there are differences in habitat occupancy by a species between mainland and island, the tendency is towards niche expansion on islands coupled with much higher densities there (e.g. Blondel, 1985; Prodon *et al.*, 2002).

Species restricted to mountains in part of their range

Differences in altitudinal distribution of species across Europe are frequent. Several species confined in Switzerland to mountains (Table 3.1) breed extensively elsewhere in lowland north and central Europe. To some extent this could be due to altitudinal shifts of vegetation belts with changing latitude. For example, spruce *Picea*-dominated coniferous forests covering lowlands in the boreal zone are found mostly at higher elevations in south Europe. Thus to occupy the same macrohabitat a species would have to breed at different altitudes in different parts of Europe. This may be the case for ptarmigan *Lagopus muta* and three-toed woodpecker *Picoides tridactylus* (Table 3.1). Similarly, middle spotted woodpecker *Dendrocopos medius* is a lowland bird in east and central Europe, but confined to mountain forests at 700–1700 m in Italy and Spain (Pasinelli, 2003). In other cases this situation does not apply.

Table 3.1 *Examples of variation in use of altitudinal ranges within Europe*

Species	Mountains	Lowlands
Mergus merganser	forested lakes and rivers in plateaux and foothills	N and C Europe: forested lakes and rivers
Aquila chrysaetos	semi-open habitats, mostly between 1500–3000 m asl	N Europe: tundra, bogs, boreal forest
Lagopus mutus	alpine tundra above timberline, 1900–2600 m asl	boreal: tundra, N Europe, N of 60°
Glaucidium passerinum	coniferous forest, 1000–2100 m asl	boreal: coniferous and mixed forests
Aegolius funereus	*Picea* dominated forest, 1200–1800 m asl	Boreal: coniferous forest with *Picea*
Picoides tridactylus	coniferous forest, 1200–1800 m asl	boreal: coniferous forest with *Picea*
Anthus pratensis	alpine meadows 800–1600 m asl	N and C Europe: range of damp open habitats, with short vegetation
Luscinia s. svecica	recently colonising above tree line, dwarf bushes, bogs, tundra like vegetation, 1500–2100 m asl	boreal: damp tundra with sparse bushes and trees
Oenanthe oenanthe	above tree line	N Europe: open heath and grasslands with some stones
Turdus torquatus	semi-open coniferous forests, 1000–2600 m asl	Britain: treeless moorland, also Scandinavia in *Picea* or *Betula* forests
Sylvia curruca	dwarf forest at timber line, 1200–2400 m asl	throughout most of Europe: open scrub, dispersed bushes
Nucifraga caryocatactes	mixed and coniferous forests, 1200–2400 m asl	Boreal: coniferous forest with *Coryllus avellana*
Pyrrhocorax pyrrhocorax	rocks, 1600–2800 m asl	Brittany to Scotland: coastal cliffs; Spain: pastoral, low intensity agriculture
Carduelis cabaret	light alpine coniferous forests, in 'Krummholz' zone, 1400–2100 m asl	Britain and Ireland: young coniferous woods and scrub; coastal dune scrub along North Sea and Baltic coasts

Mountains – species limited to high altitudes in Switzerland (Schmid *et al.*, 1998). Lowlands – based on Hagemeijer and Blair (1997).

Black redstart *Phoenicurus ochruros*, originally a montane species, spread to the lowlands and colonised urban habitats in Europe in the nineteenth century (Glutz von Blotzheim and Bauer, 1988; Tomiałojć and Stawarczyk, 2003). In Mediterranean areas, song thrush *Turdus philomelos* breeds only in the mountains, despite having no shortage of apparently suitable woods in the neighbouring lowlands (Tomiałojć, 1992).

Wetland birds

Wetland birds provide abundant examples of spatial variation in habitat and nest site use across Europe. They are limited to coastal areas in some parts of the continent, but can breed inland in other parts, nest exclusively on the ground in some areas, but use tree crowns in other regions (Table 3.2). The most versatile of European gulls, common gull *Larus canus*, can somewhere in Europe use all 'gull nesting habitats' except deserts. However, within smaller areas, they are more restricted, using locally only a few habitat types, such as rocky offshore islands in Estonia, dunes in the Netherlands, maritime meadows on White Sea islands, or islands in the Vistula River, Poland (Bukaciński and Bukacińska, 2003). In the latter area, as long as it is an island, common gulls occupy both sandbars and areas overgrown with low grass or sparse clumped vegetation, even *Salix* thickets. Occasionally they place nests on stumps of broken trees or even, more rarely, several meters above the ground on flat tree branches (Fig. 3.2). Apart from herring gull *Larus argentatus* (Table 3.2), several other species of gulls (Raven and Coulson, 1997; Bukaciński and Bukacińska, 2003) and terns (Fasola, *et al.*, 2002; Becker and Ludwigs, 2004) have colonised urban areas in disparate parts of Europe.

Macrohabitat associations of forest birds

There are good reasons to argue that the prehistoric western European lowland forests and their avifauna were similar to those persisting in a near-primeval condition in the Białowieża Forest (Wesołowski, 2007). Therefore bird–habitat relationships found in Białowieża may be treated as broadly ancestral for birds found nowadays in anthropogenic lowland landscapes. A comparison of birds' habitat associations in eastern Poland and England (Table 3.3) demonstrates an array of differences in habitat associations. These are close to the extremes of what is probably an east–west gradient in patterns of habitat association in European forest birds (Fuller *et al.*, 2007). Numerous species which in eastern Europe are confined to large forest tracts (e.g. woodpigeon *Columba palumbus*, dunnock *Prunella modularis*, song thrush and mistle thrush *Turdus viscivorus*), are widespread in anthropogenic habitats and landscapes of western Europe, including small woods, gardens and parks. Some of these species – wren, robin and blackbird – are actually regarded in Britain as the most widespread habitat generalists.

Table 3.2 *Examples of variation in habitat/nest site use by waterbirds, larids and shorebirds*

Species	Main/traditional places	Alternative/new places	Source
Egretta garzetta	Italy: nests in riverine woods, in trees	France: frequently nests in reed beds	Hafner *et al.* (2002)
Ardea cinerea	Europe: most frequently nests in canopy of riverine woods (Italy)	Poland, France: sometimes nests in reed beds; Scottish islands: on cliffs	Czapulak and Adamski, (2002); J. Blondel and I. Newton, pers comm.)
Anser brachyrhynchus	Iceland: inaccessible upland places	Iceland: sedge meadows at coast	Fox *et al.* (1997)
Anser anser	C Europe and Britain: mostly nests in reed beds, small islands, on the ground	W Poland: floodplains, nests in trees; Norway: often heather, *Betula* forest, even in *Picea* plantations	Nowysz and Wesołowski (1972); Kempe-Persson (2002)
Haematopus ostralegus	Europe incl. Britain: shore and estuaries	Britain: inland crops and pastures; Poland: river valleys, several hundred km from coast	Safriel (1985); Tomiałojć and Stawarczyk (2003)
Chroicocephalus ridibundus	Europe: along edges of shallow water bodies, on the ground, in emergent vegetation, also saltmarshes	W Poland: floodplains, nests in *Salix* bushes and rafts made of broken reed stems	Nowysz and Wesołowski (1972); Bukaciń-ski and Bukaciń-ska (1993)
Larus argentatus	Britain: coastal, rocky islands, shingle banks, sand dunes	Britain: urban breeding, roof tops	Monaghan (1980); Raven and Coulson (1997)
Sternula albifrons	W Europe: coastal beaches	C and E Europe: riverine sand bars and islets	Wesołowski *et al.* (1985), Fasola *et al.* (2002)

Striking contrasts are evident in the use of broadleaved and coniferous forest between lowland Britain and Białowieża (Fuller, 2002; Table 3.3). Several species strongly depend on conifers in the latter area (e.g. goldcrest *Regulus regulus*, coal tit, bullfinch *Pyrrhula pyrrhula*, redstart *Phoenicurus phoenicurus*), but use a wider range of woodland types in Britain, including purely

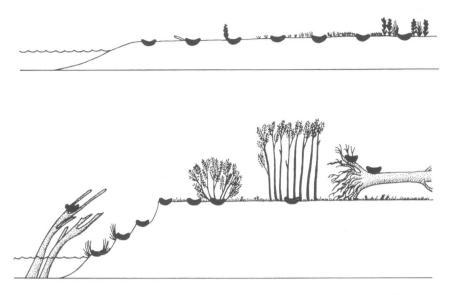

Figure 3.2 Types of nest sites used by common gull *Larus canus* on islands of the Vistula river (from Wesołowski *et al.*, 1985). Birds nest on the ground on bare sand/soil, amongst ruderal vegetation and bushes, and on dead trees. Some of these nest sites contrast strikingly with those used by the species in other parts of its range, for example in Scotland most birds nest on open moorland, in dune systems and on shingle shores.

deciduous. Some other species (e.g. wood warbler *Phylloscopus sibilatrix*, willow tit *Poecile montanus*, pied flycatcher *Ficedula hypoleuca*) in the east or north of Europe use both broadleaves and conifers, but are strongly dependent on broadleaves in the extreme west of their range. Cantabrian capercaillie *Tetrao urogallus* live in pure broadleaved forest, whereas across most of their range they are coniferous species (Blanco-Fontao *et al.*, 2010).

Nightingale *Luscinia megarhynchos* is largely confined to dense thickets in the north of its range, but in the south it uses a wider range of structures, including very sparse scrub (Fuller, 2002). White-backed woodpecker *Dendrocopos leucotos* occurs throughout its range in different types of deciduous forests containing large amounts of decaying wood, but in the coastal and middle fjordlands in western Norway it breeds also in pine forests (Haland and Ugelvik, 1990). Three-toed woodpecker depends on dying and dead *Picea* throughout its range, however in areas of north east Poland where dead wood is removed from managed conifer stands, it breeds in less intensively managed riverine and *Alnus* stands (Wesołowski *et al.*, 2005; Tumiel, 2008).

Several species that are typically confined to forest in some parts of their range, breed also in treeless or almost treeless areas in other parts of their range. These include some island populations of wren (see above),

Table 3.3 *Contrasts in breeding habitat associations and nest sites used by birds in a primeval forest, Białowieża National Park (E Poland) and in Britain*

Species	Białowieża Forest	Britain
Buteo buteo	inside extensive old-growth stands, forage under tree canopy, nests high in trees (Jędrzejewski *et al.*, 1994)	nests in mature woodlands, mainly forage outside woodland; in open country also nests on cliffs or isolated trees and bushes and in Outer Hebrides (no *Vulpes vulpes*) on ground (Newton, 1979)
Columba palumbus	as above, nests in trees above 10 m, forages in and under canopy, rarely in fields (Tomiałojć, 1982)	wide range of woodland and scrub, also outside woodland, in hedgerows and parkland; forages mostly outside woods, nests in bushes and trees, usually up to 10 m
Columba oenas	mostly in coniferous forest; forages under tree canopy, nests in tree-holes (mainly excavated by *Dryocopus martius*)	woodland and farmland with some trees, nests in tree holes, also in cliffs or rabbit holes; forages mainly outside woodland
Apus apus	nests in holes in emergent trees inside extensive old-growth stands	nests entirely in buildings in towns and villages, absent from woods, except in Speyside
Troglodytes troglodytes	mostly in riverine or other broadleaved forests, nests in root pads of fallen trees, fallen logs etc. (Wesołowski, 1983)	wide range of woodland, scrub, gardens, hedgerows, uses wide range of nest sites in dense vegetation and artefacts; occurs in treeless habitats in coastal areas and moorland
Prunella modularis	mostly riverine forests, sites with lush ground vegetation	scrub, young woodland, gardens, hedges etc., in mature woodland often confined to the edge
Erithacus rubecula	all old-growth forest types, nests on the ground, in root pads of uprooted trees, commonly in tree holes	all types of woodland, scrub, gardens, hedgerows, other places with bushes and trees, typically nests on or close to the ground
Phoenicurus phoenicurus	mature coniferous and some deciduous (with sparse understorey) stands	mature open woodland, upland *Betula* and *Quercus petraea*, wood-pasture and northern *Pinus sylvestris* woods, also

Table 3.3 (*cont.*)

Species	Białowieża Forest	Britain
		southern heaths with mature *Pinus*
Turdus merula	mostly deciduous (riverine and oak-hornbeam) old-growth forests, often in tree-holes and root pads of uprooted trees (Tomiałojć, 1993)	in all rural and urban habitats with trees or bushes, in many woods highest densities at the edge, nests usually in shrubs, below 4 m
Turdus philomelos	all types of old-growth forest, nests in tree crowns, half of them in *Picea abies* (Tomiałojć, 1992)	similar to *Turdus merula*
Turdus viscivorus	mature coniferous forest	wide range of woodland and lightly wooded country, feeding also on open land, avoids extensive forest
Regulus regulus	mature coniferous and broadleaved with admixture of *Picea abies*	highest densities in mature coniferous forest, but breeds also in pure broadleaved woods
Regulus ignicapillus	mostly mature riverine deciduous-coniferous forest	woods with mature conifers, rarely in broadleaved woods with *Ilex aquifolium*
Periparus ater	old-growth coniferous forest, temporary colonisation of *Quercus – Carpinus* habitats with admixture of *Picea*	coniferous woodland, common also in a wide range of pure broadleaved and mixed woods
Poecile palustris	broadleaved old-growth forest with sparse understorey	broadleaved woodland, avoids sites with very little understorey (Hinsley *et al.*, 2007)
Poecile montanus	mainly coniferous stands with admixture of *Betula*	broadleaved woodland and scrub with a preference for damp woodland
Pyrrhula pyrrhula	mature coniferous and broadleaved with admixture of spruce *Picea abies*	scrub, hedgerows and woodland; mainly in broadleaved woods, but also in thicket-stage conifers
Sturnus vulgaris	mature broadleaved stands along forest edge, in natural holes, forage in forest glades or in tree crowns	mostly human settlements, also woodland; feeds mainly on farmland

Table 3.3 (*cont.*)

Species	Białowieża Forest	Britain
Corvus corax	inside extensive old-growth stands, nests high in trees, forage mostly in forest (Rösner *et al.*, 2005)	moorland, bogs, coast, increasingly in wooded landscapes: nests either on tall trees or cliffs

If not shown otherwise, data from Białowieża extracted from Tomiałojć *et al.* (1984), Tomiałojć and Wesołowski (1990) and Wesołowski *et al.* (2003) and data for Britain extracted from Fuller (1995) and Robinson (2005).

town-breeding swift *Apus apus*, stock dove *Columba oenas* nesting in rabbit holes in Frisian Islands' dunes (Plaisier, 1992) or in cliff crevices in the Mediterranean (J. Blondel, pers comm.), osprey *Pandion haliaetus* breeding on electric pylons among fields in Germany (Meyburg *et al.*, 1996) or on cliffs and rock pinnacles in the Mediterranean (Terrasse and Terrasse, 1977), raven *Corvus corax* nesting on pylons in western Poland (Bednorz, 2000), saker falcon *Falco cherrug* using old corvid nests on pylons in Hungary (Baumgart and Haraszthy, 1997) or blue tit breeding at high densities under window sills of flats in downtown Warsaw (P. Rowiński, pers comm.).

Urban colonisation

Urban areas provide relatively recent habitats (many towns in central and eastern Europe are less than 1000 years old) so all bird species breeding in towns originally used other habitats. Some, like house sparrow *Passer domesticus* colonised human settlements so long ago, and with such success, that it is difficult to determine their ancestral habitats (Summers-Smith, 1988; Glutz von Blotzheim and Bauer, 1997). However, detailed documentation is available for a number of species that colonised towns recently.

Woodpigeon (review in Tomiałojć, 1976) first bred in Paris parks in the 1830s–1840s and shortly after (in the 1850s) in several towns in Germany and Poland. During 1870–1890 it colonised numerous towns in the north west and central European plains. Similarly, by the late 1800s it was nesting in London parks (Holloway, 1996). By the mid 1970s urban nesting birds were found widely within the north western part of the species range. As not every town had been colonised within this area, the distribution of urban birds is quite irregular (Tomiałojć, 1976). Urban nesting developed, apparently independently, also in Vienna and in Baghdad, Iraq. Blackbird began to colonise towns in Germany in the first half of the nineteenth century. By the beginning of the twentieth century, urban birds were found in numerous towns in western and central Europe, reaching western Poland. In Britain the spread into urban areas started in the mid nineteenth century (Holloway, 1996). By the mid 1980s urban birds occurred everywhere within the European subspecies range except the far north and east. The process of town colonisation was patchy; some towns within this area were long unoccupied. Independently, in the mid twentieth century *T. m. aterrimus* started colonising towns in Turkey, Georgia and Azerbaijan, and *T. m. intermedius* towns in Kazakhstan (Tomiałojć, 1985; Luniak *et al.*, 1990). This habitat expansion is likely to have been driven by independent colonisation events (Evans *et al.*, 2009). Goshawk *Accipiter gentilis* (Rutz *et al.*, 2006) already bred in Moscow at the end of the nineteenth century, but only colonised towns elsewhere (Germany, the Netherlands) since the 1980s (Table 3.4). Sparrowhawk *Accipiter nisus* colonised many towns in Britain during the 1980s (Newton, 1986) and in the Netherlands in the 1990s (Bijlsma *et al.*, 2001).

These cases share several features: (i) expansion occurred within the existing range; (ii) by colonising urban habitat, the species broadened its spectrum of utilised habitats; (iii) synurbisation occurred only in parts of the species range; (iv) urban populations have often arisen independently in disparate parts of the species range.

Temporal shifts in habitat use and habitat-specific density

Habitat associations are far from immutable and can change quickly. This phenomenon was described above for urban environments, but is far more widespread. Some of the habitat shifts summarised in Table 3.4 were accomplished in barely two generations. In other cases population establishment took longer, but still resulted in major habitat shifts, even in long-lived slowly reproducing species. The examples in Table 3.4 relate to habitat expansion, but abandonment can also occur, such as with hen harrier *Circus cyaneus* in Britain. Although now confined to uplands in the north and west, up until the early 1800s this species occurred in a wider range of habitats, including lowland heath and fen (Brown and Grice, 2005). We return to the subject of habitat shifts later, where we discuss some of the behavioural constraints and mechanisms involved.

Although not so dramatic as wholesale colonisation of new habitat, or the withdrawal from a particular habitat, the distribution of a species across a spectrum of occupied habitats may shift, sometimes involving large changes in density within particular habitats. Two examples from Britain illustrate this point. Newson *et al.* (2009) examined population changes for 23 species over a 13 year period across 12 broad habitat types. They detected a high proportion of significant habitat-specific population changes with over 75% of species showing variation in trends across habitats. Surveys of nightingale in 1980 and 1999 in England showed that by the second survey the species had become relatively more abundant in scrub than woodland habitats (Wilson *et al.*, 2002).

Table 3.4 *Examples of rates of colonisation of new habitat by individual species*

Species	Rate of establishment	Sources
Circus pygargus	France, cereal crops: first breeding after 1950s. By the late twentieth century 70–80% of birds bred in this habitat type	Arroyo *et al.* (2003)
Accipiter gentilis	Germany, town colonisation: Hamburg, since 1985, 22 pairs in 2000, Cologne since 1987, *c.* 40 pairs in 2000	Rutz *et al.* (2006)
Pandion haliaetus	Germany, Mecklenburg, breeding on pylons in farmland: first record in 1938, over 75% of birds in 1990s	Meyburg *et al.* (1996)
Larus argentatus	Britain, roof nesting: rare before 1940, 3000 pairs in 1976, 17 000 pairs in 1994. Started to breed in coastal towns in Finland and Poland after 1980s	Monaghan (1980); Raven and Coulson (1997); Kilpi and Ost (1998); Tomiałojć and Stawarczyk (2003)
Larus fuscus	Britain, urban population: 3200 pairs in 1994, increase by 17% $year^{-1}$ between 1976 and 1994, both increases in existing colonies and colonisation of new towns	Raven and Coulson (1997).
Columba palumbus	Several parts of Europe, urban nesting: usually 35–50 years between the first record of breeding and the onset of explosive increase	Tomiałojć (1976)
Luscinia s. svecica	Since 1980 a small isolated population has become established in the Swiss Alps using livestock resting places with lush vegetation and damp ground; contrasts with *Rhododendron ferrugineum* heaths used by other Alpine populations	Cereda and Posse (2002)
Pica pica	First started nesting in British and Irish cities 1950s–1960s. In Sheffield population density doubled between 1975 and 1986; in Dublin it increased four-fold between 1970 and 1983	Birkhead (1991)
Corvus corax	W Poland, nesting on pylons in farmland: first breeding in 1983, in 1996–1998 already *c.* 115 pairs, almost all nests in farmland. USA, Oregon and Idaho, nesting on pylons: 80–81 breeding pairs only six years after the first record	Bednorz (2000)

Table 3.4 (*cont.*)

Species	Rate of establishment	Sources
Corvus cornix	SW Poland, Wrocław, town colonisation: first downtown breeding in the early 1970s, by 2003 everywhere including densely built up areas – 219 breeding pairs within an 18 km^2 fragment, since 1983 nesting on buildings	Udolf (2005)

Consequences for modelling and applying bird–habitat relationships

Many of the above examples derive from disparate comparisons drawn from the literature or personal knowledge. These general observations are supported by more rigorous quantitative evidence from studies both in North America (Collins, 1983a,b; Dunning and Watts, 1990; Grzybowski *et al.*,1994; Willson and Comet, 1996; Dettmers *et al.*, 2002; Nur *et al.*, 2008) and Europe (Peach *et al.*, 2004; Väli *et al.*, 2004; Graf *et al.*, 2007; Sánchez *et al.*, 2009). The implication is that models of bird–habitat relationships established in one place at one time will not necessarily apply in other regions, even within similar landscapes (Fielding and Haworth, 1995; Whittingham *et al.*, 2007; Anderson *et al.*, 2009). More generally, conclusions drawn from studies of forest birds in Britain do not necessarily apply in other regions of Europe and vice versa (Fuller *et al.*, 2007). Clearly, geographical variation in habitat relationships of birds is a fact that cannot be ignored by ecologists and conservation managers. It is worth noting that this phenomenon may be widespread in nature, having also been recorded in plants, invertebrates and mammals (Gaston, 2003; Murphy and Lovett-Doust, 2007; McAlpine *et al.*, 2008; Oliver *et al.*, 2009).

Extrapolation of bird–habitat relationships from short-term, localised studies to larger regions or longer periods of time cannot be legitimate without separate validation studies. This relates not just to individual species, but also to the definition of functional groups. If differences in habitat occupancy are evident over relatively small spatial scales, then the implications for developing robust conservation management guidelines are potentially serious. As an example, in the Białowieża Forest, young-growth habitats created by natural treefalls contain somewhat different bird communities to those in nearby young-growth created by forest management (Fuller, 2000). Whilst this fact may be accounted for partly by differences in vegetation structure, the differences in bird communities were more pronounced than would have been expected based on general knowledge of the habitat requirements of the species involved.

There are also potential limitations in using contemporary bird–habitat relationships in studies that make historical assessments or future predictions of distribution. Ideally in such cases one has to account for temporal changes in habitat association. These changes can involve unpredictable (non-linear, qualitative) habitat shifts. Currently it is impossible to predict when and where such switches would occur, therefore forecasting future distributions of birds from present-day habitat associations has attendant risks. In some cases, such as prediction of distributional responses to climate change, there may be little alternative but to acknowledge that this is one of several factors hindering accurate forecasts.

Some comments seem appropriate about the interpretation of an apparent absence of a species from habitats with respect to conservation applications. Studies that compare features of habitats occupied by birds with those unoccupied, treat the latter as not acceptable. This may not be true for several reasons (Chapter 2). Numerical undersaturation may be quite common (Brown, 1969; Tomiałojć et al., 1984). For example in Białowieża Forest territories of nuthatch do not occupy all available suitable space, even in years of relatively high numbers (Wesołowski and Stawarczyk, 1991) and in some years great tit Parus major is insufficiently numerous to fill the available area (Wesołowski et al., 1987). This situation could occur regularly in threatened species, with reduced population sizes. Thus a relatively weakly occupied habitat does not necessarily mean it is not usable. Furthermore, the habitat in which a rare species has survived is not necessarily optimal. This is well illustrated by the red kite Milvus milvus in Britain, which for many years hung on only in poor habitats in central Wales (Davis and Newton, 1981). Similarly an apparent preference by goshawk for extensive forests in some regions appears to be largely a consequence of human persecution. Rutz et al. (2006) conclude a review of habitat relationships of this species as follows: 'the nest-site preferences reported for European populations may not always or entirely represent natural ecological needs, but partly reflect choices imposed on the species by human activities . . . Rather, they almost certainly evidence behaviour selected partly by past human persecution.' In cases where the major reason of population decline has been human persecution or over-exploitation, the species has most probably survived in places and habitats least accessible for humans, which are not necessarily the highest-quality habitats. Therefore using current habitat usage of such species as a template for their restoration would be ill conceived.

Potential causes of variation in spatial habitat occupancy

An array of mechanisms could explain observed spatial differences in habitat occupancy (Fuller et al., 2007). The processes discussed here do not represent a complete list, for example several plant and invertebrate species show habitat shifts towards the edge of their range, though the evidence for birds is less clear (Gaston, 2003; Oliver *et al.*, 2009). It is also possible that a species may be limited by different factors in different parts of its range, with consequences for habitat occupancy (Whittingham *et al.*, 2007). The question of whether evolved differences in fundamental habitat selection behaviours underlie phenotypic variations in habitat use has not been widely addressed. Evidence of adaptation to local habitat conditions comes from Paridae on Mediterranean islands (e.g. Blondel *et al.*, 1999; 2006) and apparent micro-evolution in urban blackbirds (e.g. Partecke and Gwinner, 2007). Adaptation to local or regional conditions is not, however, an essential element; factors such as the types of habitat available in a particular region, behavioural flexibility and variations in population density are likely to account for much of the variability. Many of the factors potentially causing spatial differences could equally drive temporal shifts in habitat use.

In some cases, differences may be more apparent than real. Variation in patterns of habitat use among areas could merely be due to details of study design and perceptions of habitat by human observers, or indeed to under-saturation (see above). What appear to be two different habitats for the researcher could be perceived by the bird as the same habitat because critical resources are provided in each case. Where these resources are provided by different habitat components (the landscape complementation model of Dunning *et al.*, 1992), any spatial variation in the relative proportions of these components can give the impression of a different pattern of habitat association. For example, in northern and eastern Europe, hazel grouse *Bonasa bonasia* uses *Picea* and *Alnus* for cover and winter food, respectively (Swenson, 1993). Relative availability of these trees differs regionally and this may affect human perceptions of habitat associations. In Sweden, where *Picea* is relatively abundant and *Alnus* relatively scarce, distribution of the species will appear to be linked with *Alnus* (Swenson, 1993) but in Białowieża, where *Picea* often occurs in patches among deciduous trees, the presence of *Picea* would appear to be critical (T.W., unpublished data). We are unaware of any studies that determine whether variation in the habitat associations among areas results from divergent sets of cues used by birds. 'Natural experiments' occasionally cast light on the key elements of habitat selection. Until recently, middle spotted woodpecker was considered an obligate '*Quercus* woodpecker' (Pasinelli, 2003). However, studies in central and eastern Europe show that this species can breed in woods without *Quercus* as long as there are other trees with rough bark and deep crevices to provide the main foraging substrate (Wesołowski and Tomiałojć, 1986; Weiß, 2003; Flade *et al.*, 2004). Such bark texture develops quite early in *Quercus*, but only at a very old age on *Alnus*, *Fraxinus* and *Fagus* trees. Overmature trees are usually rare in managed woodland, which led to the conclusion that *Quercus* was selected to the exclusion of all other trees.

Microclimate may occasionally be relevant. The effects of temperature and other climatic factors on breeding bird distributions are probably mostly indirect, acting, for instance, through their influence on vegetation zones, but there are a few instances where habitat occupancy is affected directly by microclimate. Near the southern border of their range in Norway, snow buntings *Plectrophenax nivalis* tend to settle on the northern slopes of ravines and valleys, with the coldest microclimate and snow drifts persisting in summer (Hildén, 1965). The breeding distribution of song thrush could be limited by low humidity (Tomiałojć, 1992). In dry conditions the species would be unable to find enough soft rotten wood and mud to plaster the inner parts of its nest with wood pulp. Apparently for this reason it is restricted to mountain forests in south Europe and failed to invade urban areas in central Europe.

As food supplies vary enormously across space and time it is possible that regional differences in habitat occupancy could reflect food availability; habitats in some regions may not be occupied because food supply is too low. At a proximate level, however, the majority of birds do not appear to include information on food availability in their settlement decisions (Svärdson, 1949; Hildén, 1965). Those species that do track varying food supply are mainly birds of prey and owls dependent on rodents and boreal seedeaters (Hildén, 1965; Newton, 1998) though one European insectivore, brambling *Fringilla montifringilla* selects breeding areas with defoliating caterpillar outbreaks (Enemar *et al.*, 2004). Recent declines of goshawk in its core habitat (coniferous forest) in the Netherlands since the early 1990s may be linked with precipitous declines in major prey species (Rutz and Bijlsma, 2006). By contrast, increases in numbers and diversity of breeding herons and other piscivorous birds in the Camargue (France) could be largely due to a novel and abundant food provided by the invasion of non-native crayfish *Procambarus clarkii* (Blondel *et al.*, 2010).

Predation risks vary in space and time. Some nest sites are more secure (Lack, 1954: Payevski, 1985; Wesołowski and Tomiałojć, 2005), some microhabitats, such as cliffs or islets are inherently safer (Hildén, 1965) and some regions have a permanently impoverished predator fauna (Fuller *et al.*, 2007). Humans behave as predators (hunting, persecuting, collecting eggs) in some places, whereas they become inadvert protectors in others (e.g. urban areas, Tomiałojć, 1982). Moreover, there are numerous observations indicating that the presence of predators and/or perceived threats of predation influence the settlement decisions of birds (Chapter 2). Habitat-specific differences in predation risk could, therefore, result in spatially varying habitat occupancy. Similarly, changes in predation pressure may sometimes alter fitness of individuals in the traditional habitat. Safriel (1985) suggested that increasing numbers of coastal-nesting gulls in Britain may have been an important trigger in the shift to inland breeding by oystercatchers *Haematopus ostralegus*.

In some habitats the risk of disease or parasitic infection may be continuously so high that it could prevent occupation by birds. Two examples can be given. First, exposure to parasites is likely to have been a strong factor in the evolution of habitat selection in waders (see Chapter 1). Second, the introduction of avian malaria and avian pox, along with their mosquito vector, to the Hawaiian islands led to large-scale extinctions of indigenous birds and their retreat from low- and mid-altitude forests (Newton, 1998; van Riper *et al.*, 2002). Though no example of this type has been documented for European birds, this possibility should be considered when trying to understand patterns of habitat occupancy.

Most areas of Europe have undergone immense anthropogenic changes since the last glaciation. The longest lasting and most intensive landscape transformations occurred over large tracts of temperate western Europe and in the Mediterranean Basin, where there is hardly a square metre of land not directly and repeatedly manipulated by humans (Blondel *et al.*, 2010). Birds living in these areas have either become extinct (Mikusiński and Angelstam, 1997; Tomiałojć, 2000a; 2000b) or adapted to new landscape structures. Numerous species confined to large forest tracts in primeval forests are widespread in anthropogenic habitats and landscapes in western Europe (Table 3.3). Differing rates of landscape change may, therefore, influence present habitat associations at a regional scale (Fig. 3.3).

Interspecific competition has been frequently proposed to explain spatial differences in habitat occupancy and niche shifts (Chapter 2). There have been few critical tests, however, and the difficulties of demonstrating interspecific competition are great. However, there is perhaps more compelling evidence that intraspecific competition, through the effects of crowding, can influence habitat occupancy (Chapter 2). The effects of increasing numbers of individuals in traditionally used habitats or ones of highest quality can lead to saturation, overcrowding and expansion into new habitats (Svärdson, 1949; Hildén, 1965; Tomiałojć, 1985; Blondel *et al.*, 1988; Newton, 1998). Conversely, declining populations or range contractions may result in withdrawal from some habitats. It should be recognised that habitat saturation does not always lead to habitat expansion. Queuing for territories by non-breeders (Ens *et al.*, 1995) or co-operative breeding could constitute alternative options (Brown, 1987; Koenig and Dickinson, 2004), though the latter is infrequent among European birds. Birds expanding their geographical ranges may initially use a narrow spectrum of habitats in newly colonised areas, appearing to be habitat 'specialists'. With increasing numbers, they may

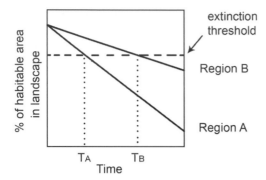

Figure 3.3 Conceptual model of how differing rates of change in the habitat composition of two regions may result in different patterns of habitat occupancy of a hypothetical species. The change in landscape composition could, for example, involve a reduction in cover of forest and extent of wetlands. The species has an extinction threshold at a certain point in the landscape change gradient indicated by the broken line. If it is to persist in region A, the species has to adapt to the new range of habitats much earlier than it does in region B. Observations made in the period between T_A and T_B would therefore give different pictures of broad habitat use in the two regions.

spread to a wider set of habitats and appear as 'generalists'. Hildén (1965) provides numerous examples of range expansions followed by habitat expansion. Habitat expansion can also occur where populations increase within the breeding range (Table 3.5). Increasing intraspecific pressure, forcing birds to settle in new places, was probably involved in many cases of urban colonisation (Tomiałojć, 1985).

Behavioural processes in colonisation of new habitats

As a result of man-made landscape transformations, birds have colonised habitats which were non-existent in the near past. They occupy new niches and live in conditions that to our eyes are quite different from those in which they evolved. What makes birds invade new habitats? What mechanisms underlie successful, sustained colonisations? Population pressure and reduced predation pressure are two potential triggers of habitat expansion (see above), but behavioural factors determine whether populations are maintained and eventually thrive in the new habitat.

For a habitat to be occupied, it has first to be visited by a bird, and second to be recognised as suitable. Many species of birds regularly visit different habitats prospecting for future breeding sites, often well before the actual settlement (Reed *et al.*, 1999; Boulinier *et al.*, 2008). The second requirement appears to constitute a far greater obstacle than the first. Perceptual ('psychological') factors play a role in the habitat selection of birds and proximate cues used for making choices are not in themselves necessarily essential to survival (Chapter 1). Therefore, potential habitats may not always be recognised as useable, even though they contain all essential resources (food, nest sites, cover). Lack (1937) gives the example of tree pipit *Anthus trivialis* using typical

Table 3.5 *Examples of apparent colonisation of new habitats following saturation of the traditional (ancestral) habitats*

Species (location)	Evidence	Sources
Anser brachyrhynchus (Iceland)	With recent increase in population, breeding range expansion has brought increasing numbers into the lowland areas, into habitats formerly associated with *Anser anser*, even down to sedge bogs at sea level (after 1980s)	Fox *et al.* (1997)
Cygnus olor (Poland)	In 1959 bred almost exclusively on large open lakes, with increase of population and range started to occupy smaller water bodies closer to humans; in 1998 only 24% on lakes	Wieloch *et al.* (2004)
Accipiter gentilis (Netherlands)	From *c.* 100 pairs around 1970 increased to *c.* 2000 pairs in 2000. In 1970 largely confined to areas with high proportion of coniferous forest, they subsequently spread to new habitats in almost treeless areas	Rutz *et al.* (2006)
Larus argentatus (Britain)	The high rate of increase of urban nesting birds appears to be due, in part at least, to the saturation or near saturation of more traditional colonies and natal dispersal into urban colonies	Monaghan (1980)
Corvus corax (W Poland)	At the beginning of the 1990s, the number of pairs in forest reached relative stability and a further increase in the number of birds occurred mostly in open farmland	Bednorz (2000)

meadow pipit *A. pratensis* habitats, provided that a single tall tree (or telegraph pole) was available as a song post. Similarly, to be acceptable, a chiffchaff *Phylloscopus collybita* territory has to contain a small gap free of trees and bushes, even though such openings are not used for singing, feeding or nesting (Piotrowska and Wesołowski, 1989). On migration, northern breeding birds fly over suitable breeding areas (as proved by successful nesting of conspecifics) without accepting them. Perhaps they do not even attempt to assess these areas as potential places to settle as their 'breeding time window' has not yet opened. A shift in the time window of a migratory species could, without any change in habitat selection mechanisms, nor in the habitats themselves, result in large-scale shifts in bird distributions (see also Chapter 17). For example, white stork *Ciconia ciconia* and bee-eater *Merops apiaster* now regularly breed on the wintering grounds in South Africa (Harrison *et al.*, 1997), barnacle goose *Branta leucopsis* breeds in a former staging area on Gotland, some 1200 km southwest of its former range (Larsson *et al.*, 1988) and dotterel *Charadrius morinellus* bred in the Netherlands, *c.* 800 km SW from the Scandinavian breeding grounds (Bijlsma *et al.*, 2001).

Cognitive change leading to modification of habitat selection templates does not come easily: 'expanding populations often keep stubbornly to their familiar habitat even in the new areas' (Hildén, 1965). It seems that really strong stimuli are needed to break this 'ecological inertia' (Peitzmeier, 1942), to force birds to conquer new habitats. Breaking the recognition barrier and settling in a novel habitat for the first time would constitute the most difficult stage. Increases in numbers, resulting in habitat saturation, may 'push' birds into new habitats (examples in Table 3.5). Changes in the habitats themselves, could also facilitate colonisation, for example the establishment of parks in towns has probably made urban areas more attractive to woodland birds.

If, maybe after initial hesitation, birds do breed in a novel habitat it often appears far more productive than the ancestral habitats (Table 3.6). Such cases demonstrate that the earlier rejection of the habitat was perceptual. After initial settlement, habitat colonisation could be facilitated by at least three different processes: social attraction, site tenacity and habitat imprinting. The presence of a group of successfully reproducing birds can make a new place much more attractive for prospecting birds and encourage them to settle (Hildén, 1965; Morse, 1980; Boulinier *et al.*, 2008). Especially in colonial birds, a newly established population can potentially increase at a fast rate through social attraction. Many birds tend to come back to their former breeding sites, even nests, in consecutive seasons, so in subsequent seasons they do not select habitat so much as return to the same location. The tendency is greatly enhanced by successful breeding (Reed *et al.*, 1999; Newton, 2008). This positive feedback encourages accumulation of birds in areas of successful reproduction. This mechanism could be especially important in long-lived birds colonising stable habitats. Very strong site tenacity can override changing habitat suitability. For example, individual pairs of *Larus canus* nesting on Vistula River islands can use the same spot for up to eight consecutive years (M. Bukacińska and D. Bukaciński, pers. comm.), despite rapid succession over this period from bare sand to dense *Salix* bushes (Fig. 3.2).

Natal experience can influence later breeding habitat choice (Davis, 2008). The mechanism of natal habitat learning (imprinting) has been frequently proposed to account for patterns of avian habitat selection (Hildén, 1965). However, it is difficult to disentangle site tenacity and natal habitat choice. Knowing, for instance, that most urban recruits of goshawk in Hamburg had fledged in the city (Rutz, 2008), how can we decide whether the birds have returned to their birth places or to natal habitat? Nest site choice by peregrine falcon *Falco peregrinus* in northern Europe offers a rare

Table 3.6 *Contrasts in the productivity of birds breeding in ancestral and newly occupied habitats or using new nest types*

Species	Ancestral	New	New/ancestral ratio	Sources
Accipiter gentilis	forests, 1.8 fledg/nest	urban, *c.* 2.3 fledg/nest	1.3	Rutz *et al.* (2006)
Pandion haliaetus	trees, 1.5 fledg/nest	electric pylons, 1.8 fledg/pair	1.4	Meyburg *et al.* (1996)
Haematopus ostralegus	shore, 0.2 fledg/nest	inland, 0.6 fledg/nest	3.0	Safriel (1985)
Larus argentatus	sea coast, *c.* 0.8 fledg/pair	towns, roofs *c.* 1.2 fledg/pair	1.5	Monaghan (1980)
Columba palumbus	old-growth forest, nest success *c.* 3%	old urban parks, without predators, nest success *c.* 50%	17.0	Tomiałojć (1999)
Megascops (otus) asio	riparian woodland, 1 fledg/pair	suburbia, 2 fledg/pair	2.0	Gehlbach (1996)
Troglodytes troglodytes	bottom layer of extensive old-growth forest, nest success 40%	wide range of woodland, scrub, hedgerows, nest success 60%	1.5	Wesołowski (1983)
Turdus merula	natural forests, nest success *c.* 28%	anthropogenic habitats, mean nest success *c.* 39%	1.4	Tomiałojć (1994)
Pica pica	rural, nest success 35%	urban, nest success 53%	1.5	Antonov and Atanasova (2003)
Corvus cornix	gallery forest, fish ponds *c.* 26%	urban, city park, *c.* 70%	2.7	Grabiński (1996); Udolf (2005)
Corvus corax	extensive forest, nest success *c.* 60%	electric pylons in farmland, nest success <85%	1.4	Bednorz (2000); Rösner *et al.* (2005)

Mean values of several years or study sites are shown. Values are partially extracted from the papers, partially calculated from the data provided in them. In all species except *Larus argentatus*, breeding densities were much higher in new than in ancestral habitats. Fledg = number of fledged young.

example of a well-documented case of habitat learning. Tree-nesting populations became extinct in the DDT era and Kirmse (2008) summarised attempts to re-establish a tree-nesting habit in eastern Germany. Falcons hacked/reared in tree nests (descendants of rock-nesters) tended to use tree nests or building/rock nests, whereas birds reared on buildings/rocks hardly used tree nests at all. This strongly suggests that tree-nesting was a culturally learned tradition. Such regional traditions are common among birds of prey (Newton, 1979). Birds become so attached to the learned type of site that they reject nest sites commonly used by the species in other regions (Newton, 2008). In the case of inland breeding by oystercatchers, learning may have affected habitat choice by acting through diet. Safriel (1985) proposed that intensified predation by coastal gulls provided the initial stimulus for birds moving inland. However, most individual oystercatchers show feeding specialisms learned from their parents, with just a small proportion of chicks becoming diet-generalists. Safriel suggests that these generalists may have been the ones best adapted to exploiting inland terrestrial food resources.

After colonisation of new habitat in one area, the habit often spreads, sometimes rapidly. The geographical expansion of urban-nesting blackbirds in Europe was as fast as the European range expansion of collared doves *Streptopelia decaocto* or the spread of starlings *Sturnus vulgaris* when introduced to North America (Luniak *et al.*, 1990). Did the habitat shift occur once, in a single place, with new places settled by dispersing descendants of the first colonisers (Steinbacher, 1942; review in Tomiałojć, 1985) or did it arise independently in many places? The first 'monopyhyletic' or 'leapfrog' model sees the habitat expansion as an instance of sympatric speciation: a new ecotype (ecospecies) originates and increases its range by colonising formerly unused habitats within the range of the ancestral species (e.g. urban and rural ecotypes of blackbird). The case of recent invasion by *Luscinia s. svecica* (northern European 'red-spotted' bluethroat subspecies) of the range of *L. s. cyanecula* (central European 'white-spotted') appears to conform to the leapfrog model. *L. s. svecica* breeds nowadays above the tree line in several central European mountains (Meijer and Štastny, 1997). The two forms are isolated by habitat; they do not interbreed, despite being separated in places by a distance of only 10 km (Krkonoše Mts, K. Dobrowolska pers. comm.).

It remains to be seen (molecular studies would be helpful) if the leapfrog model of habitat shift is frequent, but the available data from intensively studied species is not supportive. Urban populations of blackbird, woodpigeon and goshawk have arisen independently in several places within the species range (see above). In all these species, regular exchange of individuals between urban and rural areas is observed (Mulsow, 1976; Tomiałojć, 1982; Rutz, 2008). Recent genetic evidence supports the independent colonisation model for urban blackbird (Evans *et al.*, 2009). So, the colonisation was driven by flexible responses of birds to changes in local ecological conditions and was not due to immigration of new 'ecotypes' from somewhere else. This does not exclude the possibility of some dispersal of individuals specialised on new habitat types, their purposeful introductions by humans (Tomiałojć, 1985), nor that populations do not develop specific adaptations to new environments (Partecke and Gwinner, 2007).

All the mechanisms of habitat colonisation discussed so far rely on the ecological flexibility of birds, their facultative responses to changing environmental conditions. Large-scale habitat shifts have often occurred within a few generations (Table 3.4). The rapidity of these changes indicates that these were phenotypic reactions to prevailing conditions rather than genetically driven changes (although genetic change may follow). It seems probable that the large differences in macrohabitat use shown by several species in eastern and western Europe are based on evolved differences in habitat preferences, but the recent habitat shifts provide abundant evidence that large-scale habitat switches can occur without genetic change.

Final remarks/conclusions/summary

We have stressed the difficulties of predicting from contemporary bird–habitat associations in one region, the patterns of habitat occupancy in distant places or in the future. Making forecasts is especially risky, as qualitative shifts in habitat occupancy are to be expected, which no amount of modelling and extrapolation from current data could predict. However, we stress that there are situations where it is very easy to make predictions, and unfortunately they would be mostly correct. These concern the consequences of rapid loss or degradation of currently utilised habitats. Almost invariably the outcome is population decline, as evidenced by ongoing large-scale forest destruction (Asner *et al.*, 2009) and agricultural intensification in western Europe (Wilson *et al.*, 2009). Ecologists should not be deterred from predicting the consequences for nature of future habitat change, but need to acknowledge that there will always be a level of uncertainty.

There is also a more optimistic conclusion to be drawn. We know that a large amount of geographic variation in habitat use exists and that rapid changes in habitat occupancy are possible. We can cautiously expect that many birds would cope, in some way, with future changes in habitats, including those brought about by climate change. Much, of course, would depend on the scale of habitat change. Species certainly vary in their ability to make facultative adjustments to habitat change; some species may be insufficiently versatile. Critical examination of species traits in relation to responses to urbanisation and forest fragmentation could be helpful in identifying which these species might be.

This chapter shows that plasticity in habitat use is widespread. It is observed in birds from different taxonomic groups, living in various habitats and displaying contrasting life-histories. One could expect habitat specialists to be less flexible, but being a specialist or generalist is not necessarily a fixed species-specific trait. Every species appears 'specialist' when rare, but when their numbers increase, many spread to a wider spectrum of habitats. Of course some species are more restricted to a narrower set of resource needs than others, and this may help to predict consequences of habitat change. This is a good time to study habitat selection and other mechanisms producing habitat occupation patterns. As a result of enormous man-made landscape transformations, birds are faced with challenges and opportunities they may never have previously experienced. Studying how birds respond to these large-scale 'experiments', and comparing them with data from long-established cultural landscapes, as well as remnants of pristine areas, could be greatly informative.

Acknowledgements

We are grateful to Jacques Blondel, Ian Newton and Ludwik Tomiałojć for comments on an earlier draft of this chapter and useful literature suggestions. We thank Dariusz Bukaciński, Monika Bukacińska, Chris Hewson, Patryk Rowiński, Luc Schifferli and Niklaus Zbinden for discussion and sharing unpublished data.

References

Anderson, B. J., Arroyo, B. E., Collingham, Y. C. et al. (2009). Using distribution models to test alternative hypotheses about a species' environmental limit and recovery prospects. *Biol. Conserv.*, **142**, 488–499.

Antonov, A. and Atanasova, D. (2003). Re-use of old nests versus the construction of new ones in the Magpie *Pica pica* in the city of Sofia (Bulgaria). *Acta Ornithol.*, **38**, 1–4.

Armstrong, E. A. (1955). *The Wren*. London: Collins.

Arroyo, B. E., Bretagnolle, V. and Garcia, J. T. (2003). Land use, agricultural practices and conservation of Montagu's Harrier. In *Birds of Prey in a Changing Environment*, ed. D. B. A. Thompson, S. M. Redpath, A. H. Fielding, M. Marquiss and C. A. Galbraith, pp. 449–463. Edinburgh: The Stationery Office.

Asner, G. P., Rudel, T. K., Aide, T. M., Defries, R. and Emerson, R. (2009). A contemporary assessment of change in humid tropical forests. *Conserv. Biol.*, **23**, 1386–1395.

Baumgart, W. and Haraszthy, L. (1997). *Falco cherrug* Saker Falcon. In *The EBCC Atlas of European birds*, ed. E. J. M. Hagemeijer and M. J. Blair, pp. 190–191. London: Poyser.

Becker, P. H. and Ludwigs, J.-D. (2004). *Sterna hirundo* Common tern. *BWP Update*, **6**, 91–137.

Bednorz, J. (2000). Ravens *Corvus corax* Linnaeus, 1758, nesting on electricity pylons in the Wielkopolska region. *Acta Zool. Cracov.*, **43**, 177–184.

Bijlsma, R. G., Hustings, F. and Camphuysen, C. J. (2001). *Common and scarce birds of the Netherlands*. Utrecht: KNNV Uitgeverij. [Dutch, English Summary]

Birkhead, T. R. (1991). *The Magpies*. London: Poyser.

Blanco-Fontao, B., Fernández-Gil, A., Obeso, J. and Quevedo, M. (2010). Diet and habitat selection in Cantabrian Capercaillie (*Tetrao urogallus cantabricus*): ecological differentiation of a rear-edge population. *J. Ornithol.*, **151**, 269–277.

Blondel, J. (1985). Habitat selection in island versus mainland birds. In *Habitat Selection in Birds*, ed. M. L. Cody, pp. 477–516. New York: Academic Press.

Blondel, J., Aronson, J., Bodiou, J.-Y. and Boeuf, G. (2010). *The Mediterranean Region. Biological Diversity in Space and Time*. Oxford: Oxford University Press.

Blondel, J., Chessel, D. and Frochot, B. (1988). Bird species impoverishment, niche expansion, and density inflation in Mediterranean island habitats. *Ecology*, **69**, 1899–1917.

Blondel, J., Dias, P. C., Perret, P., Maistre, M. and Lambrechts, M. M. (1999). Selection-based biodiversity at a small spatial scale in a low-dispersing insular bird. *Science*, **285**, 1399–1402.

Blondel, J., Thomas, D. W., Charmantier, A. *et al.* (2006). A thirty-years study of phenotypic and genetic variation of blue tits in Mediterranean habitat mosaics. *BioScience*, **56**, 661–673.

Boulinier, T., Mariette, M., Doligez, B. and Danchin, E. (2008). Choosing where to breed: breeding habitat choice. In *Behavioural ecology*, ed. E. Danchin, L-A. Giraldeau and F. Cézilly, pp. 285–321. Oxford: Oxford University Press.

Brown, A. and Grice, P. (2005). *Birds in England*. London: Poyser.

Brown, J. L. (1969). Territorial behaviour and population regulation in birds. *Wilson Bull.*, **81**, 293–329.

Brown, J. L. (1987). *Helping and Communal Breeding in Birds*. Princeton: Princeton University Press.

Bukaciński, D. and Bukacińska, M. (1993). Colony site and nest-site selection in the Black-headed Gulls (*Larus ridibundus*) at the middle course of the Vistula river. *Ring*, **15**, 208–215.

Bukaciński, D. and Bukacińska, M. (2003). *Larus canus* Common Gull. *BWP Update*, **5**, 13–47.

Cereda, A. and Posse, B. (2002). Habitats et reproduction de la Gorgebleue à miroir roux *Luscinia svecica svecica* au Tessin (Alpes suisses). Réflexions sur le status de la sous-espèce en Europe moyenne. *Nos Oiseaux*, **49**, 215–228.

Collins, S. L. (1983a). Geographic variation in habitat structure for the wood warblers in Maine and Minnesota. *Oecologia*, **59**, 246–252.

Collins, S. L. (1983b). Geographic variation in habitat structure of the Black-throated Green Warbler (*Dendroica virens*). *Auk*, **100**, 382–389.

Czapulak, A. and Adamski, A. (2002). Reproduction biology of the Grey Heron *Ardea cinerea* nesting in reed rushes. *Notatki Ornithol*, **43**, 207–217. [Polish, English summary]

Davis, J. (2008). Patterns of variation in the influence of natal experience on habitat choice. *Q. Rev. Biol.*, **83**, 363–380.

Davis, P. E. and Newton, I. (1981). Population and breeding of Red Kites in Wales over a 30-year period. *J. Anim. Ecol.*, **50**, 759–772.

Dettmers, R., Buehler, D. A. and Franzreb, K. A. (2002). Testing habitat-relationships models for forest birds of the southeastern United States. *J. Wildlife Manage.*, **66**, 417–424.

Dunning, J. B., Danielson, B. J. and Pulliam, H. R. (1992). Ecological processes that affect populations in complex landscapes. *Oikos*, **65**, 169–175.

Dunning, J. B. and Watts, B. D. (1990). Regional differences in habitat occupancy by Bachman's Sparrow. *Auk*, **107**, 463–472.

Enemar, A., Sjöstrand, B., Andersson, G. and von Proschwitz, T. (2004). The 37-year dynamics of a subalpine passerine bird community, with special emphasis on the influence of environmental temperature and *Epirrita autumnata* cycles. *Ornis Svecica*, **14**, 63–106.

Ens, B. J., Weissing, F. J. and Drent, R. H. (1995). The despotic distribution and deferred maturity: two sides of the same coin. *Am. Nat.*, **146**, 625–650.

Evans, K. L., Gaston, K., Franz, A. C. *et al.* (2009). Independent colonization of multiple urban centres by a formerly forest specialist bird species. *Proc. R. Soc. B*, **276**, 2403–2410.

Fasola, M., Guzman, J. M. S. and Rosleaar, C. S. (2002). *Sterna albifrons* Little Tern. *BWP Update*, **4**, 89–114.

Fielding, A. H. and Haworth, P. F. (1995). Testing the generality of bird-habitat models. *Conserv. Biol.*, **9**, 1466–1481.

Flade, M., Hertel, F., Schumacher, H. and Weiß, S. (2004). Einer, der auch anders kann: Der Mittelspecht und seine bisher unbeachteten Lebensräume. *Der Falke*, **51**, 82–86.

Fox, A. D., Mitchell, C., Madsen, J. and Boyd, H. (1997). *Anser brachyrhynchus* Pink-footed Goose. *BWP Update*, **1**, 37–48.

Franco, A. M. A., Anderson, B. J., Roy, D. B. *et al.* (2009). Surrogacy and persistence in reserve selection: landscape prioritization for multiple taxa in Britain. *J. Appl. Ecol.*, **46**, 82–91.

Fuller, R. J. (1995). *Bird Life of Woodland and Forest.* Cambridge: Cambridge University Press.

Fuller, R. J. (2000). Influence of treefall gaps on distributions of breeding birds within interior old-growth stands in Białowieża Forest, Poland. *Condor*, **102**, 267–274.

Fuller, R. J. (2002). Spatial differences in habitat selection and occupancy by woodland bird species in Europe: a neglected aspect of bird-habitat relationships. In *Avian Landscape Ecology*, ed. D. Chamberlain and A. Wilson, pp. 101–111. Thetford: IALE (UK).

Fuller, R. J., Gaston, K. J. and Quine, C. P. (2007). Living on the edge: British and Irish woodland birds in a European context. *Ibis*, **149** (supp.2), 53–63.

Gaston, K. J. (2003). *The Structure and Dynamics of Geographic Ranges.* Oxford: Oxford University Press.

Gehlbach, F. R. (1996). Eastern Screech Owls in suburbia: a model of raptor urbanization. In *Raptors in Human Landscapes*, ed. D. Bird, D. Varland and J. Negro, pp. 69–74. London: Academic Press.

Gilbert, G., Tyler, G. and Smith, K. W. (2005). Behaviour, home-range size and habitat use by male Great Bittern *Botaurus stellaris* in Britain. *Ibis*, **147**, 533–543.

Glutz von Blotzheim, U. N. and Bauer, K. M. (eds) (1988). *Handbuch der Vögel Mitteleuropas* Volume 11/1. Wiesbaden: AULA-Verlag.

Glutz von Blotzheim, U. N. and Bauer, K. M. (eds) (1997). *Handbuch der Vögel Mitteleuropas* Volume 14/1. Wiesbaden: AULA-Verlag.

Grabiński, W. (1996). Breeding ecology of the Hooded Crow *Corvus corone cornix* in a fish-pond habitat. *Ptaki Śląska*, **11**, 5–38. [Polish, Engish summary]

Graf, R. F., Bollmann, K., Bugmann, H. and Suter, W. (2007). Forest and landscape structure as predictors of capercaillie occurrence. *J. Wildlife Manage.*, **71**, 356–365.

Grzybowski, J. A., Tazik, D. J. and Schnell, G. D. (1994). Regional-analysis of black-capped vireo breeding habitats. *Condor*, **96**, 512–544.

Hafner, H., Fasola, M., Voisin, C. and Kayser Y. (2002). *Egretta garzetta* Little Egret. *BWP Update*, **4**, 1–19.

Hagemeijer, W. J. M. and Blair, M. J. (1997). *The EBCC Atlas of European Birds.* London: Poyser.

Haland, A. and Ugelvik, M. (1990). The status and management of the White-Backed Woodpecker *Dendrocopos leucotos* (L.) in Norway. In *Conservation and Management of Woodpecker Populations*, ed. A. Carlson and G. Aulén, pp. 29–35. Uppsala: Swedish Univ. of Agricultural Sciences.

Harrison, J. A., Allan, D. G., Underhill, L. G. *et al.* (1997). *The Atlas of Southern African Birds.* Johannesburg: BirdLife South Africa.

Hildén, O. (1965). Habitat selection in birds – a review. *Ann. Zool. Fenn.*, **2**, 53–75.

Hinsley, S. A., Carpenter, J. E., Broughton, R. K. *et al.* (2007). Habitat selection by Marsh Tits *Poecile palustris* in the UK. *Ibis*, **149** (suppl.2), 224–233.

Holloway, S. (1996). *The Historical Atlas of Breeding Birds in Britain and Ireland 1875–1900.* London: Poyser.

Jędrzejewski, W., Szymura, A. and Jędrzejewska, B. (1994). Reproduction and food of the Buzzard *Buteo buteo* in relation to the abundance of rodents and birds in Białowieża National Park, Poland. *Ethol. Ecol. Evol.*, **6**, 179–190.

Kempe-Persson, H. (2002). Greylag Goose *Anser anser*. *BWP Update*, **4**, 181–216.

Kilpi, M. and Ost, M. (1998). Reduced availability of refuse and breeding output in a herring gull (*Larus argentatus*) colony. *Ann. Zool. Fenn.*, **35**, 37–42.

Kirmse, W. (2008) Changed behaviour being the pacemaker in isolation of a subpopulation exemplified by tree-nesting Peregrines *Falco peregrinus*. *Orn. Mitt.*, **60**, 229–237. [German, English summary]

Koenig, W. D. and Dickinson, J. L. (ed.) (2004). *Ecology and Evolution of Cooperative Breeding in Birds*. Cambridge: Cambridge University Press.

Lack, D. (1937). The psychological factor in bird distribution. *Brit. Birds*, **31**, 130–136.

Lack, D. (1954). *The Natural Regulation of Animal Numbers*. Oxford: Oxford University Press.

Larsson, K., Forslund, P., Gustafsson, L. and Ebbinge, B. (1988). From the high Arctic to the Baltic: the successful establishment of a Barnacle Goose *Branta leucopsis* population on Gotland, Sweden. *Ornis Scand.*, **19**, 182–189.

Luniak, M., Mulsow, R. and Walasz, K. (1990). Urbanization of the European blackbird – expansion and adaptations of urban population. In *Urban Ecological Studies*, ed. M. Luniak, pp. 187–199. Wrocław: Wydawnictwo Polskiej Akademii Nauk.

Mayr, E. (1963). *Animal Species and Evolution*. London: Belknap Press.

McAlpine, C. A., Rhodes, J. R., Bowen, M. E. *et al.* (2008). Can multiscale models of species' distribution be generalized from region to region? A case study of the koala. *J. Appl. Ecol.*, **45**, 558–567.

Meijer, R. and Štastny, K. (1997). *Luscinia svecica* Bluethroat. In *The EBCC Atlas of European birds*, ed. E. J. M. Hagemeijer and M. J. Blair, pp. 520–521. London: Poyser.

Meyburg, B.-U., Malanowsky, O. and Meyburg, Ch. (1996). The Osprey in Germany: its adaptations to environments altered by man. In *Raptors in Human Landscapes*, ed. D. Bird, D. Varland and J. Negro, pp. 125–136. London: Academic Press.

Mikusiński, G. and Angelstam, P. (1997). Economic geography, forest distribution, and woodpecker diversity in Central Europe. *Conserv. Biol.*, **12**, 200–208.

Monaghan, P. (1980). The breeding ecology of urban nesting gulls. In *Urban Ecology*, ed. J. A. Bornkamp and M. R. D. Seaward, pp. 111–121. Oxford: Blackwell.

Morse, D. H. (1980). *Behavioral Mechanisms in Ecology*. Cambridge, Mass.: Harvard University Press.

Mulsow, R. (1976). Amsel (*Turdus merula* L.): Daten zur Fortpflanzungsbiologie aus dem Jahre 1975 im Raum Hamburg. *Hamburger Avifaun. Beitr.*, **14**, 135–146.

Murphy, H. T. and Lovett-Doust, J. (2007). Accounting for regional niche variation in habitat suitability models. *Oikos*, **116**, 99–110.

Newson, S. E., Ockendon, N., Joys, A., Noble, D. G. and Baillie, S. R. (2009). Comparison of habitat-specific trends in the abundance of breeding birds in the UK. *Bird Study*, **56**, 233–243.

Newton, I. (1979). *Population Ecology of Raptors*. Berkhamsted: Poyser.

Newton, I. (1986). *The Sparrowhawk*. Calton: Poyser.

Newton, I. (1998). *Population Limitation in Birds*. London: Academic Press.

Newton, I. (2008). *The Migration Ecology of Birds*. London: Academic Press.

Nowysz, W. and Wesołowski, T. (1972). The birds of Kostrzyn retention reservoir and its environs in the breeding season. *Notatki Przyrod.*, **6**, 1–31. [Polish, English Summary]

Nur, N., Ballard, G. and Geupel, G. R. (2008). Regional analysis of riparian bird species response to vegetation and local habitat features. *Wilson J. Ornithol.*, **120**, 840–855.

Oliver, T., Hill, J. K., Thomas, C. D., Brereton, T. and Roy, D. B. (2009). Changes in habitat specificity of species at their climatic range boundaries. *Ecol. Lett.*, **12**, 1091–1102.

Pasinelli, G. (2003). *Dendrocopos medius* Middle Spotted Woodpecker. *BWP Update*, **5**, 49–99.

Partecke, J. G. and Gwinner, E. (2007). Increased sedentariness in European blackbirds following urbanization: a consequence of local adaptation *Ecology*, **88**, 882–890.

Payevski, W. A. (1985). *Birds' Demography*. Leningrad: Nauka. [In Russian].

Peach, W. J., Denny, M., Cotton, P. A. *et al.* (2004). Habitat selection by song thrushes in stable and declining farmland populations. *J. Appl. Ecol.*, **41**, 275–293.

Peitzmeier, J. (1942). Die Bedeutung der oekologischen Beharrungstendenz für faunistische Untersuchungen. *J. Ornithol.*, **90**, 311–322.

Plaisier, F. (1992). Zur Bionomie der Hohltaube (*Columba oenas*) auf der Nordseeinsel Langeoog. *Beitr. Vogel.*, **38**, 167–174.

Piotrowska, M. and Wesołowski, T. (1989). The breeding ecology and behaviour of the chiffchaff *Phylloscopus collybita* in primaeval and managed stands of Białowieża Forest (Poland). *Acta Ornithol.*, **25**, 25–76.

Prodon, R., Thibault, J.-C. and Dejaifve, P.-A. (2002). Expansion vs. compression of bird altitudinal ranges on a Mediterranean island. *Ecology*, **83**, 1294–1306.

Raven, S. J. and Coulson, J. C. (1997). The distribution and abundance of *Larus* gulls nesting on buildings in Britain and Ireland. *Bird Study*, **44**, 13–34.

Reed, J. M., Boulinier, T., Danchin, E. and Oring, L. W. (1999). Informed dispersal. Prospecting by birds for breeding status. *Curr. Ornithol.* **15**, 189–259.

Robinson, R. A. (2005). BirdFacts: species profiles of birds occurring in Britain and Ireland. *BTO Res. Rep.*, **407**, BTO, Thetford (http://www.bto.org/birdfacts).

Rösner, S., Selva, N., Müller, T., Pugacewicz, E. and Laudet, F. (2005). Raven *Corvus corax* ecology in a primeval temperate forest. In *Corvids of Poland*, ed. L. Jerzak, B. P. Kavanagh and P. Tryjanowski, pp. 385–405. Poznań: Bogucki Wydawnictwo Naukowe.

Rutz, C. (2008). The establishment of an urban bird population. *J. Anim. Ecol.*, **77**, 1008–1019.

Rutz, C. and Bijlsma, R. G. (2006). Food-limitation in a generalist predator. *Proc. R. Soc. B*, **273**, 2069–2076.

Rutz, C., Bijlsma, R. G., Marquiss, M. and Kenward, R. E. (2006). Population limitation in the Northern Goshawk in Europe: a review with case studies. *Stud. Avian. Biol.*, **31**, 158–197.

Safriel, U. N. (1985). 'Diet dimorphism' within an Oystercatcher *Haematopus ostralegus* population – adaptive significance and effects on recent distribution dynamics. *Ibis*, **127**, 287–305.

Sánchez, S., Václav, R. and Prokop, P. (2009). An inter-regional approach to intraspecific variation in habitat association: Rock Buntings *Emberiza cia* as a case study. *Ibis*, **151**, 88–98.

Schmid, H., Luder, R., Naef-Daenzer, B., Graf, R. and Zbinden, N. (1998). *Schweitzer Brutvogelatlas*. Sempach: Schweizerische Vogelwarte.

Steinbacher, C. (1942). Die Siedlungsdichte in der Parklandschaft. *J. Ornithol.*, **90**, 342–360.

Summers-Smith, J. D. (1988). *The Sparrows*. London: A&C Black Publishers Ltd.

Svärdson, G. (1949). Competition and habitat selection in birds. *Oikos*, **1**, 157–174.

Swenson, J. E. (1993). The importance of alder to hazel grouse in Fennoscandian boreal forests: evidence from four levels of scale. *Ecography*, **16**, 37–46.

Terrasse, J.-F. and Terrasse, M. (1977). Le Balbuzard pêcheur *Pandion haliaetus* (L.) en Méditerranée occidentale. Distribution, essai de recensement reproduction, avenir. *Nos Oiseaux*, **34**, 111–127.

Tomek, T., Bocheński, Z. and Bocheński, Z. M. (2003). Birds (Aves). In *Obłazawa Cave: Human Activity, Stratigraphy and Palaeoenvironment*, ed. P. Valde-Novak, A. Nadachowski and T. Madeyska, pp 102–113. Kraków: Institute of Archaeology and Ethnology Polish Academy of Sciences.

Tomiałojć, L. (1976). The urban population of the Woodpigeon *Columba palumbus* Linnaeus, 1758, in Europe – its origin, increase and distribution. *Acta Zool. Cracov.*, **21**, 585–632.

Tomiałojć, L. (1982). Synurbanization of birds and the prey-predator relations. In *Animals in Urban Environment*, ed. M. Luniak and B. Pisarski, pp. 131–139. Wrocław: Ossolineum.

Tomiałojć, L. (1985). Urbanization as a test of adaptive potential in birds. In *Acta XVIII International Ornithological Congress* ed. V. D. Ilyichev and V. M. Gavrilov, vol **II**, pp. 608–614. Moscow: Nauka.

Tomialojć, L. (1992). Colonization of dry habitats by the Song Thrush *Turdus philomelos*: is the type of nest material an important constraint? *Bull. Brit. Orn. Club.*, **112**, 27–34,

Tomiałojć, L. (1993). Breeding ecology of the blackbird *Turdus merula* studied in the primaeval forest of Białowieża, Poland. Part I. Breeding numbers, distribution and nest sites. *Acta Ornithol.*, **27**, 131–157.

Tomiałojć, L. (1994). Breeding ecology of the Blackbird *Turdus merula* studied in the primaeval forest of Białowieża (Poland). Part 2. Reproduction and mortality. *Acta Ornithol.*, **29**, 101–121.

Tomiałojć, L. (1999). A long-term study of changing predation impact on the breeding woodpigeons. In *Advances in Vertebrate Pest Management*, ed. P. D. Cowan and C. J. Feare, pp. 205–218. Fürth: Filander Verlag.

Tomiałojć, L. (2000a). An East-West gradient in the breeding distribution and species richness of the European woodland avifauna. *Acta Ornithol.*, **35**, 3–17.

Tomiałojć, L. (2000b). Did White-backed Woodpeckers ever breed in Britain? *Brit. Birds*, **93**, 452–456.

Tomiałojć, L. and Stawarczyk, T. (2003). *The Avifauna of Poland. Distribution, Numbers and Trends*. Wrocław: PTPP "pro Natura". [Polish, English summary]

Tomiałojć, L. and Wesołowski, T. (1990). Bird communities of the primaeval temperate forest of Białowieża, Poland. In *Biogeography and Ecology of Forest Bird Communities*, ed. A.

Keast, pp. 141–165. The Hague: SPB Academic Publishers.

Tomiałojć, L., Wesołowski, T. and Walankiewicz, W. (1984). Breeding bird community of a primeval temperate forest (Białowieża National Park, Poland). *Acta Ornithol.*, **20**, 241–310.

Tumiel, T. (2008). Abundance and distribution of the Three-toed Woodpecker in the Puszcza Knyszyńska in 2005–2007. *Notatki Ornithol.*, **49**, 74–80. [Polish, English Summary]

Udolf, J. (2005). Progress of synurbization and habitat preferences of the urban population of the Hooded Crow *Corvus cornix* in Wrocław (SW Poland). In *Corvids of Poland*, ed. L. Jerzak, B. P. Kavanagh and P. Tryjanowski, pp. 355–366. Poznań: Bogucki Wydawnictwo Naukowe.

Väli, U., Treinys, R. and Lõhmus, A. (2004). Geographical variation in macrohabitat use and preferences of the Lesser Spotted Eagle *Aquila pomarina*. *Ibis*, **146**, 661–671.

van Riper III, C., van Riper, S. G. and Hansen, W. R. (2002). Epizootiology and effect of avian pox on Hawaiian forest birds. *Auk*, **119**, 929–942.

von dem Bussche, J., Spaar, R., Schmid, H. and Schröder, B. (2008). Modelling the recent and potential future spatial distribution of the Ring Ouzel (*Turdus torquatus*) and Blackbird (*T. merula*) in Switzerland. *J. Ornithol.*, **149**, 529–544.

Weiß, S. (2003). Alder forests as hitherto neglected breeding habitat of the middle spotted woodpecker *Dendrocopos medius*. *Vogelwelt*, **124**, 177–192. (German, English summary)

Wesołowski, T. (1983). The breeding ecology and behaviour of Wrens *Troglodytes troglodytes* under primaeval and secondary conditions. *Ibis*, **125**, 499–515.

Wesołowski, T. (1989). Nest-sites of hole-nesters in a primaeval temperate forest (Białowieża National Park, Poland). *Acta Ornithol.*, **25**, 321–351.

Wesołowski, T. (1996). Natural nest sites of marsh tit (*Parus palustris*) in a primeval forest

(Białowieża National Park, Poland). *Vogelwarte*, **38**, 235–249.

Wesołowski, T. (2007). Primeval conditions – what can we learn from them? *Ibis*, **149** (Suppl. 2), 64–77.

Wesołowski, T., Czeszczewik, D., Mitrus, C. and Rowiński, P. (2003). Birds of the Białowieża National Park. *Notatki Ornithol.*, **44**, 1–31. [Polish, English summary]

Wesołowski, T., Czeszczewik, D. and Rowiński, P. (2005). Effects of forest management on Three-toed Woodpecker *Picoides tridactylus* distribution in the Białowieża Forest (NE Poland): conservation implications. *Acta Ornithol.*, **40**, 53–60.

Wesołowski, T., Głażewska, E., Głażewski, L. *et al.* (1985). Size, habitat distribution and site turnover of gull and tern colonies on the middle Vistula. *Acta Ornithol.*, **21**, 45–61.

Wesołowski, T. and Rowiński, P. (2004). The breeding behaviour of the Nuthatch *Sitta europaea* in relation to natural hole attributes in a primeval forest. *Bird Study*, **51**, 143–155.

Wesołowski, T. and Stawarczyk, T. (1991). Survival and population dynamics of Nuthatches *Sitta europaea* breeding in natural cavities in a primeval temperate forest. *Ornis Scand.*, **22**, 143–154.

Wesołowski, T. and Tomiałojć, L. (1986). The breeding ecology of woodpeckers in a temperate primaeval forest – preliminary data. *Acta Ornithol.*, **22**, 1–22.

Wesołowski, T. and Tomiałojć, L. (2005). Nest sites, nest predation, and productivity of avian broods in a primeval temperate forest: do the generalisations hold? *J. Avian Biol.*, **36**, 361–367.

Wesołowski, T., Tomiałojć, L. and Stawarczyk, T. (1987). Why low numbers of *Parus major* in Białowieża Forest – removal experiments. *Acta Ornithol.*, **23**, 303–316.

Whittingham, M. J., Krebs, J. R., Swetnam, R. D. *et al.* (2007). Should conservation strategies consider spatial generality? Farmland birds show regional not national patterns of habitat association. *Ecol. Lett.*, **10**, 25–35.

Wieloch, M., Włodarczyk, R. and Czapulak, A. (2004). *Cygnus olor* Mute Swan. *BWP Update*, **6**, 1–38.

Wilson, A. M., Fuller, R. J., Day, C. and Smith, G. (2005). Nightingales *Luscinia megarhynchos* in scrub habitats in the southern fens of East Anglia, England: associations with soil type and vegetation structure. *Ibis*, **147**, 498–511.

Wilson, A. M., Henderson, A. C. B. and Fuller, R. J. (2002). Status of the Nightingale *Luscinia megarhynchos* in Britain at the end of the 20th Century with particular reference to climate change. *Bird Study*, **49**, 193–204.

Wilson, J. D., Evans, A. D. and Grice, P. V. (2009). *Bird Conservation and Agriculture*. Cambridge: Cambridge University Press.

Willson, M. F. and Comet, T. A. (1996). Bird communities of northern forests: patterns of diversity and abundance. *Condor*, **98**, 337–349.

Yalden, D. W. and Albarella, U. (2008). *The History of British Birds*. Oxford: Oxford University Press.

CHAPTER FOUR

Mechanisms and processes underlying landscape structure effects on bird populations

PAUL M. DOLMAN

University of East Anglia

Many studies have related assemblage richness, or the incidence and abundance of individual bird species, to landscape structure. But without understanding the ecological mechanisms and processes underlying observed effects, this remains a description of pattern. Where such patterns are inconsistent among species, landscapes or regions, conceptual advance is limited. Despite this, few studies have tested hypotheses underlying these effects (Thompson *et al.*, 2000). This chapter summarises patterns of avian response to landscape structure and critically examines the evidence for different mechanisms that have been proposed to cause such effects. I focus on avian studies from semi-arid, temperate and boreal regions.

Much landscape-scale research has been driven by urgent concerns over the recent fragmentation of contiguous or extensive natural ecosystems (Andrén, 1994; Thompson *et al.*, 2000; Schmiegelow and Mönkkönen, 2002; Fahrig, 2003). However, faunal composition and responses to patch size, isolation, edges and context may differ between recently fragmented landscapes and ancient mosaics created by millennia of human land use (see also Chapters 3 and 19). Where possible, therefore, I try to contrast evidence from temperate and boreal regions of North and South America, Finland and Scandinavia, with research from southern and western Europe.

Understanding such effects is important for strategic conservation planning. When conservation activity is focused on stemming immediate habitat loss in relatively unfragmented landscapes (Sala, 2000), the arrangement of remaining patches may be less important than limiting the reduction in extent (Andrén, 1999; Fahrig, 2003). By contrast, to maximise biodiversity benefits of habitat creation or restoration in cultural landscapes retaining little semi-natural vegetation, new habitats and landscape elements should be located strategically. However, there is scant evidence available on which to build sound policy. For example, in the UK, paradigms of connectivity and ecological networks are increasingly widely adopted (Watts *et al.*, 2004;

Birds and Habitat: Relationships in Changing Landscapes, ed. Robert J. Fuller. Published by Cambridge University Press. © Cambridge University Press 2012.

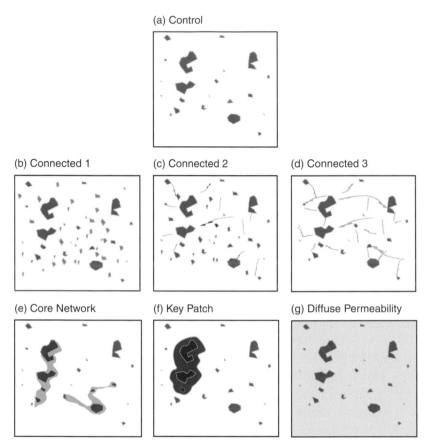

Figure 4.1 Alternative scenarios for deploying habitat creation. Six possible configurations are contrasted for habitat creation in a highly fragmented landscape: (a) Control landscape: isolated patches, wider countryside inhospitable; (b) Connected 1: stepping stones to facilitate dispersal and thus patch occupancy; (c) Connected 2: both linear elements and stepping stones to facilitate dispersal; (d) Connected 3: connectivity from linear elements only; (e) Network creation (linking the closest largest patches by continuous or permeable habitat); (f) Key patch creation: targeting habitat creation to buffer the largest patches to provide contiguous habitat for large-area species, a resilient sedentary population for dispersal-limited species or maximal area of core habitat for edge-sensitive species; (g) Diffuse permeability (broad and shallow prescription), no additional patches, but increased countryside permeability to enhance dispersal and mitigate edge effects. No one scenario can benefit all species, as these differ in responses to edges, area requirements, dispersal and gap-crossing ability.

Catchpole, 2006; Lawton *et al.*, 2010), but generally lack evidence of effectiveness (Dolman and Fuller, 2003; Dolman *et al.*, 2007). Deciding whether to use scarce conservation resources to enhance functional connectivity or buffer existing core areas (see Fig. 4.1), requires understanding how landscape structure affects local habitat suitability and the regional population processes of species of concern.

I evaluate the diverse mechanisms and hypotheses that have been proposed as explanations of landscape effects and attempt to address a number of questions. Which processes, operating at what scales, are most important to the distribution and abundance of species and the composition of local assemblages? Have we successfully moved from studying pattern to studying processes? Are processes and landscape structure effects similar among geographic regions? Or are responses to landscape structure species-specific, context-specific and individualistic, as suggested by Villard (2002)? Are landscape structure mechanisms operating in forest habitats similar to those affecting birds in other habitats? Lastly, the chapter suggests further research directions to advance understanding of processes underlying landscape effects.

Defining and measuring landscape attributes

Two main attributes of a landscape are its composition (the extent of different habitat types) and its configuration (how individual habitat patches are arranged) (Dunning *et al.*, 1992; Fahrig, 2003). Key aspects of these, and approaches to their measurement, are described in Appendix E4.1. Heterogeneity relates to diversity in habitat composition, while complexity relates to the spatial structure and intermingling of these habitat elements. Landscapes containing the same relative proportions of habitats may be either fine- or coarse-grained, depending on the degree to which different habitat patches are subdivided, perforated or intermixed, or aggregated in large blocks. Perceptions and measurements of landscape structure depend on the resolution at which it is examined, in terms of both the physical scale and the classification of habitats (Olff and Ritchie, 2002; Lindenmayer *et al.*, 2007). For example, fine-grained regenerating patches from group selection cuts or tree-fall gaps may exist within individual woods, with this heterogeneity affecting their quality for gap-sensitive species. But these woods can themselves be perceived as individual patches in a coarse-grained landscape comprising scattered woodland within an open habitat or farmland matrix (Dolman *et al.*, 2007). The spatial and ecological scale at which grain should be classified depends on traits (e.g. ecological requirements, mobility, home-range size) of the species of interest (Lindenmayer *et al.*, 2007) and whether the focus is on individual movements within a home range, in relation to gap-crossing and fine-grained habitat quality, or structure and dispersal among subpopulations (see Fig. 4.2). Complex landscapes are not static, with dynamics determined by the ecological magnitude, spatial extent and frequency of change; agricultural landscapes and forest wildfires exemplify such temporal dynamism.

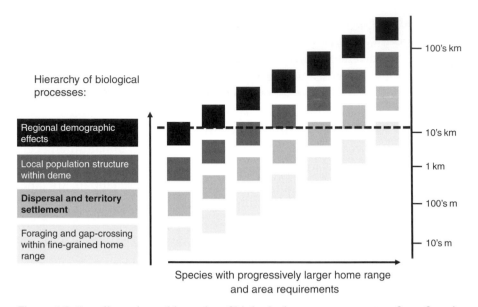

Figure 4.2 For all species, a hierarchy of biological processes operates, from foraging and provisioning movements and gap-crossing decisions within home ranges, through patterns of dispersal, territory occupancy and local density, up to population (demographic) processes at the regional scale. However, species differ in their intrinsic area requirements and mobility, so that the processes operating at a given spatial scale will differ among species (dashed line). The same physical arrangement of habitat patches may be perceived as a fine-grained landscape by large-area species, for which individual patches might form feeding sites, or as coarse-grained by species with much smaller home range area requirements, when the same individual patches may support territories or local subpopulations. Thus when a landscape is examined at a single physical scale or ecological resolution, different species exhibit different levels of biological process and patterns of response. This is illustrated for contrasting hypothetical species in landscapes of differing degrees of habitat subdivision or landscape grain in Fig. 4.3.

A hierarchy of nested biological processes underlie effects at contrasting landscape scales

There are challenges and sophisticated solutions to studying the effects of landscape structure on patterns of assemblage composition and richness, species incidence or population abundance (see Appendix E4.2). There is a huge body of evidence for landscape structure effects across a wide range of bird species, habitats and regions (Tables 4.1 and 4.2). For example, Bayard and Elphick (2010) examined 2700 area sensitivity tests, from more than 870 bird species; incidence–area patterns were found commonly in tests of forest species, and in at least half the tests of shrubland and wetland species, though less commonly for grassland birds. But despite this multitude of studies, in

Table 4.1 *Potential patterns of responses to landscape structure in bird assemblage richness and species incidence or abundance*

Edge-Sensitivity	Edge sensitive species have lower density near edges; while 'edge species' either preferentially settle on or near edges (Andrén, 1994) or have higher territory packing near edges.
Fine-grain Dependent Species	Some edge species, or other complementing species, have higher incidence or abundance in heterogeneous landscapes that are fine-grained relative to their home range extent.
Area-Sensitivity: Incidence-Area	Individual species may have greater incidence in larger patches (Freemark and Collins, 1992; Hinsley *et al*., 1996; Andrén, 1999). Species-specific minimum area-requirements and thresholds (e.g. 'large area species') can result in *Incidence-Area* patterns and can generate nested patterns of *Richness-Area*. Strongly supported for forest, grassland and wetland birds.
Area-Sensitivity: Abundance-Area	Species populations often show positive or inverse abundance-area effects, with greater or lower density in larger patches respectively (Ambuel and Temple, 1983; Hinsley *et al*., 1996; Bender *et al*., 1998; Bellamy *et al*., 2000; Lehnen and Rodewald, 2009). Strongly supported for forest, grassland and shrubland birds.
Richness-Area	Greater species density in patches of greater area (Connor and McCoy, 1979). Strongly supported for forest and grassland birds.
Landscape Diversity	Not surprisingly, landscapes with more diverse habitat composition support richer regional assemblages (Andrén, 1994). Strong support.
Habitat Extent	Effects of habitat extent are stronger than effects of configuration (Andrén, 1994; Fahrig, 2003). Strongly supported for forest birds.
Non-linear Fragmentation Effects	Initial effects of habitat fragmentation are due to loss of habitat area; but configuration effects are important in landscapes of low habitat extent e.g. <10–30% (Andrén, 1994). Strongly supported for forest birds.

Detailed evidence and examples of studies are available in Appendix E4.3A.

most instances it is still not clear what mechanisms and processes cause the observed patterns of response.

Effects of landscape structure are often taxa-specific, scale-specific and vary among landscape types (Villard, 2002; Bayard and Elphick, 2010). Although species may be attributed to a functional group according to a shared pattern of landscape response (e.g. edge, interior or area-sensitive species), individual

Table 4.2 *An overview of potential mechanisms underlying effects of landscape structure, listing key references and synthesising the strength of evidence for their importance to temperate and boreal birds.*

Hypothesis and key references	Strength of Evidence
a) Processes at the scale of individual home ranges	
Species-specific Minimum Area Requirements: of large-area species contribute to incidence-area patterns (Andrén, 1994; Hinsley *et al*., 1996)	Strong support
Reduced Edge Quality: edges are avoided by interior specialists due to lower habitat quality (McCollin, 1998; Ortega and Capen, 1999)	Some support
Passive Displacement: settlement constraints reduce territory density near edges causing apparent edge-sensitivity (Kroodsma, 1984; McCollin, 1998; Lehnen and Rodewald, 2009)	Lacks support
Edge Truncation: provisioning birds (central point foragers) avoid settlement near edges due to energetic and provisioning constraints (Huhta *et al*., 1999)	Some support
Edge- and Patch Area Effects on Nest Failure Rates: failure rates due to nest predation and/or parasitism are greater at or near edges and in smaller patches (Gates and Gysel, 1978)	Region, landscape, habitat and species-specific (Box 4.1)
Edge Contrast: greater contrast between patch and matrix increases nest failure rates (Schmiegelow and Mönkkönen, 2002)	Some support
Conspecific Attraction: settlement in response to existing conspecific territories contributes to richness-area and area-sensitivity (Svärdson, 1949; Smith and Peacock, 1990; chapter 2)	Strong support
Heterospecific Attraction: spring settlement by migrants in response to cues of surviving over-wintered residents, contributes to richness-area and area-sensitivity (Mönkkönen *et al*., 1990, 1997; chapter 2)	Strong support
Territory Packing and *Phenotype-based Territorial Compressibility*: greater territory packing near edges or in smaller patches may result from despotic settlement of core habitat by higher quality individuals; resulting in apparent inverse edge- or area-sensitivity despite lower habitat quality or underlying preference (source: this review)	Evidence consistent, requires explicit testing
Area-Quality Hypothesis: large patches are preferred as they are of better quality, due to resources, lower nest predation rates, or environmental edge effects (Ambuel and Temple, 1983; Matter, 1997)	Strong evidence in some (not all) studies

Table 4.2 (cont.)

Hypothesis and key references	Strength of Evidence
Edge Exploitation: specialists using edge habitats preferentially settle, or have higher density, at edges due to abundant food and complex structure (Strelke and Dickson, 1980; Jokimäkl *et al.*, 1998; see also chapter 5)	Strong support
Complementing Species: require juxtaposition or proximity of complementing resources available in other habitats, or contrasting landscape elements, within heterogeneous mosaics (Dunning *et al.*, 1992)	Strong support
Supplementing Species: mobile species are able to meet resource needs by exploiting multiple habitat fragments within an extensive home range larger than landscape grain (Rolstad, 1991; Dunning *et al.*, 1992; Andrén, 1994)	Strong support
Gap Sensitive Species: benefit from continuous habitat and are detrimentally affected by fine-grained perforation due to energetic costs and/or predation risk (Desrochers and Hannon, 1997; Hinsley, 2000); conversely *Perforation Insensitive Species:* are wide ranging species insensitive to fine-scale perforation within home range (Andrén, 1994)	Strong support
b) Processes at the scale of individual dispersal	
Patch Isolation Impedes Dispersal: and therefore reduces recolonisation and local patch occupancy rates (Hanski, 1994). For gap sensitive or dispersal limited species 'Barrier Effects' (whereby isolation or gaps prevent dispersal) can cause individuals to become 'Gap Locked' and trapped in low-quality isolated fragments, with important fitness consequences (Lens and Dhondt, 1994; Matthysen *et al.*, 1995; Turcotte and Desrochers, 2005).	Strong support
Physical Connectivity Enhances Dispersal: greater physical connectivity enhances functional connectivity, dispersal and colonisation, increasing local patch occupancy (Harrison, 1994)	Supported by observational studies, limited demographic evidence
Matrix Quality Hypothesis: reduced patch-matrix contrast or better matrix quality increases functional connectivity, reducing isolation effects (Åberg *et al.*, 1995; Kupfer *et al.*, 2006), and enhancing patch colonisation and metapopulation dynamics (Moilanen and Hanski, 1998; Pither and Taylor, 1998)	Some support

Table 4.2 *(cont.)*

Hypothesis and key references	Strength of Evidence
c) Processes at the scale of regional populations	
Island Biogeography: isolated assemblages in fragments are subject to species extinction and colonisation dynamics (MacArthur and Wilson, 1967)	Relevant to regional archipelagos
Density Compensation: lower species richness and thus reduced interspecific competition in smaller patches results in higher densities of those species present (MacArthur *et al.*, 1972)	Untested at landscape scales?
Metapopulation Theory: regional species populations persist by extinction / colonisation dynamics of semi-isolated sub populations in discrete patches; regional persistence depends on regional extent and dispersal (Hanski, 1998, 1999)	Not supported
Rescue Effects: local and thus regional persistence is enhanced by dispersal from nearby sub populations (Brown and Kodric-Brown, 1977; Hanski and Gyllenberg, 1993)	Some support
Mainland-island Metapopulation / Key Patch Theory: regional persistence is greatly increased by a resilient/ persistent core population in a large habitat patch (Verboom *et al.*, 2001), that may repeatedly re-colonise ephemeral sub populations in small satellite patches (Harrison, 1994)	Some support
Regional Population Effects: local persistence depends on large region-wide source populations in extensive habitat (Virkkala, 1991)	Strong support
Filtering of Assemblages: regions with greater habitat extent retain large-area dependent species, mediating richness-area species accumulation rates (Virkkala, 1991; Dolman *et al.*, 2007)	Strong support
Regional Landscape Structure Affects Nest Failure Rates: abundance of ubiquitous generalist predators is increased by matrix character and extent, causing higher nest predation rates throughout patches, irrespective of edge proximity (Robinson *et al.*, 1995; Kurki *et al.*, 2000; Stephens *et al.*, 2003)	Strong support (Box 4.1)
Source–Sink Population Dynamics: sink populations in poor quality habitat or landscape elements only persist through dispersal from viable source populations in better habitat (Pulliam, 1988; Robinson *et al.*, 1995)	Some support
Buffer Effect: ideal free or ideal despotic territory settlement across landscape elements of differing	Strong evidence for habitats; likely also to

Table 4.2 (cont.)

Hypothesis and key references	Strength of Evidence
quality regulates mean demographic rates in relation to overall population size, resulting in density-dependence (Fig. 4.4) (Kluijver and Tinbergen, 1953; Brown, 1969)	be important for landscape structure elements

Mechanisms are presented in a hierarchy of biological scales, considering processes at the scale of: a) individual home ranges; b) individual dispersal; c) structured regional populations. For each hypothesis, assumptions, predictions and evidence are detailed in Appendix E4.3B.

species within such a group may differ in the strength of effect. Even more confusing, the same species may show contrasting responses in different contexts (Sisk *et al.*, 1997; Watson *et al.*, 2005; Renfrew and Ribic, 2008; Bayard and Elphick, 2010). To explain such apparently contradictory responses, it is necessary to move beyond description of patterns to understanding mechanisms.

These mechanisms are consistently nested. Within an individual home range, territory settlement, foraging and provisioning movements, and responses to predators, may be affected by edges, gaps, habitat quality, matrix contrast and heterogeneity. At a larger scale, individual dispersal is affected by landscape structure, with multiple dispersal events then scaling up to determine regional population structure. The relative importance of these mechanisms differs among species, due to species-specific habitat and resource requirements, dispersal ability, susceptibility to predation and thus sensitivity to grain, gaps and edges. Furthermore, a particular process may operate at a greater or lesser physical scale for different species, depending on intrinsic mobility and area requirements (see Figs. 4.2 and 4.3).

Inconsistent patterns of responses are therefore to be expected among co-occurring species, particularly when a landscape is defined and examined at a single physical scale and resolution. Although there is an increasing trend for single-species studies to examine habitat associations or incidence at multiple scales (Chapter 1), landscape responses of multi-species assemblages have rarely been examined at nested scales. In Chile, forest bird species showed contrasting responses to nested scales of landscape structure (Vergara and Armesto, 2009). Some species responded most strongly to local patch configuration, others to local or regional extent, and some showed effects at more than one scale; however, body size or ecological correlates of response scales were not straightforward.

Table 4.2 summarises differing ecological processes proposed as mechanisms explaining landscape structure effects, reviewing 27 hypotheses. These are grouped according to the biological scale at which they operate,

Species Attribute: Increasing species-specific home range size

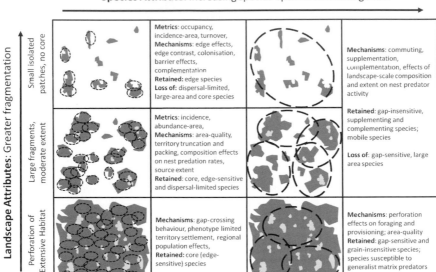

Figure 4.3 Potential processes and mechanisms underlying responses (shown as territories or home ranges) to landscape structure may differ depending both on the degree of habitat subdivision and on intrinsic species-specific differences in area requirements (see Fig. 4.2). The *y* axis represents a fragmentation gradient from contiguous but perforated, through a landscape comprising large patches retaining core areas, to a highly fragmented landscape of small scattered habitat patches. The *x* axis contrasts species with a small territory or home-range extent and large-area species (e.g. large raptors, forest grouse, large woodpeckers or complementing passerines that undertake long foraging commutes). For combinations of landscape structure and species scale, metrics for the patterns of response and potential processes underlying these are listed. Examples of types of species that may be retained in, or lost from, the landscapes are also shown.

from influences on territory settlement and individual fitness, through dispersal movements, scaling up to structured regional populations. To examine the evidence in support of each hypothesis, published literature was reviewed, using a combination of key search terms in on-line bibliographic databases (Web of Science, Scopus) and studies cited in relevant papers (e.g. Andrén, 1994; Bennett *et al.*, 2006; Wilkin *et al.*, 2007; Lehnen and Rodewald, 2009). Where studies capable of discriminatory tests provided evidence consistent with the hypothesis, this is considered to be strongly supported. Inconsistent or variable findings are also reported. Hypotheses for which tests have failed to demonstrate evidence are considered to lack support, while for others sufficient tests do not yet appear to have been conducted. A detailed synthesis of assumptions, predictions and evidence used to evaluate hypotheses is presented in Appendix E4.3. The following sections discuss the relevance and importance of each hypothesis.

Processes at the scale of individual territories or home ranges
Mechanisms underlying edge- and area-sensitivity

Patch area may affect the incidence or abundance of individual species (two forms of area-sensitivity) and consequently the richness of local assemblages (area-richness) (Table 4.1). There is strong evidence that incidence–area relationships may result from species-specific minimum-area thresholds. Large-bodied species and those subsisting on sparsely distributed food resources tend to have large-area requirements; examples include large raptors, forest grouse and large-bodied woodpeckers. Whether large home-range requirements necessitate large single patches or whether a species can supplement resources across numerous scattered patches or landscape elements depends on its mobility and gap-crossing ability. Nevertheless, threshold area–incidence requirements for some species greatly exceed territory area (Herkert, 1994; Caplat and Fonderflick, 2009). This may indicate edge-sensitivity, or may result from within-site heterogeneity so that only a small proportion represents suitable habitat (Herkert, 1994; Mallord *et al.*, 2007). At a larger scale than that of individual territories, habitat subdivision may disrupt social structure of populations, for example, in species with exploded leks.

Within the range of patch sizes commonly occupied, many species preferentially settle on larger or smaller habitat patches so that density varies with area (positive or inverse abundance–area relationships, respectively). Such patterns are frequent in forest (Bender *et al.*, 1998; Bellamy *et al.*, 2000) and grassland (Johnson and Igl, 2001) species. Positive incidence–area and abundance–area patterns can result from edge avoidance. This may arise from a response to reduced habitat quality at edges (McCollin, 1998), edge truncation that imposes constraints for provisioning nestlings (Huhta *et al.*, 1999), or perceived predation risk (Fletcher and Koford, 2003). Note that a variety of responses to edges – both negative and positive – is possible (see below and Chapter 5).

Nest predation as a mechanism of edge avoidance

It has been suggested that nest location relative to forest–field ecotones and other types of habitat edge, can result in increased failure rates due to predation or brood parasitism (Gates and Gysel, 1978). This became a major focus of study in North America, in the context of concern over declining abundance of many neotropical migrant forest bird species (Chapter 19). However, effects of local landscape structure, edge proximity or patch area are highly inconsistent among species, regions and habitats (Thompson, 2007). The emerging evidence is that although local-scale effects may sometimes occur, for some species in some landscapes, these are generally uncommon and are mediated by stronger effects at larger spatial scales, where the composition of regional landscapes determines the nature of the nest predator fauna (Box 4.1; Chapter 5).

Box 4.1 Nest predation mediated by edge proximity, patch-area and landscape-scale habitat extent

Concern that fragmentation had reduced the breeding abundance of North American forest-interior species through increased rates of nest predation and brood parasitism has driven much landscape-scale research. However, understanding has been greatly impeded by the continued use of artificial nests. These fail to measure the rates of predation affecting real nests, or the relative importance of different predators; overestimating the impact of birds and visual-searching predators, underestimating carnivores and potentially failing to detect predation by snakes or small mammals (Storaas, 1988; Willebrand and Marcström, 1988; Roper, 1992; Haskell, 1995; King et al., 1999; Thompson et al., 2000). Artificial nest studies cannot, therefore, be used to investigate effects of landscape structure on nest predation rates, as predators differ in numerical, behavioural and functional responses to landscape elements, habitats and edges.

Well-replicated studies of real nests are now accumulating, though to date most are from North America (Stephens et al., 2003). These show landscape effects are inconsistent, varying among regions, landscapes, habitats and species. Across bio-regions, differences in predator faunas can mediate (Thompson et al., 2002; Thompson, 2007) and even reverse the direction of landscape effects (Tewksbury et al., 1998). At regional scales nest predation may be greater in landscapes with greater extent of farmland and/or less contiguous forest (Robinson et al., 1995; Kurki et al., 2000; Stephens et al., 2003; Driscoll and Donovan, 2004). Meta-analysis across studies shows that effects of regional landscape composition on predation rates are stronger and more frequent than effects of local landscape structure, such as edge proximity or patch size (Stephens et al., 2003).

Understanding how different nest-predators respond to habitat extent and edges is critical to understanding mechanisms of landscape effects on predation rates (Lahti, 2001; Chalfoun et al., 2002). However, this has rarely been achieved (Larivière, 2003), with far fewer studies of predator responses to landscape structure than studies of nest success. In addition, when responses of predators to landscape structure have been examined, this has often considered predator species that are perceived as important and are easy to monitor, but rarely those species that are actually important, according to evidence from nest cameras (Chalfoun et al., 2002).

Effects of territory settlement and packing on apparent area-sensitivity

Conspecific or heterospecific attraction (Table 4.2; Chapter 2) may amplify existing area preference (for example if initial settlement responds to area quality), or lead to higher density in larger patches, even if initial settlement is random with respect to area (such that larger patches are more likely to be settled by chance). While in theory, constraints of territory placement could result in passive displacement and lower density near edges or in small patches (Lehnen and Rodewald, 2009), this may result from visualising territories as roughly circular polygons (e.g. King *et al.*, 1997; Ortega and Capen, 1999). Edge avoidance commonly penetrates much greater distances than predicted from such simulations (Kroodsma, 1984; Ortega and Capen, 1999). Conversely, territory density may often be higher in small patches or close to edges, despite positive area preference, due to truncation of territories at edges or closer territory packing. For example, although Bellamy *et al.* (2000) found that most common bird species occurred at greater densities in smaller woods in eastern England, this was only confirmed as an active preference for blackbird *Turdus merula* and dunnock *Prunella modularis*. Whilst great tit *Parus major*, blue tit *Cyanistes caeruleus*, chaffinch *Fringilla coelebs* and robin *Erithacus rubecula* also had greater density in relatively small woods, they had proportionately lower numbers in these woods in years of low regional abundance, indicating an underlying preference for larger woods. Similarly, great tit density in Wytham Woods was greater at edges, due to settlement of immigrants from external and hedgerow territories, although territories in core habitat were better quality and supported greater productivity (Wilkin *et al.*, 2007). I suggest that a potential mechanism may be greater elasticity and compressibility of marginal territories or those held by individuals of lower phenotypic quality, compared to more effective defence of territories occupied by high-quality individuals in better habitat.

Area quality

The 'area-quality' hypothesis proposes that larger patches are preferentially selected because they provide better-quality habitat, for example in terms of greater resource availability, breeding productivity or survival. The corollary is that areas in proximity to edges are poor-quality habitat, though for other species an opposite area effect may occur, where the best-quality habitat is frequently close to edges (Chapter 5). Adult ovenbirds *Seiurus aurocapillus* settle in large patches away from edges, with negative fitness effects penetrating far beyond forest boundaries, implicating habitat quality rather than settlement constraints or local edge avoidance (Kroodsma, 1984; Villard *et al.*, 1993; Ortega and Capen, 1999). In Britain, based on abundance/incidence patterns, several woodland species appear to prefer larger woodlands (Krebs, 1971;

Hinsley *et al.*, 1996, 1999; Bellamy *et al.*, 2000). For great tits, edge effects penetrate so deeply that they may affect reproduction throughout a wood smaller than 80 ha (Wilkin *et al.*, 2007). Demographic effects of patch area on breeding or survival have been shown for other forest species (Lens and Dhondt, 1994; Doherty and Grubb, 2002), but are not always found, even when there is clear area preference (Huhta and Jokimäki, 2001; Robles *et al.*, 2008). Area-quality effects may also result from the greater range and complexity of habitats, and thus resources, available within larger patches that sample a greater range of variable habitats and microhabitats. Area quality can be hard to distinguish from reduced edge quality, and edge and area effects are often conflated.

Edge exploitation

Despite a general presumption that edges provide poor-quality habitat or increase predation risk, assemblages often include edge-exploiters and edge-neutral or generalist species, as well as interior specialists that avoid edges (Kroodsma, 1984; Chapter 5). Across Californian oak woodland patches (>100 ha) edge avoidance was rarer (only 18% of 50 instances examined) than edge-exploiting (44%) or edge-neutral (38%) distributions (Sisk *et al.*, 1997). In Finland, most boreal forest insectivores and migrants occurred at higher density at edges, while old-growth specialists such as treecreeper *Certhia familiaris* and Siberian jay *Perisoreus infaustus* showed edge avoidance (Schmiegelow and Mönkkönen, 2002). In Mediterranean pine-shrubland mosaics, forest canopy species had greater relative frequency in forest patches with greater edge density (Herrando and Brotons, 2002), while in agricultural landscapes in Poland length of woody edge habitat explained total species richness and richness of species of conservation concern (Sanderson *et al.*, 2009). Species that actively exploit edge habitats, as well as complementing species, may have higher densities in small patches (Bender *et al.*, 1998; McCollin, 1998; Bellamy *et al.*, 2000).

Complementing species in mosaic landscapes

Complementing species obtain different resources from contrasting habitats within heterogeneous landscapes. Such species require contagion, juxtaposition or proximity of contrasting patches, as shown by studies of settlement patterns in response to landscape structure (Pino *et al.*, 2000; Robinson *et al.*, 2001; Brotons *et al.*, 2005b; Barbaro *et al.*, 2007) and studies of individual movements (Dale and Manceau, 2003). Preferential settlement of complementing species near edges suggests they may benefit from complex landscapes with heterogeneity at a finer grain than their territory or home range. However, complementing species may commute over scales of kilometres between nesting and foraging sites, as shown for ortolan bunting *Emberiza hortulana* (Dale and Manceau, 2003), golden plover *Pluvialis apricaria* (Whittingham *et al.*, 2000) and twite *Carduelis flavirostris* (Raine, 2006). Complementarity may also operate for poorly dispersing resident species requiring access to contrasting resources in breeding and non-breeding seasons.

Gap-crossing and foraging movements within an individual home range

Contiguity, linkage or perforation of habitat can affect foraging movements within home ranges, with potential consequences for fitness and productivity. Some strongly flying supplementing species may be able to exploit multiple scattered patches to meet their resource requirements and do not require aggregated habitat. In contrast, many smaller species may be gap sensitive, due to non-trivial costs in terms of energy, time and predation risk. Gap-crossing within territories comprising discontinuous habitat may impose energetic and time costs, selecting for smaller brood size and/or smaller adult body size (Hinsley, 2000). Gap-crossing potentially exposes individuals to predation (Rodríguez *et al.*, 2001) and willingness to cross gaps varies among species according to both body size and relative manoeuvrability (Creegan and Osborne, 2005). While mid-sized European birds such as robin, blackbird and chaffinch readily cross gaps or open fields rather than detouring through cover, many smaller forest species are reluctant to cross gaps of 50 m, while others are reluctant to break cover at all.

For gap-sensitive species, there may be a trade-off between predation risk and energetic or nutritional stress, so that decreased body condition and/or increased mortality are predicted in fragmented landscapes (Turcotte and Desrochers, 2008). In Quebec, black-capped chickadees *Poecile atricapillus* receiving *ad libitum* food during winter did not venture more than 4 m into the open, but otherwise moved up to 40 m into the open to obtain supplementary food, indicating a trade-off between food and predation risk (Turcotte and Desrochers, 2003). Chickadees also ventured further into the open in landscapes with less forest cover, suggesting that habitat subdivision increased energetic stress and risk-taking behaviour. Chickadees caching food from feeders placed close to forest edges redistributed it towards the interior, presumably to avoid exposure to wind chill or predator risk close to edges when retrieving food (Brotons *et al.*, 2001). In Spain, although blue tits did not differ in mean winter body mass between small fragments and continuous forest, body mass appeared to be more carefully regulated in fragments, suggesting management of predator risk in the context of unpredictable resource availability (Tellería *et al.*, 2001). For crested tit *Lophophanes cristatus*, willow tit *Poecile montanus*, coal tit *Periparus ater* and goldcrest *Regulus regulus* in Sweden, movement rates were affected by predation risk and matrix composition, such that even small-scale perforation of closed forest reduced its favourability (Rodríguez *et al.*, 2001).

Scaling up to dispersal: isolation, connectivity and dispersal

The contiguity or isolation of habitat has the potential to affect dispersal, and thus patterns of territory settlement, incidence in small patches and the reinforcement or re-colonisation of local populations, with consequences for regional genetic structure and demography. Connectivity among network elements is widely adopted as a guiding principle for landscape restoration (Peterken, 2000; Peterken, 2003; Watts *et al.*, 2004), on the assumption that structural habitat networks and/or increased landscape permeability enhance functional connectivity and facilitate colonisation. However, for many wood-land birds, narrow linear elements may provide lower-quality habitat than contiguous woodland (Krebs, 1971; Riddington and Gosler, 1995; Verhulst *et al.*, 1997; Major *et al.*, 1999). Unless linear elements do offer dispersal opportunities, enhancing connectivity may therefore be counter-productive compared to buffering core patches (Dolman *et al.*, 2007).

Enhancing local connectivity by linking individual patches is unlikely to be important for large-bodied birds for which natal dispersal distances are rela-tively large (Paradis *et al.*, 1998). Intuitively the same could be assumed for settlement patterns of returning migrants. However, migrants may return to a site chosen during local dispersal in their first summer (Morton *et al.*, 1991; Betts *et al.*, 2008) or following exploratory dispersal within their first breeding season (Dale *et al.*, 2006). Many small-bodied resident species do have limited natal dispersal – typically on average a few km – similar to the scale of local habitat networks (Paradis *et al.*, 1998). Does connectivity actually benefit such species? Some species will overfly unsuitable habitat when dispersing, as shown for ortolan bunting (Dale *et al.*, 2006). However, patterns of patch occupancy and colonisation provide evidence for isolation effects (van Dorp and Opdam, 1987; Dunning *et al.*, 1995; Jansson and Anglestam, 1999; Brotons *et al.*, 2003; Watson *et al.*, 2005; Rodríguez *et al.*, 2007) and, more rarely, connectivity benefits (Groom and Grubb, 2006) to some resident species in some contexts. Conclusions from individual-based simulations as to whether linear elements and enhanced landscape connectivity, or buffering of core patches best enhances regional persistence of dispersal-limited resident spe-cialist forest species entirely depend on assumptions made for dispersal behaviour (Alderman *et al.*, 2005; Schippers *et al.*, 2009).

There have been surprisingly few empirical tests of corridor and matrix use by dispersing birds (Schmiegelow and Mönkkönen, 2002). More field studies of movement behaviour and dispersal are clearly required, though valuable insights have already been gained. In eastern England the number of birds observed moving between paired woods was related to availability of woody field boundary features, rather than the distance between the woods, suggesting that boundaries facilitated movement (Bellamy and Hinsley, 2005). Differences in age-specific survival of Carolina chickadee *Poecile carolinensis* among landscape elements led Doherty and Grubb (2002) to suggest that riparian corridors in Ohio acted as dispersal conduits for transient juveniles. Large numbers of juvenile forest birds caught in linear riparian strips connecting retained forest blocks in Alberta pointed to their use as dispersal conduits (Machtans *et al.*, 1996). In Belgium, dispersal of juvenile crested tits away from their natal territory was delayed in fragments compared with continuous forest (Lens and Dhondt, 1994). Adult nuthatches *Sitta europaea* in small forest fragments were less likely to disperse to a new territory in a subsequent year than individuals in a forested landscape (Matthysen *et al.*, 1995), suggesting they may also have been 'gap-locked'. In Quebec, overwinter abundance of black-capped chickadees was positively related to forest cover across replicate landscapes with food supplementation (Turcotte and Desrochers, 2005). Interestingly, the opposite was found in control landscapes with no supplementary feeding, where abundance was less with greater forest integrity. This was interpreted as reflecting easier dispersal of juveniles and transient adults through more continuous forest, whether inward to the higher-quality (supplemental feed) sites or outward from the control sites, compared to gap-locked birds in fragmented landscapes that accumulated or exported fewer individuals. Doherty and Grubb (2002) attributed high mortality of Carolina chickadees in small woodlots to low food availability and greater exposure to windchill, combined with low gap-crossing ability that restricted movements out of these poor-quality patches.

Such studies strongly indicate that connectivity may be important to the dispersal of small and gap-sensitive species in highly perforated landscapes. Such effects may not be restricted to specialist forest birds; within 15 days of leaving the nest, radio-tagged dickcissels *Spiza americana* had moved further in larger grassland patches, suggesting barrier or entrapment effects in smaller patches (Berkeley *et al.*, 2007).

It has been proposed that decreasing the structural contrast between patch and matrix reduces the hostility of the matrix to dispersal, thus weakening isolation effects (Schmiegelow and Mönkkönen, 2002; Kupfer *et al.*, 2006). There is some evidence that the ability to cross inhospitable matrix habitats may be mediated by a dispersal–competition trade-off. In Swedish boreal forest two competitively dominant species (willow tit and crested tit) had lower dispersal abilities and greater sensitivities to isolation, than the smaller but more mobile coal tit and goldcrest. The latter two species were, however, excluded from predator-safe microhabitats by the dominant species (Rodríguez *et al.*, 2007). Thus landscape structure may mediate species composition within functional guilds.

Processes at the scale of regional populations

Processes of dispersal and colonisation across complex landscapes determine patterns of territory settlement that, with density- and patch-dependent productivity and survival, scale up to population dynamics and regional persistence. Regional populations are generally continuous, albeit patchy, demes with local aggregations and territories often embedded in a landscape grain finer than that at which adult or natal dispersal operates (see above). Lower occupancy rates in smaller patches are predicted from spatially explicit meta-population theory, where extinction rates are greater in smaller patches. However, lower incidence in smaller patches may also result from area quality and preferences at settlement (see above). Bird populations rarely persist at the regional scale by a critical balance of extinction and re-colonisation among semi-isolated local populations. I suggest that bird populations in fragmented landscapes rarely form a metapopulation, despite the widespread appeal of this conceptual model (Box 4.2). However, regional persistence is more likely where there are one or more large source patches (Alderman *et al.*, 2005), as predicted by the 'mainland-island' or 'key-patch' variants of meta-population theory (Harrison, 1994; Verboom *et al.*, 2001).

For ephemeral post-disturbance habitats, variable availability of source populations may contribute to heterogeneity in assemblage composition, as found among post-burn sites in the Iberian Peninsula (Brotons *et al.*, 2005a). Here source availability was important at local scales for most species, but linnet *Carduelis cannabina* and rock bunting *Emberiza cia* showed stronger effects across buffers of 5–10 km.

At larger scales, rescue effects and extensive regional source populations may be important in maintaining local populations and patch occupancy. This is exemplified by studies from recently fragmented boreal forest land-scapes in Finland (Box 4.3). The large extent of regional habitat required for source populations to maintain local specialist assemblages in these boreal systems, is orders of magnitude greater than scales usually considered for woodland assemblages in western Europe. It is not clear whether this reflects intrinsically low densities of taiga specialists (Virkkala, 1991), or could the contemporary forest biota of western Europe comprise a filtered subset, that lacks large-area species?

In a meta-analysis of 14 European species-area studies, rates of species loss with exponentially decreasing fragment area were greater in landscapes with less forest extent (Tellería *et al.*, 2003). This is consistent with the basic prediction that landscapes retaining greater forest cover, and thus having larger regional source populations, will have lower rates of local extirpation as there is more potential for rescue effects. Interestingly, fewer species were recorded in fragments of a given area in landscapes with greater extent of forest cover (while controlling for both regional species richness and

Box 4.2 Island biogeography and metapopulation perspectives: mismatch of landscape and avian population scales?

Preoccupation with habitat fragmentation encouraged use of models that consider patches as 'islands' of habitat in an inhospitable matrix. Island biogeography considers how the area and isolation of oceanic islands affect their species richness, through the interplay of extinction and colonisation rates (MacArthur and Wilson, 1967). A similar perspective on single species gave rise to metapopulation theory (Levins, 1969, 1970). This considers the persistence of regional populations through a dynamic balance of extinctions and colonisations of local populations within individual habitat patches. Extending Levins' classic metapopulation model to spatially explicit or real landscapes, the probability of patch occupancy may be positively related to patch area, due to reduced extinction risk, and negatively to isolation, due to increased re-colonisation rates as in island biogeography theory (Harrison, 1991; Hanski, 1998, 1999). Immigration may also reduce extinction probability through the 'rescue effect' (Brown and Kodric-Brown, 1977).

Metapopulation dynamics have been applied to bird populations to examine single species extinction/colonisation dynamics, or 'turnover' of local-patch occupancy (Opdam et al., 1995; Major et al., 1999; Foppen et al., 2000; Verboom et al., 2001; Schippers et al., 2009). However, in many cases patches are so small that occupancy involves successive settlement of individual territories within a wider continuous population deme. For example, over three years Bellamy et al. (1996) examined turnover in local occupancy for eight species of woodland birds across 145 woodlands in eastern England (range 0.02 ha to 10.3 ha). Most 'extinctions' occurred in woods containing just one to three breeding pairs, rather than local 'subpopulations', while 'persistence' in consecutive years generally involved re-colonisation by non-natal individuals (Hinsley et al., 1994). Similarly, in Finnish forest fragments (range 0.7 ha to 4.4 ha), annual turnover was at the individual bird scale (Haila et al., 1993). Although individual-based models of territory occupancy and dispersal may exhibit similar properties to metapopulations (Andrén, 1994; Alderman et al., 2005), individual settlement and movement occurs within patchily distributed but continuous regional populations (Andrén, 1994). This should be distinguished from metapopulation dynamics involving the extinction or re-colonisation of semi-independent subpopulations (Haila et al., 1993; Harrison, 1994; Andrén, 1994; Villard et al., 1995). There is support for 'mainland-island' or 'key-patch' models (see Table 4.2), in which regional persistence occurs through a permanent source population in a large patch, but this is distinct from idealised metapopulations in which regional persistence occurs through dynamic extinction/recolonisation of multiple ephemeral populations.

Box 4.3 Regional population effects at large spatial scales: evidence from northern Finland

The species composition of large individual patches of intact old-growth forest may be overwhelmed by large regional source populations of generalists from the surrounding managed matrix. For example, Väisänen *et al.* (1986) reported that the bird community of a *c.* 1 km² virgin forest changed considerably from 1915 to 1983, although the old forest structure was retained. By the 1980s the bird community resembled that of surrounding managed forest. Although the assemblage in larger extensive forests can remain distinct, it may nevertheless be filtered and modified. For example, the bird species composition of the 70 km² Oulanka Forest reserve, comprising undisturbed old-growth pine-spruce forest, differed substantially from that in surrounding clear-fell and young-growth mosaics; with a higher density of sedentary residents, lower densities of willow warblers *Phyllosocopus trochilus* and redwings *Turdus iliacus* and absence of open habitat species such as wheatear *O. oenanthe*, whinchat *Saxicola rubetra* and meadow pipit *Anthus pratensis* (Helle, 1986). However, specialist taiga species were almost entirely absent from both Oulanka and the surrounding managed forest. Helle concluded that even this 70 km² forest did not support 'closed' populations and had not preserved its original characteristics, due to regional-scale declines in source populations across northern Finland. In contrast, the Sompio old-growth forest reserve is contiguous with the Koillskaira National Park of > 1000 km² extent. In the 1980s Sompio still supported taiga specialists (pooled density, 7.2 pairs km^{-2}) virtually absent (0.9 pairs km^{-2}) from nearby managed forest sites (Virkkala, 1991). Densities of northern taiga species at Sompio were similar to those recorded in the same region in 1947 and 1955, prior to large-scale forest cutting. This emphasises the surprisingly large scales of source habitat required to sustain regional populations of large-area (low-density) specialist forest species.

---

biogeography). This is consistent with retention of large-area-dependent species in regions with greater forest extent, that will reduce the ability of small patches to sample the overall species pool and the rate at which richness saturates with increasing fragment area. Such evidence has also been obtained from North America (Freemark and Collins, 1992).

Buffer-effect theory: regional demographic consequences of landscape composition and structure

Buffer-effect theory (Kluijver and Tinbergen, 1953; Brown, 1969) provides a conceptual framework to predict population-level consequences of landscape heterogeneity. Competition for better quality territories or feeding areas

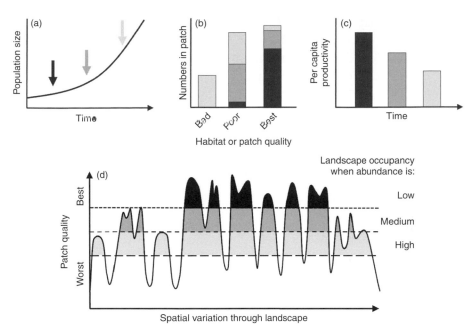

Figure 4.4 Buffer effects due to differing quality of landscape elements (for example patches differing in habitat type, area, edge effects or access to complementing resources) showing (a) hypothetical increase in population size through time, (b) corresponding changes in mean density within landscape elements of differing quality, (c) consequences of this for per capita productivity and (d) spatial pattern of patch occupancy for a schematic transect through a heterogeneous landscape. When regional population levels are low (black arrow in a, black shading in b-d) most individuals settle in better quality territories (b), mean per capita productivity is high (c), fewer patches are occupied, and habitat amplitude is less (d). When population levels increase (grey arrows and shading), saturation of good patches and intra-specific competition force a greater proportion of individuals to settle in poorer quality territories, increasing relative density in poor quality elements (b), reducing mean per capita productivity (c) and causing overspill from 'core' landscape elements into lower quality patches, resulting in wider habitat amplitude (or niche use) (d).

within heterogeneous landscapes can have important consequences for individual fitness and local demographic rates (Chapter 2). Increasing population size forces a greater proportion of individuals to occupy poorer-quality patches, reducing population-wide mean demographic rates (Fig. 4.4). This is a form of regulatory density dependence (Andrén, 1990; Both, 1998). Heterogeneity in patch quality arising from area, context, juxtaposition, configuration or edge effects may produce buffer effects in a similar way to variation in patch quality due to habitat type. In the extreme case, where individuals are excluded from breeding by saturation of available habitat, they may persist as a pool of non-breeding floaters (Newton, 1992) that 'buffers' the population (Brown, 1969). Source–sink theory (Pulliam, 1988) is a special case of the buffer effect. Examples may include Bachman's sparrow *Aimophila aestivalis* in central Florida prairie fragments (Perkins *et al.*, 2003) and woodlark *Lullula arborea* in farmland in eastern England (Wright *et al.*, 2007), both of which were thought to persist through recruitment from adjacent pine stands ('spillover'). At a finer scale, ovenbirds nesting within 100 m of clear-cut edges in Minnesota had lower production than survival, suggesting this part of the landscape supports a population sink (Manolis *et al.*, 2002). Although productivity of individuals in 'sinks' may not be sufficient to sustain a population in the absence of immigration from higher-quality landscape elements, sinks still contribute to overall regional population productivity, unlike non-breeding 'floaters'.

Buffer effects through habitat heterogeneity have been demonstrated in a very wide range of bird species and may be ubiquitous examined with appropriate ecological resolution. In addition to such buffer effects arising from different habitat types, effects of habitat configuration on patch-level quality, demography, productivity or population structure have been found in crested tit (Lens and Dhondt, 1994), great tit (Krebs, 1971; Wilkin *et al.*, 2007), pied flycatcher *Ficedula hypoleuca* (Huhta *et al.*, 1998, 1999), black-throated blue warbler *Dendroica caerulescens* (Cornell and Donovan, 2010) and red-capped robin *Petroica goodenovii* (Major *et al.*, 1999). These provide potential for density-dependent buffer effects arising through landscape structure.

Geographical variation in patterns and processes of landscape structure effects

Area-thresholds, incidence–area and abundance–area responses are not a fixed trait for individual species, but may vary geographically. For example, the magnitude and even direction of area- responses of north American grassland birds differs regionally. Some grassland bird species that were area insensitive in Illinois showed positive responses to fragment area in Maine, while others showed a positive incidence–area effect, but varied in their threshold-area requirements among studies (Herkert, 1994; Vickery *et al.*, 1994; Helzer and Jelinski, 1999). Grasshopper sparrows *Ammodramus savannarum* showed contrasting positive and negative area sensitivity across different Northern Plains regions (Johnson and Igl, 2001). Although blackbird and robin were ubiquitous in small (*c.*1 ha) woods in eastern England (Hinsley *et al.*, 1996), in eastern Europe they only reached maximum incidence in woods of 10 ha or greater (Cieslak, 1985). Similarly, while dunnock preferred small woods in eastern England (Bellamy *et al.*, 2000), in the Netherlands it only reached maximal incidence in woods of more than 5 ha (van Dorp and Opdam, 1987). This suggests geographic variation in the ecological mechanisms underlying area sensitivity, area quality or responses to patch edges. Possibilities include differences in quality of adjoining supplementary habitats, regional differences in predator assemblages (affecting edge sensitivity), or the intriguing possibility of long-term evolutionary responses in landscape of great antiquity where low compositional diversity has been replaced with complex heterogeneous mosaics with high edge density (see Chapter 3, for a more general account of regional variation in habitat use).

It is not yet clear whether the prevalence of landscape sensitivity differs for avifauna remaining in recently fragmented, compared to ancient anthropogenic, landscapes. Although differences in the frequency and strength of landscape effects have been found among continents and regions (Bender *et al.*, 1998; Bayard and Elphick, 2010), geographic contrasts are inconsistent for incidence–area and abundance–area relationships (Bayard and Elphick, 2010). Greater incidence in larger patches was more frequent among species examined in Europe and central America than Asia, North America and South America. Inverse incidence–area was more frequent in North America, however inverse abundance–area was more frequent in Europe and Australia. It is not clear whether this reflects differences in underlying mechanisms among regions or biomes, or whether contrasts are confounded by habitats, study design and varying statistical power.

For forest birds, regional-scale assemblages may be filtered as extensive forest landscapes are fragmented, with the loss of large-area species and low-density resident forest specialists (Box 4.3). Although ancient anthropogenic landscapes may have excluded large-area species, sufficient time may have elapsed for adaptation involving changes in area requirements, patch supplementation behaviour and edge responses (see also Chapter 3). Interestingly, forest interior species in North America showed stronger positive area sensitivity than forest interior species in Europe (Bender *et al.*, 1998), while for edge species the strength of inverse patch-area effects did not differ. Comparing the proportion of regional species pools showing positive or negative area sensitivity may help clarify historic effects. However, interpretation will be complicated by the smaller extent of forest refugia remaining in Europe during Pleistocene climate fluctuations compared to North America and Asia, as this is thought to have reduced Western Palearctic avifaunal diversity (Mönkkönen, 1994; Mönkkönen and Viro, 1997). Such bottle-necks and species losses could have filtered forest avifauna in a way that confounds recent differences in the timing of anthropogenic impacts between continents.

Conclusions and recommendations for future enquiry

Landscape composition and structure have profound effects on the composition of local bird assemblages and the incidence and persistence of species. There is overwhelming evidence that patch area, grain size, the arrangement and density of edges and the proximity and juxtaposition relative to other elements affect individual fitness, foraging, reproductive success, survival, dispersal, colonisation, territory settlement, demographic performance, population structure, species distributions, richness and the composition of avian assemblages. While this review has focused on birds, processes and responses to landscape structure are likely to differ for other taxa, depending on mobility and life histories.

For habitat specialists, habitat extent can be important to regional persistence at surprisingly large scales. However, binary approaches to landscape analysis are a gross oversimplification for many species (Vandermeer and Carvajal, 2001; Kupfer *et al.*, 2006) and the matrix may function as a source, resource, habitat, conduit or possible sink, not just as a barrier (Norton *et al.*, 2000; Kupfer *et al.*, 2006). Area, abundance and edge responses may differ in the context of contrasting matrix and edge habitats (Brotons *et al.*, 2005b; Watson *et al.*, 2005; Renfrew and Ribic, 2008) though causal mechanisms must often be inferred. There is a need to move beyond preoccupation with negative impacts of fragmentation to investigate processes in heterogeneous mosaics, particularly anthropogenic landscapes of great antiquity (Bennett *et al.*, 2006; see also Chapter 19). Here complexity increases regional species diversity, not just by providing new habitat elements, but also through complementarity and apparent edge specialisation (Herrando and Brotons, 2002; Fahrig *et al.*, 2011), though the latter may frequently be a case of exploiting young-growth structures rather than edges per se (e.g. Virkkala, 1991) (see also Chapter 5).

Without understanding mechanisms, optimal conservation strategies cannot be identified – for example, is it possible to ameliorate effects in small patches, or should efforts focus exclusively on larger patches? Buffer-effect theory offers a conceptual framework to predict density-dependent population dynamics resulting from landscape structure. However, this requires field studies designed to test alternative ecological mechanisms and measure the demographic consequences of landscape effects (Thompson *et al.*, 2000).

It is clear that nest predation, initially the main focus of forest fragmentation studies, is just one possible mechanism for landscape effects. Rates of nest predation may be greater closer to some edges, but such effects lack generality and are not a universal explanation for edge avoidance or patch area effects; nest predators more commonly exert effects at greater scales of landscape extent and composition. There is a real need for studies that simultaneously measure predation rates of real (not artificial) nests and the activity of confirmed nest predators, in relation to structure and composition at a hierarchy of scales (Stephens *et al.*, 2003). Such studies are particularly lacking in Europe, where understanding of nest predators is less advanced than in North America (Dolman *et al.*, 2007).

Two main focuses are needed for future applied studies of processes in heterogeneous landscapes. First, the mechanisms by which patch area, configuration, edge structures and context affect different components of habitat quality. Second, how do gap dimensions, perforation, grain and habitat contrasts affect behaviour. For example, what are the cues for territory settlement? How does landscape structure affect foraging and home-range use in the context of energetic stress and predation risk? Studies should examine mechanisms, but also the fitness and demographic consequences of these.

We know surprisingly little about how juvenile birds disperse from their natal territories, and not enough to provide reliable guidance on landscape design. The role of post-natal dispersal and exploration in determining subsequent territory settlement of both residents and long-distance migrants, is poorly understood, but can be strongly affected by landscape permeability, composition and structure. Although individual-based models can assist in exploring consequences of dispersal and territory turnover for population abundance and local patch occupancy, these require sound parameterisation based on empirical studies. To date, this is largely lacking. There is a need for further intensive studies to examine movement behaviour across contrasting landscapes that differ in structure, connectivity, perforation and grain.

At present we do not really know which types of bird species, in terms of their ecology, life-history or physiological correlates, are most strongly affected by which landscape mechanisms. Accumulating more robust knowledge about the mechanisms by which different landscape effects manifest themselves, and the contexts in which they are relevant, will ultimately allow a synthesis of understanding and evidence-based guidance for landscape design.

Acknowledgements

I am very grateful to Lluís Brotons and Erik Matthysen for their perceptive and helpful comments on an earlier version of this chapter.

References

Åberg, J., Jansson, G., Swenson, J. E. and Anglestam, P. (1995). The effect of matrix on the occurence of hazel grouse (*Bonasa bonasia*) in isolated forest fragments. *Oecologia*, **103**, 265–269.

Alderman, J., McCollin, D., Hinsley, S. A. *et al.* (2005). Modelling the effects of dispersal and landscape configuration on population distribution and viability in fragmented habitat. *Landscape Ecol.*, **20**, 857–870.

Ambuel, B. and Temple, S. A. (1983). Area-dependent changes in the bird communities and vegetation of southern Wisconsin. *Ecology*, **64**, 1057–1068.

Andrén, H. (1990). Despotic distributions, unequal reproductive success and population regulation in the jay *Garrulus glandarius* L. *Ecology*, **71**, 1796–1803.

Andrén, H. (1994). Effects of habitat fragmentation on birds and mammals in landscapes with different proportions of suitable habitat: a review. *Oikos*, **71**, 355–366.

Andrén, H. (1999). Habitat fragmentation, the random sample hypothesis and critical thresholds. *Oikos*, **84**, 306–308.

Barbaro, L., Rossi, J. P., Vetillard, F., Nezan, J. and Jactel, H. (2007). The spatial distribution of birds and carabid beetles in pine plantation forests: the role of landscape composition and structure. *J. Biogeogr.*, **34**, 652–664.

Bayard, T. S. and Elphick, C. S. (2010). How area sensitivity in birds is studied. *Conserv. Biol.*, **24**, 938–947.

Bellamy, P. E. and Hinsley, S. A. (2005). The role of hedgerows in linking woodland birds populations. In *Planning, People and Practice: The Landscape Ecology of Sustainable Landscapes. Proc. IALE(UK) Conf.*, ed. D. McCollin and J. I. Jackson, pp. 99–106. Northampton: University of Northampton.

Bellamy, P. E., Hinsley, S. A. and Newton, I. (1996). Local extinctions and recolonisations of passerine bird populations in small woods. *Oecologia*, **108**, 64–71.

Bellamy, P. E., Rothery, P., Hinsley, S. A. and Newton, I. (2000). Variation in the relationship between numbers of breeding pairs and woodland area for passerines in fragmented habitats. *Ecography*, **23**, 130–138.

Bender, D. J., Contreras, T. A. and Fahrig, L. (1998). Habitat loss and population decline: a meta-analysis of the patch size effect. *Ecology*, **79**, 517–533.

Bennett, A. F., Radford, J. Q. and Haslem, A. (2006). Properties of land mosaics: implications for nature conservation in agricultural environments. *Biol. Conserv.*, **133**, 250–264.

Berkeley, L. I., McCarty, J .P. and Wolfenbarger, L. L. (2007). Postfledging survival and

movement in Dickcissels (*Spiza americana*): implications for habitat management and conservation. *Auk*, **124**, 396–409.

Betts, M. G., Hadley, A. S., Rodenhouse, N. and Nocera, J. J. (2008). Social information trumps vegetation structure in breeding-site selection by a migrant songbird. *Proc. R. Soc. B.*, **275**, 2257–2263.

Both, C. (1998). Density dependence of clutch size: habitat heterogeneity or individual adjustment? *J. Anim. Ecol.*, **67**, 659–666.

Brotons, L., Desrochers, A. and Turcotte, Y. (2001). Food hoarding behaviour of black-capped chickadees (*Poecile atricapillus*) in relation to forest edges. *Oikos*, **95**, 511–519.

Brotons, L., Mönkkönen, M. and Martin, J. L. (2003). Are fragments islands? Landscape context and density-area relationships in boreal forest birds. *Am. Nat.*, **162**, 343–357.

Brotons, L., Pons, P. and Herrando, S. (2005a). Colonization of dynamic Mediterranean landscapes: where do birds come from after fire? *J. Biogeogr.*, **32**, 789–798.

Brotons, L., Wolff, A., Paulus, G. and Martin, J.-L. (2005b). Effect of adjacent agricultural habitat on the distribution of passerines in natural grasslands. *Biol. Conserv.*, **124**, 407–414.

Brown, J. H. and Kodric-Brown, A. (1977). Turnover rates in insular biogeography: effect of immigration on extinction. *Ecology*, **58**, 445–449.

Brown, J. L. (1969). The buffer effect and productivity in tit populations. *Am. Nat.*, **103**, 347–354.

Caplat, P. and Fonderflick, J. (2009). Area mediated shifts in bird community composition: a study on a fragmented Mediterranean grassland. *Biodivers. Conserv.*, **18**, 2979–2995.

Catchpole, R. D. J. (2006). *Planning for Biodiversity – Opportunity Mapping and Habitat Networks in Practice: a Technical Guide*. English Nature Research Reports, No 687. Peterborough: English Nature.

Chalfoun, A. D., Thompson, F. R., III, and Ratnaswamy, M. J. (2002). Nest predators and fragmentation: a review and meta-analysis. *Conserv. Biol.*, **16**, 306–318.

Cieslak, M. (1985). Influence of forest size and other factors on breeding bird species number. *Ekol. Polska*, **33**, 103–121.

Connor, E. F. and McCoy, E. D. (1979). The statistics and biology of the species-area relationship. *Am. Nat.*, **113**, 791–833.

Cornell, K. L. and Donovan, T. M. (2010). Effects of spatial habitat heterogeneity on habitat selection and annual fecundity for a migratory forest songbird. *Landscape Ecol.*, **25**, 109–122.

Creegan, H. P. and Osborne, P. E. (2005). Gap-crossing decisions of woodland songbirds in Scotland: an experimental approach. *J. Appl. Ecol.*, **42**, 678–687.

Dale, S. and Manceau, N. (2003). Habitat selection of two locally sympatric species of *Emberiza* buntings (*E. citrinella* and *E. hortulana*). *J. Ornithol.*, **144**, 58–68.

Dale, S., Steifetten, Ø., Osiejuk, T. S., Losak, K. and Cygan, J. P. (2006). How do birds search for breeding areas at the landscape level? Interpatch movements of male ortolan buntings. *Ecography*, **29**, 886–898.

Desrochers, A. and Hannon, S. J. (1997). Gap crossing decisions by forest songbirds during the post-fledging period. *Conserv. Biol.*, **11**, 1204–1210.

Doherty, P. F., Jr. and Grubb, T. C., Jr. (2002). Survivorship of permanent resident birds in a fragmented forested landscape. *Ecology*, **83**, 844–857.

Dolman, P. M. and Fuller, R. J. (2003). The processes of species colonisation in wooded landscapes: a review of principles. In *The Restoration of Wooded Landscapes*, ed. J. Humphrey, A. Newton, J. Latham *et al.*, pp. 25–36. Edinburgh: Forestry Commission.

Dolman, P. M., Hinsley, S. A., Bellamy, P. E. and Watts, K. (2007). Woodland birds in patchy landscapes: the evidence base for strategic networks. *Ibis*, **149** (Suppl. 2), 146–160.

Driscoll, M. J. L. and Donovan, T. M. (2004). Landscape context moderates edge effects: nesting success of wood thrushes in central New York. *Conserv. Biol.*, **18**, 1330–1338.

Dunning, J. B., Borgella, R., Clements, K. and Meffe, G. K. (1995). Patch isolation, corridor effects and colonization by a resident sparrow in a managed pine woodland. *Conserv. Biol.*, **9**, 542–550.

Dunning, J. B., Danielson, B. J. and Pulliam, H. R. (1992). Ecological processes that affect populations in complex landscapes. *Oikos*, **65**, 169–175.

Fahrig, L. (2003). Effects of habitat fragmentation on biodiversity. *Annu. Rev. Ecol. Syst.*, **34**, 487–515.

Fahrig, L., Baudry, J., Brotons, L. *et al.* (2011). Functional landscape heterogeneity and animal biodiversity in agricultural landscapes. *Ecol. Lett.*, **14**, 101–112.

Fletcher Jr., R. J. and Koford, R. R. (2003). Spatial responses of Bobolinks (*Dolichonyx oryzivorus*) near different types of edges in northern Iowa. *Auk*, **120**, 799–810.

Foppen, R. F. B., Chardon, J. P. and Liefveld, W. (2000). Understanding the role of sink patches in source-sink metapopulations: reed warbler in an agricultural landscape. *Conserv. Biol.*, **14**, 1881–1892.

Freemark, K. E. and Collins, B. (1992). Landscape ecology of birds breeding in temperate forest fragments. In *Ecology and Conservation of Neotropical Migrant Landbirds*, ed. J. M. Hagan and D. W. Johnston, pp. 443–454. Washington, DC: Smithsonian Institution Press.

Gates, J. E. and Gysel, L. W. (1978). Avian nest dispersion and fledging success in field-forest ecotones. *Ecology*, **59**, 871–883.

Groom, J. D. and Grubb Jr, T. C. (2006). Patch colonization dynamics in Carolina chickadees (*Poecile carolinensis*) in a fragmented landscape: a manipulative study. *Auk*, **123**, 1149–1160.

Haila, Y., Hanski, I. and Raivio, S. (1993). Turnover of breeding birds in small forest fragments:

the "sampling" colonization hypothesis corroborated. *Ecology*, **74**, 714–725.

Hanski, I. (1994). A practical model of metapopulation dynamics. *J. Anim. Ecol.*, **63**, 151–162.

Hanski, I. (1998). Metapopulation dynamics. *Nature*, **396**, 41–49.

Hanski, I. (1999). *Metapopulation Ecology*. Oxford: Oxford University Press.

Hanski, I. and Gyllenberg, M. (1993). Two general metapopulation models and the core-satellite species hypothesis. *Am. Nat.*, **142**, 17–41.

Harrison, S. (1991). Local extinction in a metapopulation context: an empirical evaluation. *Biological Journal of the Linnean Society*, **42**, 73–88.

Harrison, S. (1994). Metapopulations and conservation. In *Large-Scale Ecology and Conservation Biology*, ed. P. J. Edwards, R. M. May and N. R. Webb, pp. 111–128. Oxford: Blackwell Scientific Publications.

Haskell, D. G. (1995). A reevaluation of the effects of forest fragmentation on rates of bird nest predation. *Conserv. Biol.*, **9**, 1316–1318.

Helle, P. (1986). Bird community dynamics in a boreal forest reserve: the importance of large-scale regional trends. *Ann. Zool. Fenn.*, **23**, 157–166.

Helzer, C. J. and Jelinski, D. E. (1999). The relative importance of patch area and perimeter-area ratio to grassland breeding birds. *Ecol. Appl.*, **9**, 1448–1458.

Herkert, J. R. (1994). The effects of habitat fragmentation on Midwestern grassland bird communities. *Ecol. Appl.*, **4**, 461–471.

Herrando, S. and Brotons, L. (2002). Forest bird diversity in Mediterranean areas affected by wildfires: a multi-scale approach. *Ecography*, **25**, 161–172.

Hinsley, S. A. (2000). The costs of multiple patch use by birds. *Landscape Ecology*, **15**, 765–775.

Hinsley, S. A., Bellamy, P. E. and Newton, I. (1994). Persistence, loss and replacement of woodland birds in habitat patches in an arable landscape. In *Fragmentation in Agricultural Landscapes*, ed. J. W. Dover, pp. 161–167. Aberdeen: IALE(UK).

Hinsley, S. A., Bellamy, P. E., Newton, I. and Sparks, T. H. (1996). Influences of population size and woodland area on bird species distributions in small woods. *Oecologia*, **105**, 100–106.

Hinsley, S. A., Rothery, P. and Bellamy, P. E. (1999). Influence of woodland area on breeding success in Great Tits *Parus major* and Blue Tits *Parus caeruleus*. *J. Avian Biol.*, **30**, 271–281.

Huhta, E. and Jokimäki, J. (2001). Breeding occupancy and success of two hole-nesting passerines: the impact of fragmentation caused by forestry. *Ecography*, **24**, 431–440.

Huhta, E., Jokimäki, J. and Rahko, P. (1998). Distribution and reproductive success of the pied flycatcher *Ficedula hypoleuca* in relation to forest patch size and vegetation characteristics; the effect of scale. *Ibis*, **140**, 214–222.

Huhta, E., Jokimäki, J. and Rahko, P. (1999). Breeding success of pied flycatchers in artificial forest edges: the effect of a suboptimally shaped foraging area. *Auk*, **116**, 528–535.

Jansson, G. and Anglestam, P. (1999). Threshold levels of habitat composition for the presence of the long-tailed tit (*Aegithalos caudatus*) in a boreal landscape. *Landscape Ecol.*, **14**, 283–290.

Johnson, D. H. and Igl, I. D. (2001). Area requirements of grassland birds: a regional perspective. *Auk*, **118**, 24–34.

Jokimäki, J., Huhta, E., Itämies, J. and Rahko, P. (1998). Distribution of arthropods in relation to forest patch size, edge, and stand characteristics. *Can. J. For. Res.*, **28**, 1068–1072.

King, D. I., DeGraaf, R. M., Griffin, C. R. and Maier, T. J. (1999). Do predation rates on artificial nests accurately reflect predation rates on natural bird nests? *J. Field Ornithol.*, **70**, 257–262.

King, D. I., Griffin, C. R. and DeGraaf, R. M. (1997). Effect of clearcut borders on distribution and abundance of forest birds in northern New Hampshire. *Wilson Bull.*, **109**, 239–245.

Kluijver, H. N. and Tinbergen, L. (1953). Territory and the regulation of density in titmice. *Arch. Neérl. Zool.*, **10**, 266–287.

Krebs, J. R. (1971). Territory and breeding density in the great tit, *Parus major L. Ecology*, **52**, 2–22.

Kroodsma, R. L. (1984). Effect of edge on breeding forest bird species. *Wilson Bull.*, **96**, 426–436.

Kupfer, J. A., Malanson, G. P. and Franklin, S. B. (2006). Not seeing the ocean for the islands: the mediating influence of matrix-based processes on forest fragmentation effects. *Global Ecol. Biogeogr.*, **15**, 8–20.

Kurki, S., Nikula, A., Helle, P. and Lindén, H. (2000). Landscape fragmentation and forest composition effects on grouse breeding success in boreal forests. *Ecology*, **81**, 1985–1997.

Lahti, D. C. (2001). The "edge effect on nest predation" hypothesis after twenty years. *Biol. Conserv.*, **99**, 365–374.

Larivière, S. (2003). Edge effects, predator movements and the travel-lane paradox. *Wildlife Soc. Bull.*, **31**, 315–320.

Lawton, J. H., Brotherton, P. N. M., Brown, V. K. *et al.* (2010). *Making Space for Nature: A review of England's Wildlife Sites and Ecological Network*. London: Defra.

Lehnen, S. E. and Rodewald, A. D. (2009). Investigating area-sensitivity in shrubland birds: responses to patch size in a forested landscape. *For. Ecol. Manage.*, **257**, 2308–2316.

Lens, L. and Dhondt, A A. (1994). Effects of habitat fragmentation on the timing of crested tit *Parus cristatus* natal dispersal. *Ibis*, **136**, 147–152.

Levins, R. (1969). Some demographic and genetic consequences of environmental heterogeneity for biological control. *B. Entomol. Soc. Am.*, **15**, 237–240.

Levins, R. (1970). Extinction. In *Lectures on Mathematics in the Life Sciences, Vol 2: Some Mathematical Questions in Biology*, ed. M. Gerstenhaber, pp. 75–107. Providence, Rhode Island: American Mathematical Society.

Lindenmayer, D., Hobbs, R. J., Montague-Drake, R. *et al.* (2007). A checklist for ecological management of landscapes for conservation. *Ecol. Lett.*, **10**, 1–14.

MacArthur, R. H., Diamond, J. M. and Karr, J. R. (1972). Density compensation in island faunas. *Ecology*, **53**, 330–342.

MacArthur, R. H. and Wilson, E. O. (1967). *The Theory of Island Biogeography*. Princeton: Princeton University Press.

Machtans, C. S., Villard, M.-A. and Hannon, S. J. (1996). Use of riparian buffer strips as movement corridors by forest birds. *Conserv. Biol.*, **10**, 1366–1379.

Major, R. E., Christie, F. J., Gowing, G. and Ivison, T. J. (1999). Age structure and density of red-capped robin populations vary with habitat size and shape. *J. Appl. Ecol.*, **36**, 901–908.

Mallord, J. W., Dolman, P. M., Brown, A. F. and Sutherland, W. J. (2007). Quantifying density dependence in a bird population using human disturbance. *Oecologia*, **153**, 49–56.

Manolis, J. C., Andersen, D. E. and Cuthbert, F. J. (2002). Edge effect on nesting success of ground nesting birds near regenerating clearcuts in a forest-dominated landscape. *Auk*, **119**, 955–970.

Matter, S. F. (1997). Population density and area: the role of between- and within-patch processes. *Oecologia*, **10**, 533–538.

Matthysen, E., Adriaensen, F. and Dhondt, A. A. (1995). Dispersal distances of nuthatches, *Sitta europaea*, in a highly fragmented forest habitat. *Oikos*, **72**, 375–381.

McCollin, D. (1998). Forest edges and habitat selection in birds: a functional approach. *Ecography*, **21**, 247–260.

Mönkkönen, M. (1994). Diversity patterns in Palearctic and Nearctic forest bird assemblages. *J. Biogeogr.*, **21**, 183–195.

Mönkkönen, M., Helle, P., Niemi, G. J. and Montgomery, K. (1997). Heterospecific attraction affects community structure and migrant abundances in northern breeding bird communities. *Can. J. Zool.*, **75**, 2077–2083.

Mönkkönen, M., Helle, P. and Soppela, K. (1990). Numerical and behavioural responses of migrant passerines to experimental manipulation of resident tits (*Parus* spp.): heterospecific attraction in northern breeding bird communities? *Oecologia*, **85**, 218–225.

Mönkkönen, M. and Viro, P. (1997). Taxonomic diversity of the terrestrial bird and mammal fauna in temperate and boreal biomes of the northern hemisphere. *J. Biogeogr.*, **24**, 603–612.

Morton, M. L., Wakamatsu, M. W., Pereyra, M. E. and Morton, G. A. (1991). Postfledging dispersal, habitat imprinting, and philopatry in a montane, migratory sparrow. *Ornis Scand.*, **22**, 98–106.

Newton, I. (1992). Experiments on the limitation of bird numbers by territorial behaviour. *Biol. Rev.*, **67**, 129–173.

Norton, M. R., Hannon, S. J. and Schmiegelow, F. K. A. (2000). Fragments are not islands: patch vs. landscape perspectives on songbird presence and abundance in a harvested boreal forest. *Ecography*, **23**, 209–223.

Olff, H. and Ritchie, M. E. (2002). Fragmented nature: consequences for biodiversity. *Landscape Urban Plan.*, **58**, 83–92.

Opdam, P., Foppen, R., Reijnen, R. and Schotman, A. (1995). The landscape ecological approach in bird conservation: integrating the metapopulation concept into spatial planning. *Ibis*, **137** (suppl.), 139–146.

Ortega, Y. K. and Capen, D. E. (1999). Effects of forest roads on habitat quality for Ovenbirds in a forested landscape. *Auk*, **116**, 937–946.

Paradis, E., Baillie, S. R., Gregory, R. D. and Sutherland, W. J. (1998). Patterns of natal and breeding dispersal in birds. *J. Anim. Ecol.*, **67**, 518–536.

Perkins, D. W., Vickery, P. D. and Shriver, W. G. (2003). Spatial dynamics of source-sink habitats: effects on rare grassland birds. *J. Wildlife Manage.*, **67**, 588–599.

Peterken, G. F. (2000). Rebuilding networks of forest habitats in lowland England. *Landscape Res.*, **25**, 291–303.

Peterken, G. F. (2003). Developing forest habitat networks in Scotland. In *The Restoration of Wooded Landscapes*, ed. J. Humphrey, A. Newton, J. Latham *et al.*, pp. 85–91. Edinburgh: Forestry Commission.

Pino, J., Roda, F., Ribas, J. and Pons, X. (2000). Landscape structure and bird species richness: implications for conservation in rural areas between natural parks. *Landscape Urban Plan.*, **49**, 35–48.

Pither, J. and Taylor, P. D. (1998). An experimental assessment of landscape connectivity. *Oikos*, **83**, 166–174.

Pulliam, H. R. (1988). Sources, sinks and population regulation. *Am. Nat.*, **132**, 652–661.

Raine, A. F. (2006). The breeding ecology of Twite *Carduelis flavirostris* and the effects of upland agricultural intensification. PhD Thesis. University of East Anglia, Norwich.

Renfrew, R. B. and Ribic, C. A. (2008). Multi-scale models of grassland passerine abundance in a fragmented system in Wisconsin. *Landscape Ecol.*, **23**, 181–193.

Riddington, R. and Gosler, A. G. (1995). Differences in reproductive success and parental quality between habitats in the Great Tit *Parus major*. *Ibis*, **137**, 371–378.

Robinson, R. A., Wilson, J. D. and Crick, H. Q.P. (2001). The importance of arable habitat for farmland birds in grassland landscapes. *J. Appl. Ecol.*, **38**, 1059–1069.

Robinson, S. K., Thompson, F. R., III., Donovan, T. M., Whitehead, D. R. and Faaborg, J. (1995). Regional forest fragmentation and the nesting success of migratory birds. *Science*, **267**, 1987–1990.

Robles, H., Ciudad, C., Vera, R., Olea, P. P. and Matthysen, E. (2008). Demographic responses of middle spotted woodpeckers (*Dendrocopos medius*) to habitat fragmentation. *Auk*, **125**, 131–139.

Rodríguez, A., Andrén, H. and Jansson, G. (2001). Habitat-mediated predation risk and decision making of small birds at forest edges. *Oikos*, **95**, 383–396.

Rodríguez, A., Jansson, G. and Andrén, H. (2007). Composition of an avian guild in spatially structured habitats supports a competition-colonization trade-off. *Proc. R. Soc. B*, **274**, 1403–1411.

Rolstad, J. (1991). Consequences of forest fragmentation for the dynamics of bird populations: conceptual issues and the evidence. *Biol. J. Linn. Soc.*, **42**, 149–163.

Roper, J.J. (1992). Nest predation experiments with quail eggs: too much to swallow? *Oikos*, **65**, 528–530.

Sala, O.E., Chapin, F.S., III, Armesto, J.J. *et al.* (2000). Global Biodiversity Scenarios for the Year 2100. *Science*, **287**, 1770–1774.

Sanderson, F.J., Kloch, A., Sachanowicz, K. and Donald, P.F. (2009). Predicting the effects of agricultural change on farmland bird populations in Poland. *Agr. Ecosyst. Environ.*, **129**, 37–42.

Schippers, P., Grashof-Bokdam, C.J., Verboom, J. *et al.* (2009). Sacrificing patches for linear habitat elements enhances metapopulation performance of woodland birds in fragmented landscapes. *Landscape Ecol.*, **24**, 1123–1133.

Schmiegelow, F.K.A. and Mönkkönen, M. (2002). Habitat loss and fragmentation in dynamic landscapes: avian perspectives from the boreal forest. *Ecol. Appl.*, **12**, 375–389.

Sisk, T.D., Haddad, N.M. and Ehrlich, P.R. (1997). Bird assemblages in patchy woodlands: modelling the effects of edge and matrix habitats. *Ecol. Appl.*, **7**, 1170–1180.

Smith, A.T. and Peacock, M.M. (1990). Conspecific attraction and the determination of metapopulation colonization rates. *Conserv. Biol.*, **4**, 320–323.

Stephens, S.W., Koons, D.N., Rotella, J.J. and Willey, D.W. (2003). Effects of habitat fragmentation on avian nesting success: a review of the evidence at multiple spatial scales. *Biol. Conserv.*, **115**, 101–110.

Storaas, T. (1988). A comparison of losses in artificial and naturally occuring

Capercaillie nests. *J. Wildlife Manage.*, **52**, 123–126.

Strelke, W.K. and Dickson, J.G. (1980). Effect of forest clear-cut edge on breeding birds in east Texas. *J. Wildlife Manage.*, **44**, 559–567.

Svärdson, G. (1949). Competition and habitat selection in birds. *Oikos*, **1**, 157–174.

Tellería, J.L., Baquero, R. and Santos, T. (2003). Effects of forest fragmentation on European birds: implications of regional differences in species richness. *J. Biogeogr.*, **30**, 621–628.

Tellería, J.L., Virgos, E., Carbonell, R., Pérez-Tris, J. and Santos, T. (2001). Behavioural responses to changing landscapes: flock structure and anti-predator strategies of tits wintering in fragmented forests. *Oikos*, **95**, 253–264.

Tewksbury, J.J., Hejl, S.J. and Martin, T.E. (1998). Breeding productivity does not decline with increasing fragmentation in a western landscape. *Ecology*, **79**, 2890–2903.

Thompson, F.R., III (2007). Factors affecting nest predation on forest songbirds in North America. *Ibis*, **149** (suppl 2), 98–109.

Thompson, F.R., III, Brawn, J.D., Robinson, S., Faaborg, J. and Clawson, R.L. (2000). Approaches to investigate effects of forest management on birds in eastern deciduous forests: how reliable is our knowledge? *Wildlife Soc. Bull.*, **28**, 1111–1122.

Thompson, F.R., III, Donovan, T.M., DeGraaf, R.M., Faaborg, J. and Robinson, S.K. (2002). A multi-scale perspective of the effects of forest fragmentation on birds in eastern forests. *Stud. Avian Biol.*, **24**, 8–19.

Turcotte, Y. and Desrochers, A. (2003). Landscape-dependent response to predation risk by forest birds. *Oikos*, **100**, 614–618.

Turcotte, Y. and Desrochers, A. (2005). Landscape-dependent distribution of northern forest birds in winter. *Ecography*, **28**, 129–140.

Turcotte, Y. and Desrochers, A. (2008). Forest fragmentation and body condition in wintering black-capped chickadees. *Can. J. Zool.*, **86**, 572–581.

Väisänen, R.A., Järvinen, O. and Rauhala, P. (1986). How are extensive, human-caused habitat alterations expressed on the scale of local populations in boreal forests? *Ornis Scand.*, **17**, 282–292.

van Dorp, J. and Opdam, P. F. M. (1987). Effects of patch size, isolation and regional abundance on forest bird communities. *Landscape Ecol.*, **1**, 59–73.

Vandermeer, J. and Carvajal, R. (2001). Metapopulation dynamics and the quality of the matrix. *Am. Nat.*, **158**, 211–220.

Verboom, J., Foppen, R., Chardon, P., Opdam, P. and Luttikhuizen, P. (2001). Introducing the key patch approach for habitat networks with persistent populations: an example for marshland birds. *Biol. Conserv.*, **100**, 89–101.

Vergara, P. M. and Armesto, J. J. (2009). Responses of Chilean forest birds to anthropogenic habitat fragmentation across spatial scales. *Landscape Ecol.*, **24**, 25–38.

Verhulst, S., Perrins, C. M. and Riddington, R. (1997). Natal dispersal of Great Tits in a patchy environment. *Ecology*, **78**, 864–872.

Vickery, P. D., Hunter, M. L. Jr. and Melvin, S. M. (1994). Effects of habitat area on the distribution of grassland birds in Maine. *Conserv. Biol.*, **8**, 1087–1097.

Villard, M.-A. (2002). Habitat fragmentation: major conservation issue or intellectual attractor? *Ecol. Appl.*, **12**, 319–320.

Villard, M.-A., Martin, P. R. and Drummond, C. G. (1993). Habitat fragmentation and pairing success in the ovenbird (*Seiurus aurocapillus*). *Auk*, **110**, 759–768.

Villard, M.-A., Merriam, G. and Maurer, B. A. (1995). Dynamics in subdivided populations of Neotropical migratory birds in a temperate fragmented forest. *Ecology*, **76**, 27–40.

Virkkala, R. (1991). Population trends of forest birds in a Finnish Lapland landscape of large habitat blocks: Consequences of stochastic environmental variation or regional habitat alteration? *Biol. Conserv.*, **56**, 223–240.

Watson, J. E. M., Whittaker, R. J. and Freudenberger, D. (2005). Bird community responses to habitat fragmentation: how consistent are they across landscapes? *J. Biogeogr.*, **32**, 1353–1370.

Watts, K., Griffiths, M., Quine, C., Ray, D. and Humphrey, J. (2004). *Towards a Woodland Habitat Network for Wales (Report to Countryside Council for Wales and Forestry Commission Wales)*. Alice Holt, UK: Forest Research.

Whittingham, M. J., Percival, S. M. and Brown, A. F. (2000). Time budgets and foraging of breeding golden plover *Pluvialis apricaria*. *J. Appl. Ecol.*, **37**, 632–646.

Wilkin, T. A., Garant, D., Gosler, A. G. and Sheldon, B. C. (2007). Edge effects in the great tit: analyses of long-term data with GIS techniques. *Conserv. Biol.*, **21**, 1207–1217.

Willebrand, T. and Marcström, V. (1988). On the danger of using dummy nests to study predation. *Auk*, **105**, 378–379.

Wright, L. J., Hoblyn, R. A., Sutherland, W. J. and Dolman, P. M. (2007). Reproductive success of Woodlarks *Lullula arborea* in traditional and recently colonised habitats. *Bird Study*, **54**, 315–323.

Supplementary material: Additional information relating to this chapter is presented in an electronic appendix (Appendices E4.1–E4.3) at www.cambridge.org/9780521897563.

CHAPTER FIVE

Avian responses to transitional habitats in temperate cultural landscapes: woodland edges and young-growth

ROBERT J. FULLER

British Trust for Ornithology

Various kinds of edges and early successional vegetation are characteristic elements of human-modified landscapes. These landscape elements have large effects on the local composition of bird communities and can be thought of as contrasting types of transition. Edges are the spatial transition at the boundary zone between two different vegetation types, whereas land abandonment and woodland management trigger a temporal vegetation transition. This chapter discusses factors influencing variation in the bird communities associated with woodland edges, lowland scrub and young managed woodland. The emphasis is on north west Europe, but extensive comparison is made with processes operating in North America. Bird communities of edges and different types of young-growth are superficially similar, but their associated resources and the processes operating within them may vary substantially.

In recent decades a huge research effort has focused on avian edge effects for the reason that these are widely considered to be one of the main mechanisms by which habitat fragmentation reduces habitat quality for interior forest species (see also Chapter 4). Surprisingly little work on edge effects has been undertaken in Europe, where forest fragmentation is predominantly an ancient phenomenon. By comparison with edges, young-growth habitats have received relatively little attention from ecologists, though this has recently started to change in North America, where reduction of early successional habitats and declines in associated bird species are evident (Askins, 2001; Brawn *et al.*, 2001; Hunter *et al.*, 2001). There is also a growing concern that population declines are emerging in several young-growth species in Britain (Fuller *et al.*, 2007). Looking to the future, it will become important to develop a more refined understanding of how birds and other organisms use and respond to young-growth. The creation of habitat networks designed as climate change adaptation measures will need to encompass diverse habitat structures of which young-growth will probably form a major component (Ausden and Fuller, 2009).

Figure 5.1 Examples of transitional habitats. (a) Typical woodland edge in agricultural landscape showing sharply defined edge; note recent tree planting in foreground designed to improve connectivity between scattered woods – Lincolnshire, England 2006. (b) Mediterranean landscape showing mosaic of cultivations, garrigue and young forest developing following reduction of traditional grazing – Languedoc, France, 2007. (c) Birch *Betula* spp. shrubland regenerating on moorland – Scottish Highlands, 2009. (d) Recently established broadleaved tree plantation showing low structural complexity – Norfolk, England, 2007. (e) Coppiced woodland with high spatial complexity with patches at different stages of growth and abundant internal edges – Suffolk, England, 2004. (f) Shrubland–grass mosaic showing high patchiness of vegetation and gradients in physical complexity – Buckinghamshire, England, 2011. Photos: Rob Fuller.

Definitions, origins and processes

I define 'young-growth' as the early stages of woodland development up to and including the immediate post-canopy closure period, but with trees no more than 6 m tall. This definition includes pioneering woody vegetation developing under secondary succession (i.e. seral woody shrubs) and the early phases of tree growth in managed woodland (Fig. 5.1). The terms 'scrub' and 'shrubland' are widely used to denote similar types of early successional bushy vegetation, mainly in Europe and North America, respectively. Hereafter I use 'shrubland', rather than 'scrub', to denote early successional bushy habitats. Most young-growth within managed woodland exists as coppice (re-growth from stumps cut rotationally) or as young plantations (growth of planted trees). These habitats are often referred to as 'ecotones', but I reserve that term for the particular situation where there is a gradient of bushes and small trees between open land and closed-canopy forest. Ecotones are uncommon in anthropogenic landscapes, where edges tend to be abrupt.

The nature of transitional habitats in pre-agricultural temperate Holocene Europe is strongly debated. Traditionally, 'gap-phase' dynamics were considered to have driven regeneration within extensive closed forests (Peterken, 1996). Young-growth was confined to tree-fall gaps, unproductive soils, exposed areas, high altitudes and unstable, dynamic environments such as sand dunes and flood plains. Edges may have occurred mainly as ecotones between mature forest and young-growth, though sharp, but temporary, edges may have occurred in tree-falls created by storms. This view has been challenged by Vera's (2000) model of a dynamic cycle of wooded patches and open space driven by the activities of large herbivores. Thorny shrubland is an integral part of the Vera wood–pasture concept, for this protects saplings from browsing and is the focal centre of regeneration of wooded groves, which in turn are eventually overgrazed and return to open grassland. 'Soft shrubby edges' would therefore have been more strongly evident and continuously available under Vera's hypothesis. Strong arguments prevail that north west Europe was predominantly forested (Svenning, 2002; Kirby, 2004; Birks, 2005). Nonetheless, large herbivores probably contributed to habitat diversity and may have sustained young-growth and openness under some conditions (Kirby, 2004). For overviews of historical disturbance regimes in North America see Lorimer (2001) and Lorimer and White (2003).

Under both of these hypotheses, young-growth vegetation, especially in the form of regenerating trees and ecotones, would probably have been far more frequent than abrupt or 'hard' edges in primeval landscapes. Species associated with transitional habitats would probably therefore have been mainly adapted to young-growth vegetation structures. It seems likely, therefore, that the subsequent fragmentation of forest resulted in many young-growth species adapting to edge conditions rather than the reverse. One might expect there to have been few specialist species of edges in the primeval wooded landscapes, but many more that lived in bushy transitional vegetation. This has implications for the origins and possibly habitat preferences of many so-called 'edge species' in contemporary landscapes.

The shift to open cultural landscapes containing managed woodland started several thousand years ago and since then transitional habitats in cultural landscapes have been in a state of flux. For example, in north west Europe there were major phases of land abandonment following the collapse of the Roman empire, after episodes of plague in the Middle Ages (Yeloff and van Geel, 2007), and in the twentieth century when old grazing systems became economically unsustainable (Fuller and Ausden, 2008). The Mediterranean region has seen extensive land abandonment in recent decades resulting in landscape transformation and large shifts in bird assemblages (Sirami et al., 2008; Gil-Tena et al., 2010). In Australia and North America the use of fire by native people to manage the land (Chapters 18 and 19) extensively created early successional vegetation. Use of fire as a management tool in Europe is likely to have been more restricted in recent millennia, but wildfires generate young-growth, especially in boreal and Mediterranean systems. Species have therefore had extensive opportunities, over a long period of time, to adapt to transitional habitats, but it seems likely that most of these species were originally associated with natural young-growth and ecotonal vegetation.

Habitat requirements of breeding birds using edges and young-growth

A substantial terminology has developed to classify species according to their use or avoidance of edges (Villard, 1998; Imbeau *et al.*, 2003). Terms like 'edge species', 'edge specialist', 'interior edge generalist' and 'edge-exploiter' imply a strong association with edges, even a preference for them. The common assumption is that, unlike species that avoid edges or that depend mainly on interior habitats, many so-called 'edge species' can readily locate suitable habitat in fragmented environments. This view is superficially reinforced by the broad similarities between the assemblages of bird species that occur at woodland edges, especially external ones, and in young-growth (Fuller and Warren, 1991; Imbeau *et al.*, 2003). There are, however, several reasons for thinking that most species apparently associated with edges in north west Europe and North America should be regarded primarily as young-growth specialists.

Ecotones and young-growth, rather than abrupt edges, are likely to have been more prominent in the post-glacial landscapes and therefore in the evolutionary history of most of these species (see above). The critical resources required by early successional species are generally more limited at most modern edges compared with extensive young-growth. These resources include a diversity of bushy vegetation structures which are associated with nest site provision, predator avoidance and food availability, especially high insect biomass and berry abundance. Large seasonal variations occur in bird usage of edges and young-growth, evidenced particularly by influxes of migrant and wintering frugivorous birds, some of which have bred in other habitat types. Resource availability and habitat quality are discussed below.

Imbeau *et al.* (2003) argued that apparent associations with edges commonly arise where species are forced to use forest edges as substitutes for their preferred young-growth habitats, which are generally lacking in agricultural landscapes. Schlossberg and King (2008) pointed out that young-growth species are regarded as edge specialists in fragmentation studies. Using results from studies in North American clear-cut forests they assessed the extent to which 17 such species associate with the interior or the edges of young-growth stands. The data showed that edges were avoided and that in all cases abundances were higher in the centre of young-growth areas. In a study in Missouri, Fink *et al.* (2006) found that most shrubland species used shrubby glades and young forest regeneration more than woodland–pasture edges. In British woods, Fuller and Warren (1991) considered that 14 species use both edges and young-growth and a further 10 frequently reach relatively high densities at external woodland edges. None of the latter species, however, are obligate edge species and several can be widely distributed within woodland. All species that use edges in British woods will also occur in non-cdgc habitats. Furthermore, several young-growth species appear not to make particular use of woodland edges, notably nightingale *Luscinia megarhynchos*, lesser whitethroat *Sylvia curruca* and whitethroat *Sylvia communis*.

So what exactly is an edge species? It is clearly not adequate to equate a local spatial association with edges to a preference for edges. For many species, edges may merely be a poor substitute for young-growth. Alternatively some woodland species may reach higher densities towards the edge because of the existence of a resource gradient towards the edge. In neither of these situations are we dealing with 'true edge species', which, I suggest, are ones requiring a combination of resources uniquely provided by the close juxtaposition of different habitat types abutting the edge. Landscape complementation (*sensu* Dunning *et al.*, 1992) is therefore an intrinsic attribute of most true edge species, though it is possible that some edges could provide a particular unique resource, e.g. a specific food.

Defined in this way, true edge species may be rather uncommon (though note that Ries and Sisk (2010) propose a broader concept of edge species based on edge sensitivity). Black grouse *Tetrao tetrax* may be one of the best European examples (Chapter 8), but other apparent examples of edge species do not withstand close examination, as illustrated by two examples from English woodland. In conifer plantations, tree pipit *Anthus trivialis* territories are confined to the extreme edges of recently cut coupes, where mature trees meet open ground. This is presumably because the mature trees provide song posts and the open ground provides feeding sites. This edge dependence is temporary because as the trees grow within the felled coupe, so territories become established within it (Burton, 2007). The territories of chiffchaffs *Phylloscopus collybita* are often located along edges where tall trees are used as song posts and rank low vegetation provides nest sites at the extreme margin. The requirements of chiffchaffs are not met exclusively by edges, for young coppice growth with scattered trees can also provide the necessary combination of resources (Fuller, 1995).

Several conclusions can be drawn at this point. The first is that the great majority of 'edge species' are not confined to edges. Their habitat needs can often be met away from edges, especially in young-growth, which often provides more extensive areas of preferred habitat structures. It seems sensible to avoid using the term 'edge species' unless it is carefully defined in a particular context. The second conclusion is that many species associated with edges are best regarded primarily as young-growth specialists. In the following sections I discuss how birds respond to resource availability in both young-growth and edges which embrace an extremely diverse range of habitats (Fig. 5.1).

Young-growth: variation in bird assemblages and resources
Broad patterns

Large variation in the plant composition of young-growth, especially in shrubland, is evident within quite small parts of Europe, such as Britain, and can be associated with large differences in bird assemblages (Appendix E5.1). On a continental scale, the most striking differences in shrubland bird assemblages are those between the temperate and Mediterranean zones. Matorral, garrigue and maquis hold a higher diversity of *Sylvia* warblers than shrubland in other European bioclimatic zones; 14 of 19 species in this genus are Mediterranean endemics (Blondel *et al.*, 2010). A higher proportion of warblers are resident in Mediterranean than temperate shrubland, and several of the characteristic warblers of temperate shrubland are scarce or absent from the Mediterranean (Fuller, 1995).

Ecotonal species have widely adapted to the open stages of managed woodland and forests, and most of these species will also use woodland edges. The match between bird communities in shrubland and managed woodland, however, is not perfect. For example, in southern Britain, turtle dove *Streptopelia turtur*, nightingale, lesser whitethroat and Dartford warbler *Sylvia undata* are more strongly associated with shrubland, whereas nightjar *Caprimulgus europaeus* and woodlark *Lullula arborea* are almost exclusive to conifer plantations (Appendix E5.2). In eastern Poland, Fuller (2000) recorded differences between young-growth bird assemblages in natural tree-fall gaps and nearby forestry plantations with eight species occurring in plantations, but not in gaps. There have been very few direct comparisons of bird assemblages in different kinds of young-growth, but it is clear that young managed woodlands are not always equivalent to shrublands as bird habitats; this theme is developed further below. Throughout Europe, however, a general characteristic of young-growth is that long-distance migrants typically make up a high proportion of the overall breeding bird community (Helle and Fuller, 1988).

In the absence of grazing, fire or severe climatic exposure, young-growth vegetation is dynamic, undergoing complex structural changes as the height and cover of shrubs and trees increase. Canopy openness is a useful indicator of habitat development from the perspective of bird populations because this determines levels of shading and the character of the vegetation. The number of species and overall abundance of birds generally increases with canopy closure (Fig. 5.2). During this period of habitat change, there is large turnover in the composition of breeding bird communities that follows a similar

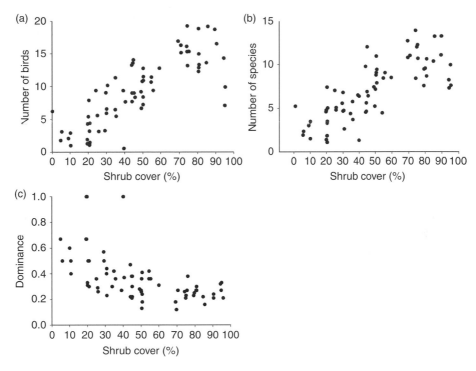

Figure 5.2 Relationships between bird community structure and cover of bushes in the Chiltern Hills, southern England. The data are derived from single 20 minute point counts of 50 m radius conducted in May and June 1980 at 70 locations in shrubland (from Fuller, 1987). For each point, panels show the total number of pairs of birds (a), the number of species (b) and a dominance index (c). The latter is the proportion of total individuals contributed by the most abundant species. The cover of bushes was estimated to the nearest 5%. The dominant shrub was hawthorn *Crataegus monogyna*, with privet *Ligustrum vulgare*, dogwood *Cornus sanguinea*, buckthorn *Rhamnus catharticus*, roses *Rosa* spp. and wayfaring tree *Viburnum lantana* also common.

pattern in shrubland and young managed woodland (Fuller, 1995). Individual bird species tend to prefer particular stages of canopy openness (Appendix E5.2). These individualistic preferences appear to be linked mainly with availability of specific structures in terms of height, openness, density and fine-grain structure of low vegetation. In the northeastern USA, individual shrubland bird species respond in diverse ways to both vegetation structure and plant species composition (Schlossberg *et al.*, 2010).

The speed of bird community turnover depends on how long it takes for canopy closure to occur. Coppiced woodland can reach a closed-canopy state after as few as six years of tree growth, most plantations take a few years longer (Fuller and Warren, 1991), but shrubland can remain open for two or three decades after the initial shrub colonisation, or even longer where succession is arrested by grazing. Differences in the duration of open habitat conditions between different types of North American young-growth have been described by Thompson and DeGraaf (2001) who point out that forest regeneration following clear-cutting changes more rapidly than in secondary successional habitats. Bird community turnover should therefore be measured in relation to change in vegetation structure, rather than years, because the length of time that the habitat remains suitable for a given species may vary substantially. The rate of change in bird communities with succession tends to be most rapid in the very earliest stages of habitat development, though there are several difficulties in measuring this (Helle and Mönkkönen, 1990). Resources such as fruits and complex habitat structures (see below), are probably available at high levels within many shrubland habitats for relatively prolonged periods due to the slowness of canopy closure compared with much managed forest. However, rotational coppicing or clear-cutting in managed woodland periodically renews the resources associated with young-growth, whereas seral shrubland is more likely to be a once-only transitional event.

Resource availability and contrasts among young-growth habitats

Knowledge about resource availability and habitat use by birds in different kinds of young-growth is more advanced in North America than in temperate Europe (Thompson and DeGraaf, 2001; Fink *et al.*, 2006). Nonetheless, based on personal observation, it appears that in much of western Europe, three features of particular significance to resource availability for birds distinguish shrubland from young managed woodland. Seral or invasive shrubland tends to have a relatively slow rate of physical development, a higher spatial complexity or patchiness, and probably higher abundance of berries. By comparison, young-growth habitat structures within stands of young managed woodland are frequently more ephemeral and spatially uniform, with relatively consistent canopy height and tree cover across the stand. This generalisation probably holds true for much of lowland western Europe, though the situation may be somewhat different in parts of North America (see below).

Fruit is one of the main food resources of birds that are provided by young-growth habitats. The fruits of woody plants form a critically important food source for migrant and wintering land birds in Europe and North America, though in the breeding season many of these species are primarily insectivorous (Thompson and Willson, 1979; Herrera, 1984; Snow and Snow, 1988). In the stages leading up to and just after canopy closure, shrubland typically provides far larger quantities of berries than does an equivalent area of woodland, where berries are often localised in tree-fall gaps and at edges (Fuller, 1995). Shrubland is usually composed of plants carrying fleshy fruits and the protracted open-canopy phase benefits flowering and fruiting. Shrub-dominated habitats appear to be strongly and widely used by frugivorous migrants in North America (Suthers *et al.*, 2000; Smith *et al.*, 2007) and Europe (Fuller, 1995; Tellería *et al.*, 2005). In contrast, most trees of commercial value planted in European temperate woodland do not bear berries; further-more, there may be limited fruit on non-crop shrubs due to shading or 'crop cleaning'. In eastern North America high fruit abundance has been reported in some young forests (Rodewald and Brittingham, 2004; Greenberg *et al.*, 2007), but not in others (Suthers *et al.*, 2000). Fruit availability in Mediterranean forests can be high where shrubs are not cleaned out (Tellería *et al.*, 2005).

The selection and use of young-growth habitats by migrant birds appears to be strongly linked with the spatial distribution of food resources, especially insects in spring and fruits in autumn. Resource availability explains why young-growth, rather than mature forests, becomes important to migrant birds and to birds in the post-breeding period (Blake and Hoppes, 1986; Martin and Karr, 1986). In autumn, those habitat types and patches with the highest concentrations of fruits are used the most, including tree-fall gaps, shrubland, forest edges and some young woodland (Rodewald and Brittingham, 2004). One study has indicated that insect availability accounts for a strong preference for use of shrubland by spring migrants (Smith and Hatch, 2008). Frugivores wintering in Mediterranean shrublands and forests are able to track spatial variation in fruit availability between years (Tellería *et al.*, 2005, 2008). It seems likely that resource-tracking ability is a general trait of species that depend on resources provided by young-growth due to its ephemeral nature. However, experimental reduction of invertebrates in young forest gaps in South Carolina was unable to demonstrate that use of gaps by insectivorous birds was consistently related to food (Champlin *et al.*, 2009). This suggests that absolute abundance of food does not necessarily always drive habitat selection.

Another set of important resources is connected with the architecture of young-growth habitats, both in terms of spatial pattern and vertical complex-ity of foliage. Vegetation structure is generally recognised as important in providing preferred habitat structures to birds in the breeding season, but it may also be an important factor in habitat selection at other times of the year. For example, in the immediate post-breeding period, young-growth habitats appear to become especially attractive for a wide range of insectivorous song-birds. This may be partly because the dense cover provides some safety from predators, but possibly also because high concentrations of insects occur there (Anders *et al.*, 1998; Pagen *et al.*, 2000; Vitz and Rodewald, 2007).

Structural complexity in shrubland can be higher than in other forms of young-growth. The physical development of shrubland depends on factors affecting seed dispersal, predation and germination, coupled with the ability of shrubs to sucker and resist browsing. Birds are principal seed dispersers of most berry-bearing shrubs (Johnston and Odum, 1956; Jordano, 1982; Finegan, 1984; Herrera, 1984; Snow and Snow, 1988; Santos *et al.*, 1999). The inherent patchiness of much shrubland, compared with other types of young-growth, may have much to do with the behaviour of birds in terms of where they roost, shelter and how they select feeding sites. The availability of perches is probably a critical factor determining exactly where seeds are deposited and how thickets develop (McClanahan and Wolfe, 1993).

This process of seed dispersal, together with the suckering habit of shrubs such as *Prunus spinosa*, are major drivers of the complex shrub–grassland mosaics that may persist for considerable lengths of time in developing shrubland. Individual patches of shrubs may differ in extent, species composition, canopy openness and height. Further complexity is created by the vegetation at the edges of shrub thickets, often being far denser than that in the thicket interior (Wilson *et al.*, 2005). Tracts of developing shrubland can therefore offer a higher diversity of foraging, nesting and resting niches for birds than much managed woodland. The birds themselves appear to be partly instrumental in the creation of this complexity of habitat structure. These observations relate principally to berry-bearing shrubs; wind-dispersed shrubs tend not to form such complex spatial patterns. This may be one of the reasons why northern British shrubland, dominated by birch *Betula* spp., supports relatively simple bird assemblages compared with most seral shrubland further south (Gillings *et al.*, 1998). Examples of how birds respond to these complex structures are given in the following section.

Shrubland mosaics and microstructures

Within managed forest, species with somewhat different habitat needs may be segregated into areas containing trees at different growth stages. But within complex shrub mosaics the same species may show an exceptional degree of territory overlap. This overlap probably arises because individuals may actually depend on several different spatially discrete patches within their territory (Haila and Hanski, 1987). Within groups of closely related species, coexistence may be facilitated by the physical complexity of the vegetation. Habitat selection by *Sylvia* warblers has generated particular interest because several can co-occur in quite small areas of shrubland. Two studies are especially informative about the underlying mechanisms. Working on islands in the Baltic, Haila and Hanski (1987) concluded that the high degree of territory overlap among five *Sylvia* species could be attributed to the existence of a fine-scale habitat mosaic that simultaneously satisfied the differing structural requirements of each species. The other study was conducted on four *Sylvia* species in Mediterranean matorral (Martin and Thibault, 1996). Here a detailed examination of foraging habitat found that warblers exploited the vegetation individualistically, differing in use of plant species, plant height and the physical elements of the shrubs selected.

The conclusion of these two studies was that physical, and to some extent floristic, complexity in shrubland mosaics enabled species to coexist through fine-scale differences in the ways that each exploited the mosaic. The assertion (summarised in Cody, 1985) that interspecific competition, resulting in territory segregation, is widely responsible for coexistence of European warbler species was refuted. Strong evidence for interspecific interactions as determinants of habitat use, has to be based on removal experiments or detailed behavioural observation, but some studies still draw conclusions based on analysis of spatial pattern (Elle, 2002). What is not disputed, however, is the fact that warblers are distributed in species-specific ways across structural shrubland gradients with varying degrees of apparent overlap in habitat use (Bairlein *et al.*, 1980; Cody, 1985; Elle, 2002, 2003; Chapter 14).

An example of warbler distribution with respect to habitat structure in seral shrubland is shown in Fig. 5.3. Whitethroat and blackcap *Sylvia atricapilla* are at the two extremes, the former occupying the most open and lowest shrubland, the latter occurring in the tallest and most closed shrubland. Willow warbler *Phylloscopus trochilus* is widely distributed across the gradient. Garden warbler *Sylvia borin* and lesser whitethroat overlap substantially with blackcap, though tend to occupy lower vegetation. Above approximately 60% bush cover, four species can occur. Three of these species (willow warbler, garden warbler and blackcap) frequently occupy the same patch of bushes. There appears to be substantial overlap in fine-scale spatial use by most of these species. It seems likely that differences in preferred microhabitat are the primary mechanism by which these species coexist in shrubland mosaics.

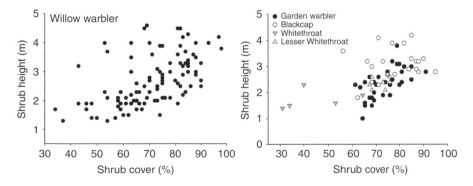

Figure 5.3 Habitat use by five warbler species in downland scrub in the Chiltern Hills, southern England, mid 1980s. Locations of singing warblers are plotted in a habitat space defined by cover and height of woody shrubs estimated for a 10 m radius around each bird. R.J. Fuller unpublished data.

The preferred habitat structure of a species may encompass several structural elements necessary for different functional needs. Examples of European species for which shrubland forms one of several functional landscape elements include linnet *Carduelis cannabina* (Eybert *et al.*, 1995), black grouse (Parr and Watson, 1988) and turtle dove (Browne and Aebischer, 2004). The proximity of different patch types *within* shrubland mosaics may be an important aspect of habitat quality for species that obtain their needs from different patches or different structures within patches. This is a fine-scale analogue of the notion of landscape complementation (Dunning *et al.*, 1992).

Edges: factors influencing use and quality for birds

The proximity of an external edge – where woodland meets open country – can affect the woodland environment in numerous ways, by altering microclimate, vegetation, species assemblages and ecosystem processes such as pollination and seed dispersal (Murcia, 1995; McCollin, 1998; Laurence, 2000). In recently intact vast forests, edge-related effects on vegetation and biodiversity can be evident kilometres from the edge (Laurance, 2000), but many studies document edge effects penetrating no more than 100 m and frequently far less (Fuller and Whittington, 1987; Paton, 1994; Murcia, 1995; Esseen and Renhorn, 1998; Moen and Jonsson, 2003), while others have recorded edge effects up to several hundred metres (Flaspohler *et al.*, 2001; Wilkin *et al.*, 2007). There is huge variety in the responses of birds and other organisms to habitat edges (Murcia, 1995; Ries and Sisk, 2004). Edge effects are highly variable (Fig. 5.4) and context-dependent; generalisations about their uniformity and universality are unwarranted. Nonetheless, in the specific context of edge effects and forest/young-growth birds, three general observations can be made.

1. The diversity of edge effects

Edge effects manifest themselves in a variety of ways. There is a large literature demonstrating that edges influence distributions, predation rates and movements. But edges can have other pervasive subtle effects. For example, great tits *Parus major* can show complex relationships of edges with population structure and individual performance (Wilkin *et al.*, 2007). Density and the number of immigrant individuals were higher close to edges, but clutch sizes were smaller and laying date later. The exact causes of these effects were unclear.

Distributions can be affected because some species are attracted to edges and others avoid them. These can be termed 'edge-exploiters' and 'edge-avoiders', respectively (Lindell *et al.*, 2007), though many of the former are essentially species adapted to young-growth (see above). The fact that the proximity of an edge alters the composition of bird communities within woodland has been long appreciated (Lay, 1938; Johnston, 1947) though the

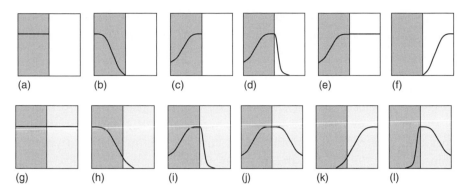

Figure 5.4 Birds can show a large range of possible distributional responses to edges, some of which are illustrated here for external (upper) and internal (lower) woodland edges within the breeding season (adapted from the model of Ries and Sisk, 2004). Dark grey represents mature woodland; pale grey is young woodland and white is farmland. Neutral responses (a, g) occur because species are not affected by resources at edges or where resources are not concentrated at edges. Edge-avoidance (b, f, h, k) occurs where species respond negatively to conditions at edges or have needs that are only met in one particular habitat. Edge-exploitation is evident where resources are concentrated at edges (c, i, j, l) and also where complementary resources are used outside the woodland (d, e). The extent to which a species is confined to one side of an edge depends on the degree of habitat specialism, but habitat specialists may show more overspill into the less-preferred habitat at internal than external edges (compare, for example, b and h, c and i, f and k).

functional basis has only recently received attention (McCollin, 1998; Ries and Sisk, 2004). Edges are widely regarded as 'problem habitats' for forest birds because they can affect the probability of nest predation. They may even be ecological traps where a species is attracted to nest there, but suffers elevated rates of predation and nest parasitism (Gates and Gysel, 1978). Alternatively relatively large numbers of generalist predators may occur on agricultural land with the result that some woodland birds nesting close to edges may be more susceptible to predation (Andrén, 1992, 1995). Some authors have attributed declines in forest-nesting migratory birds in eastern North America mainly to this mechanism (Robinson *et al.*, 1995).

   Both distributional and predation effects of edges are discussed further below; clearly they are not necessarily independent because some species may avoid edges in order to reduce predation risk. An additional type of edge effect concerns how they influence movements of birds outside the breeding season. Internal forest fragmentation can affect movement and localisation of some species within the landscape, though this can be a response to the presence of a gap rather than to an edge per se (Desrochers and Hannon,

1997; Creegan and Osborne, 2005). Predation risk seems to be an important factor influencing behavioural responses (Rodríguez *et al.*, 2001), but edges may also act as movement conduits (Desrochers and Fortin, 2000).

2. *The importance of landscape and habitat context*

Edge effects are closely linked with landscape type (see also Chapter 4). Higher predator effects are generally evident in predominantly agricultural land-scapes and where the remaining forest cover is fragmented into patches (Robinson *et al.*, 1995; Donovan *et al.*, 1997; Chalfoun *et al.*, 2002a; Rodewald, 2002). Such effects are, in some landscapes and for some species, probably mediated by elevated predation rates at edges.

Forest management often creates internal edges by clear-cutting and by the creation of forest roads. Compared with external edges, these internal edges are not generally associated with the high predation rates, or with the very pronounced distributional edge effects, that often occur at the interface of farmland and woodland (Fuller and Whittington, 1987; Andrén, 1995; Hanski *et al.*, 1996; Huhta *et al.*, 1998; Rodewald and Yahner, 2001a, b; Rodewald, 2002; Wilkin *et al.*, 2007). Nonetheless, there is evidence that internal edges can have diverse, sometimes subtle, influences on bird distribution (Hansson, 1983; Bamford, 1986; DeGraaf, 1992; Hawrot and Niemi, 1996; Brazaitis *et al.*, 2005; Rodewald and Vitz, 2005) and predation (Fenske-Crawford and Niemi, 1997; Woodward *et al.*, 2001).

Most edge studies have focused on forests, but edge effects may occur within young-growth. In central Europe, increased edge predation on rose-finch *Carpodacus erythrinus* nests has been reported where shrubby meadows adjoin arable farmland (Albrecht, 2004). A variety of edge responses has been reported for young-growth species in North American regenerating forests. Rodewald and Vitz (2005) found that seven out of eight shrubland specialists avoided mature forest edges. Woodward *et al.* (2001), however, determined that some species preferred patch edges adjacent to mature forest, while others avoided them, and that the latter had higher nesting success away from edges.

3. *Large-scale regional differences in edge effects*

Edge effects may vary depending on regional, biogeographical and evolution-ary context. There appear, for example, to be differences between neotropical and American temperate birds in their responses to edges. Lindell *et al.* (2007) found that a higher proportion of neotropical species are edge avoiders than is the case for temperate species and a higher proportion of temperate species are edge exploiters. There may be regional variations both in predator responses to landscape fragmentation (Chalfoun *et al.*, 2002b) and in edge responses of birds (Sisk and Battin, 2002; Bátáry and Báldi, 2004).

It should not be assumed that edge effects are geographically universal, nor that we can generalise about which types of species may be most sensitive. Different species complexes have different histories of exposure to landscape and habitat change. It is interesting that in Britain, and probably much of western Europe, there are few forest species that actually avoid edges, i.e. obligate forest interior species (Fuller, 1995). In North America, edge avoidance appears to be more widespread amongst forest birds, though many species also actively select edges and total density can be higher than in the interior (e.g. Johnston, 1947). Adaptation patterns to predator avoidance may vary between regions. In particular there is an unresolved question about how forest and young-growth species have adapted to landscapes that have been fragmented by agriculture for thousands of years. This contrasts with the frequent North American perception of recent man-made edges as ecological traps (Gates and Gysel, 1978), though subsequent research has not always supported this view.

Distributional edge effects: effects of vegetation and associated resources

Distributional responses to edges are mainly driven by resource availability, although predation risk and intrinsic habitat needs (which themselves can be partly resource based) may also be influential. Key resources are ones relating to preferred vegetation structures and food. Ries and Sisk (2004) developed a resource-based conceptual model to predict how species might be distributed across edges. This model provides a theoretical framework for understanding how different patterns of resource distribution at edges can potentially result in very different types of edge effects, even within the same species. A range of possible responses of bird species to external and internal woodland edges is illustrated in Fig. 5.4. Here I discuss processes that affect the selection or avoidance of edges in the context of external woodland edges.

McCollin (1998) reviewed the functional basis of edge effects in birds and identified four groups of relevant processes: (1) individualistic responses of species, (2) interspecific interactions, (3) microclimate modification and (4) vegetation modification. The first of these recognises that some species react to edges in fundamentally different ways. Some avoid edges, including some forest interior species, while others depend on them because of the particular combination of resources that occur there (the true edge species). Interspecific interactions primarily concern predation and, in North America, brood parasitism. Microclimate gradients across woodland edges could affect habitat quality, directly through physiological tolerance and indirectly through insect food supplies (McCollin, 1998). It seems likely, however, that many of the associations with edges are driven by the presence of different vegetation structures at woodland edges compared with the woodland interior.

The particular microclimate and light conditions at external edges can result in very different conditions for plant growth to those occurring under the woodland canopy. There is often substantial growth of dense, low vegetation and shrubs close to the edge. This was illustrated by Fuller and Whittington (1987) in woodland in eastern England. Although the boundary between farmland and woodland was abrupt, there was a transition in vegetation structure within the wood as one moved away from the edge. Vegetation density within 3 m of ground level was extremely high within 20 m of the edge and tended to be higher up to 60 m from the edge than in the interior. This pattern of vegetation density closely matched the distribution of several breeding bird species (notably warblers, thrushes, wren *Troglodytes troglodytes* and chaffinch *Fringilla coelebs*), which frequently reached highest density within 50 m of the edge. The positive association of these species with external edges was probably linked with preferred vegetation structures occurring there. There were, by comparison, hardly any cases where species avoided the edge, but several cases where species were neutral to edges.

Most attention on avian responses to edges has focused on nesting birds. However, structurally diverse woodland edges in eastern North America are used more heavily than the interior of woodland by flocks of migrant birds in autumn (Rodewald and Brittingham, 2002, 2004). In this region, migrating insectivores in spring also make especially high use of the edges of mature forest (Rodewald and Brittingham, 2007). This is presumably a response to higher food abundance at the woodland edge. Little seems to have been recorded about usage of European edges by migrant and wintering birds.

External edges vary greatly in vegetation structure and in the resources they provide birds. Edges that are allowed to form a shrubby margin, a 'soft-edge' structure, as opposed to a sharply defined 'hard edge', can be used by a range of shrubland and farmland species that would otherwise be absent (Berg and Pärt, 1994). Edge orientation, browsing pressure, tree species composition and forest management all affect vegetation complexity at the edge. The age of woodland edges may be relevant. With time, vegetation growth can gradually 'seal' a newly created edge (Murcia, 1995). Many individual woodland edges in cultural landscapes have been present for hundreds of years and these have probably tended to develop more complex communities of shrubs than recent edges in similar locations. Effects also depend on the nature of the forest adjacent to the edge; greater edge–interior contrasts in vegetation structure are evident where uniform mature forest, rather than young-growth, abuts the edge.

Predation edge effects: causes of variation

Although predation rates are widely considered to be relatively high at habitat edges, this is not supported by all studies (see also Chapter 4). Different reviews of the prevalence of edge effects have reached rather different conclusions. Paton (1994) concluded that edge effects were common, but not consistent, and that they mainly occurred within 50 m of the edge. By contrast, Lahti (2001) found that a majority of studies did not provide evidence for elevated predation rates at edges. These reviews drew on studies from a range of habitats and landscapes, using various methodologies. Two reviews of relationships between habitat fragmentation and nesting success or predator responses (Chalfoun *et al.*, 2002b; Stephens *et al.*, 2003) concluded that effects critically depend on the scale at which systems are examined. When fragmentation is measured on large spatial scales, effects on predators and nesting success are more likely to be evident. Small-scale studies are most likely to detect predation effects at external woodland edges in predominantly agricultural landscapes (Chalfoun *et al.*, 2002b).

Predator species often differ at habitat edges and the interior of woodland (Nour *et al.*, 1993; Chalfoun *et al.*, 2002a). However, predator assemblages can also vary greatly according to habitat, landscape context and region (Thompson, 2007). The exact types of predators present will have an important influence on the nature of predation impacts at habitat edges (Chalfoun *et al.*, 2002a). Snakes, birds and mammals can all be significant edge predators, varying in behaviour and potential impacts on prey species. However, avian predators generally appear to respond especially strongly to landscape-scale fragmentation (Chalfoun *et al.*, 2002b). On the other hand, snakes, a dominant shrubland nest predator in Midwestern North America, appear to respond to local edges and within-patch heterogeneity (Thompson, 2007; Sperry *et al.*, 2009; Weatherhead *et al.*, 2010). In Europe, the generalist predator probably having the widest effect on predation rates at external edges is the crow *Corvus corone* (Andrén, 1992; Smedshaug *et al.*, 2002) and one study has reported high edge usage by magpies *Pica pica* (Møller, 1989). It should be noted that most studies of predation at edges were based on use of artificial nests, which are open to a range of serious biases and assumptions, and that research is increasingly dependent on camera monitoring of real nests (Thompson and Burhans, 2004; see also Chapter 4).

Finally, the vegetation structure at edges may modify predation impacts. This was found in a study of indigo bunting *Passerina cyanea* (Suarez *et al.*, 1997). Predation rates at abrupt woodland edges were twice as high as at 'softer' more gradual edges with regeneration or shrubby re-growth.

Conclusions: implications for habitat creation and future research

Bird assemblages in different transitional habitats show superficial similarities at a regional level, but there can be large variation in habitat quality for individual species, both within edges and young-growth. Most woodland edges in agricultural landscapes are unlikely to offer such high-quality habitat for early successional species as shrubland and other young-growth habitats. This is because most such edges form an abrupt boundary between woodland and farmland. Nonetheless, these edges sometimes provide narrow bands of resources (e.g. fruit, nest sites) that may be scarce elsewhere in the landscape. High predation rates are not omnipresent; there appears to be much variation among species, landscapes and edge structures. Woodland edges have become widely regarded as poor-quality habitat and often perceived as ecological traps for nesting birds. It is clear, however, that not all edges are bad; they can provide local concentrations of resources that are potentially important to birds at all times of the year. The dearth of extensive areas of young-growth in many agricultural landscapes potentially makes woodland edges all the more important in this context.

The decline in North American shrubland birds has kindled a growing interest in the ecology of successional habitats and their birds (Hunter *et al.*, 2001; Thompson and DeGraaf, 2001; Rodewald and Vitz, 2005; Fink *et al.*, 2006; Chandler *et al.*, 2009). Unfortunately, there has been no comparable research effort in Europe, but it is likely that similar patterns would be evident to those emerging from North America. Different types of young-growth vary in habitat structures, ephemerality and usage by birds. In particular, managed forest regeneration offers rather different structures to those in seral vegetation, which tend to be more complex and less ephemeral. Just as concepts of 'forest-interior species' and 'old-growth specialists' are now widely accepted, so there should be greater recognition that there are many 'shrubland specialists' with critical vegetation dependencies.

Habitat creation and management

Conservation management plans should ideally recognise the ecological importance of ecotonal habitats (Askins, 2001; Thompson and DeGraaf, 2001). These are complementary to more mature woodland in both the species and resources they provide. In Europe, management for early successional species tends to focus on the requirements of grassland, heathland and fen species for which seral processes are often considered a threat. However, maintaining successional gradients and a complementary range of habitats at different scales is more important now than ever because we cannot predict whether and how climate change will alter the realised niches of species and the make-up of communities. Future responses of species to climate change are so uncertain that maintaining habitat heterogeneity, of which successional complexity is a critical part, is essential (Ausden and Fuller, 2009). A multi-scale approach to conservation planning is highly desirable in working towards such heterogeneity (Fuller and Peterken, 1995; Thompson and DeGraaf, 2001).

From a British perspective, four main opportunities would seem to exist for young-growth provision. First, large-scale development of shrubland and woodland mosaics through natural regeneration is occurring in some upland regions, mainly in Scotland (Fuller *et al.*, 1999; Gillings *et al.*, 2000). Second, many protected areas already support substantial areas of shrubland that need to be maintained through appropriate management. Protected areas offer one of the best ways of securing long-term complex shrub structures, which tend to be very scarce in the wider landscape. Third, young managed woodland is likely to continue to provide much of the young-growth in most regions. The extent of young woodland regeneration may actually increase in future decades as a result of management for woodfuel (see also Chapter 14). Fourth, large-scale habitat creation schemes are being widely advocated and implemented, partly as a means to increase resilience of ecosystems and permeability of landscapes to enable dispersal in the face of climate change (Hopkins *et al.*, 2007). In these schemes the potential value of creating complex ecotonal structures through natural regeneration at the interface of farmland and semi-natural habitats should be recognised (see, for example, the edge structures advocated by Pietzarka and Roloff, 1993). The potential biodiversity benefits are broad; in addition to birds, many plants, invertebrates and mammals can be supported by these vegetation structures (Mortimer *et al.*, 2000). A commitment to ecotones inevitably requires long-term management. There is much to be learnt about how best to manage shrubland habitats – simply cutting vegetation on a rotation does not maintain the intricate vegetation patterns and mosaics that are so desirable (Fuller and Peterken, 1995).

Knowledge gaps and future research

The literature on transitional habitats is dominated by North American research. It is unclear how well the conclusions from this work relate to the old cultural landscapes of Europe, where species have had millennia to adapt to human-induced landscape fragmentation and exploitation. I conclude with some suggested areas for research in a European context.

1. Successional changes in year-round usage of shrubland environments by birds and in the resources available to birds (also relevant to a wider range of taxa).
2. Comparison of year-round bird usage of shrubland and young managed woodland, controlling for growth stage.
3. The processes of shrubland development and the role of bird behaviour in creating spatial pattern within shrubland.
4. How does spatial pattern in shrubland (mosaics) affect habitat quality for birds? In particular, how do processes at micro versus macro edges differ (i.e. edges within shrubland mosaics and woodland edges)?

5. How will management of woodland for woodfuel affect habitat quality for birds dependent on young-growth?
6. How do species distributions respond to different vegetation structures at woodland edges and what are the effects on resources?
7. Can predation impacts at woodland edges be minimised by certain vegetation structures?
8. How widespread are relationships between edges, population structures and individual life-history traits, such as those detected by Wilkin *et al.* (2007).

Acknowledgements

I thank Chris Cheffings and Frank R. Thompson for comments. This chapter was written under a partnership between BTO and the UK Joint Nature Conservation Committee (on behalf of Natural England, Scottish Natural Heritage, the Countryside Council for Wales and the Council for Nature Conservation and the Countryside).

References

Albrecht, T. (2004). Edge effect in wetland-arable land boundary determines nesting success of Scarlet Rosefinches (*Carpodacus erythrinus*) in the Czech Republic. *Auk*, **121**, 361–371.

Anders, A. D., Faaborg, J. and Thompson, F. R., III. (1998). Postfledging dispersal, habitat use, and home-range size of juvenile Wood Thrushes. *Auk*, **115**, 349–358.

Andrén, H. (1992). Corvid density and nest predation in relation to forest fragmentation: a landscape perspective. *Ecology*, **73**, 794–805.

Andrén, H. (1995). Effects of landscape composition on predation rates at habitat edges. In *Mosaic Landscapes and Ecological Processes*, ed. L. Hansson, L. Fahrig and G. Merriam, pp. 225–255. London: Chapman and Hall.

Askins, R. A. (2001). Sustaining biological diversity in early successional communities: the challenge of managing unpopular habitats. *Wildlife Soc. Bull.*, **29**, 407–412.

Ausden, M. and Fuller, R. J. (2009). Birds and habitat change in Britain. Part 2: past and future conservation responses. *Brit. Birds*, **102**, 52–71.

Bairlein, F., Berthold, P., Querner, U. and Schlenker, R. (1980). Die Brutbiologie der Grasmücken *Sylvia atricapilla, borin, communis* und *curruca* in Mittel- und N-Europa. *J. Ornithol.*, **121**, 325–369.

Bamford, R. (1986). Broadleaved edges within conifer forest. The importance to bird life. *Q. J. Forestry*, **80**, 115–121.

Bátáry, P. and Báldi, A. (2004). Evidence of an edge effect on avian nest success. *Conserv. Biol.*, **18**, 389–400.

Berg, Å. and Pärt, T. (1994). Abundance of breeding farmland birds on arable and set-aside fields at forest edges. *Ecography*, **17**, 147–152.

Birks, H. J. B. (2005). Mind the gap: how open were European primeval forests? *Trends Ecol. Evol.*, **20**, 154–156.

Blake, J. G. and Hoppes, W. G. (1986). Influence of resource abundance on use of tree-fall gaps by birds in an isolated woodlot. *Auk*, **103**, 328–340.

Blondel, J., Aronsen, J., Bodiou, J.-Y. and Boeuf, G. (2010). *The Mediterranean Region: Biological Diversity in Space and Time*. Oxford: Oxford University Press.

Brazaitis, G., Roberge, J.-M., Angelstam, P., Marozas, V. and Petelis, G. (2005). Age-related effects of clear-cut-old forest edges on bird communities in Lithuania. *Scand. J. Forest Res.*, **20** (suppl.6), 59–67.

Brawn, J. D., Robinson, S. K. and Thompson, F. R., III. (2001). The role of disturbance in the ecology and conservation of birds. *Annu. Rev. Ecol. Syst.*, **32**, 251–276.

Browne, S. J. and Aebischer, N. J. (2004). Temporal changes in the breeding ecology of European Turtle Doves *Streptopelia turtur* in Britain, and implications for conservation. *Ibis*, **146**, 125–137.

Burton, N. H. K. (2007). Influences of restock age and habitat patchiness on Tree Pipits *Anthus trivialis* breeding in Breckland pine plantations. *Ibis*, **149** (suppl. 2), 193–204.

Chalfoun, A. D., Ratnaswamy, M. J. and Thompson, F. R., III. (2002a). Songbird nest predators in forest-pasture edge and forest interior in a fragmented landscape. *Ecol. Appl.*, **12**, 858–867.

Chalfoun, A. D., Thompson, F. R., III and Ratnaswamy, M. J. (2002b). Nest predators and fragmentation: a review and meta-analysis. *Conserv. Biol.*, **16**, 306–318.

Champlin, T. B., Kilgo, J. C. and Moorman, C. E. (2009). Food abundance does not determine bird use of early-successional habitat. *Ecology*, **90**, 1586–1594.

Chandler, R. B., King, D. I. and DeStefano, S. (2009). Scrub-shrub bird habitat associations at multiple spatial scales in beaver meadows in Massachusetts. *Auk*, **126**, 186–197.

Cody, M. L. (1985). Habitat selection in the Sylviine warblers of western Europe and north Africa. In *Habitat Selection in Birds*, ed. M. L. Cody, pp. 85–129. London: Academic Press.

Creegan, H. P. and Osborne, P. E. (2005). Gap-crossing decisions of woodland songbirds in Scotland: an experimental approach. *J. Appl. Ecol.*, **42**, 678–687.

DeGraaf, R. M. (1992). Effects of even-aged management on forest birds at northern hardwood stand interfaces. *For. Ecol. Manage.*, **47**, 95–110.

Desrochers, A. and Fortin, M. J. (2000). Understanding avian responses to forest boundaries: a case study with chickadee winter flocks. *Oikos*, **91**, 376–384.

Desrochers, A. and Hannon, S. J. (1997). Gap crossing decisions by forest songbirds during the post-fledging period. *Conserv. Biol.*, **11**, 1204–1210.

Donovan, T. M., Jones, P. W., Annand, E. M. and Thompson, F. R., III. (1997). Variation in local scale edge effects: mechanisms and landscape context. *Ecology*, **78**, 2064–2075.

Dunning, J. B., Danielson, B. J. and Pulliam, H. R. (1992). Ecological processes that affect populations in complex landscapes. *Oikos*, **65**, 169–175.

Elle, O. (2002). Microhabitat selection and dispersion suggest interspecific competition between Blackcap *Sylvia atricapilla* and Garden Warbler *S. borin* in a wood-meadow ecotone. *Vogelwelt*, **123**, 9–16.

Elle, O. (2003). Quantification of the integrative effect of ecotones as exemplified by the habitat choice of Blackcap and Whitethroat (*Sylvia atricapilla* and *S. communis*, Sylviidae). *J. Ornithol.*, **144**, 271–283.

Esseen, P.-A. and Renhorn, K.-E. (1998). Edge effects on an epiphytic lichen in fragmented forests. *Conserv. Biol.*, **12**, 1307–1317.

Eybert, M. C., Constant, P. and Lefeuvre, J. C. (1995). Effects of changes in agricultural landscape on a breeding population of linnets *Acanthis cannabina* L. living in adjacent heathland. *Biol. Conserv.*, **74**, 195–202.

Fenske-Crawford, T. J. and Niemi, G. J. (1997). Predation of artificial ground nests at two types of edges in a forest-dominated landscape. *Condor*, **99**, 14–24.

Finegan, B. (1984). Forest succession. *Nature*, **312**, 109–114.

Fink, A. D., Thompson, F. R., III and Tudor, A. A. (2006). Songbird use of regenerating forest, glade, and edge habitat types. *J. Wildlife Manage.*, **70**, 180–188.

Flaspohler, D. J., Temple, S. A. and Rosenfield, R. N. (2001). Species-specific edge effects on nest success and breeding bird density in a forested landscape. *Ecol. Appl.*, **11**, 32–46.

Fuller, R. J. (1987). *Composition and structure of bird communities in Britain*. PhD Thesis, University of London.

Fuller, R. J. (1995). *Bird Life of Woodland and Forest.* Cambridge: Cambridge University Press.

Fuller, R. J. (2000). Influence of treefall gaps on distributions of breeding birds within interior old-growth stands in Białowieża Forest, Poland. *Condor*, **102**, 267–274.

Fuller, R. J. and Ausden, M. (2008). Birds and habitat change in Britain. Part 1: a review of losses and gains in the twentieth century. *Brit. Birds*, **101**, 644–675.

Fuller, R. J., Gillings, S. and Whitfield, D. P. (1999). Responses of breeding birds to expansion of scrub in the eastern Scottish Highlands: preliminary implications for conservation strategies. *Vogelwelt*, **120** (suppl.), 53–62.

Fuller, R. J. and Peterken, G. F. (1995). Woodland and scrub. In *Managing Habitats for Conservation*, ed. W. J. Sutherland and D. A. Hill, pp. 327–361. Cambridge: Cambridge University Press.

Fuller, R. J., Smith, K. W., Grice, P. V., Currie, F. A. and Quine, C. P. (2007). Habitat change and woodland birds in Britain: implications for management and future research. *Ibis*, **149** (Suppl.2), 261–268.

Fuller, R. J. and Warren, M. S. (1991). Conservation management in ancient and modern woodlands: responses of fauna to edges and rotations. In *The Scientific Management of Temperate Communities for Conservation*, ed. I. F. Spellerberg, F. B. Goldsmith and M. G. Morris, pp. 445–472. Oxford: Blackwell Scientific Publications.

Fuller, R. J. and Whittington, P. A. (1987). Breeding bird distribution within Lincolnshire ash-lime woodlands: the influence of rides and the woodland edge. *Acta Oecol.*, **8**, 259–268.

Gates, J. E. and Gysel, L. W. (1978). Avian nest dispersion, and fledging success in field-forest ecotones. *Ecology*, **59**, 871–883.

Gillings, S., Fuller, R. J. and Balmer, D. E. (2000). Breeding birds in scrub in the Scottish Highlands: variation in community composition between scrub type and successional stage. *Scott. Forestry*, **54**, 73–85.

Gillings, S., Fuller, R. J. and Henderson, A. C. B. (1998). Avian community composition and patterns of bird distribution within birch-heath mosaics in north-east Scotland. *Ornis Fennica*, **75**, 27–37.

Gil-Tena, A., Brotons, L. and Saura, S. (2010). Effects of forest landscape change and management on the range expansion of forest bird species in the Mediterranean region. *For. Ecol. Manage.*, **259**, 1338–1346.

Greenberg, C. H., Levey, D. J. and Loftis, D. L. (2007). Fruit production in mature and recently regenerated forests of the Appalachians. *J. Wildlife Manage.*, **71**, 321–335.

Haila, Y. and Hanski, I. K. (1987). Habitat and territory overlap of breeding passerines in the mosaic environment of small islands in the Baltic. *Ornis Fennica*, **64**, 37–49.

Hanski, I. K., Fenske, T. J. and Niemi, G. J. (1996). Lack of edge effect in nesting success of breeding birds in managed forest landscapes. *Auk*, **113**, 578–585.

Hansson, L. (1983). Bird numbers across edges between mature conifer forest and clearcuts in central Sweden. *Ornis Scand.*, **14**, 97–103.

Hawrot, R. Y. and Niemi, G. J. (1996). Effects of edge type and patch shape on avian communities in a mixed conifer-hardwood forest. *Auk*, **113**, 586–598.

Helle, P. and Fuller, R. J. (1988). Migrant passerine birds in European forest successions in relation to vegetation height and geographical position. *J. Anim. Ecol.*, **57**, 565–579.

Helle, P. and Mönkkönen, M. (1990). Forest successions and bird communities: theoretical aspects and practical implications. In *Biogeography and Ecology of Forest Bird Communities*, ed. A. Keast, pp. 299–318. The Hague: SPB Academic Publishing bv.

Herrera, C. M. (1984). A study of avian frugivores, bird-dispersed plants, and their interaction in Mediterranean scrublands. *Ecol. Monogr.*, **54**, 1–23.

Hopkins, J. J., Allison, H. M., Walmsley, C. A., Gaywood, M. and Thurgate, G. (2007). *Conserving biodiversity in a Changing Climate: Guidance on Building Capacity to Adapt.* London: Department for Environment and Rural Affairs.

Huhta, E., Jokimäki, J. and Helle, P. (1998). Predation on artificial nests in a forest dominated landscape – the effects of nest type, patch size and edge structure. *Ecography*, **21**, 464–471.

Hunter, W. C., Buehler, D. A., Canterbury, R. A., Confer, J. L. and Hamel, P. B. (2001). Conservation of disturbance-dependent birds in eastern North America. *Wildlife Soc. Bull.*, **29**, 440–455.

Imbeau, L., Drapeau, P. and Mönkkönen, M. (2003). Are forest birds categorised as "edge species" strictly associated with edges. *Ecography*, **26**, 514–520.

Johnston, D. W. and Odum, E. P. (1956). Breeding bird populations in relation to plant succession on the Piedmont of Georgia. *Ecology*, **37**, 50–62.

Johnston, V. R. (1947). Breeding birds of the forest edge in Illinois. *Condor*, **49**, 45–53.

Jordano, P. (1982). Migrant birds are the main seed dispersers of blackberries in southern Spain. *Oikos*, **38**, 183–193.

Kirby, K. J. (2004). A model of a natural wooded landscape in Britain as influenced by large herbivore activity. *Forestry*, **77**, 405–420.

Lahti, D. C. (2001). The "edge effect on nest predation" hypothesis after twenty years. *Biol. Conserv.*, **99**, 365–374.

Laurance, W. F. (2000). Do edge effects occur over large spatial scales? *Trends in Ecol. Evol.*, **15**, 134–135.

Lay, D. W. (1938). How valuable are woodland clearings to birdlife? *Wilson Bull.*, **50**, 254–256.

Lindell, C. A., Riffell, S. K., Kaiser, S. A. *et al.* (2007). Edge responses of tropical and temperate birds. *Wilson J. Ornithol.*, **119**, 205–220.

Lorimer, C. G. (2001). Historical and ecological roles of disturbance in eastern North American forests: 9000 years of change. *Wildlife Soc. Bull.*, **29**, 425–439.

Lorimer, C. G. and White, A. S. (2003). Scale and frequency of natural disturbances in the northeastern US: implications for early successional forest habitats and regional age distributions. *For. Ecol. Manage.*, **185**, 41–64.

Martin, J. L. and Thibault, J. C. (1996). Coexistence in Mediterranean warblers: ecological differences or interspecific territoriality? *J. Biogeogr.*, **23**, 169–178.

Martin, T. E. and Karr, J. R. (1986). Patch utilization by migrating birds: resource orientated? *Ornis Scand.*, **17**, 165–174.

McClanahan, T. R. and Wolfe, R. W. (1993). Accelerating forest succession in a fragmented landscape: the role of birds and perches. *Conserv. Biol.*, **7**, 279–288.

McCollin, D. (1998). Forest edges and habitat selection in birds: a functional approach. *Ecography*, **21**, 247–260.

Moen, J. and Jonsson, B. G. (2003). Edge effects on liverworts and lichens in forest patches in a mosaic of boreal forest and wetland. *Conserv. Biol.*, **17**, 380–388.

Møller, A. P. (1989). Nest site selection across field-woodland ecotones: the effect of nest predation. *Oikos*, **56**, 240–246.

Mortimer, S. R., Turner, A. J., Brown, V. K. *et al.* (2000). *The Nature Conservation Value of Scrub in Britain.* JNCC Report No.308. Peterborough: Joint Nature Conservation Committee (UK).

Murcia, C. (1995). Edge effects in fragmented forests: implications for conservation. *Trends Ecol. Evol.*, **10**, 58–62.

Nour, N., Matthysen, E. and Dhondt, A. A. (1993). Artificial nest predation and habitat fragmentation: different trends in bird and mammal predators. *Ecography*, **16**, 111–116.

Pagen, R. W., Thompson, F. R., III and Burhans, D. E. (2000). Breeding and post-breeding habitat use by forest migrant songbirds in the Missouri Ozarks. *Condor*, **102**, 738–747.

Parr, R. and Watson, A. (1988). Habitat preferences of Black Grouse on moorland-dominated ground in North-east Scotland. *Ardea*, **76**, 175–180.

Paton, P. W. C. (1994). The effect of edge on avian nest success: how strong is the evidence? *Conserv. Biol.*, **8**, 17–26.

Peterken, G. F. (1996). *Natural Woodland: Ecology and Conservation in Northern Temperate Regions.* Cambridge: Cambridge University Press.

Pietzarka, U. and Roloff, A. (1993). Forest edge management in consideration of natural vegetation dynamics. *Forstarchiv*, **64**, 107–113.

Ries, L. and Sisk, T. D. (2004). A predictive model of edge effects. *Ecology*, **85**, 2917–2926.

Ries, L. and Sisk, T. D. (2010). What is an edge species? The implications of sensitivity of habitat edges. *Oikos*, **119**, 1636–1642.

Robinson, S. K., Thompson, F. R., III, Donovan, T. M., Whitehead, D. R. and Faaborg, J. (1995). Regional forest fragmentation and the nesting success of migratory birds. *Science*, **267**, 1987–1990.

Rodewald, A. D. (2002). Nest predation in forested regions: landscape and edge effects. *J. Wildlife Manage.*, **66**, 634–640.

Rodewald, A. D. and Brittingham, M. C. (2002). Habitat use and behaviour of mixed species landbird flocks during fall migration. *Wilson Bull.*, **114**, 87–98.

Rodewald, P. G. and Brittingham, M. C. (2004). Stopover habitats of landbirds during fall: use of edge-dominated and early-successional forests. *Auk*, **121**, 1040–1055.

Rodewald, P. G. and Brittingham, M. C. (2007). Stopover habitat use by spring migrant landbirds: the roles of habitat structure, leaf development, and food availability. *Auk*, **124**, 1063–1074.

Rodewald, A. D. and Vitz, A. C. (2005). Edge-and area-sensitivity of shrubland birds. *J. Wildlife Manage.*, **69**, 681–688.

Rodewald, A. D. and Yahner, R. H. (2001a). Avian nesting success in forested landscapes: influence of landscape composition, stand and nest-patch microhabitat, and biotic interactions. *Auk*, **118**, 1018–1028.

Rodewald, A. D. and Yahner, R. H. (2001b). Influence of landscape composition on avian community structure and associated mechanisms. *Ecology*, **82**, 3493–3504.

Rodriguez, A., Andrén, H. and Jansson, G. (2001). Habitat-mediated predation risk and decision making of small birds at forest edges. *Oikos*, **95**, 383–396.

Santos, T., Tellería, J. L. and Virgos, E. (1999). Dispersal of Spanish juniper *Juniperus thurifera* by birds and mammals in a fragmented landscape. *Ecography*, **22**, 193–204.

Schlossberg, S. and King, D. I. (2008). Are shrubland birds edge specialists? *Ecol. Appl.*, **18**, 1325–1330.

Schlossberg, S., King, D. I., Chandler, R. B. and Mazzei, B. A. (2010). Regional synthesis of habitat relationships in shrubland birds. *J. Wildlife Manage.*, **74**, 1513–1522.

Sirami, C., Brotons, L., Burfield, I., Fonderflick, J. and Martin, J.-L. (2008). Is land abandonment having an impact on biodiversity? A meta-analytical approach to bird distribution changes in the north-western Mediterranean *Biol. Conserv.*, **141**, 450–459.

Sisk, T. D. and Battin, J. (2002). Habitat edges and avian ecology: geographic patterns and insights for western landscapes. *Stud. Avian Biol.*, **25**, 30–48.

Smedshaug, C. A., Lund, S. E., Brekke, A., Sonerud, G. A. and Rafoss, T. (2002). The importance of the farmland-forest edge for area use of breeding Hooded Crows as revealed by radio telemetry. *Ornis Fennica*, **79**, 1–13.

Smith, R. J. and Hatch, M. I. (2008). A comparison of shrub-dominated and forested habitat use by spring migrating landbirds in northeastern Pennsylvania. *Condor*, **110**, 682–693.

Smith, S. B., McPherson, K. H., Backer, J. M. *et al.* (2007). Fruit quality and consumption by songbirds during autumn migration. *Wilson J. Ornithol.*, **119**, 419–428.

Snow, B. and Snow, D. (1988). *Birds and Berries: A Study of an Ecological Interaction*. Calton: Poyser.

Sperry, J. H., Cimprich, D. A., Peak, R. G. and Weatherhead, P. J. (2009). Is nest predation on two endangered bird species higher in habitats preferred by snakes? *Ecoscience*, **16**, 111–118.

Stephens, S. E., Koons, D. N., Rotella, J. J. and Willey, D. W. (2003). Effects of habitat fragmentation on avian nesting success. *Biol. Conserv.*, **115**, 101–110.

Suarez, A. V., Pfennig, K. S. and Robinson, S. K. (1997). Nesting success of a disturbance-dependent songbird on different kinds of edges. *Conserv. Biol.*, **11**, 928–935.

Suthers, H. B., Bickal, J. M. and Rodewald, P. G. (2000). Use of successional habitat and fruit resources by songbirds during autumn migration in central New Jersey. *Wilson Bull.*, **112**, 249–260.

Svenning, J.-C. (2002). A review of natural vegetation openness in north-western Europe. *Biol. Conserv.*, **104**, 133–148.

Tellería, J. L., Ramirez, A. and Pérez-Tris, J. (2005). Conservation of seed-dispersing migrant birds in Mediterranean habitats: shedding light on patterns to preserve processes. *Biol. Conserv.*, **124**, 493–502.

Tellería, J. L., Ramirez, A. and Pérez-Tris, J. (2008). Fruit tracking between sites and years by birds in Mediterranean wintering grounds. *Ecography*, **31**, 381–388.

Thompson, F. R., III. (2007). Factors affecting nest predation on forest songbirds in North America. *Ibis*, **149** (Suppl. 2), 98–109.

Thompson, F. R., III and Burhans, D. E. (2004). Differences in predators of artificial and real songbird nests: evidence of bias in artificial nest studies. *Conserv. Biol.*, **18**, 373–380.

Thompson, F. R., III and DeGraaf, R. M. (2001). Conservation approaches for woody, early successional communities in the eastern United States. *Wildlife Soc. Bull.*, **29**, 483–494.

Thompson, J. N. and Willson, M. F. (1979). Evolution of temperate fruit/bird interactions: phenological strategies. *Evolution*, **33**, 973–982.

Yeloff, D. and van Geel, B. (2007). Abandonment of farmland and vegetation succession following the Eurasian plague pandemic of AD1347–52. *J. Biogeogr.*, **34**, 575–582.

Vera, F. W. M. (2000). *Grazing Ecology and Forest History*. Wallingford: CABI Publishing.

Villard, M.-A. (1998). On forest-interior species, edge avoidance, area sensitivity, and dogmas in avian conservation. *Auk*, **115**, 801–805.

Vitz, A. C. and Rodewald, A. D. (2007). Vegetative and fruit resources as determinants of habitat use by mature-forest birds during the postbreeding period. *Auk*, **124**, 494–507.

Weatherhead, P. J., Carfagno, G. L. F., Sperry, J. H., Brawn, J. D. and Robinson, S. K. (2010). Linking snake behavior to nest predation in a Midwestern bird community. *Ecol. Appl.*, **20**, 234–241.

Wilkin, T. A., Garant, D., Gosler, A. G. and Sheldon, B. C. (2007). Edge effects in the Great Tit: analyses of long-term data with GIS techniques. *Conserv. Biol.*, **21**, 1207–1217.

Wilson, A. M., Fuller, R. J., Day, C. and Smith, G. (2005). Nightingales *Luscinia megarhynchos* in scrub habitats in the southern fens of East Anglia, England: associations with soil type and vegetation structure. *Ibis*, **147**, 498–511.

Woodward, A. A., Fink, A. D. and Thompson, F. R., III. (2001). Edge effects and ecological traps: effects on shrubland birds in Missouri. *J. Wildlife Manage.*, **65**, 668–675.

Supplementary material: Further information is available for this chapter in an electronic appendix (Appendix E5.1–E5.2) at www.cambridge.org/9780521897563.

CHAPTER SIX

Habitat associations of birds in complex changing cultural landscapes

SHELLEY A. HINSLEY

Centre for Ecology and Hydrology, UK

and

SIMON GILLINGS

British Trust for Ornithology

Habitat is a key factor limiting the distribution of bird species, but how we define species habitat selection depends on the scale of the analysis and the structure of the environment (Chapter 1). In regions such as western Europe where the landscape is highly man-modified, the scale and configuration of habitat patches is usually markedly different from that in more natural landscapes, with a corresponding difference in how birds respond and in our perceptions of their habitat associations. In such historically fragmented and modified landscapes, species may have been forced to adapt to a wider range of habitats than is the case in less-modified landscapes (Chapter 3). This may have consequences for the extent to which many species in long-established cultural landscapes can be regarded as true habitat specialists.

This chapter discusses how birds use European cultural landscapes, taking Britain as an example. We first outline the processes that have operated within these landscapes to influence the pattern, availability and quality of habitat for birds. We then discuss approaches and constraints to classifying birds by their apparent habitat associations. Finally, we analyse patterns of habitat use at different scales for species widely considered as generalists and specialists of certain habitats, and assess the robustness of these classifications. Classically, specialist species are those whose survival and/or breeding performance depends on a relatively narrow resource base or whose impact or functional role within their environment is relatively narrow, whereas generalists utilise a wider range of resources or have wider or multiple functional roles (reviewed by Devictor *et al.*, 2010). However, as discussed by Devictor *et al.* (2010), the use of these terms in practice has been complicated by numerous re-definitions and permutations (at multiple levels, from individuals through to populations, and across spatial scales) by many different authors. Recent work (Julliard *et al.*, 2006; Devictor *et al.*, 2008) has been

Birds and Habitat: Relationships in Changing Landscapes, ed. Robert J. Fuller. Published by Cambridge University Press. © Cambridge University Press 2012.

successful in applying a particular definition of a species specialisation index in relation to responses to habitat fragmentation and disturbance, but this still required a priori definition of habitat types.

An overview of processes affecting habitat structures and birds in cultural landscapes

The dominant role of agriculture in landscape transformation

In common with much of Europe, Britain has a long history of habitat and landscape modification driven by human use of resources and population growth (Darby, 1951; Johnston and Doornkamp, 1982). Cultural landscapes are the realised consequences of both planned and incidental changes at a range of scales from individual actions to national and global policies. British landscapes have been altered by people for at least 6000 years (Simmons, 2001). Major changes included clearance of the original post-glacial land cover (probably dominated by mature forest), widespread drainage and drastic modification of the native fauna. Persecution and exploitation of wildlife has had severe impacts on many bird species across the centuries, especially raptors and seabirds. Despite this history of modification, it is possible that the rate and extent of landscape change, and its impact on birds, may have been at least as great within the last 100 years as at any time in the past, and especially so since the advent of agricultural intensification in the 1950s (Fuller and Ausden, 2008). The British countryside has been manufactured by the necessity to feed and house its people, and the concomitant political and industrial demands on resources coupled with technological develop-ment and population growth. From 1901 to 2005, the population increased from 38.2 to 60.2 million (ESRC, 2009). Although urban and industrial devel-opment and its associated infrastructure (c. 10% of land cover), have a large visual impact, agriculture (c. 74%) has had by far the largest influence on landscape structure and composition. By contrast, forest and woodland cover only some 12%, but are likely to increase in future decades. Despite the predominance of agriculture, the less extensive land uses may have had disproportionate effects on certain habitats, such as heathland, mires and estuaries, by virtue of their locations. Drainage and reclamation of unculti-vated lands have been widely undertaken since at least the Roman occupation and gained momentum, from the twelfth century onwards (Purseglove, 1988; Wilson *et al.*, 2009). Thus, the familiarity of long-established agricultural land-scapes as 'the countryside' can cause misinterpretation of our 'green and pleasant land' which is now largely a product of human activity.

Certain types of ancient landscape structures and low-intensity manage-ment practices are now associated with high biodiversity (Bignal and McCracken, 2000), but preserving these landscapes and practices carries both economic and social costs. The difficulties of balancing the conflicting requirements of biodiversity, social change, and agricultural and economic development are exemplified by the extensive grazing systems typical of semi-arid and upland areas of Europe (Bignal, 1991). Many of these maintain habitats with an ecological value that has been lost elsewhere and whose associated bird species are declining or globally threatened (Tucker and Heath, 1994) through intensification and/or land abandonment (Scozzafava and De Sanctis, 2006). Europe's most abundant and diverse farmland bird populations are now found in extensively, rather than intensively, farmed landscapes (Tucker and Heath, 1994; Doxa *et al.*, 2010).

Originally, forest clearance and the spread of agriculture would have created new opportunities for a wide range of species associated with open habitats and the cropland itself (Wilson *et al.*, 2009). Species such as quail *Coturnix coturnix*, corncrake *Crex crex* and stone-curlew *Burhinus oedicnemus* could nest in the fallows and crops with others such as harriers, grouse, great bustard *Otis tarda*, wheatear *Oenanthe oenanthe* and whinchat *Saxicola rubetra* exploiting open heaths and downland. Thus the initial introduction of crops into the landscape can increase habitat diversity, facilitating population increase and colonisation by various species. However, such benefits are usually lost following intensification – for example, the spread of little bustards *Tetrax tetrax* into the steppe habitat of La Crau in southern France in the 1950s was associated with the presence of extensive agriculture; intensive areas are avoided (Wolff *et al.*, 2001). Tubbs (1997) suggested that a period of maximum biodiversity may have existed around the middle of the eighteenth century through a mix of low-input, low-output farming systems. With certain caveats related to scale (see below), landscape and habitat heterogeneity are generally positively associated with species diversity and ecosystem stability. Relatively fine-grained habitat diversity around settlements (e.g. small fields, woods, scrub, hedges) combined with tracts of open cultivation and extensive grazing land probably supplied such a structure. These landscapes provided resources for a larger range of bird species, and larger populations of many species, than do the same areas today. Heterogeneity across the farmed land (Chapter 7) would have been high, benefiting many species depending on fallow, crops, grassland and rough grazing. Some wetland species that are rare today (see Chapter 10), such as bittern *Botaurus stellaris* and marsh harrier *Circus aeruginosus* were probably widespread. Woodland within these landscapes would have been worked for woodfuel, food/fodder and coppice products, as well as for timber (Rackham, 1987), generating a heterogeneous internal structure of different growth stages favourable for a diverse avifauna (Chapter 14).

The massive changes in farming practices in the second half of the twentieth century, and consequences for birds, have been extensively reviewed elsewhere (Stoate, 1996; Donald *et al.*, 2001; Robinson and Sutherland, 2002;

Shrubb, 2003; Wilson *et al.*, 2009). Agricultural intensification has decreased the heterogeneity of British farmland at all scales by removing many remaining fragments of semi-natural habitat, increasing field sizes, promoting large-scale monoculture, reducing mixed farming and developing practices that maximise yields (Chapter 7). Land drainage and flood control have removed or modified much wet meadow habitat to the detriment of its breeding birds (Chapter 11). Drier landscapes may also reduce the abundance and availability of invertebrates in the semi-natural habitat patches embedded within farmland, as well as in the crops (Field and Anderson, 2004; Peach *et al.*, 2004).

The consequences of modern farming for biodiversity in western Europe have been typified by huge population declines, and in some cases range retractions, of many bird species living in farmland (Donald *et al.*, 2001; Wilson *et al.*, 2009). As many as 28 of the 52 species currently included in the most recent *UK Red List of Birds of Conservation Concern* (Eaton *et al.*, 2009) have at least some association with farmed landscapes. The high profile of these declines resulted in a *Farmland Bird Index* (FBI, Defra, 2009) being adopted as one of 18 UK biodiversity indicators. The FBI averages the population trends of 19 species of farmland birds (both perceived generalists and specialists) as a means of monitoring the effectiveness of measures to improve the sustainability of British agriculture (Gregory *et al.*, 2004). A large part of UK Government policy effort to mitigate habitat loss and degradation in farmland, and specifically to reverse farmland bird declines, has involved various agri-environment schemes. The most recent scheme, Environmental Stewardship (ES), was made available to all farmers in England in 2005. Such efforts can have beneficial effects at local and farm scales (Hinsley *et al.*, 2010), but as yet it is too soon to know if management under ES will influence bird populations at a national scale and reverse the current declining trend in the FBI (Davey *et al.*, 2010). It should also be noted that factors other than agriculture and land-use change may influence farmland bird populations. For example, cirl buntings *Emberiza cirlus* are increasing in France in the absence of any specific conservation measures, an effect possibly linked to climate warming (Jiguet and Julliard, 2005). Such a response may also favour British populations both directly and via immigration.

Habitat fragmentation and mosaics

European landscapes are often referred to as 'fragmented', but the process of fragmentation typically occurred many centuries ago and we now see patch mosaics that are the result of a long history of land use involving both habitat loss and creation (Boxes 6.1–6.3). Therefore, we use the term fragmentation here in this historic cultural context. This is a rather different process to the fragmentation of pristine habitat, where patchiness is created by habitat loss followed by isolation and modification of the patches that survive. Given the dominance of agriculture, modern habitat mosaics now frequently arise through small-scale additions or replacements to cropland. For example, the bird-food and wild-flower patches created under ES are typically 0.25–1.0 ha and uncultivated field margins 6–10 m wide. Heterogeneous habitat mixes, especially those typified by extensive mixed farming, have relatively high biodiversity (Chapter 7). However, the structure of an intensively farmed landscape with small, scattered semi-natural or managed patches is unlikely to approach this quality of habitat provision for birds; the patches will usually be too small, too scattered and too disparate (and possibly ephemeral) in their composition and management to provide a stable, coherent environment at a landscape, rather than patch or local, scale. For mobile species, such as many

---

Box 6.1 Landscape structural complexity I

Woodwalton Fen (208 ha, Cambridgeshire, England) surrounded by arable farmland interspersed with occasional small woods, hedgerows, buildings and road and rail infrastructure. The heterogeneous internal structure of grasslands, wet fen, scrub and woodland is clearly visible. The larger wood towards the top is Holme Fen (266 ha), the largest pure birch woodland in lowland Britain. The Great Fen Project aims to reconnect these two reserves by restoring 3000 ha of the intervening farmland to fenland (http://www.greatfen.org.uk/about.introduction) (photo: Shelley Hinsley).

Box 6.2 Landscape structural complexity II

This image of farmland near Buckingham in central England is derived from the airborne remote-sensing technique of Light Detection and Ranging (LiDAR, Vierling *et al.*, 2008) which provides a means of measuring the heights (and hence volumes) of surface features such as hedgerows, individual trees and woodland on a landscape scale, but at high resolution (cm). The image is presented using false shading to accentuate the topography and clearly shows the interspersion of hedges and trees in the farmland matrix. This landscape, along with the photograph of Woodwalton Fen in Box 6.1, illustrates the typical structure of lowland farming landscapes in England. Although structurally complex at a field scale, the larger landscape is dominated by the highly managed requirements of intensive agriculture within which other habitat types exist only as relatively small, rare and scattered remnants.

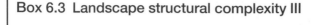

Box 6.3 Landscape structural complexity III

This image is a classification of land use derived from airborne reflectance data (Fuller and Parsell, 1990) for the same location as in Box 6.2. The large blocks of light and mid-grey shading show the dominant land uses of grass and arable crops respectively. Within this, the darker grey lines and patches show the hedgerow network and occasional small woods and, in particular, the small size and scattered distribution of managed habitats (field margins, corners and strips) created under agri-environment regulations including Environmental Stewardship (see also Chapter 7).

farmland birds, moving between small patches is compatible with their natural ability to track shifting resources and exploit small, scattered and ephemeral food sources (Newton, 1972). In contrast, less-mobile species and those with large area requirements may struggle or disappear from such landscapes. Thus modern agricultural landscapes dominated by large field sizes and low crop diversity and with semi-natural or managed agri-environment habitats dominated by edges and small patch sizes are likely to favour generalists at the expense of specialists (Devictor *et al.*, 2008).

Within such landscapes, relationships between habitat structure, management and the ability of birds to thrive (or decline) can be complex. A good example is the red-backed shrike *Lanius collurio*, now virtually extinct as a breeding species in Britain, but still abundant in Europe (Pain *et al.*, 1997). In mixed farmland in southern Austria, shrikes use habitat mosaics comprising extensively grazed grassland for foraging, and scrub for nesting (Vanhinsbergh, 1999). Foraging efficiency depends on a mixture of sward heights and the availability of taller plants within the mixture to act as perches from which the birds can hunt. Adult diet comprises mostly Coleoptera and Hymenoptera, but Orthoptera are important for nestlings. Extensive cattle grazing maintains these structures and also supplies dung, which enhances invertebrate availability, especially of the beetles eaten by adults. Similar results have been reported from the Italian Apennines where shrike habitat, typified by a mixture of grazed/cultivated land plus shrubs and hedges, was identified as structurally intermediate between land uses classed as 'abandoned' and as 'intensive' (Brambilla *et al.*, 2007). Mosaic habitats supplying contrasting foraging and nesting habitats, and a range of food supplies are important for many species (Law and Dickman, 1998), but breeding success may be modified by additional factors. For more discussion of fragmentation and edge effects see Chapters 4 and 5.

In a landscape context, it might be argued that in the last 50 years, woodland and hedgerows have changed more slowly than the rest of the landscape matrix. As agricultural management has intensified, woodland and hedgerows have been lost and fragmented, and new woodland has been planted, but the intrinsic nature of woodland and hedgerow habitat has changed considerably less than that of the productive agricultural matrix. A pre-intensification cereal field bears little resemblance to its modern counterpart, the latter typically having relatively high crop density, few weeds, high nutrient levels maintained by inorganic fertilisers and compacted soils. However, a wood at a given stage of growth shows much the same characteristics as it did 50 years ago. Cropland has become more uniform and homogenised, whereas the distribution of woodland has become patchier through fragmentation of existing woods and the planting of new, usually small, ones that are frequently dominated by exotic species. In terms of structure, hedges are similar to woodland edge habitat, the similarity increasing as hedge height and volume, and the numbers of trees, increase (Hinsley and Bellamy, 2000). Such edge habitat is favoured by generalists and thus the structure of agricultural mosaic landscapes again favours generalists, possibly at the expense of specialists (Hinsley *et al.*, 2009). There is substantial overlap in the bird species associated with woodland and hedgerows, indicating that simple classification of species by broad habitat type in complex cultural landscapes is not straightforward (Fuller *et al.*, 2001).

Habitat fragmentation may be more severe than is apparent from patch size and distribution alone; internal structure and vegetation composition can be critical. For example, at a landscape scale, much recent woodland planting in Britain has comprised exotic conifer plantations. Although some are large in extent, they offer different opportunities to a somewhat different range of bird species than do deciduous woodlands. As with coppice woodland (Chapter 14), much of the diversity value of plantations lies in their management and the mixture of compartments of different ages from clear-fell through various thicket and pole stages to eventual maturity (Avery and Leslie, 1990). In the lowlands, clear-felled and newly replanted conifer stands provide important habitat for nightjars *Caprimulgus europaeus*, tree pipits *Anthus trivialis* and woodlarks *Lullula arborea* (Langston *et al.*, 2007; Burton, 2007). In the uplands, conifer plantations have benefited species such as hen harrier *Circus cyaneus* and black grouse *Tetrao tetrix*, but this is related to growth stage; maturing plantations become increasingly unsuitable e.g. a decline of 78% in black grouse in Scotland attributed to forest maturation (Pearce-Higgins *et al.*, 2007). Whilst afforestation creates habitat for some species, it potentially removes habitat for open heath and moorland species such as red grouse *Lagopus lagopus*, golden plover *Pluvialis apricaria* and greenshank *Tringa nebularia*.

Urban and suburban landscapes

The built environment and its infrastructure currently occupies about 10% of UK land cover and is an increasing component of cultural landscapes in much of western Europe. Away from large parks and suburban gardens, the urban avifauna is dominated by a relatively small number of species (Chapter 19). Along a gradient from rural fringe to city centre, species diversity may show a small initial increase in response to a moderate increase in habitat heterogeneity, but then declines. The first species to disappear are small, arboreal insectivores, probably reflecting the lack of food supplies due to reduced volumes of vegetation and replacement of native plant species with exotics (Clergeau *et al.*, 1998; Crooks *et al.*, 2004). Gardens and parks are dominated by exotic plant species, which may support few invertebrates and hence create functional foraging gaps for higher taxa such as birds (Reichard *et al.*, 2001;

Hinsley *et al.*, 2008). Exotic plant species may also present birds and other animals with phenological gaps – even if they support significant invertebrate populations, their timing of flowering or leafing may be inappropriate for some breeding native bird species.

The breeding species characteristic of urban areas are usually ground feeders, generalists, granivores and exotics with the ability to tolerate human presence and activity, exploit abundant and often novel food supplies and to utilise buildings and other structures as nest sites in preference or in addition to trees and other vegetation. In Britain such species include feral pigeon *Columba livia*, collared dove *Streptopelia decaocto*, starling *Sturnus vulgaris*, house sparrow *Passer domesticus* and magpie *Pica pica*.

At least four species of parrot now breed in Britain and in various European cities, the most abundant by far being the ring-necked parakeet *Psittacula krameri* with population centres in south London and north Kent (Pithon and Dytham, 2002). Their increase from first records in the wild in 1969 to over 6000 by 2002 (Butler, 2002) has been less spectacular than that of some other arrivals, for example, collared doves (albeit a 'natural' invader) increasing from four birds in Norfolk in 1955 to about 250 000 pairs (Mead, 2000). Evidence of detrimental effects of parrots on native species is sparse, but results from Belgium suggest that nest site competition by parakeets can reduce numbers of nuthatches *Sitta europaea* (Strubbe and Matthysen, 2009). In contrast to urban parrots, house sparrows have declined in various British and European cites (De Laet and Summers-Smith, 2007). When horses were replaced by the internal combustion engine at the beginning of the twentieth century, birds were deprived of access to grain from horse nose-bags and droppings. London's sparrow population may have decreased by as much as two thirds between 1900 and 1925 (Bergtold, 1921). More recently, the British house sparrow population has declined by more than 60% over the last 25 years and by 65% in London between 1994 and 2005 (Summers-Smith, 1988; Robinson *et al.*, 2005). Reasons for this are unclear, but may include lack of invertebrate food for nestlings, fewer nest sites in modern buildings, air pollution related to traffic and isolation of urban from rural populations (Peach *et al.*, 2008; Shaw *et al.*, 2008). Relationships between urban and rural populations are not well understood for any species (Chamberlain *et al.*, 2009) and it is possible that persistence of some urban populations may depend on immigration. Thus reductions in rural populations could have knock-on consequences for populations within towns and cities if such a source–sink relationship exists.

Consequences and perceptions of landscape modification

It is entirely possible to preserve some aspects of 'historical' landscapes, embracing both their management and birds, as shown by the success of programmes designed to recover populations of cirl bunting and stone-curlew (Aebischer *et al.*, 2000). But such action is costly and can usually only be targeted at iconic species in selected locations. Throughout human history, people have modified their environment. Birds (and other wildlife) have either adapted and survived, or disappeared. Every change in circumstances (habitat, landscape, climate, exploitation, pollution) causes concomitant changes in the bird fauna. Such changes can be conspicuous, such as population growth in woodpigeons *Columba palumbus* in response to the introduction of autumn-sown oil-seed rape, providing a reliable winter food source (Inglis *et al.*, 1990; Isaacson *et al.*, 2002). Another example is the almost total loss of sparrowhawks *Accipiter nisus* from eastern and central England due to organochlorine pesticide poisoning in the 1960s (Newton, 1986). In contrast, increased winter mortality and population decline in small seed-eaters due to the loss of winter stubbles and other seed-rich habitat in farmland were probably less noticeable to the casual observer. The British skylark *Alauda arvensis* population has declined from 2–2.5 million to 0.8–1 million since the early 1980s (Browne *et al.*, 2000), but skylarks can still be heard singing in much of the countryside and without comprehensive monitoring that change could easily have been greatly underestimated.

As we change the landscape, the birds will inevitably change, which presents the problem of how to evaluate the consequences. If we change grassland to woodland, should we accept the change in the avifauna, and as the woodland matures do we accept that early successional species will decline? How, and over what spatial and temporal scales, do we determine relative avifaunal value? Whatever the answers to these questions, in heavily populated countries, the impact of human cultural practices on landscapes, in combination with climate effects, are likely to be the main drivers of bird–habitat associations.

Classification of bird–habitat associations: limitations and problems

Birds are frequently referred to as 'farmland' or 'woodland' species. Such categories provide a convenient means of assigning species to groups which appear to be easily understood across geographical scales, help to quantify changes in avian communities and aid in interpreting bird–habitat relationships. Knowledge of such broad relationships, not least because the habitat a bird occupies defines much of its ecology, is key to understanding the processes by which population changes occur, and for managing and evaluating the consequences of habitat creation, destruction and alteration for bird populations. A species may be impacted by many factors, such as predators, disease and climate change, but ultimately most major population impacts will be mediated through changes in habitat availability, composition and quality. Having defined such groups, their population trends can be aggregated and used as indicators of habitat change; this is the principle underlying the Farmland Bird Index (see above). However, there are a number of difficulties with this approach relating to the fact that the habitats used by bird species are not necessarily sharply defined entities due to a large range of factors. Many of these are outlined in Chapter 2, some of the most pertinent being the consequences of predator pressure and competition.

In addition, in the same locality, species can frequently occur in more than one habitat category, even when such categories are as broad as 'farmland' or 'woodland'. Species may use different habitats for different purposes (i.e. landscape complementation *sensu* Dunning *et al.*, 1992); for example, starlings that nest in woodland typically feed in farmland. They may use different habitats at different times of year, e.g. altitudinal movements in winter by meadow pipits *Anthus pratensis* and their predators, merlins *Falco columbarius*. Habitat mosaics arising from fragmentation, as discussed above, increase the difficulties of both identifying and defining habitat preferences and blur the distinctions between different types. As an example, the tawny owl *Strix aluco* is widely considered to be a 'woodland bird', but it also occurs commonly in suburban areas and farmland with scattered trees (Redpath, 1995).

Large-scale processes affecting habitat classifications

Wesołowski and Fuller (this volume) give examples of how several species that are confined to forest in east Poland are widely distributed across different habitat types in Britain. Examples are also given of species confined to conifers in central and eastern Europe that occur in a wider range of woodland habitats in Britain. Wesołowski and Fuller also point out that the longer the history of landscape change, the more likely it is that surviving species will occupy different and/or additional habitats. The long history of deforestation in western Europe, and the post-enclosure structure of British farmland, may have contributed to the large numbers of species which, while still largely confined to forest in other parts of Europe, now commonly occupy secondary habitats such as farmland, parks and gardens in Britain. Difficulties may also arise from the taxonomic classification of species, whereby, in the absence of additional information, similarities are simply inferred across subspecies or races which may in reality have been shaped by very different landscape and habitat histories.

The location of Britain on the north western fringe of Europe also contributes to the species complement of its habitats, with many species ranges failing to extend this far and even fewer reaching as far as Ireland (Fuller *et al.*, 2007). For bird species typical of small farm woods (*c.* 1 ha), across a gradient from the southern Netherlands to Norway, species richness declined at a rate of approximately 0.8 per degree of increasing latitude (Hinsley *et al.*, 1998). However, species distributions are not static and there is potential for range shifts in the future, especially in relation to climate change (Jiguet and Julliard, 2005). For example, Huntley *et al.* (2007) have used climate change predictions to forecast the northerly spread of potential colonists into Britain (e.g. hoopoe *Upupa epops* and melodious warbler *Hippolais polyglotta*) and to highlight the pressures on montane species whose climate space could disappear entirely (see also Chapter 9). Current distributions and patterns of habitat occupancy should not be regarded as stable end points.

Scale of habitat definition

Considerations of scale also operate for definitions of habitat types. For example, woodland may be subdivided into deciduous, conifer and mixed, and then further divided by species composition, vertical structure, age class, elevation, wetness etc. Although complex, these factors may have very real consequences for their bird populations. Crossbills *Loxia* spp. are generally considered as coniferous woodland birds, but at the finer scale, tree species composition in relation to seed production, cone type and seed size may determine relative species population abundances and distributions (Benkman, 1993). Hence, perceptions of specialisation depend on the scale at which habitat relationships are viewed, an effect that is probably true for all species to some degree. Variation affecting habitat use may also occur across temporal scales, for example in differences between years in resource availability in different habitats. In Sweden, annual variation in invertebrate abundance on different species of deciduous trees can affect the distribution and survival of lesser spotted woodpeckers *Dendrocopos minor* (Olsson *et al.*, 2001).

Ability to adapt: a shift towards generalisation?

Adaptation to habitat and landscape change depends on the rate of change coupled with species' innate abilities to adapt. Landscape modification will have contributed to the invasion of secondary habitats (parks and gardens) by great tits *Parus major* and blue tits *Cyanistes caeruleus*, but the absence of marsh tits *Poecile palustris* from such habitats indicates that behavioural change is also required. Nuthatch has successfully colonised small farm woods, parkland and suburban gardens, despite sharing several ecological traits (i.e. short dispersal distances, food storage) with marsh tits (Matthysen, 1998). Studies of great tits in the Netherlands have shown consistent, and heritable, differences in exploratory behaviour between individuals from wild populations, indicating a genetic component to this behaviour (Dingemanse *et al.*, 2002; Drent *et al.*, 2003). However, behavioural traits will not act in isolation. The ready adoption of nest-boxes (and other 'artificial' nest sites) by great and blue tits has undoubtedly enhanced their spread into secondary habitats. Marsh tits in Britain seldom use nest-boxes, but do so readily in Sweden, suggesting that other factors such as social learning and competition interact with innate behavioural tendencies. Therefore, the pattern of exploitation of habitats by a species will be due to a combination of historical factors (including founder effects) and behavioural flexibility, as well as external factors including climate, competition and predation. There might be a danger that we modify our bird fauna towards a small number of species with certain traits allowing them to tolerate humanity and exploit opportunities provided by human activities. Less-adaptable species may be banished to dwindling semi-natural resources, small, heavily managed populations and perhaps ultimately to extinction. Evidence from France (Devictor *et al.*, 2007) suggests that as urbanisation increases, the proportion of specialist species in bird communities decreases and the rate of community turnover increases. Such effects, whereby habitat fragmentation and disturbance associated with human activities have greater impacts on specialists than generalists, and may even favour certain of the latter, have been termed biotic homogenisation and are recognised as a global threat to biodiversity (McKinney and Lockwood 1999; Olden and Rooney, 2006). It has also been suggested that certain specialist species may respond to habitat degradation by becoming more generalist, further increasing the trend towards community homogenisation (Barnagaud *et al.*, 2011). Recent trends of increasing alpha diversity, but decreasing community specialisation, in British breeding birds have been interpreted mainly as a consequence of climate warming (Davey *et al.*, 2011).

Recent analysis of bird population abundance in Britain found no consistent evidence for more positive population trends in apparently preferred habitat compared to trends in secondary or avoided habitats (Newson *et al.*, 2009). This was contrary to the expectation that as populations increase they expand from preferred habitat into less preferred ones and vice versa. In this case, preference was based on abundance, and it should be borne in mind that abundance is not necessarily an indicator of habitat quality (Chapter 2). Nonetheless, one interpretation of these results might be that overall habitat quality has declined to the extent that the distinction between 'good' and 'poor' is no longer detectable; all habitats have become generally mediocre. It is also possible that the mosaic habitat structure of modern landscapes and the dominance of generalist species are not compatible with classic definitions of bird–habitat associations.

An analysis of commonly used bird–habitat associations

The problem of defining bird–habitat associations in complex cultural landscapes was examined in a study of habitat use by 'farmland birds' in Britain by Fuller *et al.* (2004). Breeding bird occurrence in 10 km squares was compared with the incidence of farmland at three proportions of coverage (low: 0–30%, medium: 31–70%, high: 71–100%) within the same squares, with the expectation that high proportions of farmland bird species' ranges ought to coincide with high proportions of farmland. However, for 16 out of the 28 species categorised as farmland birds, less than half the breeding range was associated with high coverage of farmland. The generality of this finding across other cultural habitat types is unclear. Furthermore, the farmland analysis was undertaken at a single spatial scale, and it is likely that the results would have differed at finer scales as the measurement of habitat approached the scale of territory use by individual birds. The following analysis extends the approach of Fuller *et al.* (2004) in two ways; first by also considering 'woodland' and 'urban' bird species groups and, second, by examining how scale influences the apparent breeding season associations of species distributions with particular habitat classifications.

Methods

We used a combination of British national bird monitoring datasets to assess the association of bird species with different habitat types at three spatial scales: 10 km, 1 km and 200 m square resolutions. For 'farmland' and 'woodland' habitat categories we used the species listed as specialists and generalists in the national Farmland and Woodland Bird Indices (Gregory *et al.*, 2005). At present, no 'standard list' of urban species exists. Therefore, from the remaining unclassified and regularly monitored species, we selected those we considered to be common inhabitants of urban and suburban landscapes based on the literature and personal experience. Lists of species (with scientific names) and their designated habitat types are given in Table 6.1. The development of these lists over recent years and their mutually exclusive nature inevitably meant that some species considered as characteristic of a particular habitat were already assigned to another category but, in a sense, this is the root of the problem of categorisation that we are addressing. The bird distribution data were as follows:

10 km   10 km distribution data from the 1988–1991 breeding bird atlas (Gibbons *et al.*, 1993). With the exception of gulls, we identified all 10 km squares with probable or confirmed breeding evidence for each species. For gulls, to ensure adequate coverage of the range of habitats used in the breeding season, we also included records away from breeding colonies.

1 km   Spring–summer 2000 data from the BTO/RSPB/JNCC Breeding Bird Survey (BBS), the national bird monitoring scheme, were used to identify the 1 km sample squares occupied by each species.

200 m   Spring–summer 2000 data from the two transects undertaken within each BBS sample square were used to identify the 200 m transect sections (200 m long by 200 m wide, hence 200 m square) occupied by each species.

Table 6.1 *Species used in the analysis of habitat associations and their classification according to the UK Farmland and Woodland Bird Indicators, and our selection of remaining unassigned species associated with urban habitat*

Farmland specialists: lapwing *Vanellus vanellus*, stock dove *Columba oenas*, turtle dove *Streptopelia turtur*, grey partridge *Perdix perdix*, starling *Sturnus vulgaris*, skylark *Alauda arvensis*, whitethroat *Sylvia communis*, linnet *Carduelis cannabina*, goldfinch *C. carduelis*, tree sparrow *Passer montanus*, yellowhammer *Emberiza citrinella*, corn bunting *E. calandra*.

Farmland generalists: kestrel *Falco tinnunculus*, woodpigeon *Columba palumbus*, rook *Corvus frugilegus*, jackdaw *C. monedula*, yellow wagtail *Motacilla flava*, greenfinch *Carduelis chloris*, reed bunting *Emberiza schoeniclus*.

Woodland specialists: sparrowhawk *Accipiter nisus*, jay *Garrulus glandarius*, great spotted woodpecker *Dendrocopos major*, lesser spotted woodpecker *D. minor*, tree pipit *Anthus trivialis*, nightingale *Luscinia megarhynchos*, redstart *Phoenicurus phoenicurus*, nuthatch *Sitta europaea*, treecreeper *Certhia familiaris*, blackcap *Sylvia atricapilla*, garden warbler *S. borin*, chiffchaff *Phylloscopus collybita*, willow warbler *P. trochilus*, goldcrest *Regulus regulus*, spotted flycatcher *Muscicapa striata*, coal tit *Periparus ater*, marsh tit *Poecile palustris*, willow tit *P. montanus*, redpoll *Carduelis flammea*, hawfinch *Coccothraustes coccothraustes*.

Woodland generalists: tawny owl *Strix aluco*, green woodpecker *Picus viridis*, dunnock *Prunella modularis*, wren *Troglodytes troglodytes*, blackbird *Turdus merula*, song thrush *T. philomelos*, robin *Erithacus rubecula*, great tit *Parus major*, blue tit *Cyanistes caeruleus*, long-tailed tit *Aegithalos caudatus*, lesser whitethroat *Sylvia curruca*, chaffinch *Fringilla coelebs*, bullfinch *Pyrrhula pyrrhula*.

Urban specialists: black-headed gull *Chroicocephalus ridibundus*, lesser black-backed gull *Larus fuscus*, herring gull *L. argentatus*, feral pigeon *Columba livia*, collared dove *Streptopelia decaocto*, swift *Apus apus*, carrion crow *Corvus corone*, magpie *Pica pica*, house martin *Delichon urbica*, house sparrow *Passer domesticus*.

We identified all the squares at each scale that had a 'high' cover of each of seven broad habitat types (farmland, broadleaved woodland, all woodland, built environment, moorland, coastal and miscellaneous). The difficulty was to produce a threshold defining 'high cover' that could be applied across habitats that varied widely in their overall availability. For example, at the 10 km square scale, urban habitat is considerably scarcer than farmland habitat: 75% of 10 km squares have less than 7.5% cover of urban habitat and none would have been classified as 'high' if using the absolute threshold of 70% cover, as used for farmland by Fuller *et al.* (2004). A re-analysis of data used by Fuller *et al.* (2004) showed that the threshold of 70% farmland cover corresponded to the 69th percentiles of non-zero farmland cover values.

Therefore, we used this percentile to categorise squares as 'high cover' for each habitat type. Data sources and derivations for habitat types were as follows:

10 km   The percentage cover of each broad habitat type in each 10 km square in Britain was derived from the Land Cover Map 1990 (LCM1990, Fuller and Parsell, 1990) which was contemporary with the 1988–1991 atlas data. For each habitat in turn, the 69th percentile of non-zero percentage cover values was determined and used to identify 'high cover' squares. For example, the 'high' farmland category was all 10 km squares with more than 69.9% farmland cover, whereas the 'high' urban category was all 10 km squares with more than 6.1% urban cover.

1 km   The percentage cover of each broad habitat type in each 1 km square in Britain was derived from the Land Cover Map 2000 (LCM2000, Fuller *et al.*, 2002) which was contemporary with the 2000 BBS data. As above, the 69th percentile was derived and used to classify squares according to habitat availability. Whereas the 10 km analysis included all 10 km squares in Britain, the BBS is a sample survey (2301 squares in 2000) stratified by human population density. Therefore, the percentage cover figures used at this scale did not represent the whole country, but since the bird data come from the same stratified sample, the habitat versus bird comparisons were valid.

200 m   Each of the two 1 km transects of a BBS square are divided into five 200 m sections. It was not possible to assign the LCM2000 data to each of these; instead we used the habitat classifications given by BBS observers that described the two most important habitats in each section. An initial analysis found a high correlation between the LCM2000 estimates of percentage cover of broad habitat types at the 1 km scale and the percentage of the 20 habitat codes given by the observers ($r > 0.7$ for each habitat except the 'miscellaneous' category where $r = 0.12$). This suggested that the categories used to describe BBS transect sections approximated well to those used in the larger-scale analyses. Thus, for the main habitat types considered, any differences in results between scales ought to have been due to scale effects, rather than methodology.

At the 10 km and 1 km scales, the proportion of squares classified as 'high cover' occupied by each species was determined for each habitat type. Results were then summarised to obtain a mean and standard error (SE) for each of the five bird categories, i.e. farmland specialists and generalists, woodland specialists and generalists, and urban birds. For each species, the habitat type coinciding with the greatest proportion of the breeding range was identified. The species with the greatest and the lowest proportions of their ranges associated with farmland, woodland and urban habitats were also identified. For the 200 m analysis, we calculated the percentage occupancy of habitat sections by counting the number of times each habitat code was assigned to a transect section occupied by a species and dividing that value by the number of times each habitat code was used across all surveyed squares. For each species, the two habitats with the highest percentage occupancy were identified as primary and secondary habitats. For example, blackbirds occupied 86% of built environment transect sections, and 67% of woodland sections.

Note that detailed results for the 200 m scale are presented as tables in an electronic appendix (Appendices E6.1–E6.4).

Results and discussion

At the 10 km scale, the breeding ranges of all farmland specialists and generalists had their greatest percentage occurrences within high-cover farmland squares. However, for woodland specialists and generalists, only 55% and 15% respectively of species ranges were most closely associated with high-cover woodland squares, with farmland being the most frequent dominant habitat type in the mismatched cases. Only one of the urban species, feral pigeon, had urban habitat as the dominant habitat type and for six species farmland squares dominated their breeding ranges. The importance of farmland at the 10 km scale was also apparent for the mean proportions of the breeding ranges of the five bird categories within each habitat type (Table 6.2). Although farmland and woodland specialists occupied, on average, 45% of high-coverage squares of their designated habitats, farmland was also well occupied by woodland and urban species. This response reflects the dominance of farmland as the majority land cover in Britain and suggests that at a 10 km scale, habitat is highly heterogeneous and mixed within the farmland matrix. This potential 'homogenisation' of habitat into a landscape blend implies that, at this scale, 'farmland' and 'woodland' birds may respond to habitat changes that do not directly affect their designated primary habitat, for example through edge, isolation and source–sink effects (Hansen and di Castri, 1992; Mazerolle and Villard, 1999; Chalfoun et al., 2002; Swift and Hannon, 2010). A third or more of the breeding range of all five bird categories was associated with the built environment, suggesting that buildings are well distributed across the whole landscape at the 10 km scale.

At the 1 km scale, the results were slightly more in line with expectation, with a match between designated and observed habitats occurring for 100% of farmland specialists and generalists, 85% of woodland specialists, 46% of woodland generalists and 30% of urban species. Where mismatching occurred, farmland was again the observed dominant habitat in all cases.

Table 6.2 *Associations of bird species categories with 'high' cover of different habitat types at 10 km and 1 km scales*

| Habitat type | Scale, km | Threshold, % cover | Percentage of breeding range, mean (SE) | | | | |
| | | | Farmland birds | | Woodland birds | | Urban birds |
			Specialists *n* = 12	Generalists *n* = 7	Specialists *n* = 20	Generalists *n* = 13	Specialists *n* = 10
Farmland	10	>69.9	**45 (2.9)**	**41 (2.8)**	41 (2.1)	38 (1.6)	35 (3.0)
	1	>87.6	**45 (2.9)**	**39 (3.9)**	22 (1.8)	29 (1.4)	30 (0.7)
Deciduous woodland	10	>4.6	34 (1.1)	34 (0.8)	**45 (2.1)**	**36 (1.6)**	32 (2.5)
	1	>13.8	19 (1.7)	21 (2.6)	**40 (2.3)**	**31 (2.1)**	21 (1.2)
All woodland	10	>8.0	30 (1.1)	31 (2.0)	**40 (1.3)**	**34 (0.9)**	30 (1.4)
	1	>17.4	18 (1.4)	20 (2.7)	**46 (2.4)**	**30 (1.9)**	20 (1.1)
Built environment	10	>6.1	41 (2.8)	38 (3.2)	38 (2.4)	35 (1.8)	**33 (2.4)**
	1	>17.1	16 (1.7)	18 (2.1)	15 (1.7)	22 (1.2)	**31 (2.1)**
Moorland	10	>17.6	16 (2.8)	21 (2.1)	21 (3.1)	24 (2.2)	23 (2.6)
	1	>10.0	5 (1.1)	7 (1.4)	10 (2.5)	6 (0.7)	6 (1.0)
Coastal	10	>81.2	4 (0.6)	3 (0.5)	2 (0.2)	4 (0.5)	6 (1.3)
	1	>44.7	1 (0.2)	2 (0.4)	1 (0.2)	1 (0.1)	2 (0.3)
Miscellaneous	10	>2.7	24 (1.6)	27 (2.0)	29 (1.3)	29 (1.0)	29 (1.1)
	1	>4.9	2 (0.3)	3 (0.9)	3 (0.3)	3 (0.1)	4 (0.3)

For each category, the mean percentage of the constituent species' ranges that occurred in high coverage squares of each habitat type is shown. Numbers shown in bold are where a high association was expected (e.g. of farmland specialists in farmland habitats). Threshold, % cover gives the values of land cover used to determine 'high' cover of each habitat at each scale (see methods for more details).

For deciduous woodland at the 1 km scale (Table 6.2), the mean proportion of the breeding range of woodland specialists (40%) in woodland-dominated squares was much greater than that of the other four bird categories (about 20%). This relatively strong association with woodland is probably due to the relationship between woodland size and landscape structure at the 1 km scale. Most woodland occurs in small patches, usually tens of hectares or less, but selecting squares with a high woodland cover will tend to select for larger woods. Extensive woodland should be favourable for all woodland species, but especially so for specialists with minimum area requirements that preclude them from breeding in small woods (Hinsley et al., 1998). Farmland and urban birds showed similar responses within their respective habitat types, presumably for similar reasons. After urban birds, woodland generalists had the next greatest proportion of their breeding range within the built environment. This was not surprising, given that many of the bird species commonly regarded as 'garden birds' are included in this category.

We might expect the closest association between bird categories and their designated habitat types to occur at the 200 m scale, this level of resolution more closely matching that at which habitats are actually used. The match for woodland and urban species did indeed improve (woodland specialists, 90%; woodland generalists, 69%; urban, 70%), but was poorer for farmland species (specialists, 42%; generalists, 43%) compared to the larger scales. This may have been partly related to prevalence. For example, skylark occupies 12 to 44% of all habitat types, whereas corn bunting occupies only 2 to 6% of three types (Appendix E6.1). The scale of woodland and urban habitats within the larger agricultural matrix may also approximate most closely to the 200 m scale, improving the match between species and habitat.

Considering all species at the 200 m scale, the most widespread across all habitat types were wren, woodpigeon, blackbird and carrion crow, closely followed by chaffinch, robin, blue tit and skylark (Appendix E6.4). Six of these species probably originated in woodland. If pre-historical landscapes in Britain were dominated by woodland, then woodland species may have had longer to adapt to habitat modification. It also strongly suggests that woodland, and other habitats with at least some of its attributes (e.g. hedges and scrub), are the most widely distributed in Britain. The appearance of skylark in this group is interesting. Despite being relatively widespread across habitat types it is generally accepted as one of the archetypal declining farmland bird specialists.

Considering the individual species with the greatest proportions of their breeding ranges in their designated habitat types, the species which appear to be the most appropriate to be considered habitat specialists are generally consistent at both the 10 km and 1 km scales (Table 6.3). Thus, corn bunting,

Table 6.3 *Individual species in each bird category with the highest and lowest percentages of their breeding ranges in high coverage squares of each specified habitat type at the 10 km and 1 km scales. Full names of species are given in Table 6.1*

10 km scale				1 km scale			
Highest percentages		Lowest percentages		Highest percentages		Lowest percentages	
FARMLAND – Farmland specialists							
Turtle dove	64	Skylark	32	Corn bunting	65	Starling	32
Corn bunting	58	Lapwing	34	Tree sparrow	60	Goldfinch	35
Tree sparrow	56	Starling	35	Grey partridge	53	Skylark	39
FARMLAND – Farmland generalists							
Yellow wag.	57	Kestrel	36	Yellow wag.	60	Woodpigeon	31
Rook	43	Woodpigeon	37	Reed bunting	43	Greenfinch	32
Greenfinch	40	Jackdaw	38	Rook	39	Jackdaw	33
		Reed bunting	38				
DECIDUOUS WOODLAND – Woodland specialists							
Hawfinch	66	Redpoll	31	Nightingale	60	Redpoll	25
Nuthatch	57	Willow warb.	32	Nuthatch	56	Willow warb.	27
Marsh tit	57	Spotted fly.	35	Marsh tit	55	Redstart	27
DECIDUOUS WOODLAND – Woodland generalists							
Green wdpk.	50	Wren	30	Tawny owl	50	L. whitethroat	21
L. Whitethroat	41	Blackbird	31	Green wdpk.	40	Wren	26
Long-tailed tit	39	Song thrush	31	Bullfinch	36	Dunnock	26
						Blackbird	26
						Chaffinch	26
ALL WOODLAND – Woodland specialists							
Hawfinch	55	Willow warb.	33	Hawfinch	60	Sparrowhawk	26
Tree Pipit	49	Blackcap	34	Tree pipit	60	Blackcap	31
Redstart	49	Spotted fly.	35	Nightingale	57	Willow warb.	32
ALL WOODLAND – Woodland generalists							
Green wdpk.	41	L. whitethroat	29	Tawny owl	45	L. whitethroat	18
Tawny owl	38	Wren	30	Green wdpk.	38	Dunnock	25
Long-tailed tit	36	Blackbird	31	Bullfinch	38	Blackbird	27
Bullfinch	36					Blue tit	27
						Wren	27
BUILT ENVIRONMENT – Urban birds							
Magpie	42	Herring gull	20	Feral pigeon	46	Carrion crow	23
Swift	41	L. black-b. gull	25	Swift	36	Herring gull	26
Collared dove	40	Black-h. gull	28	Collared dove	35	Black-h. gull	27

tree sparrow, turtle dove and grey partridge appear to have the greatest association with farmland, the first two rating highly at both scales. The results at the 200 m scale also concur with this, these same four species being those with the lowest occurrence in habitats other than farmland (Appendix E6.1).

Woodland species were highly consistent between 10 and 1 km scales, but results differed somewhat between deciduous and all woodland (Table 6.3). For deciduous woodland, the most specialist species were nuthatch and marsh tit at both scales, plus hawfinch at 10 km and nightingale at 1 km. For all woodland, the specialists were hawfinch and tree pipit at both scales, plus redstart at 10 km and nightingale at 1 km. In part this difference may reflect geographical differences in species ranges in that the all woodland category is likely to include more upland sites (and hence also western and northern sites) than deciduous woodland. This probably accounts for the appearance of tree pipit and redstart as specialists within the all woodland category. At the 200 m scale, specialist woodland species – those with the lowest occurrence in other habitats (Appendix E6.2) – were identified as hawfinch and lesser spotted woodpecker, neither of which were actually recorded in any habitat category at this scale, followed by nightingale, willow tit and tree pipit, the former two appearing only in woodland, and then marsh tit and redpoll which, with the exception of the miscellaneous category, also appear in only one other habitat category. This list of species is again reasonably consistent with the woodland specialists identified at the 10 km and 1 km scales.

For urban birds, swift and collared dove appeared as specialists at both scales, with the addition of magpie at 10 km and feral pigeon at 1 km (Table 6.3). The absence of house sparrow from these lists is probably due to the species decline in a number of British towns and cities (reducing its urban connections) coupled with its association with buildings and human habitation in farmland. Urban birds at the 200 m scale show a different pattern of response in that all the species in this category were recorded to some extent in all the habitat types (Appendix E6.3). This was perhaps as expected because, historically, these species are a subset drawn from a range of other habitats. Without the miscellaneous category, the species with the least representation in other habitats were collared dove, swift, feral pigeon and house martin, the first three being the same as those identified as urban specialists at the 10 km and 1 km scales.

From the above analyses, the species in Britain most dependent on the broad habitats of farmland, woodland and urban areas, and thus potentially most at risk from changes in these habitats, are given in Table 6.3 and Appendices E6.1–E6.3. The most widespread species across a range of broad habitat types are also identified (Appendix E6.4). Of these latter species, those associated with woodland-edge-type habitats and with the ability to exploit cropland are probably most likely to prosper in complex cultural landscapes.

The results of this analysis are obviously dependent on the habitat types and bird categories selected; different groupings might well produce differences in detail. Nonetheless, the overall picture demonstrating the difficulties of simplistic assignment of species to habitat types within patchy, complex cultural landscapes should be similar.

Conclusions

Assigning species to habitat categories is undoubtedly useful (Brown and Grice, 1993), but in landscapes with a long history of modification many such categories will be far from exclusive. Highly modified habitats such as farmland are difficult to define because they are an amalgam of cover types spread across the matrix of cropland. Similarly, suburban and urban areas comprise a mix of habitat types within an abiotic matrix of roads and buildings, and, in turn, contribute to the complexity of farmland and other landscapes. A fine-grained mixture of habitat types provides opportunities for birds to exploit a range of novel resources, blurring the boundaries of habitat use and increasing the difficulties of accurate categorisation. Thus adequate monitoring and interpretation of bird population changes requires knowledge of individual species behaviour and ecology, and how this translates into population trends in relation to habitat modification, across the whole range of habitat types used by each species.

One of the main implications of the findings presented in this chapter is that far more attention should be paid to the actual patterns of habitat use by birds at a landscape scale. This is true at both the individual bird scale and the population scale. Neglecting such considerations may underestimate the value of certain habitats and the importance of habitat mosaics and networks, and result in omission or misinterpretation of species requirements. The ways in which individual birds may use different habitat components for different purposes, both within seasons (complementation) and between seasons (seasonal shifts) have been documented for rather few species. More studies are needed of habitat-specific fitness, potential source–sink dynamics and of dispersal between habitat types.

Acknowledgements

We thank the volunteers who contributed to the surveys that provide the data analysed in the last part of this chapter. The Breeding Bird Survey is funded by the British Trust for Ornithology, the Joint Nature Conservation Committee and the Royal Society for the Protection of Birds. Thanks also to Andy Brown and Frédéric Jiguet for helpful comments, to David Noble for discussion at various stages and Rob Fuller for editorial advice, all much improving the manuscript.

References

Aebischer, N. J., Green, R. E. and Evans, A. D. (2000). From science to recovery: four case studies of how research has been translated into conservation action in the UK. In *Ecology and Conservation of Lowland Farmland Birds*, ed. N. J. Aebischer, A. D. Evans, P. V. Grice and J. A. Vickery, pp. 43 54. Tring: British Ornithologists' Union.

Avery, M. and Leslie, R. (1990). *Birds and Forestry*. London: Poyser.

Barnagaud, J. Y., Devictor, V., Jiguet, F. and Archaux, F. (2011). When species become generalists: on-going large-scale changes in bird habitat specialization. *Global Ecol. Biogeogr.*, **20**, 630–640.

Benkman, C. W. (1993). Logging, conifers, and the conservation of crossbills. *Conserv. Biol.*, **7**, 473–479.

Bergtold, W. H. (1921). The English Sparrow (*Passer domesticus*) and the motor vehicle. *Auk*, **38**, 244–250.

Bignal, E. (1991). Transhumance in Spain. In *Birds and Pastoral Agriculture in Europe*, ed. D. J. Curtis, E. M. Bignal and M. A. Curtis, pp. 18–21. Port Erin, Isle of Man: European Forum Birds and Pastoralism.

Bignal, E. M. and McCracken, D. I. (2000). The nature conservation value of European traditional farming systems. *Environ. Rev.*, **8**, 149–171.

Brambilla, M., Rubolini, D. and Guidali, F. (2007). Between land abandonment and agricultural intensification: habitat preferences of Red-backed Shrikes *Lanius collurio* in low-intensity farming conditions. *Bird Study*, **54**, 160–167.

Brown, A. F. and Grice, P. V. (1993). *Birds in England, Context and Priorities*. English Nature Research Report no. 62. Peterborough: English Nature.

Browne, S., Vickery, J. and Chamberlain, D. (2000). Densities and population estimates of breeding Skylarks *Alauda arvensis* in Britain in 1997. *Bird Study*, **47**, 52–65.

Burton, N. H. K. (2007). Influences of restock age and habitat patchiness on Tree Pipits *Anthus trivialis* breeding in Breckland pine plantations. *Ibis*, **149** (Suppl. 2), 193–204.

Butler, C. (2002). Breeding parrots in Britain. *Brit. Birds*, **95**, 345–348.

Chalfoun, A. D., Thompson, F. R. and Ratnaswamy, M. J. (2002). Nest predators and fragmentation: a review and meta-analysis. *Conserv. Biol.*, **16**, 306–318.

Chamberlain, D. E., Cannon, A. R., Toms, M. P. et al. (2009). Avian productivity in urban landscapes: a review and meta-analysis. *Ibis*, **151**, 1–18.

Clergeau, P., Savard, J.-P. L., Mennechez, G. and Falardeau, G. (1998). Bird abundance and diversity along an urban-rural gradient: a comparative study between two cities on different continents. *Condor*, **100**, 413–425.

Crooks, K. R., Suarez, A. V. and Bolger, D. T. (2004). Avian assemblages along a gradient of urbanization in a highly fragmented landscape. *Biol. Conserv.*, **115**, 451–462.

Darby, H. C. (1951). The changing English landscape. *Geogr. J.*, **67**, 377–398.

Davey, C. M., Chamberlain, D. E., Newson, S. E., Noble, D. G. and Johnston, A. (2011). Rise of the generalists: evidence for climate driven homogenization in avian communities. *Global Ecol. Biogeogr.*, **21**, 568–578.

Davey, C. M., Vickery, J. A., Boatman, N. D. et al. (2010) Assessing the impact of Entry Level Stewardship on lowland farmland birds in England. *Ibis*, **152**, 459–474.

Defra (2009) http://www.defra.gov.uk/environment/statistics/wildlife/kf/wdkf03.htm, accessed May 2009.

De Laet, J. and Summers-Smith, D. (2007). The status of the urban house sparrow *Passer domesticus* in north-western Europe: a review. *J. Ornithol.*, **148** Suppl. 2, S275–S278.

Devictor, V., Clavel, J., Julliard, R. et al. (2010). Defining and measuring ecological specialization. *J. Appl. Ecol.*, **47**, 15–25.

Devictor, V., Julliard, R., Couvet, D., Lee, A. and Jiguet, F. (2007). Functional homogenization effect of urbanization on bird communities. *Conserv. Biol.*, **21**, 741–751.

Devictor, V., Julliard, R. and Jiguet, F. (2008). Distribution of specialist and generalist species along spatial gradients of habitat disturbance and fragmentation. *Oikos*, **117**, 507–514.

Dingemanse, N. J., Both, C., Drent, P. J., van Oers, K. and van Noordwijk, A. J. (2002). Repeatability and heritability of exploratory behaviour in great tits from the wild. *Anim. Behav.*, **64**, 929–938.

Donald, P. F., Green, R. E. and Heath, M. F. (2001). Agricultural intensification and the collapse of Europe's farmland bird populations. *Proc. R. Soc.*, **268**, 25–29.

Doxa, A., Bas, Y., Paracchini, M. L. *et al.* (2010). Low-intensity agriculture increases farmland bird abundance in France. *J. Appl. Ecol.*, **47**, 1348–1356.

Drent, P. J., van Oers, K. and van Noordwijk, A. J. (2003). Realized heritability of personalities in the great tit (*Parus major*). *Proc. R. Soc. B*, **270**, 45–51.

Dunning, J. B., Danielson, B. J. and Pulliam, H. R. (1992). Ecological processes that affect populations in complex landscapes. *Oikos*, **65**, 169–175.

Eaton, M. A., Brown, A. F., Noble, D. G. *et al.* (2009). Birds of Conservation Concern 3: the population status of birds in the United Kingdom, Channel Islands and the Isle of Man. *Brit. Birds*, **102**, 296–341.

ESRC (2009). http://www.esrc.ac.uk/ESRCInfoCentre/facts/index20.aspx?ts=1 accessed August 2009.

Field, R. H. and Anderson, G. Q. A. (2004). Habitat use by breeding Tree Sparrows *Passer montanus*. *Ibis*, **146** (Suppl. 2), 60–68.

Fuller, R. J., and Ausden, M. (2008). Birds and habitat change in Britain. Part 1: a review of losses and gains in the twentieth century. *Brit. Birds*, **101**, 644–675.

Fuller, R. J., Chamberlain, D. E., Burton, N. H. K. and Gough, S. J. (2001). Distributions of birds in lowland agricultural landscapes of England and Wales: how distinctive are bird communities of hedgerows and woodland? *Agr. Ecosyst. Environ.*, **84**, 79–92.

Fuller, R. J., Gaston, K. J. and Quine, C. P. (2007). Living on the edge: British and Irish woodland birds in a European context. *Ibis*, **149** (Suppl.2), 53–63.

Fuller, R. J., Hinsley, S. A. and Swetnam, R. D. (2004) The relevance of non-farmland habitats, uncropped areas and habitat diversity to the conservation of farmland birds. *Ibis*, **146** (Suppl. 2), 22–31.

Fuller, R. M. and Parsell, R. J. (1990). Classification of TM imagery in the study of land use in lowland Britain, practical considerations for operational use. *Int. J. Remote Sens.*, **10**, 1901–1919.

Fuller, R. M., Smith, G. M., Sanderson, J. M., Hill, R. A. and Thompson, A. G. (2002). Land Cover Map 2000: a general description of the UK's new vector GIS based on classification of remotely sensed data. *Cartogr. J.*, **39**, 15–25.

Gibbons, D. W., Reid, J. B. and Chapman, R. A. (1993). *The New Atlas of Breeding Birds in Britain and Ireland: 1988–1991*. London: Poyser.

Gregory, R. D., Noble, D. G. and Custance, J. (2004). The state of play of farmland birds: population trends and conservation status of lowland farmland birds in the United Kingdom. *Ibis*, **146** (Suppl. 2), 1–13.

Gregory, R. D., van Strien, A., Vorisek, P. *et al.* (2005). Developing indicators for European birds. *Phil. Trans. R. Soc. B*, **360**, 269–288.

Hansen, A. J. and di Castri, F. (eds.) (1992). *Landscape Boundaries: Consequences for Biodiversity and Ecological Flows*. New York: Spring-Verlag.

Hinsley, S. A. and Bellamy, P. E. (2000). The influence of hedge structure, management and landscape context on the value of hedgerows to birds: a review. *J. Environ. Manage.*, **60**, 33–49.

Hinsley, S. A., Bellamy, P. E., Enoksson, B. *et al.* (1998). Geographical and land-use influences on bird species richness in small woods in agricultural landscapes. *Global. Ecol. Biogeogr.*, **7**, 125–135.

Hinsley, S. A., Hill, R. A., Bellamy, P. E. *et al.* (2008). Effects of structural and functional habitat gaps on breeding woodland birds: working harder for less. *Landscape Ecol.*, **23**, 615–626.

Hinsley, S. A., Hill, R. A., Bellamy, P. E. *et al.* (2009). Do highly modified landscapes favour generalists at the expense of specialists? An example using woodland birds. *Landscape Res.*, **34**, 509–526.

Hinsley, S. A., Redhead, J. W., Bellamy, P. E. *et al.* (2010). Testing agri-environment delivery for farmland birds at the farm scale: the Hillesden experiment. *Ibis*, **152**, 500–514.

Huntley, B., Green, R. E., Collingham, Y. C. and Willis, S. G. (2007). *A Climatic Atlas of European Breeding Birds*. Barcelona: Lynx Edicions.

Inglis, I. R., Isaacson, A. J., Thearle, R. J. P. and Westwood, N. J. (1990). The effects of changing agricultural practice upon woodpigeon numbers. *Ibis*, **132**, 262–272.

Isaacson, A. J., Inglis, I. R. and Hayes, P. J. (2002). A long-term study of the woodpigeon in relation to changes in agricultural practice. *Aspects Appl. Biol.*, **67**, 51–58.

Jiguet, F. and Julliard, R. (2005). The status and distribution of the Cirl Bunting in France in 2003. *Brit. Birds*, **98**, 216–217.

Johnston, R. J. and Doornkamp, J. C. (ed.) (1982). *The Changing Geography of the United Kingdom*. London: Methuen.

Julliard, R., Clavel, J., Devictor, V., Jiguet, F. and Couvet, D. (2006). Spatial segregation of specialists and generalists in bird communities. *Ecol. Lett.*, **9**, 1237–1244.

Langston, R. H. W., Wotton, S. R., Conway, G. J. *et al.* (2007) Nightjar *Caprimulgus europaeus* and Woodlark *Lullula arborea* – recovering species in Britain? *Ibis*, **149** (Suppl. 2), 250–260.

Law, B. S. and Dickman, C. R. (1998). The use of habitat mosaics by terrestrial vertebrate fauna: implications for conservation and management. *Biodivers. Conserv.*, **7**, 323–333.

Matthysen, E. (1998). *The Nuthatches*. London: Poyser.

Mazerolle, M. J. and Villard, M-A. (1999). Patch characteristics and landscape context as predictors of species presence and abundance: a review. *Ecoscience*, **6**, 117–124.

McKinney, M. L. and Lockwood, J. L. (1999). Biotic homogenization: a few winners replacing many losers in the next mass extinction. *Trends Ecol. Evol*, **14**, 450–453.

Mead, C. (2000). *The State of the Nation's Birds*. Stowmarket: Whittet Books.

Newson, S. E., Ockendon, N., Joys, A., Noble, D. G. and Baillie, S. R. (2009). Comparison of habitat-specific trends in the abundance of breeding birds in the UK. *Bird Study*, **56**, 233–243.

Newton, I. (1972). *Finches*. London: Collins.

Newton, I. (1986). *The Sparrowhawk*. Calton: Poyser.

Olden, J. D. and Rooney, T. P. (2006). On defining and quantifying biotic homogenization. *Global Ecol. Biogeogr.*, **15**, 113–120.

Olsson, O., Wiktander, U., Malmqvist, A. and Nilsson, S. G. (2001). Variability of patch type preferences in relation to resource availability and breeding success in a bird. *Oecologia*, **127**, 435–443.

Pain, D. J., Hill, D. and McCracken, D. I. (1997). Impact of agricultural intensification of pastoral systems on bird distributions in Britain 1970–1990. *Agr. Ecosyst. Environ.*, **64**, 19–32.

Peach, W. J., Robinson, R. A. and Murray, K. A. (2004). Demographic and environmental causes of the decline of rural Song Thrushes *Turdus philomelos* in lowland Britain. *Ibis*, **146** (Suppl. 2), 50–59.

Peach, W. J., Vincent, K. E., Fowler, J. A. and Grice, P. V. (2008). Reproductive success of house sparrows along an urban gradient. *Anim. Conserv.*, **11**, 493–503.

Pearce-Higgins, J. W., Grant, M. C., Robinson. M. C. and Haysom, S. L. (2007). The role of forest maturation in causing the decline of Black Grouse *Tetrao tetrix*. *Ibis*, **149**, 143–155.

Pithon, J. A. and Dytham, C. (2002). Distribution and development of introduced Ring-necked Parakeets *Psittacula krameri* in Britain between 1983 and 1998. *Bird Study*, **49**, 110–117.

Purseglove, J. (1988). *Taming the Flood. A History and Natural History of Rivers and Wetlands*. Oxford: Oxford University Press.

Rackham, O. (1987). *The History of the Countryside*. London: Dent.

Redpath, S. M. (1995). Habitat fragmentation and the individual – Tawny Owls *Strix aluco* in woodland patches. *J. Anim. Ecol.*, **64**, 652–661.

Reichard, S. H., Chalker-Scott, L. and Buchanan, S. (2001). Interactions between non-native plants and birds. In *Avian Ecology and conservation in an Urbanizing World*, ed. J. M. Marzluff, R. Bowman and R. Donnelly, pp. 179–223. Dordrecht: Kluwer Academic Publishers.

Robinson, R. A., Siriwardena, G. M. and Crick, H. Q. P. (2005). Size and trends of the House Sparrow *Passer domesticus* population in Great Britain. *Ibis*, **147**, 552–562.

Robinson, R. A. and Sutherland, W. J. (2002). Post-war changes in arable farming and biodiversity in Great Britain. *J. Appl. Ecol.*, **39**, 157–176.

Scozzafava, S. and De Sanctis, A. (2006). Exploring the effects of land abandonment on habitat structures and on habitat suitability for three passerines species in a highland area of Central Italy. *Landscape Urban Plan.*, **75**, 23–33.

Shaw, L. M., Chamberlain, D. and Evans, M. (2008). The House Sparrow *Passer domesticus* in urban areas: reviewing a possible link between post-decline distribution and human socioeconomic status. *J. Ornithol.*, **149**, 293–299.

Shrubb, M. (2003). *Birds, Scythes and Combines: a History of Birds and Agricultural Change*. Cambridge: Cambridge University Press.

Simmons, I. G. (2001). *An Environmental History of Great Britain from 10,000 Years Ago to the Present*. Edinburgh: Edinburgh University Press.

Stoate, C. (1996). The changing face of lowland farming and wildlife. *Brit. Wildlife*, **7**, 162–172.

Strubbe, D. and Matthysen, E. (2009). Experimental evidence for nest-site competition between invasive ring-necked parakeets (*Psittacula krameri*) and native nuthatches (*Sitta europaea*). *Biol. Conserv.*, **142**, 1588–1594.

Summers-Smith, J. D. (1988). *The Sparrows*. Calton, Poyser.

Swift, T. L. and Hannon, S. J. (2010). Critical thresholds associated with habitat loss: a review of the concepts, evidence, and applications. *Biol. Rev.*, **85**, 35–53.

Tubbs, C. R. (1997). A vision for rural Europe. *Brit. Wildlife*, **9**, 79–85.

Tucker, G. M. and Heath, M. F. (1994). *Birds in Europe: Their Conservation Status*. Cambridge: BirdLife International.

Vanhinsbergh, D. (1999). The breeding ecology and behaviour of the Red-backed Shrike *Lanius collurio*. PhD Thesis, University of Sheffield.

Vierling, K. T., Vierling, L. A., Gould, W. A., Martinuzzi, S. and Clawges, R. M. (2008). Lidar: shedding new light on habitat characterization and modelling. *Front. Ecol. Environ.*, **6**, 90–98.

Wilson, J. D., Evans, A. D. and Grice, P. V. (2009). *Bird Conservation and Agriculture*. Cambridge: Cambridge University Press.

Wolff, A., Paul, J.-P., Martin, J.-L. and Bretagnolle, V. (2001). The benefits of extensive agriculture to birds: the case of the little bustard. *J. Appl. Ecol.*, **38**, 963–975.

Supplementary material: Additional results for this chapter are presented in an electronic appendix (Appendices E6.1–E6.4) at www.cambridge.org/9780521897563.

CHAPTER SEVEN

The importance of habitat heterogeneity at multiple scales for birds in European agricultural landscapes

JULIET VICKERY

British Trust for Ornithology and Royal Society for the Protection of Birds

and

RAPHAËL ARLETTAZ

University of Bern and Swiss Ornithological Institute

Farmland throughout the world is frequently likened to a mosaic or patchwork and this heterogeneity is widely recognised as strongly influencing the abundance and diversity of species that these landscapes support. Globally, modern intensive agriculture has greatly reduced this 'patchiness' at a range of spatial and temporal scales. This change has been particularly well documented in temperate Europe (Benton *et al.*, 2003; Báldi *et al.*, 2005; Roschewitz *et al.*, 2005; Wretenberg *et al.*, 2006; Stoate *et al.*, 2009). The fine-grained, diverse habitat mosaic, typical of much 'traditional agriculture', has become increasingly uniform under modern agricultural management. This reduction in habitat complexity has been linked, at least in part, to declines in farmland biodiversity, including plants and invertebrates (Smart *et al.*, 2000; Sotherton and Self, 2000; Oliver *et al.*, 2010), mammals (Smith *et al.*, 2005) and birds (Donald *et al.*, 2001a; Benton *et al.*, 2003; Wilson *et al.*, 2005).

In general, the more habitat elements a farmed landscape contains, the wider the range of resources on offer and the higher the diversity and abundance of organisms supported. This may be due, in part, simply to the increased likelihood of a given farmed landscape containing a key habitat type (Heikkinen *et al.*, 2004). However, many species require a diversity of resources to complete their life cycle. At its most basic, birds require two essential resources: a suitable nest site and sufficient food throughout the year. These basic nesting and foraging requirements often vary within and between seasons. Bird-rich farmland should provide safe foraging habitats, offering abundant and accessible food in relatively close proximity to suitable cover for nesting and/or protection from predators or harsh weather. The extent to which farmland birds require a diverse landscape matrix, containing

Birds and Habitat: Relationships in Changing Landscapes, ed. Robert J. Fuller. Published by Cambridge University Press. © Cambridge University Press 2012.

both semi-natural and cultivated habitat components, is illustrated by many examples in the following sections.

This chapter focuses on the importance of heterogeneity in the context of the requirements of individual species, rather than farmland bird communities as a whole. We demonstrate that avian life histories, even the simplest ones, require access to a broad range of resources over spatial and temporal gradients and we show how this is more likely to be delivered by a heterogeneous than a homogeneous landscape. Since this heterogeneity is scale-dependent, we examine bird requirements for, and responses to, heterogeneity at three scales: within fields (e.g. swards), between fields or at the farm scale (in cropped and non-cropped habitats), and at the landscape scale (between farms). We then briefly consider some approaches that could restore heterogeneity in areas where it has been reduced by intensive agriculture and the ways in which such restoration may benefit wider biodiversity and some key ecosystem services.

There are several caveats that should be made at the outset. First, we provide a broad overview of the importance of heterogeneity at different scales, rather than a comprehensive review. Second, the text has a temperate and lowland northwest European bias, since this is where the majority of the work has been undertaken and these are the systems with which we are most familiar. We acknowledge that patterns and processes may not be generic across all regions, particularly between the more intensively managed landscapes of northwest Europe and those of south and east Europe (Reif *et al.*, 2008; Erdös *et al.*, 2009; Stoate *et al.*, 2009; Batáry *et al.*, 2011a). Third, the distinctions between field, farm and landscape scale are not always clear cut, particularly at the farm and landscape scales. The issue of scale is further complicated by the fact that, while quantifying environmental heterogeneity depends on the scale of measurement, an organism's response to it actually depends on its perception of the environment, something that remains poorly understood and will vary between species (Wiens, 1989).

Heterogeneity within fields

A common impact of agricultural intensification is a marked reduction in variation in grass and arable crop structure within and between fields (Tallowin *et al.*, 2005; Wilson *et al.*, 2005). Drainage, mechanised uniform sowing, intense agro-chemical use, efficient harvesting and increases in grazing and cutting intensity all tend to result in greater structural simplification and/or increasing sward density. There are two key sets of interactions in the way that crop structure affects birds. First, the interaction between the extent to which a sward provides concealment from predators and the extent to which it impacts on the detection of these predators; this applies to both foraging and nesting. Second, for foraging birds there is also an interaction between the extent to which the sward structure affects the abundance or diversity of prey and the accessibility of those prey (Wilson *et al.*, 2005; Schaub *et al.*, 2010). From a mechanistic perspective, there are also two parallel processes with respect to the effects of vegetation heterogeneity, namely whether they have functional or ecological significance. For example, dense swards may be needed to support invertebrate prey that only become accessible to birds when they move to more open areas (ecological significance). For some species, however, open sparse vegetation may be uniformly 'better' or preferred than tall dense vegetation, and heterogeneity is then only important insofar as the preferred habitat becomes scarce in the landscape (functional significance). We consider these interactions and mechanisms illustrated by a number of species-specific examples.

Sward heterogeneity and foraging success

Heterogeneity in sward structure within fields, caused by factors such as differential seed set or plant growth, or variation in management regimes, can result in patchiness in abundance, visibility and/or accessibility of potential prey (Vickery *et al.*, 2001; Morris *et al.*, 2002). The structure of the vegetation affects foraging efficiency directly, through physical obstruction and its impact on the detectability and accessibility of prey, and indirectly through its impact on the trade-off between time allocated to feeding versus vigilance for predators. In general, food abundance is highest, accessibility lowest and predator detection poorest in structurally complex swards that are rich in plant species.

Within cereal crops, several species feeding on ground- or sward-dwelling invertebrates select short, sparse patches within the sward, often directing foraging towards tram lines (e.g. yellowhammers *Emberiza citrinella*: Morris *et al.*, 2002; Douglas *et al.*, 2009; and skylarks *Alauda arvensis*: Odderskær *et al.*, 1997; Schön, 1999). Douglas *et al.* (2009) showed that *c.* 87% of foraging sites for yellowhammers were along tram lines which, given that these account for a very small field area, suggests dense cereal swards offer poor foraging habitat. In the case of skylarks, several studies have shown positive effects of small patches of short swards or bare ground within fields, perhaps because these allow access to prey in the otherwise taller vegetation (Odderskær *et al.*, 1997; Schön, 1999; Buckingham, 2001). The creation of undrilled open patches within a cereal sward was developed as an agri-environment scheme option to enhance late-season foraging (and hence nesting) opportunities for skylarks in winter cereals in several countries (Morris *et al.*, 2004; Fischer *et al.*, 2009). In the absence of these undrilled patches, late-breeding pairs are forced to forage outside the nest field, increasing the energetic costs and decreasing reproductive success (Fig. 7.1). For birds foraging within cereal stubbles in winter, areas of bare ground facilitate access to seeds. Indeed, a preference shown by a number of granivorous birds for barley over wheat stubbles has been attributed to a combination of higher weed seed abundance and more bare ground, enhancing accessibility of

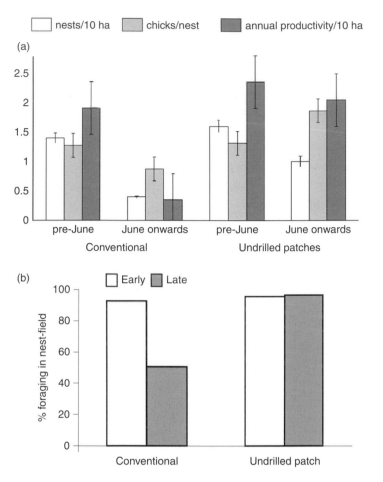

Figure 7.1 (a) Effects of undrilled patches on skylark nest density, number of chicks per nest and annual productivity compared to conventional cereal fields in the UK, before June and after June. (b) Foraging activity of skylarks within the field where the nest is located with respect to season and management (undrilled patches vs conventional). In both graphs the positive effects of undrilled patches are particularly marked later in the season when the cereal sward is very dense, impeding access to key food sources. Based on unpublished data provided by Tony Morris; see further details in Morris *et al.* (2004).

seeds (Moorcroft *et al.*, 2002). Differences in anti-predation strategies also affect stubble use by different species. Starling *Sturnus vulgaris* and blackbird *Turdus merula* prefer shorter stubble, where the need for vigilance is less and so foraging more efficient. In contrast, skylarks, grey partridges *Perdix perdix* and meadow pipits *Anthus pratensis*, that tend to rely on camouflage rather than early detection of predators, prefer plots with taller stubble. It is possible, however, that stubbles varying locally in height and density provide better overall cover and camouflage for most species regardless of their anti-predation strategies (Whittingham *et al.*, 2006).

Within grasslands, heterogeneity is probably most important for species that obtain food from within the sward itself, such as larks, finches and buntings. Relatively tall heterogeneous swards support abundant invertebrates and seeds but these are mostly accessible only from patches of bare ground (Perkins *et al.*, 2000; Buckingham *et al.*, 2006; Menz *et al.*, 2009a; Martinez *et al.*, 2010; Schaub *et al.*, 2010). The importance of providing so-called 'kitchen dining room' swards for ground and foliar foraging passerines is well accepted in both grassland and arable contexts (Odderskær *et al.*, 1997; Whittingham and Markland, 2002; Bradbury and Bradter, 2004; Devereux *et al.*, 2004; Hoste-Danylow *et al.*, 2010; Schaub *et al.*, 2010; Arlettaz *et al.*, 2012). Two experimental studies demonstrate well the effect of food accessibility mediated by vegetation height. Douglas *et al.* (2009) found that the attractiveness of field margins to foraging yellowhammers could be increased by cutting patches within them, which rendered insect food more 'accessible' than was the case in uncut margins. The relative use of the cut margins by foraging birds was especially high in late summer when the uncut sward was tall and dense elsewhere. An experiment with captive redstarts *Phoenicurus phoenicurus* showed preferential hunting in short swards with bare ground, even if the adjacent high sward offered much more insect prey (Martinez *et al.*, 2010). The results of these experiments probably apply to a number of birds that feed on foliar or surface-dwelling invertebrates (e.g. Douglas *et al.*, 2009).

Radio-tracking studies in fruit-tree plantations, orchards and vineyards in continental Europe on insectivorous species such as hoopoes *Upupa epops* and wrynecks *Jynx torquilla* also suggest a preference for a mix of vegetation and bare ground (Tagmann-Ioset *et al.*, 2012, Fig. 7.2). The latter enhances prey accessibility for terrestrially foraging species such as the hoopoe (Arlettaz *et al.*, 2010b) and may also increase prey detectability for wrynecks and redstarts hunting visually from perches (Schaub *et al.*, 2010; Weisshaupt *et al.*, 2011). Similarly, woodlarks *Lullula arborea* foraging in vineyards prefer sites with around 55% vegetation cover at the foraging site scale (Arlettaz *et al.*, 2012). The common practice of removing grass, chemically or mechanically, along every second tree or vine row provides an ideal mix in which the grassy rows provide a good food supply, whilst bare rows ensure prey accessibility (Sierro and Arlettaz, 2003; Schaub *et al.*, 2010, Fig. 7.3).

Several studies have demonstrated a preference for set-aside or fallow-land equivalents, such as sown or naturally regenerated wildflower areas, over a range of other crop types in winter and summer. Species such as stonechat *Saxicola torquatus*, whitethroat *Sylvia communis* and corn bunting *Emberiza calandra* thrive in Swiss agricultural matrices revitalised with a network of wildflower areas (Birrer *et al.*, 2007; Revaz *et al.*, 2008). These essentially

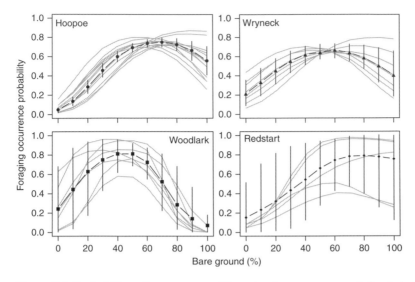

Figure 7.2 Probability of occurrence of foraging hoopoe, wryneck (both in fruit-tree plantations), woodlark (vineyards) and redstart (orchards) with respect to the availability of bare ground at the site scale, i.e. foraging location (obtained from radio-tracking data). All data are from study sites in Switzerland. The bold curve shows the marginal (i.e. mean specific) value, the thin curves the individual responses. Adapted from Schaub *et al.* (2010).

uncultivated fallows support abundant plant and invertebrate resources (Revaz *et al.*, 2008). They may also enhance nesting opportunities, at least in part, because the patchiness of the sward (e.g. Wilson *et al.*, 2005) increases accessibility of prey and/or concealment from predators. This is supported by the fact that preferences are particularly marked for rotational rather than non-rotational set-aside, and younger rather than older non-rotational set-aside; both preferences being for the more heterogeneous sward (Henderson *et al.*, 2000a, 2000b). Similarly, within set-aside several species prefer a mixture of bare ground and vegetation. The abundance of granivores, for example, peaks at around 17% bare ground, whilst gamebird abundance peaks at around 40% at the foraging-site scale (Henderson and Evans, 2000; Henderson *et al.*, 2001). Interestingly, the abundance of skylarks in other non-cropped habitats, such as wildflower strips and fallow land, peaks at similar levels of percentage bare ground to those observed in set-aside (Wakeham-Dawson and Aebischer, 1998; Toepfer and Stubbe, 2001).

Sward heterogeneity and nesting success of ground-breeding birds

The risk of failure for a nest within ground vegetation is determined by a trade-off between the extent to which the site protects it from adverse

(a)

Figure 7.3 'Kitchen–dining room' configurations in different habitat types which favour terrestrially foraging farmland birds (Valais, southwestern Switzerland). (a) Fruit-tree plantations with herbicide application (or mechanical removal of grass, not illustrated as this is rare) at the foot of tree rows: typical habitat of wryneck and hoopoe; (b) conventional vineyards with a mineral appearance (systematic application of herbicides over the whole surface) and (c) novel management practices with chemical removal of grass every second row, which provides ideal foraging conditions for woodlark. Photos: Raphaël Arlettaz and Antoine Sierro.

weather or visually hunting predators, and the extent to which it obscures the view afforded to the parent birds on the nest (Wilson *et al.*, 2005). The outcome of this trade-off differs between species. Those, such as gamebirds, that rely on avoiding detection by predators often nest (and forage) in dense vegetation. However, species like lapwings *Vanellus vanellus* and stone-curlews *Burhinus oedicnemus* that rely on early detection of predators require open ground. In some cases the uniformity of vegetation cover might, in itself, make nests or birds more conspicuous to predators perhaps by reducing the effectiveness of camouflage (Baines, 1990). The preference shown by little bustard *Tetrax tetrax* females for set-aside as nesting habitat has, for example, been attributed to structural heterogeneity, which affords better concealment from predators (Salamolard and Moreau, 1999). Similarly, the preference of lapwings for nesting in short patchy vegetation or bare ground may be because this background increases the crypticity of nests (Galbraith, 1988; Wilson *et al.*, 2001; Sheldon *et al.*, 2005).

To summarise, sward heterogeneity can enhance foraging and nesting success for a range of species. In the case of foraging this tends to be because the structural complexity has an ecological function, namely the provision of so-called 'kitchen and dining room' swards. When nesting, species tend to prefer either tall/closed or short/open swards, depending on their predator avoidance strategy, but a heterogeneous sward may enhance crypticity or camouflage.

Between-field or farm-scale heterogeneity

Between-field heterogeneity arises mainly as a result of differences in the cropped habitat types within fields and the presence of non-cropped boundary habitats such as margins, ditches and hedgerows between them. Here we focus on the availability of different boundary features and crops. Because these differences also account largely for heterogeneity at the landscape scale, in this section we consider the particular value of these components occurring in close proximity, often the within-territory scale and usually of no more than a few hectares.

Heterogeneity at the farm scale: non-cropped boundary habitats

The overall value of features such as hedgerows, field margins, ditches and banks for farmland birds is well recognised. The composition of these uncropped, rather than cropped, habitats often has the largest effect on bird species composition and abundance in farmed landscapes (Fuller *et al.*, 1997). They are important nesting and foraging habitats (Macdonald and Johnson, 1995; Jobin *et al.*, 2001; Batáry *et al.*, 2007), providing cover and rich invertebrate prey (Maudsley, 2000) and plant food (seeds, fruits and berries) (Snow and Snow, 1988; Moorcroft *et al.*, 1997). They may also have a role in providing dispersal routes for birds (Hinsley and Bellamy, 2000) and insects (Joyce *et al.*, 1999).

Numerous declining farmland bird species benefit from sympathetic management of hedgerows and field margins (Rands and Sotherton, 1987; Bradbury and Stoate, 2000; Birrer *et al.*, 2007; Brambilla *et al.*, 2007; Vickery *et al.*, 2009). Heterogeneity within boundary features can also enhance resource provision for birds. For example, variation in hedge management and structure can enhance bird species richness and abundance (Parish *et al.*, 1994, 1995; Fuller *et al.*, 2001), and nest concealment and survival (Evans, 2004). Furthermore, where a boundary comprises a hedge and an uncultivated margin in combination, the abundance of plant and invertebrate food for birds is often higher in both, with positive effects on the abundance of passerines such as the yellowhammer (Bradbury and Stoate, 2000; Vickery *et al.*, 2009). Hedgerows and margins may also enhance weeds and/or invertebrate food resources within adjacent fields and/or enable birds favouring concealment to forage close to cover (Moorcroft *et al.*, 1997; Vickery *et al.*, 2002). Experiments have shown that local skylark density can be increased in homogeneous high-intensity farmland by introducing set-aside strips or margins, coupled with extensively managed meadows (Weibel *et al.*, 2001; Jenny *et al.*, 2002).

As well as their intrinsic value, boundary features often help birds to exploit food resources in adjacent crops. Many hedgerow nesting species are limited to foraging in crops within 500 m of the nest site (e.g. grey partridge – Green, 1984; tree sparrow *Passer montanus* – Field and Anderson, 2004; red-backed shrike *Lanius collurio* – Brambilla *et al.*, 2007; yellowhammer – Douglas *et al.*, 2009). Grey and red-legged partridge *Alectoris rufa* require hedgerows with good base vegetation in which to nest and nearby weedy cereal crops as foraging habitat (Rands, 1985). The length of permanent field boundary correlates closely with breeding densities and abundance of these species (Rands, 1986; Vargas *et al.*, 2006). Similarly, turtle doves *Streptopelia turtur* require large mature hedges for nesting close to weed-rich habitats for foraging (Browne *et al.*, 2004), and the abundance of yellowhammers also increases with increasing length of hedgerows with herbaceous basal vegetation (Stoate *et al.*, 1998). Red-backed shrikes in mixed grassland and arable land avoid both totally open areas (characteristic of modern agricultural management) and abandoned farmland where forest has encroached (a widespread situation in some European mountainous areas). The optimum appears to be around 15–35% of area covered by hedges and bushes within their breeding territories, a mix often found in low-intensity farmland (Brambilla *et al.*, 2007, 2010). Less commonly, the crop may be the nesting habitat and the margin the foraging habitat. For example yellow wagtails *Motacilla flava* and corn buntings in arable landscapes nest in crops, but may forage on emergent insects from water-filled boundary ditches (Anderson *et al.*, 2002; Bradbury and Bradter, 2004; Gilroy *et al.*, 2009) or in grass field margins, respectively (Brickle *et al.*, 2000), which may be a consequence of low food supply in crops with heavy chemical inputs.

Hedges and margins close to crops also facilitate hunting for some birds of prey. For example, in Switzerland, freshly mown grassland adjacent to wildflower strips provides preferred hunting habitat for kestrels *Falco tinnunculus* and long-eared owls *Asio otus*, possibly because voles from these strips invade the more open grassland where they become easy prey (Aschwanden *et al.*, 2005), though a similar effect is not evident for barn owls *Tyto alba* (Arlettaz *et al.*, 2010c). For woodchat shrikes *Lanius senator* a combination of scattered trees, which serve as nest sites and perches for hunting, and grassland with a heterogeneous sward structure appears to be beneficial (Schaub, 1996). Hedges or isolated boundary trees provide song posts and/or feeding perches for a variety of other species (ortolan bunting *Emberiza hortulana* – Goławski and Dombrowski, 2002; Vepsäläinen *et al.*, 2005; Menz *et al.*, 2009a, 2009b; wryneck – Mermod *et al.*, 2009; roller – *Coracias garrulus*: Avilés and Costillo, 1998; Avilés *et al.*, 2000; red-backed shrike – Brambilla *et al.*, 2007, 2009a).

Farm-scale heterogeneity does not benefit all species. Several avoid tall structures such as hedges and require large open fields, particularly skylark, lapwing and stone-curlew (Donald *et al.*, 2001b; Sheldon, 2002; Sheldon *et al.*,

2004; Batary *et al.*, 2007, 2011a). These species will suffer from encroachment of trees and shrubs, which effectively fragment their habitat (Atauri and de Lucio, 2001; Moreira *et al.*, 2005). This seems to be, at least in part, because such ground-nesters suffer higher predation in or close to field margins, as these act as a source of ground predators or provide perches from which crows, birds of prey or cuckoos *Cuculus canorus* can hunt or prospect (Roskaft *et al.*, 2002; Sheldon *et al.*, 2004; Morris and Gilroy, 2008). Landscapes with diverse crops, but lacking vertical boundary structures, can support exceptionally high skylark densities; landscapes with similar crop diversity, but many hedgerows and trees, carry lower densities (Batary *et al.*, 2011a).

Heterogeneity at the farm scale: cropped habitats

At the farm scale, a diversity of crops may benefit breeding birds by increasing the range of available foraging and nesting opportunities at any given time, especially as resource requirements may change and/or vegetation and crops develop through the season. The precise mechanisms by which mixed farming benefits species will depend on their ecology and are thus likely to be species-specific (Siriwardena *et al.*, 2000). A number of species require different crop types in close proximity in order to meet different foraging resource requirements throughout the year. Relatively few studies have documented a need for habitat heterogeneity at the farm scale in winter, probably because birds are, generally, more mobile in winter and requirements for different habitats may be met at the landscape scale. Perhaps the most important benefit of between-field heterogeneity in crop type is the provision, in close proximity, of resources required for both breeding and foraging. Lapwings, for example, will use spring cereal as nesting habitat and grassland as chick-foraging habitat. The occupancy of, and productivity in, spring tillage is heavily influenced by its proximity to grassland, with spring till adjacent to grassland significantly more likely to be occupied (Wilson *et al.*, 2001). Furthermore, the fledging success of lapwing broods hatched in spring till is much higher where chicks have direct access to pasture rather than having to cross an intervening field (Galbraith, 1988). The grain of the agricultural matrix may also be important, i.e. the size and number of parcels per unit area. In a wryneck population inhabiting mixed farmland dominated by fruit trees, the occupancy of a given territory over several years depended on the number of cropping units within the territory, demonstrating a positive effect of a fine-grained mosaic (Mermod *et al.*, 2009).

The importance of breeding and foraging resources in close proximity is even greater for species in which foraging or nesting requirements vary within the breeding season. This may result from changes in requirements at different stages of the breeding cycle or because habitats change in their suitability. Vegetation growth can result in some habitats becoming unsuitable late in the season. This is true for the lesser grey shrike *Lanius minor* that hunts large insects on open soil during the early breeding season, but selects mown meadows later in the season, when vegetation elsewhere is tall (Wirtitsch *et al.*, 2001).

Many pairs of skylarks fail to raise a second brood (or late replacement brood) in modern arable monocultures because of a lack of late-nesting habitat. For populations to be self-sustaining, pairs must make two or three nesting attempts per season, but this requires structurally diverse crop mosaics (Wilson *et al.*, 1997). Foraging efficiency, breeding density and productivity of skylarks are enhanced with increasing spatial and seasonal diversity of crops and crop structures (Schläpfer, 1988; Jenny, 1990; Chamberlain *et al.*, 1999, 2000). Yellow wagtails in eastern England may have a similar requirement, because as the breeding season progresses they switch their nesting habitat from winter-sown cereals to crops of potatoes and beans that have a more open structure (Gilroy *et al.*, 2010).

Farm-scale heterogeneity appears to be important to little bustards by providing suitable habitats for the entire courtship period, and habitat diversity is greater around centres of male activity (leks) than at randomly selected sites (Salamolard and Moreau, 1999). Interestingly, for this species seasonal vegetation development may result in a habitat that was originally suitable for displaying subsequently becoming suitable for nesting (Wolff *et al.*, 2002).

In summary, between-field complexity arising from differences between cropped and uncropped habitats, or from the fine-grained structure of the cultivated matrix, can enhance the foraging efficiency and breeding success of farmland birds. In many cases this is because such heterogeneity consistently provides nesting and foraging habitats in close proximity, which is essential where habitats change throughout the season. Where habitats have become homogeneous they frequently support much lower bird densities and, for some passerines, may also be characterised by lower overall reproductive success as a result of reduced numbers of nesting attempts. There are circumstances where heterogeneity is not beneficial, notably for some open-country species where the presence of tall boundary structures can reduce habitat suitability at both farm and landscape scales.

Landscape-scale heterogeneity

At the landscape scale, habitat heterogeneity affects birds through two main mechanisms. First, the relative quantities of different habitat types, such as woodland and hedgerows, within landscapes has a large effect on the composition and diversity of bird communities (Fuller *et al.*, 1997; Berg, 2002; Winqvist *et al.*, 2011). Second, species with large home ranges or territories may benefit from being able to exploit widely spaced feeding and nesting opportunities. For relatively small farmland birds, factors at the local scale (field or farm) may be generally more important than factors at landscape scales.

Several authors have suggested that landscape-scale heterogeneity has less influence on species abundance than on species richness (Petersen, 1998; Siriwardena et al., 2000; Moreira et al., 2005). Increased species diversity frequently correlates positively with landscape-scale habitat heterogeneity (Preiss et al., 1997; Delgado and Moreira, 2000; Verhulst et al., 2004; Sierro et al., 2009; Winqvist et al., 2011). This pattern seems to be particularly pronounced in winter, perhaps reflecting a shift of some invertebrate feeding species towards mixed landscapes in winter as they become more reliant on grain and weed seed in the winter (Wilson et al., 1996; Atkinson et al., 2002).

Regarding abundance, a British study found that seven farmland bird species increased as the proportion of arable habitat rose in an otherwise largely grassland-dominated matrix (Robinson et al., 2001). However, this relationship was much stronger where arable was scarce in the wider landscape than where arable was relatively common. Similar preferences for complex, heterogeneous habitat matrices have been found in corn and cirl buntings Emberiza cirlus in Italy (Brambilla et al., 2008, 2009b). Most of these species showing abundance–heterogeneity relationships at the landscape scale are granivorous. Their distribution is likely to reflect a need for seeds and grain in winter – a sparse resource in grassland landscapes. In a multiscale analysis of relationships between farmland habitat heterogeneity and abundance of 32 breeding bird species on British farmland, Pickett and Siriwardena (2011) found that, on average, the spatial mixing of land uses, rather than field size or density of boundaries, best explained variation in bird abundance.

The effect of the distribution and size of seed-rich habitat patches on the winter-ranging behaviour and carrying capacity is an important issue for granivorous birds. Experimental provision of seed resources in winter has been shown to positively influence local breeding population trends in several farmland passerines (Siriwardena et al., 2007). Within winter, local yellowhammer populations seem to share resources that are within a radius of 500–1000 m, suggesting this is the scale at which the birds perceive heterogeneity in the winter environment (Siriwardena et al., 2006). However, the details of the effects of resource quantity or configuration within such areas on over-winter survival and, hence, breeding population responses, remain unknown (Siriwardena et al., 2007).

Landscape diversity may also benefit a wide range of species that forage over large areas or have large territories. Swallows and martins use insect-rich features such as hedgerows and waterbodies, often at considerable distances from the nest (Evans et al., 2003). In western France, hoopoes select diverse landscape mosaics, including woods and hedges that provide nest sites, and banks of sand tracks covered with short and sparse grass that offer accessible foraging grounds (Barbaro *et al.*, 2008). In Switzerland, wrynecks inhabit complex mixed farmland landscapes, with patches of bare ground providing high availability of ants adjacent to hedges, and forests offering hollow trees as nest sites (Coudrain *et al.*, 2010). In Poland, differences in the structure of the agricultural landscape explained 79% of the variation in density of grey partridges between study areas. Higher densities were correlated with larger areas of permanent cover without trees, probably because these represent safe and insect-rich foraging sites and hence enhance chick survival (Panek, 1997; Panek and Kamieniarz, 1998). In Spanish pseudosteppe, male little bustards prefer cereal–fallow mosaics within extensive agriculture rather than entirely fallow or entirely cereal landscapes (Morales *et al.*, 2005). Great bustards *Otis tarda* in cereal-steppe in southern Portugal use different habitats throughout the year, with differences in habitat preferences reflecting both changes in food availability and specific habitat requirements for displaying and nesting (Moreira *et al.*, 2004).

Even where habitat structures appear suitable, the nature of the surrounding matrix may be important. For example, the abundance of most farmland bird species breeding on fragments of semi-natural dry pastures in Sweden was generally higher on pastures that were surrounded by agricultural land rather than forest (Söderström and Pärt, 2000). This was attributed to the fact that many of these species forage over large areas and that they were supplementing their food by using the surrounding land. In the Crau area of southern France, the abundance of little bustard is higher where natural steppe habitats occur in close association with extensive agricultural land (Wolff *et al.*, 2001). Similarly, and also in the Crau, the presence of tawny pipit *Anthus campestris*, skylark and calandra lark *Melanocorypha calandra* in natural steppe fragments is affected by the nature of the agricultural landscape in which they are embedded. The majority of individuals occur where native steppe is surrounded by extensive pasture or fallows, rather than intensive agriculture (Brotons *et al.*, 2005).

Barn owls require some degree of landscape heterogeneity, and their habitat preferences vary according to season because agricultural activities impact on the densities and accessibility of small mammals (Tome and Valkama, 2001; Arlettaz *et al.*, 2010c). Lesser kestrels *Falco naumanni* also benefit from a landscape mosaic created by low intensity agriculture. This species feeds mainly on invertebrates (Orthoptera and Coleoptera) as well as small mammals and lizards, usually within 3 km of the colony. Early in the season they use grazed fallow and ploughed fields, but during chick rearing they exploit fields being harvested, as this activity results in a sudden increase in accessible insects (Franco *et al.*, 2004). A patchier landscape mosaic may also favour kestrels because, even in poor vole years, patches with the highest prey density are likely to be closer to the nest in mosaic landscapes than in uniform farmland (Valkama *et al.*, 1995).

A few species feed in different habitats and locations at day and night. Golden plovers *Pluvialis apricaria* and lapwings wintering on arable land in eastern England disperse more widely and visit more habitat types at night than during the day, probably because of variation in prey availability, and predator activity and detectability (Gillings *et al.*, 2005). Nocturnal feeding may be essential for these species to meet their daily energy requirements.

In summary, at the landscape scale, heterogeneity has an especially strong influence on bird community composition and species richness. However, there are many examples of how landscape heterogeneity can affect the abundance and distribution of wide-ranging species by enabling them to exploit local and sometimes temporary food patches.

Restoring habitat heterogeneity in farmland

Habitat diversity and patchiness, typical under many forms of 'traditional agriculture', has become increasingly uniform and rare in more modern, intensive agricultural management (Donald *et al.*, 2001b; see overview table in Benton *et al.*, 2003). Previous sections highlighted the extent to which habitat heterogeneity, at all scales, is a key feature promoting diversity and abundance of farmland birds. The 'homogenisation' of farmland can consequently have deleterious consequences for farmland bird populations through a range of mechanisms. Large-scale restoration of traditional cultivated landscapes in order to reverse this trend is unrealistic. Agri-environment schemes offer the most widespread 'tools' for increasing habitat variation.

Agri-environment schemes and field-scale heterogeneity

Few agri-environment options explicitly address the issue of 'sward homogeneity', although general reduction in the intensity of management within grass and arable crops is likely to result in structurally more diverse and plant-species-rich swards. Subsidies for extensification of grassland management, for example, may enhance habitat suitability for foraging and nesting birds by increasing vegetation patchiness. Several European countries have already adopted such schemes. The Swiss scheme specifies that 7% of the area of a farm is devoted to Ecological Compensation Areas (ECAs), a large proportion of which takes the form of extensive (49%) and low-intensity (21%) meadows, respectively (OFAG, 2010). Encouragingly such ECAs not only provide enhanced resources *in situ*, but also lead to higher invertebrate populations in adjacent conventionally cultivated fields (Albrecht *et al.*, 2010). In addition, many terrestrially foraging birds benefit from the presence of patches of bare ground within or close to invertebrate-rich grassy habitats (Fig. 7.2). Targeted removal of grass cover on small areas represents a novel option that is worth testing experimentally.

In arable land, there are also specific options targeted at species like skylark and lapwing to create 'vegetation gaps' in crop monocultures to provide food and nest sites. Small, 4 m^2 undrilled patches within winter cereals have markedly increased the value of a field for late nesting attempts by skylark (Morris *et al.*, 2004; Fischer *et al.*, 2009; Fig. 7.1). In the case of lapwings, plots of at least 2 ha are similarly left undrilled in winter, but are cultivated in spring. This creates optimal nesting habitat in the form of sparse vegetation cover and, if managed and located appropriately, such fields can support both foraging and nesting birds (Chamberlain *et al.*, 2009). A similar approach has proved extremely successful for stone-curlews which have declined in southern England due both to mechanical destruction of nests in arable habitats and reductions in rabbit grazing that had previously maintained the sparse vegetation used for feeding and nesting. Protection of nests and creation of bare-ground nesting plots in fallow and semi-natural habitats under agri-environment schemes, underpinned the recovery of the species from 139 to 307 pairs between 1990 and 2005 (Green *at al.*, 2000; Wilson *et al.*, 2009).

Agri-environment schemes and farm-scale heterogeneity

Some agri-environment measures are designed to diversify the number of crop types at the farm scale (e.g. the Swiss scheme requires at least four types of crops per farm, in non-dairy farms larger than 3 ha), others to restore nesting and foraging opportunities. A clear vision is still lacking for optimal spatial arrangement of compositional heterogeneity (crop and cover types) and configurational heterogeneity (complexity of the spatial pattern of fields), though Fahrig *et al.* (2010) provide a framework for progress.

Options for margins and boundaries can be popular with farmers and land owners when the financial incentives are attractive. Creation of small patches of semi-natural habitat such as farm woods, ponds and boundary ditches can greatly improve farm-scale habitat diversity. Changes in the cropped habitats are often more complicated to realise because market conditions remain the main driver of their management, but they are the most valuable approaches for conserving particular bird species (Butler *et al.*, 2007). Two examples follow. The habitat needs for breeding lapwings could be provided through the creation of fields with sparse vegetation, obtained perhaps through shallow cultivation, adjacent to managed meadows (Berg *et al.*, 2002). The combined reduction of rough grass and crop stubble caused the decline of cirl buntings in the UK; these habitats are required for summer and winter foraging, respectively (Evans, 1997). Specific agri-environment measures designed to provide suitably managed grassland for summer foraging and seed-rich winter stubbles in close proximity have been extremely successful in increasing local population density. Between 1992 and 1998 the population on land under these agri-environment measures increased by 83% compared with 2% increases on land outside these agreements (Peach *et al.*, 2001; Wotton *et al.*, 2004).

Within grassland, a mix of fields that differ in sward height and complexity may be achieved by adopting different grazing or cutting management intensities and time schedules in different fields (Atkinson *et al.*, 2005). As for within-field heterogeneity, overall extensification of grassland management will again provide spatial heterogeneity between fields (Buckingham *et al.*, 2004).

Agri-environment schemes and landscape-scale heterogeneity

The 'local' addition of an arable crop or vineyard to grassland (or vice versa), for example, or a stubble followed by a fallow in cereal landscapes, will create additional and/or complementary foraging resources at a wider scale (Robinson *et al.*, 2001). However, enhancing habitat heterogeneity at a landscape scale through agri-environment measures targeted at individual farmers or land owners is difficult. In effect, birds with large territories that obtain some of their resources from farmland require measures beyond agriculture alone. For example, the density of raptors in open Mediterranean habitats in Spain varies with the nature of the forest–farmland mix. At the landscape scale, the breeding density of short-toed eagle *Circaetus gallicus*, booted eagle *Hieraaetus pennatus* and buzzard *Buteo buteo* tend to increase with forest cover, peaking in density at around 80% in the latter two species. Conservation of these raptors may thus require a regional approach towards habitat mosaics created by forestry and agriculture (Sánchez-Zapata and Calvo, 1999). This is an example of where agri-environment measures would greatly benefit from being integrated, coordinated and planned across sectors. A solution is currently implemented in Switzerland whereby a new policy provides financial incentives, on the top of other subsidies, to groups of farmers who implement local ecological networks under the supervision of agro-ecologists (OFAG, 2010).

For many species, agri-environment measures that encourage traditional low-intensity or extensive farming systems may be the most appropriate way to maintain habitat heterogeneity at a landscape scale. This sort of low intensity mixed farming is at risk of being lost either to agricultural intensification or abandonment (Britschgi *et al.*, 2006). In many marginal areas, it is frequently no longer economically viable, and will only survive with support through agri-environment, social and rural development measures (Woodhouse *et al.*, 2005; Brambilla *et al.*, 2010). The conservation of many steppe birds, such as great bustards, requires a mosaic of habitat types typical of low-profitability rotational crop systems (Moreira *et al.*, 2004). The recent increase in great bustards in Portugal can be attributed almost entirely to the increase at one key site where an agri-environment 'zonal plan' was established in 1995. This promoted a rotational cropping system with dry cereals, fallows and legumes, as well as reduced pesticide use and lower livestock densities (Pinto et al., 2005). These measures have simultaneously benefited lesser kestrels (Franco et al., 2004). For the little bustard in western France, successful schemes are being developed which improve nest survival through mowing constraints and enhance grasshopper abundance as chick food (Bretagnolle et al., 2011).

A recent meta-analysis has established that agri-environment management provides contrasting outcomes for farmland biodiversity, depending on the dominant cultivation system and on landscape context (Batáry et al., 2011b). In cropland, agri-environment measures increase species richness (but not abundance) in simple landscapes, typical of much modern farmland, but not in complex landscapes. In grassland, they enhance both species richness and abundance, irrespective of the landscape context. An example of how the relationships between birds and hedgerow length depend on landscape context is shown in Fig. 7.4 – richness and abundance are only positively affected by hedgerow length in simple landscapes. Concepcion et al. (2008) even demonstrated negative effects of agri-environment schemes in complex matrices. It seems, therefore, that agri-environmental measures are most successful when implemented in simple, homogenised farmland.

Wider benefits of habitat heterogeneity

A fine-grained mosaic within agricultural habitats can deliver additional benefits beyond simply supporting rich farmland bird populations. First, increasing the heterogeneity of farmland will benefit species across a suite of taxonomic groups (Smith et al., 2005; Winqvist et al., 2011). Second, under some circumstances the biodiversity of adjacent habitats may be enriched, for example, through 'positive spillover' of invertebrates (cf. Rand et al., 2006). Third, habitat heterogeneity may improve delivery of environmental services, including pollination, biological control, soil protection and protection of watercourses (Roschewitz et al., 2005; Tscharntke et al., 2005; Arlettaz et al., 2010a; Winqvist et al., 2011). Grass margins provide both nesting and feeding opportunities for birds, but can also act as buffer strips that reduce riparian pollution from diffuse sources by impeding water flow (Bradbury and Kirby, 2006). Similarly, small wetlands provide emergent insects as a source of food for birds and can simultaneously serve as flood regulators, slowing and holding surface water run-off and suspended solids (Bradbury and Kirby, 2006). Vegetating mineral vineyards in hilly landscapes with native herbs every second vine row not only benefits arthropods and birds such as the woodlark, but also helps reduce soil erosion (Arlettaz et al., 2012).

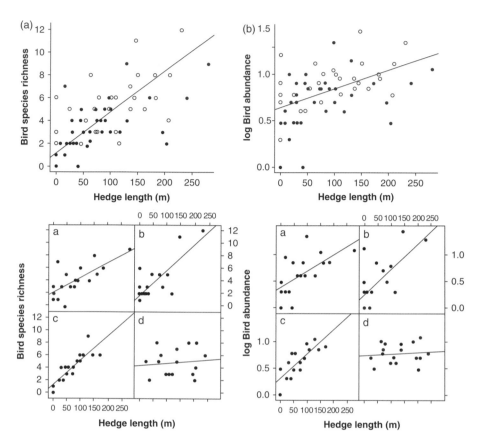

Figure 7.4 Effects of hedgerow quantity and landscape complexity on bird species richness and abundance as shown by work in Germany. Upper panel: relationship of bird species richness (a) and abundance (b) (log scale) to hedge length in organic (open circles) and conventional (closed circles) meadowland and cereals (line: regression from general linear model); note the absence of a difference in effects between the two farming systems. Lower panel: interaction plot showing the relationships between bird species richness (left) and abundance (right) and hedge length within a 500 m radius of bird point-count locations. These are shown for four different levels of landscape complexity, as measured by the proportion of semi-natural habitats around the points: (a) 0–1.5%; (b) 1.5–4.5%; (c) 4.5–17%; (d) >17%. A positive effect of hedges is only evident when the proportion of semi-natural habitat is low, at less than 17%. From Batáry *et al.* (2010).

Finally, increased heterogeneity in agricultural landscapes may prove increasingly important in the face of climate change. A diversity of habitats throughout the agricultural matrix may allow species, especially those with low mobility, to adapt to climate change by facilitating their spatial movements when they redistribute to track their climate envelope (Donald and Evans, 2006).

Concluding remarks

Cultivated landscapes have constantly changed due to evolving farming practices, but 'traditional agriculture' has contributed to the creation of a rich habitat mosaic, often associated with high levels of biodiversity. A drive for higher and higher yields has favoured specialisation in farming and the expansion of industrial agriculture. This resulted in a massive loss of habitat heterogeneity at the field, farm and landscape scales, causing a collapse of farmland wildlife. The socio-economic and ecological mechanisms behind these major changes are well documented (Vickery et al., 2001).

Over the last three decades farmland ecologists have gathered an immense knowledge about the fate of wildlife in agro-ecosystems and the basic ecological requirements of plant and animal species occurring in cultivated landscapes. A wealth of scientific evidence, originating mostly from north-west and central Europe, strongly suggests that habitat heterogeneity at multiple scales is required to maintain and enhance the quality of farmland habitats for foraging and nesting birds. Although different habitat–species associations may apply in other regions (Chapter 3), habitat heterogeneity of various kinds appears to serve a crucial set of functions everywhere for most farmland bird species. This has been particularly well documented at the field and farm scales, possibly because this is the scale at which farmland birds operate. Less work has been done, however, in relation to the ideal configuration of agricultural landscapes to promote rich communities of plants and animals. Landscape-scale conservation action is often complicated by the conflicting requirements of different potential target communities. For example, open-field species can be hampered by dense hedge networks that favour several other species. Perhaps there is a need to develop regional goals for farmland biodiversity. Maximising heterogeneity at all scales is not desirable in all contexts (Batáry et al., 2010, 2011a). We need different types of heterogeneity in different places to suit different farmland bird assemblages; a sort of diversity of diversities.

It remains to be seen which kind of financial incentives to farmers may enable agri-environment schemes to promote and sustain a sufficient spatio-temporal habitat heterogeneity for biodiversity. This requires readily-adopted approaches (political and practical) for subsidising farmers that can adapt and respond to constantly changing market conditions in a way that ensures a mix of options are adopted (Drechsler et al., 2007; Cooke et al., 2009). Biologists and agro-economists must work together to design multi-functional agricultural landscapes that are capable of maintaining optimal agricultural yield, basic environmental functions and ecosystem services, and a rich wildlife.

Acknowledgements

We thank Fiona Sanderson and Olivier Roth for extensive help with background information and references. Bertrand Posse, Antoine Sierro and Niklaus Zbinden also assisted with literature. Many thanks to Olivier Roth who managed and referenced the whole literature cited. This chapter was also greatly improved as a result of comments from András Báldi, Matthias Brambilla, Jean-Yves Humbert, Lukas Jenni, Michael Schaub, Jeremy Wilson and the editor, Rob Fuller.

References

Albrecht, M., Schmid, B., Obrist, M. K. et al. (2010). Effects of ecological compensation meadows on arthropod diversity in adjacent intensively managed grassland. *Biol. Conserv.*, **143**, 642–649.

Anderson, G. Q. A., Gruar, D. J., Wilkinson, N. and Field, R. H. (2002). Tree Sparrow *Passer montanus* chick diet and productivity in an expanding colony. *Aspects Appl. Biol.*, **67**, 35–42.

Arlettaz, R., Krähenbühl, M., Almasi, B., Roulin, A. and Schaub, M. (2010c). Wildflower areas within revitalized agricultural matrices boost small mammal populations but not breeding Barn Owls. *J. Ornithol.*, **151**, 553–564.

Arlettaz, R., Maurer, M. L., Mosimann-Kampe, P. et al. (2012). New vineyard cultivation practices create patchy ground vegetation, favouring Woodlarks. *J. Ornithol.*, **153**, 229–238.

Arlettaz, R., Reichlin, T., Schaad, M. and Schaub, M. (2010b). Impact of weather and climate variation on Hoopoe reproductive ecology and population growth. *J. Ornithol.*, **151**, 889–899.

Arlettaz, R., Schaub, M., Fournier, J. et al. (2010a). From publications to public actions: when conservation biologists bridge the gap between research and implementation. *BioScience*, **60**, 835–842.

Aschwanden, J., Birrer, S. and Jenni, L. (2005). Are ecological compensation areas attractive hunting sites for common kestrels (*Falco tinnunculus*) and long-eared owls (*Asio otus*)? *J. Ornithol.*, **146**, 279–286.

Atauri, J. A. and de Lucio, J. V. (2001). The role of landscape structure in species richness distribution of birds, amphibians, reptiles and lepidopterans in Mediterranean landscapes. *Landscape Ecol.*, **16**, 147–159.

Atkinson, P. W., Fuller, R. J. and Vickery, J. A. (2002). Large-scale patterns of summer and winter bird distribution in relation to farmland type in England and Wales. *Ecography*, **25**, 466–480.

Atkinson, P. W., Fuller, R. J., Vickery, J. A. et al. (2005). Influence of agricultural management, sward structure and food resources on grassland field use by birds in lowland England. *J. Appl. Ecol.*, **42**, 932–942.

Avilés, J. M. and Costillo, E. (1998). Selection of breeding habitats by the Roller (*Coracias garrulus*) in farming areas of the southwest of the Iberian Peninsula. *Vogelwarte*, **39**, 242–247.

Avilés, J. M., Sánchez, J. M. and Parejo, D. (2000). Nest-site selection and breeding success in the Roller (*Coracias garrulus*) in the southwest of the Iberian peninsula. *J. Ornithol.*, **141**, 345–350.

Baines, D. (1990). The roles of predation, food and agricultural practice in determining the breeding success of the lapwing (*Vanellus vanellus*) on upland grasslands. *J. Anim. Ecol.*, **59**, 915–929.

Báldi, A., Batáry, P. and Erdős, S. (2005). Effects of grazing intensity on bird assemblages and populations of Hungarian grasslands. *Agr. Ecosyst. Environ.*, **108**, 251–263.

Barbaro, L., Couzi, L., Bretagnolle, V., Nezan, J. and Vetillard, F. (2008). Multi-scale habitat selection and foraging ecology of the eurasian hoopoe (*Upupa epops*) in pine plantations. *Biodivers. Conserv.*, **17**, 1073–1087.

Batáry, P., Báldi, A. and Erdős, S. (2007). Grassland versus non grassland bird abundance and diversity in managed grasslands: local, landscape and regional scale effects. *Biodivers. Conserv.*, **16**, 871–881.

Batáry, P., Báldi, A., Kleijn, D. and Tscharntke, T. (2011b). Landscape-moderated biodiversity effects of agri-environmental management: a meta-analysis. *Proc. R. Soc. B*, **278**, 1894–1902.

Batáry, P., Fischer, J., Báldi, A., Crist, T. O. and Tscharntke, T. (2011a). Does habitat heterogeneity increase farmland biodiversity? *Front. Ecol. Environ.*, **9**, 152–153.

Batáry, P., Matthiesen, T. and Tscharntke, T. (2010). Landscape-moderated importance of hedges in conserving farmland bird diversity of organic vs. conventional croplands and grasslands. *Biol. Conserv.*, **143**, 2020–2027.

Benton, T. G., Vickery, J. A. and Wilson, J. D. (2003). Farmland biodiversity: is habitat heterogeneity the key? *Trends Ecol. Evol.*, **18**, 182–188.

Berg, Å. (2002). Composition and diversity of bird communities in Swedish farmland-forest mosaic landscapes. *Bird Study*, **49**, 153–165.

Berg, Å., Jonsson, M., Lindberg, T. and Källebrink, K. G. (2002). Population dynamics and reproduction of Northern Lapwings *Vanellus vanellus* in a meadow restoration area in central Sweden. *Ibis*, **144**, E131–E140.

Birrer, S., Spiess, M., Herzog, F. *et al.* (2007). The Swiss agri-environment scheme promotes farmland birds: but only moderately. *J. Ornithol.*, **148**, S295–S303.

Bradbury, R. B. and Bradter, U. (2004). Habitat associations of Yellow Wagtails *Motacilla flava flavissima* on lowland wet grassland. *Ibis*, **146**, 241–246.

Bradbury, R. B. and Kirby, W. B. (2006). Farmland birds and resource protection in the UK: Cross-cutting solutions for multi-functional farming? *Biol. Conserv.*, **129**, 530–542.

Bradbury, R. B. and Stoate, C. (2000). The ecology of Yellowhammers *Emberiza citrinella* on lowland farmland. In *Ecology and Conservation of Lowland Farmland Birds*, ed. N. J. Aebischer, A. D. Evans, P. V. Grice and J. A. Vickery, pp. 165–172. Tring: BOU.

Brambilla, M., Casale, F., Bergero, V. *et al.* (2009a). GIS-models work well, but are not enough: Habitat preferences of *Lanius collurio* at multiple levels and conservation implications. *Biol. Conserv.*, **142**, 2033–2042.

Brambilla, M., Casale, F., Bergero, V. *et al.* (2010). Glorious past, uncertain present, bad future? Assessing effects of land-use changes on habitat suitability for a threatened farmland bird species. *Biol. Conserv.*, **143**, 2770–2778.

Brambilla, M., Guidali, F. and Negri, I. (2008). The importance of an agricultural mosaic for Cirl Buntings *Emberiza cirlus* in Italy. *Ibis*, **150**, 628–632.

Brambilla, M., Guidali, F. and Negri, I. (2009b). Breeding-season habitat associations of the declining Corn Bunting *Emberiza calandra* – a potential indicator of the overall bunting richness. *Ornis Fennica*, **86**, 41–50.

Brambilla, M., Rubolini, D. and Guidali, F. (2007). Between land abandonment and agricultural intensification: habitat preferences of Red-backed Shrikes *Lanius collurio* in low-intensity farming conditions. *Bird Study*, **54**, 160–167.

Bretagnolle, V., Villers, A., Denonfoux, L. *et al.* (2011). Rapid recovery of a depleted population of Little Bustards *Tetrax tetrax* following provision of alfalfa through an agri-environment scheme. *Ibis*, **153**, 4–13.

Brickle, N. W., Harper, D. G. C., Aebischer, N. J. and Cockayne, S. H. (2000). Effects of agricultural intensification on the breeding success of corn buntings *Miliaria calandra*. *J. Appl. Ecol.*, **37**, 742–755.

Britschgi, A., Spaar, R. and Arlettaz, R. (2006). Impact of grassland farming intensification on the breeding ecology of an indicator insectivorous passerine, the Whinchat *Saxicola rubetra*: lessons for overall Alpine meadowland management. *Biol. Conserv.*, **130**, 193–205.

Brotons, L., Wolff, A., Paulus, G. and Martin, J. L. (2005). Effect of adjacent agricultural habitat on the distribution of passerines in natural grasslands. *Biol. Conserv.*, **124**, 407–414.

Browne, S. J., Aebischer, N. J., Yfantis, G. and Marchant, J. H. (2004). Habitat availability and use by Turtle Doves *Streptopelia turtur* between 1965 and 1995: an analysis of Common Birds Census data. *Bird Study*, **51**, 1–11.

Buckingham, D. L. (2001). Within-field habitat selection by wintering skylarks *Alauda arvensis* in southwest England. In *The Ecology and Conservation of Skylarks* Alauda arvensis, ed. P. F. Donald and J. A. Vickery, pp. 149–158. Sandy: RSPB.

Buckingham, D. L., Atkinson, P. W. and Rook, A. J. (2004). Testing solutions in grass-dominated landscapes: a review of current research. *Ibis*, **146**, 163–170.

Buckingham, D. L., Peach, W. J. and Fox, D. S. (2006). Effects of agricultural management on the use of lowland grassland by foraging birds. *Agr. Ecosyst. Environ.*, **112**, 21–40.

Butler, S. J., Vickery, J. A. and Norris, K. (2007). Farmland biodiversity and the footprint of agriculture. *Science*, **315**, 381–384.

Chamberlain, D., Gough, S., Anderson, G. *et al.* (2009). Bird use of cultivated fallow Lapwing plots within English agri-environment schemes. *Bird Study*, **56**, 289–297.

Chamberlain, D. E., Vickery, J. A. and Gough, S. (2000). Spatial and temporal distribution of breeding Skylarks *Alauda arvensis* in relation to crop type in periods of population increase and decrease. *Ardea*, **88**, 61–73.

Chamberlain, D. E., Wilson, A. M., Browne, S. J. and Vickery, J. A. (1999). Effects of habitat type and management on the abundance of skylarks in the breeding season. *J. Appl. Ecol.*, **36**, 856–870.

Concepcion, E. D., Diaz, M. and Baquero, R. A. (2008). Effects of landscape complexity on the ecologial effectiveness of agri-environment schemes. *Landscape Ecol.*, **23**, 135–148.

Cooke, I. R., Queenborough, S. A., Mattison, E. H. A. *et al.* (2009). Integrating socio-economics and ecology: a taxonomy of quantitative methods and a review of their use in agro-ecology. *J. Appl. Ecol.*, **46**, 269–277.

Coudrain, V., Arlettaz, R. and Schaub, M. (2010). Food or nesting place? Identifying factors limiting Wryneck populations. *J. Ornithol.*, **151**, 867–880.

Delgado, A. and Moreira, F. (2000). Bird assemblages of an Iberian cereal steppe. *Agr. Ecosyst. Environ.*, **78**, 65–76.

Devereux, C. L., McKeever, C. U., Benton, T. G. and Whittingham, M J. (2004). The effect of sward height and drainage on Common Starlings *Sturnus vulgaris* and Northern Lapwings *Vanellus vanellus* foraging in grassland habitats. *Ibis*, **146**, 115–122.

Donald, P. F., and Evans, A. D. (2006). Habitat connectivity and matrix restoration: the wider implications of agri-environment schemes. *J. Appl. Ecol.*, **43**, 209–218.

Donald, P. F., Evans, A. D., Buckingham, D. L., Muirhead, L. B. and Wilson, J. D. (2001a). Factors affecting the territory distribution of Skylarks *Alauda arvensis* breeding on lowland farmland. *Bird Study*, **48**, 271–278.

Donald, P. F., Green, R. E. and Heath, M. F. (2001b). Agricultural intensification and the collapse of Europe's farmland bird populations. *Proc. R. Soc. B*, **268**, 25–29.

Douglas, D. J. T., Vickery, J. A. and Benton, T. G. (2009). Improving the value of field margins as foraging habitat for farmland birds. *J. Appl. Ecol.*, **46**, 353–362.

Drechsler, M., Wätzold, F., Johst, K., Bergmann, H. and Settele, J. (2007). A model-based approach for designing cost-effective compensation payments for conservation of endangered species in real landscapes. *Biol. Conserv.*, **140**, 174–186.

Erdös, S., Báldi, A. and Batáry, P. (2009). Nest site selection and breeding ecology of Sky Larks *Alauda arvensis* in Hungarian farmland. *Bird Study*, **56**, 259–263.

Evans, A. (1997). The importance of mixed farming for seed-eating birds in the UK. In *Farming and Birds in Europe: The Common Agricultural Policy and its Implications for Bird Conservation*, ed. D. J. Pain and M. W. Pienkowski, pp. 331–357. San Diego: Academic Press.

Evans, K. L. (2004). The potential for interactions between predation and habitat change to cause population declines of farmland birds. *Ibis*, **146**, 1–13.

Evans, K. L., Bradbury, R. B. and Wilson, J. D. (2003). Selection of hedgerows by Swallows *Hirundo rustica* foraging on farmland: the influence of local habitat and weather. *Bird Study*, **50**, 8–14.

Fahrig, L., Baudry, K., Brotons, L. *et al.* (2010). Functional landscape heterogeneity and animal biodiversity in agricultural landscapes. *Ecol. Lett.*, **14**, 101–112.

Field, R. H. and Anderson, G. Q. A. (2004). Habitat use by breeding Tree Sparrows *Passer montanus*. *Ibis*, **146**, 60–68.

Fischer, J., Jenny, M. and Jenni, L. (2009). Suitability of patches and in-field strips for Sky Larks *Alauda arvensis* in a small-parcelled mixed farming area. *Bird Study*, **56**, 34–42.

Franco, A. M. A., Catry, I., Sutherland, W. J. and Palmeirim, J. M. (2004). Do different habitat preference survey methods produce the same conservation recommendations for lesser kestrels? *Anim. Conserv.*, **7**, 291–300.

Fuller, R. J., Chamberlain, D. E., Burton, N. H. K. and Gough, S. J. (2001). Distributions of birds in lowland agricultural landscapes of England and Wales: how distinctive are bird communities of hedgerows and woodland? *Agr. Ecosyst. Environ.*, **84**, 79–92.

Fuller, R. J, Trevelyan, R. J. and Hudson, R. W. (1997). Landscape composition models for breeding bird populations in lowland English farmland over a 20 year period. *Ecography*, **20**, 295–307.

Galbraith, H. (1988). Effects of agriculture on the breeding ecology of lapwings *Vanellus vanellus*. *J. Appl. Ecol.*, **25**, 487–503.

Gillings, S., Fuller, R. J. and Sutherland, W. J. (2005). Diurnal studies do not predict nocturnal habitat choice and site selection of European Golden-Plovers (*Pluvialis apricaria*) and Northern Lapwings (*Vanellus vanellus*). *Auk*, **122**, 1249–1260.

Gilroy, J. J., Anderson, G. Q. A., Grice, P. V. *et al.* (2009). Foraging habitat selection, diet and nestling condition in Yellow Wagtails *Motacilla flava* breeding on arable farmland. *Bird Study*, **56**, 221–232.

Gilroy, J. J., Anderson, G. Q. A., Grice, P. V., Vickery, J. A. and Sutherland, W. J. (2010). Mid-season shifts in the habitat associations of Yellow Wagtails *Motacilla flava* breeding in arable farmland. *Ibis*, **152**, 90–104.

Goławski, A. and Dombrowski, A. (2002). Habitat use of Yellowhammers *Emberiza citrinella*, Ortolan Buntings *E. hortulana*, and Corn Buntings *Miliaria calandra* in farmland of east-central Poland. *Ornis Fennica*, **79**, 164–172.

Green, R. E. (1984). The feeding ecology and survival of partridge chicks (*Alectoris rufa* and *Perdix perdix*) on arable farmland in East Anglia. *J. Appl. Ecol.*, **21**, 817–830.

Green, R. E., Tyler, G. A. and Bowden, C. G. R. (2000). Habitat selection, ranging behaviour and diet of the Stone Curlew (*Burhinus oecdicnemus*) in southern England. *J. Zool.*, **250**, 161–183.

Heikkinen, R. K., Luoto, M., Virkkala, R. and Rainio, K. (2004). Effects of habitat cover, landscape structure and spatial variables on the abundance of birds in an agricultural–forest mosaic. *J. Appl. Ecol.*, **41**, 824–835.

Henderson, I. G., Cooper, J., Fuller, R. J. and Vickery, J. (2000a). The relative abundance of birds on set-aside and neighbouring fields in summer. *J. Appl. Ecol.*, **37**, 335–347.

Henderson, I. G., Critchley, N. R., Cooper, J. and Fowbert, J. A. (2001). Breeding season responses of Skylarks *Alauda arvensis* to vegetation structure in set-aside (fallow arable land). *Ibis*, **143**, 317–321.

Henderson, I. G. and Evans, A. D. (2000). Responses of farmland birds to set-aside and its management. In *Ecology and Conservation of Lowland Farmland Birds*, ed. N. J. Aebischer, A. D. Evans, P. V. Grice and J. A. Vickery, pp. 69–76. Tring: BOU.

Henderson, I. G., Vickery, J. A. and Fuller, R. J. (2000b). Summer bird abundance and distribution on set-aside fields on intensive arable farms in England. *Ecography*, **23**, 50–59.

Hinsley, S. A. and Bellamy, P. E. (2000). The influence of hedge structure, management and landscape context on the value of hedgerows to birds: a review. *J. Environ. Manage.*, **60**, 33–49.

Hoste-Danylow, A., Romanowski, J. and Zmihorski, M. (2010). Effects of management on invertebrates and birds in extensively used grassland in Poland. *Agr. Ecosyst. Environ.*, **139**, 129–133.

Jenny, M. (1990). Territorialität und Brutbiologie der Feldlerche *Alauda arvensis* in einer intensiv genutzten Agrarlandschaft. *J. Ornithol.*, **131**, 241–265.

Jenny, M., Weibel, U., Lugrin, B. *et al.* (2002). *Rebhuhn: Schlussbericht 1991–2000*. Schriftenreihe Umwelt, Wildtiere Nr. 335. Bern: BUWAL.

Jobin, B., Choinière, L. and Bélanger, L. (2001). Bird use of three types of field margins in relation to intensive agriculture in Québec, Canada. *Agr. Ecosyst. Environ.*, **84**, 131–143.

Joyce, K. A., Holland, J. M. and Doncaster, C. P. (1999). Influences of hedgerow intersections and gaps on the movement of carabid beetles. *B. Entomol. Res.*, **89**, 523–531.

Macdonald, D. W. and Johnson, P. J. (1995). The relationship between bird distribution and the botanical and structural characteristics of hedges. *J. Appl. Ecol.*, **32**, 492–505.

Martinez, N., Jenni, L., Wyss, E. and Zbinden, N. (2010). Habitat structure versus food abundance: the importance of sparse vegetation for the common redstart *Phoenicurus phoenicurus*. *J. Ornithol.*, **151**, 297–307.

Maudsley, M. J. (2000). A review of the ecology and conservation of hedgerow invertebrates in Britain. *J. Environ. Manage.*, **60**, 65–76.

Menz, M. H. M., Brotons, L. and Arlettaz, R. (2009a). Habitat selection by Ortolan Buntings *Emberiza hortulana* in post-fire succession in Catalonia: implications for the conservation of farmland populations. *Ibis*, **151**, 752–761.

Menz, M. H. M., Mosimann-Kampe, P. and Arlettaz, R. (2009b). Foraging habitat selection in the last Ortolan Bunting *Emberiza hortulana* population in Switzerland: final lessons before extinction. *Ardea*, **97**, 323–333.

Mermod, M., Reichlin, T. S., Arlettaz, R. and Schaub, M. (2009). The importance of ant-rich habitats for the persistence of the Wryneck *Jynx torquilla* on farmland. *Ibis*, **151**, 731–742.

Moorcroft, D., Bradbury, R. B. and Wilson, J. D. (1997). The diet of nestling Linnets *Carduelis cannabina* before and after agricultural intensification. In *Biodiversity and Conservation in Agriculture*, ed. R. C. Kirkwood, pp. 923–928. Farnham: British Crop Protection Council.

Moorcroft, D., Whittingham, M. J., Bradbury, R. B. and Wilson, J. D. (2002). The selection of stubble fields by wintering granivorous birds reflects vegetation cover and food abundance. *J. Appl. Ecol.*, **39**, 535–547.

Morales, M. B., García, J. T. and Arroyo, B. (2005). Can landscape composition changes predict spatial and annual variation of little bustard male abundance? *Anim. Conserv.*, **8**, 167–174.

Moreira, F., Beja, P., Morgado, R. *et al.* (2005). Effects of field management and landscape context on grassland wintering birds in Southern Portugal. *Agr. Ecosyst. Environ.*, **109**, 59–74.

Moreira, F., Morgado, R. and Arthur, S. (2004). Great bustard *Otis tarda* habitat selection in relation to agricultural use in southern Portugal. *Wildlife Biol.*, **10**, 251–260.

Morris, A. J., Bradbury, R. B. and Wilson, J. D. (2002). Determinants of patch selection by yellowhammers *Emberiza citrinella* foraging in cereal crops. *Aspects Appl. Biol.*, **67**, 43–50.

Morris, A. J. and Gilroy, J. J. (2008). Close to the edge: predation risks for two declining farmland passerines. *Ibis*, **150**, 168–177.

Morris, A. J., Holland, J. M., Smith, B. and Jones, N. E. (2004). Sustainable Arable Farming For an Improved Environment (SAFFIE): managing winter wheat sward structure for Skylarks *Alauda arvensis*. *Ibis*, **146**, 155–162.

Odderskær, P., Prang, A., Poulsen, J. G., Andersen, P. N. and Elmegaard, N. (1997). Skylark (*Alauda arvensis*) utilisation of micro-habitats in spring barley fields. *Agr. Ecosyst. Environ.*, **62**, 21–29.

OFAG (2010). *Rapport agricole 2010: résumé*. Berne: Office Fédéral de l'Agriculture; Département Fédéral de l'Economie.

Oliver, T., Roy, D. B, Hill, J. K., Brereton, T. and Thomas, C. D. (2010). Heterogeneous landscapes promote population stability. *Ecol. Lett.*, **13**, 473–484.

Panek, M. (1997). The effect of agricultural landscape structure on food resources and survival of grey partridge *Perdix perdix* chicks in Poland. *J. Appl. Ecol.*, **34**, 787–792.

Panek, M. and Kamieniarz, R. (1998). Agricultural landscape structure and density of grey partridge (*Perdix perdix*) populations in Poland. *Gibier Faune Sauvage*, **15**, 309–320.

Parish, T., Lakhani, K. H. and Sparks, T. H. (1994). Modelling the relationship between bird population variables and hedgerow and other field margin attributes. I. Species richness of winter, summer and breeding birds. *J. Appl. Ecol.*, **31**, 764–775.

Parish, T., Lakhani, K. H. and Sparks, T. H. (1995). Modelling the relationship between bird population variables and hedgerow, and other field margin attributes. II. Abundance of individual species and of groups of similar species. *J. Appl. Ecol.*, **32**, 362–371.

Peach, W. J., Lovett, L. J., Wotton, S. R. and Jeffs, C. (2001). Countryside stewardship delivers cirl buntings (*Emberiza cirlus*) in Devon, UK. *Biol. Conserv.*, **101**, 361–373.

Perkins, A. J., Whittingham, M. J., Bradbury, R. B. et al. (2000). Habitat characteristics affecting use of lowland agricultural grassland by birds in winter. *Biol. Conserv.*, **95**, 279–294.

Petersen, B. S. (1998). The distribution of Danish farmland birds in relation to habitat characteristics. *Ornis Fennica*, **75**, 105–118.

Pickett, S. R. A. and Siriwardena, G. M. (2011). The relationship between multi-scale habitat heterogeneity and farmland bird abundance. *Ecography*, **34**, 955–969.

Pinto, M., Rocha, P. and Moreira, F. (2005). Long-term trends in great bustard (*Otis tarda*) populations in Portugal suggest concentration in single high quality area. *Biol. Conserv.*, **124**, 415–423.

Preiss, E., Martin, J. L. and Debussche, M. (1997). Rural depopulation and recent landscape changes in a Mediterranean region: Consequences to the breeding avifauna. *Landscape Ecol.*, **12**, 51–61.

Rand, T. A., Tylianakis, J. M. and Tscharntke, T. (2006). Spillover edge effects: the dispersal of agriculturally subsidized insect natural enemies into adjacent natural habitats. *Ecol. Lett.*, **9**, 603–614.

Rands, M. R. W. (1985). Pesticide use on cereals and the survival of grey partridge chicks: a field experiment. *J. Appl. Ecol.*, **22**, 49–54.

Rands, M. R. W. (1986). Effect of hedgerow characteristics on partridge breeding densities. *J. Appl. Ecol.*, **23**, 479–487.

Rands, M. R. W. and Sotherton, N. W. (1987). The management of field margins for the conservation of gamebirds. In *Field Margins*, ed. J. M. Way and P. W. Greig-Smith, pp. 95–104. London: British Crop Protection Council.

Reif, J., Vorisek, P., Stastny, K., Bejcek, V. and Peter, J. (2008). Agricultural intensification and farmland birds: new insights from a Central European country. *Ibis*, **150**, 596–605.

Revaz, E., Schaub, M. and Arlettaz, R. (2008). Foraging ecology and reproductive biology of the Stonechat *Saxicola torquata*: comparison between a revitalized, intensively cultivated and a historical, traditionally cultivated agro-ecosystem. *J. Ornithol.*, **149**, 301–312.

Robinson, R. A., Wilson, J. D. and Crick, H. Q. P. (2001). The importance of arable habitat for farmland birds in grassland landscapes. *J. Appl. Ecol.*, **38**, 1059–1069.

Roschewitz, I., Thies, C. and Tscharntke, T. (2005). Are landscape complexity and farm specialisation related to land-use intensity of annual crop fields? *Agr. Ecosyst. Environ.*, **105**, 87–99.

Roskaft, E., Moksnes, A., Stokke, B. G., Moskat, C. and Honza, M. (2002). The spatial habitat structure of host populations explains the pattern of rejection behaviour in hosts and parasitic adaptations in cuckoos. *Behav. Ecol.*, **13**, 163–168.

Salamolard, M. and Moreau, C. (1999). Habitat selection by Little Bustard *Tetrax tetrax* in a cultivated area of France. *Bird Study*, **46**, 25–33.

Sánchez-Zapata, J. A. and Calvo, J. F. (1999). Raptor distribution in relation to landscape composition in semi-arid Mediterranean habitats. *J. Appl. Ecol.*, **36**, 254–262.

Schaub, M. (1996). Jagdverhalten und Zeitbudget von Rotkopfwürgern (*Lanius senator*) in der Nordwestschweiz. *J. Ornithol.*, **137**, 213–227.

Schaub, M., Martinez, N., Tagmann-Ioset, A. *et al.* (2010). Patches of bare ground as a staple commodity for declining insectivorous farmland birds. *PLoS ONE*, **5**, e13115.

Schläpfer, A. (1988). Populationsökologie der Feldlerche *Alauda arvensis* in der intensiv genutzten Agrarlandschaft. *Ornithol. Beob.*, **85**, 309–371.

Schön, M. (1999). Zur Bedeutung von Kleinstrukturen im Ackerland: Bevorzugt die Feldlerche (*Alauda arvensis*) Störstellen mit Kümmerwuchs? *J. Ornithol.*, **140**, 87–91.

Sheldon, R. (2002). Lapwings in Britain – a new approach to their conservation. *Brit. Wildlife*, **14**, 109–116.

Sheldon, R., Bolton, M., Gillings, S. and Wilson, A. (2004). Conservation management of Lapwing *Vanellus vanellus* on lowland arable farmland in the UK. *Ibis*, **146**, 41–49.

Sheldon, R. D., Chaney, K. and Tyler, G. A. (2005). Factors affecting nest-site choice by Northern Lapwing *Vanellus vanellus* within arable fields: the importance of crop structure. *Wader Study Group Bull.*, **108**, 47–52.

Sierro, A. and Arlettaz, R. (2003). L'avifaune du vignoble en Valais central: évaluation de la diversité à l'aide de transects. *Nos Oiseaux*, **50**, 89–100.

Sierro, A., Frey Iseli, M., Graf, R. *et al.* (2009). Banalisation de l'avifaune du paysage agricole sur trois surfaces témoins du Valais (1988–2006). *Nos Oiseaux*, **56**, 129–148.

Siriwardena, G. M., Calbrade, N. A., Vickery, J. A. and Sutherland, W. J. (2006). The effect of the spatial distribution of winter seed food resources on their use by farmland birds. *J. Appl. Ecol.*, **43**, 628–639.

Siriwardena, G. M., Crick, H. Q. P., Baillie, S. R. and Wilson, J. D. (2000). Agricultural land-use and the spatial distribution of granivorous lowland farmland birds. *Ecography*, **23**, 702–719.

Siriwardena, G. M., Stevens, D. K., Anderson, G. Q. A. *et al.* (2007). The effect of supplementary winter seed food on breeding populations of farmland birds: evidence from two large-scale experiments. *J. Appl. Ecol.*, **44**, 920–932.

Smart, S. M., Firbank, L. G., Bunce, R. G. H. and Watkins, J. W. (2000). Quantifying changes in abundance of food plants for butterfly larvae and farmland birds. *J. Appl. Ecol.*, **37**, 398–414.

Smith, R. K., Vaughan Jennings, N. and Harris, S. (2005). A quantitative analysis of the abundance and demography of European hares *Lepus europaeus* in relation to habitat type, intensity of agriculture and climate. *Mammal Rev.*, **35**, 1–24.

Snow, B. K. and Snow, D. W. (1988). *Birds and Berries*. Calton: Poyser.

Söderström, B. and Pärt, T. (2000). Influence of landscape scale on farmland birds breeding in semi-natural pastures. *Conserv. Biol.*, **14**, 522–533.

Sotherton, N. W. and Self, M. J. (2000). Changes in plant and arthropod biodiversity on lowland farmland: an overview. In *Ecology and Conservation of Lowland Farmland Birds*, ed. N. J. Aebischer, A. D. Evans, P. V. Grice and J. A. Vickery, pp. 26–35. Tring: BOU.

Stoate, C., Báldi, A., Beja, P., Boatman, N. D. *et al.* (2009). Ecological impacts of early 21st century agricultural change in Europe – a review. *J. Environ. Manage.*, **91**, 22–46.

Stoate, C., Moreby, S. J. and Szczur, J. (1998). Breeding ecology of farmland Yellowhammers *Emberiza citrinella*. *Bird Study*, **45**, 109–121.

Tagmann-Ioset, A., Schaub, M., Reichlin, T. S., Weisshaupt, N. and Arlettaz, R. (2012). Bare ground as a crucial habitat feature for a rare terrestrially foraging farmland bird of central Europe. *Acta Oecol.*, **39**, 25–32.

Tallowin, J. R. B., Smith, R. E. N., Goodyear, J. and Vickery, J. A. (2005). Spatial and structural uniformity of lowland agricultural grassland in England: a context for low biodiversity. *Grass Forage Sci.*, **60**, 225–236.

Toepfer, S. and Stubbe, M. (2001). Territory density of the Skylark (*Alauda arvensis*) in relation to field vegetation in central Germany. *J. Ornithol.*, **142**, 184–194.

Tome, R. and Valkama, J. (2001). Seasonal variation in the abundance and habitat use of Barn Owls *Tyto alba* on lowland farmland. *Ornis Fennica*, **78**, 109–118.

Tscharntke, T., Klein, A. M., Kruess, A., Steffan-Dewenter, I. and Thies, C. (2005). Landscape perspectives on agricultural intensification and biodiversity – ecosystem service management. *Ecol. Lett.*, **8**, 857–874.

Valkama, J., Korpimäki, E. and Tolonen, P. (1995). Habitat utilization, diet and reproductive success in the Kestrel in a temporally and spatially heterogeneous environment. *Ornis Fennica*, **72**, 49–61.

Vargas, J. M., Guerrero, J. C., Farfán, M. A., Barbosa, A. M. and Real, R. (2006). Land use and environmental factors affecting red-legged partridge (*Alectoris rufa*) hunting yields in southern Spain. *Eur. J. Wildlife Res.*, **52**, 188–195.

Vepsäläinen, V., Pakkala, T., Piha, M. and Tiainen, J. (2005). Population crash of the ortolan bunting *Emberiza hortulana* in agricultural landscapes of southern Finland. *Ann. Zool. Fenn.*, **42**, 91–107.

Verhulst, J., Báldi, A. and Kleijn, D. (2004). Relationship between land-use intensity and species richness and abundance of birds in Hungary. *Agr. Ecosyst. Environ.*, **104**, 465–473.

Vickery, J., Carter, N. and Fuller, R. J. (2002). The potential value of managed cereal field margins as foraging habitats for farmland birds in the UK. *Agr. Ecosyst. Environ.*, **89**, 41–52.

Vickery, J. A., Feber, R. E. and Fuller, R. J. (2009). Arable field margins managed for biodiversity conservation: a review of food resource provision for farmland birds. *Agr. Ecosyst. Environ.*, **133**, 1–13.

Vickery, J. A., Tallowin, J. R., Feber, R. E. *et al.* (2001). The management of lowland neutral grasslands in Britain: effects of agricultural practices on birds and their food resources. *J. Appl. Ecol.*, **38**, 647–664.

Wakeham-Dawson, A. and Aebischer, N. J. (1998). Factors determining winter densities of birds on Environmentally Sensitive Area arable reversion grassland in southern England, with special reference to skylarks (*Alauda arvensis*). *Agr. Ecosyst. Environ.*, **70**, 189–201.

Weibel, U., Jenny, M., Zbinden, N. and Edwards, P. J. (2001). Territory size of skylarks *Alauda arvensis* on arable farmland in Switzerland in relation to habitat quality and management. In *The Ecology and Conservation of Skylarks* Alauda arvensis, ed. P. F. Donald and J. A. Vickery, pp. 177–187. Sandy: RSPB.

Weisshaupt, N., Arlettaz, R., Reichlin, T. S., Tagmann-Ioset, A. and Schaub, M. (2011). Habitat selection by foraging wrynecks *Jynx torquilla* during the breeding season: identifying the optimal habitat profile. *Bird Study*, **58**,111–119.

Whittingham, M. J., Devereux, C. L., Evans, A. D. and Bradbury, R. B. (2006). Altering perceived predation risk and food availability: management prescriptions to benefit farmland birds on stubble fields. *J. Appl. Ecol.*, **43**, 640–650.

Whittingham, M. J. and Markland, H. M. (2002). The influence of substrate on the functional response of an avian granivore and its implications for farmland bird conservation. *Oecologia*, **130**, 637–644.

Wiens, J. A. (1989). Spatial scaling in ecology. *Funct. Ecol.*, **3**, 385–397.

Wilson, A. M., Vickery, J. A. and Browne, S. J. (2001). Numbers and distribution of Northern Lapwings *Vanellus vanellus* breeding in England and Wales in 1998. *Bird Study*, **48**, 2–17.

Wilson, J. D., Evans, J., Browne, S. J. and King, J. R. (1997). Territory distribution and breeding success of skylarks *Alauda arvensis* on organic and intensive farmland in southern England. *J. Appl. Ecol.*, **34**, 1462–1478.

Wilson, J. D., Evans, A. D. and Grice, P. V. (2009). *Bird Conservation and Agriculture*. Cambridge: Cambridge University Press.

Wilson, J. D., Taylor, R. and Muirhead, L. B. (1996). Field use by farmland birds in winter: an analysis of field type preferences using resampling methods. *Bird Study*, **43**, 320–332.

Wilson, J. D., Whittingham, M. J. and Bradbury, R. B. (2005). The management of crop structure: a general approach to reversing the impacts of agricultural intensification on birds? *Ibis*, **147**, 453–463.

Winqvist, C., Bengtsson, J., Aavik, T. *et al.* (2011). Mixed effects of organic farming and landscape complexity on farmland biodiversity and biological control potential across Europe. *J. Appl. Ecol.*, **48**, 570–579.

Wirtitsch, M., Hoi, H., Valera, F. and Kristin, A. (2001). Habitat composition and use in the lesser grey shrike *Lanius minor*. *Folia Zool.*, **50**, 137–150.

Wolff, A., Dieuleveut, T., Martin, J. L. and Bretagnolle, V. (2002). Landscape context and little bustard abundance in a fragmented steppe: implications for reserve management in mosaic landscapes. *Biol. Conserv.*, **107**, 211–220.

Wolff, A., Paul, J. P., Martin, J. L. and Bretagnolle, V. (2001). The benefits of extensive agriculture to birds: the case of the little bustard. *J. Appl. Ecol.*, **38**, 963–975.

Woodhouse, S. P., Good, J. E. G., Lovett, A. A., Fuller, R. J. and Dolman, P. M. (2005). Effects of land-use and agricultural management on birds of marginal farmland: a case study in the Llŷn peninsula, Wales. *Agr. Ecosyst. Environ.*, **107**, 331–340.

Wotton, S. R., Rylands, K., Grice, P., Smallshire, D. and Gregory, R. (2004). The status of the Cirl Bunting in the United Kingdom and Channel Islands in 2003. *Brit. Birds*, **97**, 376–384.

Wretenberg, J., Lindström, Å., Svensson, S., Thierfelder, T. and Pärt, T. (2006). Population trends of farmland birds in Sweden and England: similar trends but different patterns of agricultural intensification. *J. Appl. Ecol.*, **43**, 1110–1120.

PART II

Case studies of habitat use and selection

Spatial variation and habitat relationships in moorland bird assemblages: a British perspective

MURRAY C. GRANT

Royal Society for the Protection of Birds Scotland and RPS Planning & Development

and

JAMES W. PEARCE-HIGGINS

Royal Society for the Protection of Birds Scotland and British Trust for Ornithology

Moorlands represent the largest extent of semi-natural habitat remaining in Britain. They provide habitat for some of Britain's most spectacular and charismatic bird species, and yet may often seem vast tracts of barren, inhospitable land, devoid of life. Moorlands occur in other temperate-zone uplands (e.g. in Scandinavia and Russia), as well as in some high-altitude tropical zones (e.g. the Andean páramos) (Holden *et al.*, 2007). Britain's moorland bird assemblages have been extensively studied and this chapter summarises current knowledge of their regional and habitat variation.

Definitions of moorland vary, but here we use the term to mean the open habitats lying between the upper edge of enclosed farmland and the original climax upper tree-line. We exclude the alpine zone (see Chapter 9). Throughout much of Britain, moorlands are found at altitudes from *c*. 300 m up to 700 m, but descend to sea level in northern Scotland. They occur in areas of high precipitation, generally on infertile acidic soils, but sometimes overlie base-rich bedrock (Thompson *et al.*, 1995). The main habitat types comprise dwarf-shrub heath, blanket bog and acid grassland (see Fig. 8.1 for examples). Dwarf-shrub heath has >25% dwarf-shrub cover, with heather *Calluna vulgaris* usually dominant. Indeed, British moorland includes the world's largest expanse of heather dominated habitats. Wet, cool climate and flat topography facilitates the development of deep peat soils on which blanket bog occurs, and where typical plants include cottongrass *Eriophorum* spp. and bog mosses *Sphagnum* spp. Acid grasslands are often dominated by mat grass *Nardus stricta* and heath rush *Juncus squarrosus*. These habitat types together cover in excess

Birds and Habitat: Relationships in Changing Landscapes, ed. Robert J. Fuller. Published by
Cambridge University Press. © Cambridge University Press 2012.

Figure 8.1 Four examples of Scottish moorland landscapes. (a) A glen in the Eastern Highlands with heather moorland on some lower slopes managed for grouse by rotational burning (photo: Sonja Ludwig). (b) Langholm Moor in the Southern Uplands – note the striking fenceline effect contrasting the rough grassland and heather-dominated moor, the former being due to heavy grazing pressure (photo: Des Thompson). (c) Deep heather, shown here in Orkney, is a preferred nesting habitat of several birds of prey (photo: Rob Fuller). (d) Blanket bog in the Outer Hebrides – a preferred nesting habitat of golden plover, dunlin and greenshank (photo: Rob Fuller).

of 5 million ha of Britain, over 20% of the total land area (Haines-Young *et al.*, 2000; Fig. 8.2).

Moorland is predominantly of anthropogenic origin as a result of woodland clearance in the Neolithic period, potentially interacting with past climate change (Tallis, 1991; Smout, 2005). Livestock grazing maintained open moorlands from the Bronze Age onwards, reaching an industrial scale in some regions by the Middle Ages (Smout, 2005). Sheep, and to a much lesser extent cattle, production remains the dominant land use. By the early 1880s large areas of heather moorland were managed specifically for shooting red grouse[1] (Lovat, 1911), which on this scale was, and continues to be, a phenomenon

---

[1] Scientific names of birds are given in Table 8.1.

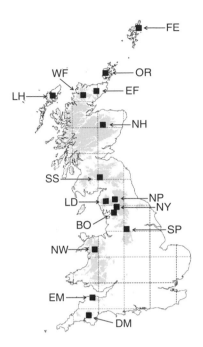

Figure 8.2 Map of the British uplands (grey shading). Regions from which data are derived for the bird community analysis presented in this chapter are indicated by black squares. Regional codes are: DM – Dartmoor, EM – Exmoor, NW – North Wales, SP – South Pennines, BO – Forest of Bowland, NY – North Yorkshire, NP – North Pennines, LD – Lake District, SS – South Scotland, NH – Northeast Highlands, LH – Lewis and Harris, EF – East Flows, WF – West Flows, OR – Orkney, FE – Fetlar.

unique to British moorlands. Today, moorlands are largely maintained through the combined effects of grazing and burning (Thompson *et al.*, 1995).

Although upland sheep numbers are currently in decline, this follows a period of substantial increase during the second half of the twentieth century (Fuller and Gough, 1999; SAC, 2008), which led to the gradual replacement of heather by grasses and sedges on many moorlands. Burning (or 'muirburn'), undertaken both to improve the quality of grazing for sheep and deer, and as management for red grouse, has also impacted moorland vegetation. Heather is the main food plant of red grouse and on moorlands managed for this species (grouse moors) is burnt in small patches (<1 ha), usually on 10–20 year rotations. This creates a patchwork of different-aged stands, where grouse can access younger, nutritious heather close to older, taller stands providing cover (Savory, 1978). Burning to improve grazing for sheep or deer involves more extensive fires, and is not rotational. Since the 1940s, grouse moors have declined in extent, but remain prevalent in the Pennines, the North York Moors, parts of southern Scotland, and the central and eastern Highlands (Hudson, 1992; Anderson *et al.*, 2009).

In the absence of grazing and burning, much moorland would revert to scrub and woodland. Although such 'natural' woodland expansion is generally suppressed, there has been extensive afforestation with commercial conifer plantations during the post-war period (Mackey *et al.*, 1998). The cutting of open drainage ditches (grips) to improve the quality of grazing was commonplace on wetter moors from the 1960s to the 1980s. Recently, considerable effort has been made to restore damp moorland habitats through large-scale drain-blocking (Armstrong *et al.*, 2009).

Moorland bird assemblages

The species associated with British moorlands include a mix of boreal, arctic, temperate and continental breeding species, with some occurring at exceptionally high densities (Thompson *et al.*, 1995). For several species, British moorland represents the edge of their range. Exmoor is the most southerly breeding location in the West Palaearctic for merlin, whilst for both golden plover and dunlin, Dartmoor is the southern limit to their world breeding distribution (Cramp and Simmons, 1980, 2001). Populations of stonechat in north Scotland are some of the most northerly in the world (Hagemeijer and Blair, 1997). It is difficult to define 'the moorland bird community' precisely, but Table 8.1 lists most of the species making substantial use of moorlands (see Appendix E8.1 for the list's derivation). In the main, moorlands are used during the breeding season, although red grouse, black grouse, golden eagle and peregrine are frequently resident, whilst Greenland white-fronted goose only occurs in winter. Amongst the species listed, several are virtually confined to moorland (e.g. red grouse and ring ouzel), whilst for some it provides habitat for much of the population e.g. curlew and meadow pipit; these species are the quintessential moorland birds.

Moorland bird communities elsewhere in Europe often share some broad similarities with those in Britain, for example a high prevalence of wader species (Boström and Nillson, 1983). The assemblage on coastal moorlands in west Norway, in particular, shows much overlap (Munkejord, 1987). Differences in species composition arise from the fact that Britain lies outside the breeding range of several species (e.g. green sandpiper *Tringa ochropus*), whilst ptarmigan is characteristic of Scandinavian moorlands, whereas it is largely restricted to the alpine zone in Britain (Boström and Nillson, 1983; Munkejord, 1987). A further difference is the absence of grousemoor management elsewhere; as a consequence many British moors carry exceptionally high densities of red grouse (the British and Irish subspecies of the Scandinavian willow grouse *Lagopus l. lagopus*).

In this chapter, we first examine regional variation in British moorland bird assemblages and then consider the habitat relationships of moorland birds, focusing on the first category of species in Table 8.1. For these species we attempt to identify aspects of habitat that strongly influence population densities.

Regional variation in moorland bird assemblages

To examine regional variation in 'the moorland bird community', data on species occurrence and density were collated from breeding season surveys in

Table 8.1 *The species considered to comprise Britain's moorland bird community, according to their use of and dependence upon moorland habitats.*

Moorlands provide both nesting and foraging resources, and hold a substantial part of the British breeding population	Hen harrier *Circus cyaneus*, golden eagle *Aquila chrysaetos*, merlin *Falco columbarius*, peregrine *Falco peregrinus*, red grouse *Lagopus lagopus scoticus*, black grouse *Tetrao tetrix*, golden plover *Pluvialis apricaria*, dunlin *Calidris alpina*, snipe *Gallinago gallinago*, whimbrel *Numenius phaeopus*, curlew *N. arquata*, greenshank *Tringa nebularia*, short-eared owl *Asio flammeus*, skylark *Alauda arvensis*, meadow pipit *Anthus pratensis*, whinchat *Saxicola rubetra*, stonechat *S. torquatus*, wheatear *Oenanthe oenanthe*, ring ouzel *Turdus torquatus*, raven *Corvus corax*, twite *Carduelis flavirostris*
Moorlands provide both nesting and foraging resources, but hold a relatively minor part of the British breeding population	Buzzard *Buteo buteo*, kestrel *Falco tinnunculus*, oystercatcher *Haematopus ostralegus*, lapwing *Vanellus vanellus*, redshank *Tringa totanus*, cuckoo *Cuculus canorus*, wren *Troglodytes troglodytes*, grasshopper warbler *Locustella naevia*, whitethroat *Sylvia communis*, willow warbler *Phylloscopus trochilus*, carrion/hooded crow *Corvus corone*
Moorlands provide nesting sites but other habitats provide major foraging (or brood-rearing) sites	Greylag goose *Anser anser*, wigeon *Anas penelope*, teal *A. crecca*, arctic skua *Stercorarius parasiticus*, great skua *S. skua*, black-headed gull *Chroicocephalus ridibundus*, common gull *Larus canus*, lesser black-backed gull *L. fuscus*, herring gull *L. argentatus*, great black-backed gull *L. marinus*, arctic tern *Sterna paradisaea*
Moorlands used for some foraging but rarely, or never, for nesting	Greenland white-fronted goose *Anser albifrons flavirostris*, red kite *Milvus milvus*, goshawk *Accipiter gentilis*

This list excludes species associated primarily with riparian and open water habitats and which make little or no use of the actual moorland habitats themselves.

15 broad regions, ranging from Britain's most southerly moors (Dartmoor and Exmoor) to some of the most northerly in Shetland (Fig. 8.2). The majority were from surveys in 2000 and 2002 and, with the exception of Orkney, all were conducted between 1999 and 2007. Not all surveys provided density or occurrence data for all moorland species, so that some regions were omitted from some analyses. Details of timing, methods and species counts are provided in the supplementary material (Appendix E8.1).

Patterns of species occurrence and breeding densities

The three regions on the north Scottish mainland supported the highest number of moorland species, with numbers being high, even after accounting

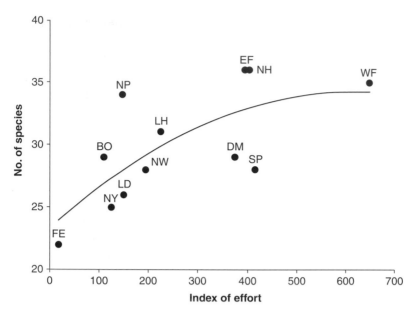

Figure 8.3 Numbers of moorland bird species (defined as all those in Table 8.1) recorded in relation to survey effort in 12 of the 15 survey regions (three regions had insufficient data). The index of effort is calculated as the product of survey area and the number of survey visits made (see supplementary material). Regression equation: No. = -0.000028*effort^2 + 0.034*effort +23.5 ($R^2 = 0.49$, $P < 0.05$). Locations and codes for regional samples are shown in Fig. 8.2.

for variation in survey effort (Fig. 8.3). Two of these regions overlap with the geographical ranges of all the species (Gibbons *et al.*, 1993), whilst several of the species are absent or rare further south (e.g. greenshank and golden eagle). Additionally, the North Pennines supported more species than expected from the survey 'effort'. The low number of species recorded on Fetlar reflects the remoteness and isolation of this island, as well as some important aspects of habitat (e.g. the absence of several small mammals and of large trees, restricting both prey and nest-sites for some raptors). Several moorland species are absent as breeders from the whole of Shetland, not just from Fetlar (Pennington *et al.*, 2004). Across the majority of mainland regions there is remarkable consistency in species occurrence.

Assemblage differences were examined in more detail by considering the proportions of species from each of six species groups present in each region (raptors and owls; grouse; waders; passerines (including corvids) and cuckoo; gulls, terns and skuas; wildfowl). Principal components analysis (PCA) highlighted two main gradients. The first, on axis 1, separated the three northern island regions, but particularly Fetlar, from the rest (Fig. 8.4). This gradient reflects the relatively low occurrence of passerines and raptors, but high occurrence of waders and moorland-nesting seabirds, on the islands. At the

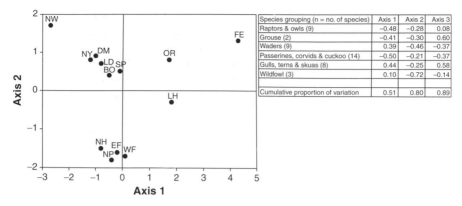

Species grouping (n = no. of species)	Axis 1	Axis 2	Axis 3
Raptors & owls (9)	−0.48	−0.28	0.08
Grouse (2)	−0.41	−0.30	0.60
Waders (9)	0.39	−0.46	−0.37
Passerines, corvids & cuckoo (14)	−0.50	−0.21	−0.37
Gulls, terns & skuas (8)	0.44	−0.25	0.58
Wildfowl (3)	0.10	−0.72	−0.14
Cumulative proportion of variation	0.51	0.80	0.89

Figure 8.4 Distribution of regions along the first two axes of a principal components analysis of the proportions of species recorded from six moorland bird species groups in those regions (see text). Coefficients are given for each group for the first three PCA axes. Locations and codes for regional samples are shown in Fig. 8.2.

other extreme, moorlands in North Wales were dominated by passerines and raptors. The second gradient, on axis 2, from high to low occurrence of all groups, particularly waterfowl and waders, largely reflects variation in species richness, and separates the North Pennines, Northeast Highlands and the two Flows regions from the rest.

Further analyses were undertaken by examining variation in breeding densities, focusing on three groups: waders, grouse, and raptors and owls. We examined each of these groups separately, but combined grouse with waders because of the broad similarities in aspects of their ecology (both being ground nesters with precocial chicks). In addition, an analysis of regional variation in passerines, for which relatively limited information was available, is presented in the supplementary material (Appendix E8.2).

A PCA of wader and grouse densities clearly separated Fetlar and, less markedly, the other two island regions (Orkney, and Lewis and Harris) from the mainland regions (axis 1, Fig. 8.5a). This is largely a consequence of the exceptional densities of several waders on the islands (see Appendix E8.1). The North Pennines was the mainland region with highest overall wader densities, but they were only one third of those on Orkney and Fetlar. The second axis in this PCA separated those regions with high densities of the three wader species most strongly associated with blanket bog (dunlin, greenshank and golden plover – Ratcliffe, 1990) from those with high densities of curlew, and to a lesser extent, lapwing and red grouse. Thus, Lewis and Harris, and the two Flow Country regions were separated from Orkney, which has a near absence of the three 'blanket-bog waders'. The remaining sites largely clustered in the middle, either as a consequence of having low densities of all species (e.g. North Wales and Exmoor), or relatively high densities of species with strong

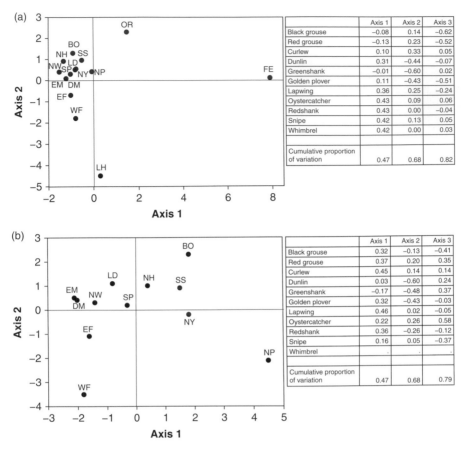

Figure 8.5 Distribution of regions along the first two axes of a principal components analysis examining variation in moorland wader and grouse densities across (a) all 15 regions and (b) excluding the three island regions. Coefficients are given for each species for the first three PCA axes. Locations and codes for regional samples are shown in Fig. 8.2.

positive or strong negative coefficients (e.g. Fetlar and North Pennines). Excluding the three island regions (to emphasise variation amongst mainland regions), the first axis distinguished regions with high wader and grouse densities, whilst the second axis was again strongly influenced by three 'blanket-bog waders' (Fig. 8.5b). Wader and grouse densities are highest in the North Pennines and lowest on Exmoor, Dartmoor, North Wales and, to a lesser extent, the Lake District.

The PCA of raptor and owl densities principally identified a gradient from low to high abundance of most species, and picked out Bowland, North Wales and the Lake District as supporting a diverse assemblage of raptors (Fig. 8.6). At the other extreme, Fetlar lacked any species – merlin is the only regularly breeding moorland raptor in Shetland (Pennington *et al.*, 2004). Short-eared

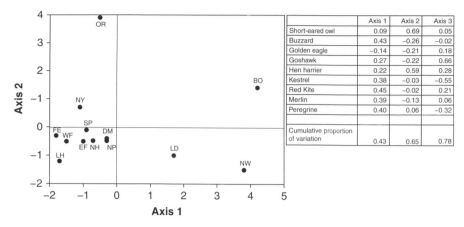

	Axis 1	Axis 2	Axis 3
Short-eared owl	0.09	0.69	0.05
Buzzard	0.43	−0.26	−0.02
Golden eagle	−0.14	−0.21	0.18
Goshawk	0.27	−0.22	0.66
Hen harrier	0.22	0.59	0.28
Kestrel	0.38	−0.03	−0.55
Red Kite	0.45	−0.02	0.21
Merlin	0.39	−0.13	0.06
Peregrine	0.40	0.06	−0.32
Cumulative proportion of variation	0.43	0.65	0.78

Figure 8.6 Distribution of regions along the first two axes of a principal components analysis examining variation in moorland raptor and owl densities across 13 regions (South Scotland and Exmoor lacked abundance data for some species). Coefficients are given for each species for the first three PCA axes. Locations and codes for regional samples are shown in Fig. 8.2.

owl and hen harrier densities were the major drivers of the second axis, which showed a marked separation of Orkney, and to a lesser extent Bowland and North Yorkshire, from the other regions. Orkney is known for high densities of both these species, due partly to the high abundance of the endemic vole *Microtus arvalis orcadensis* (Picozzi, 1980; Berry, 1985).

Causes of regional variation

The above analyses highlight two main sources of regional variation in 'the moorland bird community'. The starkest is the separation of island and mainland regions, whilst the second is a differentiation of regions supporting high densities of passerines and raptors from those supporting a diverse and high-density wader and grouse assemblage.

Two main factors probably underpin the first of these; most obviously that islands are closer to the sea, and therefore more likely to support higher densities of species that nest on moorland, but forage at sea (e.g. skuas). The high wader densities on these islands were also consistent with the absence of mammalian predators such as red fox *Vulpes vulpes* and stoat *Mustela erminea*. Predation can limit breeding wader populations on moorland (Fletcher *et al.*, 2010), with some studies suggesting that mammals are the most important predators (Grant *et al.*, 1999). High densities of ground-nesting birds such as willow ptarmigan have been noted on other islands free of such predators (Watson and Moss, 2008).

Variation in environmental conditions and land management is likely to play a major role in determining regional differences in moorland bird assemblages. Thus, moorlands in North Wales and the Lake District tend to have relatively steep terrain, less suitable for breeding waders (Stillman and Brown, 1994; Tharme *et al.*, 2001), whilst the North Pennines, East and West Flows and Lewis and Harris have deep peat, dominated by bog and wet heath favoured by golden plover, dunlin and, in the north, greenshank (Ratcliffe, 1990). Such broad-scale factors appeared to be important on Norwegian moorlands, where between-site variation in bird assemblages was attributed largely to differences between flat sites with short vegetation and topographically 'rough' sites, with taller shrubs (Munkejord, 1987). Some of the highest mainland wader densities occur where grouse moors are prevalent (e.g. North Pennines), whilst they are lowest in regions with few or no grouse moors, notably Dartmoor, Exmoor and North Wales (Fig. 8.5b). Illegal persecution associated with grouse moors limits the distribution and densities of several raptors (Etheridge *et al.*, 1997; Whitfield *et al.*, 2004), further contributing to regional differentiation, as does persecution of ravens and crows. The fact that some regions (notably Bowland) were relatively rich in raptors, waders and grouse suggests that these different components of moorland bird assemblages are not mutually exclusive.

Superimposed on these habitat and management differences is variation due to species ranges. For example, all three island regions are at high latitudes and within the geographical range of several boreal and arctic breeding species absent from southern regions (Hagemeijer and Blair, 1997). Such large-scale processes may also influence species abundance, because breeding densities tend to be higher at the centre of a species' global range relative to the range margins (Gaston, 2003). This is illustrated by the contrasting latitudinal gradients in golden plover (at its southern range margin in Britain) and stonechat (at its northern range margin in Britain) densities, with the former positively correlated with latitude ($r = 0.39$, $P = 0.14$) and the latter negatively so ($r = -0.45$, $P = 0.12$). Latitudinal gradients in wader densities occurred on Norwegian moors, with northern sites having high densities of golden plover, dunlin and whimbrel, whilst southern sites had high densities of lapwing, curlew, redshank and snipe (Munkejord, 1987).

The following sections review the habitat relationships of moorland birds and consider the role of different aspects of habitat in determining species breeding densities, thereby expanding on some of the issues that determine regional variation in moorland bird assemblages.

Habitat relationships of grouse

Red grouse are heather moorland specialists, being ubiquitous in such habitat from the lower moorland edge to its upper limits, with densities increasing with altitude on many moorlands (Stillman and Brown, 1994; Pearce-Higgins and Grant, 2006). By contrast, black grouse primarily occupy the moorland edge, generally occurring at altitudes of 250–450 m asl and rarely above 500 m asl (Sim *et al.*, 2008; Watson and Moss, 2008). They occupy habitats that are transitional between woodland and open moorland or grassland. In Britain they usually exploit moorland near to woodland (Pearce-Higgins *et al.*, 2007a; Watson and Moss, 2008). However, in some upland areas, notably the North Pennines, they occupy a transition zone between farmland and moorland (Starling-Westerberg, 2001).

Both species nest on the ground in tall, dense vegetation. Red grouse select mature or degenerate heather for nesting, which on grouse moors may hold over 90% of all nests (Campbell *et al.*, 2002). They also select vegetation that is taller (averaging *c.* 30–40 cm) than in surrounding areas (Campbell *et al.*, 2002). Similarly, black grouse select nest sites in tall, dense vegetation (often 40–50 cm in height), tending to use heather or other dwarf shrubs where available (Picozzi, 1986; Parr and Watson, 1988). Black grouse nest success may be higher in habitats or areas providing greater nesting cover (Picozzi, 1986; Brittas and Willebrand, 1991).

Young chicks of both species feed on invertebrates, and this has a major influence on brood habitat selection. After the first two to three weeks, black grouse chicks progressively switch to a herbivorous diet (Picozzi and Hepburn, 1986; Wegge and Kastdalen, 2008). Young broods often show selection for flushes and other wet grass or rush-dominated habitats, where invertebrate prey (particularly lepidopteran and sawfly caterpillars) is often abundant (Parr and Watson, 1988; Picozzi, 1986; Starling-Westerberg, 2001). Older broods select drier areas, including those with high blaeberry *Vaccinium myrtillus* cover (Parr and Watson, 1988; McFarlane, 2002). Black grouse broods select relatively tall ground vegetation, usually 25–40 cm high, which may reflect availability both of invertebrates and cover from predators. Invertebrates make a smaller contribution to chick diet in the red grouse and, even for young chicks, relatively protein-rich plant foods such as young heather shoots and moss capsules comprise the bulk of the diet (Savory, 1977). However, invertebrates are still important: chicks with less access to invertebrate prey (most notably craneflies) have relatively low growth rates and poor survival (Park *et al.*, 2001). Therefore, flushes and other wet habitats are often also important to young red grouse (Savory, 1977; Palmer and Bacon, 2001). Older red grouse broods (>1 month) prefer taller heather stands. Irrespective of age, red grouse broods select areas of edge habitat, presumably because this affords feeding areas in proximity to cover (Palmer and Bacon, 2001).

Heather is a staple food for adults of both species, but to a greater extent in red grouse, where it forms the vast bulk of the diet (Savory, 1978). Adult red grouse select tall heather in autumn and winter (Palmer and Bacon, 2001). However, in spring, the hens in particular need access to protein-rich foods to improve body condition prior to breeding. Where available, red grouse often exploit cottongrass flowers, because of their high nutritional value, but on drier moors birds rely on younger (2–5 years) heather plants, which have more nutritious shoots than older heather (Savory, 1978; Watson and Moss, 2008). At this time, red grouse may select grass-heather mixes in wetter areas where cottongrass is abundant, or edge zones between stands of young, short heather and older, taller heather (Palmer and Bacon, 2001). Adult black grouse use a wider range of habitats, including woodland and meadows, reflecting their dependence upon complementary habitats to provide a more varied diet. Trees and shrubs provide important food sources in winter and spring, particularly when snow cover is extensive (Picozzi and Hepburn, 1986). Heather-dominated moorland may be used in autumn and winter (Baines, 1994; Starling-Westerberg, 2001; Beeston et al., 2005), although open wood-land with heather and blaeberry field layers is often preferred where available (Picozzi, 1986). Wet moor, bog and acid grassland are often selected in spring, where female black grouse feed heavily on cottongrass flowers (Baines, 1994; Starling-Westerberg, 2001).

Given the dependence of red grouse on heather, it is no surprise that their densities increase with heather cover (Brown and Stillman, 1993; Stillman and Brown, 1994), and that heather loss is a cause of long-term population declines (Thirgood et al., 2000). However, detailed quantitative measures of heather cover reveal that densities only increase up to c. 50–60% heather cover, beyond which they plateau, indicating the benefits of some heteroge-neity in the vegetation (Pearce-Higgins and Grant, 2006). Surprisingly, habitat-association models provide no evidence for additional positive effects of wet habitats on densities. As described above, such habitats are sources of inver-tebrate foods for chicks and of protein-rich food for hens in spring, and so may influence breeding success, either through direct effects on chick survival or via maternal condition (Moss et al., 1975; Park et al., 2001). Red grouse densities are not only affected by heather quantity, but also by its nutrient status and productivity (Watson and O'Hare, 1979). Moors overlying base-rich bedrock often hold higher densities than those overlying acidic granite (with heather on the former having higher N and P contents), whilst the greater heather productivity associated with warmer, drier climates also appears to be important (Picozzi, 1968; Hudson, 1992). Predation, parasites (notably *Trichostrongylus tenuis*) and disease (notably tick-borne louping ill) are further factors affecting red grouse density (Hudson, 1992; Thirgood et al., 2000; Fletcher et al., 2010), whilst interactions between testosterone levels (affecting aggressive behaviour and recruitment) and parasite burdens appear to drive the cyclical trends in high-density populations (Seivwright et al., 2005). In terms of management regimes, both rotational muirburn (producing young, nutritious heather close to cover) and the removal of generalist predators produce higher densities on heather moors (Picozzi, 1968; Miller *et al.*, 1970; Tharme *et al.* 2001; Fletcher *et al.*, 2010).

As expected from their more varied habitat requirements, black grouse densities are linked not only with the occurrence of heather moorland, but also with grass moor and non-moorland habitats, especially open woodland (Pearce-Higgins *et al.*, 2007a). Both breeding success and densities tend to be higher on moorland where grazing pressure from sheep and red deer is relatively low, and where ground vegetation is relatively tall (17–34 cm) (Baines, 1996). However, trials of livestock reductions on moorland edge habitats found that initial increases in numbers were followed by declines five to six years later (Calladine *et al.*, 2002). These findings match observed trends in black grouse abundance at other British sites where grazing has been reduced (Grant *et al.*, 2009) and with the general association of this species with transient, successional habitats (Watson and Moss, 2008). Such responses may arise from temporary increases in vegetation growth and productivity following reduced grazing or fire, which could confer benefits via improved nutritional status of plant foods of adults, or increased insect abundance for chicks. As for red grouse, black grouse populations are vulnerable to predation, which may limit both breeding success and density (Marcström *et al.*, 1988; Summers *et al.*, 2004). Within Britain, clear associations between black grouse abundance and the occurrence and intensity of predator control and grousemoor management are lacking (Baines, 1996; Tharme *et al.*, 2001), but this could merely reflect the difficulty of disentangling complex habitat relationships for this species.

Habitat relationships of raptors and owls

Of the moorland raptors and owls, golden eagle, peregrine, kestrel and buzzard are mainly cliff-, crag- or tree-nesters, whilst merlin, hen harrier and short-eared owl are mainly ground-nesters (Ratcliffe, 1990). Nest site selection is not a rigid trait for all these species. For example, merlins frequently nest in isolated trees on moorland or in trees at the edges of conifer plantations (Rebecca, 2011). In rare instances, peregrine and golden eagle may nest on the ground in Britain, and this is characteristic of both species in some other parts of their range (Ratcliffe, 1993; Watson, 1997; see also Chapter 3).

Ground-nesting raptors and owls select tall, dense vegetation for nesting, generally using stands of mature or degenerate heather (Ratcliffe, 1990). Studies, undertaken across a range of Scottish sites, show that at both landscape and local scales, nesting harriers select heather-dominated vegetation (Redpath *et al.*, 1998). Nests occur in areas where mature or degenerate heather is most extensive, whilst comparisons within vegetation types used by nesting harriers showed that nests were located in heather almost twice as high as at random locations. However, nest-site selection appears to have little or no influence on breeding success (Redpath *et al.*, 1998).

Peregrines and golden eagles select nest sites that are inaccessible to potential predators and humans; higher cliffs (60–100 m) tend to be used where available. In regions with many high cliffs, peregrines rarely use cliffs of less than 30 m, but cliffs of 10–20 m are frequently used where they are scarce (Ratcliffe, 1993). Less than 5% of Scottish golden eagle nest sites are in trees (Eaton *et al.*, 2007), which accords with the general preference elsewhere for cliff sites over trees (Watson, 1997). Spanish studies suggest that golden eagles select relatively inaccessible cliff sites that are further from human presence (e.g. tracks and villages) than are similar unoccupied cliff sites (Donázar *et al.*, 1989).

Prey availability is critical in determining the use and selection of habitats by raptors and owls. The most detailed information on foraging habitat selection by moorland raptors concerns hen harriers. Studies in three different areas of Scotland found that, during the nesting period, harriers selectively foraged in areas with a mix of heather and rough grass (with an optimum of *c.* 50% heather cover). This preference is more pronounced in males, which are less constrained to foraging close to the nest than females (Arroyo *et al.*, 2009). Selection for heather–grass mixes is consistent with the fact that the abundance of meadow pipits, which often form the main prey during the nesting period, is highest in such habitat (Madders, 1997; Redpath and Thirgood, 1999). However, in some areas or years, other prey, such as young lagomorphs or red grouse chicks may be most important during the nesting period, resulting in variation in habitat preferences (Picozzi, 1980; Redpath, 1991; Madders, 1997). For example, on Islay harriers prefer to hunt over neutral grasslands, where lagomorphs, an important prey on that island, are most abundant (Madders, 1997). Prior to nesting, voles are frequently the main prey of harriers (Redpath *et al.*, 2002a; Amar and Redpath, 2005). Vole densities on moorland are higher in grass- or sedge-dominated habitats than in heather, particularly when grazing pressure is low (Wheeler, 2008).

Habitat not only affects prey abundance, but also its availability. Prey capture rates by harriers appear to be higher on grouse moors than on other moorlands (Redpath *et al.*, 2002b). In some ways this is surprising because meadow pipit densities are lower on grouse moors, and they decrease as the extent of rotational muirburn increases (Tharme *et al.*, 2001). Although some other important prey species (notably red grouse) are more abundant on grouse moors, the high prey-capture rate seems more likely to result from aspects of the habitat or from prey behaviour. Prey capture may be facilitated by the harriers selectively hunting along the edges of muirburn patches (Redpath, 1992).

Prey abundance and the availability of preferred foraging habitat appear to have important effects on hen harrier populations. Between-site variation in breeding density is positively correlated with meadow pipit abundance, and for female harriers (more weakly) with that of voles, whilst annual variation in density within sites may be related to vole abundance (Redpath and Thirgood, 1999; Redpath *et al.*, 2002a). At Langholm Moor in southwest Scotland, annual variation in clutch-size was correlated with vole abundance, although the overall fledging success was not related to variation in the abundance of any major prey species (Redpath *et al.*, 2002a). In Orkney, the number of young produced per breeding attempt was positively correlated with the proportion of rough grass habitat (selected for foraging) at radii of 1 to 2 km around the nest (Amar *et al.*, 2008a). This was due largely to early season effects on hatching success, rather than on chick survival, and was consistent with rough grass being a key habitat in which male harriers hunt for voles, to provision females prior to laying and during incubation (Amar and Redpath, 2005). A decline in the Orkney harrier population from the late 1970s to 2000 was associated with increased sheep numbers and the loss of rough grassland (which was converted to intensively managed grassland), and with a decrease in the contribution of voles to the diet in the early breeding period (Amar and Redpath, 2005).

Meadow pipits are also the main prey of merlins on most British moorlands, often comprising *c.* 60% of prey items during the breeding season (Newton *et al.*, 1984; Bibby, 1987; Petty *et al.*, 1995), although this varies according to the abundance of other small passerines. In Shetland, for example, skylark and wheatear predominate (Ellis and Okill, 1990). The occupancy of historical merlin breeding sites in Wales was positively related to the extent of heather cover in the surrounding area up to 4 km (Bibby, 1986). Links between habitat, diet and breeding parameters were apparent, with birds that occupied sites closer to farmland having a more varied diet and laying larger clutches and larger eggs (Bibby, 1986, 1987). The factors determining overall breeding success were, however, unknown. In the South Pennines, merlin abundance was positively correlated with the extent of both tall (>30 cm) heather and heather moor, whilst abundance was lower at higher altitudes (> 400 m asl), suggesting an avoidance of the blanket bog that dominates plateau hilltops in this region (Stillman and Brown, 1994).

Grouse moors often provide preferred hunting habitat for both peregrines and golden eagles, due to high prey densities. Where abundant, red grouse form a major part of the diet of both of these raptors, whilst mountain hares *Lepus timidus*, which also benefit from grouse moor management (Stoddart and Hewson, 1984), are similarly important to eagles (Ratcliffe, 1993; Watson *et al.*, 1993). Although eagles take a wide range of prey in Scotland, the diversity of prey taken declines as the contribution of grouse and hares increases; thus eagles become specialist hunters where preferred prey are abundant (Watson, 1997). This has important consequences at a population level because breeding success of Scottish eagles is higher in areas with more live prey (mainly red grouse, ptarmigan and lagomorphs), whilst across their world range golden eagles breed more successfully where they are specialist, rather than generalist, hunters (Watson *et al.*, 1992; Watson, 1997). Golden eagle densities in Scotland, however, may be more strongly influenced by availability of deer and sheep carrion in late winter and early spring, and densities are relatively low in the eastern Highlands where carrion is scarce, despite the greater abundance of live prey and higher breeding success (Watson *et al.*, 1989, 1992; Eaton *et al.*, 2007). However, determining the effects of food supply on distribution is difficult because the prevalence of grouse moors in the eastern Highlands appears to limit eagle distribution through associated illegal killing (Whitfield *et al.*, 2003, 2004). Nest-site availability may also limit golden eagle distribution on some British moorlands where large trees or cliffs are lacking.

Habitat relationships of waders

Waders are often a prominent feature of Britain's moorland avifauna, especially on the more gently sloping and level areas (Stillman and Brown, 1994; Tharme *et al.*, 2001). Golden plover and dunlin are associated with higher altitudes, more northerly latitudes and blanket bogs (Fig. 8.5a). Although widespread across moorland, snipe and curlew tend to occur on the lower slopes and the moorland edge (Brown and Stillman, 1993; Stillman and Brown, 1994). Greenshank are relatively thinly scattered on northern wet heaths and bogs below 450 m asl (Ratcliffe, 1990). Until recent population declines, over 90% of Britain's breeding whimbrel occurred in Shetland, with highest densities on serpentine heaths (Richardson, 1990; M. Grant, unpubl.).

In contrast to grouse and ground-nesting raptors, some moorland waders select short, open vegetation for nesting. On grouse moors, both golden plover and curlew select recent (often < *c*. 2 year old) muirburn patches (Robson, 1998; Whittingham *et al.*, 2002). In these areas, muirburns may hold over 70% of the nests of those species, despite comprising just 15–25% of the area. In other moorland habitats, golden plovers also prefer to nest in short vegetation (see below). Away from grouse moors, nesting curlews tend not to select short vegetation. In Northern Ireland, vegetation heights immediately around curlew nests averaged 16 cm, slightly higher than at nearby points (Grant *et al.*, 1999), whilst on Orkney curlews can nest in 60–70 cm tall heather (M. Grant unpubl.). Incubating adult curlews may be less able to detect predators when the nest is surrounded by very tall vegetation – curlews in Orkney may be able to nest in tall heather because predatory mammals are scarce there. Despite these patterns, there is little evidence that wader nest survival rates are influenced by vegetation height and cover around nests

(Grant *et al.*, 1999; Whittingham *et al.*, 2002; Pearce-Higgins *et al.*, 2007b). However, camouflage may be important and this is difficult to measure.

Like grouse, wader chicks are precocial, leaving the nest the day after hatching and being entirely self-feeding in most species. The mobility of broods makes studying their habitat use difficult, particularly in remote, inaccessible areas; consequently, few data are available from moorland. Two studies of golden plovers in the South and North Pennines found that broods avoided heather-dominated vegetation, although habitat selection differed between the studies in other respects. In the South Pennines, broods made greatest overall use of cottongrass-dominated vegetation, although use of this habitat declined as broods aged, and as use of blaeberry and crowberry *Empetrum nigrum* areas and bare peat increased (Pearce-Higgins and Yalden, 2004). By contrast, in the North Pennines, acid and calcareous grasslands and flushes were all selected, but cottongrass-dominated areas (comprising >30% of the study area) were not (Whittingham *et al.*, 2001). Patterns of habitat use in the South Pennines were linked to food availability, with adult craneflies (the main food of young chicks) most abundant in cottongrass areas, whilst larval craneflies (comprising the bulk of older chick diet) may have been accessed more easily on bare peat. Other prey, such as caterpillars and certain beetles were most abundant in blaeberry and crowberry areas, and became more important when adult cranefly abundance declined after May (Pearce-Higgins and Yalden, 2004). Habitat use in the North Pennines may also have been linked to prey abundance. Of the two main prey groups, beetles appeared to be most abundant in the preferred habitats, whilst adult craneflies were abundant in flushes. However, craneflies were scarce in grasslands, but abundant in unselected habitats, suggesting that other factors, possibly vegetation structure, also influenced brood habitat selection (Whittingham *et al.*, 2001). Golden plover broods may make long movements to access the required habitats and resources; South Pennines broods occupied home ranges that averaged 41 ha between hatching and fledging (at *c.* 37 days), occasionally making daily movements in excess of 1 km (Pearce-Higgins and Yalden, 2004).

The broods of moorland-breeding curlew sometimes select flushes, possibly linked to cranefly abundance (Robson, 1998). Whimbrel broods in Shetland showed less evidence of such selection, with 65% of all locations being on the main heath or bog nesting habitat (Grant *et al.*, 1992a). In contrast to golden plovers, whimbrel broods remained largely within their nesting territories until fledging, and usually used home ranges of *c.* 5 ha between hatching and fledging. These studies were undertaken in areas with high breeding densities, where the territory network may have limited brood movements.

The adults of several species, including golden plover, whimbrel and curlew, make substantial use of enclosed fields below the moorland edge, particularly during the pre-laying and incubation periods (Grant *et al.*, 1992b; Robson, 1998; Whittingham *et al.*, 2000; Pearce-Higgins and Yalden, 2003). Pastures and meadows are the main habitats used. Here these birds feed largely on subsurface prey, notably earthworms and cranefly larvae, which are generally far more abundant in these relatively fertile fields than on moorland, and presumably provide more profitable prey than surface-active invertebrates (Grant *et al.*, 1992b). Preferences for individual fields appear to be more strongly related to the densities (or biomass) of larval craneflies than of earthworms, whilst short vegetation is also an important determinant of field use (Grant *et al.*, 1992b; Pearce-Higgins and Yalden, 2003). Curlew usually use the fields closest to their nesting territories, whereas golden plover frequently over-fly fields to reach preferred foraging areas, which are often 2–6 km (sometimes >10 km) from their nests (Robson, 1998; Whittingham *et al.*, 2000; Pearce-Higgins and Yalden, 2003; M. Grant, unpubl.). Adult snipe diet is also dominated by earthworms and cranefly larvae, but, during daylight hours, snipe appear to feed largely on moorland, where they select wet rush- and grass-dominated areas, within which they forage close to ditches and pools (Hoodless *et al.*, 2007). Thus, snipe may be less dependent than the larger waders on accessing enclosed fields for foraging.

An indication of the importance of non-moorland foraging habitats for the larger waders comes from a pair of curlews that were studied on northern Swedish tundra. During incubation the female progressively lost weight (monitored using an electronic balance under the nest) until she began leaving the nesting territory when off duty, to fly over 10 km to the nearest grassland to forage, after which body weight recovered. By contrast, the smaller male fed in the nesting habitat throughout and maintained body weight (A. Swaan and J. Mulder, pers. comm.). Thus, the occurrence and distribution of some moorland waders, especially those that depend on larger subsurface invertebrates, could be partly determined by the proximity and condition of non-moorland habitats.

Various other habitat factors affect distribution and abundance of breeding waders. Across a wide range of moorlands, the densities of golden plover and dunlin are positively correlated with the extent of short, open vegetation (Pearce-Higgins and Grant, 2006; Buchanan *et al.*, 2007a, b; Hancock *et al.*, 2009). Both species are often most abundant where deer grass *Trichophorum cespitosum* is extensive and, for golden plover, cottongrass or other sedges. Local dunlin abundance can also be related to pool systems (a feature of many blanket bogs), probably because these provide abundant invertebrates, particularly chironomids (Holmes, 1970; Hancock *et al.*, 2009). Similarly, greenshank abundance is related to the extent of open-water habitats, notably bog pools, as well as river and loch margins which provide feeding habitat for adults and broods (Ratcliffe, 1990; Hancock *et al.*, 1997, 2009). Positive correlations between curlew abundance and vegetation indicative of wet flushes are frequent, whilst abundance also increases with variability in vegetation height (Stillman and Brown, 1994; Pearce-Higgins and Grant, 2006; Buchanan et al., 2007a). Higher snipe densities are also associated with wet flush and marsh vegetation (Pearce-Higgins and Grant, 2006; Hoodless et al., 2007).

Habitat manipulations testing the above, essentially correlative, associations are rare, but two examples illustrate the importance of short vegetation for golden plovers (M. Grant, unpubl.). First, in a $1 km^2$ plot on a North Pennines moor, plovers increased from one to five pairs following a muirburn that extended across the entire plot. This increase occurred within two years of the fire, and was not mirrored by any similar increase on a nearby $2 km^2$ plot unaffected by the fire. In the second example, golden plovers declined from 17 to 7 pairs over a three year period in a c. $7 km^2$ area of North Pennines moorland, following a substantial reduction in sheep numbers. On adjacent moorland, where sheep numbers remained unchanged, plovers increased from four to eight pairs. Where sheep had been reduced there was a c. 70% increase in early season (April) vegetation height, compared to a c. 4% increase on the adjacent moorland. Surprisingly, curlew showed a similar pattern of change, declining from 17 to 10 pairs where sheep were reduced and increasing from 18 to 23 pairs on the adjacent moorland. Over a period of almost 40 years, curlew increased on moorland in north east Scotland where grazing pressures had increased, causing a shift from heather to grass dominance, whilst they remained stable on nearby moorland with little change in grazing (Jenkins and Watson, 2001). In both examples from the North Pennines, the responses of golden plover and curlew were immediate, suggesting that behavioural responses to the habitat change caused a redistribution of breeding pairs, as opposed to the changes being driven by underlying demographics. Furthermore, curlew breeding success did not show any apparent response to the reduced sheep numbers (M. Grant, unpubl.).

Abundance of several species of waders is influenced by the intensity of grouse moor management. Although snipe do not appear to be affected, the densities of lapwing, golden plover and curlew can be up to almost three times higher on grouse moors than on other heather moors, after accounting for potentially confounding habitat effects (Tharme et al., 2001). Given the nesting associations of these species with recently burnt ground or short vegetation, one might expect such differences to result from the greater muirburn on grouse moors. However, this study suggested that the differences in densities were mainly attributable to the greater levels of predator control on grouse moors. Subsequent experimental tests demonstrated that predator control increases the breeding success of moorland-nesting lapwing, golden plover and curlew, leading to increased breeding densities of lapwing at least (Fletcher et al., 2010).

Habitat relationships of moorland passerines

Densities of meadow pipit and skylark on moorland are typically at least an order of magnitude higher than other passerine species. Meadow pipit densities ranged from 40 to 180 individuals km^{-2} across four upland regions, where they were about four times more numerous than skylark (Buchanan et al., 2006a). Meadow pipit and skylarks show common variation in abundance between regions ($r = 0.97$, $P < 0.001$), despite contrasting habitat relationships. Skylarks have a strong affinity with grass moorland, with densities negatively correlated with heather (Pearce-Higgins and Grant, 2006). Skylarks are often very abundant on enclosed upland grasslands, which may explain why moorland densities tend to decline with altitude and distance from such fields (Brown and Stillman, 1993; Pearce-Higgins and Grant, 2006). By contrast, meadow pipit densities are highest in grass–heather mixes, usually with 40–70% grass cover, and >15 cm tall vegetation (Pearce-Higgins and Grant, 2006; Buchanan et al., 2007a).

One explanation for the association of pipits with grass–heather mixes is that the resulting diversity of vegetation structures provides both nesting and feeding sites, with nests in the taller vegetation, but shorter vegetation preferred for foraging (Douglas et al., 2008). However, prey switching through the season may also be important. Pipits feed on a variety of insects but, where available, favour Diptera, spiders and caterpillars (Buchanan et al., 2006b). Craneflies can be an important food for first-brood chicks (Coulson and Whittaker, 1978), and may have highest availability in cottongrass bog or wet flushes (Coulson, 1962; Pearce-Higgins and Yalden, 2004), whilst second broods may rely more on foods such as caterpillars that are most abundant in drier areas. Thus, pairs breeding in habitat mosaics may have greater access to food for both first and second broods. Diet switching may therefore promote peak densities in areas of heterogeneous vegetation, but this remains to be established. Experimental studies on grass moorland indicate the importance of invertebrate availability in driving fine-scale variation in meadow pipit density. Densities increased under a regime of low-intensity cattle and sheep grazing, relative to low- and high-intensity sheep grazing, and no grazing (Evans et al., 2006). Although the overall abundance of foliar invertebrates increased with vegetation biomass, being highest under no grazing (Dennis et al., 2008), the increased heterogeneity in vegetation structure produced by cattle grazing may have increased invertebrate availability in the mixed grazing plots. Foraging pipits favoured areas of low sward height probably because prey was more accessible there (Douglas et al., 2008).

In addition to vegetation, predation pressure may affect local abundance of pipits and skylarks. Where raptor densities are high, their abundance can be reduced by the end of the breeding season, and in the subsequent breeding season (Amar et al., 2008b). However, although the control of predatory mammals and corvids by gamekeepers may increase meadow pipit nest survival rates, it does not appear to affect their densities, or indeed those of other common moorland passerines (Tharme *et al.*, 2001; Fletcher *et al.*, 2010).

Three chats – wheatear, whinchat and stonechat – are widespread on moorland. Availability of suitable holes and cavities for nest sites may restrict the distribution of wheatears, but neither whinchat nor stonechat are likely to be limited by nest sites. Wheatears tend to associate with areas of grass, or grass and bracken (Brown and Stillman, 1993; Stillman and Brown, 1994). Patches of short grass provide important foraging habitat as indicated by their preferential occupation by males in the spring, and by territory size being negatively correlated with sward height (Tye, 1992). Whinchats show a widespread association with bracken, often occurring on steep slopes at lower altitudes (Brown and Stillman, 1993; Stillman and Brown, 1994; Pearce-Higgins and Grant, 2006). Stonechats tend to occupy similar habitats, but are more strongly associated with tall dwarf-shrub vegetation than bracken (Pearce-Higgins and Grant, 2006).

Ring ouzel and twite have relatively restricted distributions and have undergone sustained population declines in Britain (Sim *et al.*, 2005, 2010). Ring ouzels tend to nest in areas of dense heather, particularly in steep-sided gullies and crags, but forage largely on short grass within 500 m of the nest for earthworms, which form the bulk of the nestling diet (Burfield, 2002). These requirements have a strong influence on distribution, with consistent associations with heather and grass vegetation (Stillman and Brown, 1994; Buchanan *et al.*, 2003). Ouzels may be vulnerable to both heavy grazing that depletes heather cover, potentially causing loss of nest sites (Sim *et al.*, 2007), and light grazing rendering grassland unsuitable for foraging. After breeding, ouzels switch to feeding on berries (I. Sim, unpubl.). Summer warming has been implicated in the decline of this species, possibly through reductions in earthworm availability or berry abundance (Beale *et al.*, 2006). Twite nest in areas of dense heather or bracken, but have a close affinity with the moorland edge where they forage for seeds in hay meadows and pastures. They often commute several kilometres from the nest to seed-rich habitats. The conversion of hay meadows to intensive silage production is one of the likely causes of decline.

Moorland habitats: issues of scale and determinants of density

The above review of habitat requirements illustrates the wide range of vegetation conditions upon which moorland birds depend. Considerable variation exists between species in the features selected for nesting, foraging and brood-rearing. Furthermore, individual species often have markedly different requirements for nest sites than for foraging or brood-rearing, and require access to these different conditions within their home range. Similarly, the review indicates the importance of complementary habitat types to several moorland birds. For example, black grouse often rely on scrub and woodland, enclosed grasslands provide foraging habitat for adult waders, and twite depend heavily on seed-rich fields.

Whilst many species require heterogeneity in moorland vegetation to meet their nesting and foraging requirements, they differ in the scale at which heterogeneity is required. For example, hen harriers and ring ouzels both select areas of tall heather for nesting but forage in grassier habitats. Whilst male harriers hunt up to several km from their nests, foraging ouzels are confined to smaller areas close to the nest. Heterogeneity in vegetation types also creates a range of foraging habitats, which can provide available food resources throughout the season, or provide different resources for the chicks of precocial species. Harrier diet early in the breeding season is dominated by voles, whilst pipits and other prey are more important at the nestling stage, and each of these prey species has different habitat preferences. Examples have also been given of how the chicks of golden plovers and grouse change their fine-scale habitat selection as the season progresses, in relation to availability of different invertebrate prey or changing dietary needs. At finer scales, the chicks of precocial species require access to food resources close to cover from predators, as described above for red grouse.

Associations between bird abundance and variation in the extent of particular vegetation attributes reflect the provision of key resources. These include increased food abundance or availability, reduced vulnerability to predation and shelter from inclement weather, particularly for precocial chicks. Further evidence of the importance of vegetation condition in determining moorland bird densities comes from examples where changes in vegetation condition produce subsequent changes in bird abundance. In some cases there are clear links with specific key resources, and evidence of the underpinning demographic changes. Two examples are the introduction of muirburn and increases of red grouse and the loss of preferred foraging habitat and hen harrier declines (Miller et al., 1970; Amar and Redpath, 2005).

Other aspects of habitat not directly linked to vegetation condition are also important determinants of moorland bird densities. Notably, predator populations may limit grouse and wader densities (Tharme et al., 2001; Fletcher et al., 2010), whilst climate may interact with habitat conditions to limit breeding success, and potentially density (Pearce-Higgins et al., 2010). The relative importance of different determinants of moorland bird density is likely to vary geographically and across a range of spatial scales. In considering regional-scale variation, our analyses are consistent with the possibility that predator populations are major broad determinants of wader densities. High wader densities are associated with island regions (lacking key predatory mammals) and, to a lesser extent, with regions where grouse moor management (and hence predator control) is prevalent. These analyses also point to latitudinal (and hence potential climatic) effects on the densities of some species. Regional-scale effects of vegetation are also apparent with the densities of some waders linked to regions with extensive blanket bog.

Outlook

Looking to the next few decades, Britain's 'moorland bird community' may go through considerable change. Having affinities with high altitudes and northerly latitudes, some moorland birds may be amongst the most vulnerable in Britain to climate change. Predictions from climate envelope models suggest many of these species will be lost from much of their current British breeding range by the late twenty-first century under 'moderate' change scenarios, whilst some may disappear entirely (Huntley *et al.*, 2007). There is much uncertainty over such predictions, but studies already indicate that rising summer temperatures may reduce moorland cranefly abundance, negatively affecting food availability for several species (Buchanan *et al.*, 2006b; Pearce-Higgins *et al.*, 2010).

Changes to land uses are also likely to have major impacts. Recent changes to agricultural subsidies and the loss of livestock headage payments mean upland farming is under increasing economic pressure, causing widespread declines in sheep numbers. In the short term, this will lead to taller swards and the consequent loss of conditions upon which some species depend. In the longer term, increases in dwarf shrub cover, and eventual scrub and woodland expansion would lead to very different assemblages of birds, but will probably benefit black grouse (Fuller *et al.*, 1999). Any reduction in the persecution of raptors on grouse moors could lead to increases in the abundance and range of raven, golden eagle and hen harrier, which in turn could have complex indirect effects resulting from changes in predation pressures on other bird species, conceivably causing land-management changes (Baines *et al.*, 2008). Current UK forestry policy aims for expansion of forest – this could potentially lead to further loss of open moorland and cause reductions in breeding wader densities on moorland close to plantations (Hancock *et al.*, 2009; Amar *et al.*, 2011).

Recognition of moorlands as important providers of ecosystem services has grown, with acknowledgement of their value as carbon stores, sources of drinking water and regulators of water flows (Holden *et al.*, 2007). Greater future attention will probably be given to the impacts of land managements on these services, with muirburn already under scrutiny (Yallop *et al.*, 2006). Such issues may eventually cause changes to grazing and burning practices, with effects on birds. Conversely, additional impetus could be given to drain-blocking programmes, potentially offsetting deleterious impacts of climate change on invertebrate food via creation of wetter conditions. Wind-farm developments are likely to increase further, including within areas of high bird importance. This will reduce habitat availability to some moorland birds (Pearce-Higgins *et al.*, 2009a, 2012) and may cause increased mortality from collisions with turbines.

At the current time, population declines appear to be widespread amongst species most dependent on moorland habitats (Sim *et al.*, 2005). The ongoing declines of black grouse, ring ouzel and twite are long term, evident since the early 1900s. For curlew and dunlin, declines are more recent, but nonetheless widespread, whilst for whimbrel, marked declines have occurred since the late 1980s, following a period of population increase. Past changes in land use and conversion of moorland to agricultural grasslands and forestry have doubtless caused some of these declines, but increasing predator populations have probably contributed (Pearce-Higgins *et al.*, 2009b). However, a detailed understanding of the relative importance of the different potential causes is lacking, as is the extent to which current drivers of decline are due to land management or environmental effects, notably climate change. Such knowledge is urgently required if moorland bird populations are to be conserved as we enter a period of likely rapid environmental and land-management change.

Acknowledgements

Thanks are due to many past colleagues at the RSPB who have helped us develop our ideas on moorland birds and their habitat requirements. The RSPB are to be thanked for providing access to various moorland bird survey data, as are the many people who contributed to the collection of these data. John Calladine, Derek Yalden and Rob Fuller provided very helpful advice and edits on previous drafts of this chapter, whilst Graeme Buchanan helped with the production of Fig. 8.2 and Innes Sim helped with accessing survey data.

References

Amar, A., Arroyo, B., Meek, E., Redpath, S. and Riley, H. (2008a). Influence of habitat on breeding performance of hen harriers *Circus cyaneus* in Orkney. *Ibis*, **150**, 400–404.

Amar, A., Grant, M., Buchanan, G. *et al.* (2011). Exploring the relationships between wader declines and current land use in the British uplands. *Bird Study*, **58**, 13–26.

Amar, A. and Redpath, S. M. (2005). Habitat use by hen harriers *Circus cyaneus* on Orkney: implications of land-use change for this declining population. *Ibis*, **147**, 37–47.

Amar, A., Thirgood, S., Pearce-Higgins, J. W. and Redpath, S. (2008b). The impact of raptors on the abundance of upland passerines and waders. *Oikos*, **117**, 1143–1152.

Anderson, B. J., Arroyo, B. E., Collingham, Y. C. *et al.* (2009). Using distribution models to test alternative hypotheses about a species' environmental limits and recovery prospects. *Biol. Conserv.*, **142**, 488–499.

Armstrong, A., Holden, J., Kay, P. *et al.* (2009). Drain-blocking techniques on blanket peat:

A framework for best practice. *J. Environ. Manage.*, **90**, 3512–3519.

Arroyo, B., Amar, A., Leckie, F., *et al.* (2009). Hunting habitat selection by hen harriers on moorland: implications for conservation management. *Biol. Conserv.*, **142**, 586–596.

Baines, D. (1994). Seasonal differences in habitat selection by black grouse *Tetrao tetrix* in the northern Pennines, England. *Ibis*, **136**, 39–43.

Baines, D. (1996). The implications of grazing and predator management on the habitats and breeding success of black grouse *Tetrao tetrix*. *J. Appl. Ecol.*, **33**, 54–62.

Baines, D., Redpath, S., Richardson, M. and Thirgood, S. (2008). The direct and indirect effects of predation by hen harriers *Circus cyaneus* on trends in breeding birds on a Scottish grouse moor. *Ibis*, **150**, 27–36.

Beale, C. M., Burfield, I. J., Sim, I. M. W. *et al.* (2006). Climate change may account for the decline in British ring ouzels *Turdus torquatus*. *J. Anim. Ecol.*, **75**, 826–835.

Beeston, R., Baines, D. and Richardson, M. (2005). Seasonal and between-sex differences in the diet of black grouse *Tetrao tetrix*. *Bird Study*, **52**, 276–281.

Berry, R. J. (1985). *The Natural History of Orkney*. London: Collins.

Bibby, C. J. (1986). Merlins in Wales: site occupancy and breeding in relation to vegetation. *J. Appl. Ecol.*, **23**, 1–12.

Bibby, C. J. (1987). Foods of breeding merlins *Falco columbarius* in Wales. *Bird Study*, **34**, 64–70.

Boström, U. and Nilsson, S. G. (1983). Latitudinal gradients and local variations in species richness and structure of bird communities on raised peat-bogs in Sweden. *Ornis Scand.*, **14**, 213–226.

Brittas, R. and Willebrand, T. (1991). Nesting habitats and egg predation in Swedish black grouse. *Ornis Scand.*, **22**, 261–263.

Brown, A. F. and Stillman, R. A. (1993). Bird-habitat associations in the eastern Highlands of Scotland. *J. Appl. Ecol.*, **30**, 31–40.

Buchanan, G. M., Grant, M. C., Sanderson, R. A. and Pearce-Higgins, J. W. (2006b). The contribution of invertebrate taxa to moorland bird diets and the potential implications of land-use management. *Ibis*, **148**, 615–628.

Buchanan, G. M., Pearce-Higgins, J. W. and Grant, M. C. (2006a). Observer variation in estimates of meadow pipit *Anthus pratensis* and skylark *Alauda arvensis* abundance on moorland. *Bird Study*, **53**, 92–95.

Buchanan, G. M., Pearce-Higgins, J. W. and Grant, M. C. (2007a). Bird modelling: bird-habitat associations. In *Environmentally Sustainable and Economically Viable Grazing Systems for Restoration and Maintenance of Heather Moorland: England and Wales – BD1228*. Final report (annex 3B.1). London: Defra.

Buchanan, G. M., Pearce-Higgins, J. W. and Grant, M. C. (2007b). Bird modelling: presence-absence models of scarcer species. In *Environmentally sustainable and economically viable grazing systems for restoration and maintenance of heather moorland: England and Wales – BD1228*. Final report (annex 3B.3). London: Defra.

Buchanan, G. M., Pearce-Higgins, J. W., Wotton, S. R., Grant, M. C. and Whitfield, D. P. (2003). Correlates of the change in ring ouzel *Turdus torquatus* abundance in Scotland from 1988–91 to 1999. *Bird Study*, **50**, 97–105.

Burfield, I. J. (2002). The breeding ecology and conservation of the ring ouzel *Turdus torquatus* in Britain. Unpublished PhD thesis, University of Cambridge.

Calladine, J., Baines, D. and Warren, P. (2002). Effects of reduced grazing on population density and breeding success of black grouse in northern England. *J. Appl. Ecol.*, **39**, 772–780.

Campbell, S., Smith, A., Redpath, S. and Thirgood, S. (2002). Nest site characteristics and nest success in red grouse *Lagopus lagopus scoticus*. *Wildlife Biol.*, **8**, 169–174.

Coulson, J. C. (1962). The biology of *Tipula subnodicornis* Zeiterstedt, with comparative observations on *Tipula paludosa* Meigen. *J. Anim. Ecol.*, **31**, 1–21.

Coulson, J. C. and Whittaker, J. B. (1978). Ecology of moorland animals. In *Production Ecology of British Moors and Montane Grasslands*, ed. O. W. Heal, and D. F. Perkins, pp. 52–93. Berlin: Springer-Verlag.

Cramp, S. and Simmons, K. E. L. (ed.) (1980, 2001). *The Birds of the Western Palearctic*, vols. II and III. Oxford: Oxford University Press.

Dennis, P., Skartveit, J., McCracken, D. I. *et al.* (2008). The effects of livestock grazing on foliar arthropods associated with bird diet in upland grasslands of Scotland. *J. Appl. Ecol.*, **45**, 279–287.

Donázar, J. A., Ceballos, O. and Fernández, C. (1989). Factors influencing the distribution and abundance of seven cliff-nesting raptors: a multivariate study. In *Raptors in the Modern World*, ed. B.-U. Meyburg and R. D. Chancellor, pp. 545–552. Berlin: WWGBP.

Douglas, D. J. T., Evans, D. M. and Redpath, S. M. (2008). Selection of foraging habitat and nestling diet by meadow pipits *Anthus pratensis* breeding on intensively grazed moorland. *Bird Study*, **55**, 290–296.

Eaton, M. A., Dillon, I. A., Stirling-Aird, P. K. and Whitfield, D. P. (2007). The status of golden eagle *Aquila chrysaetos* in Britain in 2003. *Bird Study*, **54**, 212–220.

Ellis, P. M. and Okill, J. D. (1990). Breeding ecology of the merlin *Falco columbarius* in Shetland. *Bird Study*, **37**, 101–110.

Etheridge, B., Summers, R. W. and Green, R. E. (1997). The effects of illegal killing and destruction of nests by humans on the population dynamics of the hen harrier *Circus cyaneus* in Scotland. *J. Appl. Ecol.*, **34**, 1081–1105.

Evans, D. M., Redpath, S. M., Evans, S. A. *et al.* (2006). Low intensity, mixed livestock grazing improves the breeding abundance of a common insectivorous passerine. *Biol. Lett.*, **2**, 636–638.

Fletcher, K., Aebischer, N. J., Baines, D., Foster, R. and Hoodless, A. N. (2010). Changes in breeding success and abundance of ground-nesting moorland birds in relation to the experimental deployment of legal predator control. *J. Appl. Ecol.*, **47**, 263–272.

Fuller, R. J., Gillings, S. and Whitfield, D. P. (1999). Responses of breeding birds to expansion of scrub in the eastern Scottish Highlands: preliminary implications for conservation strategies. *Vogelwelt*, **120** (suppl.), 53–62.

Fuller, R. J. and Gough, S. J. (1999). Changes in sheep numbers in Britain: implications for bird populations. *Biol. Conserv.*, **91**, 73–89.

Gaston, K. J. (2003). *The Structure and Dynamics of Geographic Ranges*. Oxford: Oxford University Press.

Gibbons, D. W., Reid, J. B. and Chapman, R. A. (1993). *The New Atlas of Breeding Birds in Britain and Ireland: 1988–91*. London: Poyser.

Grant, M. C., Chambers, R. E. and Evans, P. R. (1992a). The effects of re-seeding heathland on breeding whimbrel *Numenius phaeopus* in Shetland. III. Habitat use by broods. *J. Appl. Ecol.*, **29**, 516–523.

Grant, M. C., Chambers, R. E. and Evans, P. R. (1992b). The effects of re-seeding heathland on breeding Whimbrel *Numenius phaeopus* in Shetland. II. Habitat use by adults during the pre-laying period. *J. Appl. Ecol.*, **29**, 509–515.

Grant, M. C., Cowie, N., Donald, C. *et al.* (2009). Black grouse response to dedicated conservation management. *Folia Zool.*, **58**, 195–206.

Grant, M. C., Orsman, C., Easton, J. *et al.* (1999). Breeding success and causes of breeding failure of curlew *Numenius arquata* in Northern Ireland. *J. Appl. Ecol.*, **36**, 59–74.

Hagemeijer, W. J. M. and Blair, M. (ed.) (1997). *The EBCC Atlas of European Breeding Birds: Their Distribution and Abundance*. London: Poyser.

Haines-Young, R. H., Barr, C. J., Black, H. I. J. *et al.* (2000). *Accounting for Nature: Assessing Habitats in the UK Countryside*. London: DETR.

Hancock, M. H., Gibbons, D. W. and Thompson, P. S. (1997). The status of breeding greenshank *Tringa nebularia* in the United Kingdom in 1995. *Bird Study*, **44**, 290–302.

Hancock, M. H., Grant, M. C. and Wilson, J. D. (2009). Associations between distance to forest and spatial and temporal variation in abundance of key peatland breeding bird species. *Bird Study*, **56**, 53–64.

Holden, J., Shotbolt, L., Bonn, A. *et al.* (2007). Environmental change in moorland landscapes. *Earth-Science Rev.*, **82**, 75–100.

Holmes, R. T. (1970). Differences in population density, territoriality and food supply of dunlin on arctic and sub-arctic tundra. In *Animal Populations in Relation to their Food Resources*, ed. A. Watson, pp. 303–319. Oxford: Blackwell Scientific Publications.

Hoodless, A. N., Ewald, J. A. and Baines, D. (2007). Habitat use and diet of common snipe *Gallinago gallinago* breeding on moorland in northern England. *Bird Study*, **54**, 182–191.

Hudson, P. J. (1992). *Grouse in Space and Time*. Fordingbridge: Game Conservancy Trust.

Huntley, B., Green, R. E., Collingham, Y. C. and Willis, S. G. (2007). *A Climatic Atlas of European Breeding Birds*. Barcelona: Lynx Edicions.

Jenkins, D. and Watson, A. (2001). Bird numbers in relation to grazing on a grouse moor from 1957–61 to 1988–98. *Bird Study*, **48**, 18–22.

Lovat, Lord (1911). *The Grouse in Health and in Disease*. London: Smith, Elder and Co.

Mackey, E. C., Shewry, M. C. and Tudor, G. J. (1998). *Land Cover Change Scotland from the 1940s to the 1980s*. Edinburgh: The Stationery Office.

Madders, M. (1997). The effects of forestry on hen harriers *Circus cyaneus*. Unpublished PhD thesis, University of Glasgow.

Marcström, V., Kenward, R. E. and Engren, E. (1988). The impact of predation on boreal tetraonids during vole cycles: an experimental study. *J. Anim. Ecol.*, **57**, 859–872.

McFarlane, J. (2002). Habitat associations of black grouse *Tetrao tetrix* broods in a native pinewood forest. Unpublished MSc thesis, University of Reading.

Miller, G. R., Jenkins, D. and Watson, A. (1970). Responses of red grouse populations to experimental improvement of their food. In

Animal Populations in Relation to their Food Resources, ed. A. Watson, pp 323–325. Oxford: Blackwell Scientific Publications.

Moss, R., Watson, A. and Parr, R. (1975). Maternal nutrition and breeding success in red grouse (*Lagopus lagopus scoticus*). *J. Anim. Ecol.*, **44**, 233–244.

Munkejord, A. (1987). Bird communities in coastal heather moors in West Norway. *Fauna norv. Ser. C, Cinclus*, **10**, 73–80.

Newton, I., Meek, E. R. and Little, B. (1984). Breeding season foods of merlins *Falco columbarius* in Northumbria. *Bird Study*, **31**, 49–56.

Palmer, S. C. F. and Bacon, P. J. (2001). The utilization of heather moorland by territorial red grouse *Lagopus lagopus scoticus*. *Ibis*, **143**, 222–232.

Park, K. J., Robertson, P. A., Campbell, S. T. *et al.* (2001). The role of invertebrates in the diet, growth and survival of red grouse (*Lagopus lagopus scoticus*) chicks. *J. Zool.*, **254**, 137–145.

Parr, R. and Watson, A. (1988). Habitat preferences of black grouse on moorland-dominated ground in north-east Scotland. *Ardea*, **76**, 175–180.

Pearce-Higgins, J. W., Dennis, P., Whittingham, M. J. and Yalden, D. W. (2010). Impacts of climate on prey abundance account for fluctuations in a population of a northern wader at the southern edge of its range. *Glob. Change Biol.*, **16**, 12–23.

Pearce-Higgins, J. W., Finney, S. K., Yalden, D. W. and Langston, R. H. W. (2007b). Testing the effects of recreational disturbance on two upland breeding waders. *Ibis*, **149** (suppl.), 45–55.

Pearce-Higgins, J. W. and Grant, M. C. (2006). Relationships between bird abundance and the composition and structure of moorland vegetation. *Bird Study*, **53**, 112–125.

Pearce-Higgins, J. W., Grant, M. C., Beale, C. M., Buchanan, G. M. and Sim, I. M. W. (2009b). International importance and drivers of change of upland bird populations. In *Drivers of Environmental Changes in Uplands*, ed. A. Bonn, T. Allott, K. Hubacek and J. Stewart, pp. 209–227. Abingdon: Routledge.

Pearce-Higgins, J. W., Grant, M. C., Robinson, M. C. and Haysom, S. L. (2007a). The role of forest maturation in causing the decline of black grouse *Tetrao tetrix*. *Ibis*, **149**, 143–155.

Pearce-Higgins, J. W., Stephen, L., Douse, A. and Langston, R. H. W. (2012). Greater impacts of wind-farms on bird populations during construction than subsequent operation: results of a multi-site and multi-species analysis. *J. Appl. Ecol.*, **49**, 386–394.

Pearce-Higgins, J. W., Stephen, L., Langston, R. H. W., Bainbridge, I. P. and Bullman, R. (2009a). The distribution of breeding birds around upland wind farms. *J. Appl. Ecol.*, **46**, 1323–1331.

Pearce-Higgins, J. W. and Yalden, D. W. (2003). Variation in the use of pasture by breeding European golden plovers *Pluvialis apricaria* in relation to prey availability. *Ibis*, **145**, 365–381.

Pearce-Higgins, J. W. and Yalden, D. W. (2004). Habitat selection, diet, arthropod availability and growth of a moorland wader: the ecology of European golden plover *Pluvialis apricaria* chicks. *Ibis*, **146**, 335–346.

Pennington, M., Osborn, K., Harvey, P. *et al.* (2004). *The Birds of Shetland*. London: Christopher Helm.

Petty, S. J., Patterson, I. J., Anderson, D. I. K., Little, B. and Davison, M. (1995). Numbers, breeding performance, and diet of the sparrowhawk *Accipiter nisus* and merlin *Falco columbarius* in relation to cone crops and seed-eating finches. *For. Ecol. Manage.*, **79**, 133–146.

Picozzi, N. (1968). Grouse bags in relation to the management and geology of heather moor. *J. Appl. Ecol.*, **5**, 483–488.

Picozzi, N. (1980). Food, growth, survival and sex ratio of nestling hen harriers *Circus c. cyaneus* in Orkney. *Ornis Scand.*, **11**, 1–11.

Picozzi, N. (1986). *Black Grouse Research in NE Scotland*. Unpublished report. Banchory: Institute of Terrestrial Ecology.

Picozzi, N. and Hepburn, L. V. (1986). A study of black grouse in north-east Scotland. *Proc. 3rd Int. Grouse Symp.*, 462–480.

Ratcliffe, D. (1990). *Bird Life of Mountain and Upland*. Cambridge: Cambridge University Press.

Ratcliffe, D. A. (1993). *The Peregrine Falcon* (2nd edition). London: Poyser.

Rebecca, G. W. (2011). Spatial and habitat-related influences on the breeding performance of Merlins in Britain. *Brit. Birds*, **104**, 202–216.

Redpath, S. M. (1991). The impact of hen harriers on red grouse breeding success. *J. Appl. Ecol.*, **28**, 659–671.

Redpath, S. M. (1992). Behavioural interactions between hen harriers and their moorland prey. *Ornis Scand.*, **23**, 73–80.

Redpath, S., Amar, A., Madders, M., Leckie, F. and Thirgood, S. (2002b). Hen harrier foraging success in relation to land use in Scotland. *Anim. Conserv.*, **5**, 113–118.

Redpath, S., Madders, M., Donnelly, E. *et al.* (1998). Nest site selection by hen harriers in Scotland. *Bird Study*, **45**, 51–61.

Redpath, S. M. and Thirgood, S. J. (1999). Numerical and functional responses in generalist predators: hen harriers and peregrines on Scottish grouse moors. *J. Anim. Ecol.*, **68**, 879–892.

Redpath, S. M., Thirgood, S. J. and Clarke, R. (2002a). Field vole *Microtus agrestis* abundance and hen harrier *Circus cyaneus* diet and breeding in Scotland. *Ibis*, **144**, E33–E38.

Richardson, M. G. (1990). The distribution and status of whimbrel *Numenius p. phaeopus* in Shetland and Britain. *Bird Study*, **37**, 61–68.

Robson, G. (1998). The breeding ecology of curlew *Numenius arquata* on North Pennine moorland. Unpublished PhD thesis, University of Sunderland.

SAC (2008). *Farming's Retreat from the Hills*. Edinburgh: Scottish Agricultural College.

Savory, C. J. (1977). The food of red grouse chicks *Lagopus l. scoticus*. *Ibis*, **119**, 1–9.

Savory, C. J. (1978). Food consumption of red grouse in relation to the age and productivity of heather. *J. Anim. Ecol.*, **47**, 269–282.

Seivwright, L. J., Redpath, S. M., Mougeot, F., Leckie, F. and Hudson, P. J. (2005). Interactions between intrinsic and extrinsic mechanisms in a cyclic species: testosterone increases parasite infection in red grouse. *Proc. R. Soc. B*, **272**, 2299–2304.

Sim, I., Rollie, C., Arthur, D. *et al.* (2010). The decline of the ring ouzel in Britain. *Brit. Birds*, **103**, 229–239.

Sim, I. M. W., Burfield, I. J., Grant, M. C., Pearce-Higgins, J. W. and M Brooke, de L. (2007). The role of habitat composition in determining breeding site occupancy in a declining ring ouzel *Turdus torquatus* population. *Ibis*, **149**, 374–385.

Sim, I. M. W., Eaton, M. A., Setchfield, R. P., Warren, P. K. and Lindley, P. (2008). Abundance of male black grouse *Tetrao tetrix* in Britain in 2005, and change since 1995–96. *Bird Study*, **55**, 304–313.

Sim, I. M. W., Gregory, R. D., Hancock, M. H. and Brown, A. F. (2005). Recent changes in the abundance of British upland breeding birds. *Bird Study*, **52**, 261–275.

Smout, T. C. (2005). *Nature Contested. Environmental History in Scotland and Northern England Since 1600*. Edinburgh: Edinburgh University Press.

Starling-Westerberg, A. (2001). The habitat use and diet of black grouse *Tetrao tetrix* in the Pennine hills of northern England. *Bird Study*, **48**, 76–89.

Stillman, R. A. and Brown, A. F. (1994). Population sizes and habitat associations of upland breeding birds in the South Pennines, England. *Biol. Conserv.*, **69**, 307–314.

Stoddart, D. M. and Hewson, R. (1984). Mountain hares, *Lepus timidus*, bags and moor management. *J. Zool.*, **204**, 563–565.

Summers, R. W., Green, R. E., Proctor, R. *et al.* (2004). An experimental study of the effects of predation on the breeding productivity of capercaillie and black grouse. *J. Appl. Ecol.*, **41**, 513–525.

Tallis, J. H. (1991). Forest and moorland in the South Pennine Uplands in the Mid-Flandrian Period: III. The spread of moorland – local, regional and national. *J. Ecol.*, **79**, 401–415.

Tharme, A. P., Green, R. E., Baines, D., Bainbridge, I. P. and O'Brien, M. (2001). The effect of management for red grouse shooting on the population density of breeding birds on heather-dominated moorland. *J. Appl. Ecol.*, **38**, 439–457.

Thirgood, S. T., Redpath, S. M., Rothery, P. and Aebischer, N. J. (2000). Raptor predation and population limitation in red grouse. *J. Anim. Ecol.*, **69**, 504–516.

Thompson, D. B. A., MacDonald, A. J., Marsden, H. and Galbraith, C. A. (1995). Upland heather moorland in Great Britain: A review of international importance, vegetation change and some objectives for nature conservation. *Biol. Conserv.*, **71**, 163–178.

Tye, A. (1992). Assessment of territory quality and its effects on breeding success in a migrant passerine, the wheatear *Oenanthe oenanthe*. *Ibis*, **134**, 273–285.

Watson, A. and Moss, R. (2008). *Grouse*. London: Collins.

Watson, A. and O'Hare, P. J. (1979). Red grouse populations on experimentally treated and untreated Irish bog. *J. Appl. Ecol.*, **16**, 433–452.

Watson, A., Payne, S. and Rae, R. (1989). Golden eagles *Aquila chrysaetos*: land use and food in northeast Scotland. *Ibis*, **131**, 336–348.

Watson, J. (1997). *The Golden Eagle*. London: Poyser.

Watson, J., Leitch, A. F. and Rae, S. R. (1993). The diet of golden eagles *Aquila chrysaetos* in Scotland. *Ibis*, **135**, 387–393.

Watson, J., Rae, S. R. and Stillman, R. (1992). Nesting density and breeding success of golden eagles in relation to food supply in Scotland. *J. Anim. Ecol.*, **61**, 543–550.

Wegge, P. and Kastdalen, L. (2008). Habitat and diet of young grouse broods: resource partitioning between capercaillie (*Tetrao urogallus*) and black grouse (*Tetrao tetrix*) in boreal forests. *J. Ornithol.*, **149**, 237–244.

Wheeler, P. (2008). Effects of sheep grazing on abundance and predators of field vole (*Microtus agrestis*) in upland Britain. *Agr. Ecosyst. Environ.*, **123**, 49–55.

Whitfield, D. P., Fielding, A. H., McLeod, D. R. A. and Haworth, P. F. (2004). The effects of persecution on age of breeding and territory occupation in golden eagles in Scotland. *Biol. Conserv.*, **118**, 249–259.

Whitfield, D. P., McLeod, D. R. A., Watson, J., Fielding, A. H. and Haworth, P. F. (2003). The association of grouse moor in Scotland with the illegal use of poisons to control predators. *Biol. Conserv.*, **114**, 157–163.

Whittingham, M. J., Percival, S. M. and Brown, A. F. (2000). Time budgets and foraging of breeding golden plover *Pluvialis apricaria*. *J. Appl. Ecol.*, **37**, 632–646.

Whittingham, M. J., Percival, S. M. and Brown, A. F. (2001). Habitat selection by golden plover *Pluvialis apricaria* chicks. *Basic Appl. Ecol.*, **2**, 177–191.

Whittingham, M. J., Percival, S. M. and Brown, A. F. (2002). Nest-site selection by golden plover: why do shorebirds avoid nesting on slopes? *J. Avian Biol.*, **33**, 184–190.

Yallop, A. R., Thacker, J. I., Thomas, G. *et al.* (2006). The extent and intensity of management burning in the English uplands. *J. Appl. Ecol.*, **43**, 1138–1148.

Supplementary material: Additional material for this chapter is presented in an electronic appendix (Appendices E8.1 and E8.2) at www.cambridge.org/9780521897563.

CHAPTER NINE

Arctic-alpine mountain birds in northern Europe: contrasts between specialists and generalists

DES B. A. THOMPSON
Scottish Natural Heritage,
JOHN ATLE KÅLÅS
Norwegian Institute for Nature Research

and

INGVAR BYRKJEDAL
University Museum of Bergen

Europe's mountain regions, above and north of the natural treeline, have some of the world's most natural habitats. This is the arctic-alpine zone, and being treeless and not having experienced widespread managed fires, tree felling and associated human-related disturbance, is more 'natural' than the subalpine and lower 'upland' zones (Chapter 8). However, many arctic-alpine areas are grazed by livestock, with some experiencing acidic deposition and a range of pollutants and recreational influences, and so are 'near-natural' rather than 'natural' in the strictest sense. A small number of bird species are confined to the arctic-alpine zone – the alpine specialists (Ratcliffe and Thompson, 1988; Ratcliffe, 1990, 2005; Thompson *et al.*, 1988, 2003; Calladine, 2011). Many more generalists (which also nest at lower elevations, in a variably broader range of habitats) also breed in these areas. This chapter provides an overview of the breeding birds and their habitat use in the arctic-alpine zone of British and Scandinavian mountains. It considers conservation and management issues, as well as some broad differences between the two regions, focusing on specialists and generalists. We do not consider the wider range of species which only feed, rather than nest, in the arctic-alpine zone because most of these spend only a small amount of time foraging there (Ratcliffe, 1990; Calladine, 2011). Unlike Scandinavia, Britain has virtually no natural treeline habitat, and accordingly has a much lower structural diversity of habitats in its arctic-alpine zone (e.g. Ratcliffe, 1977, 1990, 2005; Ratcliffe and Thompson, 1988; Ashmole, 2011).

Arctic-alpine areas are influenced by changing climate, land-use practices and other factors such as pollution (Pearce and van der Wal, 2002; Thompson

Birds and Habitat: Relationships in Changing Landscapes, ed. Robert J. Fuller. Published by Cambridge University Press. © Cambridge University Press 2012.

et al., 2005; Welch *et al.*, 2005; Shaw and Thompson, 2007; Thompson and Whitfield, 2007; Armitage, 2010; Albon, 2011; Austrheim *et al.*, 2011; Pearce-Higgins, 2011a, b). It is important that we understand the nature of relationships between bird distribution and habitats in these extreme environments, where even small changes in climate or some other key variables may influence significant habitat or species responses. As many of the nesting species cannot move higher or further north, they face local or even regional losses if habitat changes are extreme.

The arctic-alpine zone occurs above the present treeline (Fig. 9.1). Subalpine woodland, mainly comprising birch *Betula* and *Salix* spp, occurs across the 'northern boreal zone' (Austrheim *et al.*, 2011). In Scandinavian mountains, at the natural treeline, woodland gives way to scrub in the low arctic-alpine zone, but this vegetation is virtually absent in Britain. The low, middle and high arctic-alpine zones cover as much as 30% of Norway;

Figure 9.1 Arctic-alpine environments in Scotland and Norway. (a) A'Mharconaich (975 m) summit plateau in western Cairngorms, Scotland – here the lower limit of the arctic-alpine zone is at approximately 750 m, and the treeless, wind-clipped and prostrate vegetation is evident (photo: Des Thompson). (b) In the far north of Scotland the arctic-alpine zone is as low as 350 m, as here on Ward Hill, Orkney (photo: Rob Fuller). (c) The extent, altitude and variation of arctic-alpine environments in Norway far exceeds that in Britain (photo: Des Thompson). (d) Natural treelines, absent in the British uplands, are widespread in Norway and frequently give way to willow and birch scrub shown in the foreground (photo: John Atle Kålås).

the low and middle arctic-alpine zone in Britain and Ireland (sometimes referred to as the 'montane' zone) covers no more than 4% of the total land surface (Thompson and Brown, 1992; Horsfield and Thompson, 1997; Averis *et al.*, 2004; Austrheim *et al.*, 2011; Speed *et al.*, in press). The boundaries between subalpine woodland and open mountain areas are, for many areas, much lower now than in former millennia because of human influences in the form of tree clearance, burning and grazing. At the other extreme, in the far north, the arctic-alpine zone grades into arctic tundra, and even coastal tundra, where there is little evidence of human influence over millennia; this chapter does not consider these habitats, except where specifically mentioned.

In Scandinavia, there are vast tracts of alpine mountain terrain above and beyond the treeline, and an extensive literature outlines the range of variation across these (e.g. Moen, 1999; Ratcliffe, 2005; Austrheim *et al.*, 2011). There, the upper limit of the low arctic-alpine zone lies at around 1400 m in Dovre in central Norway, but descends northwards, and is as low as 300 m in Finnmark, north Norway, where it merges into the low arctic zone (which is defined by the northern treeline). Britain's arctic-alpine zone begins above 650 m in the central Scottish Highlands, but only at around 350 m in the northwest Highlands (e.g. Thompson and Brown, 1992).

Much of the literature on alpine habitat composition, extent and quality has been informed by broad surveys and detailed studies at a small number of locations. In Britain, Ratcliffe (1977), Thompson *et al.* (1987), Ratcliffe and Thompson (1988), Thompson and Brown (1992), Brown *et al.* (1993), Averis *et al.* (2004), Armitage (2010) and Calladine (2011) provide overviews, with two principal findings. First, the Scottish Highlands have considerable expanses of near-natural alpine habitat, whereas the rest of alpine Britain is characterised by heavy influences of acidic deposition and grazing pressure, with a tendency for many of the alpine heaths to be fragmented and dominated by grass, rather than by moss (notably *Racomitrium lanuginosum*) and dwarf shrub-heath. Second, the Highlands represent southern and oceanic outliers of arctic-alpine fellfield and mountain tundra, reaching their greatest extent in the Cairngorms. Rising above the former treeline, there is first a zone of prostrate *Calluna* heath (rare outside Britain and Ireland), and then facies dominated by dwarf shrubs such as *Empetrum* spp, *Loiseleuria procumbens, Arctostaphylos uva-ursi, Arctous alpinus, Vaccinium myrtillus* and by *Racomitrium* often with *Carex bigelowii*. Above these are snowfields and stony ablation surfaces, often showing solifluction. In Scandinavia, the variation in vegetation is far greater, with distinctive gradations above the treeline in relation to snow cover (principally), soil moisture, frost action on the soil and soil type (e.g. Moen, 1999; Austrheim *et al.*, 2011).

Britain's arctic-alpine bird assemblage and variation in habitat use

There are 71 regularly breeding bird species associated with the British uplands (Thompson *et al.*, 1988), of which just three (4%) are alpine specialists: ptarmigan *Lagopus muta*, dotterel *Charadrius morinellus* and snow bunting *Plectrophenax nivalis* (full list of birds and sources are given in Appendix E9.1); several others are very rare, or irregularly occurring, alpine specialists (purple sandpiper *Calidris maritima*, shorelark *Eremophila alpestris*, Lapland bunting *Calcarius lapponicus*, and snowy owl *Bubo scandiacus*, the latter recorded breeding on moorland heath, which is technically not an arctic-alpine habitat, in Shetland until the mid 1970s (Thom, 1986)).

Information presented in this section is based on Thompson *et al.* (2003) who examined habitat use, species richness and abundance of birds in three arctic-alpine study sites in the Cairngorms National Park, eastern Scottish Highlands. Their findings illustrate some broad patterns of bird–habitat associations across Britain's arctic-alpine zone, with breeding bird assemblages differing in population densities and species composition between areas. Their work built on earlier studies (Watson, 1965; Nethersole-Thompson, 1973, 1993; Thompson and Whitfield, 1993, 2007; Galbraith *et al.*, 1993a, b; Thompson *et al.*, 1995; Byrkjedal and Thompson, 1998; Watson *et al.*, 2000; Whitfield, 2002).

On the most arctic-like plateau (in the western Cairngorms), densities and species numbers were low, and four of the six species recorded were alpine specialists. Some of these birds bred on other British mountains, but their preponderance on the site signified that it was more closely allied to higher latitude areas (e.g. in Scandinavia) than to other British sites. The absence from there of some species found more commonly in lower altitude uplands may have been due to an absence of suitable habitat, rather than any climatic constraints. For example, the absence of dunlin *Calidris alpina* and golden plover *Pluvialis apricaria* was probably due to these species showing a strong association with blanket bog, which was absent from the site.

On the other two sites (south west Cairngorms and eastern Cairngorms plateaux), two arctic-alpine species (dotterel and ptarmigan), and higher densities of typically lower-ground birds (e.g. golden plover and dunlin), were present. Lower altitudes, less severe weather and more fertile soils resulted in less harsh environments more suitable for a wider range of upland birds. Thus, unlike the more arctic site, the breeding bird communities showed closer affinities to those found on blanket bog and dry heath in subalpine areas (see Chapter 8). Whilst only sparse populations of waders had hitherto been believed to nest in the arctic-alpine zone, Thompson *et al.* (2003) recorded densities of 11–14 pairs km^{-2} of breeding waders on one of the sites. The densities of golden plover and dunlin (3.2 and 4.0 pairs km^{-2}, respectively) were greater than the mean densities recorded for these species by Stroud *et al.* (1987)

on the Caithness and Sutherland peatlands (2.4 and 1.8 pairs km^{-2}) and by Byrkjedal and Thompson (1998) for many other parts of the northern hemisphere. The dotterel breeding density on the southwest Cairngorms was high in comparison to other British sites (Galbraith *et al.*, 1993b), and exceeded densities found in Scandinavia (Kålås and Byrkjedal, 1984). Indeed, the estimated dotterel densities were comparable to the highest recorded (around 9–10 pairs km^{-2}) in arctic Russia (Cramp and Simmons, 1983). Ptarmigan densities on two sites (as high as 37 pairs km^{-2} in one year) were higher than those found on more northern sites (e.g. West Greenland, Baffin Island and central Alaska), and as high as those recorded in Iceland (Watson, 1965; Watson *et al.*, 2000).

Fine-scale patterns of habitat use by dotterel, which show evidence of changes in habitat preferences in relation to breeding stage, are summarised in Table 9.1. Dotterel nested, and reared their broods, on *Racomitrium*-dominated heaths and

Table 9.1 *Habitat use by breeding dotterel during the incubation and chick-rearing phases (adapted from Thompson* et al.*, 2003)*

	Site most similar to arctic heath		Site dominated by bog and *Nardus* grassland		Site dominated by *Racomitrium* heath	
Main vegetation types	Incubation	Chick-rearing	Incubation	Chick-rearing	Incubation	Chick-rearing
Racomitrium heath	+ ***	+	+ ***	+ ***	+	+ ***
Nardus grassland	− ***	− ***	0	− ***	+	− *
Vaccinium-Empetrum heath	0	− **	0	0	0	0
Carex flushes	0	− **	0	0	NP	NP
Calluna-Eriophorum bog	NP	NP	− *	−***	0	0
Prostrate *Calluna* heath	NP	NP	0	+	NP	NP
Juncus trifidus heath	+ *	+ *	NP	NP	NP	NP
Liverwort snow-bed	0	0	NP	NP	NP	NP

Habitats are preferred (+) or avoided (−). On each site birds had a choice of four or six vegetation types. 0 denotes no preference; NP denotes not present. *$P<0.05$; ** $P<0.01$; *** $P<0.001$; Chi-squared test comparing observed and (randomly) expected habitats (details given in Thompson *et al.*, 2003).

usually avoided *Nardus* grasslands (including those associated with prolonged snow-lie) and blanket bog. Of the other birds, ptarmigan showed no marked nest site preferences on any study area. However, they led their young to dwarf-shrub heath (dwarf shrubs are the main food plants of adults and older chicks (Cramp and Simmons, 1980; Watson *et al.*, 2000)) on two sites, and to *Juncus trifidus* heath on the other, where only limited dwarf-shrub heath was available. Waders showed marked habitat preferences on all three sites, and a degree of habitat partitioning was evident on one site. Dunlin nested in *Nardus* grassland patches, and then led their young into blanket bog. Golden plovers strongly preferred blanket bog and were less strongly associated with the more exposed habitats occupied by dotterel. Snow buntings and wheatears *Oenanthe oenanthe* preferred mainly rocky ground for nesting territories, whereas meadow pipits *Anthus pratensis* showed strong association with dwarf-shrub heath vegetation.

On the basis of the work described above, Thompson *et al.* (2003) reached four broad conclusions. First, the British arctic-alpine breeding bird assemblage is a distinctive collection of species which is not found at such high densities in comparable oceanic habitats elsewhere in the world, or in other arctic-alpine areas in Europe. Second, overall densities of birds are low on arctic-alpine bog and *Nardus* grasslands, and high on heaths dominated by dwarf-shrubs (*Erica* spp., *Vaccinium* spp., *Calluna vulgaris*), *Juncus trifidus* and bryophytes. Third, habitat preferences vary across sites, but the following general preferences occur: (i) alpine bog (skylark *Alauda arvensis*, golden plover and dunlin); (ii) *Nardus stricta* grassland (dunlin for nest sites); (iii) dwarf-shrub heaths (meadow pipit) and (iv) moss-dominated heaths and open fellfields (dotterel). Fourth, dotterel, dunlin and ptarmigan show differences in habitat preferences between the nesting and brood-rearing periods, whereas other species were not observed to show such preferences.

Comparisons between arctic-alpine bird assemblages in Britain and Scandinavia

We reviewed available information on habitat use by arctic-alpine breeding birds in northern Europe, drawing heavily on our own personal observations as well as published material (see Appendix E9.1). Where possible, we provide detail on the types of habitats used, and the factors affecting these and the birds (grazing, climatic factors, persecution, hunting etc). Additional information is given on the prey base, whether the birds are resident or migratory and current conservation status. Fifty-four species breed regularly in arctic-alpine environments, and of these nine (17%) are alpine specialists. The species comprise nine waterbirds, seven raptors (Accipitriformes), two owls (Strigiformes), two grouse (Tetraonidae), one crane (Gruidae), fifteen waders (Charadriiformes), one skua (Stercorariidae), one gull (Laridae), one cuckoo (Cuculidae) and fifteen passerines.

The nine alpine specialists comprise one raptor, one owl, one grouse, two waders, one skua and three passerines.

There are some marked contrasts between Britain and Scandinavia (Table 9.2). Whilst only six arctic-alpine specialists occur in both regions (with three of these very rare in Britain), Scandinavia has a further three specialists. Eleven species are generalists in both Britain and Scandinavia. The groups of generalists found in only one region's arctic-alpine zone reveal some tantalising issues. Whilst Britain has just two of these species, Scandinavia has 33 species (6 of these occur only in Scandinavia, but the other 27 species occur in Britain – but not in alpine areas). Why do so many of these birds not breed regularly in arctic-alpine areas in Britain?

An obvious reason accounting for some of the differences between Britain and Scandinavia is the absence of treeline scrub in Britain (e.g. Ratcliffe, 1977, 1990; Ratcliffe and Thompson, 1988; Ashmole, 2011). However, this applies to only part of the bird assemblage. Table 9.3 summarises habitat use. The specialists in both regions occur across arctic-alpine tundra, and alpine heaths and grasslands. The generalists show striking contrasts. Those in Britain are strongly associated with arctic-alpine tundra, heaths and grasslands, whereas in Scandinavia the generalists also occur in taiga, in treeline habitats and coastal arctic habitats in the far north (between 31% and 50% of all species). The absence of taiga and treeline habitats in Britain explains the absence of some of the generalist species, but by no means all of them. Other broad habitat differences that may partially account for regional differences are the relative scarcity of large standing and running water bodies in the British arctic-alpine zone.

In terms of feeding habits, broadly the same percentage of specialists and generalists are predators (c. 20%) and dependent on invertebrates (c. 60%) in both regions (Appendix E9.1). However, fewer herbivores are alpine specialists (7%) than generalists (19%). Each species has a suite of preferred and avoided habitats (e.g. Table 9.1), but there appear to be no fundamental differences between the suite of generalists in Scandinavia's arctic-alpine zone and those found in Britain which do not nest in the alpine zone – other than those which are reliant on the treeline habitats. Examples of the latter species include rough-legged buzzard *Buteo lagopus*, great snipe *Gallinago media*, bluethroat *Luscinia svecica*, fieldfare *Turdus pilaris* and willow warbler *Phylloscopus trochilus*. We may understand more about why some birds avoid nesting in Britain's alpine zone if we look at their feeding habits, which show some marked differences between species. For instance, some which breed in arctic-alpine tundra make use of wetter patches for chick rearing (purple sandpiper), but not for nesting, yet others avoid these areas and blanket bog almost entirely (dotterel). In Britain, some species forage away from alpine/arctic-alpine habitat (golden plover, dipper *Cinclus cinclus*, wheatear and ring ouzel *Turdus torquatus*); golden plover forage at lower altitudes in rich grasslands and pastureland (however, most alpine golden

Table 9.2 *Species regarded as arctic-alpine specialists or generalists (occurring in other zones as well) in British and Scandinavian mountain areas.*

Specialists in both regions	Ptarmigan *Lagopus muta*, dotterel *Charadrius morinellus*, (purple sandpiper *Calidris maritima*), (shore-lark *Eremophila alpestris*), snow bunting *Plectrophenax nivalis*, (Lapland bunting *Calcarius lapponicus*). **Note:** the species in parentheses are extremely scarce or irregular breeders in Britain; snowy owl *Bubo scandiacus* is not listed as it nested on sparsely vegetated moorland heath in Shetland.
Specialists, in Britain only	None
Specialists, in Scandinavia only	Gyrfalcon *Falco rusticolus*, long-tailed skua *Stercorarius longicaudus*, snowy owl *Bubo scandiacus*.
Generalists in both regions	Willow/red grouse *Lagopus lagopus*, golden eagle *Aquila chrysaetos*, ringed plover *Charadrius hiaticula*, golden plover *Pluvialis apricaria*, dunlin *Calidris alpina*, snipe *Gallinago gallinago*, common gull *Larus canus*, dipper *Cinclus cinclus*, ring ouzel *Turdus torquatus*, wheatear *Oenanthe oenanthe*, meadow pipit *Anthus pratensis*.
Generalists, in Britain only	Peregrine falcon *Falco peregrinus*, skylark *Alauda arvensis*.
Generalists, in Scandinavia only	Wigeon *Anas penelope*, teal *A. crecca*, pintail *A. acuta*, tufted duck *Aythya fuligula*, scaup *A. marila*, long-tailed duck *Clangula hyemalis**, common scoter *Melanitta nigra*, velvet scoter *M. fusca**, red-throated diver *Gavia stellata*, black-throated diver *G. arctica*, hen harrier *Circus cyaneus*, rough-legged buzzard *Buteo lagopus**, kestrel *Falco tinnunculus*, merlin *F. columbarius*, crane *Grus grus**, Temminck's stint *Calidris temminckii*, ruff *Philomachus pugnax*, great snipe *Gallinago media**, whimbrel *Numenius phaeopus*, common sandpiper *Actitis hypoleucos*, greenshank *Tringa nebularia*, wood sandpiper *T. glareola*, redshank *T. totanus*, red-necked phalarope *Phalaropus lobatus*, cuckoo *Cuculus canorus*, short-eared owl *Asio flammeus*, raven *Corvus corax*, willow warbler *Phylloscopus trochilus*, fieldfare *Turdus pilaris*, bluethroat *Luscinia svecica**, yellow wagtail *Motacilla flava*, twite *Carduelis flavirostris*, reed bunting *Emberiza schoeniclus*. **Note:** asterisks signify species not breeding in British mountain areas, the remaining species breed in Britain, but not in the arctic-alpine zone, with some local exceptions.

Source data are in Appendix E9.1.

Table 9.3 *Habitat associations of specialist and generalist species in the arctic-alpine zone of Britain and Scandinavia*

Species type	Arctic-alpine tundra	Alpine heaths and grasslands	Subalpine birch/treeline	Taiga	Rivers/lakes	Arctic coast
Specialists in Britain	6	6	0	n.a.	0	n.a.
Specialists in Scandinavia	9	9	0	0	0	3
Generalists in Britain	12	10	4	n.a.	2	n.a.
Generalists in Scandinavia	32	25	17	18	15	16

Note that many of the species breed in more than one habitat type. Source data are in Appendix E9.1. n.a. indicates that these habitat types do not occur in Britain.

plovers do not commute to pastureland in the way moorland/peatland birds do, despite the frequent close proximity of suitable fields; Byrkjedal and Thompson, 1988). There is a sense that in Britain there is an insufficient range of habitats within the arctic-alpine zone to support a wider assemblage of birds.

Conservation and management issues

The land-use impacts on birds in the arctic-alpine zone are evidently small: 28% of the specialist and 72% of the generalist species appear to suffer no adverse impacts on the breeding grounds. Of those that do so, persecution, hunting and fish-trapping locally affect five specialists and eight generalists (but probably none significantly). Grazing influences the distribution of only two species (dotterel and ptarmigan in their southerly British breeding grounds); recreational disturbance may influence the distribution of three species very locally (snowy owl and divers), and hydroelectric schemes may affect the waterfowl and dipper, but again very locally (see also Ratcliffe, 1977, 1990; Thompson *et al.*, 2003). Climate change is likely to have severe consequences for arctic-alpine environments and their associated wildlife (Chamberlain *et al.*, 2012). Climate change may influence at least four species: drier conditions for purple sandpiper, alpine fen habitat changes for great snipe, potentially losses of snow-lie for snow bunting and extreme weather conditions affecting the prey base of some snowy owls (but in all cases the evidence is anecdotal). There may, however, be subtle effects of climate change on food resources for other species that are not yet understood or researched (e.g. Selås *et al.*, 2011). The small incidence of land-use effects contrasts with that for moorland birds (e.g. Thompson *et al.*, 1988; Pearce-Higgins, 2011b; Chapter 8).

Observational and experimental studies have revealed complex interactions between two principal drivers – grazing and nitrogen deposition – influencing the composition and condition of alpine summit moss and dwarf shrub heaths (e.g. Pearce and van der Wal, 2002; Welch *et al.*, 2005; Armitage, 2010; Albon, 2011; Ross *et al.*, 2011). Williams (2006) provided the first assessment of habitat condition for montane (alpine) heaths and grasslands in 49 Special Areas of Conservation (SACs, classified under the EC Habitats Directive) in the UK (Fig. 9.2). Of these, 27% were in favourable condition, 61% were unfavourable and 12% were deemed to be unfavourable-recovering. Favourable sites were mainly in the central Scottish Highlands. Five of the unfavourable-recovering sites were in the north of England, indicating some reasonable prospects for recovery. Heavy grazing by sheep *Ovis aries* (and, in the Highlands, by red deer *Cervus elaphus*) was the principal reason for SACs being in unfavourable condition, followed by recreation/disturbance, burning, and lack of remedial management and water management (in relation to reservoirs).

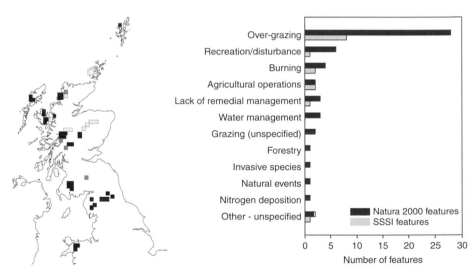

Figure 9.2 Condition of Special Areas of Conservation (SAC) features for montane heaths and grasslands in Britain. The left panel shows the distribution of SACs according to their condition. Pale grey: 80–100% assessed features in 10 km squares favourable; dark grey: 50–79% favourable; black: < 50% favourable. Note that sites that were not assessed are not shown – these were predominantly in the Scottish Highlands. Key attributes of the feature (e.g. extent, quality, supporting processes of habitats) were identified and targets set for each (given in detail in JNCC, 2009). If all targets were met, the feature was deemed to be in favourable condition. The right panel shows factors associated with the unfavourable condition of montane heaths and grasslands in the UK SACs and Sites of Special Scientific Interest (SSSIs). (Natura 2000 – European network of protected areas.) From Williams (2006).

In Norway, no comparable assessment of habitat condition has been developed. Austrheim *et al.* (2011) surmise that about 4% of threatened and near-threatened species in Norway have a significant proportion of their populations (>20%) linked to arctic-alpine areas, with bryophytes and vascular plants most threatened. Of the environmental changes, land-use change is the greatest threat, especially from increased grazing pressure by domesticated grazers in some areas.

Discussion and further research questions

We have described some striking differences between Britain and Scandinavia, notably for the generalist species. A greater number of alpine species in Scandinavia is to be expected, given its massively greater extent of arctic-alpine terrain, the presence of treeline scrub, and other tall shrub and wetland habitat types absent from Britain. Not all the differences in habitat use between regions, however, are likely to be explained simply in terms of different quantities and types of habitat available in the two regions. It is possible, for example, that in the two regions, species have evolved different adaptations to their breeding grounds to maximise fitness in the differing environments.

The reasons are unclear as to why some species are restricted in their distributions to alpine habitats while others have a broader occurrence. Amongst the waders, for instance, dotterel and purple sandpiper are alpine specialists, whereas golden plover, dunlin, Temminck's stint *Calidris temminckii*, ruff *Philomachus pugnax* and great snipe are not. For dotterel there are a few examples of birds nesting outside alpine areas, on cultivated fields in the Netherlands on migration routes (Nethersole-Thompson, 1973) and on a very few high moorland areas in England, yet they have not bred in many other 'lowland' areas where many birds pass through. Some species have a tenuous foothold in the arctic-alpine zone in Britain, of which perhaps the most puzzling is the ringed plover *Charadrius hiaticula*, which across its north European range is typically coastal or associated with stony areas by rivers and lakes, yet it also occurs well away from these in arctic-alpine areas (and, interestingly in parts of northern Scotland in peatlands, where the mineral soils base is widely exposed).

It has long been a concern that the absence of a natural treeline underpins a dearth of wildlife in the British uplands (e.g. Ratcliffe, 1977, 1990, 2005; Ashmole, 2011). A substantial number of species in Scandinavia breed in alpine scrub and heath dominated by *Salix* and *Betula nana* (Fig. 9.1d, Table 9.3, and Appendix E9.1). This surely points to a potential considerable increase in the breeding bird species richness of Britain's arctic-alpine zone if extensive scrub could be re-created. However, the absence of the treeline and associated alpine scrub is unlikely to explain why many of the birds are missing from Britain. One constraint may be the lack of key invertebrate food sources, or lack of spatial/seasonal mosaics of vegetation that provide different functional needs. This may account for the absence of some waders from the British arctic-alpine zone, such as greenshank, redshank, wood sandpiper and whimbrel. Some of these birds have breeding populations less than 1 km from alpine areas, but they do not nest in these despite flying over them. Furthermore, the relatively high densities of some alpine birds breeding in Britain (notably dotterel, golden plover, dunlin, ptarmigan) may be related to the absence of generalist competitors, or to relatively low impacts of nest and chick predators, which might be more numerous if habitat structural and species diversity was greater, as is the case in Scandinavia.

The low incidence of adverse land-use impacts on alpine birds and their habitats is striking. Indeed, so far as the birds are concerned these may be some of the least threatened of all broad habitats in Europe. Nevertheless, habitat condition assessments in Britain show that habitats exist in unfavourable conditions at the southern edge of alpine Britain (see also Ratcliffe, 1977; Thompson and Brown, 1992; Thompson *et al.*, 1987, 1995, 2001, 2005). Such edge-of-range arctic-alpine habitats should be monitored closely, as these may be the first to show responses in bird numbers to habitat improvement or deterioration (see Armitage, 2010; Ross *et al.*, 2011; Pearce-Higgins 2011a, b). Heavy grazing pressure from sheep has resulted in the replacement of moss-dominated heaths with grassy heaths in large areas of the English, Welsh and southern Scottish uplands, with some losses of breeding birds arising from this (Thompson *et al.*, 1987, 2001, 2003; Thompson and Brown, 1992; Pearce and van der Wal, 2002; Thompson and Whitfield, 2007; Armitage, 2010). Climate change, in the form of wetter spring and summer conditions (e.g. Watson, 2010; Pearce-Higgins, 2011a, b), or an increased frequency of adverse weather during the breeding season (see Shaw and Thompson, 2007), may well exacerbate these effects, with potentially important consequences for adaptive management responses such as increased predator control (Pearce-Higgins, 2011a; Thompson and Mackey, 2011). If conditions do become milder in the alpine zone, we may see an increase in the abundance of the alpine generalist species, as well as a decline in the specialists. Chamberlain *et al.* (2012) have stressed the need for improved monitoring of arctic-alpine birds to assess whether altitudinal shifts occur in bird distribution in response to climate. They also argue that more intensive fine-scale studies are needed of habitat associations and demographic mechanisms that determine distributions of arctic-alpine birds; this would help to identify which species are limited by climate rather than other factors.

Whilst no evidence points to impacts of land-use change across the north European arctic-alpine zone having adverse impacts on birds, the upward expansion of woodland in some regions (Speed *et al.*, in press) may become a significant constraint for alpine specialists, as well as for some generalists. Ironically, this expansion might benefit Britain's alpine bird fauna, if a treeline (or timberline) forms which offers greater variation in habitat structure and prey.

Some research gaps have emerged. Whilst broad habitat use by birds in alpine areas is now well understood, more fine-scale work is needed on the use of mosaics by specialists and generalists and their food requirements. Working on moorland, Pearce-Higgins (2011a) has shown how finely related the numbers and productivity of golden plovers are to the timing of tipulid emergence. We need to develop our understanding of such prey–bird productivity relationships for other species in order to predict how habitat quality will be affected by climate and land-use change (noting the importance of tipulids to alpine birds; e.g. Galbraith *et al.*, 1993a; Thompson *et al.*, 2003; Thompson and Whitfield, 2007). It would also be interesting to determine whether constraints of food availability underlie the absence of some of the alpine generalists from Britain's arctic-alpine landscape. Ross *et al.* (2011) have shown that very subtle changes in upland vegetation (through changes in species composition), rather than major changes in boundaries of habitat types, will characterise responses to changes in grazing, climate and nitrogen deposition. Whether there are thresholds beyond which particular invertebrate faunas change remains to be studied.

Given the relatively insular and fragmented nature of British arctic-alpine habitats, migrancy and movement patterns may account for some species failing to encounter suitable breeding grounds there. However, if subpopulations are adapted to particular alpine environments there may be genetic differentiation between populations, or at least behavioural differences, that preclude individuals from recognising some alpine areas as potential habitat. Assessing the extent of any dispersal and interchange between British and Scandinavian populations of arctic-alpine birds, by genetic approaches or direct tracking of individuals, would be extremely interesting. We already know that some individual dotterel nest in both Britain and Norway in the same year (e.g. Thompson and Whitfield, 2007).

Acknowledgements

We thank: Rob Fuller for patient and critical editorial work; David Stroud, James Pearce-Higgins and Phil Whitfield for critical comments; Gunnar Austrheim and DYLAN colleagues at Trondheim and Bergen for recent discussions; Heather Armitage, John Birks, Terry Burke, Keith Duncan, Hector Galbraith, Barbara Jones, Sally Johnson, Ian Owens, Louise Ross, Rick Smith, James Speed, David Stroud, Pat Thompson, Rene van der Wal, Adam Watson, David Welch and Sarah Woodin for discussions and ideas over many years; the JNCC for allowing us to reproduce results from common standards monitoring; and the late Derek Ratcliffe and Desmond Nethersole-Thompson for inspiring us to think about the contrasts between Fennoscandia and Britain.

References

Albon, S. D. (comp.) (2011). *Programme 3. Environment – land use and rural stewardship.* End of programme Report to the Scottish Government (Strategic Research for the Scottish Government: Environment, Biology and Agriculture). Edinburgh: Scottish Government.

Armitage, H. F. (2010). Assessing the influence of environmental drivers on the current condition and recovery potential of *Racomitrium* heath. Unpublished PhD thesis, University of Aberdeen.

Ashmole, P. (2011). Grass-roots contributions to woodland restoration in the Scottish uplands. In *The Changing Nature of Scotland*, ed. S. Marrs, S. Foster, C. Hendrie, E. C. Mackey and D. B. A. Thompson, pp. 355–372. Edinburgh: TSO.

Austrheim, G., Bråthen, K. A., Ims, R. A., Mysterud, A.å. and Ødegaard, F. (2011). Alpine environment. In *Environmental Conditions and Impacts for Red List Species*, ed. J. A. Kålås, S. Henriksen, S. Skjelseth and Å. Viken, pp. 107–117. Trondheim: Norwegian Biodiversity Information Centre.

Averis, A. B., Averis, A. M., Birks, H. J. B. *et al.* (2004). *An Illustrated Guide to British Upland Vegetation.* Peterborough: Joint Nature Conservation Committee.

Brown, A., Birks, H. J. B. and Thompson, D. B. A. (1993). A new bio-geographical classification of the Scottish uplands. Vegetation-environment relationships. *J. Ecol.*, **81**, 231–251.

Byrkjedal, I. and Thompson, D. B. A. (1998). *Tundra Plovers.* London: Academic Press.

Calladine, J. (2011). Seasonal variation in the apparent abundance of breeding birds in arctic-alpine habitats in Scotland: implications for their survey and monitoring. *Bird Study*, **58**, 27–36.

Chamberlain, D. E., Arlettaz, R., Caprio, E. *et al.* (2012). The altitudinal frontier in avian climate impact research. *Ibis*, **154**, 205–209.

Cramp, S. and Simmons, K. E. L. (ed.) (1980). *The Birds of the Western Palearctic Volume II.* Oxford: Oxford University Press.

Cramp, S. and Simmons, K. E. L. (ed.) (1983). *The Birds of the Western Palearctic Volume III.* Oxford: Oxford University Press.

Galbraith, H., Duncan, K., Murray, S. *et al.* (1993a). Diet and habitat use of the dotterel (*Charadrius morinillus*) in Scotland. *Ibis*, **135**, 148–155.

Galbraith, H., Murray, S., Rae, S., Whitfield, D. P. and Thompson, D. B. A. (1993b). Numbers and distribution of dotterel (*Charadrius morinellus*) breeding in Great Britain. *Bird Study*, **40**, 161–169.

Horsfield, D. and Thompson, D. B. A. (1997). The uplands: guidance on terminology regarding altitudinal zonation and related terms. *Information and Advisory Note 26.* Battleby: Scottish Natural Heritage.

JNCC (2009). *Common Standards Monitoring Guidance for Upland Habitats.* Peterborough: Joint Nature Conservation Committee.

Kålås, J. A. and Byrkjedal, I. (1984). Breeding chronology and mating system of the Eurasian Dotterel. *Auk*, **101**, 838–847.

Moen, A. (1999). *National Atlas of Norway. Vegetation.* Honefoss: Norwegian Mapping Authority.

Nethersole-Thompson, D. (1973). *The Dotterel.* London: Collins.

Nethersole-Thompson, D. (1993). *The Snow Bunting.* Reprint. Leeds: Peregrine Books.

Pearce, I. S. K. and van der Wal, R. (2002). Effects of nitrogen deposition on growth and survival of montane *Racomitrium lanuginosum* heath. *Biol. Conserv.*, **104**, 83–89.

Pearce-Higgins, J. W. (2011a). Modelling conservation management options for a southern range-margin population of golden plover *Pluvialis apricaria* vulnerable to climate change. *Ibis*, **153**, 345–356.

Pearce-Higgins, J. W. (2011b). How ecological science can help manage the effects of climate change: a case study of upland birds. In *The Changing Nature of Scotland*, ed. S. Marrs,

S. Foster, C. Hendrie, E. C. Mackey and D. B. A. Thompson, pp 330–346. Edinburgh: TSO.

Ratcliffe, D. A. (ed.) (1977). *A Nature Conservation Review Volume 1*. Cambridge: Cambridge University Press.

Ratcliffe, D. A. (1990). *Bird life of Mountain and Upland*. Cambridge: Cambridge University Press.

Ratcliffe, D. A. (2005). *Lapland: A Natural History*. London: Poyser.

Ratcliffe, D. A. and Thompson, D. B. A. (1988). The British uplands: their ecological character and international significance. In *Ecological Change In The Uplands*, ed. M. B. Usher and D. B. A. Thompson, pp. 9–36. Oxford: Blackwell.

Ross, L., Woodin, S. J., Hester, A. J., Thompson, D. B. A. and Birks, H. J. B. (2011). Is the vegetation of the north-west Highlands changing. Results from a 50 year re-visitation study of major upland vegetation types. In *The Changing Nature of Scotland*, ed. S. Marrs, S. Foster, C. Hendrie, E. C. Mackey and D. B. A. Thompson, pp. 429–434. Edinburgh: TSO Scotland.

Selås, V., Sonerud, G., Framstad, E. *et al.* (2011). Climate change in Norway: warm summers limit grouse reproduction. *Population Ecol.*, **53**, 361–371.

Shaw, P. and Thompson, D. B. A. (ed.) (2007). *The Nature of the Cairngorms: Diversity in a Changing Environment*. Edinburgh: TSO.

Speed, D. M., Austrheim, G., Birks, H. J. B. *et al.* (in press). Natural and cultural heritage in mountain landscapes: towards an integrated valuation. *Int. J. Biodivers. Sci. Ecosyst. Manage.*

Stroud, D. A., Reed, T. M., Pienkowski, M. W. and Lindsay, R. A. (1987). *Birds, Bogs and Forestry: the Peatlands of Caithness and Sutherland*. Peterborough: Nature Conservancy Council.

Thom, V. (1986). *Birds in Scotland*. Calton: Poyser.

Thompson, D. B. A. and Brown, A. (1992). Biodiversity in sub-alpine–alpine Britain: habitat variation, vegetation diversity and some objectives for conservation. *Biodivers. Conserv.*, **1**, 179–209.

Thompson, D. B. A., Galbraith, H. and Horsfield, D. H. (1987). Ecology and resources of Britain's mountain plateaux: conflicts and land use issues. In *Agriculture and Conservation in the Hills and Uplands*, ed. M. Bell and R. G. Bunce, pp. 22–31. Merlewood: Institute of Terrestrial Ecology.

Thompson, D. B. A., Gordon, J. E. and Horsfield, D. (2001). Mountain landscapes in Scotland: are these natural, artefacts or complex relics? In *Earth Science and the Natural Heritage*, ed. J. E. Gordon and K. Lees, pp. 105–119. Edinburgh: TSO.

Thompson, D. B. A., Hester, A. J. and Usher, M. B. (ed.) (1995). *Heaths and Moorland: Cultural Landscapes*. Edinburgh: HMSO.

Thompson, D. B. A. and Mackey, E. C. (2011). The changing nature of Scotland – looking ahead in a European context. In *The Changing Nature of Scotland*, ed. S. Marrs, S. Foster, C. Hendrie, E. C. Mackey and D. B. A. Thompson, pp. 487–498. Edinburgh: TSO.

Thompson, D. B. A., Nagy, L., Johnson, S. M. and Robertson, P. (2005). The nature of mountains: an introduction. In *Mountains of Northern Europe*, ed. D. B. A. Thompson, M. F. Price and C. A. Galbraith, pp. 43–55. Edinburgh: TSO.

Thompson, D. B. A., Stroud, D. A. and Pienkowski, M. W. (1988). Afforestation and upland birds: consequences for population ecology. In *Ecological Change in the Uplands*, ed. M. B. Usher and D. B. A. Thompson, pp. 237–259. Oxford: Blackwell.

Thompson, D. B. A. and Whitfield, D. P. (1993). Research on mountain birds and their habitats. *Scott. Birds*, **17**, 1–8.

Thompson, D. B. A. and Whitfield, D. P. (2007). Dotterel. In *The Birds of Scotland*, ed. R. Forrester and I. Andrews, pp. 435–442. North Berwick: Scottish Ornithologists' Club.

Thompson, D. B. A., Whitfield, D. P., Galbraith, H. *et al.* (2003). Breeding bird assemblages and habitat use of alpine areas in Scotland. In

Alpine Biodiversity in Europe, ed. L. Nagy, G. Grabherr, Ch. Korner and D. B. A. Thompson, pp. 328–338. Berlin: Springer-Verlag.

Watson, A. (1965). A population study of ptarmigan in Scotland. *J. Appl. Ecol.*, **34**, 135–172.

Watson, A., Moss, R. and Rothery, P. (2000). Weather and synchrony in ten-year population cycles of rock ptarmigan and red grouse in Scotland. *Ecology*, **81**, 2126–2136.

Watson, J. (2010). *The Golden Eagle*, 2nd edn. London: Poyser/AC Black.

Welch, D., Scott, D. and Thompson, D. B. A. (2005). Changes in the composition of *Carex bigelowii-Racomitrium lanuginosum* moss heath on Glas Maol, Scotland, in response to sheep grazing and snow fencing. *Biol. Conserv.*, **122**, 621–631.

Whitfield, D. P. (2002). Status of breeding Dotterel *Charadrius morinellus* in Britain in 1999. *Bird Study*, **49**, 237–249.

Williams, J. M. (ed.) (2006). Common Standards Monitoring for Designated Sites. First six year report. Peterborough: Joint Nature Conservation Committee. http://jncc.defra. gov.uk/page-3520.

Supplementary material: Additional material for this chapter is presented in an electronic appendix (Appendix E9.1) at www.cambridge.org/ 9780521897563.

CHAPTER TEN

Bird–habitat relationships in reedswamps and fens

GILLIAN GILBERT

Royal Society for the Protection of Birds Scotland

and

KEN W. SMITH

Hertfordshire, UK

This chapter focuses on the habitat relationships of birds that are closely associated with reedswamps and fens in western Europe. These are normally waterlogged habitats with vegetation frequently dominated by tall robust plant species. They embrace an extremely diverse range of ecological conditions, often described by tortuous technical terminology. Classification systems struggle to capture the fluid and fragile nature of these dynamic environments that change through time with hydroseral succession and frequently grade into one another in space. Water chemistry and the physical processes that create the waterlogged conditions underpin much of the complex variation in plant communities (e.g. Rodwell, 1995). Using British examples, this section introduces the variety of habitat types which, although generally very localised, support highly distinctive bird assemblages.

'Reedbeds' are dominated mainly by common reed *Phragmites australis*. The term 'reedswamp' refers to the wettest reedbeds, with at least 20 cm or more of standing water throughout the year. Early successional areas may be dominated by *Typha latifolia*, *T. angustifolia* or *Schoenoplectus lacustris* (Rodwell, 1995). Reedswamp may develop from open water, into swamp, then to waterlogged woodland ('carr') and eventually to relatively dry woodland. This succession is only arrested by grazing or cutting, or natural disturbance such as severe winter flooding. Reedswamp is not necessarily confined to peat-based, water-retentive soils; it can rapidly colonise mineral extraction sites, natural lake margins and estuaries with a variety of substrates. Reedbeds are relatively rare in Britain: a total of 5000 ha was recorded in 1993, with only 50 sites larger than 20 ha (Gilbert *et al.*, 1996). Recent creation and restoration projects are substantially increasing reedbed area. For example, three newly created sites in Somerset, Suffolk and Cambridgeshire will eventually provide at least another 1000 ha.

Birds and Habitat: Relationships in Changing Landscapes, ed. Robert J. Fuller. Published by Cambridge University Press. © Cambridge University Press 2012.

Fens are more complex and varied, both botanically and structurally, than reedswamp. Fens usually develop on peaty soils where local topography maintains summer water levels at or close to the surface. The dampest areas may be rich in sedges and a wide range of vascular plants, whereas relatively dry areas ('high marsh or fen') typically consist of tall rank mixtures often including nettles, umbellifers and meadowsweet *Filipendula ulmaria*. 'Poor fens', where the water is derived from base-poor rock, occur mainly in the uplands, or are associated with lowland infertile soils. They are characterised by shorter, less species-rich vegetation than base-rich or calcareous fens. Britain's largest base-poor fen, Insh Marshes in the floodplain of the River Spey in Scotland, covers an area of 300 ha. The most extensive area of calcareous rich fen and swamp is Broadland in Norfolk, England, covering 3000 ha. In the Outer Hebrides, extensive fens and shallow lochs are associated with the calcareous machair grasslands of the Uists.

Wetland with peat soils broadly constitute 'mires', of which there are several lowland variants, locally defined by the dominant geomorphological processes (e.g. valley bog, basin bog, open-water transition and floodplain fen). These can have complex vegetation characteristics as illustrated by two examples. Broubster Leans is a transition mire which has developed on a floodplain beside the River Forss in Caithness, Scotland. The Leans support a diversity of plant communities from open water to carr, rush-pasture and blanket bog. Rhos Goch in Powys, Wales, is a suite of poor fen swamp communities positioned between an active raised bog and a rush pasture. The communities are typical of a 'lagg zone' which classically is fed by water draining from an acidic bog into more mineral and nutrient-rich soils which carry a greater diversity of plant species, usually dominated by sedges *Carex* spp.. Raised bogs are different in several respects to other lowland mires. They depend for their water on high rainfall, rather than on a high water table and support vegetation adapted to waterlogged, acidic, nutrient-poor conditions. Many raised bogs have been seriously degraded, but habitat restoration may result in a transitory reedbed or fen stage. This chapter focuses on reedswamp and fen habitats; it does not consider acid mires, such as raised bogs or blanket bog, which are generally very different in both vegetation and bird assemblages.

Broadscale bird-habitat associations

This section gives a short overview of the bird assemblages, concentrating on Britain, but making selected comparisons with continental Europe. Structurally, reedswamp and fen can be relatively simple two-dimensional habitats supporting few, albeit specialised, bird species. Soil wetness, water, structural vegetation complexity and successional stage are major influences on the bird assemblages. The breeding birds associated with the different successional habitats of reedswamp and fens are summarised in Fig. 10.1. Early

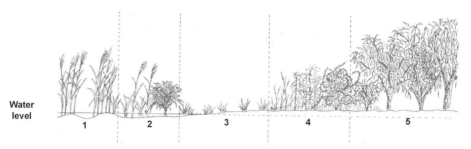

Figure 10.1 Breeding birds associated with different successional habitats of lowland reedswamp and fen. Specialists of habitats 1 to 5 are marked with asterisks. Based on an original figure in Fuller (1982).

1. **Phragmites reedswamp:** bittern *Botaurus stellaris**, marsh harrier *Circus aeruginosus**, water rail *Rallus aquaticus*, cuckoo *Cuculus canorus*, reed warbler *Acrocephalus scirpaceus*, sedge warbler *A. schoenobaenus*, bearded tit *Panurus biarmicus**

2. **Mixed fen swamp:** water rail, spotted crake *Porzana porzana**, crane *Grus grus*, Savi's warbler *Locustella luscinioides**, sedge warbler, reed warbler, reed bunting *Emberiza schoeniclus*

3. **Grazed fen:** lapwing *Vanellus vanellus*, snipe *Gallinago gallinago*, curlew *Numenius arquata*, redshank *Tringa totanus*, yellow wagtail *Motacilla flava*

4. **High marsh:** whinchat *Saxicola rubetra*, Cetti's warbler *Cettia cetti**, grasshopper warbler *Locustella naevia*, sedge warbler, reed warbler, marsh warbler *Acrocephalus palustris**, whitethroat *Sylvia communis*, reed bunting

5. **Willow scrub:** willow warbler *Phylloscopus trochilus*, blackbird *Turdus merula*, wren *Troglodytes troglodytes* plus a variety of other scrub/woodland species.

successional stages tend to have fewer breeding species than the later stages (Fuller, 1982). Pure *Phragmites* is the major breeding habitat of a few specialist species, notably marsh harrier *Circus aeruginosus*, bittern *Botaurus stellaris* and bearded tit *Panurus biarmicus* (Fig. 10.2a). Other wetland breeding species typifying a variable mix of wet reedswamp and drier fen are crane *Grus grus*, water rail *Rallus aquaticus*, reed warbler *Acrocephalus scirpaceus*, sedge warbler *A. schoenobaenus*, reed bunting *Emberiza schoeniclus*, Savi's warbler *Locustella luscinioides*, grasshopper warbler *L. naevia* and Cetti's warbler *Cettia cetti*, the latter mainly associated with scrub at the wetland margin. Because many rich fen sites consist of mixtures of swamp, dry high fen, scrub and woodland, their bird communities are often diverse, including many common woodland species.

Reed warbler and sedge warbler are two of the most characteristic and numerous species of reedswamp and fen. Where they coexist, they share similar habitat, but feed in slightly different ways. Sedge warbler feeds low down in dense vegetation, mainly by 'picking' slow moving or stationary prey. Reed warbler is more opportunist, using a variety of feeding sites in reeds,

Figure 10.2 Example reedbed and marsh habitats in the UK. (a) A recently created early successional *Phragmites* reedbed with a good ratio of reedbed edge to open water at Lakenheath, Suffolk. Wet reedbed edge is important feeding habitat for bittern and bearded tit. (Photo: Andy Hay, rspb-images.com.) (b) Harvesting reed on the Tay reedbeds, Scotland. The reed is cut and bundled using a specially adapted Seiga reed harvesting machine. Commercial reed cutting usually takes place in winter or early spring, annually or biennially and requires lowering of water levels. Relatively long intervals between cutting are most beneficial for reedbed birds. (Photo: Andy Hay, rspb-images.com.) (c) Mixed fen vegetation at Marazion marsh, Cornwall, with scrub in the background. Such fen can support rails and a variety of warblers, while wetland scrub can be attractive to a variety of breeding and migrating passerines. (Photo: Chris Gomersall, rspb-images.com.) (d) High marsh, mainly umbellifers and nettles, on a Hertfordshire sewage irrigation area in the early 1980s, holding high densities of breeding sedge warblers and reed buntings. (Photo: Rob Fuller.)

rushes, bushes and on the ground. Although many reed warbler nests are in pure reed, they frequently nest in other wet fen vegetation, usually in the vicinity of reedbeds (Catchpole, 1974). Sedge warblers breed in a wide range of low, dense vegetation usually preferring slightly drier vegetation. Together with reed buntings, sedge warblers are often the dominant species in the rank growth of dry high marshes (Fig. 10.2d).

The diversity of species breeding in these habitats is greater on mainland Europe than in Britain, though some of these species appear now to be colonising. Species that typify nearby continental, but not British, reedswamp and fen include little bittern *Ixobrychus minutus*, purple heron *Ardea purpurea*, great white egret *A. alba*, spoonbill *Platalea leucorodia*, cattle egret *Bubulcus ibis*, little crake *Porzana parva*, Baillon's crake *P. pusilla*, great reed warbler *Acrocephalus arundinaceus*, marsh warbler *A. palustris*, bluethroat *Luscinia svecica* and penduline tit *Remiz pendulinus*. Further east, paddyfield warbler *Acrocephalus agricola*, aquatic warbler *A. paludicola* and citrine wagtail *Motacilla citreola* are associated with extensive areas of fen and mire habitat. There are spatial differences in habitat use (see also Chapter 3). On the continent, hen harrier *Circus cyaneus* and short eared owl *Asio flammeus* breed in fens and swamps, but in Britain are now almost entirely confined to upland moorland. Other examples, including bittern and crane, are discussed below.

The relatively wide variety of the larger wetland bird species on the continent is especially marked. However, there are signs that this is changing. There are increasing numbers of great white egrets visiting Britain, a rash of breeding attempts by little bittern, cattle egret, purple heron, spoonbill and strong colonisation by little egret *Egretta garzetta*. The main predictor of breeding heron distribution in Europe appears to be climate (Kushlan and Hafner, 2000), but warming temperatures appear not to be the only climatic driver of recent increases in numbers of larger wetland species in Britain. Most of these species have expanded their populations elsewhere in Europe (van Turnhout *et al.*, 2010), and this has been linked to improved wintering conditions (increased rainfall in the Sahel, Fasola *et al.*, 2000). Until recently, little bittern had declined across Europe and this was thought to be due to increased mortality during migration or when wintering in Africa (Bekhuis, 1990).

Several waterbirds nest in reedswamp and fen habitats where they occur in close proximity to open waters (Fig. 10.2a). Grebes typically need emergent vegetation for nesting and shelter. Diving and dabbling ducks nest in vegetation close to water bodies and the fringing vegetation provides feeding habitats and shelter for the broods. Open water and its margins attract an array of feeding species such as several species of herons, hobbies *Falco subbuteo* and hirundines. There is a wider diversity of such species on mainland Europe, for example marsh terns *Chlidonias* spp. breed widely across Europe, but no longer do so in Britain.

Especially in northern Britain, breeding waders and gulls are characteristic of the larger nutrient-poor fen systems. Northern Scottish fens and mires hold wood sandpipers *Tringa glareola* and a range of commoner breeding waders and gulls such as redshank *T. totanus*, curlew *Numenius arquata*, snipe *Gallinago gallinago* and black-headed gull *Chroicocephalus ridibundus*. The mosaic of fens and damp grasslands of the Uists carry exceptionally high densities of breeding waders (Fuller *et al.*, 1986).

Outside the breeding season, reedswamps and fens provide feeding and roost sites for many species. Large numbers of migrating reed and sedge warblers and other warblers pass through reedbed sites where they actively feed on invertebrates such as chironomids and aphids (Bibby and Green, 1981, 1983; Chernetsov, 1998; Chernetsov and Manukyan, 2000). These habitats can provide food through the winter for resident insectivores, including blue tits *Cyanistes caeruleus* and wrens *Troglodytes troglodytes*, and also species that switch to a seed-based diet such as bearded tit and reed bunting. Other species like bittern and water rail spend the whole year resident in tall vegetation associated with water, but may disperse in winter to sites not readily used during the breeding season. They still require tall, vegetated habitat with abundant food, but sites occupied in the winter may be much more varied in character and smaller than breeding sites. In winter the numbers of these birds in Britain and north west Europe are boosted by immigration from further north and east.

The most important feature of reedswamp as roosting habitat is predator avoidance. During late summer and autumn large roosts of migrating hirundines can occur, usually in reedbeds, but other wetland vegetation may also be used (Turner, 2006). Throughout the autumn and winter, reedbed and fen vegetation is used for roosting by harriers *Circus* spp. and a range of passerines – mainly wagtails *Motacilla alba*, starlings *Sturnus vulgaris* and buntings.

Many of the species which are found in reedswamp and fen at different times of year also use other wetland habitat types, including coastal marshes, wet meadows, lakes and rivers. Others merely use reedswamp and fen for roosting, but feed in other habitat types, including farmland. A small core of species comprises obligate fen or reedswamp specialists. In Britain these include bittern, bearded tit, marsh harrier, Savi's warbler, spotted crake and, arguably, water rail and Cetti's warbler. The number of specialists is larger for mainland Europe.

Processes shaping bird assemblages

Successional stage, spatial patterns and vertical structure of vegetation, and wetness gradients are overarching drivers of variation in the bird assemblages. Different vegetation types can vary strikingly in their typical bird species (Figs. 10.1 and 10.2). Habitat complexity at different scales frequently determines suitability, as illustrated by factors influencing bird distribution within reedbeds. Fine-scale structure of vegetation, such as the density of rigid elements, vegetation height, basal vegetation and open water interface are good predictors of habitat occupancy in several species of reed passerines (Van der Hut, 1986; Leisler *et al.*, 1989). Bearded tit, reed, sedge and Savi's warblers all show preference for the reed–water interface (Báldi and Kisbenedek, 1999). At the opposite end of the successional gradient, forest-reedbed interfaces form local bird diversity hotspots, especially in winter (Vâlcu, 2006).

The extent of different vegetation types also affects species with large area requirements, such as cranes and bitterns. The vegetation and hydrological complexity of wetlands is a primary driver of species richness across different taxa. Loss of complexity in aquatic habitats, especially in terms of vegetation structure and composition, may be linked to reduction in biodiversity and the local extinction of some wetland species in Europe. Reedswamp and fen can easily become homogeneous, catering just for the habitat specialists which do not necessarily occur with great abundance. For example, the numbers of all waterbird species recorded on Lake Engure in Latvia declined as separate stands of emergent vegetation merged to form a huge, uniform sward dominated by common reed, and areas of varied meadow vegetation were reduced (Viksne *et al.*, 2005). Even reed specialists such as bittern and bearded tit may disappear when open water, or the interface between water and reed, is lost as reedbeds dry or their internal watercourses become choked with vegetation so that favoured foods decline or become unobtainable. Successional changes can result in loss of open wetlands, but changes in water quality and primary plant productivity may also be important influences on habitat structure and biodiversity.

Increased phosphate availability in particular is a major cause of change in wetland biodiversity (Kaminski and Prince, 1981; Linz *et al.*, 1996a and 1996b; Venterink *et al.*, 2003). Productivity and nutrient limitation are closely linked with plant species richness and with the occurrence of threatened species within wetlands (Venterink *et al.*, 2003). Phosphate eutrophication alters vegetation development and affects many typical reedswamp birds directly (food availability) or indirectly (habitat change). For instance, the Savi's warbler diet of freshwater snails and aquatic invertebrates and the great reed warbler diet of aquatic invertebrates are very sensitive to nutrient enrichment (Graveland, 1998). Exactly how eutrophication affects resource availability and habitat quality for birds in freshwater wetlands has not been thoroughly investigated, although some links are known (for a discussion of the Dutch situation see van Turnhout *et al.*, 2010). Whilst reed is quite capable of growing under eutrophic conditions, a eutrophic system produces a large input of dead organic material which accumulates and decomposes between the reed stems. If the water table remains stable all year round this causes anaerobic conditions and toxins will eventually cause a die-back of reed vegetation (Brix, 1999; Ostendorp, 1989). Many reedswamps in western Europe are no longer influenced by natural summer drawdown and winter flooding; such 'water table rigidity' is often a consequence of surrounding agricultural needs. This, combined with eutrophication, can also lead to the loss of early successional stages of reedswamp vegetation and a higher rate of succession in the late successional stages (R. Foppen pers. comm.).

Invasive plant species can greatly modify natural wetland habitats. Even though ≤6% of the Earth's land mass is wetland, 24% (8 of 33) of the world's most invasive plants are wetland species (Zedler and Kercher, 2004). Many wetland invaders form monotypes, which alter habitat structure, lower biodiversity (both number and 'quality' of species), change nutrient cycling and productivity (often increasing it), and modify food webs (Zedler and Kercher, 2004). British examples of problem invasive plants are Himalayan balsam *Impatiens glandulifera*, Japanese knotweed *Fallopia japonica*, Canadian pondweed *Elodea canadensis* and Australian swamp stonecrop *Crassula helmsii*. These species may rapidly form dense monocultures that force out native species in or near wetlands, and are difficult to eradicate. Exact consequences for birds are poorly understood but there is potential for modifying preferred habitat structures and mosaics.

Increased species richness with increasing wetland and reedbed size, or connectivity with other wetland patches, has been reported in several studies (Rafe *et al.*, 1985; Báldi, 2006; Naugle *et al.*, 2001; Paracuellos and Tellería, 2004). In particular there is evidence from the Netherlands for fragmentation effects on the occurrence, population dynamics and resilience of reedswamp species (Foppen *et al.*, 1999, 2000; Foppen, 2001). The relative importance of site size, habitat patchiness and structural complexity of emergent vegetation is difficult to unravel and changes seasonally. For instance, in south east Spain a study of 40 vegetated patches dominated by *Phragmites*, identified size, perimeter and isolation of reedbeds as the best predictors of avian species richness in winter and vegetative complexity as best during the breeding season (Paracuellos, 2006). Small patch size does not necessarily confer low fitness. In a Swiss study of reed buntings breeding in 18 wetland fragments, reproductive performance was equally good in small and large patches (Pasinelli *et al.*, 2008).

Habitat associations of some key species

The following sections examine habitat relationships and spatial patterns of habitat use for seven contrasting wetland species. While the context is mainly Britain, different patterns of habitat use occurring elsewhere in Europe are indicated. Each of these focal species breeds in Britain in small numbers and is a specialist of the relevant habitat. They have been chosen to illustrate the diverse niche requirements of bird species associated with these wetlands. Four of the species have been relatively well studied (bittern, marsh harrier, bearded tit and Savi's warbler), but the requirements of the others are less fully understood.

Bittern *Botaurus stellaris*

Across their global range, bitterns use a wide range of reed-dominated vegetation and wetland landscapes, including fish ponds, reed-fringed lakes and rivers. Non-*Phragmites* habitats include *Typha angustifolia*, *Schoenoplectus lacustris*, *Cladium mariscus* and even rice fields (Alessandria *et al.*, 2003; Poulin *et al.*, 2005; Puglisi and Bretagnolle, 2005; Puglisi *et al.*, 2005; White *et al.*, 2006; Longoni *et al.*, 2007). In Britain, however, most breeding bitterns are confined to large, wet *Phragmites*-dominated reedbeds. Common elements of nesting habitats across Europe are tall emergent vegetation and standing water, close to a source of food (Adamo *et al.*, 2004; Gilbert *et al.*, 2003, 2005a, b; Polak, 2007; Polak *et al.*, 2008; Poulin *et al.*, 2005; Puglisi *et al.*, 2005). Bitterns have large feet and long claws adapted to grasp a bundle of reed stems in each foot enabling them to move with speed through the reeds above deep water.

Males are polygamous. Females do not necessarily choose to nest within the male's territory, but may nest in a relatively isolated position, or in a loose group close to other nesting females (closest distances 5 m in Poland (Polak *et al.*, 2008), 19 m in Britain (Gilbert *et al.*, 2005a), 39 m in France (Puglisi and Bretagnolle, 2005)). Females incubate the eggs and feed the young on their own without any contribution from the males. They will defend the nest, but do not defend a feeding territory in the breeding season and may range very close to the nest or fly as far as 2 km to find food for the chicks. Nesting habitat choice is driven both by avoidance of predators and proximity to feeding habitat (Adamo *et al.*, 2004; Gilbert *et al.*, 2005a, b, 2007; Polak *et al.*, 2008). Nests are in areas with relatively many old reed stems, thicker, stronger vegetation and, most importantly, water at a sufficient depth such that it is likely to be maintained through the season (Gilbert *et al.*, 2005a; Polak *et al.*, 2008). Bitterns appear to recognise sites likely to stay wet through the season based on vegetation characteristics, presumably an adaption to ensure access to prey and reduce nest loss to ground predators.

In general, fish dominate the diet, the species of which vary with local abundance and availability. In Britain, native freshwater fish make up most of the chick diet biomass. Elsewhere, the diet can be dominated by amphibians, crayfish, mammals and aquatic invertebrates. Males have a breeding territory within which they feed during most of the season and 'boom' in late winter and early spring in order to attract females. The composition of habitats within these territories varies across countries, probably related to the most easily available prey species.

The most important feeding habitat in Britain is usually the flooded 30 m margin of reedbed vegetation next to open water (Fig.10.3) and the availability of this habitat drives male territory size (Gilbert *et al.*, 2005b). This is not the case at some sites in France and Italy, where the main prey is the non-native red swamp crayfish *Procambarus clarkii* (Adamo, 2002; Poulin *et al.*, 2007). Here the favoured habitat structure is rather more homogeneous, sparse open reed in shallower water, which is probably easiest for hunting crayfish. Feeding

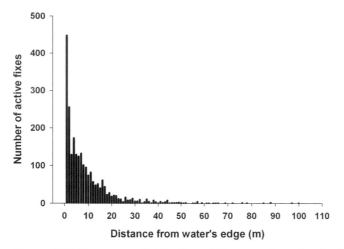

Figure 10.3 Frequency distribution of distances (m) of active bittern radio-tracking locations from the water's edge. Radio-tracking locations are from 2310 active locations of eight birds. All were within reedbed habitat and the water's edge may have been an open pool or a linear ditch. Redrawn from Gilbert *et al.* (2005b).

habitat structure, at least where fish dominate the diet, is determined by fish being able to penetrate from open water into reedbed edges and be available to the foraging bitterns; this is ideally early successional reedswamp with a complex edge structure.

Radio tracking indicates that the average size of British male breeding territories is 20 ha (Gilbert *et al.*, 2005b), though males may occupy relatively isolated sites as small as 3–4 ha, especially where these are set within a larger wetland landscape. Males normally defend a single area as a territory in continuous habitat. However, the territory may be multi-centric, consisting of several nuclei within a larger, apparently suitable, area (Puglisi *et al.*, 2005). In more fragmented wetland landscapes they may defend several patches of suitable habitat separated by woodland, river, road or path. Britain has a winter influx of continental birds and these individuals, along with some dispersing local bitterns, can be found in a broader range of wetland habitats than the favoured breeding sites.

Studies in the Netherlands have suggested that a viable 'key patch' for bitterns in a metapopulation should have carrying capacity for at least 20 pairs (Verboom *et al.*, 2001). Whether this means that many individual sites in Britain and western Europe are too small to contain viable populations in the long term remains to be seen, but it is likely that the wider metapopulation structure is crucial. Threats to populations include the lack of large wet reedbeds, problems with food availability, pollution and human recreational activities. The greatest overall threats, however, are a lack of water, drainage, seral succession, the inappropriate management of reedbeds, and the proximity of some of the most important reedbeds to the coast, where rising sea-levels and increased storminess threaten saline inundation. Bittern research results have been translated into practical habitat management advice that has been implemented since the mid 1990s (Hawke and Jose, 1996; White and Gilbert, 2003; White *et al.*, 2006) with considerable success (Wotton *et al.*, 2009).

Marsh harrier *Circus aeruginosus*

Breeding marsh harriers generally use freshwater or brackish reedswamps, where they prefer large areas of dense emergent aquatic growth, which may be *Phragmites*, *Typha* or *Carex* species (Báldi and Kisbenedek, 1998). Females nesting in *Phragmites*, rather than *Typha*, have been found to be more successful (Nemeckova *et al.*, 2008). Nests are built on the ground, usually within an area of unbroken dense vegetation. During the nest-building phase, which may take a few weeks, marsh harriers are quite vulnerable to disturbance.

The early stages of reedbed succession are preferred for nesting because the presence of water increases safety from predation (particularly foxes) and may also provide easier access to high prey abundance (Dijkstra and Zijlstra, 1997). Large reedswamps are preferred as these are less vulnerable to fluctuating water levels, to flooding from wave action and to predation from terrestrial mammals if water levels fall earlier than expected during the season (Stanevicius, 2004). Harriers occur in some British sites with small areas of emergent vegetation, especially if they are in proximity to larger wetlands or wet grassland.

The British population has increased spectacularly (from 1 to >600 pairs in 40 years) and densities in some reedbeds are now 8–10 pairs per 100 hectares. Where high densities occur, nests are within 50–300 m of each other and a loose nesting territory is defended (Clarke, 1995). Males may be polygamous, with clumped nests associated with the same male. Hunting ranges may extend up to at least 2 km away from the nesting area. Hunting ranges tend to become larger, and areas of overlap increase, as the season progresses (Altenburg *et al.*, 1982). During the breeding season they hunt regularly over agricultural land, including meadows, vineyards and ricefields. There has been a recent increase in their use of more intensive arable landscapes, for example in south west Slovakia they nest predominantly in agricultural crops (cereals, sugar beet, sunflowers and maize) (Takácsová, 2007). Whilst harriers have recently started to nest in crops in Britain, the majority continue to depend on reedbeds. As breeding numbers have increased, so too have the numbers of birds which roost in reedbeds in autumn and winter.

Bearded tit *Panurus biarmicus*

Bearded tits nest and forage throughout the year almost exclusively in reed-dominated wetlands. Their short wing length and long tail indicate a bird adapted to dense reedbed habitat, with the tail aiding balance when moving through reed stems (Pujante *et al.*, 2005; Peiro *et al.*, 2006). Nesting and feeding habitat requirements seem consistent across their range. They nest on or close to the ground among sedges or fallen reed stems and the nest may be partly concealed by leaf litter. So a drier, older area of reedbed is needed for nesting, although at some sites provision of nest-boxes has enabled nesting in wetter areas where birds are less vulnerable to predation or flooding and closer to feeding areas. The species breeds relatively early in the spring and Poulin *et al.* (2002) suggest that a dense cover of dry, thin reed stems is important for concealing nests.

Nesting areas may be well separated from feeding areas (Wawrzyniak and Sohns, 1986). They chiefly feed on invertebrates in the spring and summer and seeds in late autumn and winter. *Phragmites* seed is the principal winter food, but seed production varies between sites and seed set appears to be strongly affected by climate, especially rainfall and temperature patterns, at the time of flowering (McKee and Richards, 1996). Climate may, therefore, be a limiting factor in reedbed suitability for bearded tits. However, they frequently search for invertebrates, even in mid-winter, which is surprising, given their seasonal physiological adaptation to plant diet (Cramp and Perrins, 1993). They prefer the reedbed edge near water for foraging, as do several other species (Fig.10.4) and, in the spring and summer, fly to the wetter parts of the reedbed, especially to patches where chironomid midges are abundant. In summer, birds sometimes feed on bare soil, or from the water surface. In the autumn and winter, bearded tits extend their range and may be found in reed patches not occupied during the breeding season (Surmacki and Stepniewski, 2003). Their preference for different vegetation strata also changes through the year, independent of food availability (Hoi, 2001; Trnka and Prokop, 2006). The litter layer is an important winter foraging site and prolonged flooding that deprives birds of access to the reed litter can result in high winter mortality (Wilson and Peach, 2006).

Bearded tits do not appear to be territorial and nests may be solitary or loosely colonial. Birds breeding in loose groups may also feed together in communal feeding areas. Densities may appear very high in localised areas where breeding birds are grouped, for example 24 nests in an area 250 × 175 m in Germany (Cramp and Perrins, 1993). It seems unlikely that limited habitat availability drives colonial nesting, and female bearded tits may choose to nest colonially to increase opportunities for extra pair copulation (Hoi and Hoi-Leitner, 1997).

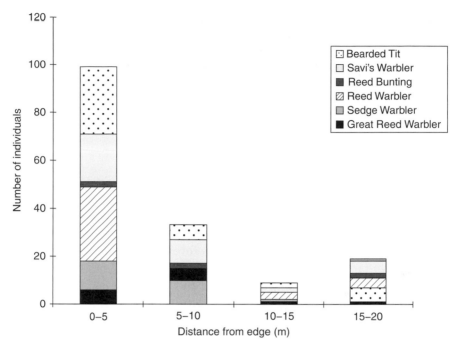

Figure 10.4 The distribution of the six most abundant bird species in the first 20 m of a reedbed edge at Lake Velence, Hungary. Based on Báldi and Kisbenedek (1999).

Savi's warbler *Locustella luscinioides*

Savi's warblers winter south of the Sahara and have become very rare breeders in Britain. The species has highly specific habitat requirements. Territories are characterised by having relatively high and dense reeds or sedge vegetation, extensive basal litter, and a thick cover of dead sedge leaves (Aebischer *et al.*, 1996; Van der Hut, 1986). Within a relatively small territory it needs both drier marsh fen in which to nest and wetter reedswamp in which to feed on their favoured prey; mainly adult and larval arthropods and snails (Neto, 2006). Hence, breeding adults defend a territory that contains all the elements required for successful nesting and feeding.

The nesting habitat is generally relatively dry mixed herbaceous fen and low scrub. The nest rests on vegetation rather than being fixed (Neto, 2006); this can be at ground level, on dense vegetation on the ground, or over standing water that has a dense mat of vegetation above (Cramp, 1992). Post-breeding birds prefer the lower strata of reedbeds (Trnka and Prokop, 2006) and there is a strong preference for the water edge when feeding (Báldi and Kisbenedek, 1999). The habits are similar to grasshopper warbler, adopting mouse-like 'creeping runs' through dense vegetation.

The confinement of Savi's warbler to places with both pure reedbeds and fens, and its dependence on litter and the presence of old vegetation, have important implications for habitat management and conservation. Cutting vegetation reduces the area available for nesting and feeding for at least two years (Neto, 2006). Drainage, successional drying out and homogeneous *Phragmites* would adversely affect the habitat conditions preferred by this species, as well as any management that cleared out the basal litter layer. As a ground-nester, it is also vulnerable to flooding from fluctuating water levels.

Crane *Grus grus*

The native and resident crane population in Britain is increasing. This is concurrent with other parts of Europe, where the population is expanding and increasing. In the main European breeding areas in the north and east, where cranes are migratory, they generally prefer large, extensive mires and other swampy habitats, including floodplain forests, providing isolated nesting territories that are free from disturbance. However, in some intensively cultivated landscapes they nest in smaller and less wild wetlands. The founder population in Britain was based in Norfolk within large areas of reedswamp over 100 ha. Recently, however, they have expanded into less wild and newly created wetlands surrounded by agricultural land and with nearby pockets of human habitation.

Cranes have an over-riding need for an inaccessible nest site on the ground and, because of the long incubation period, use areas that are free of, or inaccessible to, ground predators. Nest sites are nearly always associated with water, but can be situated in a variety of vegetation types, ranging from pure tall reed to more open mire. They prefer to have an unobstructed field of vision, except when using small swampy clearings in forests or on mire near tall scrub.

The two most important British nesting habitats for cranes appear to be reedbeds (uncut reedswamp and reed cut annually) and fen (supposedly preferring areas cut the previous summer), but they have also bred on lowland raised bog, floodplain grasslands and old flight ponds. The nests are often in close proximity to shallow water bodies, but occasionally within them. Initially after hatching, the families tend to forage within the wetland habitats, but as they get older the young are often escorted to feed in surrounding grassland and arable fields, returning to roost in the wetland at night (A. Stanbury pers. comm.).

Cranes are omnivorous in both breeding and non-breeding seasons and feed in a variety of open habitats and shallow water. Large invertebrates seem to be a key food for chicks (A. Stanbury pers. comm.). Pairs are usually solitary and territorial during the breeding season, but often feed up to 1.5 km away from the nesting territory (Moll, 1963). The size of nesting territory depends on habitat type; smaller territories of 1–10 ha are most common in fen, lakeside or within woodland, whereas territories tend to be larger (>1000 ha) in open mire habitat (Leito *et al.*, 2006).

Spotted crake *Porzana porzana*

Across Europe, spotted crakes occur in a variety of lowland swamps, fens, mires, wet grasslands and overgrown edges of lakes and rivers. The species is migratory and birds pair on arrival in the breeding area. A small breeding territory is defended that encompasses both nesting and feeding habitat, although they will also range further. Breeding territories may be as small as 0.5 ha (Bengtson, 1962) and in high-density sites, nests have been found as close as 10–15 m apart (Glutz von Blotzheim *et al.*, 1973). Radio tracking of six crakes in England and Scotland found the core area used within territories to be 0.4–2.93 ha (Mallord, 1999; Mackenzie, 2000).

Breeding territories are generally characterised by wetness and dense vegetation. However, habitat measures within core territory areas of radio-tracked birds (Schäffer, 1999; Mallord, 1999; Mackenzie, 2000) and at 63 singing positions during a national survey (Gilbert, 2002) indicate that variation or heterogeneity at a small scale is important. Territories contained a combination of permanent shallow standing water with aquatic vegetation providing nest sites, together with feeding habitat characterised by tussocks of wet sedge or grass, and drier areas of exposed substrate. Within the core territories examined in Britain, crakes occurred in a variety of different vegetation types: swamp (e.g. with *Eleocharis palustris, Equisetum fluviatile*), *Carex* beds, marsh (e.g. with *Glyceria maxima, Schoenoplectus lacustris*), mire (e.g. with *Molinia caerulea*) and grassland (e.g. with *Festuca ovina*). It is likely that across their range they utilise a wide range of vegetation types that provide the structural mosaics necessary for nesting and feeding.

Wood sandpiper *Tringa glareola*

Wood sandpipers winter in the tropics, but breed widely across the northern Palearctic, including Scotland where their preferred habitat is upland floodplain of open mire with scattered pools and marshy areas (Nethersole-Thompson and Nethersole-Thompson, 1986). The vegetation typically includes sedges, rushes and fen plants such as meadowsweet, marsh bedstraw *Galium palustre* and bog myrtle *Myrica gale* (Kalejta-Summers, 2006). More widely, wood sandpipers can use a wide range of vegetation types, with and without trees (Piersma *et al.*, 1996).

The preferred habitat structure appears to be linked to predation, providing enough vegetative cover to hide birds and their nests, but with a wide aspect from which approaching potential predators can be seen (Kalejta-Summers, 2006). Wood sandpipers breed at low density in the Scottish Highlands, where

47–50 breeding locations have been recorded since 1959 (Chisholm, 2007). Some Scottish birds form loose nesting groups (Kalejta-Summers, 2006). The highest recorded nesting density, not in Scotland, is 10 pairs on 20 ha (Kirchner, 1978), but general dispersion is 1 pair per 10–100 ha (Glutz von Blotzheim *et al.*, 1977).

Species requirements and habitat management

The seven species discussed above are all relatively rare in Britain, but have wide global distributions. Although all are specialists of particular wetland habitat types, they are to varying degrees able to adapt to available prey species and vegetation types within the constraints of required habitat structures. Savi's warbler, spotted crake and wood sandpiper require breeding territories containing a complex mix of both nesting and feeding habitat, although these are at different spatial scales. By contrast, bearded tit, bittern, marsh harrier and crane can all use spatially separated nesting and feeding areas within certain constraints. For example, during the vulnerable stage when large crane chicks can leave the nest, adults are constrained by the availability of feeding areas within walking distance. Also, female bitterns having to provision young on their own are constrained by the time spent away from the nest searching for food, as young are vulnerable to exposure.

Each of these species differs to some extent in its preferred habitat. In each case, however, the physical architecture of the substrate and the vegetation, coupled with its association with water, is paramount in providing the necessary structure for feeding, nesting and protection from predation. Some of this preferred structure comes from the presence of dead vegetation – previous years' growth that has not been cleared away by flooding, grazing or other management.

Practical habitat management decisions have to be made as to which habitats to provide; the above examples illustrate that different management approaches cannot match the requirements of all species, perhaps other than on a very large site. It is difficult to understand and control the processes and conditions necessary to provide the range of habitats required by most of these species. Consequently, these preferred structures are difficult to replicate artificially, particularly at different spatial scales within the same site. The species that probably best highlights this is Savi's warbler whose specific habitat requirements of thick fen vegetation associated with water on a small scale is not common and does not easily fit into recognised habitat-management regimes, especially on small sites. The importance of scale in wetland restoration has been emphasised by Platteeuw *et al.* (2010) who argue that very large areas provide more gradients of wetland conditions, opportunities for a greater number of species and minimise the effects of surrounding agriculture (Fig. 10.5).

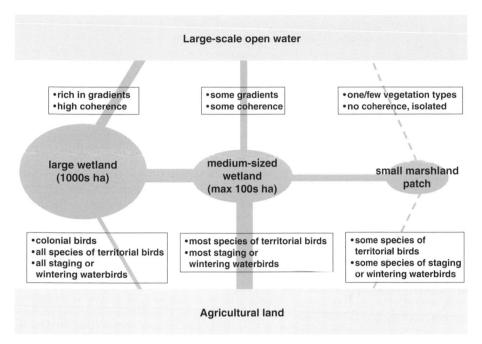

Figure 10.5 The hypothetical relationship between size and coherence of a wetland area and species richness in wetland birds. Coherence is described as the distance between different habitats that may have different ecological functions for species. Large wetlands can support birds that do not depend on agricultural land. Redrawn from Platteeuw *et al.* (2010).

Careful, targeted management will be required to retain specialist reed-swamp and fen species in western Europe. The UK programme of reed and fen creation is welcome and ambitious, but unlikely to be of sufficient scale to allow natural processes to hold sway. Figure 10.6 summarises some of the reedswamp and fen management practices advocated. In the distant past, wetlands would have been subject to natural processes and habitats would have developed in response to these. In natural floodplains, reedswamp and fen, in particular, would be dynamic habitats, colonising new areas and in turn being removed by natural flood events, or progressing to woodland. In cultural landscapes, many of the remaining wetlands are man-made and highly managed, sometimes in an attempt to mimic natural processes, but often simply to hold back or reverse vegetation succession. It is possible on larger sites to manage for a range of successional stages, but this is difficult to achieve on smaller sites. The heterogeneity of habitats that once would have been available nationally, or even within individual large natural wetlands, is probably impossible to recreate artificially on a small scale. Today in western Europe there tend to be disproportionate amounts of relatively dry, highly managed early successional habitat and late successional scrub and

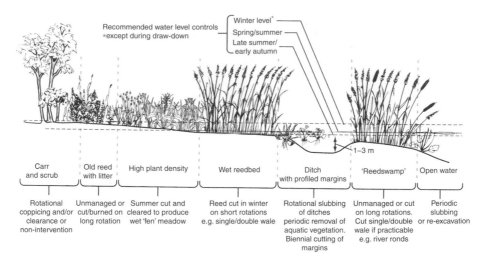

Figure 10.6 The main techniques that may be used to manage succession for a range of reedbed habitats. From Hawke and Jose (1996).

woodland. By contrast, early successional reedbed in standing water, an especially important habitat for specialist marsh birds, declined substantially during the last century, at least in the Netherlands (van Turnhout *et al.*, 2010).

Reedbed management in several parts of Europe has received particular attention in recent decades with the focus on creating high-quality bittern habitat. In the 1980s and 1990s many remnants of British reedswamp had been left unmanaged, to the detriment of the early successional reedswamp species (Bibby and Lunn, 1982; Tyler *et al.*, 1998). Several of the sites on which bittern persisted had been commercially cut, which recreated the early successional habitat favoured by the species. Reedswamp management for bitterns usually aims to keep much of the reed at an early successional stage (Burgess *et al.*, 1995; Hawke and Jose, 1996). Equally as important, however, is the surrounding standing water that has to be suitable for a healthy fish population (White *et al.*, 2006). Water regime and water quality can usually be altered and vegetation can be removed to prevent litter accumulation in the reedbed, by cutting, burning or grazing. An understanding of water balance from inputs and losses may be crucial to achieving the correct timing of lowering or raising water levels for reedswamp management (Fig. 10.7). With the aid of EU–Life funding, large-scale wetland restoration and creation has taken place, specifically aimed at bitterns, to create a strategic network of reedbeds across England. This landscape approach to ecological restoration and creation of wetlands has been adopted within national strategies in England (Hume, 2007), the Netherlands (Swart *et al.*, 2001) and elsewhere (Moser, 2001). There has also been Europe-wide collaboration on providing such reedbed management advice (White *et al.*, 2006).

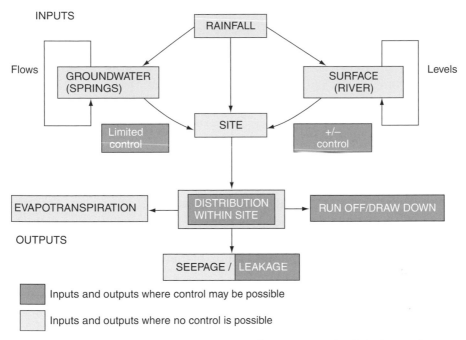

Figure 10.7 Supply, distribution and control of water on reedbeds (redrawn from White *et al.*, 2006)

Whilst it is essential to manage reedswamp to maintain wet *Phragmites* areas for specialists such as bittern, in general the abundance of birds is low during the first years after reed harvesting and burning (Vadász *et al.*, 2008; Valkama *et al.*, 2008) and the risk of predation is increased for some nesting passerines (Graveland, 1999). Food limitation through management practices might reduce the abundance of some bird species. A meta-analysis found that numbers of butterflies, beetles and some spiders, which are important prey groups for some passerines, could be substantially reduced in managed compared to unmanaged sites, but the duration of management was important, with short 1–2 year management periods within longer rotations having no effect on invertebrates (Valkama *et al.*, 2008). Long rotations, with reed cut every third year or more, are uncommon in commercially cut beds, and are more common on nature reserves (Fig. 10.2b).

The aims of management in fen habitats are usually quite different from reedswamp. In Europe, fen habitats are frequently managed to maintain floristic diversity, most commonly by mowing or extensive grazing during the summer (Middleton *et al.*, 2006). Unlike reedbeds, the emphasis is rarely on birds. Unmanaged fens tend to develop dominance by tall sedges (Bullock *et al.*, 2001) shifting to trees and shrubs which shade out the smaller and rarer species.

A balance can usually be found between managing for one specialist species and the needs of other species, but it is likely that we do not always get this right; there may be a case for reduced management of some areas. We have seen that the basal structure and coverage of vegetation is important to a number of bird species associated with these wetlands. Dead vegetation from previous years and species other than *Phragmites*, such as tussocky *Juncus*, may contribute much to these structures. Active management for dead vegetation and *Juncus* is rare. Understanding when not to interfere is probably as important as knowing when to manage.

Concluding thoughts on future research needs

Much work has focused on understanding the habitat needs of a relatively small number of specialist wetland birds. Whilst there is still much to be learnt about the preferred habitat structures of these and other wetland birds, there are some under-researched wider aspects of wetlands that are likely to be crucial in improving the conservation management of these habitats in the longer term:

(1) What is the optimal design and management approach of habitat networks for individual bird species, particularly when these species rely on dynamic, successional or even transient habitats? Dispersal behaviour in most wetland birds is poorly understood and would benefit from more attention. Factors affecting population persistence in relation to site size and spatial relationship with other sites is highly relevant (Verboom *et al.*, 2001; Vermaat *et al.*, 2008).

(2) Eutrophication, particularly in conjunction with an unnaturally rigid water table regime, has a profound effect on wetland ecosystems, yet the exact consequences for the food resources, preferred habitat structures and breeding productivity of most birds are poorly known and we do not know if these processes are reversible.

(3) The use of certain wetland habitats by birds has been poorly researched, particularly seasonally flooded grassy rush pastures, which can provide significant nesting and feeding habitat for a variety of bird species.

(4) The importance of wetlands as feeding habitats for migrating birds, especially the use of wetland scrub, has received surprisingly little attention in Europe. Similarly the extent to which species breeding in adjacent habitats utilise wetlands as feeding habitat has hardly been explored. In intensively managed landscapes, and especially if climate change widely reduces water tables, permanent wetlands may become increasingly important focal habitats for many species.

(5) In Britain there is awareness of the need to relocate reedbeds inland and towards the north west, in anticipation of increased storminess and

increasing sea levels along the south east coast and the general reduction in water tables in the south east. A European- or Palearctic-scale review of this is warranted and a realistic strategy to highlight any changing emphasis on the sustainable long-term location of such wetlands.

Acknowledgements

Many thanks to the editor Rob Fuller and the reviewers, Andy Brown and Ruud Foppen for many helpful additions and suggestions.

References

Adamo, M.C. (2002). *Il tarabuso ed il suo habitat: riflessi sul comportamento spaziale e riproduttivo.* PhD thesis, University of Pisa.

Adamo, M.C., Puglisi, L. and Baldaccini, N.E. (2004). Factors affecting Bittern *Botaurus stellaris* distribution in a Mediterranean wetland. *Bird Conserv. Int.*, **14**, 153–164.

Aebischer, A., Perrin, N., Krieg, M., Studer, J. and Myer, D.R. (1996). The role of territory choice, mate choice and arrival date on breeding success in the Savi's Warbler *Locustella luscinioides*. *J. Avian Biol.*, **27**,143–152.

Alessandria, G., Carpegna, F. and Toffola, M.D. (2003). Vocalizations and courtship displays of the Bittern *Botaurus stellaris*. *Bird Study*, **50**, 182–184.

Altenburg, W., Daan, S., Starkenburg, J. and Zijlstra, M. (1982). Polygamy in the Marsh harrier, *Circus aeruginosus*: individual variation in hunting performance and number of mates. *Behaviour*, **79**, 272–312.

Báldi, A. (2006). Factors influencing occurrence of passerines in the reed archipelago of Lake Velence (Hungary). *Acta Ornithol.*, **41**, 1–6.

Báldi, A. and Kisbenedek, T. (1998). Factors influencing the occurrence of Great White Egret (*Egretta alba*), Mallard (*Anas platyrhynchos*), Marsh Harrier (*Circus aeruginosus*) and Coot (*Fulica atra*) in the reed archipelago of Lake Velence, Hungary. *Ekol. Bratislava*, **17**, 384–390.

Báldi, A. and Kisbenedek, T. (1999). Species-specific distribution of reed-nesting passerine birds across reed-bed edges: effects of spatial scale and edge type. *Acta Zool. Hung.*, **45**, 97–114.

Bekhuis, J. (1990). How long will Little Bitterns breed in The Netherlands? *Limosa*, **63**, 47–50.

Bengtson, S.-A. (1962). The occurrence and breeding biology of the Spotted Crake *Porzana porzana* in northeastern Scania. *Vår Fågelvärld*, **21**, 253–266.

Bibby, C.J. and Green, R.E. (1981). Autumn migration strategies of Reed and Sedge Warblers. *Ornis Scand.*, **12**, 1–12.

Bibby, C.J. and Green, R.E. (1983). Food and fattening of migrating warblers in some French marshlands. *Ring. Migr.*, **4**, 175–184.

Bibby, C.J. and Lunn, J. (1982). Conservation of reed beds and their avifauna in England and Wales. *Biol. Conserv.*, **23**, 167–186.

Brix, H. (1999). The European research project on reed die-back and progression (EUREED). *Limnologia*, **29**, 5–10.

Bullock, J.M., Franklin, J., Stevenson, M.J. *et al.* (2001). A plant trait analysis of responses to grazing in a long-term experiment. *J. Appl. Ecol.*, **38**, 253–267.

Burgess, N., Ward, D., Hobbs, R. and Bellamy, D. (1995). Reedbeds, fens and acid bogs. In *Managing Habitats for Conservation*, ed. W.J. Sutherland and D.A. Hill, pp. 149–197. Cambridge: Cambridge University Press.

Catchpole, C.K. (1974). Habitat selection and breeding success in the reed warbler (*Acrocephalus scirpaceus*). *J. Anim. Ecol.*, **43**, 363–380.

Chernetsov, N. (1998). Post-breeding and post-fledging movements in the reed warbler

(*Acrocephalus scirpaceus*) and sedge warbler (*A. schoenobaenus*) depend on food abundance. *Ornis Svecica*, **8**, 77–82.

Chernetsov, N. and Manukyan, A. (2000). Foraging strategy of the Sedge Warbler (*Acrocephalus schoenobaenus*) on migration. *Vogelwarte*, **40**, 189–197.

Chisholm, K. (2007). History of the Wood Sandpiper as a breeding bird in Britain. *Brit. Birds*, **100**, 112–121.

Clarke, R. (1995). *The Marsh Harrier*. London: Hamlyn.

Cramp, S. (ed.) (1992). *The Birds of the Western Palearctic Volumes V and VI*. Oxford: Oxford University Press.

Cramp, S. and Perrins, C. M. (ed.) (1993). *The Birds of the Western Palearctic Volume VII*. Oxford: Oxford University Press.

Dijkstra, C. and Zijlstra, M. (1997). Reproduction of the Marsh Harrier *Circus aeruginosus* in recent land reclamations in the Netherlands. *Ardea*, **85**, 37–50.

Fasola, M., Hafner, H., Prosper, J., van der Kooij, H. and Schogolev, I. (2000). Population changes in European herons in relation to African climate. *Ostrich*, **71**, 52–55.

Foppen, R. (2001). *Bridging Gaps in Fragmented Marshland*. Alterra Scientific Contributions 4. Wageningen: Alterra.

Foppen, R., Ter Braak, C. J. F., Verboom, J. and Reijnen, R. (1999). Dutch Sedge Warblers *Acrocephalus schoenobaenus* and West-African rainfall: empirical data and simulation modelling show low population resilience in fragmented marshlands. *Ardea*, **87**, 113–127.

Foppen, R. P. B., Chardon, J. P. and Liefveld, W. (2000). Understanding the role of sink patches in source-sink metapopulations: reed warbler in an agricultural landscape. *Conserv. Biol.*, **14**, 1881–1892.

Fuller, R. J. (1982). *Bird Habitats in Britain*. Calton: Poyser.

Fuller, R. J., Reed, T. M., Buxton, N. E. *et al.* (1986). Populations of breeding waders (Charadrii) and their habitats on the crofting lands of the Outer Hebrides. *Biol. Conserv.*, **37**, 333–361.

Gilbert, G. (2002). The status and habitat of Spotted Crake *Porzana porzana* in Britain in 1999. *Bird Study*, **49**, 79–86.

Gilbert, G., Painter, M. and Smith, K. W. (1996). An inventory of British reedbeds in 1993. *RSPB Conserv. Rev.*, **10**, 39–45.

Gilbert, G., Tyler, G. A., Dunn, C. J., Ratcliffe, N. and Smith, K. W. (2007). The influence of habitat management on the breeding success of the Great Bittern *Botaurus stellaris* in Britain. *Ibis*, **149**, 53–66.

Gilbert, G., Tyler, G. A., Dunn, C. J. and Smith, K. W. (2005a). Nesting habitat selection by Bitterns in Britain and the implications for wetland management. *Biol. Conserv.*, **124**, 547–553.

Gilbert, G., Tyler, G. A. and Smith, K. W. (2003). Nestling diet and fish preference of Bitterns *Botaurus stellaris* in Britain. *Ardea*, **91**, 35–44.

Gilbert, G., Tyler, G. and Smith, K. W. (2005b). Behaviour, home-range size and habitat use by male Great Bittern *Botaurus stellaris* in Britain. *Ibis*, **147**, 533–543.

Glutz von Blotzheim, U. N., Bauer, K. M. and Bezzel, E. (1973, 1977). *Handbuch der Vögel Mitteleuropas Volumes 5 and 7*. Frankfurt am Main and Wiesbaden: Akademische Verlagsgesellschaft.

Graveland, J. (1998). Reed die back, water level management and the decline of the Great Reed Warbler in The Netherlands. *Ardea*, **86**, 187–201.

Graveland, J. (1999). Effects of reed cutting on density and breeding success of Reed Warbler *Acrocephalus scirpaceus* and Sedge Warbler *A. schoenobaenus*. *J. Avian Biol.*, **30**, 469–482.

Hawke, C. J. and Jose, P. V. (1996). *Reedbed Management for Commercial and Wildlife Interests*. Sandy: RSPB.

Hoi, H. (2001). The ecology of reed birds. *Biosyst. Ecol. Ser.*, **18**, 151–160.

Hoi, H. and Hoi-Leitner, M. (1997). An alternative route to coloniality in the Bearded Tit: Females pursue extra-pair fertilizations. *Behav. Ecol.*, **8**, 113–119.

Hume, C. (2007). *Wetland Vision Technical Document: Overview and Reporting of Project Philosophy and Technical Approach*. Sandy: England Wetland Vision Partnership.

Kalejta-Summers, B. (2006). Habitat preferences of Wood Sandpipers in Scotland. *Wader Study Group Bull.*, **111**, 15–16.

Kaminski, R. M. and Prince, H. H. (1981). Dabbling duck and aquatic macroinvertebrate responses to manipulated wetland habitat. *J. Wildlife Manage.*, **45**, 1–15.

Kirchner, H. (1978). *Bruchwasserlaeufer und Waldwasserlaeufer* Tringa glareola *und* Tringa ochropus. Wittenberg Lutherstadt: A. Ziemsen Verlag.

Kushlan, J. A. and Hafner, H. (2000). *Heron Conservation*. London: Academic Press.

Leisler, B., Ley, H. W. and Winkler, H. (1989). Habitat, behaviour and morphology of *Acrocephalus* warblers: an integrated analysis. *Ornis Scand.*, **20**, 181–186.

Leito, A., Truu, J., Roosaluste, E., Sepp, K. and Poder, I. (2006). Long-term dynamics of breeding birds in broad-leaved deciduous forest on Hanikatsi Island in the West-Estonian archipelago. *Ornis Fennica*, **83**, 124–130.

Linz, G. M., Blixt, D. C., Bergman, D. L. and Bleier, W. J. (1996a). Response of ducks to glyphosate-induced habitat alterations in wetlands. *Wetlands*, **16**, 38–44.

Linz, G. M., Blixt, D. C., Bergman, D. L. and Bleier, W. J. (1996b). Responses of red-winged blackbirds, yellow-headed blackbirds and marsh wrens to glyphosate-induced alterations in cattail density. *J. Field Ornithol.*, **67**, 167–176.

Longoni, V., Rubolini, D. and Bogliani G. (2007). Delayed reproduction amongst great bitterns *Botaurus stellaris* breeding in rice fields. *Bird Study*, **54**, 254–258.

Mackenzie, J. (2000). Habitat preferences of breeding Spotted Crakes *Porzana porzana,* and the implications for site selection. University of East Anglia, Dissertation.

Mallord, J. (1999). Habitat preferences and population monitoring of Spotted Crakes *Porzana porzana*. University of East Anglia, Dissertation.

McKee, J. and Richards, A. J. (1996). Variation in seed production and germinability in common reed (*Phragmites australis*) in Britain and France with respect to climate. *New Phytol.*, **133**, 233–243.

Middleton, B. A., Holsten, B. and van Diggelen, R. (2006). Biodiversity management of fens and fen meadows by grazing, cutting and burning. *Appl. Veg. Sci.*, **9**, 307–316.

Moll, K. H. (1963). Kranichbeobachtungen aus dem Miirutzgebiet. *Beitr.Vogel.*, **8**, 221–253.

Moser, M. (2001). Wetland status and trends in Europe. The case for rehabilitation and restoration of naturally functioning wetlands. In *The Role of Wetlands in River Basin Management*. Copenhagen: WWF.

Naugle, D. E., Johnson, R. R., Estey, M. E. and Higgins, K. F. (2001). A landscape approach to conserving wetland bird habitat in the prairie pothole region of Eastern South Dakota. *Wetlands*, **21**, 1–17.

Nemeckova, I., Mrlik, V. and Drozd, P. (2008). Timing of breeding habitat preference and reproductive success of Marsh Harriers *Circus aeruginosus*. *Biologia*, **63**, 261–265.

Nethersole-Thompson, D. and Nethersole-Thompson, M. (1986). *Waders – Their Breeding, Haunts and Watchers*. Calton: Poyser.

Neto, J. M. (2006). Nest-site selection and predation in Savi's warblers *Locustella luscinioides*. *Bird Study*, **53**, 171–176.

Ostendorp, W. (1989). 'Die-back' of reeds in Europe – a critical review of literature. *Aquat. Bot.*, **35**, 5–26.

Paracuellos, M. (2006). Relationships of songbird occupation with habitat configuration and bird abundance in patchy reed beds. *Ardea*, **94**, 87–98.

Paracuellos, M. and Tellería, J. L. (2004). Factors affecting the distribution of a waterbird community: the role of habitat configuration and bird abundance. *Waterbirds*, **27**, 446–453.

Pasinelli, G., Mayer, C., Gouskov, A. and Schiegg, K. (2008). Small and large wetland fragments are equally suited breeding sites for a ground nesting passerine. *Oecologia*, **156**, 703–714.

Peiro, I. G., Robledano, F. and Esteve, M. A. (2006). The effect of age and sex on wing morphology and body size of the bearded tit *Panurus biarmicus* in relation to complete moult. *Ring. Migr.*, **23**, 101–106.

Piersma, T., van Gils, J. and Wiersma, P. (1996). Family Scolopacidae (snipes, sandpipers and phalaropes). In *Handbook of the Birds of the World Volume 3*, ed. J. del Hoyo, A. Elliott and J. Sargatal, pp. 444–533. Barcelona: Lynx Edicions.

Platteeuw, M., Foppen, R. P. B. and van Eerden, M. R. (2010). The need for future wetland bird studies: scales of habitat use as input for ecological restoration and spatial water management. *Ardea*, **98**, 403–416.

Polak, M. (2007). Nest-site selection and nest predation in the Great Bittern *Botaurus stellaris* population in eastern Poland. *Ardea*, **95**, 31–38.

Polak, M., Kasprzykowski, Z. and Kucharczyk, M. (2008). Micro-habitat nest preferences of the great bittern *Botaurus stellaris* on fish ponds in central Eastern Europe. *Ann. Zool. Fenn.*, **45**, 102–108.

Poulin, B., Lefebvre, G. and Crivelli, A. J. (2007). The invasive Louisiana red-swamp crayfish as a predictor of Eurasian bittern density in the Camargue, France. *J. Zool.*, **273**, 98–107.

Poulin, B., Lefebvre, G. and Mathevet, R. (2005). Habitat selection by booming Bitterns *Botaurus stellaris* in French Mediterranean reed-beds. *Oryx*, **39**, 265–274.

Poulin, B., Lefebvre, G. and Mauchamp, A. (2002). Habitat requirements of passerines and reedbed management in southern France. *Biol. Conserv.*, **107**, 315–325.

Puglisi, L., Adamo, M. C. and Baldaccini, N. E. (2005). Man induced habitat changes and sensitive species: a GIS approach to the Eurasian Bittern (*Botaurus stellaris*) in a Mediterranean wetland. *Biodivers. Conserv.*, **14**, 1909–1922.

Puglisi, L. and Bretagnolle, V. (2005). The breeding biology of the Great Bittern. *Waterbirds*, **28**, 392–398.

Pujante, M. R., Hoi, H. and Blomquist, D. (2005). The importance of tail length for habitat use in the bearded tit *Panurus biarmicus*: an experimental study. *Ibis*, **147**, 464–470.

Rafe, R. W., Usher, M. B. and Jefferson, R. G. (1985). Birds on reserves: the influence of area and habitat on species richness. *J. Appl. Ecol.*, **22**, 327–335.

Rodwell, J. S. (1995). *British Plant Communities. Vol. 4: Aquatic Communities, Swamps and Tall-herb Fens*. Cambridge: Cambridge University Press.

Schäffer, N. (1999). Habitat use and mating systems of the Corncrake and Spotted Crake. *Ökol. Vögel*, **21**, 1–267.

Stanevicius, V. (2004). Nest site selection by Marsh Harrier (*Circus aeruginosus*) in the shore belt of helophytes on large lakes. *Acta Zool. Lituanica*, **14**, 47–53.

Surmacki, A. and Stepniewski, J. (2003). A survey of the Bearded Tit *Panurus biarmicus* during the non-breeding season in a landscape of western Poland. *Acta Ornithol.*, **38**, 53–58.

Swart, J. A. A., van der Windt, H. J. and Keulartz, J. (2001). Valuation in nature of restoration and conservation. *Restor. Ecol.*, **9**, 230–238.

Takácsová, M. (2007). On habitat selection of the Marsh Harrier (*Circus aeruginosus*) in the agricultural region (SW Slovakia, the Danubian lowland). *Acta Zool. Univ. Comenianae*, **47**, 57–63.

Trnka, A. and Prokop, P. (2006). Reedbed structure and habitat preference of reed passerines during the post-breeding period. *Biologia*, **61**, 225–230.

Turner, A. (2006). *The Barn Swallow*. London: Poyser.

Tyler, G. A., Smith, K. W. and Burgess, D. J. (1998). Reedbed management and breeding Bitterns *Botaurus stellaris* in the UK. *Biol. Conserv.*, **86**, 257–266.

Vadász, C., Német, Á., Biró, C. and Csörgő, T. (2008). The effect of reed cutting on the abundance and diversity of breeding passerines. *Acta Zool. Hung.*, **54**, 177–188.

Vâlcu, M. (2006). Seasonal changes in bird species diversity at the interface between forest and reed-bed. *Biodivers. Conserv.*, **15**, 3459–3467.

Valkama, E., Lyytinen, S. and Koricheva, J. (2008). The impact of reed management on wildlife: A meta-analytical review of European studies. *Biol. Conserv.*, **141**, 364–374.

Van der Hut, R. M. (1986). Habitat choice and temporal differentiation in reed passerines of a Dutch marsh. *Ardea*, **74**, 159–176.

van Turnhout, C. A. M., Hagemeijer, E. J. M. and Foppen, R. P. B. (2010). Long-term population developments in typical marshland birds in The Netherlands. *Ardea*, **98**, 283–299.

Venterink, H. O., Wassen, M. J., Verkroost, A. W. M. and De Ruiter, P. C. (2003). Species richness-productivity patterns differ between N-, P- and K- limited wetlands. *Ecology*, **84**, 2191–2199.

Verboom, J., Foppen, R. P. B., Chardon, P., Opdam, P. and Luttikhuizen, P. (2001). Introducing the key patch approach for habitat networks with persistent populations: an example for marshland birds. *Biol. Conserv.*, **100**, 103–113.

Vermaat, J. E., Vigneau, N. and Omtzigt, N. (2008). Viability of meta-populations of wetland birds in a fragmented landscape: testing the key-patch approach. *Biodivers. Conserv.*, **17**, 2263–2273.

Viksne, J., Mednis, A., Janaus, M. and Stipniece, A. (2005). Changes in the breeding bird fauna, waterbird populations in particular, on Lake Engure (Latvia) over the last 50 years. *Acta Zool. Lituanica*, **15**, 188–194.

Wawrzyniak, H. and Sohns, G. (1986). *Die Bartmeise*. Wittenberg Lutherstadt: A. Ziemsen Verlag.

White, G., Purps, J. and Alsbury, S. (2006). *The Bittern in Europe: A Guide to Species and Habitat Management*. Sandy: RSPB.

White, G. J. and Gilbert, J. C. (2003). *Habitat Creation Handbook for the Minerals Industry*. Sandy: RSPB.

Wilson, J. and Peach, W. (2006). Impact of an exceptional winter flood on the population dynamics of bearded tits (*Panurus biarmicus*). *Anim. Conserv.*, **9**, 463–473.

Wotton, S., Lewis, B., Pledger, E. *et al.* (2009). *Bittern* Botaurus stellaris *Monitoring in the UK: Summary of the 2009 Season*. Sandy: RSPB.

Zedler, J. B. and Kercher, S. (2004). Causes and consequences of invasive plants in wetlands: opportunities, opportunists, and outcomes. *Crit. Rev. Plant Sci.*, **23**, 431–452.

CHAPTER ELEVEN

Breeding waders on wet grassland: factors influencing habitat suitability

MALCOLM AUSDEN

Royal Society for the Protection of Birds

and

MARK BOLTON

Royal Society for the Protection of Birds

In this chapter, we describe habitat requirements of breeding waders (also known as meadow birds) on lowland grasslands in western and north western Europe. Eight wader species breed on lowland wet grassland in this region: oystercatcher *Haematopus ostralegus*, lapwing *Vanellus vanellus*, dunlin *Calidris alpina*, ruff *Philomachus pugnax*, snipe *Gallinago gallinago*, black-tailed godwit *Limosa l. limosa*, curlew *Numenius arquata* and redshank *Tringa totanus*. Populations of most of these species have declined on lowland wet grassland in recent decades (Stanbury *et al.*, 2000; Henderson *et al.*, 2002; BirdLife International, 2004; Thorup, 2004; Wilson *et al.*, 2005). The habitat requirements of several of these species have been well studied, mainly with the aim of diagnosing causes of their population declines and testing solutions for improving habitat quality. We describe the results of this research, and how they have been used to inform land management. In contrast, the habitat requirements of most other bird species on lowland wet grassland have received little attention, with the exception of those of wildfowl. For a general account of the wider breeding and wintering bird assemblages of wet grassland see Fuller (1982).

Two aspects of habitat quality are particularly significant to breeding waders. The first is the importance of agricultural management in affecting habitat suitability. The second is that breeding productivity can be strongly influenced by land management carried out after birds have settled to nest. Hence, there is the potential for birds to settle in areas that are initially of high quality, but which turn out to be of low quality because of subsequent management decisions, i.e. an ecological trap (Chapter 1).

Habitat definition

We define lowland wet grassland as low-lying grassland, periodically inundated with fresh or slightly brackish water, or that otherwise has a high water

Birds and Habitat: Relationships in Changing Landscapes, ed. Robert J. Fuller. Published by Cambridge University Press. © Cambridge University Press 2012.

table. Lowland wet grasslands are created and maintained through human land use and are commonly referred to as grazing marsh or wet meadow (examples are illustrated in Fig. 11.1). Grazing marsh refers to grassland grazed by livestock. In Britain, wet meadow refers to grassland that is mown to provide food for livestock in winter, but this term is also commonly used to describe both grazed and mown wet grasslands in the Netherlands. There are a number of distinct types of lowland wet grasslands in western and north

Figure 11.1 Example wet grassland habitats. (a) Agriculturally unimproved wet meadows containing ridge and furrow at Skrins, in the Netherlands. Dutch wet meadows support the majority of breeding *limosa* race black-tailed godwits in Europe. Photo: Graham Hirons. (b) Coastal grazing marsh at Holkham National Nature Reserve, England, containing relict, water-filled saltmarsh creeks. Such marshes, if managed appropriately, can support high densities of breeding lapwings and redshank. Photo: Malcolm Ausden. (c) Berney Marshes RSPB Reserve, England, where footdrains (just visible as narrow dark lines) have been excavated and water levels raised, to benefit feeding lapwings and redshank, and a range of other breeding and wintering waterbirds. This photograph shows the maximum extent of winter flooding. Photo: Mike Page. (d) The Ouse Washes (the extensively flooded area) is one of only two regularly flooded washlands in the UK. Washlands were created to store flood water, but the increase in frequency of late spring flooding at the Ouse Washes means that it is now often too flooded for waders to nest on. Replacement wet grassland is therefore being created outside of the Washes. A trial area, containing pools and shallow ditches, can be seen to the right of the Washes. Photo: Martin Aris.

western Europe, defined by their location and management: (i) river flood-plain grasslands; (ii) lakeshore grasslands; (iii) coastal grazing marshes, usually derived historically from saltmarsh; (iv) coastal pastures and meadows, e. g. Baltic shore meadows and Scottish machair grassland; (v) polders (land claimed from the sea), especially in the Netherlands; (vi) washlands; (vii) water meadows.

Washlands and water meadows are two ingenious systems of management that involve artificial flooding. On water meadows calcareous spring, or river, water is flowed over the grass in early spring via an elaborate network of channels, to deposit nutrients and encourage early grass growth. As a water management system, water meadows are now largely defunct. Washlands were constructed to provide flood storage and aid land drainage. They consist of a flat, embanked area lying between a river and artificial relief channel, or between two artificial relief channels, into which water is diverted and stored during periods of high river flow. Most washlands no longer regularly flood, but where they do flood, and water tables are high in spring and summer, mixtures of wet grassland, shallow water and swamp occur. Wet grassland can be regarded as one end of a continuum of wetland habitats that grade towards the managed fens and reedswamp considered in Chapter 10.

Lowland wet grasslands usually comprise relatively flat areas interspersed with water-filled ditches (dykes), excavated to provide drainage and barriers for livestock. Unlevelled coastal grazing marsh has a different topography, containing relict saltmarsh channels, which accumulate water when drainage is impeded. In the cooler and wetter north and west of the British Isles, wet grasslands also occur at higher altitude and on slopes. These upland grasslands, and lowland farmland in the same regions, support a similar assemblage of breeding wader species to that found on lowland wet grasslands, but lack breeding godwits and ruff.

Densities of breeding waders on different types of wet grassland in Britain are shown in Table 11.1. Densities vary greatly, with those on nature reserves managed to benefit breeding waders being far higher than on other types of grassland. Although not specifically dealt with in this chapter, exceptionally high densities, including dunlin which are absent from most types of wet grassland, occur on the complex machair habitats of the Outer Hebrides (Fuller *et al.*, 1986).

Agricultural and conservation management

Before considering habitat use by breeding waders, it is useful to describe how lowland wet grasslands are managed for agriculture and for conservation, since this management profoundly affects habitat quality. There are three approaches: high-input agricultural management, low-input agricultural management and conservation management. The aims of high-input, and

Table 11.1 *Densities of breeding waders on lowland wet grassland in Britain*

Habitat	Area surveyed	Year(s)	Oystercatcher	Lapwing	Snipe	Black-tailed Godwit	Curlew	Redshank
A. Lowland wet grassland in England and Wales[a]								
	1508.5 km²	2002	0.6	3.6	0.4	0.05	0.3	1.6
B. Lowland wet grassland in southern England with different protection and management[b]								
Unprotected land[c]	216.2 km²	2002	–	1.2	0.05	–	–	0.4
Entered into agri-environment schemes	168.9 km²	2002	–	4.6	0.3	–	–	2.9
Designated for its conservation interest[d]	63.7 km²	2002	–	2.5	0.2	–	–	1.9
Nature reserves	46.9 km²	2002	–	11.6	2.0	–	–	9.1
C. Lowland wet grassland nature reserves managed to benefit breeding waders[e]								
Peat washland[f]	One site, area 2.8 km²	Mean 2005–09	0.2	58.1	47.3	15.4	0.0	48.1
Coastal grazing marsh	13 sites, total area 29.0 km²	Mean 2005–09	5.6	26.6	3.1	0.1	1.0	20.6
Floodplain grassland	8 sites, total area 18.1 km²	Mean 2005–09	0.7	10.0	4.0	0.0	1.6	5.3

[a] All main areas of lowland wet grassland in England and Wales, including nature reserve and non-nature reserve land. From Wilson *et al.* (2005).
[b] From Wilson *et al.* (2007).
[c] Not entered into agri-environment schemes, nor designated for its conservation interest, nor managed as nature reserves.
[d] Sites of Special Scientific Interest.
[e] RSPB nature reserves throughout the UK.
[f] Low Wash, Nene Washes RSPB Reserve, Cambridgeshire, England.

low-input, agricultural management are to provide summer grazing for live-stock, and silage (high-input) or hay (low-input) to feed livestock in winter. In low-input agricultural management, nutrients removed in hay and lost though grazing are replaced by adding small quantities of farmyard manure. Flooded grasslands also receive inputs of nutrient-rich sediment. Drainage tends to be relatively ineffective on low-input grasslands, and consequently water levels are usually high.

On low-input grasslands, the combination of high water levels and rela-tively low nutrient levels produces a sward that is fairly unproductive, and often botanically species-rich. The high water levels provide suitable feeding conditions for waders. The low productivity of the sward means that it can only support low densities of livestock, and consequently there is only a low risk of livestock trampling waders' nests. The slow rate of vegetation growth also means that the sward is only ready to be mown after the majority of wader chicks have fledged. Hence, mowing destroys very few wader nests and kills few chicks. This low-input management thus provides good conditions for waders to rear young.

Conversion of low-input grassland to high-input grassland involves a range of measures aimed at increasing grass growth: application of inorganic fertil-iser, improvement of drainage and, on acid soils, addition of lime to neutralise soil pH. Such 'agricultural improvement' can also involve re-seeding with more agriculturally productive grasses (Williams and Bowers, 1987; Beintema *et al.*, 1997). The combination of lower water levels, more rapid grass growth, and an often denser and more structurally uniform sward, greatly reduces habitat quality for breeding waders (Fig. 11.2).

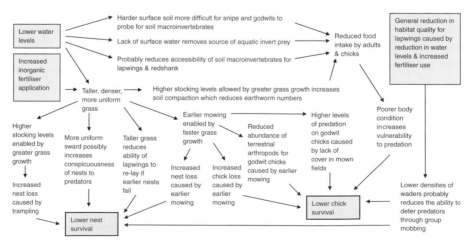

Figure 11.2 Mechanisms by which agricultural improvement is thought to affect habitat quality for breeding waders on lowland wet grassland.

The aim of conservation management on nature reserves is to maximise conservation benefits. On low-input grasslands, the approach usually involves continuing the low-input management which created and maintained the grassland, but often with slight modifications aimed at benefiting particular species, or groups of species – most commonly breeding waders, wintering wildfowl, the flora of botanically rich meadows, the ditch flora and invertebrate fauna, and water voles *Arvicola terrestris* (Ausden, 2007).

On former high-input grasslands now managed within nature reserves, several measures can be introduced to benefit waders which are described in the following sections. On non-nature-reserve land, the aim of conservation management is usually to provide more modest benefits to birds and other wildlife, using measures which can be integrated within more conventional agricultural practice. Conservation management of lowland wet grasslands is encouraged by agri-environment schemes. These provide payments to landowners to compensate for financial losses incurred through adoption of conservation measures.

Habitat selection by breeding waders

A large number of studies have investigated associations between occupancy of fields by breeding waders and measures of habitat condition. These studies have generally found that breeding waders are associated with wetter fields, avoid hedgerows, roads and power lines, and that wader species differ in their preferences for vegetation height and measures of vegetation heterogeneity (Herbert *et al.*, 1990; Green and Robins, 1993; Vickery *et al.*, 1997; Milsom *et al.*, 2000 and 2002; Kleijn and van Zuijlen, 2004; Wilson *et al.*, 2005; Smart *et al.*, 2006; Durant *et al.*, 2008a). It is also widely thought that breeding waders prefer areas grazed by cattle, rather than sheep or equines, because cattle produce a more tussocky sward, which waders prefer for feeding and nesting (Durant *et al.*, 2008b). This has not been investigated in detail, though.

The mechanisms by which habitat conditions influence habitat quality for breeding waders are discussed in the following sections, together with approaches used to improve habitat quality, which generally focus on breeding productivity. Declines on lowland wet grassland are thought to have been driven mainly by low breeding productivity, rather than by a decline in adult survival (Peach *et al.*, 1994; Schekkerman and Müskens, 2000; Ratcliffe *et al.*, 2005; Gill *et al.*, 2007; Schekkerman *et al.*, 2008).

High levels of breeding site tenacity and natal philopatry can result in birds continuing to use suboptimal habitat. Lapwings, godwits, redshank and curlews all show high site fidelity (Thompson and Hale, 1989; Groen, 1993; Berg, 1994; Berg *et al.*, 2002). In Britain, godwits continue to return to the Ouse Washes, despite insufficient productivity to maintain a stable population

(Ratcliffe *et al.*, 2005), yet over the same period have failed to colonise many apparently suitable areas of breeding habitat.

Habitat quality and feeding conditions

All lowland wet grassland waders feed entirely on invertebrates during the breeding season. They obtain these from the soil, vegetation, shallow water and mud. Chicks of lapwings, redshank, godwits and curlews all feed themselves. Chicks of oystercatchers, snipe and ruff are initially fed by their parents (Cramp, 1983). Feeding conditions for waders are influenced by the abundance and accessibility of prey, both of which are particularly affected by water levels. Verhulst *et al.* (2007) found that 82% of the variation in total numbers of breeding waders between paired plots with and without agri-environment scheme measures, was explained by variation in biomass of soil macroinvertebrates (earthworms and tipulid larvae) and water table height. In the following sections, we describe how habitat attributes affect feeding conditions for snipe, godwits, lapwings and redshank. The feeding habits of the other wet grassland waders have been less well studied.

Snipe and adult black-tailed godwits
The principal factors affecting habitat quality for snipe and, almost certainly, adult godwits are: (i) whether the upper soil is soft enough for them to probe for prey; (ii) the biomass of soil macroinvertebrates close to the surface and (iii) the height/structure of the vegetation.

Breeding snipe prefer taller swards than godwits and other grassland wader species, apart from curlew (Durant *et al.*, 2008b). Snipe consequently tend to favour uncut meadows to grazed pasture (Herbert *et al.*, 1990), although swards grazed during the breeding season by low densities of cattle are also suitable.

Snipe and adult godwits feed mainly on soil macroinvertebrates which they obtain by probing into the top 10 cm or so of soft soil. Adult godwits also feed in pools, and godwit chicks feed mainly on terrestrial arthropods. Green (1988) found that the number of snipe chicks hatched per female over the whole breeding season was determined by the rate of failure of breeding attempts, and the duration of the breeding season. If the soil remained moist and easy to probe, then snipe were able to continue nesting until later in the summer, which could help increase their breeding success.

The softness of the upper soil is determined by its physical structure and composition, and by its moisture content. In general, the force required to probe soil declines as its moisture content increases. Breeding godwits are usually associated with fields that have a high water table (e.g. Kleijn and van Zuijlen, 2004). The extent to which the surface soil actually remains wet and soft ultimately depends on the soil type and soil structure, how high water levels are maintained in surrounding ditches, the distance from the nearest ditch, and micro-topography within the field (Box 11.1).

Lowland wet grasslands occur on a variety of different soil types – peat, marine clays, alluvial soils and peat deposits covered with thin layers of marine clay or alluvium. These soils differ in their permeability and potential to remain wet and soft during the wader breeding season (Box 11.1). In the Netherlands, the highest densities of breeding waders are found on marine clays overlying peat. This is probably because the marine clays provide high fertility, resulting in high biomass of soil macroinvertebrates (see later), while the underlying peat helps keep the clay above it wet and soft when water levels are high (Beintema *et al.*, 1997). The largest breeding populations of snipe and godwits in lowland England currently occur at the Ouse and Nene Washes, on peat overlain with fluvial deposits.

Compaction reduces the ability of soils to transmit water, and therefore to remain wet and soft close to the surface. It also reduces biomass of earthworms (see below). Compaction is caused by livestock trampling, and by use of heavy machinery in wet conditions. Drying out and oxidation of peat also destroys its structure and reduces its rate of water transmission. Water levels influence the vertical distribution and hence accessibility of earthworms. The most abundant earthworm species in wet grassland tend to avoid saturated soils (Ausden *et al.*, 2001; Zorn *et al.*, 2008). High water levels force these earthworms close to the soil surface, thereby making them more accessible to feeding birds. However, high water levels also reduce earthworm biomass. In particular, flooded grasslands contain far lower biomass of earthworms and tipulid larvae than unflooded grasslands (Ausden *et al.*, 2001). Hence, although maintaining high water levels improves habitat quality for feeding snipe and godwits by keeping the upper soil soft and concentrating prey close to the soil surface, it also reduces prey abundance. Most breeding snipe occur on soft, wet soils with low biomass of macroinvertebrates. This suggests that accessibility of prey, rather than abundance, most commonly limits habitat quality for feeding snipe (Ausden *et al.*, 2001).

Earthworm biomass tends to be highest on well-structured (i.e. uncompacted), non-acidic soils, which contain high levels of organic matter (e.g. Piearce, 1984; Standen, 1984; Pizl, 1992; Hansen, 1996; Verhulst *et al.*, 2007; Watkins 2007). Earthworm biomass is positively related to soil pH within the range of conditions found on wet grasslands (Standen, 1984; Verhulst *et al.*, 2007). Soil pH has declined in many semi-natural habitats in Europe, as a result of inputs of anthropogenic atmospheric nitrogen and sulphur (Bobbink *et al.*, 1998; Blake *et al.*, 1999; Horswill *et al.*, 2008). Earthworm biomass can potentially be increased by manipulating soil quality. Watkins (2007) found that additions of 10 to 15 tonnes of farmyard manure per ha to a range of lowland wet grasslands increased earthworm biomass in the top 10 cm of soil between 39–82%, but had no effect on biomass of tipulid larvae. Application of these rates of farmyard manure is within the levels currently permissible in agri-environment schemes. In contrast, Verhulst *et al.* (2007) found a negative relationship between total soil macroinvertebrate biomass and levels of farmyard manure application on Dutch wet grasslands.

The main conservation measures used to improve feeding conditions for snipe and adult godwits during the breeding season are to maintain high water levels to provide soft soil, and to maintain suitable sward height/structure, usually through cattle grazing or mowing. On nature reserves, introduction of these measures results in only short-term increases in numbers of breeding snipe on non-peat soils (Ausden and Hirons, 2002), but has successfully increased numbers on at least some peat sites (e.g. the RSPB's West Sedgemoor and Nene Washes Reserves). Introduction of raised water levels, suitable sward management, and control of foxes *Vulpes vulpes* and carrion crows *Corvus corone* has increased Britain's largest breeding population of godwits.

Black-tailed godwit chicks
Godwit chicks feed primarily on arthropods gleaned from tall (>*c.* 15 cm) vegetation (Beintema *et al.*, 1991; Kruk *et al.*, 1997; Schekkerman and

---

Box 11.1 The effects of water levels and soil type on conditions for feeding snipe and black-tailed godwits on lowland wet grassland

Snipe and godwits require soft, wet soil in which to probe for earthworms and tipulid larvae (see text). The wetness of the upper soil in a field is linked to water levels in surrounding ditches. The nature of this relationship depends on soil type and structure, and the time of year. In winter, inputs of water through precipitation, and in some cases direct flow, invariably exceed losses through evapotranspiration; this results in wet, soft upper soil. As the breeding season progresses, evapotranspiration increases due to rising temperature and plant growth. Once losses of water through evapotranspiration exceed inputs through precipitation, field water levels begin to fall, unless there are additional inputs of water. In general, only well-structured peats and some mineral soils have sufficient permeability to allow lateral movement of water from water-filled ditches to replenish losses through evapotranspiration. On less-permeable soils, soft, wet soil conditions are more restricted to the margins of water-filled ditches and pools. As water levels fall in late spring and summer, the water table in the centre of a field becomes lower relative to that close to the water-filled ditches. Consequently, for a given water level in

Box 11.1 (cont.)

the ditches, larger fields tend to have a lower water table than smaller fields. The water table height is also affected by small-scale topographic variation.

(a) Winter – maintaining high ditch water levels on *permeable* and *impermeable* soils
Precipitation > evapotranspiration

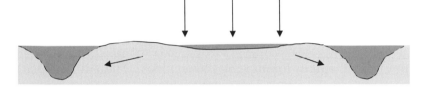

(b) Summer – maintaining high ditch water levels on *permeable* soils
Evapotranspiration > precipitation

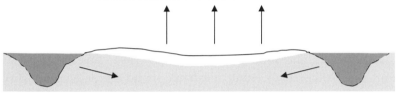

(c) Summer – maintaining high ditch water levels on *impermeable* soils
Evapotranspiration > precipitation

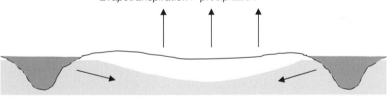

Dark grey = water in ditches; light grey = saturated soil; white = drier soil; arrows indicate net directions of water movement.

Beintema, 2007). Agricultural management influences habitat quality for chicks. Recently mown fields support lower densities of grassland arthropods than unmown fields, and chicks foraging in recently mown fields have lower intake rates than those in unmown fields (Schekkerman and Beintema, 2007). Mowing probably reduces arthropod abundance simply because it removes most of the vegetation on which arthropods live. Fertiliser inputs increase the rate of grass growth, which allows fields to be mown earlier in the season, resulting in destruction of nests and chicks (see below). More heavily fertilised fields may also support lower densities, and a reduced mean size, of the preferred arthropod prey (Siepel, 1990; Schekkerman and Beintema, 2007). A reduction in mean prey size might make it more difficult for chicks to meet their energy requirements (Beintema *et al.*, 1991). It is also likely that fertilised dense swards are more difficult for chicks to forage in. This combination of effects arising from agricultural improvement has probably caused the decline of breeding godwits in the Netherlands (Kruk *et al.*, 1997; Gill *et al.*, 2007).

The main conservation measures used to improve habitat quality for godwit chicks (and to reduce mortality from mowing, see below) are to delay and stagger mowing, and to leave areas of uncut grass ('refuge strips') to maintain a continuity of tall swards for foraging godwit chicks. There is evidence that these measures increase chick survival (Schekkerman and Müskens, 2000; Schekkerman *et al.*, 2008).

Lapwings and redshank

Adult and young lapwings and redshank feed by picking invertebrates from, or just below, the surface of the soil, from vegetation and bare ground, and from shallow water and mud (Beintema *et al.*, 1991; Ausden *et al.*, 2003; Eglington *et al.*, 2008, 2010). Adult redshank spend a greater proportion of their time feeding in shallow water, and less time feeding on grassland, than adult lapwings (Milsom *et al.*, 2002; Ausden *et al.*, 2003). Lapwings also forage in cattle dung (Beintema *et al.*, 1991), while adult redshank nesting on coastal grazing marshes feed on adjacent estuaries (Ausden *et al.*, 2003). The use of estuaries probably accounts, at least in part, for the high densities of breeding redshank on coastal grazing marsh compared to floodplain grasslands (Table 11.1).

Lapwing chicks prefer shorter vegetation than adults, and adult redshank select taller, and more heterogeneous swards than adult lapwings (Vickery *et al.*, 1997; Milsom *et al.*, 2000; Smart *et al.*, 2006; Watkins, 2007; Durant *et al.*, 2008a, 2008b). Both species feed in open conditions, which allows early visual detection of predators.

The diet of lapwings and redshank can vary greatly during the breeding season, between sites and even between years at the same site (Ausden *et al.*, 2003). There is, though, strong evidence that soil macroinvertebrates are the most profitable prey for both species on grassland during the early part of the breeding season and, at least in the case of lapwings, also prior to egg-laying (Högstedt, 1974; Baines, 1990). Watkins (2007) found that foraging female lapwings selected patches which had higher biomass of earthworms (mean of 25 g m^{-2}) than random points (mean of 13 g m^{-2}). Their chicks also selected areas with high earthworm biomass. Interestingly, there was no selection for earthworm-rich areas by foraging adult males. Adult females probably need to maximise their food intake prior to egg laying, and during periods when they are not incubating (females spend more time incubating than males). The feeding location of adult males might be more heavily influenced by their territorial and vigilance behaviour.

Feeding conditions for lapwings and redshank are, thus, influenced primarily by sward height, water levels and the abundance of prey. Because both species require relatively short and open vegetation, higher rates of grass growth caused by agricultural improvement reduce habitat suitability. Whilst the negative effects of increased grass growth can be reduced by higher-intensity grazing, this has the potential to increase the proportion of nests trampled (see below).

Habitat quality for lapwings and redshank appears to vary less in relation to soil type and structure than it does for snipe and godwits, because neither lapwings nor redshank require soft soil in which to probe. However, water is important to lapwings and redshank in several ways. Maintaining high water levels forces earthworms close to the soil surface, and thereby increases prey accessibility. High water levels also tend to reduce grass growth. This reduction in sward height undoubtedly increases the accessibility of prey for lapwings and redshank. High water levels have the effect of decreasing the biomass of soil macroinvertebrates (see above) and surface flooding can also reduce the abundance of terrestrial arthropod prey (Ausden, 1996). However, the accessibility of soil macroinvertebrate prey, rather than its abundance, probably limits habitat quality more commonly, particularly during the latter part of the breeding season (Box 11.2). Winter grazing by wigeon *Anas penelope* and geese also helps to maintain a short, open sward the following spring. Wigeon tend to concentrate grazing close to water, which provides a refuge when disturbed by people and predators (Mayhew and Houston, 1989). Shallow water in ditches and fields provides aquatic invertebrate prey, mainly non-biting midge larvae, Chironomidae, and adult and larval beetles (Ausden *et al.*, 2003). Biomass of non-biting midge larvae in pools is low in early spring, but increases as the wader breeding season progresses (Ausden, 1996). Pools left by receding river floodwaters in early spring can contain high densities of stranded, riverine invertebrates. Temporary and permanent pools probably differ in their abundance of aquatic invertebrates during the latter part of the wader breeding season, but this has been little studied. In other shallow, freshwater habitats, invertebrate productivity tends to be greatest in temporary, rather than permanent water bodies (Danell and Sjöberg, 1982). This is attributed to high overall productivity fuelled by release of soluble nutrients from freshly inundated soil and decomposition of flooded terrestrial vegetation, and low densities of predatory invertebrates and fish. Drying out of pools confines flightless aquatic invertebrates to ever-decreasing patches,

Box 11.2 Changes in feeding conditions for lapwings and redshank on lowland wet grassland during the breeding season

Soil macroinvertebrates (earthworms and tipulid larvae) are only accessible to feeding lapwings and redshank if they are close to the soil surface, and the vegetation is short and open enough for birds to find them. During the early part of the breeding season, the surface soil of unflooded grassland is still moist from winter rainfall, and supports high biomass of soil macro-invertebrates close to its surface. Providing the grassland is short (i.e. has been heavily grazed the previous autumn, and in milder areas, during the winter), this unflooded grassland can provide good feeding conditions for both species.

Early spring

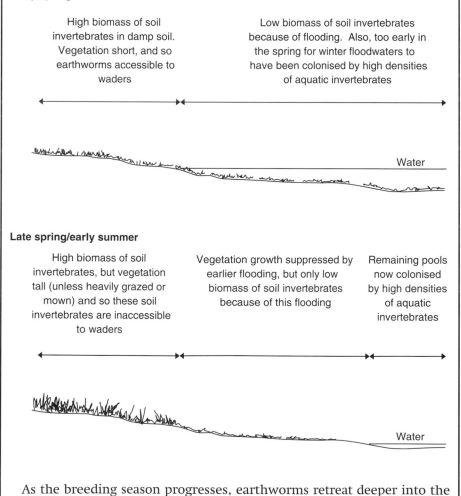

High biomass of soil invertebrates in damp soil. Vegetation short, and so earthworms accessible to waders

Low biomass of soil invertebrates because of flooding. Also, too early in the spring for winter floodwaters to have been colonised by high densities of aquatic invertebrates

Water

Late spring/early summer

High biomass of soil invertebrates, but vegetation tall (unless heavily grazed or mown) and so these soil invertebrates are inaccessible to waders

Vegetation growth suppressed by earlier flooding, but only low biomass of soil invertebrates because of this flooding

Remaining pools now colonised by high densities of aquatic invertebrates

Water

As the breeding season progresses, earthworms retreat deeper into the soil if the surface dries out (Ausden *et al.*, 2001; Watkins, 2007), while the

Box 11.2 (cont.)

increase in height of the grass (unless heavily grazed or mown) must also make soil macroinvertebrates increasingly less accessible to waders. Suitably short and open vegetation often becomes increasingly restricted to the margins of pools where flooding has suppressed growth (Ausden *et al.*, 2003). However, abundance of earthworms and tipulid larvae is greatly reduced by the flooding. As the spring progresses, abundance of aquatic invertebrate prey increases in remaining pools, as do terrestrial arthropods (Ausden, 1996, 2001).

which provide a temporary concentrated food source. The margins of more-permanent pools often develop relatively tall, swampy vegetation, especially dense stands of rushes *Juncus* spp., which makes them less suitable for feeding waders than ephemeral pools.

The accessibility of soil macroinvertebrates tends to decline as sites dry out during the breeding season. If shallow water is present, lapwings and redshank can switch to feeding more on aquatic invertebrates and terrestrial arthropods as the breeding season progresses (Ausden *et al.*, 2003; Eglington *et al.*, 2010; Box 11.2). On grasslands that lack shallow water, lapwings must eat an increasing proportion of terrestrial arthropods as soil macroinvertebrates become less accessible (Baines, 1990). Beintema *et al.* (1991) suggested that as chicks of lapwings and redshank mature on lowland wet grasslands that lack shallow water, they need to switch from feeding mainly on terrestrial arthropods, to feeding mainly on soil macroinvertebrates, in order to meet their energy demands. This change in diet has been observed in lapwings (Watkins, 2007).

The main conservation measures used to improve habitat quality for feeding lapwings and redshank are: (i) raising water levels; (ii) excavating shallow, water-filled footdrains and pools in otherwise flat grasslands and (iii) grazing to maintain a short, but heterogeneous sward, while also minimising the risk of nests being trampled. Grazing is usually carried out using cattle, or more rarely, mixed cattle and sheep. This management aims to produce a mosaic of short winter-flooded grassland, unflooded grassland and shallow water, to provide continuity of profitable feeding conditions throughout the breeding season. For a given water level, areas with more varied topography have greater variation in hydrological conditions, and are therefore more likely to maintain suitable feeding conditions as water levels fall. Raising water levels and introducing suitable sward management on nature reserves has resulted in threefold increases in numbers of breeding lapwings and fivefold increases in numbers of breeding redshank (Ausden and Hirons, 2002).

Condition of lapwing chicks can be higher in fields containing high densities of footdrains (Eglington *et al.*, 2010), which also probably benefit lapwings by concentrating birds so that they are better able to deter predators by group-mobbing (see below).

The height of water levels during the latter part of the wader breeding season is determined to some extent by management decisions taken after birds have settled to nest. There is, therefore, the potential for birds to select areas that have high water levels, but to then be left in poor-quality habitat if these areas subsequently dry out. This occurred under some early UK agri-environment prescriptions that encouraged shallow flooding in winter and early spring, thereby making areas attractive for waders to settle on. However, it was specified that flooding should not persist after April because it was thought that late flooding would damage the sward and reduce the abundance of soil macroinvertebrates.

Habitat quality, and nest and chick survival

Nest survival is affected by predation, mowing, trampling by livestock and flooding (see Appendix E11.1). Predation tends to be the main cause of nest loss on wet grassland managed for conservation (Eglington *et al.*, 2009), because nest loss caused by mowing and trampling is usually minimised using methods described below. The proportion of nests lost through flooding is usually small, although it can be important at some sites (Ratcliffe *et al.*, 2005).

Productivity of waders is more sensitive to variation in levels of chick survival, than to similar levels of variation in nest survival (Teunissen *et al.*, 2008). This is because waders will re-nest following loss of clutches early in the breeding season, but rarely do so following loss of a brood. The rate of nest loss that a wader population can withstand without declining, depends on levels of chick survival. In the case of lapwings, it appears that a population is likely to decline if fewer than about 50% of nests survive (Box 11.3).

There is limited information on the causes of chick mortality. In studies of chick predation, a large proportion of chicks disappear without their fate being known, but the available information suggests that at most sites, of the chicks whose cause of mortality has been established, the majority are predated. Mowing can also kill a significant proportion of chicks. Smaller numbers die from starvation and hypothermia, and by drowning (Kruk *et al.*, 1997; Schekkerman *et al.*, 2009). Levels of chick mortality caused by starvation are affected by feeding conditions, which may also affect the vulnerability of chicks to predation (see below).

Nest loss caused by trampling
The probability of nests being trampled depends on stocking levels and the type of livestock (Box 11.4). Habitat conditions affect stocking intensities – the

---

Box 11.3 What levels of nest predation are likely to limit the population size of breeding lapwings?

It is estimated that each pair of lapwings needs to fledge between 0.6 and 0.8 young per year in order to balance losses to mortality and maintain a stable population (Catchpole *et al.*, 1999; MacDonald and Bolton, 2008a). The nest survival rates necessary to achieve these levels of productivity depend on the extent of re-nesting following nest failure, and on chick survival rates. Measuring the latter is not easy. Broods may move considerable distances (several kilometres) in just a few days. When relying on re-sighting colour-marked chicks, those which move outside the study area may erroneously be assumed to have died. Radio tracking chicks enables brood movements to be followed and dead chicks may be recovered if the tag remains intact, allowing the cause of mortality to be determined in some cases. However, Sharpe *et al.* (2009) found that the frequent disturbance of lapwing broods commonly associated with radio tracking may impair chick condition and therefore reduce survival rate.

Among five lowland wet grassland sites in Britain that were each studied for four years when no predator control was conducted (Bolton *et al.*, 2007), chick survival rates were on average 21%. Assuming a similar effect of disturbance on chick survival to that found by Sharpe *et al.* (2009), the actual survival rate to fledging of undisturbed chicks would have been around 23%. If this percentage of chicks survive to fledging, then the population is only likely to remain stable if about 50% of nests survive to hatch. If fewer than 23% of chicks survive, then a higher proportion of nests must survive for the population to remain stable. If chick survival falls below 17%, then the population is predicted to decline irrespective of the proportion of nests that survive (MacDonald and Bolton, 2008a). Schekkerman *et al.* (2009) found that, in the Netherlands, an average of just 14% of lapwing chicks survived to fledging.

---

greater the vegetation growth, the higher the densities of livestock that can be supported. The grazing regime during the nesting and chick-rearing period depends on management decisions taken after birds have settled to nest. This creates the potential for an ecological trap; areas that appear to be of high quality at the time of settlement, may turn out to be of low quality because of high levels of nest trampling.

Grazing during the breeding season is usually necessary to keep the sward short and open enough for waders to feed in, especially lapwings. Grazing can also be important in maintaining sufficiently open conditions for lapwings to re-nest following the loss of earlier clutches (Hart *et al.*, 2002). Therefore, the

Box 11.4 Estimated levels of trampling of wader nests on lowland wet grassland

The graph below shows the relationships between the proportions of nests trampled throughout the egg-laying and incubation period at different stocking levels. These have been calculated using trampling rates from Beintema and Müskens (1987). Figures are shown for oystercatchers, which suffered the lowest rates of nest trampling, and redshank, which suffered the highest rates. Levels of nest trampling of lapwings and godwits were between these two extremes.

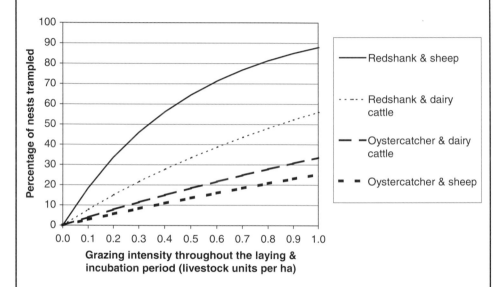

Sheep trample a higher proportion of redshank nests than dairy cattle per quantity of vegetation removed, because it requires about ten sheep (i.e. a total of 40 hooves which might tread on nests) to remove the same quantity of vegetation as one cow. In the case of oystercatchers, though, nest survival is actually slightly higher per livestock unit under sheep grazing, presumably because they are better able to defend their nests against sheep than cattle.

chosen grazing intensity is a trade-off between maintaining suitable conditions for feeding and re-nesting, and minimising trampling of nests. One approach is to avoid grazing areas with high densities of nesting waders, or to graze these at a low intensity, while heavily grazing other areas nearby to maintain short and open conditions for adults and chicks to feed on. These heavily grazed areas need to be close to nests. Lapwing broods which have to move long distances between nesting and chick-rearing habitat tend to have lower survival than those which only need to move short distances between the two (Blomqvist and Johansson, 1995).

Another technique to reduce nest trampling is to protect individual nests using nest protectors or nest exclosures. Nest protectors consist of a raised metal grille placed over a nest. Nest exclosures have a roof and sides constructed from metal bars, with the sides pushed deep into the ground. Incubating birds can enter through the gaps in the side of the exclosure, but these gaps are too narrow to allow access by foxes, crows and other larger predators (Isaksson et al., 2007). Guldemond et al. (1993) found hatching success under nest protectors to be between 61% and 76%, but there are no published studies comparing nest survival between nests with and without nest protectors.

Nest and chick loss caused by mowing

In the absence of mitigation measures, mowing destroys virtually all wader nests and kills many chicks. Agricultural improvement accelerates the rate of grass growth, resulting in earlier mowing at a time when more waders are nesting and young chicks are present (Beintema et al., 1985). Mowing also takes place earlier following warmer springs, but waders also nest earlier in warmer springs, so that the effects of earlier springs on productivity are not as severe as they might first appear (Kruk et al., 1996).

As with nest loss caused by trampling, the potential for nests and chicks to be lost during mowing depends on a management decision – if and when fields are mown. Hence, yet again there is the potential for an ecological trap (Kleijn et al., 2001). Nest and chick survival of breeding waders on mown grasslands can, however, be increased by delaying mowing (e.g. Kruk et al., 1996), and by marking nests and mowing around them. Nests of oystercatchers, lapwings, godwits and redshank that have been mown around, have a hatching success of between 64 and 83% (Guldemond et al., 1993). Flags can also be placed in fields that are about to be cut, to deter broods from entering them (Kruk et al., 1997).

Habitat quality and predation of nests and chicks

Most predation of wader nests on lowland wet grassland is by nocturnal mammals. Evidence for this comes from the results of nest camera studies (Teunissen et al., 2008; Ausden et al., 2009), and the fact that most (75–88%) nest predation occurs at night (Bolton et al., 2007; Bellebaum and Bock, 2009; Eglington et al., 2009). Most mammalian predation of lapwing and godwit nests is by foxes (Teunissen et al., 2008; Ausden et al., 2009).

The best evidence of the cause of predation of chicks comes from following radio-tagged chicks. In most cases where it has been possible to identify the species of predator, it has been a bird (Teunissen et al., 2008). However, the identity of predators is unknown in many cases. Unknown predators are probably mainly mammals, because mammals are more likely than birds to destroy radio tags or take them below ground where they cannot be located. It is comparatively easy to search for radio tags at known breeding locations of bird predators. Therefore, the results of radio tagging might over-estimate the role of birds in chick predation.

Habitat conditions are thought to affect levels of predation on wader nests and chicks by influencing: (i) densities of predators; (ii) the ability of predators to locate nests and chicks and (iii) the ability of waders to deter predators through mobbing. The mechanisms by which habitat conditions may affect predation on nests and chicks are summarised in Fig. 11.3. Habitat quality will also influence the effect that a given level of nest predation has on overall breeding productivity. The longer conditions remain suitable for re-nesting and chick-rearing, the greater potential there is to raise clutches laid to replace those lost through predation.

Many of the most important predators of wader nests and chicks – foxes, badgers *Meles meles*, crows and buzzards *Buteo buteo* (Teunissen *et al.*, 2008; Ausden *et al.*, 2009) – are generalist predators, which also use farmed and wooded habitats. The densities of these predators foraging over wet grassland will therefore probably be influenced by the habitat composition of the surrounding landscape. Densities of foxes and badgers foraging over wet

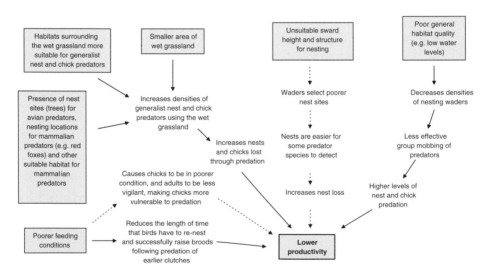

Figure 11.3 Potential mechanisms through which poor habitat quality is thought to increase levels of predation on wader nests and chicks on lowland wet grassland. Solid arrows indicate mechanisms supported by good evidence. Dotted arrows indicate mechanisms based on weaker evidence.

grassland must also be influenced by the availability of areas for them to establish earths and setts within the grassland itself. Similarly, densities of crows and buzzards on wet grassland during the breeding season must be influenced by the availability of trees for them to nest in. Extensive flooding of washlands and river floodplains reduces densities of small mammals which are an important food of these generalist predators, but mammalian predators appear to re-colonise grasslands quickly as floodwaters recede (Jacob, 2003; Bellebaum and Bock, 2009).

Sward structure affects the quality of potential nest sites for waders, and thereby presumably the vulnerability of nests to predation. For example, Baines (1990) considered that the relatively high levels of predation suffered by lapwings on structurally uniform upland grasslands, was probably because nests were more conspicuous to avian predators than on more structurally diverse, agriculturally unimproved grasslands. Wader species differ in their preferred nest sites, with respect to sward height and structure (e.g. Durant *et al.*, 2008b). The suitability of the sward for nesting is determined largely by grazing and mowing management. In the case of lapwings, which nest in open conditions and often on bare ground, the availability of nest sites is also influenced by the availability of bare and disturbed ground created by cleaning of ditches, poaching of livestock and suppression of vegetation by flooding. Earlier mowing increases the vulnerability of godwit chicks to avian predation, presumably because they have less vegetation to hide in (Schekkerman *et al.*, 2009).

The vulnerability of wader nests and chicks to avian predators is widely thought to be influenced by their proximity to trees, fences and other features providing perches for crows and buzzards (Wallander *et al.*, 2006). Studies using dummy nests show that crows, in particular, can potentially find and eat a large proportion of unprotected eggs on lowland wet grasslands (Green *et al.*, 1990). However, the fact that real wader nests usually suffer fairly low levels of predation by birds (see above), suggests that waders' strategies for reducing nest loss to avian predators are reasonably successful. Waders tend to nest away from trees and other high-predation-risk features (Wallander *et al.*, 2006), and avoid areas close to nesting crows, magpies *Pica pica* and buzzards (van der Vliet *et al.*, 2008). Most studies have actually found no effect of distance to the nearest potential avian look-out post on nest survival of waders (Ottvall *et al.*, 2005; Wallander *et al.*, 2006). This is presumably because waders avoid nesting in high-predation-risk areas. The main effect of raised features in the grassland landscape is probably to reduce the area of habitat available for nesting and feeding.

Most studies have also found no relationship between how conspicuous nests appear (to us at least) and how likely they are to be predated (Macdonald and Bolton, 2008a). This suggests that a large proportion of nests which are predated (i.e. by mammals – see above) are detected using non-visual cues, or are discovered incidentally. Thus, strategies that waders use to protect their nest from avian predation appear to be less successful against mammals. There has been concern that linear features, which attract high densities of nesting waders and chicks, might increase levels of nest and chick predation, due to mammalian predators concentrating their hunting along them. This was investigated by Eglington *et al.* (2009), who found that although lapwings did preferentially nest close to linear footdrains, there was no evidence that foxes concentrated their hunting activity along them, or that lapwing nests placed close to footdrains suffered higher levels of predation than those further away.

Breeding lapwings, redshank, godwits and oystercatchers deter predators by mobbing. Several studies have found that lapwings nesting at high densities have higher levels of nest survival than those nesting at low densities (Hart *et al.*, 2002; Seymour *et al.*, 2003; MacDonald and Bolton, 2008b; Eglington *et al.*, 2009). This might be because higher densities of lapwings settle on areas with lower densities of predators, or because higher densities of lapwings are more effective at mobbing and deterring predators, or a combination of the two. Higher densities of lapwing broods also have higher levels of survival (Eglington *et al.*, 2009), probably because of more effective group-mobbing. Hence, aspects of habitat quality that increase densities of lapwings probably also act to reduce levels of nest and chick predation.

A variety of measures are used to reduce levels of predation on wader nests and chicks. Lapwing nests can be protected from larger predators using nest exclosures (see above), fences can be used to exclude mammalian predators (Jackson, 2001; Moseby and Read, 2006) and foxes and crows can be killed (Bolton *et al.*, 2007; Ausden *et al.*, 2009).

Human disturbance

Densities of breeding waders are reduced by disturbance from people and vehicles. Reijnen *et al.* (1996) found that densities of breeding waders were lower within the following distances of roads used by *c.* 50 000 cars per day, than on similar grassland further away: lapwing 560 m; black-tailed godwit 940 m; oystercatcher 3530 m. An estimated 10% of the area of land entered into agri-environment schemes aimed at benefiting breeding waders in the Netherlands, is thought to support reduced densities of breeding waders due to its proximity to roads (Melman *et al.*, 2008). Experimental disturbance by walkers reduced densities of breeding godwits at distances of up to 500 m from routes used by seven walkers per day (Holm and Laursen, 2009). Conservation management seeks to minimise these effects of disturbance at key breeding wader sites by managing access.

Effects of climate change on habitat quality

Changes in climate have the potential to markedly affect habitat quality for lowland wet grassland waders. There is, though, a greater potential to mitigate negative effects of climate change on lowland wet grassland waders through habitat management, than is the case for most groups of birds in other habitats. The main projected changes in climate in Britain with potential consequences for breeding waders are higher winter rainfall, reduced water availability in summer, more frequent heavy rainfall events and higher temperatures (www.ukclimateprojections.defra.gov.uk).

There are unlikely to be major implications of changes in precipitation on habitat quality when waders settle to nest, apart from at sites: (i) where flood risk management responses to projected increases in the frequency of extreme flood events impact on water levels in early spring; (ii) in the far south east of England where, despite a predicted increase in winter rainfall, there is predicted to be a reduction in the extent and duration of winter flooding due to lower water levels in autumn (Thompson *et al.*, 2009).

The main impact of climate change on breeding waders is likely to be through an increase in drawdown of water levels once birds have settled to nest. This will reduce the length of time that feeding conditions are suitable for chicks. Population impacts of predation (and other causes of loss of first clutches) will be more severe, because replacement clutches are less likely to be successful as wetlands dry out earlier. Increased frequency of heavy rainfall events in spring and early summer could increase levels of nest loss of waders through flooding. Higher temperatures will increase the rate of vegetation growth in winter and spring, making the sward longer and therefore less suitable for lapwings and possibly also redshank.

There are a number of ways that these predicted negative changes in habitat quality could be mitigated through habitat management. At some sites, effects of reduced rainfall and increased evapotranspiration in spring and early summer can be reduced by maximising inputs, and minimising losses, of water. Reservoirs can be constructed to store water abstracted from rivers in winter, which can be used to supplement water supply to the grassland in spring and summer. Such systems have already been built. Another approach is to design wet grasslands to include greater topographic variation, so that shallow pools and wet mud persist, even with increased rates of spring and summer drawdown. Water levels can also be held higher at the beginning of the breeding season. Where there is insufficient water to maintain optimal water levels across the entire site, higher levels could be maintained over only a proportion of the site, possibly flooding different parts of the site in different years. Sward height can be reduced through grazing, but winter grazing may poach wet soil, and heavier grazing in spring will increase the proportion of nests trampled.

Declines in breeding productivity caused by a reduction in the time that sites remain wet enough for waders to raise replacement clutches, could be mitigated by minimising losses of earlier clutches and broods through trampling and predation. This would mean that populations would be less dependent on raising replacement clutches to achieve sufficient levels of productivity.

The increased threat of flooding also provides opportunities to create new areas of wetland habitat through the construction of washlands for flood storage (English Nature, 2001; Morris *et al.*, 2004, 2008). The value of these washlands for breeding waders and other wetland wildlife will depend on the details of how they are designed and managed. If water levels are kept relatively high throughout the year, and the washland is subject to periodic winter flooding, then it should provide valuable breeding wader habitat. However, if, in order to maximise flood storage capacity, water levels are kept low for much of the year, then new washlands would provide few, if any, benefits to wetland birds and other wildlife. Flooding during the breeding season would also destroy birds' nests (Ratcliffe *et al.*, 2005) potentially creating an ecological trap situation.

Conclusions

There is a considerable amount of information regarding how habitat conditions affect habitat quality for waders breeding on lowland wet grassland in western Europe. Key features influencing habitat quality for this group are water levels, sward height and structure, the effects of grazing, mowing and predation on nest and chick survival, and human disturbance. Our understanding of how habitat conditions affect breeding productivity has been used to develop management prescriptions aimed at increasing breeding populations of waders. It is important to recognise, though, that maintenance of suitable conditions for breeding waders depends to a great extent on the skilled judgement of land managers and advisors.

Despite many notable successes, there are still several uncertainties and gaps in knowledge that hinder attempts to improve habitat quality for these birds. First, we have only partial understanding of the factors limiting breeding populations of snipe. The success of measures aimed at benefiting breeding snipe, principally raised water levels, has been variable. The lack of a general increase in breeding populations at sites where habitat-based conservation measures have been applied suggests that other factors might be limiting snipe populations, including those operating outside the breeding season.

Second, reducing levels of chick predation is especially important, because overall wader productivity is so sensitive to small variations in levels of chick survival. At present, the only way to determine the cause of chick mortality is by following the fate of radio-tagged individuals, but our knowledge is hampered by the unknown fate of a high proportion of chicks. Advances in tracking technology are required to enable us to identify the causes of mortality of a higher proportion of chicks.

Third, how can existing knowledge be most effectively applied outside nature reserves? Agri-environmental schemes have been largely unsuccessful at conserving the formerly large populations of many wader species in the wider countryside (Kleijn *et al.*, 2001 and 2004; Kleijn and van Zuijlen, 2004; Wilson *et al.*, 2007). This contrasts with the success of similar habitat-based measures (sometimes accompanied by control of foxes and crows) when applied within nature reserves. We need to better understand how to apply these and other measures in the wider countryside, including how best to use incentives to deliver suitable habitat conditions on the ground (e.g. Musters *et al.*, 2001; Merricks, 2008; Swagemakers *et al.*, 2009).

Finally, climate change will reduce the quality of some lowland wet grassland currently supporting breeding waders, principally through changes in hydrology and growing conditions, but could also provide opportunities to improve habitat quality in some other areas. Climate change is also likely to increase pressure on land for production of food and biofuels, thereby increasing pressure on unprotected wetland habitats. As with other habitats, a key challenge will be to ensure that protected area networks as a whole continue to support breeding waders and other wildlife, even though the value of individual sites for particular species will inevitably change.

Acknowledgements

Thanks to Graham Hirons and Ken Smith for discussions about the habitat requirements of wet grassland waders over many years, and to Rob Fuller and Sarah Eglington for comments on an earlier draft of this chapter.

References

Ausden, M. (1996). The effects of raised water levels on food supply for breeding waders on lowland wet grassland. PhD thesis, University of East Anglia.

Ausden, M. (2007). *Habitat Management for Conservation: A Handbook of Techniques*. Oxford: Oxford University Press.

Ausden, M., Bolton, M., Butcher, N. *et al.* (2009). Predation of breeding waders on wet grassland – is it a problem? *Brit. Wildlife*, **21**, 29–38.

Ausden, M. and Hirons, G. J. M. (2002). Grassland nature reserves for breeding waders in England and the implications for the ESA

agri-environment scheme. *Biol. Conserv.*, **106**, 279–291.

Ausden, M., Rowlands, A., Sutherland, W. J. and James, R. (2003). Diet of breeding Lapwing *Vanellus vanellus* and Redshank *Tringa totanus* on coastal grazing marsh and implications for habitat management. *Bird Study*, **50**, 285–293.

Ausden, M., Sutherland, W. J and James, R. (2001). The effects of flooding lowland wet grassland on soil macroinvertebrate prey of breeding wading birds. *J. Appl. Ecol.*, **38**, 320–338.

Baines, D. (1990). The roles of predation, food and agricultural practice in determining the breeding success of the lapwing (*Vanellus vanellus*) on upland grasslands. *J. Anim. Ecol.*, **59**, 915–929.

Beintema, A. J., Beintema-Hietbrink, R. J. and Müskens, G. J. D. M. (1985). A shift in the timing of breeding in meadow birds. *Ardea*, **73**, 83–89.

Beintema, A. J., Dunn, E. and Stroud, D. A. (1997). Birds and wet grasslands. In *Farming and Birds in Europe: The Common Agricultural Policy and its Implications for Bird Conservation*, ed. D. J. Pain and M. W. Pienkowski, pp. 269–296. San Diego: Academic Press.

Beintema, A. J. and Müskens, G. J. D. M. (1987). Nesting success of birds breeding in Dutch grasslands. *J. Appl. Ecol.*, **24**, 743–758.

Beintema, A. J., Thissen, J. B., Tensen, D. and Visser, G. H. (1991). Feeding ecology of Charadriiform chicks in agricultural grassland. *Ardea*, **79**, 31–44.

Bellebaum, J. and Bock, C. (2009). Influence of ground predators and water levels on Lapwing *Vanellus vanellus* breeding success in two continental wetlands. *J. Ornithol.*, **150**, 221–230.

Berg, Å. (1994). Maintenance of populations and causes of population changes of curlews *Numenius arquata* breeding on farmland. *Biol. Conserv.*, **67**, 233–238.

Berg, Å., Jonsson, M., Lindberg, T. and Källebrink, K. G. (2002). Population dynamics and reproduction of Lapwings *Vanellus vanellus* in a meadow restoration area in central Sweden. *Ibis*, **144**, E131-E140.

BirdLife International (2004). *Birds in Europe: Population Estimates, Trends and Conservation Status*. BirdLife Conservation Series No. 12. Cambridge: Birdlife International.

Blake, L., Goulding, K. W. T., Mott, C. J. B. and Johnston, A. E. (1999). Changes in soil chemistry accompanying acidification over more than 100 years under woodland and grass at Rothamsted Experimental Station, UK. *Eur. J. Soil Sci.*, **50**, 401–412.

Blomqvist, D. and Johansson, O. C. (1995). Trade-offs in nest site selection in coastal populations of Lapwings *Vanellus vanellus*. *Ibis*, **137**, 550–558.

Bobbink, R., Hornung, M. and Roelofs, J. G. M. (1998). The effects of air-borne nitrogen pollutants on species diversity in natural and semi-natural European vegetation. *J. Ecol.*, **86**, 717–738.

Bolton, M., Tyler, G., Smith, K. and Bamford, R. (2007). The impact of predator control on lapwing *Vanellus vanellus* breeding success on wet grassland nature reserves. *J. Appl. Ecol.*, **44**, 534–544.

Catchpole, E. A., Morgan, B. J. T., Freeman, S. N. and Peach, W. J. (1999). Modelling the survival of British Lapwings *Vanellus vanellus* using ring-recovery data and weather covariates. *Bird Study*, **46** (suppl), 5–13.

Cramp, S. (ed.) (1983). *The Birds of the Western Palearctic*. Vol. III. Oxford: Oxford University Press.

Danell, K. and Sjöberg, K. (1982). Successional patterns of plants, invertebrates and ducks in a man-made lake. *J. Appl. Ecol.*, **19**, 395–409.

Durant, D., Tichit, M., Fritz, H. and Kernéis, E. (2008a). Field occupancy by breeding lapwings *Vanellus vanellus* and redshanks *Tringa totanus* in agricultural wet grasslands. *Agr. Ecosyst. Environ.*, **128**, 146–150.

Durant, D., Tichit, M., Kernéis, E. and Fritz, H. (2008b). Management of agricultural wet grasslands for breeding waders: integrating ecological and livestock system perspectives – a review. *Biodivers. Conserv.*, **17**, 2275–2295.

Eglington, S. M., Bolton, M., Smart, M. A. *et al.* (2010). Managing water levels on wet grasslands to improve foraging conditions for breeding northern lapwing *Vanellus vanellus*. *J. Appl. Ecol.*, **47**, 451–458.

Eglington, S. M., Gill, J. A., Bolton, M. *et al.* (2008). Restoration of wet features for breeding waders on lowland grassland. *J. Appl. Ecol.*, **45**, 305–314.

Eglington, S. M., Gill, J. A., Smart, M. A. *et al.* (2009). Habitat management and patterns of predation of Northern Lapwings on wet grasslands: The influence of linear habitat structures at different spatial scales. *Biol. Conserv.*, **142**, 314–324.

English Nature (2001). *Sustainable Flood Defence: the Case for Washlands*. No. 406 Research Report No. 406. Peterborough: English Nature.

Fuller, R. J. (1982). *Bird Habitats in Britain*. Calton: Poyser.

Fuller, R. J., Reed, T. M., Buxton, N. E. *et al.* (1986). Populations of breeding waders (Charadrii) and their habitats on the crofting lands of the Outer Hebrides. *Biol. Conserv.*, **37**, 333–361.

Gill, J. A., Langston, R. H. W., Alves, J. A. *et al.* (2007). Contrasting trends in two Black-tailed Godwit populations: a review of causes and recommendations. *Wader Study Group Bull.*, **114**, 43–50.

Green, R. E. (1988). Effects of environmental factors on the timing and success of breeding snipe *Gallinago gallinago* (Aves: Scolopacidae). *J. Appl. Ecol.*, **25**, 79–93.

Green, R. E., Hirons, G. J. M. and Kirby, J. S. (1990). The effectiveness of nest defence by black-tailed godwits *Limosa limosa*. *Ardea*, **78**, 405–413.

Green, R. E. and Robins, M. (1993). The decline of the ornithological importance of the Somerset Levels and Moors, England and changes in the management of water levels. *Biol. Conserv.*, **66**, 95–106.

Groen, N. M. (1993). Breeding site tenacity and natal philopatry in the black-tailed godwit *Limosa l. limosa*. *Ardea*, **81**, 107–113.

Guldemond, J. A., Parmentier, F. and Visbeen, F. (1993). Meadow birds, field management and nest protection in a Dutch peat soil area. *Wader Study Group Bull.*, **70**, 42–48.

Hansen, S. (1996). Effects of manure treatment and soil compaction on plant production of a dairy farm system converting to organic farming practice. *Agr. Ecosyst. Environ.*, **56**, 173–186.

Hart, J. D., Milsom, T. P., Baxter, A., Kelly, P. F. and Parkin, W. K. (2002). The impact of livestock on Lapwing *Vanellus vanellus* breeding densities and performance on coastal grazing marsh. *Bird Study*, **49**, 67–78.

Henderson, I. G., Wilson, A. M., Steele, D. and Vickery, A. (2002). Population estimates, trends and habitat associations of breeding Lapwing *Vanellus vanellus*, Curlew *Numenius arquata* and Snipe *Gallinago gallinago* in Northern Ireland in 1999. *Bird Study*, **49**, 17–25.

Herbert, I. J., Heery, S. and Meredith, C. R. M. (1990). Distribution of breeding waders in relation to habitat features on the River Shannon callows at Shannon harbour, Ireland, 1987–89. *Irish Birds*, **4**, 203–215.

Högstedt, G. (1974). Length of the pre-laying period in the Lapwing *Vanellus vanellus* L. in relation to its food resources. *Ornis Scand.*, **5**, 1–4.

Holm, T. E. and Laursen, K. (2009). Experimental disturbance by walkers affects behaviour and territory density of nesting Black-tailed Godwit *Limosa limosa*. *Ibis*, **151**, 77–87.

Horswill, P., O'Sullivan, O., Phoenix, G. K., Lee, J. A. and Leake, J. R. (2008). Base cation depletion, eutrophication and acidification of species-rich grasslands in response to long-term simulated nitrogen deposition. *Environ. Pollut.*, **155**, 336–349.

Isaksson, D., Wallander, J. and Larsson, M. (2007). Managing predation on ground-nesting birds: the effectiveness of nest exclosures. *Biol. Conserv.*, **136**, 136–152.

Jackson, D. B. (2001). Experimental removal of introduced hedgehogs improves wader nest success in the Western Isles, Scotland. *J. Appl. Ecol.*, **38**, 802–812.

Jacob, J. (2003). The response of small mammal populations to flooding. *Mamm. Biol.*, **68**, 102–111.

Kleijn, D., Berendse, F., Smit, R. and Gilissen, N. (2001). Agri-environment schemes do not effectively protect biodiversity in Dutch agricultural landscapes. *Nature*, **413**, 723–725.

Kleijn, D., Berendse, F., Smit, R. *et al.* (2004). Ecological effectiveness of agri-environment schemes in different agricultural landscapes in the Netherlands. *Conserv. Biol.*, **18**, 775–786.

Kleijn, D. and van Zuijlen, G. J. C. (2004). The conservation effects of meadow bird agreements on farmland in Zeeland, The Netherlands, in the period 1989–1995. *Biol. Conserv.*, **117**, 443–451.

Kruk, M., Noordervliet, A. A. W. and ter Keurs, W. J. (1996). Hatching dates of waders and mowing dates in intensively exploited grassland areas in different years. *Biol. Conserv.*, **77**, 213–218.

Kruk, M., Noordervliet, M. A. W. and ter Keurs, W. J. (1997). Survival of black-tailed godwit chicks *Limosa limosa* in intensively exploited grassland areas in the Netherlands. *Biol. Conserv.*, **80**, 127–133.

Macdonald, M. A. and Bolton, M. (2008a). Predation on wader nests in Europe. *Ibis*, **150** (Suppl. 1), 54–73.

Macdonald, M. A. and Bolton, M. (2008b). Predation of Lapwing *Vanellus vanellus* nests on lowland wet grassland in England and Wales: effects of nest density, habitat and predator abundance. *J. Ornithol.*, **149**, 555–563.

Mayhew, P. and Houston, D. (1989). Feeding site selection by Wigeon *Anas penelope* in relation to water. *Ibis*, **131**, 1–8.

Melman, C. P., Schotman, A. G. M., Hunink, S. and De Snoo, G. R. (2008). Evaluation of meadow bird management, especially black-tailed godwit (*Limosa limosa* L.) in the Netherlands. *J. Nature Conserv.*, **16**, 88–95.

Merricks, P. (2008). Environmental Stewardship and HLS – Achieving better outcomes for breeding waders. *ECOS*, **29**, 77–80.

Milsom, T. P., Hart, J. D., Parkin, W. K. and Peel, S. (2002). Management of coastal grazing marshes for breeding waders: the importance of surface topography and wetness. *Biol. Conserv.*, **103**, 199–207.

Milsom, T. P., Langton, S. D., Parkin, W. K. *et al.* (2000). Habitat models of bird species' distribution: an aid to the management of

coastal grazing marshes. *J. Appl. Ecol.*, **37**, 706–727.

Morris, J., Bailey, A. P., Lawson, C. S. *et al.* (2008). The economic dimensions of integrating flood management and agri-environment through washland creation: a case study from Somerset, England. *J. Environ. Manage.*, **88**, 373–381.

Morris, J., Hess, T. M., Gowing, D. J. *et al.* (2004). *Integrated Washland Management for Flood Defence and Biodiversity*. Report to Department for Environment, Food and Rural Affairs and English Nature. Silsoe: Cranfield University.

Moseby, K. E. and Read, J. L. (2006). The efficacy of feral cat, fox and rabbit exclusion fence designs for threatened species. *Biol. Conserv.*, **127**, 429–437.

Musters, C. J. M., Kruk, M., De Graaf, H. J. and Ter Keurs, W. J. (2001). Breeding birds as a farm product. *Conserv. Biol.*, **15**, 363–369.

Ottvall, R., Larsson, K. and Smith, H. G. (2005). Nesting success in Redshank *Tringa totanus* breeding on coastal meadows and the importance of habitat features used as perches by avian predators. *Bird Study*, **52**, 289–296.

Peach, W. J., Thompson, P. S. and Coulson, J. C. (1994). Annual and long-term variation in the survival rates of British lapwings *Vanellus vanellus*. *J. Anim. Ecol.*, **63**, 60–70.

Piearce, T. G. (1984). Earthworm populations in soils disturbed by trampling. *Biol. Conserv.*, **29**, 241–252.

Pizl, V. (1992). Effect of soil compaction on earthworms (Lumbricidae) in apple orchard soil. *Soil Biol. Biochem.*, **24**, 1573–1575.

Ratcliffe, N., Schmitt, S. and Whiffin, M. (2005). Sink or swim? Viability of a black-tailed godwit population in relation to flooding. *J. Appl. Ecol.*, **42**, 834–843.

Reijnen, R., Foppen, R. and Meeuwsen, H. (1996). The effects of traffic on the density of breeding birds in Dutch agricultural grasslands. *Biol. Conserv.*, **75**, 255–260.

Schekkerman, H. and Beintema, A. J. (2007). Abundance of invertebrates and foraging success of Black-tailed Godwit *Limosa limosa* chicks in relation to agricultural grassland management. *Ardea*, **95**, 39–54.

Schekkerman, H. and Müskens, G. (2000). Produceren Grutto's *Limosa limosa* in agarisch grasland voldoende jongen voor een duurzame populatie. *Limosa*, **73**, 121–134.

Schekkerman, H., Teunissen, W. and Oosterveld, E. (2008). The effect of 'mosaic management' on the demography of black-tailed godwit *Limosa limosa* on farmland. *J. Appl. Ecol.*, **45**, 1067–1075.

Schekkerman, H., Teunissen, W. and Oosterveld, E. (2009). Mortality of Black-tailed Godwit *Limosa limosa* and Northern Lapwing *Vanellus vanellus* chicks in wet grasslands: influence of predation and agriculture. *J. Ornithol.*, **150**, 133–45.

Seymour, A. S., Harris, S., Ralston, C. and White, P. C. L. (2003). Factors influencing the nesting success of Lapwings *Vanellus vanellus* and behaviour of Red Fox *Vulpes vulpes* in Lapwing nesting sites. *Bird Study*, **50**, 39–46.

Sharpe, F., Bolton, M., Sheldon, R. and Ratcliffe, N. (2009). Effects of color banding, radio tagging, and repeat handling on the condition and survival of Lapwing chicks and consequences for estimates of breeding productivity. *J. Field Ornithol.*, **80**, 101–110.

Siepel, H. (1990). The influence of management on food size in the menu of insectivorous animals. In *Experimental and Applied Entomology*, ed. M. J. Sommeijer and J. van der Blom, pp. 101–143. Amsterdam: Nederlandse Entomologische Vereniging.

Smart, J., Gill, J. A., Sutherland, W. J. and Watkinson, A. R. (2006). Grassland-breeding waders: identifying key habitat requirements for management. *J. Appl. Ecol.*, **43**, 454–463.

Stanbury, A., O'Brien, M. and Donaghy, A. (2000). Trends in breeding wader populations in key areas within Northern Ireland between 1986 and 2000. *Irish Birds*, **6**, 513–526.

Standen, V. (1984). Production and diversity of enchytraeids, earthworms and plants in fertilized hay meadow plots. *J. Appl. Ecol.*, **21**, 293–312.

Swagemakers, P., Wiskerke, H. and Van Der Ploeg, J. D. (2009). Linking birds, fields and farmers. *J. Environ. Manage.*, **90**, S185–S192.

Teunissen, W., Schekkerman, H., Willems, F. and Majoor, F. (2008). Identifying predators of eggs and chicks of Lapwing *Vanellus vanellus* and Black-tailed Godwit *Limosa limosa* in the Netherlands and the importance of predation on wader reproductive output. *Ibis*, **150**, 74–85.

Thompson, J. R., Gavin, H., Refsgaard, A. *et al.* (2009). Modelling the hydrological impacts of climate change on UK lowland wet grassland. *Wetlands Ecol. Manage.*, **17**, 503–523.

Thompson, P. S. and Hale, W. G. (1989). Breeding site fidelity and natal philopatry in the Redshank *Tringa totanus*. *Ibis*, **131**, 214–224.

Thorup, O. (2004). Status of populations and management of Dunlin *Calidris alpina*, Ruff *Philomachus pugnax* and Black-tailed Godwit *Limosa limosa* in Denmark. *Dansk Orn. Foren. Tidsskr.*, **98**, 7–20.

Van der Vliet, R. E., Schuller, E. and Wassen, J. (2008). Avian predators in a meadow landscape: consequences of their occurrence for breeding open-area birds. *J. Avian Biol.*, **39**, 523–529.

Verhulst, J., Kleijn, D. and Berendse, F. (2007). Direct and indirect effects of the most widely implemented Dutch agri-environment schemes on breeding waders. *J. Appl. Ecol.*, **44**, 70–80.

Vickery, J. A., Sutherland, W. J., O'Brien, M. and Yallop, A. (1997). Managing coastal grazing marshes for breeding waders and overwintering geese: is there a conflict? *Biol. Conserv.*, **79**, 23–34.

Wallander, J., Isaksson, D. and Lenberg, T. (2006). Wader nest distribution and predation in relation to man-made structures on coastal pastures. *Biol. Conserv.*, **132**, 343–350.

Watkins, C. M. H. (2007). Farmyard manure application as a management tool for conserving breeding waders on lowland wet grassland. PhD thesis, Harper Adams University College.

Williams, G. and Bowers, J. K. (1987). Land drainage and birds in England and Wales. *RSPB Conserv. Rev.*, **1**, 25–30.

Wilson, A. M., Vickery, J. A., Brown, A. *et al.* (2005). Changes in the numbers of breeding waders on lowland wet grasslands in England and Wales between 1982 and 2002. *Bird Study*, **52**, 55–69.

Wilson, A., Vickery, J. and Pendlebury, C. (2007). Agri-environment schemes as a tool for reversing declining populations of grassland waders: mixed benefits from Environmentally Sensitive Areas in England. *Biol. Conserv.*, **136**, 128–135.

Zorn, M. I., Van Gestel, C. A. M., Morrien, E., Wagenaar, M. and Eijsackers, H. (2008). Flooding responses of three earthworm species, *Allolobophora chlorotica*, *Aporrectodea caliginosa* and *Lumbricus rubellus*, in a laboratory-controlled environment. *Soil Biol. Biochem.*, **40**, 587–593.

Supplementary material: Additional material for this chapter is presented in an electronic appendix (Appendix E11.1) at www.cambridge.org/9780521897563.

CHAPTER TWELVE

Processes influencing bird use of estuarine mudflats and saltmarshes in western Europe

JENNIFER A. GILL
University of East Anglia

The intertidal zone between land and sea provides some of the most productive and complex of habitats, supporting vast numbers of birds of many species. This chapter explores patterns of use of estuarine mudflats and saltmarshes by birds, drivers of within- and between-estuary variation in use of estuarine resources by these species, and consequences of recent environmental changes on estuaries. A series of case studies of anthropogenic impacts on estuarine habitats and their implications for bird populations is described. Although the primary geographic focus of these examples is western Europe, and particularly Britain, estuaries across the globe are experiencing similar threats and impacts. There are also large intertidal areas outside estuaries that provide rather different environments for birds; these are discussed in Chapter 13.

The estuarine environment and its bird assemblages

Estuarine mudflats and sandflats typically occur in areas of shallow, sheltered tidal water, where currents from rivers and tidal movements slow sufficiently to allow settlement of particles of sediment. Sand and gravel particles are typically large enough to settle out of the water column directly, but the settlement of finer particles of silt and clay is aided by the surface attraction displayed by these fine sediments when in salt water, in a process known as flocculation. The resulting formation of extensive areas of mud and sandflat creates a habitat of extreme importance for many intertidal species and communities (Fig. 12.1).

Estuaries typically form in low-lying areas, often as a result of river valleys being 'drowned' by rising sea levels (McLusky and Elliott, 2004). Many originated as drowned river valleys, although Europe also has examples of barrier beaches and embayments, in which sediment build-up occurs as a result of an offshore barrier or between rocky headlands (Davidson *et al.*, 1991). The tidal rhythms of estuaries create a highly dynamic yet predictable system. In Britain, the tidal period typically results in two high tides per day, and the

Birds and Habitat: Relationships in Changing Landscapes, ed. Robert J. Fuller. Published by Cambridge University Press. © Cambridge University Press 2012.

Figure 12.1 (a) Intertidal mudflats at Breydon Water, eastern England. The east coast estuaries of Britain tend to have muddy sediments supporting relatively high biomass of invertebrates that are exploited by extremely large populations of wintering waterbirds. (b) Intertidal sandflats, North Uist, Scotland. Densities of wintering waterbirds on sandy estuaries tend to be lower than those of invertebrate-rich mudflats. (c) Saltmarsh, North Norfolk, eastern England – an important and highly dynamic wintering habitat for seed-eating passerines. Photos: Rob Fuller.

tidal amplitudes are amongst the largest in the world; that of the Severn Estuary is second only to that of the Bay of Fundy in eastern Canada. Individual estuaries also vary in their tidal ranges, with strong influences on plant and animal assemblages.

Estuaries are widespread around the British coast and throughout the Atlantic coast of Europe. Britain contains approximately one quarter of the estuarine area of Europe, and the influence of the Gulf Stream means that its estuaries are less prone to freezing during winter than those on mainland Europe (Davidson *et al.*, 1991). Daily fluctuations in salinity, temperature, inundation and the continuous erosion and settlement of sediments through tidal, wind and wave energy have led to high levels of specialisation among the plants and animals of estuaries. However, the features of estuaries that make them physically extreme environments also make them rich in resources. The continuous and dynamic flow and settlement of sediments from marine and terrestrial sources results in a highly productive and nutrient-rich environment, and nutrient loads are often enhanced by inputs from human settlements (Hill *et al.*, 1993; McLusky and Elliott, 2004). The communities of algae and invertebrates are typically highly abundant, but low in diversity. Mudflats can support densities of tens of thousands of individual invertebrates per square metre, but the number of species is generally lower by two to three orders of magnitude (McLusky and Elliott, 2004). The high densities of polychaetes, molluscs, crustaceans and other invertebrates that mudflats can support provide rich resources for a wide range of bird and fish predators (Prater, 1981; van de Kam *et al.*, 2004).

The deposition and consolidation of sediments in estuaries can lead to vegetation development in the form of saltmarshes. The current European coastline formed approximately 6000 years ago, following the last glaciation and the resulting rapid sea level rise (Allen, 2000). The structure and distribution of European saltmarshes have subsequently been greatly influenced by human activities such as embankment and land claim, grazing, cultivation, mining, sea-salt production and coastal protection (Davy *et al.*, 2009). Land claim for agricultural development has occurred throughout the southern North Sea countries, particularly in the Netherlands, Germany and Denmark, but also along much of the eastern coast of England. Extensive land claim has taken place around the Wash, Humber and Thames estuaries, and also on large estuaries in western Britain, such as the Severn, the Ribble and Morecambe Bay. An estimated 53 400 hectares of saltmarsh has been lost to land claim in Britain (Doody, 1992). The development of new marshes on the seaward side of land claims frequently occurs, but these marshes are typically of lower diversity than the original marsh (Davy *et al.*, 2009). The complex vegetation of saltmarshes provides nesting and roosting habitats and a variety of food resources for birds. Although the densities of invertebrates on saltmarsh habitats are generally far lower than those available on mudflats, saltmarsh plants are extensively grazed by wildfowl and their seeds attract many passerines.

Range of bird species using estuarine habitats in Britain

The large area of diverse saltmarsh habitats supports breeding populations of several bird species. Higher areas of saltmarsh, where inundation is restricted to infrequent high spring tides, can support breeding populations of passerines such as skylark *Alauda arvensis*, reed bunting *Emberiza schoeniclus* and meadow pipit *Anthus pratensis*, and colony-nesting species such as black-headed gulls *Chroicocephalus ridibundus*, and common *Sterna hirundo* and little *Sternula albifrons* terns (Fuller, 1982). Frequent tidal inundation of mudflats and lower areas of saltmarsh prevents most birds from nesting in these zones. However, in east and south east England, the low-mid saltmarsh zone (frequently dominated by saltmarsh plants such as *Atriplex portulacoides*, *Puccinellia maritima* and *Elymus pycnanthus*) supports significant breeding populations of redshank *Tringa totanus* (Norris *et al.*, 1997; Smart, 2005). Declines in British numbers of saltmarsh-breeding redshank in recent decades have been linked to changes in grazing regimes on saltmarsh (Norris *et al.*, 1998). Redshank nests are typically placed in small patches of tall vegetation within areas containing a mosaic of sward structure and height, and high levels of grazing pressure can result in uniform, short swards that are unsuitable for nesting (Norris *et al.*, 1997; Smart, 2005).

While changes in sward structure resulting from grazing activities by livestock and geese may have driven recent changes in numbers of saltmarsh-nesting redshank in Britain, the threat of saltmarsh erosion as a consequence of sea level rise is a greater future threat to these populations (Norris and Buisson, 1994; Norris *et al.*, 1998; Smart and Gill, 2003a). This is in part because most saltmarsh-breeding redshank are concentrated in south east England, and rates of saltmarsh loss and relative sea level rise are greatest in this part of the country (Burd *et al.*, 1989; UKCIP, 2005).

Estuarine habitats worldwide provide resources and shelter for a vast diversity of bird species during the non-breeding season. Mudflats support a wide range of wading bird species, many of which have evolved specific morphological adaptations for exploiting the riches buried within estuarine sediments (see below). In addition, many species of wildfowl occur on mudflats and saltmarshes. Estuaries are particularly important for species such as shelduck *Tadorna tadorna*, teal *Anas crecca* and wigeon *Anas penelope*, but many other wildfowl use estuarine habitats, both as foraging and roosting locations. While waders and wildfowl may be the most well-known bird inhabitants of estuaries, these habitats are also important for a range of other species during the non-breeding season. Large numbers of lesser black-backed *Larus fuscus*, herring *L. argentatus*, common *L. canus*, and black-headed gulls use estuaries in winter (Burton *et al.*, 2003). The huge flocks of waders inevitably attract birds of prey, and many peregrine falcons *Falco peregrinus*, merlins *F. columbarius* and sparrowhawks *Accipiter nisus* move to coastal zones throughout Europe during winter (Wernham *et al.*, 2002; Whitfield, 2003). Passerines also make use of estuarine resources in winter (Kalejta-Summers, 1997; Dierschke and Bairlein, 2004). The seeds of saltmarsh plants in Britain provide key resources for seed-eating species such as twite *Carduelis flavirostris*, skylarks and reed buntings (Brown and Atkinson, 1996; Gillings and Fuller, 2001).

Geographic variation in estuarine bird assemblages

The majority of bird species that inhabit estuarine mudflats and saltmarshes are migratory, with vast numbers arriving from Arctic and sub-Arctic breeding grounds each autumn, at the same time as many of the species breeding on western European estuaries are migrating into southern Europe and Africa (Wernham *et al.*, 2002). While the communities of birds on estuaries around western Europe may appear superficially similar, the origins of the birds can vary greatly. Distinct breeding populations of many shorebird and wildfowl species arrive each autumn from Siberia, Scandinavia, mainland Europe, Iceland, Greenland and Canada (Wernham *et al.*, 2002). Although there is a tendency for birds from westerly breeding locations to winter on north- and west-coast estuaries of Britain, and birds from easterly breeding locations to winter in the east and south, birds from different breeding locations are frequently found in the same estuaries (Wernham *et al.*, 2002; Delany *et al.*, 2009).

Among the clearest examples of different breeding populations having distinct wintering grounds are several goose species. For example, three populations of brent geese *Branta bernicla* winter in Britain and Ireland; the Siberian breeding population occurs on estuaries in south and east England, the Svalbard breeding population winters in north east England and the Canadian breeding population is found almost exclusively in Ireland (Madsen *et al.*, 1999; Wernham *et al.*, 2002). Similarly, barnacle geese *Branta leucopsis* from Svalbard winter almost exclusively around the Solway Firth, whereas barnacle geese from Greenland winter in Ireland and the Western Isles of Scotland (Madsen *et al.*, 1999; Wernham *et al.*, 2002).

Many species of shorebirds and ducks show a higher degree of mixing of breeding populations. For example, redshank from breeding populations in Britain and Ireland (the *totanus* race) and from Iceland (the *robusta* race) frequently occur on the same estuaries in Britain, although in varying proportions (Summers *et al.*, 1988; Derrett and Smith, 2001; Burton *et al.*, 2002). However, the timing of use of British estuaries by different breeding populations of the same species often varies. For example, dunlin *Calidris alpina* of the *schinzii* race breed in Iceland and south east Greenland, and use these estuaries extensively on autumn passage, en route to African wintering grounds. During autumn, the same estuaries are used by dunlin of the *alpina* race, which breed in Scandinavia and Siberia, but these birds remain in Britain throughout the winter (Wernham *et al.*, 2002).

These broad differences between waders and geese in the extent of overlap of different breeding populations in the non-breeding season may in part be a consequence of differences in the extent of their winter range. Whereas most goose populations in western Europe winter over rather narrow latitudinal ranges, wader populations typically have much more extensive non-breeding distributions. Most of the wader populations that winter in coastal habitats occur throughout Europe and often well into Africa, whereas most goose populations occupy a much smaller number of sites, often within one country (Fig. 12.2). This difference may be related to the differing mechanisms by

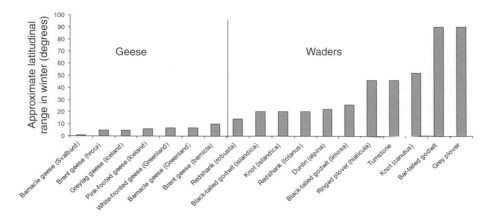

Figure 12.2 Estimated latitudinal ranges of the winter distribution of different breeding populations of geese and waders that occur within the UK (collated from Madsen *et al.*, 1999; Wernham *et al.*, 2002; Delany *et al.*, 2009).

which migration routes are learned by individuals. Geese typically migrate as family parties and thus there is extensive cultural transmission of migration routes and winter location information (Cramp and Simmons, 1977). By contrast, waders migrate independently of the family structure, with juvenile birds typically leaving the breeding grounds after their parents (Reynolds and Székely, 1997; Gunnarsson *et al.*, 2005). Consequently, migration routes and winter locations are likely to be determined through a mix of genetically based orientation, learning from flock-mates, and trial and error, which might be expected to result in a wider range of sites being occupied in winter. Alternatively, the patchy nature of coastal habitats may result in waders wintering over broader geographic areas than herbivorous goose species, for which agricultural landscapes can provide suitable foraging conditions within a relatively small area.

Within-estuary patterns and drivers of distribution and abundance

While mudflats and sandflats may appear, to the human eye at least, to be highly uniform in structure, the frequently patchy distribution of the birds foraging on these habitats suggests otherwise. The distribution of foraging birds on mudflats is influenced by patchiness in the distribution and availability of their prey, but also by constraints on where the birds themselves are prepared to forage. On most tidal systems, birds are able to forage during the low-tide period, but at high tide, when the mudflats are unavailable, they typically gather at nearby roosting sites (usually saltmarshes or beaches) which will not be inundated. The location and availability of these roosting sites can be a major driver of the distribution of birds across an estuary, and the proximity of roost sites can influence their foraging distribution. For example, Dias *et al.* (2006) showed that dunlin foraging densities on the Tagus estuary in Portugal declined with distance from roost, and that few dunlin ever foraged more than 5 km from suitable roosting sites. In the Dutch Wadden Sea, van Gils *et al.* (2006a) showed that red knot *Calidris canutus* trade-off travel distance and the quality of foraging locations; sites that are close to roosts but of low energetic value are typically avoided, while higher-quality foraging sites are used more often if roosting sites are nearby (see also Chapter 15). The foraging and roosting locations of estuarine birds can vary between day and night (Sitters *et al.*, 2001; Burton and Armitage, 2005), as the trade-offs between foraging profitability and safety from predators can differ diurnally and nocturnally. In Roebuck Bay, an area of tropical mudflats in north western Australia, during the daytime great knot *Calidris tenuirostris* and red knot foraged closer to roosts with cool, damp substrates, which may reduce heat stress (Rogers *et al.*, 2006a). However, at night-time, birds were prepared to undertake the energetically expensive longer commute to distant but safer roost sites, highlighting the fine-scale energetic decisions that are necessary in selecting roosting and foraging sites in a tidal environment.

Roosting locations are often used repeatedly within and between years, which may indicate that suitable roosting sites are typically limited in availability (Rehfisch *et al.*, 1996, 2003; Peters and Otis, 2007). Although relatively few studies of roost site quality and the features influencing their selection have been conducted (but see Rogers *et al.*, 2006b; Rosa *et al.*, 2006; Peters and Otis, 2007), there are clear indications that the availability of suitable roosting locations can potentially constrain the use of foraging locations and thus the number of individuals that can be supported by the resources on individual estuaries. Consequently, the identification and protection of roosting locations is likely to be just as important as the protection of foraging sites in estuarine habitats.

While roost site availability and quality can influence the distribution of foraging birds across an estuary, bird distribution within mudflats is likely to be influenced by spatial variation in the abundance and quality of prey. Simple correlations of invertebrate and bird abundance across estuaries generally fail to find clear patterns of association because most species show high levels of prey specialisation and selection. Waders, in particular, display wide morphological adaptation for prey location, with large differences in bill and leg length, variation in bill structure and even highly evolved seasonal changes in gut physiology (Burton, 1974; van de Kam *et al.*, 2004). Thus, despite the very high densities of invertebrate prey that are often present on mudflats, the proportion that is available and profitable for any particular species can vary greatly.

Constraints on the size of prey that can be consumed are often set at the upper limit by bill structure, particularly maximum gape size, and at the lower end by prey profitability (van de Kam *et al.*, 2004). Prey detectability can also influence the types and sizes of prey that are consumed. Wading birds have evolved a variety of mechanisms to enhance prey detectability, including eye shape and structure (Martin and Piersma, 2009) and pressure-sensory mechanisms within the bill (Piersma *et al.*, 1998). Many of the invertebrates on estuarine mudflats are hard-shelled, and thus the birds that consume them must be able to either extract the prey from the shell or to crush the shell internally. Most wading birds have a muscular gizzard and strong, muscular stomachs to provide the force needed to crush hard-shelled prey (van de Kam *et al.*, 2004). Extracting prey from the shells prior to consumption is only likely to be profitable for large molluscs, and consequently only larger waders tend to have evolved methods of prey extraction from shells.

The adaptations of wader species to particular prey types have clear consequences for their foraging distribution. Estuarine wader species typically vary in abundance and distribution, primarily in relation to sediment type and structure. For example, bivalves such as *Scrobicularia plana* and *Macoma balthica* and polychaetes such as the ragworm *Hediste diversicolor* tend to thrive in soft, silty sediments, while cockles *Cerastoderma edule* and lugworms *Arenicola marina* are typically more abundant in coarser-grained sandy sediments (Yates *et al.*, 1993). Consequently, the distribution of estuarine bird species is often directly related to the distribution of prey and sediment type (Yates *et al.*, 1993). An example is illustrated in Fig. 12.3 for two species of godwits *Limosa* spp.

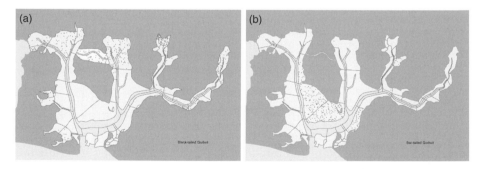

Figure 12.3 Differences in the distribution of (a) black-tailed godwits *Limosa limosa* and (b) bar-tailed godwits *Limosa lapponica* during low tide on Chichester Harbour, south England. The counts were made in winter 2005/2006 using methods described in Musgrove *et al.* (2003). The small dots are proportionate to the densities of feeding birds in different sections of the estuary. Bar-tailed godwits frequently forage on the outer shore of estuaries where coarser-grained sediments provide appropriate conditions for the annelid worms upon which they typically feed, while black-tailed godwits are generally more abundant on inner mudflats where silty sediments and high bivalve densities are often located.

A key driver of spatial and temporal variation in bird abundance within and between estuaries is the seasonal depletion of food resources. At temperate latitudes, seasonal productivity of invertebrate and plant populations can result in a bonanza of foraging opportunities for birds returning from Arctic breeding grounds in the autumn. However, the vast numbers of birds can reduce prey resources rapidly (Mendonca *et al.*, 2007), which can result in a redistribution of birds to alternative foraging locations. For example, brent geese in north Norfolk forage preferentially on saltmarsh plants during autumn and winter, but the depletion of these food sources results in an enforced move to inland sites, where geese forage on the growing tips of cereals and grasses, resulting in unfortunate conflicts with farming activities (Vickery *et al.*, 1995). Wading bird distribution is also strongly influenced by seasonal depletion of prey resources; black-tailed godwits *Limosa limosa* in eastern England severely reduce densities of their bivalve prey during autumn and early winter (Gill *et al.*, 2001a), and subsequently move inland to exploit prey populations on wet grasslands (Gill *et al.*, 2008). Seasonal prey depletion can also drive much larger-scale movements. Van Gils *et al.* (2005) suggest that rapid seasonal depletion of crustacean prey on the Wadden Sea means that only the first red knot to return from the breeding grounds can exploit this resource, and later individuals tend to skip the Wadden Sea and move straight to alternative winter locations.

Predation risk can have a significant impact on foraging distributions within estuaries. Locations at which the risk of predation may be relatively high, for example coastal habitats that are adjacent to woodlands or sea walls, which can conceal approaching predators can be avoided, and the birds that do forage in these locations can be disproportionately vulnerable to predation (Whitfield, 2003; Quinn and Cresswell, 2004).

Between-estuary patterns and drivers of distribution and abundance

While the distribution of birds within an estuary is largely determined by the location of foraging and roosting sites of suitable quality and safety, the distribution of birds between estuaries is typically influenced by larger-scale processes. As previously described, the geographic location of individual estuaries can greatly affect the community that is likely to occur there. In addition, variation in the relative abundance of different sediment types between estuaries can greatly influence the resulting invertebrate and bird communities (Hill *et al.*, 1993). For example, large, open embayment estuaries in Britain, like Morecambe Bay and the Wash, typically contain vast areas of sandflats, which can be dominated by polychaete prey. Consequently, specialist polychaete-feeders, such as bar-tailed godwit *Limosa lapponica* and grey plover *Pluvialis squatarola* are often concentrated around these estuaries. By contrast, narrow, sinuous estuaries, such as the Thames Estuary and Chichester

Harbour, typically contain a higher proportion of muddier sediments, with high densities of molluscs and mollusc specialists, such as oystercatchers, red knot, dunlin and black-tailed godwits (Fig. 12.3).

Weather is also thought to influence the large-scale distribution of estuarine birds, both through mortality and, indirectly, through impacts on prey. Severe weather events, usually prolonged periods of freezing temperatures, can have dramatic effects on estuarine bird populations of particular estuaries. Mass mortality events have been recorded during periods of severe weather and count information suggests that it can take many years for numbers of birds to recover on affected winter sites (Clark, 2009). Estuarine birds may be particularly prone to severe weather because the tidal nature of the habitat can prevent birds from feeding for several hours per day, which may reduce their ability to meet daily energetic demands. Weather can also influence invertebrate prey abundance and quality. For example, several mollusc species at north west European latitudes have metabolic systems that are adapted to cold winters; increased metabolic activity during periods of warm winter weather can reduce body condition and subsequent breeding success (Beukema, 1992; Philippart et al., 2003). The behaviour of prey species can also change with weather conditions. For example, the burrowing depth of the ragworm H. diversicolor increases when sea temperatures are low (Esselink and Zwarts, 1989). While the decline in the frequency of severe winter weather events in Britain in recent decades may have reduced the probability of mass mortality events among birds, the consequences for invertebrate prey populations are less easily predicted.

Recent evidence of an impact of predators on the distribution of birds between estuaries has also been reported. Long-term monitoring of the migration of western sandpipers Calidris mauri through western Canada has indicated that stop-over duration on one of the major estuaries has declined sharply as numbers of peregrine falcons increased, following reductions in pesticide use (Ydenberg et al., 2004). The shortened stop-over duration has resulted in steep declines in the overall use of the estuary by western sandpipers. The mortality costs to estuarine birds of wintering in particular localities are clearly important drivers of large-scale distribution patterns, however, the processes that govern recruitment to winter locations are much less well understood (Gunnarsson et al., 2005). Consequently, patterns of recovery of populations on estuaries that have experienced severe weather, or other extreme events influencing mortality rates, are currently very difficult to predict.

Approaches to understanding the consequences of environmental change on estuaries and saltmarshes

The coastal zone of western Europe can appear relatively pristine, with large areas of 'natural' mudflats and saltmarsh that can sharply contrast with the highly structured agricultural habitats that frequently surround them. However, in reality most of these estuaries and saltmarshes have been heavily modified as a consequence of many different human activities (Davy *et al.*, 2009). The loss and degradation of estuarine habitat through impacts ranging from over-exploitation of estuarine resources (Lotze *et al.*, 2006) to wholesale loss of estuarine ecosystems through land claim (Lie *et al.*, 2008) is ongoing throughout the world. This section outlines some of these human-induced changes and the approaches that have been used to identify their impacts on bird populations.

The development and use of individual-based modelling approaches on estuaries

The juxtaposition of British estuaries as key areas for wildlife and for the development of trade and industry, through port developments, fishing activities and so on, has resulted in frequent battles between developers and conservationists. The pressure for development of estuarine ports for shipping activities is ongoing and the resulting conflict with nature-conservation interests resulted in a need for detailed understanding of the potential impact of these developments on the internationally important bird populations that these sites support. The migratory nature of most estuarine bird populations led to a perception of high mobility of these species, and developers frequently argued that birds could simply move to alternative locations if an area of mudflat or saltmarsh were developed for human uses. This debate led to a series of detailed and intensive empirical studies allied with elegant modelling approaches which have greatly improved our understanding of population-scale responses to environmental changes.

The issue at the heart of many debates between developers and conservationists was whether the loss and degradation of estuarine habitats would result in population decline or population redistribution. There was concern that the loss of access to food supplies resulting from coastal developments would directly increase bird mortality rates and that redistribution to alternative locations could also increase mortality rates if those sites did not contain sufficient resources to support the displaced birds (e.g. Burton *et al.*, 2006). However, even if mortality rates increased either directly through habitat loss or indirectly through redistribution, the overall population size could be unaffected if the reduced density of birds in the breeding season led to increased *per capita* breeding success. These density-dependent responses were thus the key issues to be quantified – would habitat loss result in increased mortality and would such an effect be buffered by increased breeding success. These questions are extremely difficult to address because of the scale at which density and demography have to be measured, and because density-dependence is notoriously difficult to quantify in wild populations

(Sutherland and Norris, 2002). The approach taken by estuarine bird ecologists has focused on understanding the behavioural responses of birds to changing environmental conditions. Behavioural responses such as competition for limited food resources and territorial exclusion of competitors are key mechanisms by which a change in density can alter individual fitness. The development of behaviour-based models provided tools for linking these responses to survival and breeding success probabilities, and thus for predicting the consequences of environmental change for a population. Behaviour-based models are constructed around the fitness consequences of the decisions made by individuals, and they operate by calculating the optimal decision for each individual to maximise its fitness, given the decisions made by other individuals in the population (the evolutionarily stable strategy). One of the major advantages of behaviour-based models over traditional techniques of statistical or demographic modelling is that constructing models around individual decision-making processes allows the consequences of novel environmental conditions to be assessed (Norris, 2004).

Much of the empirical and theoretical development of behaviour-based models focused on studies of foraging waders, in particular through the detailed work of John Goss-Custard and colleagues on the Exe Estuary in Devon (Goss-Custard, 1996; Stillman et al., 2000; Norris, 2004). Oystercatchers on the Exe forage primarily on mussels Mytilus edulis, and the success of individual birds in exploiting this resource is influenced by prey abundance and quality, dominance behaviour and the risk of kleptoparasitism, the technique used to extract the animal from its shell and individual efficiency at foraging on this resource. These parameters were included within a behaviour-based model which was subsequently able to accurately predict levels of mortality resulting from a population increase, and to predict the consequences of issues such as shellfish harvesting and recreational disturbance on oystercatcher populations in the Exe and elsewhere (Stillman et al., 2000, 2001).

Behaviour-based models have generally been constructed around responses to competition for resources, and the majority have been applied to waterbird systems (e.g. Percival et al., 1998; Gill et al., 2001a; Stillman et al., 2001; Goss-Custard et al., 2006). Thus the issues that have arisen as a result of the conflicting demands of humans and birds for estuarine resources have resulted in the development of powerful tools for predicting ecological responses to environmental change.

Identifying and quantifying cross-season links in relation to estuarine habitat quality

Behaviour-based models have been an extremely important development in understanding the local consequences of environmental change. However, at the whole-population scale, the effect of environmental change on particular winter or breeding sites will depend on the consequences for processes operating throughout the annual cycle (Ratikainen *et al.*, 2008). Of particular importance is the extent to which cross-season links are present in populations. If the conditions experienced by individuals in one season 'carry over' and influence their demography in the subsequent season, then the effects of local environmental change can potentially be magnified or reduced.

Establishing migratory connectivity has traditionally relied on bird-ringing to track the movements of individuals between different parts of the migratory range. However, recoveries of ringed birds provide limited opportunities for establishing links between breeding and winter locations, or for quantifying individual habitat use, body condition and demography to identify carry-over effects. However, the widespread use of colour-ringing and tagging studies and the development of intrinsic markers such as stable isotope ratios and genetic markers have aided this field greatly (Webster *et al.*, 2002).

There is a growing body of evidence to suggest that migratory connectivity and carry-over effects are widespread among migratory species, including those occupying estuarine habitats (Gill *et al.*, 2001b; Gunnarsson *et al.*, 2005). In several species of goose, identifying links between the conditions experienced in winter and spring, and subsequent breeding success has been possible because of the fact that geese migrate as family parties, and hence breeding success can be assessed during autumn migration (Ebbinge and Spaans, 1995; Madsen, 1995).

Establishing between-season carry-over effects in species that do not migrate in family parties is more complex, as individuals need to be tracked throughout the annual cycle. However, if the demographic consequences of occupying different types of habitat within each season can be quantified, then tools such as stable isotope analyses of feather or tissue samples can provide a means of remotely quantifying individual habitat use. For example, tracking of colour-marked individuals and stable isotope analyses of feather samples in Icelandic black-tailed godwits wintering in the estuaries of northwestern Europe have shown that individuals wintering on sites with better foraging conditions tend to also breed in habitats in which breeding success is highest (Fig. 12.4; Gill *et al.*, 2001b; Gunnarsson *et al.*, 2005). These links have important implications for demography, as individuals with the highest survival are also those with highest breeding success (Gunnarsson *et al.*, 2005; Ratikainen *et al.*, 2008).

Case studies of anthropogenic issues influencing bird populations on estuaries in Britain

Industrial and urban impacts

Industrial developments on estuaries can result in the loss and degradation of estuarine habitats and their resources. The invertebrate, plant and algal

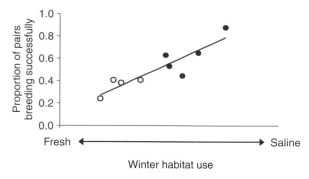

Figure 12.4 Links between winter habitat use and breeding success in migratory Icelandic black-tailed godwits. Godwits foraging on better-quality saline winter sites tend to also breed in better-quality marsh (filled circles) sites, while those on poorer-quality freshwater winter habitats are more likely to breed on poorer-quality dwarf birch bog (open circles) sites (redrawn from Gunnarsson *et al.*, 2005).

populations upon which the bird populations depend are strongly influenced by sediment type and water quality, both of which can be greatly influenced by activities such as dredging for shipping access and the development of ports and harbours. Dredging of mudflats can directly impact invertebrates, as well as increasing turbidity and so reducing light penetration, altering nutrient flow and releasing contaminants from sediments (Johnston, 1981; Knott *et al.*, 2009). Even though these activities are widespread in European estuaries, the impacts on invertebrate and bird populations are not always clear (McLusky and Elliott, 2004). Dredging of sediments may also influence the erosion and accretion of saltmarshes, although this complex issue is also poorly understood. Undoubtedly, more research into the effects of dredging on estuarine ecosystems is needed.

The impact of water quality on estuarine invertebrate populations has received more attention in recent years. The abundance of urban developments along many of the estuaries of Europe has resulted in a long history of waste-water discharge into estuarine waters. Many major British cities are adjacent to estuaries, and estuarine catchments typically contain a high proportion of urban, industrial and agricultural land (McLusky and Elliott, 2004). The potential impact of urban discharge and agricultural runoff on estuarine invertebrates can be severe; high nutrient loadings can lead to hyperabundance of diatoms and phytoplankton, and many invertebrate populations flourish under these rich food conditions (Beukema, 1991; Cardell *et al.*, 1999; Savage *et al.*, 2002). In particular, pollution-tolerant and opportunistic annelid worms can thrive in areas with high nutrient inputs (McLusky and Elliott, 2004). The bird predators of these invertebrate populations can therefore potentially benefit from waste water discharge into estuarine waters, but the extent to which bird abundance and community structure are influenced by water quality impacts on estuarine macrozoobenthos is another complex issue (van de Kam *et al.*, 2004). In recent decades, extensive efforts to reduce nutrient inputs into estuarine systems have taken place throughout Europe, in part as a consequence of the EU Water Framework Directive (and its predecessor, the Urban Waste Water Treatment Directive), which requires member states to achieve 'good ecological status' for all coastal and inland waters by 2015.

Increased abundance and foraging activity of waders and wildfowl close to sewage outfalls has been reported (Pounder, 1976; Campbell, 1984; Alves, 2012), and some studies have reported reductions in numbers of birds when organic loading is reduced (Campbell, 1984; Raven and Coulson, 2001; Burton *et al.*, 2005). However, alternative food sources are likely to have been available in at least some of these cases (Raven and Coulson, 2001; Alves, 2012). Improving the quality of water sources discharging into estuaries is clearly desirable and, while specific components of the invertebrate and bird communities may alter as a result, the available evidence suggests that these effects may be limited, especially in comparison to the likely substantial overall benefits to estuarine ecosystems.

Urban and agricultural development on the lands adjacent to estuaries throughout Europe has resulted in increased demand for freshwater sources, and consequently high levels of abstraction of freshwater sources destined for estuarine systems. Although birds have been shown to aggregate around freshwater streams on estuarine mudflats (Ravenscroft and Beardall, 2003), it is not yet known whether this is a consequence of higher prey densities or availability or whether access to freshwater sources is important for drinking and preening. The consequences of reductions in freshwater inputs into estuaries for invertebrate and plant populations are therefore poorly understood, but are potentially important processes worthy of further study.

Shell fishing

One of the main ways in which human activities on estuarine habitats can directly conflict with bird populations is through shellfish harvesting. The shellfish populations that thrive in the shallow, warm waters of estuarine habitats are a key source of protein for many human societies, and many countries engage in international trade in shellfish. In north western European estuaries, shellfishing is primarily for mussels and cockles, and harvesting techniques range from hand-collecting in some traditionally managed fisheries, to mechanical dredging of large areas of soft sediments. The consequences of shellfishing activities for the bird populations are potentially severe. Some species compete directly with humans for access to these mussels and cockles; oystercatchers frequently forage on mussel and cockle beds and the younger age classes of both species are a key food source for species such as red knot and turnstone *Arenaria interpres*. In addition, mechanical dredging of sediments can lead to extensive damage to non-target invertebrate populations (Ferns *et al.*, 2000), such as polychaetes (e.g. ragworms *H. diversicolor* and catworms *Nephythys caeca*), crustaceans (e.g. shrimps *Corophium volutator*), decapods (e.g. common crab *Carcinus edulis*) and smaller bivalves (e.g. Baltic tellin *Macoma balthica*, peppery furrow shell *Scrobicularia plana* and sandgapers *Mya arenaria*), which are the main prey species for many of the waders inhabiting these estuaries.

The conflict between birds and shellfishers has been explored in detail in Britain and the Netherlands (see also Chapter 15). In the Wadden Sea, mechanical dredging for shellfish has occurred extensively, despite national and international Marine Protected Area status because of its extreme importance for many European migratory bird populations (Verhulst *et al.*, 2004). Detailed studies of invertebrate and shorebird responses to mechanical dredging in the Wadden Sea have shown that both the abundance and the quality of invertebrate prey decline significantly in areas subject to dredging, and that these declines are sufficient to severely impact the population of red knots that uses the area (van de Kam *et al.*, 2004). In addition to declines in shellfish abundance following dredging, studies on the Wadden Sea have shown that the quality of the small cockles that remain after dredging also declines, because the coarser grain sizes of the sediment following dredging reduce the filtering efficiency of bivalves, resulting in a reduced flesh-to-shell ratio (van Gils *et al.*, 2006b). Red knots are capable of adjusting the size of the gizzard in response to the quality of the prey that they are exploiting, and a gradual decline in shellfish quality on the Wadden Sea during the late 1990s and early 2000s was matched by increases in gizzard size among red knots, although these physiological changes do not appear to have been sufficient to prevent significant increases in mortality (van Gils *et al.*, 2006b).

In Britain, the potential impact of shellfishing on waders, particularly oystercatchers, has been the source of long-running debate (Goss-Custard, 1996; Atkinson *et al.*, 2003). Behaviour-based models of oystercatcher distribution and foraging success, and the consequent risk of starvation, have indicated that shellfishing with low-intensity techniques such as hand-collecting and hand-raking has no major impact on oystercatcher mortality, but that mechanical suction dredging has potential to substantially increase oystercatcher mortality (Stillman *et al.*, 2001). These models have also been used to explore the consequences of future fishery management options such as setting harvest limits (Goss-Custard *et al.*, 2003) and minimum sizes for harvesting (Stillman *et al.*, 2001). On the Wash Estuary, years with low abundance of cockles and mussels as a consequence of widespread shellfishing and poor recruitment have been associated with severe mortality of oystercatchers, emigration of red knot (Atkinson *et al.*, 2003) and switching to wheat grain as an alternative prey resource in turnstone (Smart and Gill, 2003b).

Mechanical dredging for cockles and mussels also reduces the abundance of other non-fished bivalves, many of which are the main prey for waders (Piersma *at al.*, 2001; Kraan *et al.*, 2007). Consequently, shellfishing may impact species that do not consume cockles or mussels (e.g. Kraan *et al.*, 2009). Shifts in the community composition of waterbirds on major European estuaries on which intensive commercial shellfishing takes place have recently been noted. On both the Wash Estuary and the Wadden Sea, the abundance of bivalve-feeding species has declined and consequently the community structure has shifted towards polychaete-feeding species (van Roomen *et al.*, 2005; Atkinson *et al.*, 2010). Suction-dredging for shellfish is an activity that does not appear to be compatible with maintaining populations of waterfowl on European estuaries. Given the protected status of most of these sites, this is an issue which seems likely to continue to cause serious concern.

Recreational activities

Coastal zones are popular areas for human recreational activities throughout the world. While sandy beaches undoubtedly hold greater attraction for humans than mudflats and saltmarshes, nonetheless recreational activities on estuaries are common and have rapidly increased in some areas. Coastal paths for walkers, water-borne activities such as sailing and windsurfing, and wildfowling occur on estuaries throughout Britain, leading to concerns that the presence of humans may discourage birds from foraging and roosting on sites that would be used in the absence of these activities. Understanding the magnitude of any such effect therefore ideally requires information on the distribution of birds in the absence of humans. Experimental approaches to understanding the impacts of human presence on bird populations are of particular value. Experimental manipulation of hunting activities on coastal marshes in Denmark has indicated that quite rapid increases in the use of areas from which hunting is excluded can occur, both for hunted and non-hunted species (Madsen, 1998; Bregnballe *et al.*, 2004). However, the consequences of such shifts in distribution for individual fitness and population-scale processes are not known.

Opportunities for the experimental manipulation of human activities in coastal habitats are rare, particularly over the large spatial and temporal scales necessary to identify changes in distribution in highly mobile species within tidal environments. An alternative approach is to relate the distribution and abundance of resources used by the birds to the presence of human activities, in order to assess whether resources are underused in response to human presence. For example, comparison of levels of use of prey resources by black-tailed godwits on mudflats with differing levels of human presence indicated no consistent differences among sites (Gill *et al.*, 2001c). This lack of any effect of human presence on resource use could arise either from godwit distribution being unaffected by human activities, or through any changes in distribution being temporary (Gill, 2007). For example, avoidance of disturbed areas at the start of the season may result in depletion of the available resources within the undisturbed sites and consequent movement into areas that were previously avoided.

During the breeding season, human presence in coastal zones may have greater potential to impact breeding success of species nesting in coastal habitats, either through avoidance of areas with human activity, or more direct effects such as trampling of nests or increased risk of predation (Gill, 2007). For example, a study of ground-nesting ringed plovers *Charadrius hiaticula* in eastern England showed that birds avoided nesting in areas with high levels of human activity (Liley and Sutherland, 2007). Detailed analyses of the quality of nesting territories in this study indicated that some areas that were avoided contained high-quality territories which, in the absence of human presence, would have been expected to be occupied and productive, and thus that the population of plovers would be significantly larger were humans to be excluded from these sites.

It is clearly important to identify the cases where human presence is likely to be a threat to bird populations (Bathe, 2007; Gill, 2007). The evidence to date suggests that human activities during the breeding season have the potential to impact populations of birds nesting in coastal habitats that are attractive to humans, such as beaches. However, during the non-breeding season, estuarine bird populations are likely to face more severe threats from habitat loss and degradation through activities such as land-claim, dredging and shell fishing than from human recreational activities.

Sea-level rise

Against the backdrop of coastal development, sediment dredging, shellfishing and pollution is a new and potentially even more severe threat to coastal habitats. Rising sea levels as a consequence of thermal expansion of the oceans and increased Arctic ice and glacial melt are already impacting low-lying areas around the world (IPCC, 2007). The coastline of Britain is no exception, with rising sea levels likely to result in increased flood risk and coastal erosion (Watkinson *et al.*, 2004). Ongoing isostatic adjustment following glacial retreat means that relative rates of sea-level rise are greatest in south eastern England (Davy *et al.*, 2009), and saltmarsh habitats on many estuaries in these low-lying regions have already experienced severe rates of erosion (Burd, 1989; Wolters *et al.*, 2005). Landward migration of saltmarsh habitats in response to rising sea levels is typically impossible because of the presence of hard sea defences around most low-lying regions of Europe.

Consequently, saltmarsh habitats have been described as experiencing 'coastal squeeze', with rising sea levels moving the lower limit of saltmarshes landwards, but sea walls preventing the movement of the upper regions of saltmarsh. The causes of the rapid erosion of saltmarshes in many of the estuaries of south eastern England are not yet clear, but strong winds and increased wave heights appear to play an important role (Wolters *et al.*, 2005).

The consequences of continued loss of saltmarshes for bird populations could be severe. Increased rates of erosion and tidal inundation are likely to impact the important breeding redshank populations in south east England (Brindley *et al.*, 1998; Smart, 2005). Redshank also breed on wet grassland habitats, both in the coastal zone and further inland, and increasing the area and improving the management of wet grasslands may therefore be the most effective means of maintaining breeding redshank populations (Smart *et al.*, 2006; see also Chapter 11).

Saltmarshes provide key resources for several bird species in winter. In particular, the twite population that breeds in the English uplands relies heavily on the seed resources on saltmarshes in south eastern England during winter (Norris *et al.*, 2004). This twite population has declined rapidly in recent decades, with changes in the availability of both breeding and wintering habitat being implicated in the declines (Norris and Atkinson, 2000), thus the continued loss of saltmarsh habitats in south eastern England may pose a severe threat to this dwindling population.

Saltmarsh erosion may also have important consequences for the availability and quality of roosting sites for waterbirds on estuaries. Saltmarsh roosts are common throughout British estuaries, but the extent to which their availability is limited is currently unknown. However, given the influence of roost locations on patterns of exploitation of mudflat resources by waterbirds (see above), the loss of saltmarsh has clear potential to directly influence the numbers of birds supported by these key habitats.

Managed re-alignment

After centuries of land claim and embankment of British estuaries, the last few years have witnessed a radical change in estuarine management, particularly in south eastern England. Concerns have arisen over the cost-effectiveness of using hard sea defences such as sea walls to defend low-lying coastal areas from flooding (Turner *et al.*, 2007), particularly in the face of rising sea levels, increased wave heights and the widespread erosion of saltmarshes, which can increase the tidal impact on sea walls (Möller *et al.*, 1999). Consequently, recent significant resources and efforts have gone into developing techniques and strategies for managed re-alignment – the deliberate removal or breaching of sea defences to allow tidal flooding of previously protected land (Atkinson *et al.*, 2004; Davy *et al.*, 2009). The intertidal habitats in re-aligned areas can potentially reduce the costs of sea defence by providing protection for the new sea walls and the lands that they protect, particularly if saltmarshes develop. The saltmarsh communities that have developed on sites that were historically breached, usually through major flooding events, suggest that differences from surrounding natural marshes can persist for many decades (Atkinson *et al.*, 2004; Smart, 2005). Studies of re-alignment sites have highlighted the importance of elevation relative to the tidal range, sediment type and drainage capacity in determining the saltmarsh community that is likely to form following sea wall breaching (Atkinson *et al.*, 2001). Nonetheless, the ecological and physical processes determining saltmarsh development on re-alignment sites are still not fully understood and require further study.

Managed re-alignment has real potential to provide important new habitats for estuarine bird populations (Atkinson *et al.*, 2004). Although saltmarsh formation has been the goal of many re-alignment projects to date, intertidal habitats of any type can potentially provide resources for estuarine birds. For example, the creation of a saltmarsh and saline lagoon as part of a re-alignment project at Freiston Shore on the Wash Estuary, eastern England has been extremely successful at attracting large numbers of a wide range of waterbirds (Badley and Allcorn, 2006). The potential for re-alignment projects to be engineered to produce suitable roosting and foraging habitats for waterbirds makes them a very exciting development, and offers a potential means of maintaining and enhancing estuarine bird populations, while also providing important ecosystem services in low-lying coastal zones.

Conclusions and future research directions

Estuarine mudflats, sandflats and saltmarshes provide key habitats for a wide range of bird species throughout the annual cycle. Within Britain, these environments are particularly important for migratory birds during the non-breeding season, when they support internationally important populations of a wide range of species. The migratory and highly mobile nature of these species creates particular complexities in understanding how populations are likely to respond to the many anthropogenic impacts on estuarine habitats. While the development and application of behaviour-based modelling approaches has allowed many issues to be explored at the estuary level, we are only beginning to understand the implications of within-estuary changes for the larger-scale dynamics of these populations.

A major focus of recent research has been to explore the evidence for cross-season carry-over effects that influence individual fitness and demography. Carry-over effects highlight the need to integrate studies at a range of spatial scales in order to understand population-scale consequences of environmental changes within one part of the migratory range. As the site and prey-choice

decisions made by individuals may influence not only their overwinter survival, but also their subsequent body condition in spring, timing of migration,
territory quality and breeding success (Newton, 2008), future research is
needed to quantify the nature, strength and extent of these links.
Addressing these issues will therefore require the integration of small-scale
studies of individual behaviour allied with larger-scale tracking of individual
migration patterns and their consequences. The growing range of technolo-
gies through which patterns of habitat use and distribution can be remotely
assessed is making these complex issues increasingly tractable.

Quantifying the demographic consequences of occupying particular
breeding and non-breeding locations is a major challenge. Predicting
responses to environmental changes in particular sites also requires an
understanding of factors influencing site choice and site fidelity (e.g.
Burton and Armitage, 2008), which is perhaps an even greater challenge.
Constraints on site choice and high levels of site fidelity would imply potentially strong limits on the capacity of a population to locate alternative sites,
but at present we know very little about the factors influencing these
decision-making processes.

Estuaries may be a particularly important habitat in which to address these
issues because of the high levels of anthropogenic activity that they experience and because of their inherently patchy distribution. Among the most
widespread of human activities on estuaries, particularly those supporting
urban and industrial developments, is dredging of sediments. Very little is
currently known about the impacts of dredging and removing large volumes
of sediment on estuarine habitats and communities. The processes driving the
ongoing and rapid erosion of saltmarshes in some parts of Britain are also
poorly understood.

In addition to the threats facing estuaries at present, there are also real
opportunities for habitat creation. Managed re-alignment is increasingly used
as a means of mitigating for loss of habitats to industrial development, and
the mudflats and saltmarshes that can develop on these sites can provide
significant biodiversity benefits, as well as potentially reducing the costs of
coastal protection. Future research that aims to quantify the environmental
services provided by existing and re-created coastal habitats can thus provide
a potentially powerful tool for encouraging the long-term protection of these
habitats and the wonderful array of bird life that they support.

References

Allen, J. R. L. (2000). Morphodynamics of
Holocene saltmarshes: A review sketch from
the Atlantic and Southern North Sea coasts of
Europe. *Quaternary Sci. Rev.*, **19**, 1155–1231.

Alves, J. A., Sutherland, W. J. and Gill, J. A.
(2012). Will improving wastewater
treatment impact shorebirds? Effects of
sewage discharges on estuarine

invertebrates and birds. *Anim. Conserv.*, **15**, 44–52.

Atkinson, P. W., Clark, N. A., Bell, M. C. *et al.* (2003). Changes in commercially fished shellfish stocks and shorebird populations in the Wash, England. *Biol. Conserv.*, **114**, 127–141.

Atkinson, P. W., Crooks, S., Drewitt, A. *et al.* (2004). Managed realignment in the UK – the first 5 years of colonization by birds. *Ibis*, **146** (Suppl.1), 101–110.

Atkinson, P. W., Crooks, S., Grant, A. and Rehfisch, M. M. (2001). *The Success of Creation and Restoration Schemes in Producing Intertidal Habitat Suitable for Waterbirds*. English Nature Research Reports. Peterborough: English Nature.

Atkinson, P. W., Maclean, I. M. D. and Clark, N. A. (2010). Impacts of shellfisheries on waterbird community composition in the Wash, England. *J. Appl. Ecol.*, **47**, 191–199.

Badley, J. and Allcorn, R. I. (2006). The creation of a new saline lagoon as part of a flood defence scheme at Freiston Shore RSPB Reserve, Lincolnshire, England. *Conserv. Evidence*, **3**, 99–101.

Bathe, G. (2007). Political and social drivers for access to the countryside: the need for research on birds and recreational disturbance. *Ibis*, **149** (Suppl. 1), 3–8.

Beukema, J. J. (1991). Changes in composition of bottom fauna of a tidal-flat area during a period of eutrophication. *Mar. Biol.*, **111**, 293–301.

Beukema, J. J. (1992). Expected changes in the Wadden Sea benthos in a warmer world: lessons from periods with mild winters. *Neth. J. Sea Res.*, **30**, 73–79.

Bregnballe, T., Madsen. J. and Rasmussen, P. (2004). Effects of temporal and spatial hunting control in waterbird reserves. *Biol. Conserv.*, **119**, 93–104.

Brindley, E., Norris, K., Cook, T. *et al.* (1998). The abundance and conservation status of redshank *Tringa totanus* nesting on saltmarshes in Great Britain. *Biol. Conserv.*, **86**, 289–297.

Brown, A. F. and Atkinson, P. W. (1996). Habitat associations of coastal wintering passerines. *Bird Study*, **43**, 188–200.

Burd, F. (1989). *The Saltmarsh Survey of Great Britain*. Research and Survey in Nature Conservation No. 17. Peterborough: Nature Conservancy Council.

Burton, P. J. K. (1974). *Feeding and the Feeding Apparatus in Waders*. London: British Museum (Natural History).

Burton, N. H. K and Armitage, M. J. S. (2005). Differences in the diurnal and nocturnal use of intertidal feeding grounds by Redshank *Tringa totanus*. *Bird Study*, **52**, 120–128.

Burton, N. H. K. and Armitage, M. J. S. (2008). Settlement of Redshank *Tringa totanus* following winter habitat loss: effects of prior knowledge and age. *Ardea*, **96**, 191–205.

Burton, N. H. K., Dodd, S. G., Clark, N. A. and Ferns, P. N. (2002). Breeding origins of Redshank *Tringa totanus* wintering at two neighbouring sites on the Severn Estuary: evidence for partial racial segregation. *Ring. Migr.*, **21**, 19–24.

Burton, N. H. K, Fuller, R. A. and Eaton, M. A. (2005). Between-year changes in the wintering sites of Ruddy Turnstones *Arenaria interpres*: a response to diminished food resources? *Wader Study Group Bull.*, **107**, 36–39.

Burton, N. H. K., Musgrove, A. J., Rehfisch, M. M., Sutcliffe, A. and Waters, R. (2003). Numbers of wintering gulls in the United Kingdom, Channel Islands and Isle of Man: a review of the 1993 and previous Winter Gull Roost Surveys. *Brit. Birds*, **96**, 376–401.

Burton, N. H. K, Rehfisch, M. M., Clark, N. A. and Dodd, S. G. (2006). Impacts of sudden winter habitat loss on the body condition and survival of redshank *Tringa totanus*. *J. Appl. Ecol.*, **43**, 464–473.

Campbell, L. H. (1984). The impact of changes in sewage treatment on seaducks wintering in the Firth of Forth, Scotland. *Biol. Conserv.*, **28**, 173–180.

Cardell, M. J., Sardà, R. and Romero, J. (1999). Spatial changes in sublittoral soft-bottom polychaete assemblages due to river inputs and sewage discharges. *Acta Oecol.*, **20**, 343–351.

Clark, J. A. (2009). Selective mortality of waders during severe weather. *Bird Study*, **56**, 96–102.

Cramp, S. and Simmons, K. E. L. (ed.) (1977). *The Birds of the Western Palearctic Volume I*. Oxford: Oxford University Press.

Davidson, N. C. D., d'A Laffoley, D., Doody, J. P. *et al.* (1991). *Nature Conservation and Estuaries in Great Britain*. Peterborough: Nature Conservancy Council.

Davy, A. J., Bakker, J. P. and Figueroa, M. E. (2009). Human Modification of European Saltmarshes. In *Human Impacts on Salt Marshes: A Global Perspective*, ed. B. R. Silliman, E. D. Grosholz and M. D. Bertness, pp. 311–336. Berkeley, California: University of California Press.

Delany, S., Scott, D., Dodman, T. and Stroud, D. (ed.) (2009). *An Atlas of Wader Populations in Africa and Western Eurasia*. Wageningen: Wetlands International.

Derrett, K. and Smith, R. (2001). The status of Icelandic Redshank *Tringa totanus robusta* in north Kent during autumn. *Ring. Migr.*, **20**, 338–343.

Dias, M. P., Granadeiro, J. P., Lecoq, M., Santos, C. D. and Palmeirim, J. M. (2006). Distance to high-tide roosts constrains the use of foraging areas by dunlins: implications for the management of estuarine wetlands. *Biol. Conserv.*, **131**, 446–453.

Dierschke, J. and Barlein, F. (2004). Habitat selection of wintering passerines in saltmarshes of the German Wadden Sea. *J. Ornithol.*, **145**, 48–58.

Doody, J. P. (1992). The conservation of British saltmarshes. In *Saltmarshes: Morphodynamics, Conservation and Engineering Significance*, ed. J. R. L. Allen and K. Pye, pp. 80–114. Cambridge: Cambridge University Press.

Ebbinge, B. S. and Spaans, B. (1995). The importance of body reserves accumulated in spring staging areas in the temperate zone

for breeding in dark-bellied brent geese in the high Arctic. *J. Avian Biol.*, **26**, 105–113.

Esselink, P. and Zwarts, L. (1989). Seasonal trend in burrow depth and tidal variation in feeding activity of *Nereis diversicolor*. *Mar. Ecol. Prog. Ser.*, **56**, 243–254.

Ferns, P. N., Rostron, D. M. and Siman, H. Y. (2000). Effects of mechanical cockle harvesting on intertidal communities. *J. Appl. Ecol.*, **37**, 464–474.

Fuller, R. J. (1982). *Bird Habitats in Britain*. Calton: Poyser.

Gill, J. A. (2007). Approaches to measuring the effects of human disturbance on birds. *Ibis*, **149**, (Suppl. 1), 9–14.

Gill, J. A., Langston, R. H. W., Alves, J. A. *et al.* (2008). Contrasting trends in two Black-tailed Godwit populations: a review of causes and recommendations. *Wader Study Group Bull.*, **114**, 43–50.

Gill, J. A., Norris, K., Potts, P. M. *et al.* (2001b). The buffer effect and large-scale population regulation in migratory birds. *Nature*, **412**, 436–438.

Gill, J. A., Norris, K. and Sutherland, W. J. (2001c). The effects of disturbance on habitat use by black-tailed godwits, *Limosa limosa*. *J. Appl. Ecol.*, **38**, 846–856.

Gill, J. A., Sutherland, W. J. and Norris, K. (2001a). Depletion models can predict shorebird distribution at different spatial scales. *Proc. R. Soc. B*, **268**, 369–376.

Gillings, S. and Fuller, R. J. (2001). Habitat selection by skylarks *Alauda arvensis* wintering in Britain in 1997/98. *Bird Study*, **28**, 293–307.

Goss-Custard, J. D. (ed.) (1996). *The Oystercatcher: From Individuals to Populations*. Oxford: Oxford University Press.

Goss-Custard, J. D., Burton, N. H. K., Clark, N. A. *et al.* (2006). Test of a behavior-based individual-based model: response of shorebird mortality to habitat loss. *Ecol. Appl.*, **16**, 2215–2222.

Goss-Custard, J. D., Stillman, R. A., West, A. D. *et al.* (2003). When enough is not enough:

shorebirds and shellfishing. *Proc. R. Soc. B*, **271**, 233–237.

Gunnarsson, T. G., Gill, J. A, Newton, J., Potts, P. M. and Sutherland, W. J. (2005). Seasonal matching of habitat quality and fitness in migratory birds. *Proc. R. Soc. B*, **272**, 2319–2323.

Hill, D., Rushton, S. P., Clark, N. A., Green, P. and Prys-Jones, R. (1993). Shorebird communities on British estuaries: factors affecting community composition. *J. Appl. Ecol.*, **30**, 220–234.

IPCC (2007). *Climate change 2007: Synthesis Report*. Contribution of Working Groups I, II, and III to the 4th Assessment Report of the Intergovernmental Panel on Climate Change. Geneva: IPCC.

Johnston, S. A. (1981). Estuarine dredge and fill activities: a review of impacts. *Environ. Manage.*, **5**, 427–440.

Kalejta-Summers, B. (1997). Diet and habitat preferences of wintering passerines on the Taff/Ely saltmarshes. *Bird Study*, **44**, 367–373.

Knott, N. A., Aulbury, J. P., Brown, T. H. and Johnston, E. L. (2009). Contemporary ecological threats from historical pollution sources: impacts of large-scale resuspension of contaminated sediments on sessile invertebrate recruitment. *J. Appl. Ecol.*, **46**, 770–781.

Kraan, C., Piersma, T., Dekinga, A., Koolhas, A. and van der Meer, J. (2007). Dredging for edible cockles (*Cerastoderma edule*) on intertidal flats: short-term consequences of fisher patch-choice decisions for target and non-target benthic fauna. *ICES J. Mar. Sci.*, **64**, 1735–1742.

Kraan, C., van Gils, J. A., Spaans, B. *et al.* (2009). Landscape-scale experiment demonstrates that Wadden Sea intertidal flats are used to capacity by molluscivore migrant shorebirds. *J. Anim. Ecol.*, **78**, 1259–1268.

Lie, H. J., Cho, C. H., Lee, S. *et al.* (2008). Changes in marine environment by a large coastal development of the Saemangeum Reclamation Project in Korea. *Ocean Polar Res.*, **30**, 373–545.

Liley, D. and Sutherland, W. J. (2007). Predicting the population consequences of human disturbance for Ringed Plovers *Charadrius hiaticula*: a game theory approach. *Ibis*, **149**, (Suppl. 1): 82–94.

Lotze, H. K., Lenihan, H. S., Bourque, B. J. *et al.* (2006). Depletion, degradation, and recovery potential of estuaries and coastal seas. *Science*, **213**, 1806–1809.

Madsen, J. (1995). Impacts of disturbance on migratory waterfowl. *Ibis*, **137**, 67–74.

Madsen, J. (1998) Experimental refuges for migratory waterfowl in Danish wetlands. II. Tests of hunting disturbance effects. *J. Appl. Ecol.*, **35**, 398–417.

Madsen, J., Cracknell, G. and Fox, A. D. (1999). *Goose Populations of the Western Palearctic: A Review of Status and Distribution*. Wageningen: Wetlands International.

Martin, G. R. and Piersma, T. (2009). Vision and touch in relation to foraging and predator detection: insightful contrasts between a plover and a sandpiper. *Proc. R. Soc. B*, **276**, 437–445.

McLusky, D. S. and Elliott, M. (2004). *The Estuarine Ecosystem: Ecology, Threats and Management*. Oxford: Oxford University Press.

Mendonca, V. M., Raffaelli, D. G. and Boyle, P. R. (2007). Interactions between shorebirds and benthic invertebrates at Culbin Sands lagoon, NE Scotland: effects of avian predation on their prey community density and structure. *Sci. Mar.*, **71**, 579–591.

Möller, I., Spencer, T., French, J. R., Leggett, D. J. and Dixon, M. (1999). Wave transformation over salt marshes: a field and numerical modelling study from North Norfolk, England. *Estuar. Coast. Shelf Sci.*, **49**, 411–426.

Musgrove, A. J., Langston, R. H. W., Baker, H. and Ward, R. M. (2003). *Estuarine Waterbirds at Low Tide: the WeBS Low Tide Counts 1992/93 to 1998/99*. Thetford: WSG/BTO/WWT/RSPB/JNCC.

Newton, I. (2008). *The Migration Ecology of Birds*. London: Academic Press.

Norris, K. (2004). Managing threatened species: the ecological toolbox, evolutionary theory and declining-population paradigm. *J. Appl. Ecol.*, **41**, 413–426.

Norris, K. and Atkinson, P. W. (2000). Declining populations of coastal birds in Great Britain: victims of sea-level rise and climate change? *Environ. Res.*, **8**, 303–323.

Norris, K., Atkinson, P. W. and Gill, J. A. (2004). Climate change and coastal waterbird populations – past declines and future impacts. *Ibis*, **146** (Suppl. 1), 83–90.

Norris, K., Brindley, E., Cook, T. *et al.* (1998). Is the density of redshank *Tringa totanus* nesting on saltmarshes in Great Britain declining due to changes in grazing management? *J. Appl. Ecol.*, **35**, 621–634.

Norris, K. and Buisson, R. (1994). Sea-level rise and its impact upon coastal birds in the UK. *RSPB Conserv. Rev.*, **8**, 63–71.

Norris, K., Cook, T., O'Dowd, B. and Durdin, C. (1997). The density of redshank *Tringa totanus* breeding on the salt-marshes of the Wash in relation to habitat and its grazing management. *J. Appl. Ecol.*, **34**, 999–1013.

Percival, S. M., Sutherland, W. J. and Evans, P. R. (1998). Intertidal habitat loss and wildfowl numbers: applications of a spatial depletion model. *J. Appl. Ecol.*, **35**, 57–63.

Peters, K. A. and Otis, D. L. (2007). Shorebird roost-site selection at two temporal scales: is human disturbance a factor? *J. Appl. Ecol.*, **44**, 196–209.

Philippart, C. J., van Aken, H. M., Beukema, J. J. *et al.* (2003). Climate-related changes in recruitment of the bivalve *Macoma balthica*. *Limnol.Oceanogr.*, **48**, 2171–2185.

Piersma, T., Koolhaas, A., Dekinga, A. *et al.* (2001). Long-term indirect effects of mechanical cockle-dredging on intertidal bivalve stocks in the Wadden Sea. *J. Appl. Ecol.*, **38**, 976–990.

Piersma, T., van Aelst, R., Kurk, K., Berkhoudt, K. and Maas, L. R. M. (1998). A new pressure sensory mechanism for prey detection in birds: the use of principles of seabed dynamics? *Proc. R. Soc. B*, **265**, 1377–1383.

Pounder, B. (1976). Wintering flocks of Goldeneyes at sewage outfalls in the Tay estuary. *Bird Study*, **23**, 121–131.

Prater, A. J. (1981). *Estuary Birds of Britain and Ireland*. Calton: Poyser.

Quinn, J. L. and Cresswell, W. (2004). Predator hunting behaviour and prey vulnerability. *J. Anim. Ecol.*, **73**, 143–154.

Ratikainen, I. I., Gill, J. A., Gunnarsson, T. G., Sutherland, W. J. and Kokko, H. (2008). When density-dependence is not instantaneous: theoretical developments and management implications. *Ecol. Lett.*, **11**, 184–198.

Raven, S. J. and Coulson, J. C. (2001). Effects of cleaning a tidal river of sewage on gull numbers: a before-and-after study of the River Tyne, northeast England. *Bird Study*, **48**, 48–58.

Ravenscroft, N. O. M. and Beardall, C. H. (2003). The importance of freshwater flows over estuarine mudflats for wintering waders and wildfowl. *Biol. Conserv.*, **113**, 89–97.

Rehfisch, M. M., Clark, N. A., Langston, R. H. W. and Greenwood, J. J. D. G. (1996). A guide to the provision of refuges for waders: an analysis of 30 years of ringing data from the Wash, England. *J. Appl. Ecol.*, **33**, 673–687.

Rehfisch, M. M., Insley, H. and Swann, B. (2003). Fidelity of overwintering shorebirds to roosts on the Moray Basin, Scotland: implications for predicting impacts of habitat loss. *Ardea*, **91**, 53–70.

Reynolds, J. D. and Székely, T. (1997). The evolution of parental care in shorebirds: life histories, ecology, and sexual selection. *Behav. Ecol.*, **8**, 126–134.

Rogers, D. I., Battley, P. F., Piersma, T., van Gils, J. A. and Rogers, K. G. (2006a). High-tide habitat choice: insights from modeling roost selection by shorebirds around a tropical bay. *Anim. Behav.*, **72**, 563–575.

Rogers, D. I., Piersma, T. and Hassell, C. J. (2006b). Roost availability may constrain shorebird distribution: exploring the energetic costs of roosting and disturbance around a tropical bay. *Biol. Conserv.*, **133**, 225–235.

Rosa, S., Encarnação, A. L., Granadeiro, J. P. and Palmeirim, J. M. (2006). High-tide roost selection by waders: maximizing feeding opportunities or avoiding predation? *Ibis*, **148**, 88–97.

Savage, C., Elmgren, R. and Larsson, U. (2002). Effect of sewage-derived nutrients on an estuarine macrobenthic community. *Mar. Ecol. Prog. Ser.*, **243**, 67–82.

Sitters, H., González, P., Piersma, T., Baker, A. J. and Price, D. J. (2001). Day and night feeding habitat of red knots in Patagonia: profitability versus safety? *J. Field Ornithol.*, **72**, 86–95.

Smart, J. (2005). Strategies of sea-level rise mitigation for breeding redshank. Unpublished PhD Thesis, University of East Anglia, UK.

Smart, J. and Gill, J. A. (2003a). Climate change and the potential impact on breeding waders in the UK. *Wader Study Group Bull.*, **100**, 80–85.

Smart, J. and Gill, J. A. (2003b). Non-intertidal habitat use by shorebirds: a reflection of inadequate intertidal resources? *Biol. Conserv.*, **111**, 359–369.

Smart, J., Gill, J. A., Sutherland, W. J. and Watkinson, A. R. (2006). Predicting the habitat requirements of waders breeding on grassland. *J. Appl. Ecol.*, **43**, 454–463.

Stillman, R. A., Goss-Custard, J. D., West, A. D. *et al.* (2000). Predicting mortality in novel environments: tests and sensitivity of a behaviour-based model. *J. Appl. Ecol.*, **37**, 564–588.

Stillman, R. A., Goss-Custard, J. D., West, A. D. *et al.* (2001). Predicting shorebird mortality and population size under different regimes of shellfishery management. *J. Appl. Ecol.*, **38**, 857–868.

Summers, R. W., Nicoll, M., Underhill, L. G. and Petersen, A. (1988). Methods for estimating the proportions of Icelandic and British redshanks *Tringa totanus* in mixed populations wintering on British coasts. *Bird Study*, **35**, 169–180.

Sutherland, W. J. and Norris, K. (2002). Behavioural models of population growth rates: implications for conservation and prediction. *Phil. Trans. R. Soc. B*, **357**, 1273–1284.

Turner, R. K., Burgess, D., Hadley, D., Coombes, E. and Jackson, N. (2007). A cost–benefit appraisal of coastal managed realignment policy. *Global Environ. Change*, **17**, 397–407.

UKCIP (2005). *Updates to Regional Net Sea-Level Change Estimates for Great Britain*. Report Number 124. Oxford: UKCIP.

van de Kam, J., Ens, B. J., Piersma, T. and Zwarts, L. (2004). *Shorebirds: An illustrated Behavioural Ecology*. Utrecht: KNNV Publishers.

van Gils, J. A., Dekinga, A. Spaans, B., Vahl, W. T and Piersma, T. (2005). Digestive bottleneck affects foraging decisions in red knots *Calidris canutus*. II. Patch choice and length of working day. *J. Anim. Ecol.*, **74**, 120–130.

van Gils, J. A., Spaans, B., Dekinga, A. and Piersma, T. (2006a). Foraging and a tidally structured environment by red knots (*Calidris canutus*): ideal, but not free. *Ecology*, **87**, 1189–1202.

van Gils, J. A., Piersma, T., Dekinga, A., Spaans, B. and Kraan, C. (2006b). Shellfish dredging pushes a flexible avian top predator out of a Marine Protected Area. *PLOS Biol.*, **4**, 2399–2404.

van Roomen, M., van Turnhout, C., van Winden *et al.* (2005). Trends in benthivorous waterbirds in the Dutch Wadden Sea 1975–2002: large differences between shellfisheaters and worm-eaters. *Limosa*, **78**, 21–38.

Verhulst, S., Oosterbeek, K., Rutten, A. L. and Ens, B. J. (2004). Shellfish fishery severely reduces condition and survival of oystercatchers despite creation of large marine protected areas. *Ecol. Society*, **9**, 17.

Vickery, J. A., Sutherland, W. J., Watkinson, A. R., Rowcliffe, J. M. and Lane, S. J. (1995). Habitat switching by dark-bellied brent geese *Branta b. bernicla* (L.) in relation to food depletion. *Oecologia*, **103**, 499–508.

Watkinson, A. R., Gill, J. A. and Hulme, M. (2004). Flying in the face of climate change: a review of climate change, past, present and future. *Ibis*, **146** (Suppl. 1), 4–10.

Webster, M. S., Marra, P. P., Haig, S. M., Bensch, S. and Holmes, R. T. (2002). Links between worlds: unraveling migratory connectivity. *Trends Ecol. Evol.*, **17**, 76–83.

Wernham, C.V., Toms, M.P., Marchant, J.H. *et al.* (ed). (2002). *The Migration Atlas: Movements of the Birds of Britain and Ireland*. London: Poyser.

Whitfield, D.P. (2003). Predation by Eurasian sparrowhawks produces density-dependent mortality of wintering redshanks. *J. Anim. Ecol.*, **72**, 27–35.

Wolters, M., Bakker, J.P., Bertness, M.D., Jefferies, R.L. and Möller, I. (2005). Saltmarsh erosion and restoration in south-east England:

squeezing the evidence requires realignment. *J. Appl. Ecol.*, **42**, 844–851.

Yates, M.G., Goss-Custard, J.D., McGrorty, S. *et al.* (1993). Sediment characteristics, invertebrate densities and shorebird densities on the inner banks of the Wash. *J. Appl. Ecol.*, **30**, 599–614.

Ydenberg, R.C., Butler, R.W., Lank, D.B., Smith, B.D. and Ireland, J. (2004). Western sandpipers have altered migration tactics as peregrine falcon populations have recovered. *Proc. R. Soc. B*, **271**, 1263–1269.

CHAPTER THIRTEEN

Avian habitat use on the non-estuarine intertidal coast

NIALL H. K. BURTON

British Trust for Ornithology

Non-estuarine ('open') coasts provide extensive and varied habitats for birds. Rocky intertidal shores, in particular, can provide abundant food resources for several species, notably waders (Feare and Summers, 1985). These resources and the bird assemblages that use them are fundamentally different in several respects to those occurring within estuaries (Chapter 12). This chapter reviews the bird assemblages that use intertidal habitats outside estuaries, habitat associations and constraining factors, interactions between the use of the open coast and supratidal and other adjacent habitats, and the impacts of recent environmental changes on avian assemblage composition and habitat relationships. The focus is on intertidal habitats and not other open coast habitats such as dune systems, coastal scrub and cliffs; this wider, highly varied range of coastal environments supports diverse assemblages of migrating and breeding birds, most notably of passerines and breeding seabirds. While the chapter primarily considers the avian assemblages that use non-estuarine intertidal habitats in Europe, in particular Britain, I also draw on studies from elsewhere in reviewing the factors and environmental changes that affect habitat use.

Non-estuarine intertidal habitats and their bird assemblages

The intertidal habitats found on the open coast include both soft-substrate (typically sandy) shores and rocky shores of exposed bedrock, boulders and shingle (gravel), the character of which depends greatly on the prevailing rock type and the shore's exposure (Little *et al.*, 2009). Rocky shore habitats can be highly varied and complex, and in Britain, at least, may be extensively covered by beds of mussels (chiefly *Mytilus edulis*), limpets, barnacles and seaweed (including brown algae such as *Fucus*, *Ascophyllum* and *Pelvetia*, and green algae such as *Ulva*), while subtidal areas can support dense beds of kelp (e.g. *Laminaria*) (Connor *et al.*, 2004). These habitats support a varied avifauna, both in the breeding and, notably, the non-breeding seasons – a previous review of bird species utilising rocky shores, for example, reported that a total of 47 species fed in the rocky intertidal zone at Robin Hood's Bay, Yorkshire (Feare and Summers, 1985).

Birds and Habitat: Relationships in Changing Landscapes, ed. Robert J. Fuller. Published by Cambridge University Press. © Cambridge University Press 2012.

Waders represent probably the most significant species group using non-estuarine intertidal habitats. A total of *c.* 790 000 waders of 27 species was recently estimated to winter on the non-estuarine coasts of 12 countries extending from southern Sweden to Croatia (Burton *et al.*, 2008). The most abundant species were oystercatcher *Haematopus ostralegus*, dunlin *Calidris alpina*, curlew *Numenius arquata* and lapwing *Vanellus vanellus* (Fig. 13.1). Species for which non-estuarine habitats were estimated to hold over 25% of biogeographic populations, and thus which may be viewed as being particularly dependent on these habitats, were ringed plover *Charadrius hiaticula*, sanderling *Calidris alba*, purple sandpiper *C. maritima* and turnstone *Arenaria interpres*. The former two species, together with Kentish plover *Charadrius alexandrinus*,

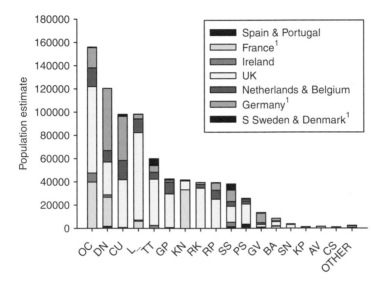

Figure 13.1 Estimates of the numbers of waders using northwest Europe's non-estuarine coast in winter (derived from Burton *et al.*, 2008; note, no estimates were produced for Norway, Iceland or the Faeroes).[1] = minimum population estimates. OC = oystercatcher *Haematopus ostralegus*, DN = dunlin *Calidris alpina*, CU = curlew *Numenius arquata*, L_ = lapwing *Vanellus vanellus*, TT = turnstone *Arenaria interpres*, GP = golden plover *Pluvialis apricaria*, KN = knot *Calidris canutus*, RK = redshank *Tringa totanus*, RP = ringed plover *Charadrius hiaticula*, SS = sanderling *Calidris alba*, PS = purple sandpiper *Calidris maritima*, GV = grey plover *Pluvialis squatarola*, BA = bar-tailed godwit *Limosa lapponica*, SN = snipe *Gallinago gallinago*, KP = Kentish plover *Charadrius alexandrinus*, AV = avocet *Recurvirostra avosetta*, CS = common sandpiper *Actitis hypoleucos*; other species recorded were greenshank *Tringa nebularia*, black-tailed godwit *Limosa limosa*, whimbrel *Numenius phaeopus*, little stint *Calidris minuta*, grey phalarope *Phalaropus fulicarius*, spotted redshank *Tringa erythropus*, jack snipe *Lymnocryptes minimus*, green sandpiper *Tringa ochropus*, black-winged stilt *Himantopus himantopus* and ruff *Philomachus pugnax*.

are particularly associated with sandy shores and the latter two with rocky shores (Summers *et al.*, 1988, 2002).

Several wader species also breed on open coasts. In Europe, sandy coasts represent a particularly important breeding habitat for Kentish and ringed plovers (Schulz and Stock, 1993; Conway *et al.*, 2008; Liley and Sutherland, 2007). Oystercatchers may also nest on rocky coasts, shingle beaches and dunes, as well as saltmarshes (Heppleston, 1972). Such habitats provide foraging opportunities for young, while providing adults with access to intertidal prey. In Britain, ringed plovers and oystercatchers occur in particularly high densities on the coastal machair of the Outer Hebrides (Fuller *et al.*, 1986), though the extent to which breeding adults use or require the adjacent beaches is limited.

Open coasts are also of considerable importance for a number of species of seaduck which dive in shallow water to forage on invertebrate prey, most notably mussels. Previously, at least 120 000 scaup *Aythya marila*, 1 700 000 eiders *Somateria mollissima*, 2 100 000 long-tailed ducks *Clangula hyemalis*, 610 000 common scoters *Melanitta nigra*, 140 000 velvet scoters *M. fusca* and 89 000 red-breasted mergansers *Mergus serrator* wintered in Europe (BirdLife International, 2004), the majority associated with open coasts, though there have been recent declines in some of these populations. In addition to these species, significant numbers of pochards *Aythya ferina*, tufted ducks *A. fuligula* and goldeneyes *Bucephala clangula* also winter off the open coast. Eiders forage largely on mussels and are most associated with intertidal zones, having an exclusively coastal distribution throughout the year. An estimated 840 000–1 200 000 pairs breed in Europe (BirdLife International, 2004).

Within Europe, the majority of these wader and wildfowl populations are found in the north. Britain (including the Isle of Man) holds 50% of the total estimated number of non-breeding waders occurring on Europe's non-estuarine coasts, France 19%, Germany 14% and Ireland 12% (Burton *et al.*, 2008). This pattern applies for most species, though Kentish plover *Charadrius alexandrinus*, little stint *Calidris minuta* and whimbrel *Numenius phaeopus* have a more southerly distribution. The largest numbers of wintering seaduck on Europe's open coasts are typically found in the Baltic (BirdLife International, 2004).

Significant numbers of gulls also use non-estuarine coasts in the non-breeding seasons. During the 2003/04–2005/06 UK Winter Gull Roost Survey, for example, 534 616 black-headed gulls *Chroicocephalus ridibundus*, 198 457 common gulls *Larus canus*, 13 576 lesser black-backed gulls *L. fuscus*, 211 211 herring gulls *L. argentatus* and 17 880 great black-backed gulls *L. marinus* were counted across estuarine and non-estuarine coasts, though these raw counts underestimate the total numbers using these habitats (Banks *et al.*, 2007). Cormorants *Phalacrocorax carbo*, grey herons *Ardea cinerea* and little egrets *Egretta garzetta* also exploit the fish and crustacean populations found on rocky shores (Carss and Elston, 2003).

Amongst the passerines, as a breeding species, the rock pipit *Anthus petrosus* is almost exclusively found on the non-estuarine coast, nesting in tussocks and crevices on rock cliffs and other slopes and preferentially feeding in the intertidal zone, though the species also uses saltmarshes in the winter (Gibb, 1956; Feare, 1970; Kalejta-Summers, 1997; Dierschke, 2002). Corvids may also forage extensively on invertebrate prey on intertidal shores (Robinette and Ha, 2000; Hori and Noda, 2001a, 2001b), in Europe, most notably hooded crows *Corvus cornix* (Berrow, 1992a, b) and jackdaws *C. monedula* (Burnett, 2009). In addition, the food resources of non-estuarine intertidal habitats may be exploited at times by many other passerine species, including wagtails, wheatears *Oenanthe oenanthe*, blackbirds *Turdus merula* and starlings *Sturnus vulgaris* (Backlund, 1945; Feare and Summers, 1985; Hori and Noda, 2001a; Burnett, 2009). Burnett (2009), for example, observed a total of 21 species, including 14 passerines, feeding on strandlines in the Firth of Clyde during a breeding season study.

Habitat associations and constraining factors

The densities of birds found on non-estuarine intertidal habitats may vary considerably, both between and within habitats (Hubbard and Dugan, 2003), though they are typically greater on rocky as opposed to sandy shores (Lafferty, 2001; Figs. 13.2 and 13.3). This variation chiefly reflects the densities and distribution of food resources, but also a number of further constraints (Feare and Summers, 1985; see also Chapter 12). Invertebrate prey densities, particularly on rocky shores, may be extremely high and these habitats can thus support very high densities of birds. In turn, these species may have a considerable impact on the size and structure of the invertebrate populations and ecosystems that they exploit (Feare, 1967; Marsh, 1986; Wootton, 1992, 1997; Ellis *et al.*, 2005, 2007; Hori *et al.*, 2006).

The habitat preferences of waders utilising non-estuarine coasts in Britain in the non-breeding seasons are well documented. In the Orkney Islands, sandy shores were preferred by ringed plovers, sanderlings and bar-tailed godwits *Limosa lapponica*; oystercatchers, golden plovers *Pluvialis apricaria* and purple sandpipers preferred rocky shores, while turnstones preferred gravel and rocky shores (Summers *et al.*, 2002); other wader species selected muddy, more typically estuarine, substrates). Purple sandpipers, ringed plovers and bar-tailed godwits additionally preferred exposed shores, and curlews and redshanks *Tringa totanus* sheltered shores, while sanderlings, purple sandpipers, dunlins, bar-tailed godwits and turnstones also showed a preference for wider shores (i.e. broad rock platforms, up to 200 m wide). These habitat preferences are typical for the species, though it should be noted that preferences may also be affected by geology. In Shetland, where rocky shores are predominantly comprised of metamorphic and igneous rocks in contrast to

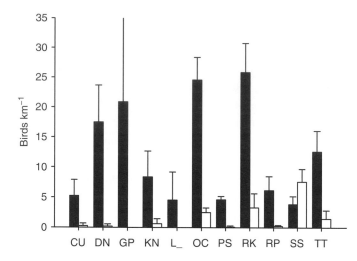

Figure 13.2 Lowtide densities (birds km^{-1}) of wader species on rocky (black bars) and sandy (white bars) intertidal shores along a 39 km stretch of the Northumberland coast, UK (data are means ± 1 SD of 10 counts across winter 2005/06). CU = curlew, DN = dunlin, GP = golden plover, KN = knot, L_ = lapwing, OC = oystercatcher, PS = purple sandpiper, RK = redshank, RP = ringed plover, SS = sanderling, TT = turnstone. See Fig. 13.1 for scientific names. The data are derived from surveys undertaken as part of a project funded by Northumbrian Water Limited.

the sedimentary rocks found in Orkney, ringed plovers preferred sandy shores, and golden plovers and purple sandpipers shallow-sloping bedrock, whereas oystercatchers, curlews and turnstones showed no clear preferences (Summers *et al.*, 1988). On the Isles of Scilly, Kirby (1990) similarly reported that ringed plovers, sanderlings, dunlins and to a lesser extent, turnstones, preferred sandy shores, whereas purple sandpipers preferred shores with boulders, and all species avoided shores of exposed igneous bedrock. Summers and Nicoll (2004) further reported that purple sandpipers avoided areas where channel wrack *Pelvetia canaliculata* was abundant and thus preferred lower intertidal zones. These preferences reflect the species' diets and the breadth of the food resources they exploit – turnstones, for example, being more catholic in their diet than purple sandpipers (Cramp and Simmons, 1983).

The habitat preferences of grey herons on rocky coasts in Scotland have been investigated by Carss and Elston (2003) who found that adults preferred algae-dominated shores, particularly those dominated by the kelp *Ascophyllum nodosum*. Herons primarily fed on small fish in these habitats e.g. fifteen-spined sticklebacks *Spinachia spinachia*, butterfish *Pholis gunnellus* and viviparous blenny *Zoarces viviparous*. Fish species richness and abundance were greater on *Ascophyllum*-dominated shores than on those dominated by bladder-wrack *Fucus vesiculosus*.

Feare and Summers (1985) have previously outlined the constraints that affect the use of rocky shore intertidal habitats by feeding birds. Use of the

Figure 13.3 (a) Knot *Calidris canutus* feeding on a rocky shore, northeastern England – densities of waders are typically much higher on rocky than sandy shores (see Fig. 13.2). (b) Seaweed deposit, South Uist, Scotland. Strandline accumulations of seaweed such as this attract large numbers of feeding waders. (c) A rocky outcrop on an otherwise sandy beach in North Uist, Scotland which provides the focal centre for most of the waders feeding on this beach during migration and in winter. (d) An open sandy beach, North Uist, Scotland which attracts few feeding waders with the exception of sanderling *Calidris alba*. Photos: (a) Niall Burton, (b)–(d) Rob Fuller.

intertidal is chiefly limited by the tidal cycle, but also by other physical factors such as climate and weather. Except for seaduck, which dive for their prey when it is covered by water, prey only becomes available to birds as it is uncovered by the tide and certain prey species may only become available at low tide, or even only on the lowest spring tides. For example, on rocky coasts in Japan, sea urchins are a favoured prey of gulls and crows, and are only accessible at low tide in shallow subtidal areas and rock crevices (Hori and Noda, 2001a). Many bird species prefer prey that are active and consequently move up and down the shore with the tide, consuming different prey in different zones (Feare, 1966; Feare and Summers, 1985; Hori and Noda, 2001a). The use of different habitats or zones of the shore is primarily driven by the need of species to meet their energy requirements as efficiently as possible. For example, seaduck such as eider tend to select feeding habitats characterised by high (invertebrate) prey density and shallow water in order to minimise the time and energy spent while diving (Guillemette *et al.*, 1993). Similarly, in California, sanderlings switched between open coast sandy beaches and estuarine sand-flats over the tidal cycle according to the availability of prey in order to max-imise their feeding efficiency (Connors *et al.*, 1981).

At northerly latitudes short day-length and the timing of tides may restrict the time available for foraging during the day. Consequently, many wader species also need to forage at night to meet their energetic requirements. The extent of nocturnal foraging may also be influenced by moonlight (Heppleston, 1971), though this may be more true for visual predators, such as plovers, than *Calidris* and *Tringa* spp., that are tactile feeders at night (Pienkowski, 1981). Evidence suggests that some species, such as purple sandpiper, may spend less of their time at night foraging, indicating that the intake rates achievable may be lower and that the species probably favours diurnal foraging (Eaton, 2001). Nevertheless, populations of this spe-cies and its close relative, the rock sandpiper *Calidris ptilocnemis*, are able to winter north of the Arctic circle (Summers *et al.*, 1990b) and thus must clearly be able to meet their energy requirements through nocturnal foraging. At such latitudes, the energetic requirements imposed by the severe climate, as well as the formation of ice on open shores (Smith and Bleakney, 1969; Ruthrauff and Eskelin, 2009) restrict the species that are able to overwinter. Even at more temperate latitudes, increased wave intensity associated with stormy weather may also limit the time available for feeding where coasts are exposed (Feare, 1966; Dierschke, 1993; Hori and Noda, 2001a).

Imposed on these general patterns are further constraints, most notably the need to avoid areas where the risk of predation or levels of disturbance are high. Studies of purple sandpipers and turnstones in rocky shore habitats have shown how vigilance levels increase when birds' views of their surround-ings are impaired (Metcalfe, 1984). This is because the risk of predation is typically greatest in areas that are close to cover and consequently such areas may be avoided or occupied by subordinate individuals (Cresswell, 1994; Hilton *et al.*, 1999). Fitzpatrick and Bouchez (1998) reported that the vigilance of wintering waders in relation to human activity tends to be greatest in higher shore zones and on the ebb tide birds may delay their arrival to areas where disturbance levels are high and similarly depart from such areas earlier on the flood tide.

A number of studies have examined how the intra- and interspecific density-dependent competition for the rich, but patchily distributed, food resources found in rocky shore systems may limit species use of this environ-ment. Guillemette and Himmelman (1996), for example, examined how patch use by eiders feeding on mussels compared with models of the dispersion of individuals in relation to their resources. They found that eiders initially crowded into a small number of food-rich patches when their densities increased, indicating that interference competition did not affect their distribution. However, as prey was depleted, birds became more dispersed and patch use was correlated with food availability and thus followed a simple 'ideal free distribution'. In contrast, Summers *et al.* (1990a) reported that a degree of resource partitioning existed between the sexes in purple sandpipers, as longer-billed females took larger prey items (mussels and littorinids) than shorter-billed males. It was concluded that this sexual dimorphism may have evolved, or at least been maintained or enhanced, due to competitive displacement on the wintering grounds. Intraspecific competition, and so in turn the numbers of individuals that are able to use particular areas of habitat, may be affected by the spatial distribution of food resources. In a field experiment, Vahl *et al.* (2007) found that competition between turnstones was reduced if food patches were more evenly distributed and as a consequence a greater number of birds were able to use the area. Similarly, interspecific competition may also be a driver of habitat use: Rome and Ellis (2004), for instance, found that aggression by great black-backed gulls prevented herring gulls from foraging on crabs in shallow subtidal zones.

The seasonal depletion of prey in coastal areas by birds may lead to changes in the prey species or size classes taken by particular species (Cayford and Goss-Custard, 1990) and thus the habitats they use. O'Connor and Brown (1977) reported how depletion of cockle stocks by oystercatchers on Strangford Lough, Northern Ireland, led to significant movements away from the site by the end of the winter. The foraging preferences of one species may also indirectly affect the habitat use of another: Hori and Noda (2001b), for example, reported how consumption of green algae by gulls during winter actually helped to increase the number of algal mats during spring and so limited the accessibility of chitons for foraging crows.

The use of supratidal and other habitats adjacent to the intertidal zone

Species utilising intertidal rocky shore food resources, such as turnstone and purple sandpiper, show a high degree of within- and between-year site fidelity (Metcalfe and Furness, 1985; Summers *et al.*, 1990b, 2001; Burton and Evans, 1997; Dierschke, 1998) likely reflecting the predictability of the food resources found in this habitat. Nevertheless, many species may also exploit other habitats and resources and their availability may be important in determining the populations that non-estuarine coasts are able to support, and assemblage composition.

Supratidal (i.e. strandline) food resources, in particular, may be used extensively by waders that are more typically associated with intertidal foraging habitats and probably are important in allowing them to meet their energy demands. Deposits of beach-cast seaweed (i.e. brown *Fucus*, *Ascophyllum*, *Pelvetia* and *Laminaria*) are not only important components of productivity and nutrient cycling in open coast systems but, due to the rich invertebrate fauna that these beds support as they decompose, also represent a valuable habitat for foraging birds (Dugan *et al.*, 2003; Fuller, 2003), though the ecological importance of this resource has received little study (Kirkman and Kendrick, 1997). In Britain, kelp flies *Coelopa frigida* typically represent the most abundant fauna in these deposits and may be exploited by turnstones and purple sandpipers (Summers *et al.*, 1990a; Dierschke, 1993; Fuller, 2003). Banks of beach-cast seaweed vary in extent and distribution according to weather patterns and season, with the amount of stranded material being closely correlated to storms and thus greatest in winter (Rodil *et al.*, 2008). Nevertheless, seaweed banks are probably an extensive and predictable enough resource on open coasts for supratidal feeding to play a much more important role in open coast systems than in estuarine systems (Fuller, 2003). In Britain, banks of beach-cast seaweed are an important habitat for waders staging in the Orkneys and Outer Hebrides prior to their migrations to their Arctic breeding grounds (Prŷs-Jones *et al.*, 1992; Corse and Summers, 1999; Fig. 13.3). Dugan *et al.* (2003) reported that numbers of grey plovers *Pluvialis squatarola* and Kentish plovers on sandy beaches in California were positively correlated with the extent of beach-cast seaweed, while Bradley and Bradley (1993) found that numbers of turnstones, both *Arenaria melanocephala* and *A. interpres*, wintering in California increased after the recovery (from pollution) of kelp beds offshore, which presumably influenced quantities of beach-cast seaweed, though this was not directly measured.

Fuller (2003) explored the use of supratidal habitats, specifically beach-cast seaweed, by turnstones in northeast England. In his study, the energy content of prey items in beach-cast seaweed was on average three times that of items found in intertidal habitats (see also Summers *et al.*, 1990a; Dierschke, 1993) and the habitat was used more by birds of higher dominance rank. This, and the extensive use of beach-cast seaweed, suggests that this habitat is not simply used to compensate for inadequate energy intake during the intertidal period. Indeed, Dierschke (1993) reported that purple sandpipers may at times feed on seaweed banks in preference to rocky intertidal habitats in order to fulfil their energy demands more quickly and so reduce the time that they spend exposed to wind. Use of this habitat, however, potentially exposes birds to an increased predation risk, as shown by increased levels of vigilance (Fuller, 2003).

Many waders also make extensive use of other habitats adjacent to the open coast (Goss-Custard, 1969; Heppleston, 1971; Townshend *et al.*, 1981; Evans Ogden *et al.*, 2005). The resources found in wet grassland may be particularly important in contributing to the energy demands of coastal wintering waders (see Chapter 12 for discussion of black-tailed godwits *Limosa limosa*). In northeast England turnstones frequently fed on playing fields or other areas of short grass in suburban areas immediately adjacent to the coast over winter high-tide periods and, particularly, while building up resources prior to spring migration (Burton, 1995). On the Wash Estuary, Smart and Gill (2003) found that use of superabundant food resources in non-intertidal habitats by turnstones increased over the winter and was greater on colder days, suggesting that intertidal resources could not support the local population throughout the winter.

Environmental changes affecting avian use of non-estuarine intertidal habitats
Climate change

The distributions of several wader species wintering on British estuaries have changed in association with climate change, count data suggesting that less severe recent winters have allowed greater proportions of British wader populations to winter on the generally richer, but traditionally colder, east coast estuaries (Austin and Rehfisch, 2005). A similar pattern has been seen across northwest Europe as a whole, with the non-breeding distributions of waders shifting to the north and east as winter temperatures have increased (Maclean *et al.*, 2008). Eastward and northward shifts in the distributions of wader species on Britain's non-estuarine coast have likewise been linked with increasingly mild and less extreme winter temperatures (Rehfisch *et al.*, 2004).

While the decreasing severity of winter weather has been suggested as one potential direct driver of these shifts, climate change might also affect the birds wintering on open coasts indirectly through effects on their food supplies. Of particular concern is the possibility that the abundance and productivity of brown algae (i.e. wrack and kelp) will decrease due to increasing sea and air temperatures, the loss of cover potentially being exacerbated by the increases in storminess that are also predicted as a consequence of global warming (Kendall *et al.*, 2004). This would directly affect the rocky shore feeding habitats of some species, such as grey herons (see above), and also reduce the availability of beach-cast seaweed and so potentially have significant effects on species such as turnstone (see above). Further, reductions in the abundance and productivity of brown algae are predicted to have knock-on effects for the productivity of open coast systems because of the nutrients supplied by decaying algae (Kendall *et al.*, 2004).

Sea defences and beach-cleaning

In the developed world, in particular, an increasing proportion of the open coast has been modified by coastal development and the construction of sea defences against sea-level rise (Thompson *et al.*, 2002), though the effects of this on avian assemblages have received little attention. In estuarine habitats, the combination of sea-level rise as a consequence of the thermal expansion of oceans and the presence of hard sea defences potentially threatens the extent of saltmarsh through 'coastal squeeze' (see also Chapter 12). On open sandy coasts, Dugan and Hubbard (2006) outlined how the imposition of hard sea defences would first impact sand-stabilising vegetation and the supratidal zone before leading to accelerated erosion and beach narrowing. This in turn would impact the retention of beach-cast seaweed. Their study in California found that the species richness and abundance of waders, and the abundance of gulls, were significantly greater on 'unarmoured' as opposed to 'armoured' segments of beach.

Beach-cleaning – i.e. the regular mechanical removal of strandline deposits such as beach-cast seaweed – may severely reduce the density and diversity of supratidal invertebrates (Llewellyn, 1996) and is potentially a significant issue for birds on open coasts (Defoe et al., 2009), though to date has been the subject of little study (Burnett, 2009). Guidelines for the 'Blue Flag' scheme that promotes environmental management of beaches state that 'algae vegetation or natural debris should be left on the beach' . . . . 'as long as it does not present a nuisance' (http://www.blueflag.org/Menu/Criteria/Beach+Criteria/Beach_Criteria_Explanatory_Notes_2010.pdf).

Human recreational activities

Open coasts, particularly sandy beaches, are subject to considerable pressure from recreational activities. Species that breed on open coasts, such as plovers and terns, may be particularly susceptible, either because disturbance leads to avoidance of potential nesting areas, or because of the increased probability of nests or young being accidentally destroyed or exposed to predators. A great many studies have thus shown how recreational disturbance may impact the abundance and aspects of the breeding performance (nest and chick survival) and the overall breeding productivity of beach-nesting plover species, including ringed plover (Liley and Sutherland, 2007), Kentish plover (Schulz and Stock, 1993; Ruhlen et al., 2003), piping plover Charadrius melodus (Flemming et al., 1988; Melvin et al., 1994), Malaysian plover C. peronii (Yasué and Dearden, 2006) and white-fronted plovers C. marginatus (Baudains and Lloyd, 2007). Although high recreational pressure generally has negative consequences for populations of these birds, in some cases quite subtle relationships have been shown. Baudains and Lloyd (2007), for example, examined the reproductive success of white-fronted plovers at two South African sites, one with low and one with high recreational activity. Nest mortality (from mammalian and corvid predators) was significantly lower at the site with high recreation, whereas chick mortality (mostly from dogs) was significantly greater at that site. As a consequence, per capita annual productivity was substantially higher at the more disturbed site.

Liley and Sutherland (2007) and Yasué and Dearden (2006) used modelling approaches to identify the factors, including human disturbance, that influenced the habitat selection and breeding success of, respectively, ringed plover and Malaysian plover. In each of these studies, the species preferred wide beaches. Based on their models, and information on adult mortality, Liley and Sutherland (2007) were able to predict the impacts of different levels of disturbance and concluded that the local population was reduced in size by recreational pressure excluding birds from some potential breeding habitat. Understanding of the potential effects of recreational disturbance on breeding plovers has directly informed management strategies for these species (e. g. Lafferty *et al.*, 2006).

There has similarly been considerable research on the behavioural responses of non-breeding coastal waterbirds to disturbance (e.g. for non-estuarine habitats: Burton *et al.*, 1996; Fitzpatrick and Bouchez, 1998). However, simple behavioural measures such as flushing distances do not necessarily reflect the potential costs of human disturbance and thus may be misleading indicators of likely impacts (Gill *et al.*, 2001; Beale and Monaghan, 2004; Yasué, 2006). Furthermore, a number of studies have shown that the abundance of waders using open coastal habitats may not always be related to the level of human activity observed (e.g. Lafferty, 2001; Neuman *et al.*, 2008). The potential for disturbance during the non-breeding seasons to impact coastal bird populations has been explored through individual-based models, which relate the observed behavioural responses of individuals to disturbance to their fitness (body condition and survival) costs and thus population consequences (West *et al.*, 2002; Goss-Custard *et al.*, 2006; Stillman *et al.*, 2007).

Changes in water quality

Sewage and other waste water discharges can provide foraging opportunities for a wide variety of bird species in both freshwater and coastal habitats. Several previous studies have highlighted their particular importance for coastal waterbirds – for example, in directly providing food for gulls (Ferns and Mudge, 2000) and seaduck (e.g. Campbell, 1978; Campbell *et al.*, 1986), or by enhancing the invertebrate food supplies (e.g. Savage *et al.*, 2002) of waders and wildfowl through nutrient and organic enrichment (reviewed by Burton *et al.*, 2002).

Considerable efforts have been made to reduce nutrient and organic inputs (from both point sources and from diffuse agricultural run-off) into European coastal systems, most recently through the EU Water Framework Directive and its predecessor, the Urban Waste Water Treatment Directive (UWWTD). While improving coastal water quality is clearly a desirable aim, there is some evidence that bird numbers may be reduced following such improvements

(Campbell, 1984; Raven and Coulson, 2001; Burton *et al.*, 2005). Burton and Goddard (2007) investigated the effects of the UWWTD for waders wintering in northeast England. Following changes in sewage disposal, the percentage of particulate organic matter attributable to sewage, and thus probably the total organic matter available to filter-feeding invertebrates such as mussels, declined. Reductions in the numbers of turnstones and purple sandpipers coincided with this decline, local changes appearing dependent on the positions of outfalls relative to the intertidal zone. The effects of reductions in nutrient and organic inputs on waterbirds will typically be highly localised, and often hard to disentangle from other factors.

Conclusions

Much has been learnt in recent decades about the ecology of birds on non-estuarine coasts and it is now appreciated that these environments provide complementary habitats to those occurring within estuaries. They support considerable populations of wintering waders and wildfowl, with a number of species being particularly dependent on these habitats. Nonetheless, the waterbird populations wintering on open coasts remain less frequently and less comprehensively covered by monitoring schemes in comparison to those in estuarine and freshwater habitats. There is also a need for a better understanding of the importance of open coasts and their habitats for a range of other species – notably gulls and passerines.

It is apparent that strandlines, in particular deposits of beach-cast seaweed, can support a wide range of bird species. There is considerable scope for developing a better understanding of the importance of this resource for waders and other species (Kirkman and Kendrick, 1997). Fuller (2003) suggested a latitudinal gradient in the use of beach-cast seaweed by turnstones, whereby birds wintering further north may need to utilise this or other non-intertidal habitats more than those wintering in the tropics or southern hemisphere, due to greater energy demands and shorter day-length (though this does not appear to be the case for purple sandpipers: Strann and Summers, 1990). Understanding such interactions would be valuable in predicting the implications of environmental change. Further work is also desirable on the extent to which waterbirds wintering along open coasts depend on supplementary or complementary resources from nearby terrestrial or estuarine habitats.

Among the environmental issues discussed here, the effects of the construction of sea defences and beach-cleaning on the avian assemblages of open coasts have received least attention, and would be particularly worthy of future research. The wider population-level implications of essentially local issues such as recreational disturbance and changes in water quality also remain to be explored.

Acknowledgements

My thanks to Ron Summers and Jenny Gill for their useful comments on an earlier draft of this chapter.

References

Austin, G. E. and Rehfisch, M. M. (2005). Shifting nonbreeding distributions of migratory fauna in relation to climatic change. *Glob. Change Biol.*, **11**, 31–38.

Backlund, H. O. (1945). Wrack fauna of Sweden and Finland: ecology and chorology. *Opuscula Entomol. Suppl.*, **5** (Suppl.), 1–256.

Banks, A. N., Burton, N. H. K., Calladine, J. R. and Austin, G. E. (2007). *Winter Gulls in the UK: Population Estimates from the 2003/04–2005/06 Winter Gull Roost Survey*. BTO Research Report No. 456. Thetford: BTO.

Baudains, T. P. and Lloyd, P. (2007). Habituation and habitat changes can moderate the impacts of human disturbance on shorebird breeding performance. *Anim. Conserv.*, **10**, 400–407.

Beale, C. M. and Monaghan, P. (2004). Behavioural responses to human disturbance: a matter of choice? *Anim. Behav.*, **68**, 1065–1069.

Berrow, S. D., Kelly, T. C. and Myers, A. A. (1992a). The diet of coastal breeding Hooded Crows *Corvus corone cornix*. *Ecography*, **15**, 337–346.

Berrow, S. D., Kelly, T. C. and Myers, A. A. (1992b). The mussel caching behaviour of Hooded Crows *Corvus corone cornix*. *Bird Study*, **39**, 115–119.

BirdLife International. (2004). *Birds in Europe: Population Estimates, Trends and Conservation Status*. Cambridge: BirdLife International.

Bradley, R. A. and Bradley, D. W. (1993). Wintering shorebirds increase after kelp (*Macrocystis*) recovery. *Condor*, **95**, 372–376.

Burnett, H. (2009). The use of strandlines as a foraging habitat by birds on the Isle of Cumbrae. MSc Thesis, Queen Mary University of London.

Burton, N. H. K. (1995). Roosting and associated feeding behaviour of Turnstones *Arenaria interpres* and Purple Sandpipers *Calidris maritima* in north-east England. PhD Thesis, University of Durham.

Burton, N. H. K., Blew, J., Colhoun, K. *et al.* (2008). Population status of waders wintering on Europe's non-estuarine coasts. In *The European Non-Estuarine Coastal Waterbird Survey*, ed. N. H. K. Burton, M. M. Rehfisch, D. A. Stroud and C. J. Spray, pp. 95–101. Thetford: International Wader Study Group.

Burton, N. H. K. and Evans, P. R. (1997). Survival and winter site-fidelity of Turnstones *Arenaria interpres* and Purple Sandpipers *Calidris maritima* in north-east England. *Bird Study*, **44**, 35–44.

Burton, N. H. K., Evans, P. R. and Robinson, M. A. (1996). Effects on shorebird numbers of disturbance, the loss of a roost site and its replacement by an artificial island at Hartlepool, Cleveland. *Biol. Conserv.*, **77**, 193–201.

Burton, N. H. K., Fuller, R. A. and Eaton, M. A. (2005). Between-year changes in the wintering sites of Ruddy Turnstones *Arenaria interpres*: a response to diminished food resources? *Wader Study Group Bull.*, **107**, 36–39.

Burton, N. H. K. and Goddard, A. P. (2007). *Impacts of Changes in Sewage Disposal on Populations of Waterbirds Wintering on the Northumbrian Coast*. Final report. BTO Research Report No. 442. Thetford: BTO.

Burton, N. H. K., Paipai, E., Armitage, M. J. S. *et al.* (2002). *Effects of Reductions in Organic and Nutrient Loading on Bird Populations in Estuaries and Coastal Waters of England and Wales. Phase 1 Report*. BTO Research Report No. 267. BTO, Thetford.

Campbell, L. H. (1978). Patterns of distribution and behaviour of flocks of seaducks wintering at Leith and Musselburgh, Scotland. *Biol. Conserv.*, **14**, 111–123.

Campbell, L. H. (1984). The impact of changes in sewage treatment on seaducks wintering in the Firth of Forth, Scotland. *Biol. Conserv.*, **28**, 173–180.

Campbell, L. H., Barrett, J. and Barrett, C. F. (1986). Seaducks in the Moray Firth: a review of their current status and distribution. *Proc. R. Soc. Edinb.*, **91B**, 105–112.

Carss, D. N. and Elston, D. A. (2003). Patterns of association between algae, fishes and Grey Herons *Ardea cinerea* in the rocky littoral zone of a Scottish sea loch. *Estuar. Coast. Shelf Sci.*, **58**, 265–277.

Cayford, J. T. and Goss-Custard, J. D. (1990). Seasonal changes in the size selection of Mussels, *Mytilus edulis* by Oystercatchers, *Haematopus ostralegus*: an optimality approach. *Anim. Behav.*, **40**, 609–624.

Connor, D. W., Allen, J. H., Golding, N. *et al.* (2004). *The Marine Habitat Classification for Britain and Ireland. Version 04.05.* Peterborough: JNCC. http://www.jncc.gov.uk/MarineHabitatClassification/.

Connors, P. G., Myers, J. P., Connors, C. S. W. and Pitelka, F. A. (1981). Interhabitat movements by Sanderlings in relation to foraging profitability and the tidal cycle. *Auk*, **98**, 4–64.

Conway, G. J., Burton, N. H. K., Austin, G. E. and Handschuh, M. (2008). *UK Population Estimates from the 2007 Breeding Little Ringed Plover and Ringed Plover Surveys.* BTO Research Report No. 510. BTO, Thetford.

Corse, C. J. and Summers, R. W. (1999). The seasonal pattern of numbers, population structure and migration of Purple Sandpipers in Orkney. *Ring. Migr.*, **19**, 275–282.

Cramp, S. and Simmons, K. E. L. (ed.) (1983). *The Birds of the Western Palearctic. Vol. III.* Oxford: Oxford University Press.

Cresswell, W. (1994). Age-dependent choice of Redshank (*Tringa totanus*) feeding location: profitability or risk? *J. Anim. Ecol.*, **63**, 589–600.

Defoe, O., McLachlan, A., Schoeman, D. S. *et al.* (2009). Threats to sandy beach ecosystems: a review. *Estuar. Coast. Shelf Sci.*, **81**, 1–12.

Dierschke, J. (2002). Occurrence and habitat use of Rock Pipit *Anthus petrosus* in the German Wadden Sea. *Vogelwelt*, **123**, 125–134.

Dierschke, V. (1993). Food and feeding ecology of Purple Sandpipers *Calidris maritima* on rocky intertidal habitats (Helgoland, German Bight). *Neth. J. Sea Res.*, **31**, 309–317.

Dierschke, V. (1998). Site fidelity and survival of Purple Sandpipers *Calidris maritima* at Helgoland (SE North Sea). *Ring. Migr.*, **19**, 41–48.

Dugan, J. E. and Hubbard, D. M. (2006). Ecological responses to coastal armoring on exposed sandy beaches. *Shore and Beach*, **74**, 10–16.

Dugan, J. E., Hubbard, D. M., McCrary, M. and Pierson, M. (2003). The response of macrofauna communities and shorebirds to macrophyte wrack subsidies on exposed sandy beaches of southern California. *Estuar. Coast. Shelf Sci.*, **58**, 133–148.

Eaton, M. A. (2001). **Determinants of habitat and site use by Turnstones and Purple Sandpipers in N.E. England, and possible effects of the removal of coastal nutrients.** PhD Thesis, University of Durham.

Ellis, J. C., Chen, W., O'Keefe, B., Shulman, M. J. and Witman, J. D. (2005). Predation by gulls on crabs in rocky intertidal and shallow subtidal zones of the Gulf of Maine. *J. Exp. Mar. Biol. Ecol.*, **324**, 31–43.

Ellis, J. C., Shulman, M. J., Wood, M., Witman, J. D. and Lozyniak, S. (2007). Regulation of intertidal food webs by avian predators on New England rocky shores. *Ecology*, **88**, 853–863.

Evans Ogden, L. J., Hobson, K. A., Lank, D. B. and Bittman, S. (2005). Stable isotope analysis reveals that agricultural habitat provides an important dietary component for nonbreeding Dunlin. *Avian Conserv. Ecol.*, **1**, http://www.ace-eco.org/vol1/iss1/art3/.

Feare, C. J. (1966). The winter feeding of the Purple Sandpiper. *Brit. Birds*, **59**, 165–179.

Feare, C. J. (1967). The effect of predation by shorebirds on a population of Dogwhelks *Thais lapillus. Ibis*, **109**, 474.

Feare, C. J. (1970). Aspects of the ecology of an exposed shore population of Dogwhelks *Nucella lapillus* (L.). *Oecologia*, **5**, 1–18.

Feare, C. J. and Summers, R. W. (1985). Birds as predators on rocky shores. In *The Ecology of Rocky Coasts*, ed. P. G. Moore and R. Seed, pp. 249–264. London: Hodder and Stoughton.

Ferns, P. N. and Mudge, G. P. (2000). Abundance, diet and *Salmonella* contamination of gull feeding at sewage outfalls. *Water Res.*, **34**, 2653–2660.

Fitzpatrick, S. and Bouchez, B. (1998). Effects of recreational disturbance on the foraging behaviour of waders on a rocky beach. *Bird Study*, **45**, 157–171.

Flemming, S. P., Chiasson, R. D., Austin-Smith, P. J. and Bancroft, R. P. (1988). Piping Plover status in Nova Scotia related to its reproductive and behavioral responses to human disturbance. *J. Field Ornithol.*, **59**, 321–330.

Fuller, R. A. (2003). Factors influencing foraging decisions in Ruddy Turnstones *Arenaria interpres* (L.). PhD Thesis, University of Durham.

Fuller, R. J., Reed, T. M., Buxton, N. E. *et al.* (1986). Populations of breeding waders (Charadrii) and their habitats on the crofting lands of the Outer Hebrides. *Biol. Conserv.*, **37**, 333–361.

Gibb, J. (1956). Food, feeding habits and territory of the Rock Pipit *Anthus spinoletta*. *Ibis*, **98**, 506–530.

Gill, J. A., Norris, K. and Sutherland, W. J. (2001). Why behavioural responses may not reflect the population consequences of human disturbance. *Biol. Conserv.*, **97**, 265–268.

Goss-Custard, J. D. (1969). The winter feeding ecology of the Redshank *Tringa totanus*. *Ibis*, **111**, 338–356.

Goss-Custard, J. D., Triplet, P., Sueur, F. and West, A. D. (2006). Critical thresholds of disturbance by people and raptors in foraging wading birds. *Biol. Conserv.*, **127**, 88–97.

Guillemette, M. and Himmelman, J. H. (1996). Distribution of wintering Common Eiders over mussel beds: does the ideal free distribution apply? *Oikos*, **76**, 435–442.

Guillemette, M., Himmelman, J. H., Barette, C. and Reed, A. (1993). Habitat selection by common eiders in winter and its interaction with flock size. *Can. J. Zool.*, **71**, 1259–1266.

Heppleston, P. B. (1971). The feeding ecology of Oystercatchers *Haematopus ostralegus* L. in winter in northern Scotland. *J. Anim. Ecol.*, **40**, 651–672.

Heppleston, P. B. (1972). The comparative ecology of Oystercatchers (*Haematopus ostralegus*) in inland and coastal habitats. *J. Anim. Ecol.*, **41**, 23–51.

Hilton, G. M., Ruxton, G. D. and Cresswell, W. (1999). Choice of foraging area with respect to predation risk in Redshanks: the effects of weather and predator activity. *Oikos*, **87**, 295–302.

Hori, M. and Noda, T. (2001a). Spatio-temporal variation of avian foraging in the rocky intertidal food web. *J. Anim. Ecol.*, **70**, 122–137.

Hori, M. and Noda, T. (2001b). An unpredictable indirect effect of algal consumption by gulls on crows. *Ecology*, **82**, 3251–3256.

Hori, M., Noda, T. and Nakao, S. (2006). Effects of avian grazing on the algal community and small invertebrates in the rocky intertidal zone. *Ecol. Res.*, **106**, 768–775.

Hubbard, D. M. and Dugan, J. E. (2003). Shorebird use of an exposed sandy beach in southern California. *Estuar. Coast. Shelf Sci.*, **58**, 169–182.

Kalejta-Summers, B. (1997). Diet and habitat preferences of wintering passerines on the Taff/Ely saltmarshes. *Bird Study*, **44**, 367–373.

Kendall, M. A., Burrows, M. T. and Hawkins, S. J. (2004). Predicting the effects of marine climate change on the invertebrate prey of the birds of rocky shores. *Ibis*, **146** (Suppl. 1), 40–47.

Kirby, J. S. (1990). Numbers, distribution and habitat preferences of waders wintering on the Isles of Scilly. *Wader Study Group Bull.*, **57**, 47–52.

Kirkman, H. and Kendrick, G. A. (1997). Ecological significance and commercial harvesting of drifting and beach-cast macro-algae and seagrasses in Australia: a review. *J. Appl. Phycol.*, **9**, 311–326.

Lafferty, K. D. (2001). Birds at a Southern California beach: seasonality, habitat use and disturbance by human activity. *Biodivers. Conserv.*, **10**, 1949–1962.

Lafferty, K. D., Goodman, D. and Sandoval, C. P. (2006). Restoration of breeding by Snowy Plovers following protection from disturbance. *Biodivers. Conserv.*, **15**, 2217–2230.

Liley, D. and Sutherland, W. J. (2007). Predicting the population consequences of human disturbance for Ringed Plovers *Charadrius hiaticula*: a game theory approach. *Ibis*, **149** (Suppl. 1), 82–94.

Little, C., William, G. A. and Trowbridge, C. D. (2009). *The Biology of Rocky Shores*. Second edition. Oxford: Oxford University Press.

Llewellyn, P. (1996). The effects of beach cleaning on invertebrate populations. *Brit. Wildlife*, **7**, 147–155.

Maclean, I. M. D., Austin, G. E., Rehfisch, M. M. *et al.* (2008). Climate change causes rapid changes in the distribution and site abundance of birds in winter. *Glob. Change Biol.*, **14**, 2489–2500.

Marsh, C. P. (1986). Rocky intertidal community organization: the impact of avian predators on mussel recruitment. *Ecology*, **67**, 771–786.

Melvin, S. M., Hecht, A. and Griffin, C. R. (1994). Piping Plover mortalities caused by off-road vehicles on Atlantic coast beaches. *Wildlife Soc. Bull.*, **22**, 409–414.

Metcalfe, N. B. (1984). The effects of habitat on the vigilance of shorebirds: is visibility important? *Anim. Behav.*, **106**, 981–985.

Metcalfe, N. B. and Furness, R. W. (1985). Survival, winter population stability and site-fidelity in the Turnstone *Arenaria interpres*. *Bird Study*, **32**, 207–214.

Neuman, K. K, Henkel, L. A. and Page, G. W. (2008). Shorebird use of sandy beaches in central California. *Waterbirds*, **31**, 115–121.

O'Connor, R. J. and Brown, R. A. (1977). Prey depletion and foraging strategy in the Oystercatcher *Haematopus ostralegus*. *Oecologia*, **27**, 75–92.

Pienkowski, M. W. (1981). How foraging plovers cope with environmental effects on invertebrate behaviour and availability. In *Feeding and Survival Strategies of Estuarine Organisms*, ed. N. V. Jones and W. J. Wolff, pp. 179–192. New York: Plenum Press.

Prŷs-Jones, R. P., Corse, C. J. and Summers, R. W. (1992). The role of the Orkney Islands as a staging post for Turnstones *Arenaria interpres*. *Ring. Migr.*, **13**, 83–89.

Raven, S. J. and Coulson, J. C. (2001). Effects of cleaning a tidal river of sewage on gull numbers: a before-and-after study of the River Tyne, northeast England. *Bird Study*, **48**, 48–58.

Rehfisch, M. M., Austin, G. E., Freeman, S. N., Armitage, M. J. S. and Burton, N. H. K. (2004). The possible impact of climate change on the future distributions and numbers of waders on Britain's non-estuarine coast. *Ibis*, **146** (Suppl. 1), 70–81.

Robinette, R. L. and Ha, J. (2000). Beach-foraging behavior of Northwestern Crows as a function of tide height. *Northwest. Nat.*, **81**, 18–21.

Rodil, F. I., Olabarria, C., Lastra, M. and Lopez, J. (2008). Differential effects of native and invasive algal wrack on macrofaunal assemblages inhabiting exposed sandy beaches. *J. Exp. Mar. Biol. Ecol.*, **358**, 1–13.

Rome, M. S. and Ellis, J. C. (2004). Foraging ecology and interactions between Herring Gulls and Great Black-backed Gulls in New England. *Waterbirds*, **27**, 200–210.

Ruhlen, T. D., Abbott, S., Stenzel, L. E. and Page, G. W. (2003). Evidence that human disturbance reduces Snowy Plover chick survival. *J. Field Ornithol.*, **74**, 300–304.

Ruthrauff, D. and Eskelin, T. (2009). Observations of body-icing on Rock Sandpipers during winter in upper Cook Inlet, Alaska. *Wader Study Group Bull.*, **116**, 88–90.

Savage, C., Elmgren, R. and Larsson, U. (2002). Effect of sewage-derived nutrients on an estuarine macrobenthic community. *Mar. Ecol. Prog. Ser.*, **243**, 67–82.

Schulz, R. and Stock, M. (1993). Kentish plovers and tourists: competitors on sandy coasts? *Wader Study Group Bull.*, **68**, 83–91.

Smart, J. and Gill, J. A. (2003). Non-intertidal habitat use by shorebirds: a reflection of inadequate intertidal resources? *Biol. Conserv.*, **106**, 359–369.

Smith, P. C. and Bleakney, J. S. (1969). Observations on oil pollution and wintering Purple Sandpipers, *Erolia maritima* (Brunnich), in Nova Scotia. *Can. Field Nat.*, **83**, 19–22.

Stillman, R. A., West, A. D., Caldow, R. W. G. and Durell, S. E. A. le V. dit (2007). Predicting the effect of disturbance on coastal birds. *Ibis*, **149** (Suppl. 1), 73–81.

Strann, K-B. and Summers, R. W. (1990). Diet and diurnal activity of Purple Sandpipers *Calidris maritima* wintering in northern Norway. *Fauna norv. Ser. C, Cinclus*, **13**, 75–78.

Summers, R. W., Ellis, P. M. and Johnston, J. P. (1988). Waders on the coast of Shetland in winter: numbers and habitat preferences. *Scott. Birds*, **15**, 71–79.

Summers, R. W., Underhill, L. G. and Simpson, A. (2002). Habitat preferences of waders (Charadrii) on the coast of the Orkney Islands. *Bird Study*, **49**, 60–66.

Summers, R. W., and Nicoll, M. (2004). The dispersion of wintering Purple Sandpipers *Calidris maritima* in relation to the tidal cycle and shore zonation. *Wader Study Group Bull.*, **103**, 32–35.

Summers, R. W., Nicoll, M. and Peach, W. (2001). Numbers, migration phenology and survival of Purple Sandpipers *Calidris maritima* at Gourdon, eastern Scotland. *Bird Study*, **48**, 139–146.

Summers, R. W., Smith, S., Nicoll, M. and Atkinson, N. K. (1990a). Tidal and sexual differences in the diet of Purple Sandpipers *Calidris maritima* in Scotland. *Bird Study*, **37**, 187–194.

Summers, R. W., Strann, K.-B., Rae, R. and Heggås, J. (1990b). Wintering Purple Sandpipers *Calidris maritima* in Troms county, northern Norway. *Ornis Scand.*, **21**, 248–254.

Thompson, R. C., Crowe, T. P. and Hawkins, S. J. (2002). Rocky intertidal communities: past environmental changes, present status and predictions for the next 25 years. *Environ. Conserv.*, **29**, 168–191.

Townshend, D. J. (1981). The importance of field feeding to the survival of wintering male and female Curlews *Numenius arquata* on the Tees Estuary. In *Feeding and Survival Strategies of Estuarine Organisms*, ed. N. V. Jones and W. J. Wolff, pp. 261–273. New York: Plenum Press.

Vahl, W. K., van der Meer, J., Meijer, K., Piersma, T. and Weissing, F. J. (2007). Interference competition, the spatial distribution of food and free-living foragers. *Anim. Behav.*, **74**, 1493–1503.

West, A. D., Goss-Custard, J. D., Stillman, R. A. *et al.* (2002). Predicting the impacts of disturbance on shorebird mortality using a behaviour-based model. *Biol. Conserv.*, **106**, 319–328.

Wootton, J. T. (1992). Indirect effects, prey susceptibility, and habitat selection: impacts of birds on limpets and algae. *Ecology*, **73**, 981–991.

Wootton, J. T. (1997). Estimates and tests of per capita interaction strength: diet abundance and impact of intertidally foraging birds. *Ecol. Monogr.*, **67**, 45–64.

Yasué, M. (2006). Environmental factors and spatial scale influence shorebirds' responses to human disturbance. *Biol. Conserv.*, **128**, 47–54.

Yasué, M. and Dearden, P. (2006). The potential impact of tourism development on habitat availability and productivity of Malaysian Plovers *Charadrius peronii*. *J. Appl. Ecol.*, **43**, 978–989.

CHAPTER FOURTEEN

Temperate western European woodland as a dynamic environment for birds: a resource-based view

ROBERT J. FULLER

British Trust for Ornithology

KEN W. SMITH

Hertfordshire, UK

and

SHELLEY A. HINSLEY

Centre for Ecology and Hydrology, UK

Woodland bird communities are immensely variable in the number and composition of species and the overall density. Some of this variation is essentially biogeographic. For example, the species pool in most taxonomic and ecological avian groups increases from Ireland through to central Europe (Fuller *et al.*, 2007a). At more local scales, variation is driven mainly by environmental attributes that influence the resources available and consequently determine fitness of individual birds within habitat patches (Holmes, 1990; Chapter 2).

The context for this chapter is long-established woodland in landscapes that have been heavily populated and modified by people for hundreds, even thousands, of years. These woods are predominantly broadleaved, often with a recently introduced coniferous element. Mountain and conifer forests lie outside the scope of the chapter, but for a discussion of northern conifer forests see Chapter 19. In western Europe, a long history of human-related disturbance has produced woodland that is far removed from any 'natural' state. Historical interactions between socio-economic processes and environmental factors have produced great diversity of woodland types of varying habitat quality for birds. Regional traditions, differences in management systems and markets, spatial variation in grazing pressure, even neglect, all contribute to this heterogeneity. Whilst some heavily wooded landscapes have persisted, much woodland exists merely as fragments in agricultural landscapes and its plant and animal communities are strongly affected by the surroundings (Chapters 4–6).

Birds and Habitat: Relationships in Changing Landscapes, ed. Robert J. Fuller. Published by Cambridge University Press. © Cambridge University Press 2012.

Forests throughout Europe face a dynamic future. Greater demands are likely to be placed on them for fuel, timber and other wood-based products. The forest area will expand in many regions, partly as planned climate change mitigation, but also as a result of agricultural abandonment (Rounsevell *et al.*, 2006). Climate change is expected to drive shifts in tree distribution and forest structure, most severely in Mediterranean forests through drought stress and fire (Lindner *et al.*, 2010). Although it is unclear how forest biodiversity will respond, it should be possible to develop management approaches that maintain a diversity of structures and habitat types across forests, providing continuity of key resources for birds and other forest wildlife.

This chapter considers critical resources used by woodland birds and the factors that determine their availability, taking three contrasting groups of birds as examples. We concentrate on the breeding season and on those species that obtain their resources mainly from woodland. Human actions are central to the character of most European woodland and it is, therefore, appropriate that the consequences of past and current woodland management form a major part of this chapter.

Critical resources for woodland birds

Figure 14.1 summarises major components of forest structures and their determinants at three broad scales – global/continental, regional/landscape and individual woodlands. At the largest scales, climate and soils are the main drivers of forest character. Climate is also important at regional and woodland scales, especially in combination with topography, soils and water availability, but at these scales the over-riding influence on location, extent, composition and structure of woodland is human activity. In this section, we consider how the main structural components at the woodland scale influence resources for birds.

Tree canopy

The tree canopy influences woodland structure by modifying light penetration to lower levels (Barbier *et al.*, 2008). It may also affect the distribution and chemistry of throughfall rain and can dominate overall soil moisture characteristics through evapotranspiration (van Oijen *et al.*, 2005; Levia and Frost, 2006). Leaf-fall, along with twigs, bud scales and frass, affect soil and litter-layer pH and nutrient status (Hansen *et al.*, 2009), which in turn influence plant growth. Canopy structure, particularly its density and continuity, and interaction with internal gaps, also determines the microclimate at lower levels and thus is a key determinant of overall woodland structure and resource availability. These effects are common to all woodland, but the details vary with canopy tree species.

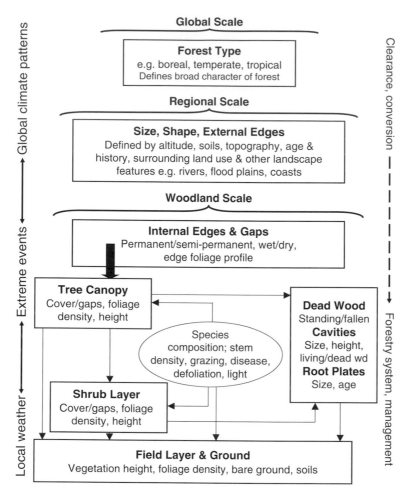

Figure 14.1 Conceptual diagram of factors influencing availability of structural woodland components providing resources for woodland birds. Structure is considered at three broad scales. The influence of the major drivers of change – climate and human activity – is indicated by the vertical text. The boxes and text show the main structural determinants and components of woodland and the arrows the major direction of the interactions. The large arrow indicates the major effect of internal edges and gaps on the continuity and overall character of the canopy. The text in the oval shows the main modifiers of the structural components.

Leaves in the upper canopy provide a huge potential area of invertebrate habitat and hence foraging substrate for insectivorous birds. In oak-hickory forest in Georgia, Monk *et al.* (1970) estimated the upper leaf surface area of individual hardwood trees of trunk diameter 36 cm to be 235 m². However, leaves were estimated to account for only 3% of total above-ground biomass,

85% being contributed by wood. Litter fall from the canopy in northern temperate woodland was estimated at 3200–3800 kg ha^{-1} with non-leaf material comprising 21–45% (Gorham and Bray, 1964; Carlisle et al., 1966). For a *Quercus petraea* wood (40–120 years old) in northwestern England, leaf number, dry weight and upper surface area were estimated at 22–23 × 10^6 ha^{-1}, 2202–2476 kg ha^{-1} and 4.8–5.5 m^2 per square metre of ground, respectively (Carlisle et al., 1966).

Additional resources are provided by the trunks, branches and twigs for both wood-boring and surface-dwelling invertebrates. The abundance of the latter can be influenced by bark architecture, which varies with species and changes with tree age; a preference of bark foragers for large trees with rough-textured bark is well known (Adamik and Kornan, 2004). The tree canopy also provides seed and fruit resources (Laiolo, 2002), though productivity can be sporadic. In mast years, seed crops may significantly enhance overwinter survival in some bird species (Perdeck et al., 2000), but this must be balanced against lean years. A mix of tree species may help reduce annual fluctuation in seed availability. The physical complexity of the canopy and provision of food resources may be further enhanced by epiphytes (Nadkarni, 1994).

The physical structure of the canopy provides nest and roost sites (e.g. for birds of prey), selection of which usually involves some degree of cover and/or shelter (North et al., 2000). Aspect, field of view and solar radiation may also be important (Fisher et al., 2004). Canopy height appears to act as a surrogate for a suite of characters associated with woodland maturation and can be used to predict woodland bird community structure (Fig. 14.2), especially when combined with information on canopy cover (Hinsley et al., 2009). Other canopy attributes, such as volume and density, have also been related to bird community composition and diversity (Diaz et al., 2005; Goetz et al., 2010).

Shrub and field layers

The 'shrub layer' or understorey is typically composed of small trees up to *c.* 5 m in height, beneath which there may be a distinct 'field layer' consisting of low shrubs such as *Rubus* spp., grasses, sedges and herbs rarely growing above 1 m in height. Although contributing less biomass than the canopy, the shrub layer is no less complex, and interacts with the canopy via light/shading, and nutrient and water cycling (Beckage et al., 2008). The shrub layer can suppress canopy tree regeneration through shading and, in concert with the canopy, affects field layer characteristics through light, moisture and nutrient input. In heavy shade, the field layer may be reduced to mosses or bare ground, whereas vegetation may be tall and dense if the canopy is open and/or with high N/P inputs. Low vegetation is also heavily modified by large herbivores (see below; Fig. 14.3).

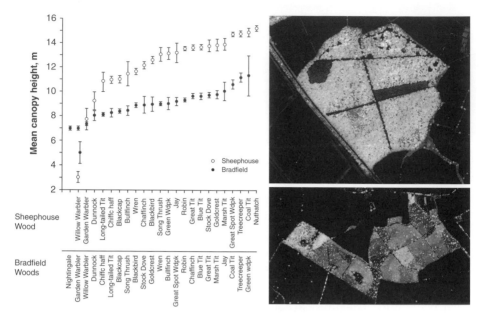

Figure 14.2 Mean canopy height (± SE) measured by LiDAR at locations occupied by breeding bird species at two English woods, each less than 80 ha. The LiDAR images are of Sheephouse Wood (upper) and Bradfield Woods (lower); lighter shading indicates greater canopy height. Sheephouse is mainly closed canopy high forest oak and ash (modal canopy height 16 m) with two clear-cuts and several group-fells visible as dark patches. Bradfield is coppice (modal canopy height 9 m) and individual compartments at different stages of growth are visible with scattered standard trees showing as white dots. From Hinsley *et al.* (2009).

For many small, open-nesting birds in European forests, complex low vegetation provides preferred nest sites, being more sheltered than the tree canopy and offering greater cover from predators. The shrub layer also provides foraging substrates for insectivores and frequently also flower, fruit and seed resources, which may complement those of the trees in both quality and quantity (Laiolo, 2002). Low perennials such as *Rubus* spp. can also supply seeds and fruits which affect small mammal populations, these in turn affecting avian predators. Fruit and seed resources may be of particular importance to migrating birds in autumn (Suthers *et al.*, 2000) and to food storers such as marsh tits *Poecile palustris* (Sherry and Hoshooley, 2007). Some shrubs and trees extract calcium from deeper soil layers and make it available through leaf-fall, potentially increasing snail abundance and hence providing an important calcium resource for birds (Nation, 2007). In general, the absence or removal of shrubs reduces bird species richness and abundance (Camprodon and Brotons, 2006; De la Montana *et al.*, 2006; Seavy *et al.*, 2008).

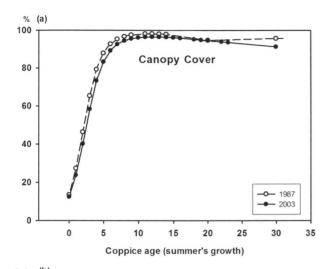

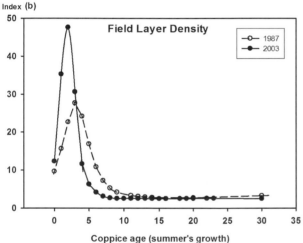

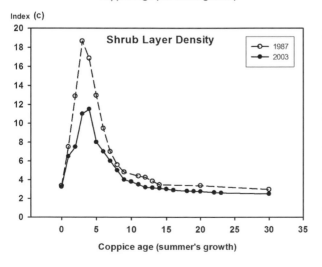

Figure 14.3 Changes in vegetation structure of coppiced woodland in Suffolk, England, in relation to time after cutting in 1987 and 2003: (a) closure of the tree canopy progresses rapidly and open habitat has disappeared in less than 10 years of growth, (b) the density of the field layer, measured here at 0.5 m above ground, peaks within 5 years of growth and rapidly shades out, (c) the density of the shrub layer foliage, measured at 1.5 m above ground, also peaks early. Differences in low-foliage density are probably a consequence of intensified deer browsing between the two years. Redrawn from Fuller and Rothery (2010).

Edges and gaps

Edge vegetation and microclimate frequently differ from that of the interior (Chapter 5). Edges tend to offer a higher density of shrub and herbaceous growth with concomitant potential increases in nesting cover and foraging opportunities (De Casenave *et al.*, 1998). Large internal edges and open spaces can provide focal centres for hunting, territory delimitation and display (e.g. roding woodcock *Scolopax rusticola*). Food and nesting resources on external edges may also be used by birds from the surrounding landscape (Hinsley *et al.*, 1995), including predators less typical of the interior (Andrén and Angelstam, 1988). External land use may impact edges, for example through spray drift, which can result in domination by nitrogen- and phosphate-tolerant species (Willi *et al.*, 2005).

Depending on the slope and aspect of the edge, differences in solar radiation, coupled with shelter, may influence microclimate and therefore the phenology and abundance of both plant and invertebrate resources (Kuhrt *et al.*, 2006). Such effects, coupled with physical aspects of canopy structure, may also influence winter habitat use in relation to thermoregulation (Huertas and Díaz, 2001) and timing of breeding by birds (Wilkin *et al.*, 2007) and other taxa. In microclimate terms, many small woods are essentially entirely edge.

Canopy gaps create a range of different structures depending on their origin, size and management (Fuller, 2000; Zmihorski, 2010). Colonisation of gaps by light-demanding shrubs and herbs create nesting and foraging opportunities which, although localised in the case of small gaps, provide resources for birds that may otherwise be rare in mature forest (Bowen *et al.*, 2007; Lain *et al.*, 2008).

Deadwood and cavities

Deadwood, both standing dead trees and coarse woody debris, is greatly reduced in managed relative to 'natural' stands (Kirby *et al.*, 1998). Dead wood in its various forms, is host to a huge invertebrate resource which may be especially important for birds in winter. Tree species differ in their deadwood faunas in both space and time (see below). Thus a mix of species may offer greater continuity in supply of invertebrates (Olsson *et al.*, 2001). Where fire is a regular part of forest ecology, for example in many North American conifer forests, recently burned trees provide massively increased food resources for many woodpeckers and seed-eaters (Hutto, 2006). In broadleaved forests, storms are the main natural disturbance creating occasional pulses of dead wood. Drought and disease also contribute to deadwood volume.

Dead and decaying wood, especially on live and diseased trees (Steeger and Hitchcock, 1998; Witt, 2010), also offers nest sites for secondary cavity nesters through the development of rot holes and other defects. Nest holes are frequently considered as a limiting resource for secondary users, but in mature woodland, holes appear to be abundant, at least for smaller species (Wesołowski, 2007; Blakely *et al.*, 2008). A wide range of nest sites within the woody portion of trees may be used by birds, including exposed root plates of fallen trees, woodpecker excavations, fissures in and under loose bark, rot holes and cavities in coppice stools, tree stumps and in/under fallen timber. Primary excavators, mainly woodpeckers, use both living and deadwood and provide an important resource for the non-excavators (Bai *et al.*, 2005). Some species will nest in remarkably small stems. For example, mean stem diameter used by willow tits *Poecile montanus* in the UK was 12 cm, but the smallest diameter recorded was 5 cm (Lewis *et al.*, 2009). Large cavities, and large trees suitable for primary excavation by species such as black woodpecker *Dryocopus martius*, may be more limiting (Summers, 2004). Nest hole quality also varies with respect to risk of predation, flooding and collapse.

Modifiers of resource availability at the stand scale
Tree species composition
The influence of vegetation composition on forest bird communities has received relatively little attention compared with woodland structure. Many studies have recorded differences in bird communities of coniferous and broadleaved forests, both in Europe and North America (e.g. James and Wamer, 1982; Tomiałojć and Wesołowski, 1990; Donald *et al.*, 1998; du Bus de Warnaffe and Deconchat, 2008). Differences in food resources, the physical structure of the trees and availability of year-round cover can make conifers and broadleaves very different environments for birds. Whilst it is often assumed that conifers are poorer habitats than broadleaves, this is not consistently supported by the evidence (Willson and Comet, 1996; Archaux and Bakkaus, 2007). This is not surprising because there is much variation within both broadleaves and conifers in the traits of individual tree species. Foraging birds show tree species preferences which are probably related to variations in food availability and to microstructural variation influencing foraging efficiency and safety from predators (Holmes and Robinson, 1981; Morrison *et al.*, 1985; Peck, 1989; Whelan, 1989; Parrish, 1995; Gabbe *et al.*, 2002).

Tree species vary in growth form, physical structure and foliage characteristics, which determine light penetration and affect the vertical foliage profile beneath. For instance, canopies of beech *Fagus sylvatica* and hornbeam *Carpinus betulus* cast deeper shade than ash *Fraxinus excelsior*. Biomass of foliage invertebrates also varies with tree species according to leaf chemistry and structure (Kennedy and Southwood, 1984; Alexander *et al.*, 2006). Native oaks *Quercus* spp. have relatively high biomass compared with beech and hornbeam, which is reflected in their typical densities of breeding insectivores. In both Europe and North America, many breeding woodland birds depend on defoliating lepidoptera larvae and their availability, largely determined by tree species, is a main driver of breeding productivity (Holmes, 1990). Variations in bark texture can be important for bark-gleaning species; preference of nuthatches *Sitta europaea* for mature oak may be related to availability of food in the highly fissured bark (Matthysen, 1998). Rather little is known of the relative value of different tree species for decayed-wood invertebrates, although the fauna depends crucially on the fungi involved and the mode of decay (Bobiec *et al.*, 2005). For instance the bark and sapwood of oak branch wood decay rapidly and are important for foraging great spotted woodpeckers *Dendrocopos major* (Smith, 2007), but the heartwood of these branches can persist for many years. Beech and hornbeam by contrast show rapid decay of both sapwood and heartwood, except for the largest diameter trunks. Outside the breeding season certain tree species provide important seed resources, notably pines *Pinus* spp., spruces *Picea* spp., birch *Betula* spp., alder *Alnus glutinosa* and beech.

In a study of the breeding bird community along a gradient from oak to beech in northern France, Smith (1992) found that, in spite of the massive differences in insect food resources between the two tree species, the trends in breeding bird density and diversity were very modest. There was a suggestion that pure beech stands had lower density and species richness than any stands which included oak, but there were no overall trends with percentage of oak. The most significant variables related to density and richness were ones reflecting woodland structure and it was not possible to disentangle the effects of tree species and habitat structure. By contrast, an extensive study of species-specific habitat associations in woodland stands in Britain, found that tree species composition was a frequent predictor of the occurrence of some species, independently of vegetation structure (Hewson *et al.*, 2011). The mechanisms by which tree species affected birds were unclear. However, this work indicated that both tree species and habitat structure are likely to be important determinants of bird community composition. Taken together, these two studies suggest that tree species effects may be detected more readily at the level of individual species, rather than in total abundance or diversity.

Succession and growth stage

The maturity of woodland is fundamental in determining the types of resources likely to be available for birds. Whether woodland vegetation is developing as a consequence of natural succession or woodland management, there are broadly predictable changes in the character of the stand and resource availability which are driven by tree growth, canopy closure and shading (Quine *et al.*, 2007). Open space becomes filled with regenerating trees (and other vegetation). These early open stages often support ephemeral concentrations of foliar insects, fruits and (in tree-falls) deadwood. Sapling growth, low vegetation and fruits are rapidly reduced by shading once the canopy starts to close. As trees mature, cavities become more available and some under-storey regeneration may occur as canopy gaps start to develop and deadwood volumes increase. These dynamics are accompanied by turnover in bird com-munities such that the species characteristic of late stages are typically com-pletely different to those of the early stages. Several features appear to be general. First, the turnover rate of bird species is considerably higher in the early stages than later (Helle and Mönkkönen, 1990). This is probably caused by the rapid growth of field and shrub layer vegetation that is soon shaded out (Fig. 14.3). Thereafter the vegetation structure may be relatively stable and change slowly. Second, the early flush of low vegetation can provide habitat for early successional species that will be absent or rare after canopy closure until such time as the stand is felled or canopy gaps appear. Third, with increasing maturity, resources usually become more abundant for cavity nesters, species that require large trees and ones using decaying wood.

Large herbivores

Domestic ungulates, especially sheep, have long shaped the foliage profiles of woodland in some regions e.g. western Britain. However, recent interest has focused on wild deer populations, which have increased substantially in both North America and Europe, generating cascading impacts on plant, inverte-brate, small mammal and bird populations (Côté *et al.*, 2004; Suhoninen and Danell, 2006; Martin *et al.*, 2010).

Deer can reduce habitat quality for birds that depend on understorey structures, mainly by removing preferred nesting and feeding sites. The natural experiment offered by the Canadian Haida Gwaii achipelago, where introduced black-tailed deer *Odocoileus hemionus* colonised some, but not all, islands, shows that shrub-dependent, but not canopy-dependent, birds are much reduced on islands with deer relative to deer-free islands (Allombert *et al.*, 2005). Two North American experiments using fenced plots to either exclude or simulate different densities of white-tailed deer *O. virginianus*, also show large effects on summer bird abundance (deCalesta, 1994; McShea and Rappole, 2000). Both studies showed that numbers of songbirds depending on the lower foliage layers were reduced by deer browsing. A similar finding was obtained in an exclosure experiment in English coppiced woodland where low foliage complexity and abundance of shrub-dependent breeding song-birds were higher in plots where deer were excluded than in matched plots to which deer had access (Gill and Fuller, 2007). Using the same experiment, Holt *et al.* (2010, 2011) showed that breeding nightingales *Luscinia megarhynchos*, garden warblers *Sylvia borin* and dunnocks *Prunella modularis* were especially affected by deer browsing, being more dependent on the unbrowsed plots.

Management policy

Changing markets and uses of woodland can drive massive changes (Mason, 2007). In lowland Britain, for example, there has been a shift from systems dominated by mixed-species coppice, essentially of medieval origin, towards plantation forestry designed to produce uniform timber, in which broad-leaves were widely replaced by fast-growing conifers. In the late twentieth century, lack of demand resulted in active management ceasing in many woods, causing loss of open space and heavy shading in woodland stands. More recently, emerging markets for firewood may bring neglected woods back into management. Few woods are managed primarily for nature conservation, or under ecological forestry principles (Seymour and Hunter, 1999; Lindenmayer et al., 2006). Consequently, markets are a fundamental driver of resource availability for woodland birds, especially by affecting the openness of woodland and the diversity of growth stages. The imperative to make future woodland resilient to climate change, to maximise carbon storage, and to provide substitutes for fossil fuels will have large implications for future management (Read et al., 2009). Mason (2007) suggests that a greater diversity of systems may characterise woodland in future.

All the major elements depicted in Fig. 14.1 at the woodland scale are influenced by woodland management to some degree. Management has a pervasive influence on vegetation structure and tree composition, and hence on availability of food, nest sites, feeding sites and roost sites (Quine et al., 2007). Specific silvicultural management activities, such as removal of dead or diseased trees, cutting out understorey shrubs (e.g. Rodewald and Smith, 1998; Camprodon and Brotons, 2006) and removal of deciduous trees from managed conifer forests (Easton and Martin, 1998), can impact negatively on resource availability. There is mixed evidence as to how birds respond to the periodic tree thinning widely used in commercial woodland. Two British studies found little effect of thinning on bird communities, probably because the thinning did not open the canopy sufficiently to stimulate large understorey regeneration (Fuller and Green, 1998; Calladine et al., 2009). Habitat quality for Siberian jays Perisoreus infaustus in boreal forests is reduced by thinning (Griesser et al., 2007). However, redstarts P. phoenicurus and spotted flycatchers Muscicapa striata can show rapid but temporary increases in breeding densities in thinned oak stands in central France (Lovaty, 2004). North American studies also indicate that some species respond positively to thinning (DeGraaf et al., 1991; Wilson and Watts, 1999; Hayes et al., 2003).

Irrespective of these within-stand silvicultural treatments, the broad management system adopted sets fundamental constraints on the relative extent of different growth stages and determines light penetration through the canopy with consequences for field and shrub layer development (Figs. 14.1 and 14.3). Systems vary in rotation length and the size of individual management units. Early successional species are obviously favoured by short rotations, and late successional species by long rotations. Size of management unit may be important where species have minimum area requirements (Bayard and Elphick, 2010) or where species derive complementary resources from patches differing in structure or age.

The spatial characteristics of four management systems are contrasted in Fig. 14.4. Coppice systems are unique in having a relatively high proportion of young-growth, but lack stages dominated by large trees. Consequently their bird communities tend to be dominated by early successional species with

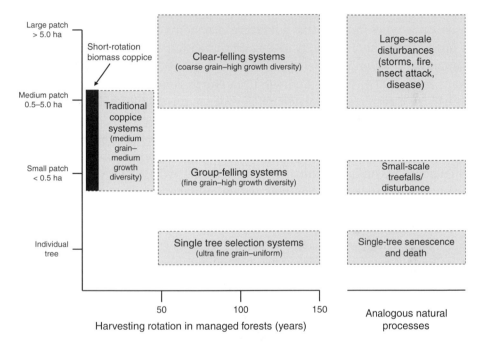

Figure 14.4 Spatial characteristics of forests as determined by management (left) or natural gap dynamics (right). Four management systems are shown in terms of rotation length (this influences the relative availability of different growth stages) and the size of individual management units or patches (this affects the grain size of the managed forest mosaic). 'Growth diversity' is the diversity or range of growth stages in terms of tree age. Coppice systems are fundamentally different to other managed systems in their spatial characteristics, having relatively short rotations. The only natural analogy to coppice is riparian woodland subject to regular devastating disturbance from flooding or beaver *Castor fiber* activity. The other management systems are all variants of high forest management within which conifers tend to have shorter rotations than broadleaves. Single tree selection systems aim to maintain high canopy cover through the management of individual trees. Clear-felling is also known as clear-cutting, and group-felling as group selection. These three systems have natural analogies in terms of gap creation.

relatively low densities of hole-nesters. Many high forest systems will have more nest sites for hole-nesters, though in commercially managed systems high quality timber trees may offer fewer nest sites than trees of similar age with dead branches, rot holes etc. Clear-felling and group-felling systems can both have high diversity of growth stages, but the larger patch sizes of clear-felling tend to benefit scrub/thicket species more than the small canopy openings created by group-felling (Costello *et al.*, 2000; R.J.F. pers. obs.). Single tree selection systems are unlikely to offer suitable habitat for early successional species because the canopy openings are even more limited than in group-felling. There are few, if any, European comparisons of bird responses to these different broadleaved management systems. North American studies indicate that a mixture of systems creating a range of sizes of open canopy areas is likely to sustain the widest diversity of bird species (Annand and Thompson, 1997; Chambers *et al.*, 1999; Costello *et al.*, 2000; Gram *et al.*, 2003). Whilst findings from North American managed forests cannot be directly extrapolated to Europe, it would be surprising if this general conclusion did not apply to both continents.

Lack of management, as much as active management, has consequences for bird communities. For example, actively managed coppice has a far more diverse bird assemblage than abandoned coppice, which typically has a uniformly closed canopy and minimal understorey (Fuller and Green, 1998; Fig. 14.3). In the long term, formerly managed woodland left to succession will gradually assume a more natural structure with a diversity of tree sizes, an abundance of dead and decaying wood, and canopy gaps created by the death of individual trees and storms. Natural tree-fall gaps can provide localised patches of deadwood and dense regeneration providing concentrations of fruits and invertebrates that create hotspots for some early successional bird species (Blake and Hoppes, 1986; Fuller, 2000). Windthrow or insect attack sometimes creates large tracts of flattened or dead forest, potentially diversifying habitat structures within managed forests if they are left undisturbed and allowed to naturally regenerate (Glutz von Blotzheim, 2001; Müller *et al.*, 2010). In the absence of a catastrophic reduction of the human population, it is unlikely that managed woods in western Europe will ever fall into a lasting unmanaged state on a large scale.

Case studies of resource use

In this section we provide examples of the resource requirements of three groups of species, focusing on the situation in British woodland and nearby areas of Europe. The species within these groups show loose similarities in their habitat and resource needs, but there are striking differences between groups. In each case we consider nesting and foraging requirements, followed by a short discussion about how woodland management affects habitat suitability.

Woodpeckers: keystone species

By foraging on dead and decaying wood, and excavating nesting and roosting cavities, woodpeckers (Picidae) play a key role in woodland ecosystems by creating cavities for other species and by cycling deadwood. In general, dead and decaying wood in its various manifestations is the critical resource for woodpeckers, but the exact relationships depend on the species of both the woodpecker and the wood. There are 10 woodpecker species in Europe many of which are habitat specialists, but the numbers of species decrease from east to west, with only three species in Britain. In this section we mainly compare resource needs of great spotted and lesser spotted woodpecker *Dendrocopos minor*, with briefer observations on middle spotted *D. medius*, green *Picus viridis* and black woodpeckers. All five species are widespread in western and central Europe, though black and middle spotted do not occur in Britain.

Woodpeckers excavate a new nest cavity in most years, with a relatively low level of reuse of old cavities from one year to the next (Hansen, 1989; Smith, 1997). For the black woodpecker this has been suggested as an adaptation against nest predation (Nilsson *et al.*, 1991). The cavities can be excavated in living or dead wood. Glue and Boswell (1994) found that roughly half of green and great spotted nests were in 'live/mature' trees, whereas 75% of lesser spotted nests were in 'dead/decaying' trees. In a more restricted study in southern England, Smith (2007) reported 50% of lesser spotted woodpecker nests in dead trees compared with 34% for great spotted and 8% for green woodpecker. The smaller woodpeckers, such as middle and lesser spotted tend to be more likely to nest in dead trees (Hagvar *et al.*, 1990; Kosiński and Winiecki, 2004). Even when nests are placed in living trees, the actual site used is often a dead limb, so that Smith (2007) found that overall, 94% of lesser spotted woodpecker nests were in deadwood compared with 48% for great spotted and 14% for green woodpecker. If a dead tree is used for nesting, birch is particularly favoured, as other species may be prohibitively hard. When nesting in living trees, most woodpecker species select mature trees (Smith, 1997; Pasinelli, 2000; Kosiński and Winiecki, 2004). The minimum diameter at breast height of great spotted nest trees was about 30 cm which implies a minimum age of about 70 years for oak (Smith, 1997). For dead birch, the minimum diameter was 20 cm which could be achieved in about 30 years. For black woodpeckers, Johansen (1989) found that beech trees used for nesting were at least 90 years old.

Outside the breeding season, the *Dendrocopos* species depend heavily on invertebrates excavated from dead and decaying wood, as well as gleaning from the surface of live branches and trunks of trees. In Britain, great spotted tends to forage on larger-diameter dead branches lower down in the tree than lesser spotted (Smith, 2007). Great spotted regularly forages on deadwood on the ground, but lesser and middle spotted rarely do so (Hertel, 2003; Smith,

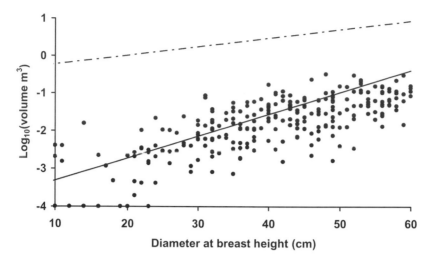

Figure 14.5 Estimated volume of dead branch wood on live oak trees, Wormley Wood, Hertfordshire, UK, 2006. The points are the estimated volume for individual trees ($n = 288$) and the solid line the best fit to these data. The dashed line is the modelled dead branch wood volume per hectare based on the relationship for individual trees and the stocking density from Forestry Commission yield class models (YC 6 assumed). Even though the density of trees per hectare declines as the stand matures, the overall volume of dead branch wood increases. Data collected by Ken W. Smith.

2007). In terms of resource availability, the estimated volume of deadwood on standing living trees increases with tree diameter. If allowance is made for stem density in managed stands, the overall volume of deadwood on living trees per hectare also increases with stand age (Fig. 14.5). Thus, mature stands are likely to provide more resources for foraging woodpeckers than young ones. During the breeding season all three western European spotted woodpeckers feed on surface-dwelling invertebrates, especially defoliating lepidoptera larvae (see above). Unlike the other species, green woodpeckers are mainly ground feeders, eating ants in woodland rides, glades and outside woodland. Radio-tracking studies have shown strong selection for unimproved pastures, presumably because of the high ant numbers (Alder and Marsden, 2010). Black woodpeckers in Scandinavian forests feed on carpenter ants *Camponotus* spp. excavated from spruce snags and cut stumps (Rolstad *et al.*, 1998).

Both for nest sites and foraging resources, mature trees are important for most woodpeckers; even fast growing tree species such as birch do not provide nest sites until at least 30 years old. Longer rotation high forest systems are likely to provide higher densities of mature trees, but habitat quality will depend on the extent to which silvicultural treatments allow deadwood to be created and maintained. Where stands are managed by low intervention, self thinning will provide a continuity of supply of standing and fallen deadwood.

Tits: the principal group of resident insectivores

The family Paridae, comprises 56 species of which 6 (great tit *Parus major*, blue tit *Cyanistes caeruleus*, marsh tit *Poecile palustris*, willow tit *Poecile montanus*, coal tit *Periparus ater* and crested tit *Lophophanes cristatus*) occur in western Europe and Britain and are the focus of this section. These species form the main group of resident arboreal foliage-gleaning insectivorous woodland birds in the region. Most tit species are secondary cavity nesters, but willow and crested excavate their own holes in living (usually soft or partially rotted) and dead wood. Thus the major constraint on secondary users is the availability of cavities, which in turn is largely dependent on woodland age (Wesołowski, 2007). Up to an age of approximately 30 years, most woods are deficient in natural holes, but regenerating woodland may offer alternatives if stumps and fallen timber are present (see above). Primary excavators are less restricted by tree age once a certain minimum size is achieved, but may be hindered by a lack of dead or decaying wood. Primary excavators can also constitute a resource for secondary users via usurpation of freshly dug holes, as well as the use of abandoned sites. Willow tits can lose nest sites to great and blue tits (Maxwell, 2002) and their current British stronghold in scrub-dominated sites may be associated with low population densities of these secondary users. Evolution of cavity exacavation in North American *Poecile* species has been linked to competition from larger species for nest holes (Dhondt, 2007).

In woodland, most tits nest in tree holes, an exception being the coal tit which frequently uses holes in the ground. When using trees, most species favour higher sites with the smallest possible accessible hole (to exclude predators and larger competitors, Dhondt, 2010), harder wood and sufficient internal space to place the nest away from the hole (to reduce predation) (Christman and Dhondt, 1997; Wesołowski, 2002). Marsh tits in Britain (and many species in North America) seldom use nest-boxes or woodpecker holes (K.W.S. unpubl.) and frequently select tight-fitting holes probably to reduce nest site loss to great and blue tits (Alderman *et al.*, 2011). Holes are used at all times of year and their availability can influence natal dispersal distances (Dhondt and Adriaensen, 1999) and may be a limiting resource in winter (Dhondt *et al.*, 1991). Roosting in holes throughout the year may help birds select breeding sites with respect to thermal properties and flooding risk. Dense vegetation, especially evergreen or conifer, can also provide roost sites and may be used in preference to holes, the quality of which, for both roosting and nesting, may be modified by the presence of parasites (Dhondt *et al.*, 2010).

The production of one large brood per season is achieved by targeting the brief spring population peak of defoliating caterpillar larvae. Timing of breeding is crucial, to match the peak of food availability to the period of greatest demand from young in the nest (Chapter 17). Classically, woodland foraging niches are considered to be divided according to body mass, morphology (e.g. tits favouring conifers have relatively longer and narrower bills) and foraging techniques (Lack, 1971). In deciduous woodland, the smaller, more agile species such as blue tits (and coal tits in the UK) occupy the upper/outer canopy with the larger great tit using branches, trunks and the ground. Marsh tits typically occupy the mid foliage layers, especially the shrub layer, between blue and great tit, to which they are subdominant (Broughton *et al.*, 2006). When spring caterpillars are superabundant these distinctions break down, as many species use the canopy to exploit this ephemeral resource.

Tits use many foraging techniques and exploit a wide range of substrates e.g. buds, flowers, leaves, twigs, branches, trunks, bark, deadwood, epiphytic growth, galls, herbaceous vegetation and the ground (Gosler and Clement, 2007). In addition to caterpillars, diverse invertebrates, including eggs, pupae, larvae and adults, are taken. Calcium can be a limiting resource during egg laying (Gosler *et al.*, 2005); typical sources include snails taken from trunks/branches and the ground and shell fragments from thrush anvils. In winter, more vegetable matter, especially fruits and seeds, is used as invertebrate availability declines. When available, mast crops, especially beech, will be exploited by all species capable of opening the seed and/or benefiting from such activities by others. In the Netherlands, the size of the beech seed crop was the most important environmental variable correlated with winter survival in great tits (Perdeck *et al.*, 2000). A larger proportion of the Swedish blue tit population migrated south in winters when beech crops were relatively small (Nilsson *et al.*, 2000). About 20 species of tits, including all North American species and marsh tit, willow tit, coal tit and crested tit in Europe, regularly store food, usually seeds and nuts, particularly in late summer and through the winter (Sherry and Hoshooley, 2007).

Even-aged young plantations will be generally unfavourable for breeding due to the lack of natural nest cavities. However, young woodland and scrub may be suitable if managed to provide dead and decaying wood, and may provide foraging habitat for species with relatively large winter home ranges, such as blue and great tits. Nest-box provision in young woodland will bias populations in favour of box-users and potentially inhibit colonisation by non-users. Traditional coppice systems provide nest sites in the standard trees and old coppice stools, but short-rotation energy coppice is likely to lack nest sites.

In general, mature woodland favours most tits, but heavy shading leading to a sparse shrub layer will reduce quality for some, such as marsh tit (Hinsley *et al.*, 2007). Most studies of effects on tits of high forest management systems have been conducted in North America, so assessing the consequences in a European context is difficult. Selective felling, group-felling and partial clearance appear to have less immediate impact on habitat quality than clear-cutting (Norton and Hannon, 1997). However, the consequences of management depend on many factors, including the proportion of canopy removed, tree species composition, amounts of deadwood and the structural attributes of retained trees (e.g. Weakland *et al.*, 2002; Jobes *et al.*, 2004; Vanderwel *et al.*, 2009). Given the habitat flexibility of European tits and their long history of exposure to woodland modification, it seems likely that low or even moderate (up to *c.* 30%?) canopy loss might be tolerated by most species, depending on the age and species of the trees both harvested and retained. Some effects might even be beneficial if increased light penetration maintains or stimulates growth of the shrub layer. For sedentary species, such as marsh tit, with short dispersal distances, there is also an important land-scape-scale perspective to woodland management. Habitat quality should be preserved in key woods that act as source populations for less favourable surrounding sites and potential dispersal corridors maintained (Broughton *et al.*, 2010). Removal of standing dead trees, deadwood in living trees and fallen wood will remove nest sites and food resources. In contrast, leaving standing stumps when thinning, particularly in conifers, can provide forag-ing, caching and nest excavation sites (Denny and Summers, 1996).

Migrant songbirds: 'young-growth' and 'mature-growth' species

There is a dichotomy in habitat use of migrant species that breed in woodland in Britain (Fuller and Crick, 1992) and this is broadly true of Europe more widely (e.g. Fuller, 2000). One group uses 'young-growth' habitats associated with early stages of managed woods, tree-falls or woodland edges and other areas with dense low vegetation. The other consists of species that associate with stands of older trees, often with a very sparse understorey. We discuss the resource requirements of these two loose groups of species, starting with the young-growth species.

The species in the young-growth group include three trans-Saharan migrants – nightingale, garden warbler and willow warbler *Phylloscopus trochilus*. There are also two short-distance migrants – blackcap *S. atricapilla* and chiffchaff *P. collybita* – for which woodland does not form a major winter habitat in western Europe, although they overwinter there. Despite super-ficial similarities in habitat selection, these five species show individual differences in preferred vegetation structures. Nightingale, willow warbler and chiffchaff all nest on or close to the ground in, or under, field-layer herbage. Garden warbler and blackcap nest higher, usually in shrubs, bram-ble, tall nettles etc. Availability of concealed nest sites is probably a critical factor in habitat selection of these species (Weidinger, 2000). Nightingales feed on the ground, while the other species all glean insects from foliage in the field layer, shrub layer and the low canopy. More general characteristics of territories are as follows. Nightingale and garden warbler territories are typically centred on thickets of shrubs. Nightingale territories often contain a particular set of features: dense thicket providing cover for singing and feeding birds, a fringing field layer giving cover for nests and young, and a dense canopy casting sufficient shade to ensure that patches of ground are sufficiently bare to enhance foraging efficiency (Wilson et al., 2005). Garden warbler and willow warbler tend to avoid locations with a tall canopy (Bellamy et al., 2009). Blackcaps and chiffchaffs will also use similar habitats, but they also widely use taller canopy woodland (Fig. 14.2). For blackcaps, a dense shrub layer is a prerequisite under taller canopies (Carbonell and Telleria, 1998; Weidinger, 2000), while for chiffchaffs a complex field layer and the presence of canopy gaps is more important (Piotrowska and Wesołowski, 1989; R.J.F., pers. obs.).

Woodland management systems (Fig. 14.4) differ considerably in the relative extent of potentially suitable habitat they offer these young-growth species in the order: coppice systems > clear-felling > group-felling > single tree selection. Single tree selection offers very little suitable habitat for nightingale, garden warbler and willow warbler due to the closed uniform canopy structure. Blackcap and chiffchaff may be more able to exploit group-felling and selection systems than the other species, depending on low vegetation structure. Within all systems, the edges of glades and wide tracks can provide strips of dense bramble and other vegetation offering semipermanent nest and feeding sites, especially for the four sylviid warblers (R.J.F. pers. obs.). Although coppice systems can support exceptionally high densities of these species, the period of optimal habitat is narrow and the impacts of deer on habitat quality can be severe (see above and Fig. 14.6).

The second distinct group of long-distance migrant birds characteristic of mature woodland habitats contains three long-distance migrants in Britain: redstart, wood warbler *Phylloscopus sibilatrix* and pied flycatcher *Ficedula hypoleuca*. Elsewhere in Europe, Bonelli's warbler *P. bonelli*, collared flycatcher *F. albicollis* and red-breasted flycatcher *F. parva* also use similar mature forest stands. In Britain, redstart, wood warbler and pied flycatcher are now strongly associated with, though not confined to, oak woods in the north and west uplands (Amar et al., 2005). They are, however, widely distributed throughout northern Europe and Scandinavia where they appear to occupy a wider range of habitats.

Both pied flycatcher and redstart are hole-nesters, which occur in higher densities in broadleaved than coniferous woods (Lundberg and Alatalo, 1992; Taylor and Summers, 2009; though see Chapter 17). The density of both species can be increased by provision of nest-boxes, suggesting that high-quality nesting sites may be limited in many otherwise suitable habitats (Enemar and Sjöstrand, 1972; Järvinen, 1978; Currie and Bamford, 1982).

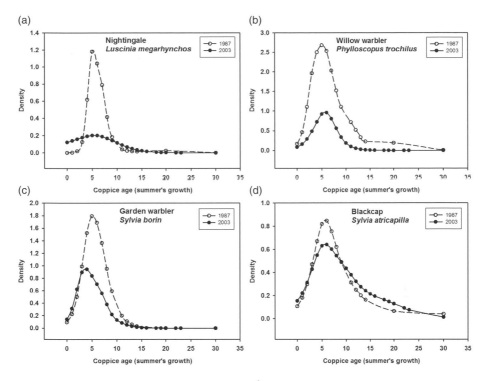

Figure 14.6 Territory density (territories ha^{-1}) of four species of migrants in coppiced woodland in Suffolk, England, in relation to time after cutting in 1987 and 2003. All species reach peak densities in growth stages when the field and shrub layers are most strongly developed (see Fig. 14.3). Densities of all species were lower in 2003 partly due to increased pressure from deer. Redrawn from Fuller and Rothery (2010).

The wood warbler nests on or near the ground, often amongst mosses and short grasses. It also prefers woods with few or no shrubs below 4 m in height (Cody, 1978). Redstart and pied flycatcher forage mainly from the ground and by catching flying invertebrates between the ground and the canopy (Edington and Edington, 1972). By contrast wood warblers forage mainly on invertebrates gleaned from leaves, although they too catch some flying invertebrates. In some parts of their range wood warblers appear to be nomadic, settling to breed where perceived predation pressure is low or potential food supply high (Wesołowski *et al.*, 2009).

As with most of the tits, young woodland offers very limited resources for these species each of which requires mature woodland with many tree cavities, high invertebrate numbers and an open structure beneath the canopy. They need an open air space between the lower canopy and the ground in which to forage for flying insects and, in the case of wood warbler, a sparse ground cover of mosses and grass. This combination of conditions is most likely to be provided in grazed woodlands, particularly oak woods. The highest densities of these species in Britain tend to be in sheep-grazed western woodland; interestingly, intense deer browsing of woodland further east has not yet benefited these species.

Conclusions and future issues

The title of this chapter refers to woodland as a dynamic environment for birds. This partly alludes to the fact that woodland management systems are never static. The growing and harvesting of trees usually creates spatial patchiness and temporal turnover in woodland structure within patches, albeit at different scales, depending on the system. Climate change will introduce a new dynamic. By the end of this century the climate in southern Britain will probably be unsuitable for several native and non-native tree species that are currently widely planted (Read *et al.*, 2009). The likely response of forestry will involve trialling new types of tree mixtures, with non-native trees being increasingly planted. It will be important to understand how well these future forests and their management will provide resources for birds and other wildlife. Much as at present, the question will be to what extent can the habitat needs of wildlife be integrated into the management practices of productive stands, or will they be met mainly through provision of 'conservation areas' or confined to 'wildlife management' of edge habitats?

In Europe, in contrast to North America, there have been few systematic comparisons of avian responses to different woodland management systems. This is especially the case for high forest systems. Although there have been several detailed studies of particular systems (e.g. Ferry and Frochot, 1990), there is poor understanding of how the bird assemblages of clear-felling, group-felling, selection systems and their variants compare. Woodfuel production will probably become a major future use of established woodland, but we cannot yet predict what the implications might be for birds (Fuller *et al.*, 2007b; Fuller and Rothery, 2010). This is partly because of uncertainty about the systems likely to be used, but also because knowledge is lacking of how thinning treatments affect habitat quality. There is also uncertainty about how interactions between management treatments and deer pressure affect vegetation structures. DeGraaf *et al.* (1991) suggested that in Massachusetts oak forest, effects of deer browsing could be mitigated by manipulating canopy cover and shade levels through thinning. In Europe it is questionable whether conventional levels of thinning would produce sufficient response in understorey structures to improve habitat conditions (see above). Deer browsing will probably continue to intensify as a widespread constraint on woodland structure and habitat quality for many birds in North America and Europe.

Species respond individually to the forest environment and their distribution and abundance is affected by a wide range of factors (Holmes, 1990;

Chapter 2). No single woodland type, structure or management system can provide resources for all species. Conversely, managing woods for one or a very small number of species is unlikely to sustain a spectrum of conditions that will benefit a wide range of species. It is unclear exactly what habitats may be occupied by woodland species under future climate regimes. These observations suggest that using different management treatments to maintain complementary structures, and hence resources, would provide an appropriate basis for conservation strategy. The question then to be answered is what is the right scale for provision of resource heterogeneity through management?

Acknowledgements

We thank Elisabeth Charman and John Calladine for comments.

References

Adamík, P. and Kornan, M. (2004). Foraging ecology of two bark foraging passerine birds in an old-growth temperate forest. *Ornis Fennica*, **81**, 13–22.

Alder, D. and Marsden, S. (2010). Characteristics of feeding-site selection by breeding green woodpeckers *Picus viridis* in a UK agricultural landscape. *Bird Study*, **57**, 100–107.

Alderman, J., Hinsley, S. A., Broughton, R. K. and Bellamy, P. E. (2011). Local recruitment in woodland birds: habitat fragmentation interacts with natal territory location and timing of fledging. *Landscape Res.*, **36**, 553–571.

Alexander, K., Butler, J. and Green, T. (2006). The value of different tree and shrub species to wildlife. *Brit. Wildlife*, **18**, 18–28.

Allombert, S., Gaston, A. J. and Martin, J.-L. (2005). A natural experiment on the impact of overabundant deer on songbird populations. *Biol. Conserv.*, **126**, 1–13.

Amar, A., Smith, K. W. and Lindsell, J. (2005). Population changes of some bird species in Scottish and Welsh Atlantic Oakwoods between the 1980s and 2003/4 using data from the Repeat Woodland Bird Survey. *Bot. J. Scotland*, **57**, 179–185.

Andrén, H. and Angelstam, P. (1988). Elevated predation rates as an edge effect in habitat islands: experimental evidence. *Ecology*, **69**, 544–547.

Annand, E. M. and Thompson, F. R. (1997). Forest bird response to regeneration practices in central hardwood forests. *J. Wildlife Manage.*, **61**, 159–171.

Archaux, F. and Bakkaus, N. (2007). Relative impact of stand structure, tree composition and climate on mountain bird communities. *For. Ecol. Manage.*, **247**, 72–79.

Bai, M. L., Wichmann, F. and Muhlenberg, M. (2005). Nest-site characteristics of hole-nesting birds in a primeval boreal forest of Mongolia. *Acta Ornithol.*, **40**, 1–14.

Barbier, S., Gosselin, F. and Balandier, P. (2008). Influence of tree species on understory vegetation diversity and mechanisms involved – a critical review for temperate and boreal forests. *For. Ecol. Manage.*, **254**, 1–15.

Bayard, T. S. and Elphick, C. S. (2010). How area sensitivity in birds is studied. *Conserv. Biol.*, **24**, 938–947.

Beckage, B., Kloeppel, B. D., Yeakley, J. A. Taylor, S. F. and Coleman, D. C. (2008). Differential effects of understory and overstory gaps on tree regeneration. *J. Torrey Bot. Soc.*, **135**, 1–11.

Bellamy, P. E., Hill, R. A., Rothery, P. *et al.* (2009). Willow Warbler *Phylloscopus trochilus* habitat in woods with different structure and management in southern England. *Bird Study*, **56**, 338–348.

Blake, J. G. and Hoppes, W. G. (1986). Influence of resource abundance on use of tree-fall gaps by birds in an isolated woodlot. *Auk*, **103**, 328–340.

Blakely, T. J., Jellyman, P. G., Holdaway, R. J. *et al.* (2008). The abundance, distribution and structural characteristics of tree-holes in Nothofagus forest, New Zealand. *Austral Ecol.*, **33**, 963–974.

Bobiec, A., Gutowski, J. M., Laudenslayer, W. F., Pawlaczyk, P. and Zub, K. (2005). *The Afterlife of a Tree*. Warszawa: WWF Poland.

Bowen, L. T., Moorman, C. E. and Kilgo, J. C. (2007). Seasonal bird use of canopy gaps in a bottomland forest. *Wilson J. Ornithol.*, **119**, 77–88.

Broughton, R. K., Hill, R. A., Bellamy, P. E. and Hinsley, S. A. (2010). Dispersal, ranging and settling behaviour of Marsh Tits *Poecile palustris* in a fragmented landscape in lowland England. *Bird Study*, **57**, 458–472.

Broughton, R. K., Hinsley, S. A., Bellamy, P. E., Hill, R. A. and Rothery, P. (2006). Marsh Tit territories in a British broad-leaved wood. *Ibis*, **148**, 744–752.

Calladine, J., Humphreys, E. M., Strachan, F. and Jardine, D. C. (2009). Forestry thinning in commercial conifer plantations has little effect on bird species richness and breeding abundance. *Bird Study*, **56**, 137–141.

Camprodon, J. and Brotons, L. (2006). Effects of undergrowth clearing on the bird communities of the North Western Mediterranean coppice Holm Oak forests. *For. Ecol. Manage.*, **221**, 72–82.

Carbonell, R. and Telleria, J. L. (1998). Selection and habitat use by five Iberian Blackcap (*Sylvia atricapilla*) populations. *Ardeola*, **45**, 1–10.

Carlisle, A., Brown, A. H. F. and White, E. J. (1966). Litter fall, leaf production and the effects of defoliation by *Tortrix viridana* in a Sessile Oak (*Quercus petraea*) woodland. *J. Ecol.*, **54**, 65–85.

Chambers, C. L., McComb, W. C. and Tappeiner, J. C. (1999). Breeding bird responses to three silvicultural treatments in the Oregon coast range. *Ecol. Appl.*, **9**, 171–185.

Christman, B. J. and Dhondt, A. A. (1997). Nest predation in black-capped chickadees: How safe are cavity nests? *Auk*, **114**, 769–773.

Cody, M. L. (1978). Habitat selection and interspecific territoriality among the Sylviid warblers in England and Sweden. *Ecol. Monogr.*, **48**, 351–396.

Costello, C. A., Yamasaki, M., Pekins, P. J., Leak, W. B. and Neefus, C. D. (2000). Songbird response to group selection harvests and clearcuts in a New Hampshire northern hardwood forest. *For. Ecol. Manage.*, **127**, 41–54.

Côté, S. D., Rooney, T. P., Tremblay, J.-P., Dussault, C. and Waller, D. M. (2004). Ecological impacts of deer overabundance. *Annu. Rev. Ecol. Evol. Syst.*, **35**, 113–147.

Currie, F. A. and Bamford, R. (1982). Songbird nest-box studies in forests in north Wales. *Q. J. Forestry*, **76**, 250–255.

deCalesta, D. S. (1994). Effect of white-tailed deer on songbirds within managed forests in Pennsylvania. *J. Wildlife Manage.*, **58**, 711–718.

De Casenave, J. L., Pelotto, J. P., Caziani, S. M. *et al.* (1998). Responses of avian assemblages to a natural edge in a Chaco semiarid forest in Argentina. *Auk*, **115**, 425–435.

DeGraaf, R. M., Healy, W. M. and Brooks, R. T. (1991). Effects of thinning and deer browsing on breeding birds in New England oak woodlands. *For. Ecol. Manage.*, **41**, 179–191.

De la Montana, E., Rey-Benayas, J. M. and Carrascal, L. M. (2006). Response of bird communities to silvicultural thinning of Mediterranean maquis. *J. Appl. Ecol.*, **43**, 651–659.

Denny, R. E. and Summers, R. W. (1996). Nest site selection, management and breeding success of Crested Tits *Parus cristatus* at Abernethy Forest, Strathspey. *Bird Study*, **43**, 371–379.

Dhondt, A. A. (2007). What drives differences between North American and Eurasian tit studies? In *Ecology and Behaviour of Chickadees and Titmice: An integrated approach*, ed.

K. A. Otter, pp. 299–310. Oxford: Oxford University Press.

Dhondt, A. A. (2010). Effects of competition on great and blue tit reproduction: intensity and importance in relation to habitat quality. *J. Anim. Ecol.*, **79**, 257–265.

Dhondt, A. A. and Adriaensen, F. (1999). Experiments on competition between Great and Blue Tit: effects on Blue Tit reproductive success and population processes. *Ostrich*, **70**, 39–48.

Dhondt, A. A., Blondel, J. and Perret, P. (2010). Why do Corsican Blue Tits *Cyanistes caeruleus ogliastrae* not use nest-boxes for roosting? *J. Ornithol.*, **151**, 95–101.

Dhondt, A. A., Kempenaers, B. and De Laet, J. (1991). Protected winter roosting sites as a limiting resource for blue tits. *Acta XX Congr. Int. Ornithol.*, pp. 1436–1443.

Diaz, I. A., Armesto, J. J., Reid, S. *et al.* (2005). Linking forest structure and composition: avian diversity in successional forests of Chiloe Island, Chile. *Biol. Conserv.*, **123**, 91–101.

Donald, P. F., Fuller, R. J., Evans, A. D. and Gough, S. J. (1998). Effects of forest management and grazing on breeding bird communities in plantations of broadleaved and coniferous trees in western England. *Biol. Conserv.*, **85**, 183–197.

du Bus de Warnaffe, G. and Deconchat, M. (2008). Impact of four silvicultural systems on birds in the Belgian Ardenne: implications for biodiversity in plantation forests. *Biodivers. Conserv.*, **17**, 1041–1055.

Easton, W. E. and Martin, K. (1998). The effect of vegetation management on breeding bird communities in British Columbia. *Ecol. Appl.*, **8**, 1092–1103.

Edington, J. M. and Edington, M. A. (1972). Spatial patterns and habitat partitioning in the breeding birds of an upland wood. *J. Anim. Ecol.*, **41**, 331–357.

Enemar, A. B. and Sjöstrand, B. (1972). Effects of the introduction of Pied Flycatchers *Ficedula hypoleuca* on the composition of a passerine bird community. *Ornis Scand.*, **3**, 79–87.

Ferry, C. and Frochot, B. (1990). Bird communities of the forests of Burgundy and the Jura (Eastern France). In *Biogeography and Ecology of Forest Bird Communities*, ed. A. Keast, pp. 183–195. The Hague: SPB Academic Publishing bv.

Fisher, R. J., Fletcher, Q. E., Willis, C. K. R. and Brigham, R. M. (2004). Roost selection and roosting behavior of male common nighthawks. *Am. Midl. Nat.*, **151**, 79–87.

Fuller, R. J. (2000). Influence of treefall gaps on distributions of breeding birds within interior old-growth stands in Białowieża Forest, Poland. *Condor*, **102**, 267–274.

Fuller, R. J. and Crick, H. Q. P. (1992). Broad-scale patterns in geographical and habitat distribution of migrant and resident passerines in Britain and Ireland. *Ibis*, **134** (suppl.1), 14–20.

Fuller, R. J., Gaston, K. J. and Quine, C. P. (2007a). Living on the edge: British and Irish woodland birds in a European context. *Ibis*, **149** (Suppl.2), 53–63.

Fuller, R. J. and Green, G. H. (1998). Effects of woodland structure on breeding bird populations in stands of coppiced lime (*Tilia cordata*) in western England over a 10-year period. *Forestry*, **71**, 199–218.

Fuller, R. J. and Rothery, P. (2010). Woodfuel management: prospects for reversing declines in woodland birds. *BOU Proc. – Climate Change and Birds*. www.bou.org.uk/bouproc-net/ccb/fullerandrothery.pdf.

Fuller, R. J., Smith, K. W., Grice, P. V., Currie, F. A. and Quine, C. P. (2007b). Habitat change and woodland birds in Britain:implications for management and future research. *Ibis*, **149** (Suppl.2), 261–268.

Gabbe, A. P., Robinson, S. K. and Brawn, J. D. (2002). Tree-species preferences of foraging insectivorous birds: implications for floodplain forest restoration. *Conserv. Biol.*, **16**, 462–470.

Gill, R. M. A. and Fuller, R. J. (2007). The effects of deer browsing on woodland structure and songbirds in lowland Britain. *Ibis*, **149** (Suppl. 2), 119–127.

Glue, D. E. and Boswell, T. (1994). Comparative nesting ecology of the three British breeding woodpeckers. *Brit. Birds*, **87**, 253–269.

Glutz von Blotzheim, U. N. (2001). Breeding bird dynamics within up to 18 years after extensive windthrow in Norway spruce-dominated fir-beech woodland on the northern edge of the Alps of Central Switzerland. *Ornithol. Beob.*, **98**, 81–112.

Goetz, S. J., Steinberg, D., Betts, M. G. *et al.* (2010). Lidar remote sensing variables predict breeding habitat of a Neotropical migrant bird. *Ecology*, **91**, 1569–1576.

Gorham, E. and Bray, J. R. (1964). Litter production in forests of the world. *Adv. Ecol. Res.*, **2**, 101–57.

Gosler, A. G. and Clement, P. (2007). Family Paridae (Tits and Chickadees). In *Handbook of the Birds of the World*. Vol. **12**, ed. J. del Hoyo, A. Elliott and D. A. Christie, pp. 662–709. Barcelona: Lynx Edicions.

Gosler, A. G., Higham, J. P. and Reynolds, S. J. (2005). Why are birds' eggs speckled? *Ecol. Lett.*, **8**, 1105–1113.

Gram, W. K., Porneluzi, P. A., Clawson, R. L., Faaborg, J. and Richter, S. C. (2003). Effects of experimental forest management on density and nesting success of bird species in Missouri Ozark forests. *Conserv. Biol.*, **17**, 1324–1337.

Griesser, M., Nystrand, M., Eggers, S. and Ekman, J. A. N. (2007). Impact of forestry practices on fitness correlates and population productivity in an open-nesting bird species. *Conserv. Biol.*, **21**, 767–774.

Hågvar, S., Hågvar, G. and Mønness, E. (1990). Nest site selection in Norwegian woodpeckers. *Holarctic Ecol.*, **13**, 156–165.

Hansen, F. (1989). Sortspættens *Dryocopus martius* udmejsling og genbrug af redehuller på Bornholm. *Dansk. Orn. Foren. Tidsskr.*, **83**, 125–129.

Hansen, K., Vesterdal, L., Schmidt, I. K. *et al.* (2009). Litterfall and nutrient return in five tree species in a common garden experiment. *For. Ecol. Manage.*, **257**, 2133–2144.

Hayes, J. P., Weikel, J. M. and Huso, M. M. P. (2003). Response of birds to thinning young Douglas-fir forests. *Ecol. Appl.*, **13**, 1222–1232.

Helle, P. and Mönkkönen, M. (1990). Forest successions and bird communities: theoretical aspects and practical implications. In *Biogeography and Ecology of Forest Bird Communities*, ed. A. Keast, pp. 299–318. The Hague: SPB Academic Publishing bv.

Hertel, F. (2003). Habitatnutzung und Nahrungserwerb von Buntspecht *Picoides major*, Mittlespecht *Picoides medius* und Kleiber *Sitta europaea* in bewirtschafteten und unbewirtschafteten Buchenwäldern des nordostdeutschen Tieflandes. *Vogelwelt*, **124**, 111–132.

Hewson, C. M., Austin, G. E., Gough, S. J. and Fuller, R. J. (2011). Species-specific responses of woodland birds to stand-level habitat characteristics: the dual importance of forest structure and floristics. *For. Ecol. Manage.*, **261**, 1224–1240.

Hinsley, S. A., Bellamy, P. E., Newton, I. and Sparks, T. H. (1995). Habitat and landscape factors influencing the presence of individual breeding bird species in woodland fragments. *J. Avian Biol.*, **26**, 94–104.

Hinsley, S. A., Carpenter, J. E., Broughton, R. K. *et al.* (2007). Habitat selection by Marsh Tits *Poecile palustris* in the UK. *Ibis*, **149** suppl. 2, 224–233.

Hinsley, S. A., Hill, R. A., Fuller, R. J., Bellamy, P. E. and Rothery, P. (2009). Bird species distributions across woodland canopy structure gradients. *Community Ecol.*, **10**, 99–110.

Holmes, R. T. (1990). The structure of a temperate deciduous forest bird community: variability in time and space. In *Biogeography and Ecology of Forest Bird Communities*, ed. A. Keast, pp. 121–139. The Hague: SPB Academic Publishing.

Holmes, R. T. and Robinson, S. K. (1981). Tree species preferences of foraging insectivorous birds in a northern hardwood forest. *Oecologia*, **48**, 31–35.

Holt, C. A., Fuller, R. J. and Dolman, P. M. (2010). Experimental evidence that deer browsing reduces habitat suitability for breeding Common Nightingales *Luscinia megarhynchos*. *Ibis*, **152**, 335–346.

Holt, C. A., Fuller, R. J. and Dolman, P. M. (2011). Breeding and post-breeding responses of woodland birds to modification of habitat structure by deer. *Biol. Conserv.*, **144**, 2151–2162.

Huertas, D. L. and Díaz, J. A. (2001). Winter habitat selection by a montane forest bird assemblage: the effects of solar radiation. *Can. J. Zool.*, **79**, 279–284.

Hutto, R. L. (2006). Towards meaningful snag-management guidelines for postfire salvage logging in North American conifer forests. *Conserv. Biol.*, **20**, 984–993.

James, F. C. and Wamer, N. O. (1982). Relationships between temperate forest bird communities and vegetation structure. *Ecology*, **63**, 159–171.

Järvinen, A. (1978). Nest-box studies in mountain birch forest at Kilpisjärvi, Finnish Lapland. *Anser* (Suppl), **3**, 107–111.

Jobes, A. P., Nol, E. and Voigt, D. R. (2004). Effects of selection cutting on bird communities in contiguous eastern hardwood forests. *J. Wildlife Manage.*, **68**, 51–60.

Johansen, T. (1989). Sortspættens *Dryocopus martius* redetræer og redehuller I Tisvilde Hegn, Nordsjælland, 1977–1986. *Dansk. Orn. Foren. Tidsskr.*, **83**, 119–124.

Kennedy, C. E. J. and Southwood, T. R. E. (1984). The number of species of insects associated with British trees: a re-analysis. *J. Anim. Ecol.*, **53**, 455–478.

Kirby, K. J., Reid, C. M., Thomas, R. C. and Goldsmith, F. B. (1998). Preliminary estimates of fallen dead wood and standing dead trees in managed and unmanaged forests in Britain. *J. Appl. Ecol.*, **35**, 148–155.

Kosiński, Z. and Winiecki, A. (2004). Nest-site selection and niche partitioning among the Great Spotted Woodpecker *Dendrocopos major* and Middle Spotted Woodpecker *Dendrocopos medius* in riverine forest of central Europe. *Ornis Fennica*, **81**, 145–156.

Kuhrt, U., Samietz, J. and Dorn, S. (2006). Effect of plant architecture and hail nets on temperature of codling moth habitats in apple orchards. *Entomol. Exp. Appl.*, **118**, 245–259.

Lack, D. (1971). *Ecological Isolation in Birds*. Oxford: Blackwell Scientific Publications.

Lain, E. J., Haney, A., Burris, J. M. and Burton, J. (2008). Response of vegetation and birds to severe wind disturbance and salvage logging in a southern boreal forest. *For. Ecol. Manage.*, **256**, 863–871.

Laiolo, P. (2002). Effects of habitat structure, floral composition and diversity on a forest bird community in north-western Italy. *Folia Zool.*, **51**, 121–128.

Levia, D. F. and Frost, E. E. (2006). Variability of throughfall volume and solute inputs in wooded ecosystems. *Prog. Phys. Geog.*, **30**, 605–632.

Lewis, A. J. G., Amar, A., Charman, E. C. and Stewart, F. R. P. (2009). The decline of the Willow Tit in Britain. *Brit. Birds*, **102**, 386–393.

Lindenmayer, D. B., Franklin, J. F. and Fischer, J. (2006). General management principles and a checklist of strategies to guide forest biodiversity conservation. *Biol. Conserv.*, **131**, 433–445.

Lindner, M., Maroschck, M., Netherer, S. *et al.* (2010). Climate change impacts, adaptive capacity, and vulnerability of European forest ecosystems. *For. Ecol. Manage.*, **259**, 698–709.

Lovaty, F. (2004). Common Redstart (*P. phoenicurus*) and Spotted Flycatcher (*Muscicapa striata*) population size variations in mature oak timber forests of the Allier (France). *Alauda*, **72**, 81–86.

Lundberg, A. and Alatalo, R. (1992). *The Pied Flycatcher*. London: Poyser.

Martin, J.-L., Stockton, S. A., Allombert, S. and Gaston, A. J. (2010). Top-down and bottom-up consequences of unchecked ungulate browsing on plant and animal diversity in temperate forests: lessons from a deer introduction. *Biol. Invasions*, **12**, 353–371.

Mason, W. L. (2007). Changes in the management of British forests between 1945 and 2000 and possible future trends. *Ibis*, **149** (suppl. 2), 41–52.

Matthysen, E. (1998). *The Nuthatches*. London: Poyser.

Maxwell, J. (2002). Nest-site competition with blue tits and great tits as a possible cause of declines in willow tit numbers: observations in the Clyde area. *Glasgow Nat.*, **24**, 47–50.

McShea, W. J. and Rappole, J. H. (2000). Managing the abundance and diversity of breeding bird populations through manipulation of deer populations. *Conserv. Biol.*, **14**, 1161–1170.

Monk, C. D., Child, G. I. and Nicholson, S. A. (1970). Biomass, litter and leaf surface area estimates of an oak-hickory forest. *Oikos*, **21**, 138–141.

Morrison, M. L., Timossi, I. C., With, K. A. and Manley, P. N. (1985). The use of tree species by forest birds during winter and summer. *J. Wildlife Manage.*, **49**, 1089–1102.

Müller, J., Noss, R. F., Bussler, H. and Brandl, R. (2010). Learning from a "benign neglect strategy" in a national park: response of saproxylic beetles to dead wood accumulation. *Biol. Conserv.*, **143**, 2559–2569.

Nadkarni, N. M. (1994). Diversity of species and interactions in the upper canopy of forest ecosystems. *Am. Zool.*, **34**, 70–78.

Nation, T. H. (2007). The influence of flowering dogwood (*Cornus florida*) on land snail diversity in a southern mixed hardwood forest. *Am. Midl. Nat.*, **157**, 137–148.

Nilsson, A. L. K., Linström, A., Jönzen, N., Nilsson, S. G. and Karlsson, L. (2000). The effect of climate change on partial migration – the blue tit paradox. *Glob. Change Biol.*, **12**, 2014–2022.

Nilsson, S. G., Johnsson, K. and Tjernberg, M. (1991). Is avoidance by black woodpeckers of

old nest holes due to predators? *Anim. Behav.*, **41**, 439–441.

North, M., Steger, G., Denton, R. *et al.* (2000). Association of weather and nest-site structure with reproductive success in California spotted owls. *J. Wildlife Manage.*, **64**, 797–807.

Norton, M. R. and Hannon, S. J. (1997). Songbird response to partial-cut logging in the boreal mixed wood forest of Alberta. *Can. J. For. Res.*, **27**, 44–53.

Olsson, O., Wiktander, U., Malmqvist, A. and Nilsson, S. G. (2001). Variability of patch type preferences in relation to resource availability and breeding success in a bird. *Oecologia*, **127**, 435–443.

Parrish, J. D. (1995). Effects of needle architecture on warbler habitat selection in a coastal spruce forest. *Ecology*, **76**, 1813–1820.

Pasinelli, G. (2000). Oaks (*Quercus sp.*) and only oaks? Relations between habitat structure and home range size of the middle spotted woodpecker (*Dendrocopos major*). *Biol. Conserv.*, **93**, 227–235.

Peck, K. M. (1989). Tree species preference shown by foraging birds in forest plantations in northern England. *Biol. Conserv.*, **48**, 41–57.

Perdeck, A. C., Visser, M. E. and van Balen, J. H. (2000). Great Tit *Parus major* survival and the beech-crop cycle. *Ardea*, **88**, 99–108.

Piotrowska, M. and Wesołowski T. (1989). The breeding ecology and behaviour of the Chiffchaff *Phylloscopus collybita* in primaeval and managed stands of Białowieża Forest. *Acta Ornithol.*, **25**, 25–76.

Quine, C. P., Fuller, R. J., Smith, K. W. and Grice, P. V. (2007). Stand management: a threat or opportunity for birds in British woodland? *Ibis* (Suppl. 2), **149**, 161–174.

Read, D. J., Freer-Smith, P. H., Morison, J. I. L. *et al.* (ed). (2009). *Combating Climate Change – a Role for UK Forests*. The synthesis report. Edinburgh: The Stationery Office.

Rodewald, P. G. and Smith, K. G. (1998). Short-term effects of understory and overstory management on breeding birds in Arkansas oak-hickory forests. *J. Wildlife Manage.*, **62**, 1411–1417.

Rolstad, J., Majewski, P. and Rolstad, E. (1998). Black Woodpecker use of habitats and feeding substrates in a managed Scandinavian forest. *J. Wildlife Manage.*, **62**, 11–23.

Rounsevell, M. D. A., Reginster, I., Araújo, M. B. *et al.* (2006). A coherent set of future land use change scenarios for Europe. *Agr. Ecosyst. Environ.*, **114**, 57–68.

Seavy, N. E., Alexander, J. D. and Hosten, P. E. (2008). Bird community composition after mechanical mastication fuel treatments in southwest Oregon oak woodland and chaparral. *For. Ecol. Manage.*, **256**, 774–778.

Seymour, R. S. and Hunter, M. L. (1999). Principles of ecological forestry. In *Maintaining Biodiversity in Forest Ecosystems*, ed. M. L. Hunter, pp. 22–61. Cambridge: Cambridge University Press.

Sherry, D. F. and Hoshooley, J. S. (2007). Neurobiology of spatial behaviour. In *The Ecology and Behaviour of Chickadees and Titmice*, ed. K. A. Otter, pp. 9–23. New York: Oxford University Press.

Smith, K. W. (1992). Bird populations: effects of tree species mixtures. In *The Ecology of Mixed-Species Stands of Trees*, ed. M. G. R. Cannell, D. C. Malcolm and P. A. Robertson, pp. 233–242. Oxford: Blackwell Scientific Publications.

Smith, K. W. (1997). Nest site selection of the great spotted woodpecker *Dendrocopos major* in two oak woods in southern England and its implications for woodland management. *Biol. Conserv.*, **80**, 283–288.

Smith, K. W. (2007). The utilization of dead wood resources by woodpeckers in Britain. *Ibis*, **149** (suppl.2), 183–192.

Steeger, C. and Hitchcock, C. L. (1998). Influence of forest structure and diseases on nest-site selection by red-breasted nuthatches. *J. Wildlife Manage.*, **62**, 1349–1358.

Suominen, O. and Danell, K. (2006). Effects of large herbivores on other fauna. In *Large Herbivore Ecology, Ecosystem Dynamics and Conservation*, ed. K. Danell, R. Bergström, P. Duncan and J. Pastor, pp. 383–412. Cambridge: Cambridge University Press.

Summers, R. W. (2004). Use of pine snags by birds in different stand types of Scots Pine *Pinus sylvestris*. *Bird Study*, **51**, 212–221.

Suthers, H. B., Bickal, J. M and Rodewald, P. G. (2000). Use of successional habitat and fruit resources by songbirds during autumn migration in central New Jersey. *Wilson Bull.*, **112**, 249–260.

Taylor, S. D. and Summers, R. W. (2009). Breeding numbers and stand type preferences of Redstarts *Phoenicurus phoenicurus* and Tree Pipits *Anthus trivialis* in a Scots Pine *Pinus sylvestris* wood. *Bird Study*, **56**, 120–126.

Tomiałojć, L. and Wesołowski, T. (1990). Bird communities of the primaeval temperate forest of Białowieża, Poland. In *Biogeography and Ecology of Forest Bird Communities*, ed. A. Keast, pp. 141–165. The Hague: SPB Academic Publishing bv.

Vanderwel, M. C., Mills, S. C. and Malcolm, J. R. (2009). Effects of partial harvesting on vertebrate species associated with late-successional forests in Ontario's boreal region. *Forest. Chron.*, **85**, 91–104.

Van Oijen, D., Feijen, M., Hommel, P., den Ouden, J. and de Waal, R. (2005). Effects of tree species composition on within-forest distribution of understory species. *Appl. Veg. Sci.*, **8**, 155–166.

Weakland, C. A., Wood, P. B. and Ford, W. M. (2002). Responses of songbirds to diameter-limit cutting in the central Appalachians of West Virginia, USA. *For. Ecol. Manage.*, **155**, 115–129.

Weidinger, K. (2000). The breeding performance of blackcap *Sylvia atricapilla* in two types of forest habitat. *Ardea*, **88**, 225–233.

Wesołowski, T. (2002). Anti-predator adaptations in nesting Marsh Tits *Parus palustris*: the role of nest-site security. *Ibis*, **144**, 593–601.

Wesołowski, T. (2007). Lessons from long-term hole-nester studies in a primeval temperate forest. *J. Orn.* (suppl. 2), **148**, S395–S405.

Wesołowski, T., Rowiński, P. and Maziarz, M. (2009). Wood Warbler *Phylloscopus sibilatrix*: a nomadic insectivore in search of safe breeding grounds? *Bird Study*, **56**, 26–33.

Whelan, C. J. (1989). Foliage structure preferences and the effects of prey biomass. *Anim. Behav.*, **38**, 839–846.

Wilkin, T. A., Perrins, C. M. and Sheldon, B. C. (2007). The use of GIS in estimating spatial variation in habitat quality: a case study of lay-date in the Great Tit *Parus major*. *Ibis*, **149** (suppl. 2), 110–118.

Willi, J. C., Mountford, J. O. and Sparks, T. H. (2005). The modification of ancient woodland ground flora at arable edges. *Biodivers. Conserv.*, **14**, 3215–3233.

Willson, M. F. and Comet, T. A. (1996). Bird communities of northern forests: patterns of diversity and abundance. *Condor*, **98**, 337–349.

Wilson, A. M., Fuller, R. J., Day, C. and Smith, G. (2005). Nightingales *Luscinia megarhynchos* in scrub habitats in the southern fens of East Anglia, England: associations with soil type and vegetation structure. *Ibis*, **147**, 498–511.

Wilson, M. D. and Watts, B. D. (1999). Response of brown-headed nuthatches to thinning of pine plantations. *Wilson Bull.*, **111**, 56–60.

Witt, C. (2010). Characteristics of aspen infected with heartrot: implications for cavity-nesting birds. *For. Ecol. Manage.*, **260**, 1010–1016.

Zmihorski, M. (2010). The effect of windthrow and its management on breeding bird communities in a managed forest. *Biodivers. Conserv.*, **19**, 1871–1882.

PART III

Wider perspectives

CHAPTER FIFTEEN

What is habitat quality? Dissecting a research portfolio on shorebirds

THEUNIS PIERSMA

*University of Groningen and Royal Netherlands Institute
for Sea Research (NIOZ)*

It is intriguing that the fourth edition of the main British ecology textbook *Ecology: From Individuals to Ecosystems* (Begon *et al.*, 2006) does not include *habitat selection* or *habitat choice* amongst the keywords in the subject index. What can be found is the word *niche*. Of course, this concept is closely bound up with the concepts related to the use and selection of habitats, as discussed in the present book. Nevertheless, Begon *et al.* (2006, p. 31) have interesting things to say about the relationships between the niche concept and the use of habitat, so let's start with a citation: 'The term *ecological niche* … is often used loosely to describe the sort of place in which an organism lives, as in the sentence: "Woodlands are the niche of woodpeckers". Strictly, however, where an organism lives is its *habitat*. A niche is not a place but an idea: a summary of the organism's tolerances and requirements. The habitat of a gut micro-organism would be an animal's alimentary canal; the habitat of an aphid might be a garden; and the habitat of a fish could be a whole lake. Each habitat, however, provides many different niches: many other organisms also live in the gut, the garden or the lake – and with quite different lifestyles.'

This chapter presents a rather personal account of the attempts by myself and co-workers to explain the distribution and abundance of shorebirds, especially during the non-breeding season. We have tried to explain why non-breeding shorebirds use certain mudflats more than others, and why different individuals may use the same area in such different ways. In addition to the population and individual levels, we have also addressed questions on habitat selection at the species level, such as why some shorebird species use coastal rather than freshwater wetlands during the non-breeding season, and why some shorebird species breed on High Arctic tundra rather than in temperate grasslands (a behaviour that condemns them to very long migrations to escape the polar winters).

Of course, this work implicitly addresses the behavioural processes involved in active habitat selection, as illustrated so attractively in a diagram from Temple (2004). This diagram portrays the spatial hierarchy of decisions,

Birds and Habitat: Relationships in Changing Landscapes, ed. Robert J. Fuller. Published by Cambridge University Press. © Cambridge University Press 2012.

related to ever finer-grained space, which has to be taken by a wood thrush *Hylocichla mustelina* when selecting a place to breed (Fig. 15.1). This, and the example of starlings *Sturnus vulgaris* that face a choice between two types of prey to feed to their nestlings that are found in different habitats (Fig. 15.1; Tinbergen, 1981), illustrate how questions on habitat use very easily develop into questions on the nature of individual choice processes. This is the realm of behaviour, and may explain why Begon *et al.* (2006) in their textbook on ecology shied away from the theme of habitat selection.

In trying to answer questions on shorebird habitat use and selection, we have studied the ecological requirements of shorebirds and tried to use this knowledge to derive measurable axes of environmental variation to explain differences in occurrence and use. Over the course of the years we kept adding more axes to the picture. In fact, as I am assembling the accumulated insight, the birds' use of habitat can perhaps easiest be described as a multi-dimensional environmental hyperspace (see Fig. 15.2). This very much reflects the modern concept of niche. However, as is subtly apparent even in the citation from Begon *et al.* (2006), the niche concept has been used mainly to understand the role of interspecific competition in the occurrence of organisms (MacArthur, 1972; Schoener, 1989). The shorebird species of our shores are so

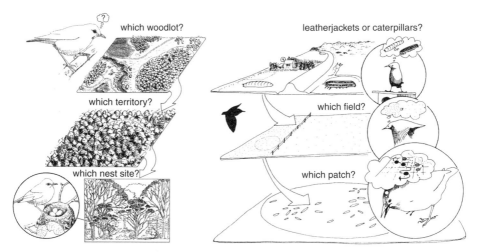

Figure 15.1 Two incarnations of the habitat selection questions that birds have to ask themselves when choosing a nest site (the example for a wood thrush *Hylocicha mustelina* on the left) or a place to find food for nestlings once a nest site, in this case a nest-box attached to a little house in a Dutch polder, has been established (the example for a starling *Sturnus vulgaris* on the right). In this chapter we are not so much asking how birds answer such questions, but addressing the criteria that birds might use to achieve answers to habitat selection questions. Compiled from Temple (2004, left) and Tinbergen (1981, right).

distinct, with such clear-cut differences in food choice and habitat selection, that interspecific competition (except sequential exploitative competition by smaller species depleting a cohort of prey before they become profitable for larger species – Zwarts and Wanink, 1984) has never struck us as the prime explanatory axis of shorebird habitat use, on ecological time scales at least. That the relevance of interspecific competition must have been considered greater in the heyday of niche theorising, is illustrated by Recher's (1966) single confirmatory analysis of a community of shorebirds. Hence, despite the obvious conceptual overlap with the ways in which I will talk about axes of explanation of habitat use, and the ways that the niche concept is used in ecology, I will refrain from using 'niche' here. What I will focus on is why some habitats are used more than others by shorebirds of a kind, using a set of explanatory variables that will be outlined below.

Embodying what is hopefully a profitable line of thought, this chapter reviews the development and growth of an increasingly worldwide research programme on shorebirds, especially on red knot *Calidris canutus* (Piersma, 2007). As participants in a tradition of studies on shorebirds foraging on intertidal flats that now goes back more than half a century (e.g. Zwarts, 1974; Ens *et al.*, 1994; van de Kam *et al.*, 2004; Colwell, 2010), since 1988 we (a team that includes undergraduate, graduate, postgraduate associates and many volunteers) have investigated the distribution and abundance of red knots in the Wadden Sea and beyond. We chose red knots as a model migrant shorebird in view of their uniform diet of hard-shelled prey, mainly molluscs, found in soft sediments, a diet that can quite easily be quantified by visual observation and faecal analyses (Dekinga and Piersma, 1993; van Gils *et al.*, 2003a). We also chose red knots because of their strict habitat choice. During the non-breeding season (i.e. most of the year, as breeding in the High Arctic takes not quite three months, and only six weeks with reproductive failure), red knots only occur on extensive coastal intertidal flats, but they do so worldwide (Piersma *et al.*, 2005; Piersma, 2007). Finally, we chose red knots because, unlike many other shorebirds, they can be kept in captivity relatively easily if the aviaries are perfectly clean, they live in social groups, and if, by being able to probe in wet sand or mud, they have the chance to exercise their specialised bill-tip organ (Piersma *et al.*, 1998).

Axes of explanation

To enable this 'dissection', i.e. a *post hoc* analysis of our work on shorebird distribution and habitat selection, I need to pull off a recursive trick. That is, we will need to begin at the very end, with a summary of the explanatory axes of habitat use (Fig. 15.2), to then relate the story of how the successive steps in developing these axes came about.

An animal that does not eat enough will eventually starve to death: sufficient food is a primary condition for survival, and if energy requirements increase, so must food intake (King, 1974). Of course, animals may be buffered against starvation for a few days to several weeks, the relative importance of energy storage going up with body size (Schmidt-Nielsen, 1984; Klaassen, 2003). The way that animals keep these budgets balanced could be termed *energy management*. In areas where daytime air temperatures exceed body temperatures, about 41 °C in the case of birds, animals can only prevent overheating by finding relatively cool shaded locations or by using body water for evaporative cooling (Williams and Tieleman, 2001; Tieleman *et al.*, 2002). Especially under such conditions, the maintenance of energy balance is closely coupled with the maintenance of a water balance (Tieleman *et al.*, 2002, 2003a, b), an aspect of organismal housekeeping we could call *water management*.

Nevertheless, the maintenance of an energy and a water balance are only two of the considerations that animals should routinely take into account. Birds that fall victim to predators such as peregrine falcon *Falco peregrinus* will not have as many descendants as birds that avoid the attentions of this dangerous beast. The inescapability of evolutionary mechanisms then ensures that animals do also take danger into account. That is, animals have to find the right balance between fear, external danger and foraging or water-saving opportunities (Brown, 1988; 1992; Lima and Dill, 1990; Cresswell, 1994; Lank and Ydenberg, 2003; Caro, 2005; Lind and Cresswell, 2006; Brown and Kotler, 2007). In short, they have to take *danger management* into account. Animals may succumb to starvation, to water loss or overheating, to a predator, but they also can get sick. The extent that birds carry out *disease management* (e.g. by avoiding habitats with lots of pathogens and parasites), seems another important explanatory axis of habitat use and selection (Tieleman *et al.*, 2005; Geue and Partecke, 2008; Råberg *et al.*, 2009; Buehler *et al.*, 2010b). The avoidance of sick-making habitats can either be subsumed under the banner of danger management (Hall *et al.*, 2008), or be raised to a category of its own. Since drawing more than four axes is problematic, in Fig. 15.2 I have put danger from predators together with disease under one axis; one could call this an axis of 'spatial avoidance'.

The fourth axis has to do with the fact that animals rarely live in social isolation. Every individual has to search for a balance between socially uncomplicated loneliness and living in pairs or groups. In the context of habitat selection, *social management* especially comes to the fore when individuals face a choice between an initially very good habitat patch that receives many conspecifics, and a lower-quality patch that has attracted fewer competitors. Thinking about these processes has generated the standard null-model of animal distribution, the so-called *ideal free distribution* model, which predicts that animals will distribute themselves in such a way that they achieve similar

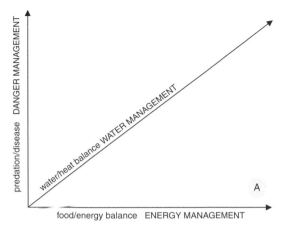

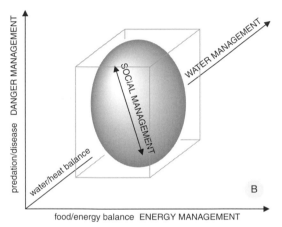

Figure 15.2 Explaining the presence or absence of a particular animal in a habitat may be represented as resolving four kinds of 'management'. Visually they could be represented as several perpendicular 'axes', which in goniometric terms would imply that the axes (or kinds of management) would be independent (which they are unlikely to be). In the top panel the three dimensions related to balancing *energy*, *water* and *danger* (here including *disease*) are visualised. In the bottom panel a fourth dimension called *social* management is additionally brought in. Dealings with conspecifics (intraspecific competition and facilitation) often determine the more precise habitat conditions that individual animals are able to live in. Note that keeping the balance of water and heat is particularly critical even at intervals of a few hours or even minutes.

intake rates at all available patches (Fretwell, 1972; Sutherland, 1996). Incorporating the other axes of explanation (Fig. 15.2), one could also state that under an ideal free distribution, the different axes, or rather the 'evolutionary outcome' (i.e. fitness) will be in balance in similar ways in all patches of habitat used (van Gils *et al.*, 2004). Obviously, if 'some animals are more equal than others' (Orwell, 1945), despotic issues come into play and animals no longer are distributed with equal fitness for everybody. Note that only animals that have full knowledge of the alternatives can be considered *ideal*. Animals that find hindrance in moving from one patch to another (a travel cost, or social obstruction) no longer are *free*, and individuals in such situations are expected to face inequalities with respect to the other three explanatory axes also.

Getting to know a study species

In 1988 we started with red knots as the focus of interest, a species for which we would like to explain foraging and roosting distributions during the non-breeding season, especially in the Wadden Sea. This implied that we would need to measure red knot distributions across mudflats. Given the *Zeitgeist*, just after the heyday of 'optimal foraging' in the context of 'behavioural ecology' (Stephens and Krebs, 1986; Krebs and Davies, 1987), we initially focused entirely on food as the single explanatory variable. We knew that red knots were molluscivores with a preference for thin-shelled, shallow-buried bivalves (Zwarts and Blomert, 1992). Thus we were required to measure food abundance for red knots at relevant spatial scales, and determine diet in areas frequented by red knots.

Getting a handle on foraging distributions was not easy, as the fashionable approach at the time, erecting watch towers on mudflats and waiting for birds to show up in fixed plots and then counting them, hardly worked for this species. Red knots move around over vaster scales than can be observed from a single hide, and they are notoriously unpredictable. We therefore simply regularly walked the *c.* 50 km^2 of intertidal flats around the islet of Griend in the western Dutch Wadden Sea, where we carried out studies in the late summers of 1988–1992, and plotted flocks of red knots on a map of the area, positioning ourselves in this landscape using compass bearings on known landmarks on the horizon (this was before GPS became available). In a summary of five years of fieldwork, we were able to correlate relative abundance across sectors of the mudflats with the densities of prey types that red knots ate most in the respective years (Fig. 15.3). Red knots, we could conclude at the time (Piersma *et al.*, 1993), generally select those parts of the intertidal flats where they find the highest densities of suitably sized shellfish. We were reluctant to conclude much more, as the scale at which we tried to link the food and the flocks of feeding red knots necessarily was very coarse. For finer, and more informative, spatial resolutions, at least on the uniform mudflats around Griend, we had to await the appearance of the Global Positioning System (GPS) in the public domain. We did not have to wait too long, and were able to start with fine-grained benthic food sampling in late 1993 (see below).

With an eye towards explaining why some red knots winter in the cold conditions in Western Europe, whereas others fly to congenially warm West Africa (Piersma *et al.*, 1991), in the meantime we tried to disentangle two processes related to energy management. Using tamed red knots in confinement, we first quantified energy loss of red knots as a function of both weather conditions (expressed in terms of wind speed, air temperature and global solar radiation, as measured by meteorologists worldwide) and habitat features (including vegetation and density of surrounding conspecifics). This work yielded equations to predict the maintenance energy requirements of free-living red knots as a function of weather and habitat (Wiersma and Piersma, 1994). Second, we tried to experimentally derive the sensory mechanism enabling red knots to find buried hard-shelled prey in soft

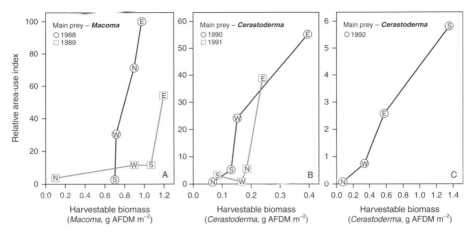

Figure 15.3 Aggregative responses of red knots on the intertidal areas around the islet of Griend (western Dutch Wadden Sea) in 1988–1992. For each year the indices of intensity of area use of the four different sectors (indicated by N for north, E for east, S for south and W for west) around Griend are plotted as a function of the harvestable biomass (measured as ash-free dry mass, AFDM) in that sector of the most commonly eaten prey in that year (*Macoma* in 1988 and 1989, panel A; *Cerastoderma* in the remaining three years, panels B and C). The intensities of area use were scaled to the maximum index of area use (100) as in the eastern sector in 1988. Since numbers of knots were very low in 1992, a separate panel (C) presents the data for that year. Note that the minimum threshold levels for harvestable biomass values in Fig. 15.4 cannot directly be applied to these plots because of scaling issues: here we have plotted averages of quarter segments of the Griend intertidal areas, which will lead to rather lower values than the point estimates that we measured from the field season of 1993 onward. From Piersma *et al.* (1993).

sediments. Our feeding experiments had suggested that, unlike oystercatchers *Haematopus ostralegus*, which detect buried shellfish if they touch them with their probing bills (Hulscher, 1982), red knots actually sense a buried bivalve (or a stone!) from some distance (Piersma *et al.*, 1995). Eventually we could come up with the strong suggestion that this 'remote sense' relies on the particular arrays of pressure sensors in the bill tip of red knots, and the ways with which their rapid and repeatedly vertically probing bill pushes interstitial water in wet sediment to generate pressure contours of which the deviations caused by buried objects can be read by the sensitive bill tip (Piersma *et al.*, 1998).

These three new elements (fine-scale grid sampling enabled by GPS, quantitative predictive models of energy expenditure, as well as empirical functional response equations), were brought together in an attempt to describe in detail the distribution of foraging red knots and their prey around Griend in August–September 1993 (Fig. 15.4). On the basis of various pieces of laboratory

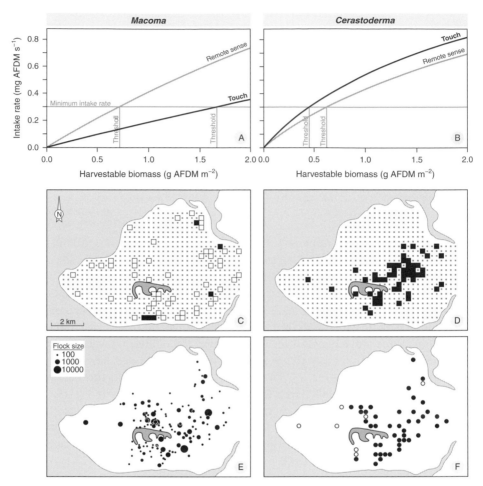

Figure 15.4 The match between predicted minimally suitable sites for red knots feeding either on Baltic tellins *Macoma balthica* or edible cockles *Cerastoderma edule* and the observed distribution of foraging flocks of red knots during all stages of the tide on intertidal flats around the islet of Griend in August–September 1993. Functional response curves are shown in panels A and B using two models ('touch' and 'remote-sensed'). Biomass is measured as ash-free dry mass (AFDM). Maps C and D show the island (small grey area) surrounded by 250 × 250 m grid sampling locations across the intertidal flats (white area). Locations predicted to support sufficient *Macoma* to meet minimum intake rates according to the two models are shown as open ('remote-sensed') and closed ('touch') squares in map C. Locations predicted to hold sufficient *Cerastoderma* by the two models, which gave similar results, are shown as closed squares in map D. The distribution of flocks of different sizes is shown in map E. The distribution of flocks of at least 500 knots is compared with the minimally suitable sites for either prey in map F, with filled dots indicating that the flocks border or overlap with a suitable site, and open circles that they do not. From Piersma *et al.* (1995).

work, we were able to suggest the minimum threshold levels of prey density to explain whether an area of intertidal mudflat was used or not (Piersma *et al.*, 1995), an approach that we could also scale up to include other areas within the international Wadden Sea (Piersma *et al.*, 1994). Such independent estimates of threshold values for harvestable food abundance are much more general (and possibly have more predictive power) than field estimates of threshold values (Gill *et al.*, 2001), for the simple reason that the field values would incorporate effects of all other selection pressures (considered below) in addition to energy management (van Gils *et al.*, 2004).

Our continued work on habitat use and selection in red knots in the Wadden Sea not only helped us understand some drivers of these patterns (limited, of course, to those that we had incorporated in our explanatory framework at that stage, mainly issues of energy management), the work also yielded many puzzling observations. Were the observations that red knots rarely used food-rich mudflats close to the islet of Griend, and the finding that the food thresholds of occurrence seemed to be much higher close to the Frisian foreshore (Zwarts *et al.*, 1992) than off Griend (Piersma *et al.*, 1993), both related to the relative risks of surprise attacks by raptors in the different areas? Why would some red knots move on from the mudflats around Griend to areas even further removed from their apparently favourable high-tide roost on the sandspit Richel, 7 km northwest of Griend, necessitating more than 30 km of flight each tide (Piersma *et al.*, 1993)? From now on, the narrative no longer is linear. I will first consider issues of individual variation in habitat use, and then examine whether the predators of red knots have any role to play in their selection and use of foraging and roosting habitats.

Individual variation in the use of non-breeding habitat

By 1996 we were well aware of the diet-selection patterns of red knots in the Wadden Sea (Zwarts and Blomert, 1992; Dekinga and Piersma, 1993; Piersma *et al.*, 1993). We also had built up the sampling techniques and logistics to sample harvestable food biomass (see Zwarts and Wanink, 1984) at the relevant spatial scale for red knots in the western Dutch Wadden Sea. Using the ships and moveable observation platforms of the NIOZ Royal Netherlands Institute for Sea Research on Texel, most of these intertidal flats had become accessible to our research team. Year after year we managed to determine the distribution of molluscs over hundreds of square kilometres of intertidal flat (Piersma *et al.*, 2001; van Gils *et al.*, 2006b; Kraan *et al.*, 2007, 2009). In a programme of laboratory and experimental field studies, Jan van Gils successfully explained diet selection for red knots, which turned out not only to be gape-limited foragers (Zwarts and Blomert, 1992), but more critically could be considered digestive-rate limited foragers because of their need to internally process the ballast that comes with ingesting hard-shelled prey whole (van Gils *et al.*, 2003a, 2003b, 2005a, 2006a, 2007; Quaintenne *et al.*, 2010). Not only did this work yield estimates of the costs of digestion (Piersma *et al.*, 2003), but the understanding of the prey selection criteria in the digestive-rate limited red knots (van Gils *et al.*, 2003a, 2005a) also provided us with the means to weigh the importance of multiple prey found at any single sampling station and derive a predicted intake rate (van Gils *et al.*, 2006b). In a resulting summary map (Fig. 15.5), the size of the black dots scales with the predicted food intake rate at each of these sampling stations: the darker an area, the more food there is for red knots to find.

To explain why only some red knots stay close to Griend for the whole low-tide period, whereas others apparently moved further east, we started to follow individual red knots throughout the day and night by applying 1.5 g radio transmitters to their backs and registering their absence or presence within a certain radius with automated radio-tracking stations (van Gils and Piersma, 1999; van Gils *et al.*, 2000). Most red knots appeared to use that great sandbank, Richel, to roost. With the outgoing tide they had to decide whether to fly to forage on the intertidal flats of Westwad, or Richelwad, or Grienderwaard or Ballastplaat (Fig. 15.5). Red knots had to ask themselves whether it was worth travelling all the way to the Ballastplaat, 20 km away

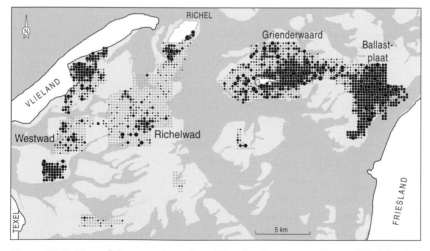

Figure 15.5 Map of the complex of mudflats in the western Dutch Wadden Sea used by red knots roosting at Richel, Griend and Vlieland, with an outline of the annual benthic sampling grid with 250 m intersections. Pale dots indicate sites where knots would not have found anything to eat in August–September 1996–2000. The size of the black dots is scaled to the predicted intake rate averaged across the five years of study (August–September 1996–2000). This map is based on van Gils *et al.* (2006b).

from Richel, or whether the poorer intertidal flats closer to Richel would be good enough. We asked ourselves whether red knots have all the relevant information to take such strategic decisions (van Gils *et al.*, 2006a). Many radio-tagged red knots remained close to the high-tide roost, whilst many birds moved to the Grienderwaard, but the rich mudflats of the Ballastplaat indeed appeared not to be particularly popular. Apparently many red knots decided against the long and costly journeys to Ballastplaat.

To evaluate these decisions, we compared the empirical distribution pattern with predicted distribution patterns, predictions made on the basis of models that either did or did not incorporate their omniscience and travel costs (van Gils *et al.*, 2006b). Red knots that did not know the distribution of their food, and did not care about travel costs, should distribute themselves across the different areas relative to the extents of these areas. Red knots that lacked information on food distribution, but did take travel costs into account, should remain close to Richel even at low tide. Red knots that knew as much about the distribution of their food as we did, but that didn't account for travel costs, should travel to the richer Ballastplaat in much larger numbers than we saw. Omniscient red knots that took travel costs into account should distribute themselves approximately according to what it turned out that real wild red knots did (van Gils *et al.*, 2006b). So, we had learned that the distribution of red knots during low tide in the western Dutch Wadden Sea is consistent with the assumption that they know the distribution of their food really well and that they incorporate flight costs into their strategic decisions.

Why some individuals bothered to go all the way to food-rich Ballastplaat (Fig. 15.5), but so many did not, could be explained on the basis of individual gizzard mass. This was measured after capture, and before release with a radio tag, using non-invasive means, i.e. ultrasound (Dietz *et al.*, 1999; Dekinga *et al.*, 2001; Starck *et al.*, 2001). These studies were carried out in late summer, during a time that red knots return from the tundra breeding grounds, often with atrophied gizzards (van Gils *et al.*, 2003a; Battley and Piersma, 2005). Initially this will limit their daily processing powers. Birds with small gizzards were therefore predicted to have to feed for longer periods each day than birds with large gizzards. Red knots roosting at Richel have the option to follow a delaying tide towards the east, the mainland coast of Friesland, and can thus lengthen their working day and indeed, they did (Fig. 15.6). Variations in habitat use were thus explained by variations in body state, particularly the size of the gizzard (van Gils *et al.*, 2005b, 2006c, 2007), but note that this state is far from constant over time scales longer than the few weeks of field studies and in continuous interaction with the environment that the animals find themselves in (Piersma and van Gils, 2011).

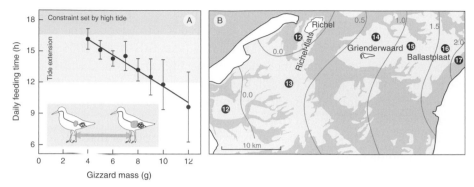

Figure 15.6 Individual variation in relation to gizzard mass differences in red knots. In the western Dutch Wadden Sea, knots can extend their daily feeding period by 4–5 h beyond the usual 12 h in tidal areas by moving eastwards with the outgoing tide. (A) The smaller their gizzard, the longer the radio-marked knots were away from their roost at Richel, feeding on mudflats instead (means ± standard errors). Inset shows knots with either a small (left) or large (right) gizzard. (B) The numbered dots show the hours of mudflat exposure and also tide isoclines, expressed in hours delay per tidal cycle relative to the tide time at Richel. Compiled from van Gils *et al.* (2005b, 2007).

The role of predation risk

Early on we suggested that red knots avoided foraging close to the higher ground of small islands and seawalls, because such obstructions can cover the approach of raptors before they launch their surprise attacks on shorebirds (Piersma *et al.*, 1993). Elsewhere in Europe, red knots were found to also keep well away from cover (McGowan *et al.*, 2002). However, the most convincing evidence that red knots and the closely related great knots *Calidris tenuirostris* indeed avoid cover, came from studies on roost-site choice by radio-tagged birds in the tropics of northwest Australia (Rogers *et al.*, 2006). Avoiding cover for potential predators, especially at night because of the danger of owl predation, seems to be the rule rather than the exception (Sitters *et al.*, 2001) and this may explain why all red knots in the western Dutch Wadden Sea seemed to leave Griend for the open sandbanks of Richel when high tides cover the most open roosting space (Piersma *et al.*, 1993).

Nevertheless, some red knots usually do forage close to obstructive cover, even at low tide. Why some individuals do this, whereas others do not (i.e. an analysis at the individual level) was the subject of Piet van den Hout's studies on the Banc d'Arguin in Mauritania, an area of extensive shallows and intertidal flats bordered by small dunes that separate sea from Sahara (van den Hout *et al.*, 2008, submitted). Here, several species of falcon hunt by stealth using the low dunes to launch their attacks (Fig. 15.7A). It could be shown that inshore foraging shorebird species were more prone to die in the claws of

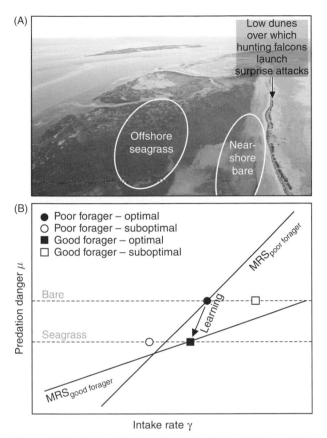

Figure 15.7 (A) Aerial view from a height of 150 m of the study area on Banc d'Arguin, Mauritania, where Piet van den Hout carried out his studies on near-shore versus offshore foraging in red knots, distinguishing near-shore bare mudflat, and offshore sea-grass habitat as indicated. (B) State space diagram illustrating two different optimal decision trajectories by poor and good foragers, respectively, with respect to the trade-off between energy intake γ and predation danger μ (adapted from Houston and McNamara, 1999). In this state space, fitness is maximised towards the lower right (where predation danger μ is lowest and intake rate γ is highest). Which of the two available options (offshore sea-grass or near-shore bare) is located 'lowest right' depends on a bird's marginal rate of substitution (MRS) of predation danger for energy intake. Birds that are rather poor foragers (which usually are in a poor energy state) experience a high MRS and should therefore feed in the near-shore bare habitat. In contrast, good foragers (which usually are in a high energy state) experience low MRS and should therefore feed in offshore sea-grass habitat. That with increasing age and experience initially poor foragers may develop into good foragers and should make a shift between the habitats is indicated by the arrow. Photo by Marion Broquère and Simon Nancy. Compiled from P.J. van den Hout *et al.* (submitted).

these falcons than offshore foragers (van den Hout *et al.*, 2008). Predation was also selective with respect to age: young birds were much more likely to die and, at least in red knots, the near-shore foragers were mostly juveniles. Although only a few per cent of winter mortality can be explained by depredation (suggesting that the anti-predation counter measures were pretty effective), red knots on the Banc d'Arguin certainly avoid predation risk at some cost, as we shall now see.

By showing an increased frequency of head-ups close to shore, foraging red knots indicated that they were well aware of the dangers of near-shore foraging (van den Hout *et al.*, submitted). Indeed, near-shore areas were avoided by experienced adult red knots, apart from the brief periods when they are pressed against the shoreline by the incoming tides. Nevertheless, the bare near-shore areas (with less but easier to detect food than in sea-grass beds) were used by some young birds. Using the state-space approach of Houston and McNamara (1999) to solve the trade-off between predation danger and intake rate for birds with different foraging proficiencies (Fig. 15.7B), we can understand why young and relatively inexperienced red knots actually did best by feeding in these near-shore areas. As finding and extracting bivalves buried among the roots of sea-grass may require some time to learn, we expect red knots, as they become more experienced with age, to move to the offshore sea-grass areas during low water. And this, it appears, is what they do (van den Hout *et al.*, submitted).

Changing criteria with changing contexts?

Depending on context (nutritional demand, time pressures, body state), animals may be expected to adjust their habitat selection criteria. With respect to the previous situation at Banc d'Arguin, where red knots have to decide whether, with the incoming tide, they still want to use near-shore habitat as a means to lengthen the number of feeding minutes, we actually have some evidence for a migration-related change in criteria. In winter, adults refrain from visiting near-shore foraging areas unless they are in very poor condition (van den Hout *et al.*, submitted). In April, however, when adults fuel up for northward migration (Zwarts *et al.*, 1990a) and have long working days (Zwarts *et al.*, 1990b), the relatively fat birds (scored on the basis of their bulging abdomens), did use near-shore foraging areas with incoming and outgoing tides. The correlative caveat here is that in spring the surprise-attacking raptors that make near-shore foraging so dangerous at this site, showed up three times less frequently than in winter.

Arguably the most celebrated example of a staging area supposedly stacked with good benthic food and swiftly refuelling shorebirds is Delaware Bay in May (Myers, 1986). This is the single site along the Atlantic coast of the northeastern USA where female horseshoe crabs *Limulus polyphemus* still come in good numbers onto coarse and steep sandy beaches to deposit their eggs in clumps and have them fertilised by males in close pursuit of the digging females (Schuster *et al.*, 2003). After good spawning events, during which egg-filled beaches get churned up by veritable masses of horseshoe crabs, shorebirds capitalise on the spilled eggs that may cover the surface. What keeps me amazed about red knots at this place is the narrowness of the beaches where they congregate to feed on the eggs, the general nervousness of the birds as they crowd in with turnstones *Arenaria interpres*, sanderling *Calidris alba* and laughing gulls *Larus atricilla* (Karpanty *et al.*, 2006; Vahl *et al.*, 2007) and the proximity to buildings and high vegetation that they appear to tolerate. Although the birds find abundant food that is relatively easy to process (A. Dekinga *et al.*, unpubl. data), and fuel up at very high rates (Atkinson *et al.*, 2007), I have the distinct impression that red knots tolerate conditions at the Delaware Bay beaches only because they have little time left for refuelling (and are thus in need of abundant high-quality prey – van Gils *et al.*, 2005c) with basically nowhere else to go (Baker *et al.*, 2004). This tallies with their propensity, even during their stay in Delaware Bay, to travel to the open Atlantic estuaries and beaches to roost, sometimes taking the opportunity to feed on small mussels *Mytilus edulis* (Cohen *et al.*, 2010a, 2010b). To go beyond such conjecture, we should probably revisit the red knots in the Wadden Sea and study the effects of changing context on habitat selection criteria in autumn, when demands are relatively low, and in midwinter, when energy demands are high (Wiersma and Piersma, 1994).

So far we have not included competitor density (i.e. social management, Fig. 15.2) as part of the explanations for why individuals vary in their use of habitat. Although red knots, by virtue of their digestive bottleneck, may not be very susceptible to intraspecific interference during foraging (van Gils and Piersma, 2004), by making them feed at different densities on small artificial indoor mudflats, we have been able to show that foraging interference and the resulting negative density-dependence does exist (Vahl *et al.*, 2005). Such interference processes would constrain densities within foraging flocks (van Gils and Piersma, 2004; Folmer *et al.*, 2010), and even help explain the distribution of overwintering red knots along the western European coastline (Quaintenne *et al.*, 2011). That competitive (despotic) processes seem to limit individual movement between alternative foraging areas and roosts on the Banc d'Arguin (Leyrer *et al.*, 2012) suggests that social management may be an important axis of habitat use, even in a flock-living and supposedly non-competitive species like the red knot.

Are water and heat ever out of balance?
During the wet hot season in the tropics of northwestern Australia, great knots fuelling for northward migration, at least during days with intense

solar radiation, will have to take heat stress into account (Battley *et al.*, 2003). They can do this by limiting their distribution to places where they can keep their legs wet to enhance heat loss. It is possible that they have to actively limit rates of energy intake and fuel deposition to what will be possible under cooler conditions (Piersma *et al.*, 2005), as these internal processes generate additional heat (cf. Petit *et al.*, 2010; Speakman and Król, 2010).

In general, however, the behavioural and physiological mechanisms to maintain water and heat balance would seem to be adequate within much of the distributional range of red knots. For example, their large salt-glands (Gutiérrez *et al.*, 2012) ensure that red knots foraging on intertidal invertebrates are able to maintain high water turnover rates with little need to drink seawater (Verboven and Piersma, 1995). A comparison of predicted evaporative water loss in the Wadden Sea and in the tropical Banc d'Arguin suggested that red knot wintering in the tropics may need only marginally more water for evaporative cooling than birds overwintering at temperate latitudes (Verboven and Piersma, 1995). Thus, except for a daytime preference for the coolest roosting sites by red and great knots in the tropics (Rogers *et al.*, 2006), issues of water and heat balance, so far, have not been much needed in explanations of the habitat use at any spatial scale.

Disease management

Red knots are rare, but occur worldwide (with the exception of Antarctica). A close look at the rather few sites where they do occur reveals a stunning pattern (Piersma, 2007). Like almost all migrating bird species breeding in the High Arctic, during the non-breeding season red knots only occur in marine shoreline habitats (Piersma, 2007). If there are reasons to think that in harsh and extreme polar climates the causes of externally induced diseases (i.e. parasites and pathogens) are rare (Ridley, 1994), then there are also reasons to think that the chicks of tundra-breeding birds may not be triggered to build up proper immune systems. These birds would then have to restrict themselves to relatively 'clean' (i.e. parasite- and pathogen-poor) habitats during the rest of their lives (Piersma, 1997, 2003). Marine, seaside and otherwise saline habitats indeed may provide such relatively clean areas, at least with respect to some disease groups (notably avian malaria, a blood parasite – Figuerola, 1999; Mendes *et al.*, 2005). The staging area in Delaware Bay, discussed above, may be an exception to the rule (Buehler *et al.*, 2010a).

We have not been able to establish examples where the presence or absence of a disease organism influences the spatial pattern of use within an intertidal area. Perhaps we have stumbled upon one smoking gun, and for this we go back to the Banc d'Arguin where red knots are not as free to move between areas as one would expect at first sight (Leyrer *et al.*, 2012). Here Buehler *et al.* (2009) examined the interaction of age and environment on immune-system indicators and found that first-year birds (but not adults) in a relatively low–quality area had higher leukocyte concentrations (i.e. were either better defended or showed higher responses) than first-year birds or adults in a higher-quality area. Although the two areas are quite comparable in structure and food, and though they differ in survival of red knot, it remains unclear whether this difference in immunity relates to the risks of disease or rather reflects the body condition of birds that find themselves in the two different areas, with condition being determined by food availability and/or predation danger (Leyrer *et al.*, 2012).

Can this research programme be applied elsewhere?

Looking back, it is clear that coming to grips with the diet selection criteria, and food and feeding of red knots was critical. Because they are digestive-rate limited foragers, we also needed to understand the dynamics of the digestive tract (Quaintenne *et al.*, 2010; Piersma and van Gils, 2011). This means that the *x*-axis of Fig. 15.2 was in fact the most crucial to understand. With information on diet and food availability, the relative distribution of red knots across mudflat areas could be understood at a correlative level. With information on organ size, body state and prey quality, an understanding of the use of staging habitats at worldwide scales was achieved (van Gils *et al.*, 2005c), and we could account for the patterns of individual variation at single sites (van Gils *et al.*, 2006a, 2006c). Subsequently, during attempts to bring in other axes of explanation in explaining habitat use, notably predation danger and social management, the food axis always needed to be accounted for (Folmer *et al.*, 2010; Quaintenne *et al.*, 2011; van den Hout *et al.*, submitted). Actually, what we have established during all this work is the parameterised 'niche' of non-breeding red knots, but not in a community ecology context (see Chase and Leibold, 2003).

Although it was the *Zeitgeist* of the late 1970s and 1980s (a time when behavioural ecology became our trade-name – Stephens and Krebs, 1986; Krebs and Davies, 1987; Danchin *et al.*, 2008), that prompted us to start with studies of food and foraging, even with hindsight this priority was spot on. For any species, knowledge of food selection criteria, food processing issues, digestive organ capacities and dynamics, and energy expenditure as a function of weather and activity, remain critical ingredients for a mechanistic understanding of habitat use. But do we need to know as much as we do about red knots to make reasonable inferences about habitat selection in the other 10 000 bird species?

A good starting point is an understanding of the prey selection criteria which enable one to select the appropriate measure for food abundance and the derivation of 'functional response curves' that describe the relationship between food abundance and intake rates (Fig. 15.4; Goss-Custard *et al.*, 2006). As shown for two subspecies of black-tailed godwits *Limosa limosa*, one eating buried bivalves in winter (Gill *et al.*, 2001) and another spilled rice kernels during northward migration (Lourenço *et al.*, 2010), on this basis, local distributions, food depletion patterns and even the movements of individuals can readily be explained. Still, one might say that without a good and complete understanding of energy management (including organ flexibility, and food quality and availability), an understanding of the roles of sociality and predation danger at the individual level is out of reach. Even when looking to explain the differential use of roosting habitats in relation to predation danger (Rogers *et al.*, 2006), it is pertinent to know the food abundance of the nearby mudflats. We should be aware that to try and understand habitat selection of a particular species the devil is likely to be in the details.

Red knots in a changing world

The reason that all this utterly specialised knowledge on the habitat selection criteria of a single species is so important is that it enables us as ecologists to be 'predictive'. In our changing modern world of increasing complexity, prediction is what societies demand of the scientists that they employ. What is requested from ecology is no different from what other sciences have to deliver. Can we predict what will happen to red knots if we know what will happen to their non-breeding habitats? I believe we can. Seasons of dredging for shellfish in formally protected areas of intertidal flat in the Dutch Wadden Sea were followed by stark decreases in bivalve food stocks (Piersma *et al.*, 2001; Kraan *et al.*, 2007). As predicted, the numbers of wintering red knots *C. c. islandica* relying on these mudflats declined in close correspondence with the decline in the area of suitable mudflat remaining (Kraan *et al.*, 2009). The declines could be attributed to a reduction in annual survival and movements away from the Wadden Sea (Kraan *et al.*, 2009). As cockle dredging negatively affected prey quality, individuals returning from the High Arctic breeding grounds with small gizzards were particularly at risk (van Gils *et al.*, 2006c). The subspecies that uses the Wadden Sea en route from Siberia to West Africa (including Banc d'Arguin), *C. c. canutus*, comes here to refuel quickly. This doubles the daily demands of these birds, the threshold food values of what is a suitable mudflat are higher also, and so were the relative population declines (Kraan *et al.*, 2010). Earlier, we showed that overharvesting of horseshoe crabs in Delaware Bay led to a precipitous decrease in the annual survival of staging red knots for a few years (Baker *et al.*, 2004).

At the time of writing, two other subspecies of red knot, *C. c. piersmai* and *rogersi* (of which the first winters mainly in northwestern Australia and the second mainly in New Zealand) are faced with the rapid reclamation of their intertidal refuelling areas along the Chinese coast of the Yellow Sea (Rogers *et al.*, 2010; Yang *et al.*, 2011). Unless these birds are able to find and exploit the remaining intertidal areas that they have not used so far, we predict their declines from 2008 onwards will mirror the rate of loss of suitable mudflat area (Yang *et al.*, 2011). For these reasons these are both daunting and interesting times, during which we should be able to further test, refine and apply the habitat-use models developed for red knots. In the meantime, we also like to use this knowledge to explore the unknown worlds of *intra*specific competition, information exchange and self-organisational processes in this highly social shorebird (Bijleveld *et al.*, 2010; Folmer *et al.*, 2010). And of course, we would like to see similar levels of detail to be achieved with other species and in other systems, to establish that the research programme is indeed generalisable, to re-examine questions on *inter*specific competition in the structuring of bird communities and simply to learn from all the comparisons that are then possible.

Acknowledgements

For a long time Rudi Drent was my gentle taskmaster. He embodied the enduring insights of his time and started a school in animal ecology in which studies on food, foraging and energetics took centre stage. I am most grateful to NIOZ and the University of Groningen for the many years of hosting and supporting the research team of which I am part, and of course the wonderful hard-working contributors who joined this long-term research endeavour for briefer or longer times, often (initially) as volunteers. A few individuals, however, have been involved for particularly long times, and in this regard I like to single out for thanks Anne Dekinga, Bernard Spaans, Jan van Gils and Maurine Dietz in view of their unrelenting enthusiasm and input. I thank Dick Visser for his usual meticulous illustrations and Christiaan Both, Jan van Gils, Piet van den Hout, Rodney West, editor Rob Fuller and reviewers Phil Atkinson and Tony Fox for feedback on drafts.

References

Atkinson, P. W., Baker, A. J., Bennett, K. A. *et al.* (2007). Rates of mass gain and energy deposition in Red Knot on their final spring staging site is both time- and condition-dependent. *J. Appl. Ecol.*, **44**, 885–895.

Baker, A. J., Gonzalez, P. M., Piersma, T. *et al.* (2004). Rapid population decline in red knots: fitness consequences of decreased refuelling rates and late arrival in Delaware Bay. *Proc. R. Soc. B*, **271**, 875–882.

Begon, M., Townshend, C. R. and Harper, J. L. (2006). *Ecology: From Individuals to Ecosystems.* Oxford: Blackwell Publishing.

Battley, P. F. and Piersma, T. (2005). Adaptive interplay between feeding ecology and features of the digestive tract in birds. In: *Physiological and Ecological Adaptations to Feeding in Vertebrates*, ed. J. M. Starck and T. Wang, pp. 201–228. Enfield: Science Publishers.

Battley, P. F., Rogers, D. I., Piersma T. and Koolhaas, A. (2003). Behavioural evidence for heat-load problems in Great Knots in tropical Australia fuelling for long-distance flight. *Emu*, **103**, 97–104.

Bijleveld, A. I., Egas, M., van Gils, J. A. and Piersma, T. (2010). Beyond the information centre hypothesis: communal roosting for information on food, predators, travel companions and mates? *Oikos*, **119**, 277–285.

Brown, J. S. (1988). Patch use as an indicator of habitat preference, predation risk, and competition. *Behav. Ecol. Sociobiol.*, **22**, 37–47.

Brown, J. S. (1992). Patch use under predation risk. 1. Models and predictions. *Ann. Zool. Fenn.*, **29**, 301–309.

Brown, J. S. and Kotler, B. P. (2007). Foraging and the ecology of fear. In *Foraging: Behaviour and Ecology*, ed. D. W. Stephens, J. S. Brown and R. C. Ydenberg, pp. 437–480. Chicago: University of Chicago Press.

Buehler, D. M., Tieleman, B. I. and Piersma, T. (2009). Age and environment affect constitutive immune function in Red Knots (*Calidris canutus*). *J. Ornithol.*, **150**, 815–825.

Buehler, D. M., Tieleman, B. I. and Piersma, T. (2010a). Indices of immune function are lower in Red Knots (*Calidris canutus*) recovering protein than in those storing fat during stopover in Delaware Bay. *Auk*, **127**, 394–401.

Buehler, D. M., Tieleman, B. I. and Piersma, T. (2010b). How do migratory species stay healthy over the annual cycle? A conceptual model for immune function and for resistance to disease. *Integr. Comp. Biol.*, **50**, 346–357.

Caro, T. M. (2005). *Antipredator Defences in Birds and Mammals*. Chicago: Chicago University Press.

Cohen, J. B., Karpanty, S. M. and Fraser, J. D. (2010a). Habitat selection and behaviour of Red Knots on the New Jersey Atlantic coast during spring stopover. *Condor*, **112**, 655–662.

Cohen, J. B., Karpanty, S. M., Fraser, J. D. and Truitt, B. R. (2010b). The effect of benthic prey abundance and size on Red Knot (*Calidris canutus*) distribution at an alternative migratory stopover site on the US Atlantic coast. *J. Ornithol.*, **151**, 355–364.

Colwell, M. A. (2010). *Shorebird Ecology, Conservation, and Management*. Berkeley: University of California Press.

Chase, J. M. and Leibold, M. A. (2003). *Ecological Niches. Linking Classical and Contemporary Approaches*. Chicago: University of Chicago Press.

Cresswell, W. (1994). Flocking is an effective anti-predator strategy in Redshanks, *Tringa totanus*. *Anim. Behav.*, **47**, 433–442.

Danchin, É., Giraldeau, L.-A. and Cézilly, F. (ed.) (2008). *Behavioural Ecology*. Oxford: Oxford University Press.

Dekinga, A. and Piersma, T. (1993). Reconstructing diet composition on the basis of faeces in a mollusc-eating wader, the Knot *Calidris canutus*. *Bird Study*, **40**, 144–156.

Dekinga, A., Dietz, M. W., Koolhaas, A. and Piersma, T. (2001). Time course and reversibility of changes in the gizzards of Red Knots alternately eating hard and soft food. *J. Exp. Biol.*, **204**, 2167–2173.

Dietz, M. W., Dekinga, A. Piersma, T. and Verhulst, S. (1999). Estimating organ size in small migrating shorebirds with ultrasonography: an intercalibration exercise. *Physiol. Biochem. Zool.*, **72**, 28–37.

Ens, B. J., Piersma, T. and Drent, R. (1994). The dependence of waders and waterfowl migrating along the East Atlantic Flyway on their coastal food supplies: what is the most profitable research programme? *Ophelia*, Suppl. 6, 127–151.

Figuerola, J. (1999). Effects of salinity on rates of infestation of waterbirds by haematozoa. *Ecography*, **22**, 681–685.

Folmer, E. O., Olff, H. and Piersma, T. (2010). How well do food distributions predict spatial distributions of shorebirds with different degrees of self-organization? *J. Anim. Ecol.*, **79**, 747–756.

Fretwell, S. D. (1972). *Populations in a Seasonal Environment*. Princeton: Princeton University Press.

Geue, D. and Partecke, J. (2008). Reduced parasite infestation in urban European Blackbirds (*Turdus merula*): a factor favoring urbanization? *Can. J. Zool.*, **86**, 1418–1424.

Gill, J. A., Sutherland, W. J. and Norris, K. (2001). Depletion models can predict shorebird distribution at different spatial scales. *Proc. R. Soc. B*, **268**, 369–376.

Goss-Custard, J. D., West, A. D., Yates, M. G. *et al.* (2006). Intake rates and the functional response in shorebirds (Charadriiformes) eating macro-invertebrates. *Biol. Rev.*, **81**, 501–529.

Gutiérrez, J. S., Dietz, M. W., Masero, J. A. *et al.* (2012). Functional ecology of saltglands in shorebirds: flexible responses to variable environmental conditions. *Funct. Ecol.*, **26**, 236–244.

Hall, S. R., Brown, J. H., Cáceres, C. E. *et al.* (2008). Is infectious disease just another type of consumer-resource interaction? In *Reciprocal Interactions between Ecosystems and Disease*, ed. R. S. Ostfeld, F. Keesing and V. T. Eviner, pp. 223–241. Princeton: Princeton University Press.

Houston, A. I. and McNamara, J. M. (1999). *Models of Adaptive Behaviour*. Cambridge: Cambridge University Press.

Hulscher, J. B. (1982). The Oystercatcher *Haematopus ostralegus* as a predator of the bivalve *Macoma balthica* in the Dutch Wadden Sea. *Ardea*, **70**, 89–152.

Karpanty, S. M., Fraser, J. D., Berkson, J. *et al.* (2006). Horseshoe Crab eggs determine Red Knot distribution in Delaware Bay. *J. Wildlife Manage.*, **70**, 1704–1710.

King, J. R. (1974). Seasonal allocation of time and energy resources in birds. In *Avian Energetics*, ed. R. A. Paynter, pp. 4–85. Cambridge, Mass.: Nuttall Onithological Club.

Klaassen, M. (2003). Relationships between migration and breeding strategies in Arctic breeding birds. In *Avian Migration*, ed. P. Berthold, E. Gwinner, and E. Sonnenschein, pp. 237–249. Berlin: Springer-Verlag.

Kraan, C., Piersma, T., Dekinga, A., Koolhaas, A. and van der Meer, J. (2007). Dredging for Edible Cockles (*Cerastoderma edule*) on intertidal flats: short-term consequences of fisher patch-choice decisions for target and non-target benthic fauna. *ICES J. Mar. Sci.*, **64**, 1735–1742.

Kraan, C., van Gils, J. A., Spaans, B. *et al.* (2009). Landscape-scale experiment demonstrates that Wadden Sea intertidal flats are used to capacity by molluscivore migrant shorebirds. *J. Anim. Ecol.*, **78**, 1259–1268.

Kraan, C., van Gils, J. A., Spaans, B., Dekinga, A. and Piersma, T. (2010). Declining refuelling opportunities for Afro-Siberian Red Knots *Calidris canutus canutus* in the western Dutch Wadden Sea. *Ardea*, **98**, 155–160.

Krebs, J. R. and Davies, N. B. (1987). *An Introduction to Behavioural Ecology*. Second edition. Oxford: Blackwell Scientific Publications.

Lank, D. B. and Ydenberg, R. C. (2003). Death and danger at migratory stopovers: problems with "predation risk". *J. Avian Biol.*, **34**, 225–228.

Leyrer, J., Brugge, M., Dekinga, A. *et al.* (2012). Small-scale demographic structure suggests pre-emptive behaviour in a flocking shorebird. *Behav. Ecol.*, in press.

Lima, S. L. and Dill, L. M. (1990). Behavioral decisions made under the risk of predation: a review and prospectus. *Can. J. Zool.*, **68**, 619–640.

Lind, J. and Cresswell, W. (2006). Anti-predation behaviour during bird migration; the benefit of studying multiple behavioural dimensions. *J. Ornithol.*, **147**, 310–316.

Lourenço, P. M., Mandema, F. S., Hooijmeijer, J. C. E. W., Granadeiro, J. P. and Piersma, T. (2010). Site selection and resource depletion in black-tailed godwits *Limosa l. limosa* eating rice during northward migration. *J. Anim. Ecol.*, **79**, 522–528.

MacArthur, R. H. (1972). *Geographical Ecology: Patterns in the Distribution of Species*. Princeton: Princeton University Press.

McGowan, A., Cresswell, W. and Ruxton, G. D. (2002). The effects of daily weather variation on foraging and responsiveness to disturbance in overwintering Red Knot *Calidris canutus*. *Ardea*, **90**, 229–237.

Mendes, L., Piersma, T. Lecoq, M., Spaans, B. and Ricklefs, R. E. (2005). Disease-limited distributions? Contrasts in the prevalence of avian malaria in shorebird species using marine and freshwater habitats. *Oikos*, **109**, 396–404.

Myers, J.P. (1986). Sex and gluttony in Delaware Bay. *Nat. Hist.*, **95**, 68–77.

Orwell, G. (1945). *Animal Farm, a Fairy Story*. London: Secker and Warburg.

Petit, M., Vézina, F. and Piersma, T. (2010). Ambient temperature does not affect fuelling rate in absence of digestive constraints in long-distance migrant shorebird fuelling up in captivity. *J. Comp. Physiol. B*, **180**, 847–856.

Piersma, T. (1997). Do global patterns of habitat use and migration strategies co-evolve with relative investments in immunocompetence due to spatial variation in parasite pressure? *Oikos*, **80**, 623–631.

Piersma, T. (2003). 'Coastal' versus 'inland' shorebird species: interlinked fundamental dichotomies between their life- and demographic histories? *Wader Study Group Bull.*, **100**, 5–9.

Piersma, T. (2007). Using the power of comparison to explain habitat use and migration strategies of shorebirds worldwide. *J. Ornithol.*, **148** (Suppl. 1), S45–S59.

Piersma, T. and van Gils, J.A. (2011). *The Flexible Phenotype: A Body-centred Integration of Ecology, Physiology, and Behaviour*. Oxford: Oxford University Press.

Piersma, T., Drent, R. and Wiersma, P. (1991). Temperate versus tropical wintering in the world's northernmost breeder, the Knot: metabolic scope and resource levels restrict subspecific options. *Acta XX Congr. Int. Ornithol. (Christchurch)*, **II**, 761–772.

Piersma, T., Hoekstra, R., Dekinga, A. *et al.* (1993). Scale and intensity of intertidal habitat use by Knots *Calidris canutus* in the western Wadden Sea in relation to food, friends and foes. *Neth. J. Sea Res.*, **31**, 331–357.

Piersma, T., Verkuil, Y. and Tulp, I. (1994). Resources for long-distance migration of Knots *Calidris canutus islandica* and *C. c. canutus*: how broad is the temporal

exploitation window of benthic prey in the western and eastern Wadden Sea? *Oikos*, **71**, 393–407.

Piersma, T., van Gils, J., de Goeij, P. and van der Meer, J. (1995). Holling's functional response model as a tool to link the food-finding mechanism of a probing shorebird with its spatial distribution. *J. Anim. Ecol.*, **64**, 493–504.

Piersma, T., van Aelst, R., Kurk, K., Berkhoudt, H. and Maas, L.R.M. (1998). A new pressure sensory mechanism for prey detection in birds: the use of principles of seabed dynamics? *Proc. R. Soc. B*, **265**, 1377–1383.

Piersma, T., Koolhaas, A., Dekinga, A. *et al.* (2001). Long-term indirect effects of mechanical cockle-dredging on intertidal bivalve stocks in the Wadden Sea. *J. Appl. Ecol.*, **38**, 976–990.

Piersma, T., Dekinga, A., van Gils, J.A., Achterkamp, B. and Visser, G.H. (2003). Cost-benefit analysis of mollusc-eating in a shorebird. I. Foraging and processing costs estimated by the doubly labelled water method. *J. Exp. Biol.*, **206**, 3361–3368.

Piersma, T., Rogers, D.I., González, P.M. *et al.* (2005). Fuel storage rates in red knots worldwide: facing the severest ecological constraint in tropical intertidal conditions? In *Birds of Two Worlds: The Ecology and Evolution of Migratory Birds*, ed. R. Greenberg and P.P. Marra, pp. 262–274. Baltimore: Johns Hopkins University Press.

Quaintenne, G., van Gils, J.A., Bocher, P., Dekinga, A. and Piersma, T. (2010). Diet selection in a molluscivore shorebird across Western Europe: does it show short- or long-term intake rate-maximization? *J. Anim. Ecol.*, **79**, 53–62.

Quaintenne, G., van Gils, J.A., Bocher, P., Dekinga, A. and Piersma, T. (2011). Scaling up ideals to freedom: are densities of Red Knots across Western Europe consistent with IFD? *Proc. R. Soc. B*, **278**, 2728–2736.

Råberg, L., Graham, A.L. and Read, A.F. (2009). Decomposing health: Tolerance and resistance to parasites in animals. *Phil. Trans. R. Soc. B*, **265**, 1637–1641.

Recher, H. F. (1966). Some aspects of the ecology of migrant shorebirds. *Ecology*, **47**, 393–407.

Ridley, M. (1994). *The Red Queen: Sex and the Evolution of Human Nature*. London: Penguin Books.

Rogers, D. I., Battley, P. F., Piersma, T., van Gils, J. A. and Rogers, K. G. (2006). High-tide habitat choice: insights from modelling roost selection by shorebirds around a tropical bay. *Anim. Behav.*, **72**, 563–575.

Rogers, D. I., Yang, Y.-H., Hassell, C. J. *et al.* (2010). Red Knots (*Calidris canutus piersmai* and *C. c. rogersi*) depend on a small threatened staging area in Bohai Bay, China. *Emu*, **110**, 307–315.

Schmidt-Nielsen, K. (1984). *Scaling: Why is Animal Size so Important?* Cambridge: Cambridge University Press.

Schoener, T. W. (1989). The ecological niche. In *Ecological Concepts: The Contribution of Ecology to an Understanding of the Natural World*, ed. J. M. Cherrett, pp. 79–113. Oxford: Blackwell Scientific Publications.

Schuster, C. N. J., Barlow, R. B. and Brockman, H. J. (2003). *The American Horseshoe Crab*. Cambridge, MA: Harvard University Press.

Sitters, H. P., Gonzalez, P. M., Piersma, T., Baker, A. J. and Price, D. J. (2001). Day and night feeding habitat of Red Knots in Patagonia: profitability versus safety? *J. Field Ornithol.*, **72**, 86–95.

Speakman, J. R. and Król, E. (2010). Maximal heat dissipation capacity and hyperthermia risk: neglected key factors in the ecology of endotherms. *J. Anim. Ecol.*, **79**, 726–746.

Starck, J. M., Dietz, M. W. and Piersma, T. (2001). The assessment of body composition and other parameters by ultrasound scanning. In *Body Composition Analysis of Animals. A Handbook of Non-destructive Methods*, ed. J. R. Speakman, pp. 188–210. Cambridge: Cambridge University Press.

Stephens, D. W. and Krebs, J. R. (1986). *Foraging Theory*. Princeton: Princeton University Press.

Sutherland, W. J. (1996). *From Individual Behaviour to Population Ecology*. Oxford: Oxford University Press.

Temple, S. A. (2004). Individuals, populations, and communities: the ecology of birds. In *Handbook of Bird Biology* (2nd edition, Cornell Laboratory of Ornithology), pp. 1–135. Princeton, NJ: Princeton University Press.

Tieleman, B. I., Williams, J. B. and Buschur, M. E. (2002). Physiological adjustments to arid and mesic environments in larks (Alaudidae). *Physiol. Biochem. Zool.*, **75**, 305–313.

Tieleman, B. I., Williams, J. B. and Bloomer, P. (2003a). Adaptation of metabolism and evaporative water loss along an aridity gradient. *Proc. R. Soc. B*, **270**, 207–214.

Tieleman, B. I., Williams, J. B., Buschur, M. E. and Brown, C. R. (2003b). Phenotypic variation of larks along an aridity gradient: are desert birds more flexible? *Ecology*, **84**, 1800–1815.

Tieleman, B. I., Williams, J. B., Ricklefs, R. E. and Klasing, K. C. (2005). Constitutive innate immunity is a component of the pace-of-life syndrome in tropical birds. *Proc. R. Soc. B*, **272**, 1715–1720.

Tinbergen, J. M. (1981). Foraging decisions in Starlings (*Sturnus vulgaris* L.). *Ardea*, **69**, 1–67.

Vahl, W. K., van der Meer, J., Weissing, F. J., van Dullemen D. and Piersma, T. (2005). The mechanisms of interference competition: two experiments on foraging waders. *Behav. Ecol.*, **16**, 845–855.

Vahl, W. K., van der Meer, J., Meijer, K., Piersma, T. and Weissing, F. J. (2007). Interference competition, the spatial distribution of food and free-living foragers. *Anim. Behav.*, **74**, 1493–1503.

van de Kam, J., Ens, B. J., Piersma, T. and Zwarts, L. (2004). *Shorebirds. An Illustrated Behavioural Ecology*. Utrecht: KNNV Publishers.

van den Hout, P. J., Spaans, B. and Piersma, T. (2008). Differential mortality of wintering shorebirds on the Banc d'Arguin, Mauritania, due to predation by large falcons. *Ibis*, **150** (Suppl. 1), 219–230.

van den Hout, P. J., van Gils, J. A., Lok, T. *et al.* (submitted – contact Theunis Piersma for details). Habitat selection mediated by individual variation in foraging and competitive skills: a study on food-safety trade-off in a shorebird.

van Gils, J. A., Battley, P. F., Piersma, T. and Drent, R. (2005c). Reinterpretation of gizzard sizes of Red Knots world-wide emphasises overriding importance of prey quality at migratory stopover sites. *Proc. R. Soc. B*, **272**, 2609–2618.

van Gils, J. A., de Rooij, S. R., van Belle, J. *et al.* (2005a). Digestive bottleneck affects foraging decisions in Red Knots *Calidris canutus*. I. Prey choice. *J. Anim. Ecol.*, **74**, 105–19.

van Gils, J. A., Dekinga, A., Spaans, B., Vahl, W. K. and Piersma, T. (2005b). Digestive bottleneck affects foraging decisions in Red Knots (*Calidris canutus*). II. Patch choice and length of working day. *J. Anim. Ecol.*, **74**, 120–130.

van Gils, J. A., Dekinga, A., van den Hout, P. J., Spaans, B. and Piersma, T. (2007). Digestive organ size and behavior of Red Knots (*Calidris canutus*) indicate the quality of their benthic food stocks. *Isr. J. Ecol. Evol.*, **53**, 329–46.

van Gils, J. A., Edelaar, P., Escudero, G. and Piersma, T. (2004). Carrying capacity models should not use fixed prey density thresholds: a plea for using more tools of behavioural ecology. *Oikos*, **104**, 197–204.

van Gils, J. A. and Piersma T. (1999). Day- and nighttime movements of radiomarked knots, *Calidris canutus*, staging in the western Wadden Sea in July-August 1995. *Wader Study Group Bull.*, **89**, 36–44.

van Gils, J. A. and Piersma T. (2004). Digestively constrained predators evade the cost of interference competition. *J. Anim. Ecol.*, **73**, 386–398.

van Gils, J. A., Piersma, T., Dekinga, A. and Battley, P. F. (2006a). Modelling phenotypic flexibility: an optimality analysis of gizzard size in Red Knots (*Calidris canutus*). *Ardea*, **94**, 409–420.

van Gils, J. A., Piersma, T., Dekinga, A. and Dietz, M. W. (2003a). Cost-benefit analysis of mollusc-eating in a shorebird. II. Optimizing gizzard size in the face of seasonal demands. *J. Exp. Biol.*, **206**, 3369–3380.

van Gils, J. A., Piersma, T., Dekinga, A. and Spaans, B. (2000). Distributional ecology of individually radio-marked knots *Calidris canutus* in the western Dutch Wadden Sea in August-October 1999. *Limosa*, **73**, 29–34.

van Gils, J. A., Piersma, T., Dekinga, A., Spaans, B. and Kraan, C. (2006c). Shellfish-dredging pushes a flexible avian top predator out of a protected marine ecosystem. *PLoS Biol.*, **4**, 2399–2404.

van Gils, J. A., Schenk, I. W., Bos, O. and Piersma, T. (2003b). Incompletely informed shorebirds that face a digestive bottleneck maximize net energy gain when exploiting patches. *Am. Nat.*, **161**, 777–793.

van Gils, J. A., Spaans, B., Dekinga, A. and Piersma, T. (2006b). Foraging in a tidally structured environment by Red Knots (*Calidris canutus*): ideal, but not free. *Ecology*, **87**, 1189–1202.

Verboven, N. and Piersma, T. (1995). Is the evaporative water loss of Knot *Calidris canutus* higher in tropical than in temperate climates? *Ibis*, **137**, 308–316.

Wiersma, P. and Piersma, T. (1994). Effects of microhabitat, flocking, climate and migratory goal on energy expenditure in the annual cycle of Red Knots. *Condor*, **96**, 257–279.

Williams, J. B. and Tieleman, B. I. (2001). Physiological ecology and behavior of desert birds. *Curr. Ornithol.*, **16**, 299–353.

Yang, H.-Y., Chen, B., Barter, M. *et al.* (2011). Impacts of tidal land claims in Bohai Bay, China: ongoing losses of critical Yellow Sea waterbird wintering and staging sites. *Bird Conserv. Int.*, **21**, 241–259. doi:10.1017/S0959270911000086

Zwarts, L. (1974). *Vogels van het brakke getijdegebied, ecologische onderzoekingen op de Ventjagersplaten*. Amsterdam: Bondsuitgeverij van de jeugdbonden voor natuurstudie.

Zwarts, L. and Blomert, A.-M. (1992). Why Knot *Calidris canutus* take medium-sized *Macoma balthica* when six prey species are available. *Mar. Ecol. Prog. Ser.*, **83**, 113–128.

Zwarts, L., Blomert, A.-M. and Hupkes, R. (1990a). Increase of feeding time in waders preparing their spring migration from the Banc d'Arguin, Mauritania. *Ardea*, **78**, 237–256.

Zwarts, L., Blomert, A.-M. and Wanink, J.H. (1992). Annual and seasonal variation in the food supply harvestable by Knot *Calidris canutus* staging in the Wadden Sea in late summer. *Mar. Ecol. Prog. Ser.*, **83**, 129–139.

Zwarts, L., Ens, B.J., Kersten, M. and Piersma, T. (1990b). Moult, mass and flight range of waders ready to take off for long-distance migrations. *Ardea*, **78**, 339–364.

Zwarts, L. and Wanink, J.H. (1984). How Oystercatchers and Curlews successively deplete clams. In *Coastal Waders and Wildfowl in Winter*, ed. P.R. Evans, J.D. Goss-Custard and W.G. Hale, pp. 69–83. Cambridge: Cambridge University Press.

CHAPTER SIXTEEN

Understanding individual life-histories and habitat choices: implications for explaining population patterns and processes

BEAT NAEF-DAENZER

Swiss Ornithological Institute

Prologue

The restoration of grey wolves *Canis lupus* to the Yellowstone ecosystem is one of the largest and best-monitored experiments addressing links between individual habitat use and processes at the population level. After some 70 wolf-free years, 31 wolves were released in 1995–1996, so that Yellowstone again hosts all native large carnivores. Although large efforts to predict the ecological effects of wolves had been made on the basis of extant evidence, models and expert knowledge (Mack and Singer, 1992; Boyce, 1993; Cook, 1993) no one expected that these few individuals would change so much of the ecosystem. After only a decade the re-introduction has given rise to manifold ecological changes. Many of these are related to individual behaviour of the new predator or individual responses of potential prey. Proximate impacts, such as predation on elk *Cervus elaphus*, the main prey, were as predicted (Boyce, 1993; Smith *et al.*, 2003). It was a surprise, however, that the re-introduction of a top predator would so quickly influence Yellowstone's vegetation. The presence of wolves had profound effects on the trophic web, operating remarkably fast and reaching down to primary production. Interestingly, these effects were mainly related to behavioural processes (such as habitat use and spatial distributions) rather than to demographic processes (for example, population sizes and survival rates) due to predation. How did these relatively few wolf individuals cause so many changes at various levels of the ecosystem? Primarily, as an anti-predator response, elk altered their habitat selection and use of resources. Simultaneous GPS tracking of wolves and elk revealed that the elk responded to the presence of wolves at a distance of up to 1 km. They moved into wooded areas, avoiding the open grassland (Creel *et al.*, 2005). The vegetation responded quickly to the resulting relief from browsing, and various plant species re-colonised areas from which they were absent for decades, for example willows *Salix* spp. and aspen *Populus* spp. (Ripple *et al.*, 2001; Ripple and Beschta, 2006; Beyer *et al.*, 2007).

The strikingly rapid changes in the Yellowstone system suggest a cascade of behavioural responses extending over many trophic levels. While the predator impact on demographic parameters was small, the presence of wolves strongly affected the spatial distribution and habitat use of the elk. The altered habitat use (not the altered abundance) of ungulates will probably continue to influence the diversity and a new succession of the vegetation, and affect nutrient flows and cycles in the soil–vegetation system (Ripple *et al.*, 2001). Many species will probably benefit from these wolf-mediated vegetation changes, including beavers *Castor canadensis*, birds and invertebrates. Various scavengers have adjusted their range use and behaviour to the altered availability and patterns of resources provided by elk carcasses (ravens *Corvus corax*, magpies *Pica pica*, golden eagles *Aquila chrysaetos*, bald eagles *Heliaeetus leucocephalus*, bears *Ursus arctos*; Stahler *et al.*, 2002; Wilmers *et al.*, 2003). In contrast to the small effect on elk population dynamics, wolves have markedly affected the population sizes and key demographic parameters of some other species. They rapidly reduced the population of coyotes *Canis latrans* to about half of the pre-wolf period (wolves kill coyotes at the prey; Crabtree and Sheldon, 1999). As coyotes are the main predator of pronghorn *Antilocapra americana*, pronghorn fawn survival improved, and pronghorn reproductive success appears positively correlated with the re-introduction of the wolf (Smith *et al.*, 2003).

Why insight into individual life-histories is a basis for understanding populations

This chapter discusses links between individual decisions involving habitat use, life-history traits and patterns and processes at the population level. Several textbooks and book chapters have addressed these issues (e.g. Sutherland, 1996; Begon *et al.*, 2006). The wolf example renews old wisdom that the life-histories and habitat use of individuals ultimately determine much of the dynamics and spatial dimensions of populations. Clearly, understanding the interaction of individuals with their environment is essential for understanding the mechanisms that shape populations in space and size (e.g. MacArthur, 1964). Yet, the subject remains complicated and confusing. One simple reason is that biological systems *are* complicated and intriguing because they are highly plastic and, in the long term, unpredictable. Here, I address some sources of this plasticity and approaches to analysing the interface between individual life-histories and population ecology. I emphasise that a general way to resolve persisting problems is through studying individuals: their needs for growth, maintenance and reproduction are all related to the habitat, and their fates essentially determine where a species persists on a long-term basis. Individual decisions and plasticity of responses to the environment, determine population parameters such as survival, reproductive rates and spatial dynamics. Thus, while *patterns* of populations (and multispecies systems) can be described and analysed without looking at individual behaviour, the *explanations* for the function of higher-level systems depend on understanding how individuals perform under varying ecological conditions. The approach to both *patterns* and *explanations* is also affected by methodological paradigms. A central issue is that knowing how the 'average' individual interacts with its 'average' habitat is insufficient for understanding what happens to populations. Within a population, individual behavioural ecology, and thus demographic parameters, can vary substantially (for example, reproductive sources and sinks). Consequently, studying this variation, specifically the ecological mechanisms operating at population limits, is a challenge for explaining population processes.

The individual scale: strategy, plasticity and personality

Even the simplest organisms, and all birds, interact permanently with their habitat, and are able to respond to changes in their environment. The basic rules directing the selection and use of habitat differ amongst species, and within species amongst life-history stages. However, interaction with the habitat is not restricted to mere response to influence from outside. As organisms also act autonomously, the variation amongst individuals in response to the same environment is large. Possibly, this plasticity is the only universal principle throughout biological systems. Obviously, it is of paramount importance in the life-history of any individual (Box 16.1).

The plasticity and autonomy in all biological systems causes a fundamental difficulty to researchers because it is somehow in contradiction with the general approach to scientific investigation. Under a general mechanistic approach it is assumed that natural phenomena are caused by universal laws that apply to all subjects identically, that is, at least to all individuals of a species. However, the mechanistic view that one cause (or constellation of multiple causes) will invariably have the same effect is challenged in biological systems. The interesting point is often that animals do *not* follow universal rules. They respond in various ways. Accordingly, different individual patterns or processes can result from similar causes. With respect to habitat use, individuals often choose among apparently equivalent solutions to a specific task (e.g. foraging) without a measurable external cause. A golden eagle can search for prey in the same area with an unchanged distribution of resources by using sit-and-wait tactics on a big boulder, by soaring close to the ground or by circling at high altitude. Moreover, the bird may change between a time-minimising and an energy-maximising strategy of foraging.

The perpetual cycle of ecological variation and evolutionary adaptation creates, but also limits, individual plasticity. The underlying mechanisms

Box 16.1 Behavioural flexibility and habitat use

The white stork *Ciconia ciconia* is able to live in very different habitats. Its highly flexible behavioural 'toolbox' allows exploitation of very different resources, types of prey and spatial patterns. During its annual life cycle it lives and survives in such contrasting habitats as wetlands and agricultural land in central and northeastern Europe, and in the arid regions of northwestern Africa. There is virtually no overlap in food resources between such contrasting habitats, and the differences in resource availability and distribution likely require profound changes in the behavioural strategies of the individual. Via differential survival and reproduction these fundamental characteristics at the individual level determine where and how well populations persist. Thus, knowledge of the plasticity of individual habitat selection and use is one key to understanding patterns and processes at the population level.

(Photos: A. Labhardt (left), W. Wisniewski (right))

are difficult to understand with a strong focus on short-term individual strategies. The reason is that ecological and evolutionary feedback mechanisms (e.g. selection) operate via demographic probabilities such as differential survival, immigration/emigration or reproductive performance. In this context quantifying plasticity is a crucial issue. The evolutionary approach considers between-individual variation in a trait as one of the pre-conditions of selection (together with heritability and differential survival or reproduction). Here, variation is the very focus of the research. This contrasts with the approach to behavioural strategies as a set of strict rules that determine the behaviour in specific life-history functions. Here, individual variation is often considered the confounding noise concealing the rules.

However, individual variation is an essential part of the system, not noise. In recent years it has become increasingly addressed by behavioural ecologists. The 'discovery' of *personality* stirred new interest in what makes individuals differ. This brought substantial advances in understanding the evolutionary forces that shape life-history traits. In behavioural ecology the term *strategy* is used to describe a set of rules determining how animals respond to specific environmental conditions to fulfil specific life-history functions. Behavioural strategies characterise species-specific behaviour, but personality can be considered as a set of traits that determine how the individual deviates from the strategy. Pioneer studies on great tits *Parus major* showed that personalities differ in how individuals respond to the same environmental stimulus (review and further references in Dingemanse and Réalc, 2005). These deviations from a general strategy are consistent for an individual's lifetime, are heritable and concern important life-history functions, such as risk-taking (van Oers *et al.*, 2004) and exploration of new habitat features (Verbeek *et al.*, 1994; Drent *et al.*, 2003). The fitness relevance of personality is via differential survival in relation to a variety of interactions with the environment (Perdeck *et al.*, 2000; Dingemanse *et al.*, 2003). For example, parental personality is a determinant of the post-fledging range use of great tit families. 'Bold' parents, i.e. those that are 'bold' in exploring an unknown standard laboratory environment, tend to guide their chicks further from the nest site, thereby potentially accessing new resources (Van Overveld *et al.*, 2011). It is likely that moving families will improve chances to find rich food resources. As the post-fledging period coincides with a strong decline in food availability (Naef-Daenzer *et al.*, 2001), the individual trees that still host many invertebrates ('feeding hotspots') are sparsely scattered over the forest. Thus, 'bold explorers' may have a considerable advantage in terms of winter survival and recruitment. On the other hand, families of prudent parents may take advantages from detailed knowledge of local conditions, better exploitation of available resources and less risk of moving through inhospitable habitat. Recent field studies suggest that heterogeneous environmental conditions result in considerable selection on personality traits. However, its direction may vary in relation to resource availability (competition), age, sex or reproductive stages (for details see Dingemanse and Réale, 2005).

The population scale: the search for broad pattern and process

A different approach to looking at populations is from a global perspective. At this scale, consistent patterns in biomes are evident and these large-scale systems are related to global conditions, especially climate and the related biogeographical zones. Climate is a set of extremely powerful fundamental environmental conditions; it determines much of the distribution, phenology and long-term trends in populations (e.g. Bolger *et al.*, 2005; Martin, 2001, 2007). Recent climate trends demonstrate that these forces can alter habitats surprisingly quickly. Huntley *et al.* (2007) give examples of how continent-wide spatial patterns in potential species distributions can be modelled using a small set of climate factors, with complete exclusion of the individual level. These models, based on general 'envelope' factors representing a set of correlated environmental variables, allow projections into the future, at least at a scale of a decade or two. Other long-term studies, (e.g. Maggini *et al.*, 2011) confirm that some range shifts are occurring, broadly as predicted by Huntley *et al.* (2007). At this general level, models ignore the mechanisms behind the changing patterns, for example whether they result from movement of individuals or from spatial differentials in reproductive rates or other demographic variables. Since early in the history of biological sciences, two major mechanisms, habitat selection and segregation, have been postulated in the interpretation of large-scale distribution patterns (Darwin, 1859; MacArthur *et al.*, 1966; MacArthur, 1968; Cody, 1985). Both imply, but do not specify, behavioural processes. The general approach reveals broad patterns and processes, however it fails to discover the core explanatory mechanisms of ecosystem structure and functionality. This is a serious drawback. Knowing the causal webs that link (changing) climate, (changing) environments and (changing) bird populations is indispensable for developing effective conservation policies.

Finding an ideal combination of scales

The complexity of scales at which within- and between-population processes operate has long been recognised as a crucial issue in ecology (e.g. Begon *et al.*, 2006). It is intriguing because ecological relationships and the rules driving them appear to differ amongst scales. Again, the apparent problem might originate from different approaches to biological systems. Finding and analysing patterns and processes, and investigating their causal mechanisms represent different steps in ecological research. For example, populations clearly 'respond' to long-term climatic trends. The effects of the climatic forcing on local habitat conditions and the ecology of species may vary amongst areas (Saether *et al.*, 2003; Both *et al.*, 2004; Chapter 17), and the effect size may vary amongst populations (Visser *et al.*, 2002; Martin, 2007). Obviously, however, individuals cannot respond directly to global climate factors such as the North-Atlantic Oscillation (Hurrell, 1995). The *pattern* of climate response is described using correlations which suggest but do not prove causal relationships. In contrast, investigating the *cause* of climate response requires following the entire cascade of interactions down to the level of the individual. In the case of how birds respond to climate change, this cascade may include the North-Atlantic Oscillation, local climate, local phenology of habitat, timing of breeding, clutch size and number of chicks fledged. The two levels of investigation do not necessarily follow in a fixed order. For the great tit, vast observational and experimental evidence on the ecological determinants of breeding performance has been collected since the

1950s, long before global climate changes were recognised. Today, this knowledge is an invaluable source for explaining the complex cascade from global climate patterns down to the performance of individuals and to key parameters of population dynamics (Naef-Daenzer *et al.*, 2012).

Morrison and Hall (2002) provided a standard terminology that helps to disentangle the various scales at which species–environment interactions can be considered. They emphasise that 'habitat' is a concept rather than a real environment (see also Chapter 1). The concept serves as an umbrella under which relationships between the individual and its environment operate. What is considered 'the habitat' of one species consists in reality of populations of other species that may, for example, represent food, predators or more distant parts of the trophic web. Such trophic chains or webs are powerful determinants of population processes because satisfying daily energy requirements is the basis for maintenance, survival and reproduction. Thus, the availability of energy and particular resources exert strong impacts at different levels of a system. Analyses of population trends in relation to habitat quality, or analyses of differential survival in relation to food availability address the same trophic web at different levels of generalisation. At all levels, a difficulty in understanding population implications of individual habitat selection lies in the many variables involved, and in their interactions. This results in an enormous range of variation in any system under consideration.

Hutchinson (1953) defined the ecological niche as an n-dimensional space in which the n dimensions correspond to the (relevant) environmental variables determining the probability for a species to persist. Unfortunately, this statistical point of view is not that close to reality. Many of these n dimensions represent other species in the ecosystem for which a different, m-dimensional, niche may be defined. Some of the variables may be the same while many may differ. Moreover, individuals of any of these populations can trade a deficit in one of these dimensions against a benefit from another. Even with the assistance of unlimited computation power, it is difficult for the human brain to understand multi-dimensional relationships between multi-dimensional ecological spaces. Techniques that reduce this complexity to the most important determinants, are invaluable aids in disentangling the crucial causal chains at the interface between individual habitat interaction and population processes (see below).

The starting point: understanding individual life-histories and habitat choices

Birth, growth, maintenance, reproduction, dispersal and death are all individual events and processes. All are related to the environment. The early concepts of habitat use considered the habitat as a clearly defined and static pattern of resources (often one single resource), and the focus was on how one (the 'average') individual makes its decision on using the resource. The quantitative investigation of animal habitat use, particularly foraging, began in the mid 1960s with some seminal empirical studies (e.g. Emlen, 1966; MacArthur and Pianka, 1966), followed by an increasing field of theoretical modelling (e.g. Schoener, 1971; Charnov, 1976).

As an example, Fig. 16.1 illustrates the rise of the 'optimal foraging' discipline since 1950. The optimal foraging approach has proved very successful for analysing individual strategies and defining habitat requirements at a local scale (see Schoener (1971) for a review of early theory). Optimal foraging theory and empirical studies have introduced a most valuable framework for rigorous tests of particular functions of habitat use and behaviour. Studies of optimal foraging have flourished over the past four decades (Perry and Pianka, 1997). Theory and empirical research primarily focused on general foraging modes and specific foraging strategies, for example maximising energy intake versus minimising foraging time (Schoener, 1971), optimal patch use (the marginal value model; Charnov, 1976), or optimal moving modes (e.g. central-place foraging, sit-and-wait; Horn *et al.*, 1978). The frequency of 'optimal foraging' articles increased in parallel with the general interest in 'resource use' (Fig. 16.1). Optimal foraging theory and empirical research were deliberately restricted to the specific task of collecting energy from the environment, and to its short-term optimisation. Typical 'one individual–one resource' problems were a good starting point, but researchers soon realised that,

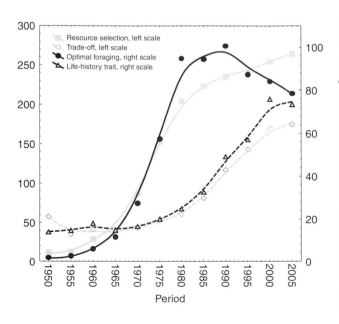

Figure 16.1 The frequency of selected key words in articles referring to 'habitat use' in the JSTOR database (biological sciences). Black dots and black solid line: frequency of papers with the keyword 'optimal foraging'. Grey squares and grey solid line: keyword 'resource selection'. Black triangles and black broken line: keyword 'life-history trait'. Grey diamonds and grey broken line: keyword 'trade-off'. Frequencies are given per 1000 articles on the basis of all papers referring to 'habitat use' or 'habitat selection' per five-year period. Curves give least-squares fits.

even in the short term, an individual has to solve more than one optimisation problem simultaneously. Since about 1985, theory and empirical research have increasingly considered the costs and benefits of foraging within a life-history context and aimed at understanding the ultimate consequences of optimisation processes in the currency of fitness. Analysis of keyword frequencies illustrates this evolution of perspective with the decline of 'optimal foraging' papers and the increasing frequencies of papers relating to 'life-history traits' or 'trade-offs' (Fig. 16.1). Hence, despite some change in the point of view, the optimisation aspect still is of central interest in ecological research.

Optimal foraging theory has faced stiff opposition, mainly because it rapidly emerged that there could be no generalised universal theory. Even in relatively simple systems there are too many foraging 'problems' and too many solutions to each of them. Stephens and Krebs (1986) advocate the explanatory power of models, listing numerous conclusive tests, while others argued against (e.g. Pierce and Ollasen, 1987), pointing out that models were unrealistic due to over-simplification. Somehow both parties were right. The models do provide *explanations* for observed foraging strategies, and may quantify how efficiently a particular foraging task is fulfilled. However, optimal foraging theory fails to *predict* how a particular pattern of resources will be exploited. A rarely addressed limitation is that animals seldom know the value of all resources (patches) within their home ranges (mainly because these are also populations of 'food' with their own dynamics) and hence the individual is necessarily operating away from the theoretical optimum. Optimal foraging theory helps to understand how far from the optimum the observed behaviour is and what the costs for probing resources are (e.g. Naef-Daenzer, 2000). Optimal foraging studies have proliferated mainly because the interesting point is often the strategy of individual–habitat interactions rather than a test of whether a theoretical optimum is met in reality.

The expectation that optimal foraging models should allow predictions for what individuals of a species will do in different habitats with different patterns and availability of resources may be unrealistic. Models primarily aim at explaining one particular strategy rather than the entire behavioural 'toolbox' of a species. Thus, they are focused on particular, well-defined 'tools' within the options available. Furthermore, the strategies observed in reality are frequently combinations of various elements that traditional optimal foraging theory addresses separately. For example, the search flights of the eagle may perfectly match with a 'random walk' strategy, but at a larger spatial scale it emerges that these random walks are oriented to patches with high prey density, while the bird flies straight from one patch to the next; and suddenly, the eagle may switch to its sit-and-wait strategy, spending hours motionless on a cliff.

Axes of increasing complexity

On the way from understanding individuals towards understanding populations, things become increasingly complicated along the four axes (or scales) discussed below. The aim is to evaluate some sources of complexity in habitat–population relationships, and to discuss how we may use current methodology and techniques to at least partially resolve the persistent problems.

Axis 1: Increasing the number of individuals and populations

Although individuals are the unit of population processes, populations and their spatial dynamics are not simply 'the sum' of all individual fates. One difficulty with relating the individual level to population processes is that many components of individual life-histories have a different significance at the two scales and are measured in different units. At the level of the individual, birth and death are dichotomous and occur only once in an individual's lifetime; these singular events do not explain anything at the level of a population. However, the multitude of individual fates matters very much at the level of the population. Birth and mortality rates, age distributions, sex ratios or dispersal frequencies can only be assessed on the basis of large samples. Conversely, the average life expectancy at age x has no relevance for a particular individual's life-history. Birth and death of individuals are the units of birth and death *rates* at the population level and the statistical distribution of births and deaths lead to estimates of age structure and life expectancies.

Since all individuals live for limited time in limited space, they typically face a more or less stable habitat. Thus, modelling how individuals use their habitat here and now is most valuable for fundamental research and conservation. All studies of individual–habitat relationships, however, are limited to restricted areas. A problem arising from this limitation is that only a part of the habitat and a very small proportion of the population can be sampled. Results obtained in one research area do not necessarily apply to other parts of the population (see Chapter 3). For example various parts of a population may differ in life-history decisions such as the start of breeding, clutch size, number of annual broods or habitat choice. Investigations can explain, but hardly predict, this variation amongst subpopulations (Saether *et al.*, 2003; Both *et al.*, 2004).

From the behavioural viewpoint it is intriguing how many individual ways of life exist – no two life-histories are identical. The closer one looks at individual histories, the more one may be confused about potential generalised conclusions for populations. However, from the statistical point of view, a large sample of individual fates sheds light on fascinating patterns and processes that cannot otherwise be detected or understood. On the condition that sufficiently large samples are collected, the intriguing variability of individual life-histories becomes tangible and measurable. The large sample informs us about probabilities of life-history events and the limits of variation. Like other variables of individual behaviour, there are reaction norms of habitat selection within which all individuals of a species will lie. This is very similar to Hutchinson's (1953) definition of the n-dimensional ecological niche. However, frequency distributions rather than sharp limits characterise the requirements of a species for each of the n dimensions. The uncomfortable consequence is that the 'niche' has diffuse borders, and limits in any of the dimensions are hard to define. Within the niche, there will be populations that experience suboptimal conditions, i.e. they are located somewhere in the vague periphery of the niche. For the individuals living at such places, the general assumption of optimally adapted behaviour and performance is likely to be untrue (Box 16.2). Unfortunately there is very scant evidence for how this affects habitat selection, species distributions and long-term persistence. In reality, many of these peripheral populations may be sinks that depend on immigration from outside.

Axis 2: Increasing the complexity of the habitat

The habitat of a bird is complex and consists of diverse resources and constraints on its use. Individuals have to trade costs and benefits of using these resources in relation to various life-history functions. The flow of energy through systems is one of the major issues. Food resources and their spatial distribution determine how energy is acquired and whether the requirements are fulfilled. Predators represent a cost in terms of survival prospects. These habitat components are interdependent and build complex trophic webs (Polis et al., 2004). Whilst it is relatively easy to quantify the flow of matter or energy through such systems, it is very difficult to establish quantitative models for the optimal performance of individuals in complex environments. Optimality models often preclude the use of multiple resources and thus are excellent to study specific aspects rather than the complex reality. With respect to understanding animal populations it is particularly important to assess the limiting factors. How much of which resource must be available to allow the start of reproduction in spring? What is the role of transient extremes in conditions for reproductive success (Coulson et al., 2001; Bolger et al., 2005)? Studying individuals under varying conditions gives insights as to where in Hutchinson's n-dimensional virtual 'niche' these limits lie. A drawback for understanding populations is that scant evidence is available on individual-habitat relationships close to the limits of the niche (Peréz-Tris et al., 2000; Carbonell et al., 2003; Box 16.2). Ecological boundaries can be viewed as large 'natural experiments' with large variations in crucial habitat factors that directly affect range use, density, survival or reproductive performance (Cadenasso et al., 2003).

Box 16.2 Life at the limits of the niche

An unpublished (and unpublishable) experience of trophic limitations at population borders. The great tit *Parus major* is one of the best-investigated organisms in general. Nevertheless, the factors limiting great tit populations in space are poorly understood. At low altitudes, the reproductive perform-ance depends much on the structure of the habitat in deciduous and mixed forests. The nestling food consists mainly of insect larvae that are collected from the leaves. The tits' timing of breeding is strongly determined by two trophic interactions: first, a strong seasonal peak in nestling food (the cater-pillar peak, Perrins, 1991) and second, another peak in predation rates on fledglings (Naef-Daenzer *et al.*, 2001). The two seasonal processes focus the tits' timing of breeding into a very narrow time window.

A subalpine coniferous forest, shown here, is an atypical habitat for great tits, but there exist small populations in this vegetation type. Here, the caterpillar peak is lacking and great tits breed less synchronously. The intri-guing point, however, is that resources for nestling food differ greatly from deciduous forests. Large prey is rare. The insect imagos and spiders are inaccessible in cold weather conditions. Consequently, a short spell of heavy precipitation exterminates all great tit broods. By contrast, the many coal tits *Periparus ater* breeding in the same forest have no trouble with feeding their chicks because they largely rely on very small, sessile prey such as plant lice *Pseudococcidae* that are ignored by the great tits. (Naef-Daenzer *et al.* unpublished data).

(Photos: S. Cordier (great tit), C. Marti (forest).)

Conspecifics are a very particular habitat factor. The rest of a population forms part of the habitat, and intraspecific interactions strongly influence individual habitat interactions (many examples are given in Newton, 1998; see also Chapters 1 and 2). The functionality and ecology of social systems is a good illustration of why Hutchinson's n-dimensional niche is an incomplete model. Most habitat components (except physical factors) consist of populations that interact at a higher level. Thus, intraspecific competition in combination with site-specific resource distributions, and factors such as the costs of using these resources may result in confusingly complex biological webs and cause enormous variation in population processes.

Axis 3: Increasing the time window

What are the implications of time scales for understanding habitat–population relationships? In the short term, individuals behave differently in relation to their ontogeny and stages of the life cycle. These aspects are perhaps less important for understanding long-term population processes. However, if the time window is larger than one reproductive cycle, factors such as differential survival and reproductive performance are important forces driving population dynamics. These characteristics of individual life-histories determine the basic demographic parameters and processes, and these in turn, affect abundance and spatial distribution patterns. One persisting difficulty at this level is that investigations of individual histories and behaviour are demanding and locally focused, and typically limited to short periods. In contrast, long-term, large-scale studies of abundance or spatial distribution are generally based on relatively simple counts. For example, distribution atlases give excellent information on the spatial extent and abundance and long-term changes in these patterns. However, the ecological mechanisms creating these patterns must be investigated mainly by local intensive studies.

Axis 4: Increasing the spatial scale

At large spatial scales, additional complexity comes into a system because populations are seldom homogeneous. For a widely distributed species, there can be large variations in physical habitat factors – for example in photoperiod, geology, altitude and climate. At this level it becomes particularly important to know the critical factors within the Hutchinsonian 'niche'. The distributional limits of a species to the north and south of its range may be determined by different factors. Many examples of population limitation are given by Newton (1998). The analysis of patterns in populations at a very large spatial scale is often facilitated by the use of meta-determinants of ecological processes such as large-scale climate conditions. Thus, the classic multidimensional habitat model is packed into a habitat 'envelope' using only a few general variables (Hampe, 2004). Using higher-order factors (such as the

North-Atlantic Oscillation) may better explain large-scale spatial patterns than would a variety of local variables (Stenseth *et al.*, 2003; Huntley *et al.*, 2007).

Shifts in large-scale spatial distributions and possible local extinction have come into focus in the context of recent climatic changes. Relatively simple climate envelopes have proved useful for modelling present and future bird distributions (Huntley *et al.*, 2007). However, the long-term accuracy of the predictions using these models is uncertain. They are imprecise in predicting the future climate-related development of habitat qualities or even ignore these altogether. They also ignore habitat-independent changes in populations, for example through variation in fecundity, dispersal ability or phenotypic plasticity. Although correlations may be highly plausible, models and predictions at such a large scale lack the link to the ecological mechanisms involved. Even for the most common bird species, insight into the environmental processes forming large-scale, long-term patterns is scant (Saether *et al.*, 2007). As outlined below, new statistical tools promise solutions to these problems by integrating both the individual and the population level.

Implications for exploring population patterns and processes

In reality, drawing conclusions on populations involves all four axes. Understanding the habitat needs of individuals is essential, but insufficient, for understanding populations. At the level of populations, information on demographic processes and the flow of energy and matter through ecosystems is required to complete the picture.

At the individual and short-term level, the habitat concept holds fairly well – an individual will need a specific quantity of a particular habitat component to survive and reproduce. Hence, this 'here and now' approach – based on the conditions that an individual encounters and has to interact with – is excellent for developing conservation measures and for analysing individual strategies. However, at larger scales in space and time the concept of a habitat and its user has drawbacks. What in models is considered constant, in reality is often dynamic and, as the wolf example at the start of the chapter illustrates, the components of the system mutually influence each other. These feedbacks between system components are difficult to measure and model, and are one source of unpredictable changes in biological systems. The methodological toolbox is therefore of great importance for quantifying, analysing and modelling the complex relationships.

Thoughts on methods

The approach to individual habitat selection and habitat–population relationships, and the insights gained, are influenced by the toolbox of methods available at the time. There have been marked methodological developments towards a synthesis of the four axes discussed above. In the mid 1970s, multi-variate statistics became widely available and gave enormous potential for solving the obviously multi-variate problems of ecology. There followed other new points of view and techniques, such as stochastic modelling (Tijms, 1986) and fractal mathematics, which originated from chaos theory (Hastings and Sugihara, 1993). Often the potential of new techniques was overestimated, and sometimes researchers were misled. The fractal dimension of a habitat pattern or a home-range proved to be very difficult to translate into biologically meaningful information. Similarly, a virtual 'factor' derived from principal components extraction may be statistically justified, but may not represent any understandable characteristic of an ecological system. However, factor analysis can be an excellent tool to reduce large sets of variables to those few real-world variables representing major habitat characteristics (Box 16.3). A whole suite of new techniques is now offered with geographic information systems (GIS) allowing spatio-temporal patterns to be modelled and graphically represented with unprecedented resolution, and spatially explicit models to be constructed. Although the opportunities and almost unlimited computation power should not tempt researchers to suppose that everything becomes predictable, GIS is indeed an excellent tool for the ecologist. Habitat suitability modelling combines multi-variate and spatial statistical techniques. Thus, these models are approaches to handling and visualising the multi-dimensional niche concept. Taken together, multi-variate mixed models and GIS tools integrate hypothesis testing, spatial statistics and visualisation, and thus provide much scope to master the methodological problems of ecological niches and bird–habitat interactions (for a methodological review see Guisan and Zimmermann, 2000). An example of how habitat suitability modelling has revealed valuable insights is given in Box 16.3.

Major steps have been made in resolving methodological issues related to linking the habitat needs of the individual and the implications at the population scale. Interestingly, both the estimation of crucial life-history parameters (the individual level) and assessing key demographic and diversity parameters (the population level) benefit from the same general approach. At both levels, the key is estimating how likely it is that animals remain undetected. At the individual level, the problem is in estimating survival (or similar data, such as the proportion of non-reproductive individuals) in relation to life-history stages. Both survival and detection probability may differ amongst life-history stages, sites and years. Quantifying the likelihood that live individuals remain undetected helps to disentangle survival rate and observation probability. Thus, unbiased survival estimates can be obtained independently of the detectability of individuals in relation to sex, stage, year or site (Lebreton *et al.*, 1992; Burnham and Anderson, 1998). Similarly,

Box 16.3 Habitat suitability modelling: an Alpine example

Since 1986 some 150 captive-bred bearded vultures *Gypaetus barbatus* have been released in the Alps (Frey, 1992). Until 2010 some 140 individuals and close to 20 breeding pairs have settled, and the small new population seems to sustain itself. Although the birds use huge areas, they are not unselective. Habitat suitability modelling has revealed valuable insights about how the species will re-colonise the Alps (Hirzel *et al.*, 2004). Bearded vultures strongly prefer a limestone environment, particularly for settlement and subsequent reproduction. The explanation is that the limestone environment is typified by many small-scale habitat features that are directly relevant to the birds' life. Craggy lime cliffs may offer a larger proportion of suitable roosts and nesting niches compared to silicate rocks, which are normally less complex structurally. In addition, fine-scale structures such as screes at the cliff foot that are used for breaking large bones and for food storage are also more frequent. Food availability appears to be a minor factor for habitat selection and settlement decisions. Although limestone has no direct relevance for the vultures' life-history functions, it represents an important 'lead habitat variable', representing a suite of geology-mediated favourable habitat characteristics. For conservation measures, the geological structure of the Alps as a whole may therefore serve as a simple and practical proxy for modelling potential for re-colonization and connectivity of areas (Hirzel *et al.*, 2004).

(Photo credit: Ch. Meier-Zwicky.)

estimating population parameters such as abundance, proportions of age categories, sex ratios and trends in these, suffer from unknown variation in the detectability of animals. Here, too, repeat counts are the key to assess the detectability of species or individuals and in turn, to correct abundance estimates for those biases. These methods are normally used in combination with an information theoretic approach for selecting the best-fitting model (Kéry and Royle, 2008). This is another welcome supplement to probabilistic statistics that offers alternatives to testing results against (often questionable) null hypotheses. In particular, the opportunity to evaluate entire models (in contrast to variance components) is an excellent addition to the toolbox (see Grueber *et al.* (2011) for a discussion of limitations).

Unbiased estimates of life-history and demographic parameters are the basis of integrated population models. These aim to combine the individual and the population scale in stage-classified models, and to quantify key population parameters and processes. This allows data from intensive, small-scale individual-based studies to be linked with larger-scale, longer-term estimates of abundance and demographic trends. Ultimately, this opens a way to determine the crucial life-history stages that are important for the growth rate and persistence of a population and how these interact with habitat. Comparisons and projections of population trends in varying habitats are far more informative than single estimates of fecundity (individuals) or abundance (population) (Caswell, 2001). Two contrasting examples of such models from central Europe are given in Box 16.4.

In conclusion, the methods and techniques that are available and 'en vogue' influence the approach to analysing biological systems at all levels. With increasing computing power, there is great scope for integrating data ranging from the individual level to demographies, and from local behavioural studies to continent-wide monitoring data. Thus, there are powerful new methods for addressing the increasing complexity along the four above axes, and for handling the different data qualities at different scales. Financial and logistic obstacles in the acquisition of data, rather than methodology and computing power, may be the main constraint limiting our ability to bridge the gap between individual life-histories and understanding population patterns and processes at large scales and over long periods of time.

Conclusions and perspectives

First, and chiefly, the individual level is crucial for explaining the mechanisms underlying population processes. For fundamental research and conservation it is important that the cascades of proximate ecological mechanisms driving population processes are examined at the level at which they operate. The ecology of key population parameters (fecundity, survival, dispersal, range) are often insufficiently understood because large-sample investigations of the

Box 16.4 Two contrasting examples of integrated population models from central Europe

These models combine data from individual and population scales to identify key parameters in population dynamics which can be used to inform conservation strategies. In the Alps, the re-introduced population of bearded vultures *Gypaetus barbatus*, although still very small, appears to sustain itself, but depends strongly on limestone areas (see Box 16.3). Its re-introduction is an extremely expensive undertaking, and thus requires careful evaluation of the right moment to stop releases. Schaub *et al.* (2009) analysed mark-resighting data of all birds and fecundity rates of the established pairs. As expected for a long-lived species, the population growth rate was mainly related to adult survival (Lebreton and Clobert, 1991). Stochastic modelling of various potential adverse effects demonstrated that the population seems to be quite robust against variation in adult survival rates. Hence the authors of the study concluded that no further releases would be required.

In contrast, Swiss populations of the far smaller and nocturnal bird of prey, the little owl *Athene noctua* are unsustainable. Schaub *et al.* (2006) showed that the mostly small populations scattered over southern Germany and Switzerland vary in relation to immigration and local juvenile survival. As none of the populations in the study was self-sustaining, the results raised questions about where those immigrants, mainly juveniles, come from and how a sufficient connectivity between the local populations may be established.

Photos: P. Keusch (vulture), B. Naef-Daenzer (little owl).

fundamental individual processes are lacking. Particular gaps persist, for example, in the relationships between fecundity, survival and abundance at the climate-ecosystem interface, in spatial variation in trophic cascades, or in the importance of dispersal for meta-population dynamics. In these fields, empirical research at the individual level often lags behind theoretical work. New methods of analysis, and of combining different levels and scales, open enormous opportunities to advance insight into these fundamental processes. Promising steps in quantifying key parameters of populations with good spatial and temporal resolution have already been made.

In the context of analysing individual–habitat relationships and their importance at the population level, two approaches to understanding this interface between individual fates and population ecology seem particularly promising. Expanding the view of life-history ecology from selected traits (such as the timing of breeding) towards entire life-histories reveals the important bottlenecks and how differential survival or reproduction in relation to habitat will affect key parameters of population dynamics. For example, Low and Pärt (2009) quantified survival rates for New Zealand stitchbirds *Notiomystis cincta* over their life. They showed that survival rates generally increased with age, but that each transition between life-history stages (e.g. hatching, fledging) caused marked drops in survival. Thus, age-related survival followed a saw-tooth function indicating several critical stages in the life cycle. Assessing entire lives instead of selected traits will greatly improve the power of behavioural ecological studies for explaining population processes. The other approach, involves maintaining investigations of selected life-history traits over many generations. Even 'simple' long-term nest record schemes are invaluable sources for explaining population consequences of environmental change, because they assess the phenology of life-history traits and crucial demographic parameters over a long period (Both *et al.*, 2004; Naef-Daenzer *et al.*, 2012). Still, studies of both kinds are spatially limited and cannot yield representative data for a continent-wide population. However, recent efforts to pool compatible basic data over the full distribution range of species with detailed studies of ecology and behaviour give further scope for understanding ecological mechanisms, trophic webs and population dynamics (Saether *et al.*, 2003, 2007; Both *et al.*, 2004).

The second conclusion is that the paradigm of optimality is challenged. In parts of a population, often at ecological borders, individuals do not perform optimally. This may result, for example, in poor reproduction, elevated mortality or a high turnover of individuals. Here, too, abundance estimates and population trends describing the spatial and long-term patterns, need to be complemented by investigations revealing the mechanisms involved. The poor reproductive performance of great tits in subalpine regions (Box 16.2) illustrates that what we observe in a limited research area may not always be the result of adaptation (from either an evolutionary or a behavioural plasticity perspective). Ecological limitation in the flexibility of response to the environment is a crucial issue for understanding population limitation. Further research is needed to understand how local populations of a species may persist in clearly unfavourable habitats. Existing theory of source–sink dynamics or metapopulation dynamics provides testable predictions at the population level. In addition, investigating why sources are productive and how individuals disappear from sinks is required to clarify the mechanisms that shape the patterns. Thus, combining metapopulation and life-history models may be a promising approach to analysing both the heterogeneity in individual habitat interactions and the resulting population patterns (Skórka et al., 2009).

Third, analysing patterns of animal abundance, population trends and spatial distributions does not necessarily require individual life-histories to be monitored. The approach of covering large areas (or the entire range of a species) over long periods reveals patterns and processes that are indispensable for building conservation policies and measures. Good examples are the country- or continent-wide bird surveys in Europe and the United States (Sauer et al., 2008; Robinson, 2010). However, to obtain the most complete understanding of systems, both approaches – one starting at the most general level and one starting at individuals – are required. The wolf example illustrates that finding an ideal combination of various levels is important. Here, good biological intuition can greatly help to disentangle the enormous complexity of relationships in such systems and to focus on the key mechanisms. An additional precondition is to find or develop the methods and techniques allowing quantification of the crucial variables. In the case of Yellowstone, cutting-edge GPS devices made it possible to simultaneously track predator and prey at high spatial resolution.

Finally, projections of future developments receive increasing attention for both research and conservation. The need to investigate and predict ecosystem structures and functionality at various scales is very real (Scott et al., 2002; Wilson et al., 2009). However, with all biological systems, the likelihood of unpredictable, discontinuous changes is high (e.g. Coulson et al., 2001; Bolger et al., 2005). Projections should not be made over excessive periods of time, nor equations extrapolated too far beyond boundaries of current knowledge (see also Chapter 3). The easiest but most uncertain way is to extrapolate counts or population indices. The hardest and most reliable way is to build models on the basis of environmental and demographic data and their relationships (equations) at different scales. Hence, research at the individual level is crucial for quantifying the causal cascades from the environment to the individual and from the individual to the population level. Integrated population models hold great potential for robust representation of major population processes because they do not rely on demographic trends alone, but integrate crucial parameters of dynamics such as fecundity, survival and dispersal rates (Lebreton and Clobert, 1991). Ironically, making conservation decisions is often most urgent in areas at the periphery of the *n*-dimensional ecological niche, where scientific knowledge of the 'average' ecology of a species may not apply. It is often the small (and endangered) populations at range extremes for which policy-makers call for hard facts, and for which this demand is hardest to fulfil.

There emerges one major implication for understanding population patterns and processes on the basis of individual habitat interactions. While variation in ecological conditions over species ranges is well documented, knowledge of the related variation in individual behavioural responses and related demographic parameters is scant. The modes of individual response to heterogeneous environmental conditions vary largely over the range of a species. Thus, subpopulations of a species occurring in a continuum of habitat conditions, differ in demography and dynamics over space and time (e.g. Fuller *et al.*, 2007). Studying the behavioural ecology at range edges will explain which ecological mechanisms act on which parameter of population dynamics. Giving behavioural ecology and population dynamics a geographical context and addressing spatial variation in plasticity may open a way to clarify the forces that shape species distributions through the multitude of individual fates and to find solutions for crucial conservation problems.

Acknowledgements

I am grateful for the invaluable inspiration and support coming from many colleagues. M. Grüebler, L. Naef-Daenzer and T. Wesołowski and an anonymous reviewer commented on various versions of the manuscript. Rob Fuller provided not only scientific advice, but also supported all editorial stages and finally amended all persisting flaws in language and style.

References

Begon, M., Townsend, C. R. and Harper, J. L. (2006). *Ecology: From Individuals to Ecosystems*. Oxford: Blackwell Publishing.

Beyer, H. L., Merrill, E. H., Varley, N. and Boyce, M. S. (2007). Willow on Yellowstone's northern range: evidence for a trophic cascade? *Ecol. Appl.*, **17**, 1563–1571.

Bolger, D. T., Patten, M. A. and Bostock, D. C. (2005). Avian reproductive failure in response to an extreme climatic event. *Oecologia*, **142**, 398–406.

Both, C., Artemyev, A. V., Blaauw, B. *et al.* (2004). Large-scale geographical variation confirms that climate change causes birds to lay earlier. *Proc. R. Soc. B*, **271**, 1657–1662.

Boyce, M. S. (1993). Predicting the consequences of wolf recovery to ungulates in Yellowstone National Park. *Wildlife Soc. Bull.*, **24**, 402–413.

Burnham, K. P. and Anderson, D. R. (1998). *Model Selection and Multimodel Inference. A Practical Information-theoretic Approach*. New York: Springer.

Cadenasso, M. L., Pickett, S. T. A. and Weathers, K. C. *et al.* (2003). An interdisciplinary and synthetic approach to ecological boundaries. *BioScience*, **53**, 717–722.

Carbonell, R., Pérez-Tris, J. and Tellería, J. L. (2003). Effects of habitat heterogeneity and local adaptation on the body condition of a forest passerine at the edge of its distributional range. *Biol. J. Linn. Soc.*, **78**, 479–488.

Caswell, H. (2001). *Matrix Population Models. Construction, Analysis and Interpretation.* Sunderland, MA: Sinauer Associates.

Charnov, E. L. (1976). Optimal foraging: attack strategy of a mantid. *Am. Nat.*, **110**, 141–151.

Cody, M. L. (ed.) (1985). *Habitat Selection in Birds.* San Diego: Academic Press.

Cook, R. S. (1993). *Ecological Issues on Reintroducing Wolves into Yellowstone National Park.* Denver, Colorado: National Park Service. NPS/NRYELL/NRSM-93/22.

Coulson, T., Catchpole, E. A., Albon, S. D. *et al.* (2001). Age, sex, density, winter weather and population crashes in Soay sheep. *Science*, **292**, 1528–1531.

Crabtree, R. L. and Sheldon, J. W. (1999). The ecological role of coyotes on Yellowstone's northern range. *Yellowstone Science*, **7**, 15–23.

Creel, S., Winnie, Jr. J., Maxwell, B., Hamlin, K. and Creel, M. (2005). Elk alter habitat selection as an antipredator response to wolves. *Ecology*, **86**, 3387–3397.

Darwin, C. R. (1859). *On the Origin of Species by Means of Natural Selection, or The Preservation of Favoured Races in the Struggle for Life.* London: John Murray.

Dingemanse, N. J., Both, C., Drent, P. J., Rutten, A. L. and Tinbergen, J. M. (2003). Fitness consequences of avian personalities in a fluctuating environment. *Proc. R. Soc. B.*, **270**, 741–747.

Dingemanse, N. J. and Réale, D. (2005). Natural selection and animal personality. *Behaviour*, **142**, 1165–1190.

Drent, P. J., van Oers, K. and van Noordwijk, A. J. (2003). Realized heritability of personalities

in the great tit (*Parus major*). *Proc. R. Soc. B.*, **270**, 45–51.

Emlen, J. M. (1966). The role of time and energy in food preference. *Am. Nat.*, **100**, 611–617.

Frey, H. (1992). Die Wiedereinbürgerung des Bartgeiers (*Gypaetus barbatus*) in die Alpen. *Egretta*, **35**, 85–95.

Fuller, R. J., Gaston, K. J. and Quine, C. P. (2007). Living on the edge: British and Irish woodland birds in a European context. *Ibis*, **149** (suppl. 2), 53–63.

Grueber, C. E., Nakagawa, S., Laws, R. J. and Jamieson, I. G. (2011). Multimodel inference in ecology and evolution: challenges and solutions. *J. Evol. Biol.*, **24**, 699–711.

Guisan, A. and Zimmermann, N. E. (2000). Predictive habitat distribution models in ecology. *Ecol. Model.*, **135**, 147–186.

Hampe, A. (2004). Bioclimate envelope models: what they detect and what they hide. *Global Ecol. Biogeogr.*, **13**, 469–471.

Hastings, H. M. and Sugihara, G. (1993). *Fractals. A User's Guide for the Natural Sciences.* Oxford: Oxford Science Publications.

Hirzel, A. H., Bosse, B., Oggier, P.-A. *et al.* (2004). Ecological requirements of reintroduced species and the implications for release policy: the case of the bearded vulture. *J. Appl. Ecol.*, **41**, 1103–1116.

Horn, D. Mitchell, R. and Stairs, G. R. (ed.) (1978). *Analysis of Ecological Systems.* Columbus: Ohio State University Press.

Huntley, B., Green, R. E., Collingham, Y. C. and Willis, S. G. (2007). *A Climatic Atlas of European Breeding Birds.* Barcelona: Lynx edicions.

Hurrell, J. W. (1995). Decadal trends in the North Atlantic Oscillation and relationships to regional temperature and precipitation. *Science*, **269**, 676–679.

Hutchinson, G. E. (1953). The concept of pattern in ecology. *P. Natl. Acad. Sci.*, **105**, 1–12.

Kéry, M. and Royle, A. J. (2008). Hierarchical Bayes estimation of species richness and occupancy in spatially replicated surveys. *J. Appl. Ecol.*, **45**, 589–598.

Lebreton, J. D., Burnham, K. P., Clobert, J. and Anderson, D. R. (1992). Modelling survival and testing biological hypotheses using marked animals: a unified approach with case studies. *Ecol. Monogr.*, **62**, 67–118.

Lebreton, J. D. and Clobert, J. (1991). Bird population dynamics, management and conservation: the role of mathematical modelling. In *Bird Population Studies*, ed. C. M. Perrins, pp. 105–125. Oxford: Oxford University Press.

Low, M. and Pärt, T. (2009). Patterns of mortality for each life-history stage in a population of the endangered New Zealand stitchbird. *J. Anim. Ecol.*, **78**, 761–771.

MacArthur, R. H. (1964). Environmental factors affecting bird species diversity. *Am. Nat.*, **68**, 387–397.

MacArthur, R. H. (1968). The theory of the niche. In *Population Biology and Evolution*, ed. R. C. Lewontin, pp. 159–176. Syracuse: Syracuse University Press.

MacArthur, R. H. and Pianka, E. R. (1966). On optimal use of a patchy habitat. *Am. Nat.*, **100**, 603–609.

MacArthur, R. H., Recher, H. and Cody, M. (1966). On the relation between habitat selection and species diversity. *Am. Nat.*, **100**, 319–332.

Mack, J. A. and Singer, F. (1992). Population models for elk, mule deer, and moose on Yellowstone's northern winter range. In *Wolves for Yellowstone? Report to the US Congress, Vol. 4*, ed. J. D. Varley and W. G. Brewster, pp. 4/3–4/31. Yellowstone National Park Service: NPS/NRYELL/NRSM-93-22.

Maggini, R., Lehmann, A., Kéry, M. *et al.* (2011). Are Swiss birds tracking climate change? Detecting elevational shifts using response curve shapes. *Ecol. Model.* **222**, 21–32.

Martin, T. E. (2001). Abiotic vs. biotic influences on habitat selection of coexisting species: climate change impacts? *Ecology*, **82**, 175–188.

Martin, T. E. (2007). Climate correlates of 20 years of trophic changes in a high-elevation riparian system. *Ecology*, **88**, 367–380.

Morrison, M. L. and Hall, L. S. (2002). Standard terminology: toward a common language to advance ecological understanding and application. In *Predicting Species Occurrences. Issues of Accuracy and Scale*, ed. J. M. Scott, P. J. Heglund, M. L. Morrison *et al.* London: Island Press.

Naef-Daenzer, B. (2000). Patch time allocation and patch sampling by foraging great and blue tits. *Anim. Behav.*, **59**, 989–999.

Naef-Daenzer, B., Luterbacher, J., Nuber, M., Rutishauser, T. and Winkel, W. (2012). Cascading climate effects and related ecological consequences during past centuries. *Clim. Past Discuss.*, **8**, 2041–2073.

Naef-Daenzer, B., Widmer, F. and Nuber, M. (2001). Differential post-fledging survival of great and coal tits in relation to their condition and fledging date. *J. Anim. Ecol.*, **70**, 730–738.

Newton, I. (1998). *Population Limitation in Birds*. London: Academic Press.

Perdeck, A. C., Visser, M. E. and van Balen, J. H. (2000). Great tits *Parus major* survival and the beech-crop cycle. *Ardea*, **88**, 99–106.

Pérez-Tris, J., Carbonell, R. and Tellería, J. L. (2000). Abundance distribution, morphological variation and juvenile condition of robins, *Erithacus rubecula*, in their Mediterranean range boundary. *J. Biogeog.*, **27**, 879–888.

Perrins, C. M. (1991). Tits and their caterpillar food supply. *Ibis*, **133**, 49–54.

Perry, G. and Pianka, E. R. (1997). Animal foraging: past, present and future. *Trends Ecol. Evol.*, **12**, 360–363.

Pierce G. J. and Ollasen, J. G. (1987). Eight reasons why optimal foraging is a complete waste of time. *Oikos*, **49**, 111–118.

Polis, G. A., Power, M. E. and Huxel, G. R. (2004). *Food Webs at the Landscape Level*. Chicago: University of Chicago Press.

Ripple, W. J. and Beschta, R. L. (2006). Linking wolves to willows via risk-sensitive foraging by ungulates in the northern Yellowstone ecosystem. *For. Ecol. Manage.*, **230**, 96–106.

Ripple, W. J., Larsen, E. J., Renkin, R. A. and Smith, D. W. (2001). Trophic cascades among wolves, elk and aspen on Yellowstone

National Park's northern range. *Biol. Conserv.*, **102**, 227–234.

Robinson, R. A. (2010). State of bird populations in Britain and Ireland. In *Silent Summer: The State of Wildlife in Britain and Ireland*, ed. N. Maclean, pp. 281–318. Cambridge: Cambridge University Press.

Saether, B. E., Engen, S., Grøtan, V. *et al.* (2007). The extended Moran effect and large-scale synchronous fluctuations in the size of great tit and blue tit populations. *J. Anim. Ecol.*, **76**, 315–325.

Saether, B. E., Engen, S., Møller, A. P. *et al.* (2003). Climate variation and regional gradients in population dynamics of two hole-nesting passerines. *Proc. R. Soc. B.*, **270**, 2397–2404.

Sauer, J. R., Hines, J. E. and Fallon, J. (2008). *The North American Breeding Bird Survey, Results and Analysis 1966–2007. Version 5.15.2008*. Laurel, MD: USGS Patuxent Wildlife Research Center.

Schaub, M., Zink, R., Beissmann, H., Sarrazin, F. and Arlettaz, R. (2009). When to end releases in reintroduction programmes: demographic rates and population viability analysis of bearded vultures in the Alps. *J. Appl. Ecol.*, **46**, 92–100.

Schaub, M., Ullrich, B., Knötzsch, G., Albrecht, P. and Meisser, C. (2006). Local population dynamics and the impact of scale and isolation: a study on different little owl populations. *Oikos*, **115**, 389–400.

Schoener, T. W. (1971). Theory of feeding strategies. *Annu. Rev. Ecol. Syst.*, **2**, 369–404.

Scott, J. M., Heglund, P. J., Morrison, M. L. *et al.* (eds.) (2002). *Predicting Species Occurrences: Issues of Accuracy and Scale*. Island Press. London.

Skórka, P., Lenda, M., Martyka, R. and Tworek, S. (2009). The use of metapopulation and optimal foraging theories to predict movement and foraging decisions of mobile animals in heterogeneous landscapes. *Landscape Ecol.*, **24**, 599–609.

Smith, D. W., Peterson, R. O. and Houston, D. B. (2003). Yellowstone after wolves. *BioScience*, **53**, 330–340.

Stahler, D., Heinrich, B. and Smith, D. (2002). Common ravens, *Corvus corax*, preferentially associate with grey wolves, *Canis lupus*, as a foraging strategy in winter. *Anim. Behav.*, **64**, 283–290.

Stenseth, N. C., Ottersen, G., Hurrell, J. W. *et al.* (2003). Studying climate effects on ecology through the use of climate indices: the North Atlantic oscillation, El Niño Southern Oscillation and beyond. *Proc. R. Soc. B*, **270**, 2087–2096.

Stephens, D. W. and Krebs, J. R. (1986). *Foraging Theory*. Princeton: Princeton University Press.

Sutherland, W. J. (1996). *From Individual Behaviour to Population Ecology*. Oxford: Oxford University Press.

Tijms, H. C. (1986). *Stochastic Modelling and Analysis: A Computational Approach*. New York: Wiley and Sons.

Van Oers, K., Drent, P. J., de Goede, P. and van Noordwijk, A. J. (2004). Repeatability and heritability of risk-taking behaviour in relation to avian personalities. *Proc. R. Soc. B.*, **271**, 65–71.

Van Overveld, Th., Adriaensen, F. and Matthysen, E. (2011). Post fledging family space use in great tits in relation to environmental and parental characteristics. *Behav. Ecol.*, **22**, 899–907.

Verbeek, M. E. M., Drent, P. J. and Wiepkema, P. R. (1994). Consistent individual differences in early exploratory behaviour of male great tits. *Anim. Behav.*, **48**, 1119–1121.

Visser, M. E., Adriaensen, F., Van Balen, J. H. *et al.* (2002). Variable responses to large-scale climate change in European *Parus* populations. *Proc. R. Soc. B*, **270**, 367–372.

Wilmers, C. C., Crabtree, R. L., Smith, D. W., Murphy, K. M. and Getz, W. M. (2003). Trophic facilitation by introduced top predators: grey wolf subsidies to scavengers in Yellowstone National Park. *J. Anim. Ecol.*, **72**, 909–916.

Wilson. J. D., Evans, A. D. and Grice, P. V. (2009). *Bird Conservation and Agriculture*. Cambridge: Cambridge University Press.

CHAPTER SEVENTEEN

Insufficient adaptation to climate change alters avian habitat quality and thereby changes habitat selection

CHRISTIAAN BOTH

University of Groningen

Before approaching the main theme of this chapter I want to start with some intriguing field observations that, by accident, set me on the track of investigating the effects of climate change on avian ecology. Checking nest-boxes is like having a birthday party: opening boxes is always a surprise. While tramping from box to box, my mind works in overdrive to find patterns. One such pattern that started to fascinate me was that pied flycatchers *Ficedula hypoleuca* seem to prefer nest-boxes occupied by tits. Flycatchers are long-distance migrants that normally arrive when the tits already have started nest-building, and often have started egg-laying as well. Upon the flycatcher's arrival, many boxes are still empty, whereas others are occupied by various tit species. Still, flycatchers consistently prefer the boxes containing nest material of tits. I have recorded this pattern over many years and in several areas (unpublished data), so I truly believe this pattern is real. This is not just a minor fact of life, but a potentially deadly adventure for a pied flycatcher. Each year we find – mostly male – flycatchers killed in nest-boxes, and often these nest-boxes had been occupied by great tits *Parus major* (Slagsvold, 1975; Ahola *et al.*, 2007). It occasionally happens that great tits are incubating on extremely smelly nests, because a decomposing pied flycatcher had been included in the nest material. A closer look at the killed flycatchers further reveals that – more often than not – the brain has been eaten, a high-energy meal for an egg-laying bird early in the season. The attraction of already occupied nest-boxes for arriving pied flycatchers must have an enormous advantage, given its frequency and potentially lethal outcome.

Habitat selection is likely to be the answer as to why pied flycatchers prefer nest-boxes already occupied by tits (Forsman *et al.*, 2002; Seppanen and Forsman, 2007). Pied flycatchers are in a hurry and have little time upon arrival to figure out what the best breeding sites are. Spring develops quickly, and flycatchers have to race the clock to be able to profit from the narrow peak in caterpillar numbers in early spring. Gathering information on habitat quality, however, takes time, and a short-cut could be to rely on information provided by other species with near-similar ecological requirements. The

Birds and Habitat: Relationships in Changing Landscapes, ed. Robert J. Fuller. Published by Cambridge University Press. © Cambridge University Press 2012.

reason why flycatchers prefer occupied nest-boxes thus may be – via information indirectly provided by tits – related to food availability, safety from predators or other important habitat features. The associated benefits clearly outweigh the chance of being killed. In the year 2000 I set out to test this idea with a simple experiment. Just before the flycatchers arrived in spring, I put moss (tit nesting material) in random nest-boxes, and kept others empty. It was an exceptionally warm April, and I did not want to start the experiment too early in order not to interfere with the tits' breeding behaviour. Therefore I waited for the first male pied flycatchers to arrive. Despite the high local temperatures, pied flycatchers arrived exceptionally late: I observed the first male on 20 April (normally 10 April), and set out to do the experiment on April 23. To my surprise, the first pied flycatcher had already an almost completely built nest! Three days after arrival of the first male, he got paired, his female immediately had built a nest and the first egg was laid on April 26! This high-speed start of the season came as a surprise, and was unlike anything I had experienced in previous years. Late arrival and early start of breeding have kept me busy ever since, whilst examining how climate change has affected the annual cycle of long-distance migrants. Interestingly, April layings of pied flycatchers in the Netherlands are no longer out of the ordinary.

In this chapter my aim is to explore how climate change affects habitats and, by inference, habitat selection of birds. Of special interest is the timing of breeding in birds relative to the timing of other trophic levels. How individuals gather information about where to settle in anticipation of climate change is an exciting new line of research, which falls outside the scope of the present study. I do acknowledge that the view presented in this chapter is highly biased towards phenology and how birds match their own breeding time with the seasonality of their environment. Other effects of climate change on avian habitat quality and use could be (at least as) important in many systems, depending on features of both the habitat and the bird species involved. One such process is the interaction between birds and their parasites, which may alter habitat suitability through changes in parasite prevalence and phenology, or range changes of parasites and/or birds as a result of climate change (see review in Merino and Møller, 2010). Also the structure of communities may change, through a differential effect of climatic variables on different (groups of) species and hence shifting the competitive balance and thereby affecting habitat suitability (Brotons and Jiguet, 2010). This could be through a change in migratory behaviour (Lehikoinen and Sparks, 2010), or due to an increase in winter survival for resident species (Robinson *et al.*, 2007), leading to a shifting balance between resident and migrant species competing for the same resources (Böhning-Gaese and Lemoine, 2004; Ahola *et al.*, 2007). With all processes involved we need to address the question of whether the observed adjustments are sufficient given the plethora of (possible) changes in the habitat and, if not, how birds could either adjust their phenotypes or their habitat selection to maintain population size. The examples given in this chapter all relate to these major questions.

Seasonally varying habitats: a matter of timing

Almost all habitats change through time, seasonally as well as over the years. This change is epitomised by vegetation structure, with its associated cycles of leafing, flowering and fruiting and, in the long run, changes in composition and density. Profound transformations of the environment, impact every living creature from bottom to top and vice versa. My research is mainly focused on the effect of seasonal variations in food availability on birds. Species that rely on seasonally fluctuating food sources have to change their diet, or switch habitat in order to find sufficient food to survive. Seasonal changes in diet have been observed in a wide range of birds, and often require profound changes in the digestive system. Bearded tits *Panurus biarmicus*, for example, switch from an insectivorous diet in summer to a granivorous diet in winter (seeds), only possible by changing their digestive tract (Spitzer, 1972). Other species do not change their diet, and have to migrate to a different habitat to survive periods of food shortage. Many, mainly insectivorous, long-distance migrants migrate from their temperate breeding habitats to tropical winter habitats.

The seasonality in habitats weighs heavily on important life-history decisions. To a large extent, the timing of life-history decisions determines fitness of individual birds, especially if habitats are strongly seasonal. Important decisions include the timing of breeding, whether birds should breed more than once in a season, how long they care for their offspring, when they moult, whether and when to migrate to distant wintering areas, and when to return to the breeding grounds (Perrins, 1970; Drent, 2006). Each decision is intricately linked with others, and has fitness consequences determined by the phenology of the habitat. Raising chicks before, during or after the food peak clearly resonates in number and condition of offspring. The timing of the annual cycle of birds thus should be adapted to the seasonality of the habitats they use. Changes in seasonality are expected to pose problems if birds cannot adjust to novel circumstances.

Climate change affects the timing of different components within the ecosystem. This effect is not always synchronous across different species, and therefore birds can get out of sync with vital resources such as food. The best examples come from long-term nest-box studies on forest-dwelling insectivorous passerines, mainly tits (*Paridae*) and *Ficedula* flycatchers. To a large extent, both groups of species feed their nestlings on caterpillars, and hence are dependent on the narrow but high peak in caterpillar abundance in forest ecosystems. The long-term studies showed that since about 1980 laying dates in many populations have advanced (Winkel and Hudde, 1997; Visser *et al.*, 1998; McCleery and Perrins, 1998; Slater, 1999), although responses differed between populations across Europe (Visser *et al.*, 2003; Both *et al.*, 2004). For collared *Ficedula albicollis* and pied flycatchers, the rate of advance was strongly correlated with the rate of local spring warming. The larger advancements were recorded in areas where it became warmer, suggesting that climate change indeed played an important role (Both *et al.*, 2004). Data on the timing of the caterpillar peak in a Dutch habitat showed that caterpillars advanced much more than annual median hatching dates of tit species and flycatchers (Fig. 17.1; Both *et al.*, 2009). Probably as a consequence, the fitness penalty of late breeding increased over the years, as late nests became progressively more mismatched with the food peak (Visser *et al.*, 1998; Both and Visser, 2001; Visser *et al.*, 2006). The breeding habitat for these species thus became less suitable over time. In contrast, the great tit population of Wytham Woods (near Oxford, UK) showed the opposite: the laying date of the birds advanced

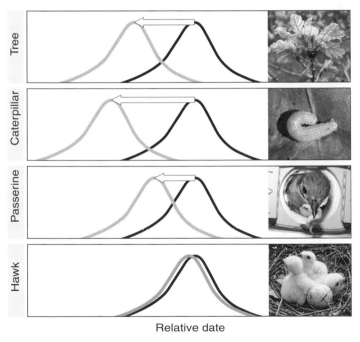

Relative date

Figure 17.1 Relative changes in timing of four trophic levels in a Dutch forest shown from top to bottom: oak budburst, caterpillar availability, passerine hatching dates, sparrowhawk hatching dates. Dark curves represent the relative timing of the trophic levels around 1985, and the grey curves at about 2005. Caterpillars changed more than budburst, passerines changed less than their caterpillar prey and sparrowhawks did not change, whereas their passerine prey did change phenology. After Both *et al.* (2009). Photos: C. Both, M.E. Visser and R.G. Bijlsma.

more than the caterpillar peak, and the average bird became better timed with the food peak (Cresswell and McCleery, 2003; Charmantier *et al.*, 2008). In the Czech Republic, advancements of laying dates in collared flycatcher and great tit were very much in synchrony with the change in the timing of the caterpillar peak between 1961–2001 (Bauer *et al.*, 2010), again showing enormous variation between geographic areas. Why the mismatches between caterpillars and birds increased in the Dutch breeding habitat, improved in the English breeding habitat and remained unaffected in the Czech habitat is not well understood, and shows that effects of climate change differ depending on either subtle variation between habitats or changes in the temporal structure of temperature change within seasons.

An advancement of the food peak in spring could lower habitat quality for birds but, in contrast, other changes may be favourable. For example, Dutch tits and flycatchers may profit from a reduction in post-fledging predation, as the breeding phenology of one of their main predators was even less affected by increased spring temperatures (Both *et al.*, 2009). At present, most tits and flycatchers fledge well in advance of the peak food demand of sparrowhawks *Accipiter nisus* (Fig. 17.1). The process of unequal trophic responses may thus also be beneficial if birds escape to some extent the brunt of predation. Nest predation is another important determinant of reproductive success (Martin, 1995), but long-term data are scarce and correlations with climate change unexplored (Wesołowski and Maziarz, 2009; Wesołowski *et al.*, 2009). Changing conditions, climatic or otherwise, are likely to also affect the abundance of nest predators (either positively or negatively), with effects on habitat choice and abundance of prey species. In this respect, the interaction between mast-seeding trees, rodents (as seed- and nest-predators) and ground-breeding passerines springs to mind (Wesołowski *et al.*, 2009). Masting frequency of trees like beech (*Fagus sylvatica*) is related to summer temperatures, and has increased over the years (Overgaard *et al.*, 2007). Overwinter survival of rodents, in its turn, is positively affected by mast seeding (Schmidt and Ostfeld, 2008). As a result, birds breeding after high mast years are confronted with high numbers of rodents, which could reduce nest success and post-fledging survival via predation (Schmidt *et al.*, 2008), or even force birds into other habitats (Wesołowski *et al.*, 2009). Climate-induced changes in one component of the habitat (increased frequency of mast seeding) could thus have cascading effects via an increase in the frequency of nest predation by rodents, finally leading to more years with a lowered breeding success.

Differential changes among habitats

Habitats may differ in how they are affected by climate change and, depending on ecology, how birds respond. One of the few examples, showing habitat-related differences in population trends of pied flycatchers, comes from the

Netherlands. Nest-box monitoring showed that in deciduous (oak) stands on fertile soils the pied flycatcher population declined strongly from the late 1980s onwards, whereas flycatchers breeding in coniferous and mixed forests were still thriving (Fig. 17.2 and Visser *et al.*, 2004). In an attempt to explain the variable patterns among habitats, we measured the timing of the caterpillar peak in nine study plots, expecting populations to decline most strongly in areas with an early food peak as opposed to areas with a more extended food peak. This was precisely what we found: population trends were strongly negative in areas with an early food peak and no change occurred in areas with a late food peak (Both *et al.*, 2006). Furthermore, in areas with an early food peak, breeding dates of birds responded least to annual variations in temperature, probably because the birds in these areas were already

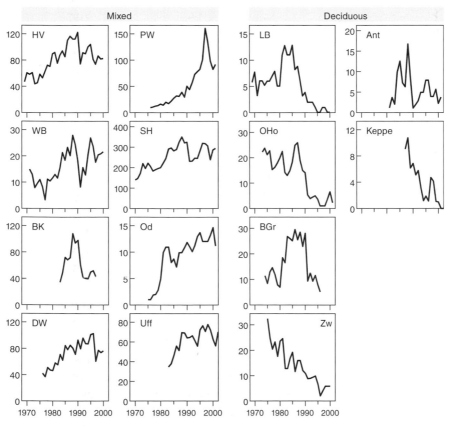

Figure 17.2 Population trends of nest-box populations of pied flycatchers across the Netherlands and northern Belgium in relation to forest habitat type. Until the late 1980s most populations grew as part of a general range expansion from east to west in the Netherlands. Thereafter, populations showed markedly different trends, depending on habitat type. Abbreviations refer to different study plots.

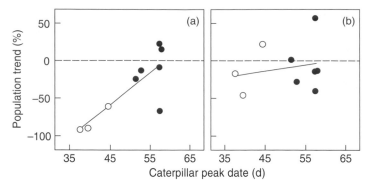

Figure 17.3 Population trends of Dutch nest-box populations of pied flycatchers (a) and great tits (b) in relation to the local date of the caterpillar peak in 2003. Population trends are expressed as the percentage change between 1983 and 2003. Open dots are deciduous habitats, filled dots mixed deciduous-coniferous habitats. Caterpillar peaks are in all cases measured under oak. After Both *et al.* (2006).

performing at the very limits of early breeding, but even so, missed the caterpillar peak and had to make do with the descending part of the food cycle. It is not likely that these areas with early food peaks had deteriorated in overall quality, because population trends of local great tits were unrelated to the date of the food peak (Fig. 17.3), and absolute peak densities of caterpillars were highest in areas with the earliest food peaks (Both *et al.*, 2006).

Interestingly, pied flycatchers are known to prefer deciduous forest over coniferous forest (Lundberg and Alatalo, 1992), and also normally reproduce better in deciduous forest (Siikamäki, 1995). We have no direct data showing that the decline in deciduous forests was caused by reduced reproductive success or by dispersal from purely deciduous to mixed and coniferous forests. In Spain, reproductive success of pied flycatchers in oak forests has declined strongly over the last decades, possibly due to an increased mismatch with the food (Sanz *et al.*, 2003). Flycatchers feed their chicks a rather diverse diet, depending on both habitat (Sanz, 1998), and timing of breeding. Early birds are known to feed their chicks mostly with caterpillars, and as caterpillar abundance drops with advancing season, so does the proportion of caterpillars in the diet. This change in diet is reflected in recruitment rates of chicks, which decline the later the chicks are born (Both, 2010b). The seasonal decline in reproductive success is typical for pied flycatchers, and for most other bird species (Smith and Moore, 2005; Verhulst and Nilsson, 2008), and indeed is caused by the seasonal decline in food abundance (Siikamäki, 1998). The reliance on caterpillars in oak forests was particularly pressed upon us when mass mortality of chicks occurred in the spring of 2009. In one of our study areas caterpillars were so abundant that they defoliated the trees just after budburst, and most caterpillars starved before the flycatcher eggs had hatched. The chicks in ten out of eleven nests all died shortly after hatching, despite the high food density earlier in the season. Tits that bred ten days earlier were hardly affected.

So far we have seen that a species like the pied flycatcher has not responded sufficiently to climate change, because its breeding phenology no longer matches the phenology of its main food. The reason why these birds got out of sync with their main food is pre-destined by their annual cycle. These birds are long-distance migrants, wintering in sub-Saharan West Africa. The evidence from western and central Europe shows that at least the males have not advanced their arrival time during the last three decades (Both *et al.*, 2005; Hüppop and Winkel, 2006). Also, for females there is some evidence that they have not advanced arrival either. The advance in breeding dates is therefore mostly due to a reduction in the interval between arrival and the start of breeding (Both and Visser, 2001). The inflexibility in arrival time has been explained by a rather rigid and photoperiodically controlled annual cycle (Gwinner, 1996; Both and Visser, 2001; Gwinner and Helm, 2003). New evidence shows, however, that pied flycatchers breeding in western and central Europe have advanced their spring migration passage through North Africa, but this advance has not led to earlier arrival at the breeding grounds because environmental constraints in southern Europe preclude uninterrupted continuation of migration (Both, 2010a). Pied flycatchers, and many other long-distance migrants that breed in more northerly regions have, however, advanced their arrival time (Ahola *et al.*, 2004; Lehikoinen *et al.*, 2004; Marra *et al.*, 2005; Jonzén *et al.*, 2006; Rubolini *et al.*, 2007), which is explained by their advanced timing of migration in response to warming temperatures in southern and central Europe during the migration window (Ahola *et al.*, 2004; Both and te Marvelde, 2007). Even so, long-distance migrants generally have responded less to warming with their arrival dates than short-distance migrants (Lehikoinen *et al.*, 2004; Rubolini *et al.*, 2007), and whether they show a response mostly depends on whether conditions en route at the time of travelling have improved.

The limited change in migration timing of long-distance migrants in comparison to the advanced phenology of their breeding habitats makes them more vulnerable to mismatches with food abundance than residents and short-distance migrants. Within migrants across Europe, species with the smallest advancement in spring arrival had declined most by the end of the twentieth century (Møller *et al.*, 2008). If a trophic mismatch with food availability for the offspring lies at the heart of the matter, we expect this to differ between habitats, depending on how food availability changes throughout the season. Fitness penalties associated with breeding at exactly the right time are most severe when the timing is out of sync. Indeed, we found evidence for habitat differences in long-term population trends of bird species that were consistent with the notion of increased trophic mismatches mainly affecting long-distance migrants in more seasonal habitats (Both *et al.*, 2010). Comparing Dutch forests and marshlands revealed narrow food peaks for insectivorous birds in the former, whereas marshland had an extended period of insect abundance over much of the spring and summer. All long-distance migrants in the forest declined; short-distance migrants and residents did not show systematic declines (Fig. 17.4a). In the less seasonal marshlands we found no systematic decline in long-distance migrants, nor any difference in trends between groups with different migration strategy. That timing relative to the food peak could be a reason for the decline in forest migrants was suggested by the strong correlation between arrival date and population trend: the later a species arrived in spring, the more it declined (Fig. 17.4c). The habitat differences in trends were also found in some generalist migratory species: they declined more in forest and increased in numbers in marshland (Fig. 17.4b). As with the habitat-related population trends of pied flycatchers, generalist species may have changed their habitat preference from forest to marsh. If so, this may have been triggered by marshland becoming better in comparison to forest, which could be due to forests deteriorating, marshlands improving, or both. Because the specialised forest species also declined, and often steeply so (up to 85% decline in the icterine warbler *Hippolais icterina*), there is reason to believe that for these species the forest habitat must have lost much of its attraction. In contrast, many resident and short-distance migrants, which generally breed earlier than long-distance migrants, have shown increases in the forest habitat, suggesting that the habitat per se did not decline in quality (Both *et al.*, 2010). It is unlikely that these effects were strongly mediated through habitat change in the winter: also within generalist species the decline was much stronger in the forest compared to the marsh. Changes in habitat suitability caused by differential phenological responses resulting from climate change are in general expected especially in habitats with strong seasonality, and for species that are least flexible in adjusting their phenology to changes at other trophic levels.

Dispersal as adaptation to climate change

If habitats become less suitable because birds increasingly miss the local food peak, then dispersal to areas where the food peak matches their breeding phenology is an option. This might take place on a small spatial scale, as was discussed for pied flycatchers that *could* choose between nearby areas differing in food peak dates. But dispersal on larger spatial scales is equally possible: if Dutch pied flycatchers arrive too late on their former breeding grounds, why then not continue migration to more northerly sites? Their migration speed is much higher than the 'speed' with which spring moves northwards, and by

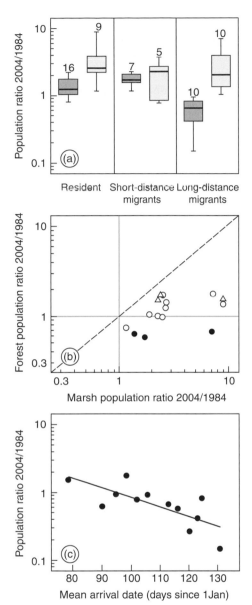

Figure 17.4 (a) Population trends of passerines in Dutch forests and marshlands between 1984 and 2004 for species with different migration behaviour. Results GLM: interaction habitat*migration status: $F_{2,51} = 6.16$, $p = 0.004$ (dark boxes: forest, pale boxes: marsh; numbers refer to number of species). (b) Within-species comparison of population trends in forests and marshes, showing that within species long-distance migrants decline stronger in forests than in marshes (open triangles: residents, open circles: short-distance migrants, filled circles: long-distance migrants). GLM: dependent variable – forest growth rate, explanatory variables: marsh growth rate: $F_{1,11} = 7.08$, $p = 0.022$, migration status: $F_{2,11} = 18.49$, $p < 0.001$, interaction: $F_{2,9} = 0.82$, $p = 0.47$. (c) Population trends of migratory passerines living in forests and their spring arrival date at the breeding grounds. Later arriving species declined most (GLM: mean arrival date: $F_{1,10} = 12.41$, $p = 0.006$). Population trends are expressed as the ratio of the densities present in 2004 relative to 1984, which is based on the annual population growth rates (1 = stable, 0.1 is a 90% decline, 10 is a tenfold increase). Population trends are from the Dutch Breeding Bird Monitoring Programme. Arrival data are based on the first three males arriving annually at a study site in Drenthe (northern Netherlands). After Both *et al.* (2010).

selecting a more northerly located breeding site they should be able to restore the match between their own phenology and the phenology of chick food (Fig. 17.5). Evidence for directional dispersal in response to phenological mismatches is non-existent, and data on long-distance dispersal are generally mostly anecdotal. Using stable isotope ratios from feathers moulted in the

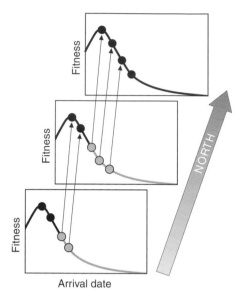

Figure 17.5 Hypothetical changes in fitness consequences of breeding date at different latitudes, and how birds may move depending on their timing of arrival. Within each area, the curve gives the hypothetical change in fitness over the date. The black part could be the realised curve, because late birds may prefer to move northwards (arrows from grey to black symbols), rather than breed too late relative to the phenology in a southern area. If birds had complete freedom to move without costs, one would expect within areas only a narrow peak of arrival and laying dates, and no decline in fitness with date.

previous breeding season could allow such long-distance dispersal to be detected (Hobson *et al.*, 2004; Hobson, 2005; Studds *et al.*, 2008). The hydrogen/deuterium ratio, in particular, changes with latitude, and therefore could be used to pinpoint the breeding/natal origin of immigrant birds. The expectation would be that in warmer years, individuals disperse more often to higher latitudes, and that these immigrants also breed earlier than the philopatric individuals at these places.

It is an alluring idea that birds could disperse to areas with a better phenological match, but in practice this may have attendant difficulties. It is important to make a distinction between the importance for individuals to improve their reproductive success by dispersing, and the importance it could have for the evolutionary dynamics of local adaptation. To begin with the second point, the movement of a rather small number of individuals to other populations may introduce new genetic material on which selection can act, allowing evolutionary change. Migratory birds that do breed more to the north not only breed later in spring, but also migrate later from their wintering sites (Bell, 1996; Studds *et al.*, 2008; Langin *et al.*, 2009; Both, 2010a). If this latitudinal variation in migration time between breeding populations has a genetic background (Pulido *et al.*, 2001; Pulido and Berthold, 2004; Pulido, 2007), individuals dispersing to more northern breeding populations could introduce genes for earlier migration. This could have a selective advantage, as climate change advances the phenology of other parts of the ecosystem. Thus, if the population in which these new genes are introduced, is also mismatched with the phenology of main food sources, the immigrants bring genes for earlier arrival and earlier breeding, and therefore have a selective premium.

Any advantage, however, depends on how well these immigrants perform relative to the original population. In other words, how important local adaptation is with respect to other heritable traits and local knowledge of the area for successful breeding. In general, local residents perform better than immigrants (Bensch *et al.*, 1998; reviewed in Marr *et al.*, 2002), although in inbred populations immigrants may entail a fitness advantage (Marr *et al.*, 2002). Interestingly, in the example of the song sparrows *Melospiza melodia* of Mandarte Island, immigrants had higher fitness in this inbred population, but their descendants had much lower fitness, which was attributed to their lack of locally adapted gene-complexes (Marr *et al.*, 2002). Philopatric individuals could have higher fitness because they have the residents' advantage of familiarity with the area, and they have lower costs in searching for important resources like nest sites (Parn *et al.*, 2009). Several studies found that immigrant males performed worse than philopatric males, whereas no difference was found among females (Bensch *et al.*, 1998; Parn *et al.*, 2009). This suggests that local experience may have a larger effect on immigrant fitness than local genetic adaptation.

As far as I know there are no studies examining fitness consequences of long-distance dispersers, because the origin of most dispersers is unknown, and most likely the majority originates from nearby sites. In contrast to short-distance dispersal, long-distance dispersers may in fact perform more poorly because they lack locally adapted genes. Long-distance dispersers could introduce new genes for earlier migration that allow a population to adapt to advances in the phenology of their habitat but, conversely, these immigrants may also have genes that are disadvantageous in their new breeding area. The success from an evolutionary perspective will evidently depend on the balance between such advantages and disadvantages, and translocation experiments are needed to examine this balance for immigrating individuals.

Another problem may arise from the spatial variation in phenology changes across the breeding areas. Whereas Dutch birds have become mismatched with their primary food source, Swedish birds probably have not, because spring temperatures did not rise so steeply there (Both *et al.*, 2004; Both and te Marvelde, 2007). In fact, if immigrants of southern origin arrive in these more northern places before the arrival of the philopatric individuals, they may encounter detrimental ecological circumstances because it is too cold for most insects to be active, and hence insectivorous birds may starve (Møller, 1994; Brown and Brown, 2000; Newton, 2007). Furthermore, in these more northern areas long-distance migrants arrive with larger body stores as an insurance against more adverse circumstances at arrival (Sandberg and Moore, 1996). This means that birds aiming to continue migration to more northern areas should obtain these stores before moving on.

The logic of latitudinal dispersal as an adaptation to climate change may be appealing, but in reality it may have drawbacks. There is abundant evidence that the decline in reproductive success over the season is a general phenomenon operating in the absence of climate change that is related to late birds being generally mismatched with the local food peak (Lack, 1966; Siikamäki, 1998; Charmantier *et al.*, 2008; Verhulst and Nilsson, 2008). Late arriving and late breeding individuals with poor success continue to persist in populations (Fig. 17.5), whereas (especially in migratory species) they also could have moved to a more northerly site and bred there in synchrony with the food peak. This suggests that the costs of continuation of migration must be rather high. However, there is some compelling evidence for latitudinal (or altitudinal) dispersal related to timing of spring migration from North America. American redstarts *Setophaga ruticilla* that spent the winter in the richest territories departed first in spring and subsequently selected breeding areas to the south of areas where they were born the previous year. In contrast, individuals wintering in low-quality habitat departed later, and tended to disperse to more northerly areas relative to their natal site (Studds *et al.*, 2008). Within the same breeding habitat, redstarts that had wintered in high-quality habitat arrived earlier in spring, bred earlier and hence fledged more offspring than those from low-quality winter habitat (Norris *et al.*, 2004). Thus, although the data on natal dispersal for this species suggested that birds can track the phenology of their breeding areas relative to their own departure date, it seems that many birds wintering in low-quality habitat should breed even further to the north in order to have timed their breeding season optimally. Their failure to do so suggests that the costs of dispersal could be too high, and/or that fitness in more southerly breeding areas is generally higher than in more northerly areas.

Habitat choice and local adaptation

Although we have little direct evidence that birds perform latitudinal dispersal to adapt to climate change, how much evidence is there in general that locally maladapted individuals show higher dispersal tendencies? The first problem we encounter here is how to define locally maladapted. Here I assume that young that grow poorly and/or hatch late in the season relative to the local food phenology are less well tuned to the local environment than other young, and therefore consider them locally maladapted. The question is whether these young are more likely to disperse to other areas? If this is so, the next question is whether these individuals are excluded from the better sites where they were born and therefore are 'forced' to disperse, or whether they disperse to areas that fit their needs better. Then we would expect that dispersal does indeed improve their fitness.

A number of studies have shown that young fledged in poor condition are more likely to disperse (Verhulst *et al.*, 1997; Tinbergen, 2005), and that individuals born late in the season disperse more (Pärt, 1990; Hansson *et al.*, 2002). However, examples for opposite patterns are available as well; sometimes early born fledglings disperse further, especially if in low condition (Altwegg *et al.*, 2000), or individuals in good condition can disperse more (Tilgar *et al.*, 2010), and date effects are not always found (Verhulst *et al.*, 1997). Most of these studies involve correlations between dispersal propensity/distance and phenotypic traits, not knowing the causes of individual variation and their effect on dispersal (but see Tinbergen, 2005). There are no studies that specifically addressed whether it is the locally maladapted individuals that disperse, which then also should show that these individuals are performing better in other habitats.

Costs and benefits of dispersal are not easily measured, especially because individuals that successfully immigrated into a population are normally compared with philopatric individuals, without taking the cost into account of finding and establishing a breeding territory elsewhere (Marr *et al.*, 2002; Møller *et al.*, 2006). Furthermore, studies of fitness consequences rarely measure all fitness components simultaneously, and again are mostly correlative (Doligez and Pärt, 2008). The fitness consequences of dispersal are variable when single fitness components are considered, but 8 out of 11 studies examining life-time reproductive success reported a decline in fitness of dispersing individuals of at least one sex (Doligez and Pärt, 2008). This suggests that dispersal is generally disadvantageous, but these fitness costs may be overestimated because dispersal tendency could have a genetic basis, and therefore young of dispersing individuals leave the study population more often, discounting the fitness of the dispersal genotype (Doligez and Pärt, 2008; Doligez *et al.*, 2009). Even if the fitness of dispersing individuals is generally lower, it still may be that for individuals that do disperse, their fitness is higher at the site of immigration, than at the natal site. Furthermore, there is the possibility that also for philopatric individuals, fitness is higher at another place, and the only way to discriminate these effects is by forcing individuals to disperse to another site, and measure the subsequent fitness consequences.

In our pied flycatcher study we found that chicks born later in the season dispersed further, which was even more pronounced in areas with an early tree phenology (Fig. 17.6). This suggests that young disperse more widely if they are locally maladapted with their hatching date to the local food peak, and therefore they grow up under low food conditions. For this reason one has to be cautious in interpreting trends towards higher local fitness penalties of breeding late as a maladaptive response to climate change (Both and Visser, 2001). Increased selection for early breeding may indeed even reduce local fitness (Charmantier *et al.*, 2008), but these changes in fitness consequences

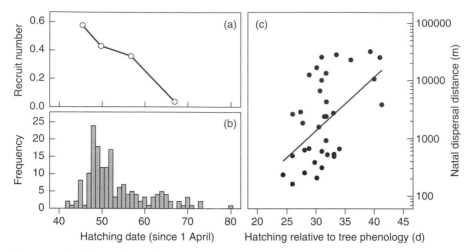

Figure 17.6 Effect of hatching date on local fitness (number of local recruits) (a) and natal dispersal distance (c) of pied flycatchers during the 2007 breeding season in Drenthe, the Netherlands. (b) gives the frequency distribution of hatching dates during this year. In 2007 the caterpillar peak was exceptionally early, with the peak date at 4 May. In (a) for each 25% percentile of hatching dates the mean number of recruits per brood is given (*y*-axis), and the mean hatch date for this group (*x*-axis). The *x*-axis in (c) gives the number of days between local budburst and hatching: higher values refer to larger asynchrony. Unpublished data.

are difficult to estimate if dispersal also changes at the same time, and especially late born young emigrate more due to their locally maladapted phenotype. The increased fitness penalty of breeding late could thus also partly be an adaptive response, because late young disperse to other habitats to which they are better adapted.

At this moment it is impossible to evaluate the different habitat selection options that birds face in order to successfully adjust their timing of breeding when they arrive too late to profit from the local food peak. Fitness evaluations can only be done if we are able to track long-distance dispersal (e.g. by using stable isotopes, Hobson, 2005) and relate this to the timing of the annual cycle. It also requires manipulation of individual birds, to force them to breed at other (more northerly) sites and compare their breeding success to that of birds breeding in their familiar area. Although this seems a daunting task for most species, we have successfully translocated pairs of pied flycatchers to other breeding sites where they eventually reproduced successfully under natural conditions (Burger and Both, 2011). This experimental setup allows the study of fitness consequences of alternative breeding sites, including the effects of unfamiliarity with the local habitat. The next step would be to perform this experiment, including controls, over longer distances: do birds translocated to more northerly breeding areas breed earlier than local birds, and what is their reproductive success in comparison to local, non-manipulated birds? For dispersal to be advantageous, and mistiming occurring at both sites, we expect translocated birds of southern origin to breed earlier at the northern release site than local birds, and to reproduce better than the controls in both capture and release sites. This result would indicate that dispersal is a viable option for adaptation to mismatched phenology resulting from climate change. The alternative would be that translocated birds perform worse than control birds, which would strongly suggest that long-distance dispersal may not be an easy way to adapt to climate change.

The evolutionary potential of long-distance dispersal not only depends on the fitness consequences for dispersers, but also on the timing of arrival and breeding being heritable. Evidence for additive genetic inheritance of laying date within populations is available for several bird species (van Noordwijk, 1984; Sheldon *et al.*, 2003), but it is not always found (Both and Visser, 2001). Within-population genetic variation, together with the among-population variation in laying date, especially along a latitudinal gradient (Sanz, 1997), would suggest that birds in the north breed later than more southerly breeding birds because they are genetically programmed to do so. For great tits there is evidence that, given exactly the same aviary conditions, individuals of southern origin do indeed breed at shorter photoperiods than individuals of northern origin (Silverin *et al.*, 1993); this difference in photoperiodic response could well have a genetic basis. For pied flycatchers, we found that the timing of spring migration through North Africa was related to latitude, but also to birth date; these effects interacted in a complicated way. In western Europe birth date had a clear positive effect on migration date, but the effect was reversed in northern Europe, where later-born individuals migrated earlier through North Africa in spring (Both, 2010a). As a potential mechanism I hypothesised that photoperiod at birth sets the individual annual clock, and birds from more southern origins (west Europe) are born before the longest day, and thus experience longer days the later they are born (Both, 2010a). For northern Europe the reverse is true: virtually all young are born after the solstice, and hence the later born birds experience shorter photoperiods. This possible effect of photoperiod at birth on annual timing has some experimental support (Coppack *et al.*, 2001), but requires further investigation. It is important in this context because if birds do disperse to more northerly sites, and the timing of the annual cycle is mostly determined by environmental conditions at the natal site, the young of these dispersers may not behave differently from the original birds at this site (apart from hatching earlier in the season). The phenotypic effect of birth date, via photoperiod on the timing of the annual cycle, may be a nice adaptation to breeding at different latitudes, and also to allow earlier migration, arrival and breeding if phenology changes directionally. But at the same time it may hamper (genetic) adaptation to changed circumstances by latitudinal dispersal, because the young of the dispersers may not be phenotypically very different from the local population.

Concluding remarks and future directions

Climate change has multiple effects on the suitability of habitats for bird species, and the change in phenology of essential resources for important life stages of birds has been emphasised here. For some bird species there is clear proof that the phenology of their food is changing at a different pace than the timing of breeding, but examples of both compensatory timing and increased mismatches are available. Meta-analyses in general show that invertebrate phenology advances more strongly than vertebrate phenology (Root *et al.*, 2003; Thackeray *et al.*, 2010), implying that trophic mismatches are expected to become more frequent with ongoing climate change (Visser and Both, 2005). The first population consequences of trophic mismatches are beginning to show themselves, albeit only in long-distance migrants because these species are probably least flexible in adjusting their timing sufficiently to changes in the underlying trophic levels (Both *et al.*, 2006; Møller *et al.*, 2008; Both *et al.*, 2010). There are several ways to adapt to changes in phenology, and a change in habitat selection is one of the most promising. This may occur at small spatial scales if phenology varies among habitats, but this would solve the problem only temporarily. Changes in habitat selection on larger spatial scales may allow birds to adapt to advances in phenology on longer time scales, but we need more data on the frequency of long-distance dispersal and the fitness consequences of the improved phenological match relative to potentially detrimental effects of lack of local (genetic) adaptation. Technological novelties to track long-distance dispersal, and translocation experiments to investigate fitness consequences of dispersal, will allow us to predict the adaptive ability of species to adjust to climate change.

Acknowledgements

Comments on earlier drafts from Rob Bijlsma, Claudia Burger, Theunis Piersma, James Pearce-Higgins and Ken Smith helped to improve this chapter. I would like to thank Rob Fuller for the invitation to contribute this chapter and for his comments. Dick Visser produced the figures.

References

Ahola, M., Laaksonen, T., Sippola, K. *et al.* (2004). Variation in climate warming along the migration route uncouples arrival and breeding date. *Glob. Change Biol.*, **10**, 1–8.

Ahola, M. P., Laaksonen, T., Eeva, T. and Lehikoinen, E. (2007). Climate change can alter competitive relationships between resident and migratory birds. *J. Anim. Ecol.*, **76**, 1045–1052.

Altwegg, R., Ringsby, T. H. and Saether, B. E. (2000). Phenotypic correlates and consequences of dispersal in a metapopulation of house sparrows *Passer domesticus*. *J. Anim. Ecol.*, **69**, 762–770.

Bauer, Z., Trnka, M., Bauerova, J. *et al.* (2010). Changing climate and the phenological response of great tit and collared flycatcher populations in floodplain forest ecosystems in Central Europe. *Int. J. Biometeorol.*, **54**, 99–111.

Bell, C. P. (1996). Seasonality and time allocation as causes of leap-frog migration in the Yellow Wagtail *Motacilla flava*. *J. Avian Biol.*, **27**, 334–342.

Bensch, S., Hasselquist, D., Nielsen, B. and Hansson, B. (1998). Higher fitness for philopatric than for immigrant males in a semi-isolated population of great reed warblers. *Evolution*, **52**, 877–883.

Böhning-Gaese, K. and Lemoine, N. (2004). Importance of climate change for the ranges, communities and conservation of birds. *Adv. Ecol. Res.*, **35**, 211–236.

Both, C. (2010a). Flexibility of timing of avian migration to climate change masked by environmental constraints en route. *Curr. Biol.*, **20**, 243–248.

Both, C. (2010b). Food availability, mistiming and climatic change. In *Effects of Climate Change on Birds*, ed. A. P. Møller, W. Fiedler and P. Berthold, pp. 129–147. Oxford: Oxford University Press.

Both, C., Artemyev, A. A., Blaauw, B. *et al.* (2004). Large-scale geographical variation confirms that climate change causes birds to lay earlier. *Proc. R. Soc. B*, **271**, 1657–1662.

Both, C., Bijlsma, R. G. and Visser, M. E. (2005). Climatic effects on spring migration and breeding in a long distance migrant. *J. Avian Biol.*, **36**, 368–373.

Both, C., Bouwhuis, S., Lessells, C. M. and Visser, M. E. (2006). Climate change and population declines in a long distance migratory bird. *Nature*, **441**, 81–83.

Both, C. and te Marvelde, L. (2007). Climate change and timing of avian breeding and migration throughout Europe. *Climate Res.*, **35**, 93–105.

Both, C., van Asch, M., Bijlsma, R. G., van den Burg, A. B. and Visser, M. E. (2009). Climate change and unequal phenological changes across four trophic levels: constraints or adaptations. *J. Anim. Ecol.*, **78**, 73–83.

Both, C., van Turnhout, C. A. M., Bijlsma, R. G. *et al.* (2010). Avian population consequences of climate change are most severe for long-distance migrants in seasonal habitats. *Proc. R. Soc. B*, **277**, 1259–1266.

Both, C. and Visser, M. E. (2001). Adjustment to climate change is constrained by arrival date in a long-distance migrant bird. *Nature*, **411**, 296–298.

Brotons, L. and Jiguet, F. (2010). Bird communities and climate change. In *Effects of Climate Change on Birds*, ed. A. P. Møller, W. Fiedler and P. Berthold, pp. 275–294. Oxford: Oxford University Press.

Brown, C. R. and Brown, M. B. (2000). Weather-mediated natural selection on arrival time in cliff swallows (*Petrochelidon pyrrhonota*). *Behav. Ecol. Sociobiol.*, **47**, 339–345.

Burger, C. and Both, C. (2011). Translocation as a novel approach to study effects of (dispersal to) a new breeding habitat on reproductive output in wild birds. *Plos One*, **6**(3) e18143. doi:10.1371/journal.pone.0018143

Charmantier, A., McCleery, R. H., Cole, L. R. *et al.* (2008). Adaptive phenotypic plasticity in response to climate change in a wild bird population. *Science*, **320**, 800–803.

Coppack, T., Pulido, F. and Berthold, P. (2001). Photoperiod response to early hatching in a migratory bird species. *Oecologia*, **128**, 181–186.

Cresswell, W. and McCleery, R. H. (2003). How great tits maintain synchronization of their hatch date with food supply in response to long-term variability in temperature. *J. Anim. Ecol.*, **72**, 356–366.

Doligez, B., Gustafsson, L. and Pärt, T. (2009). 'Heritability' of dispersal propensity in a patchy population. *Proc. R. Soc. B*, **276**, 2829–2836.

Doligez, B. and Pärt, T. (2008). Estimating fitness consequences of dispersal: a road to 'know-where'? Non-random dispersal and the underestimation of dispersers' fitness. *J. Anim. Ecol.*, **77**, 1199–1211.

Drent, R. H. (2006). The timing of birds' breeding seasons: the Perrins hypothesis revisited especially for migrants. *Ardea*, **94**, 305–322.

Forsman, J. T., Seppanen, J.-T. and Mönkkönen, M. (2002). Positive fitness consequences of interspecific interaction with a potential competitor. *Proc. R. Soc. B*, **269**, 1619–1623.

Gwinner, E. (1996). Circannual clocks in avian reproduction and migration. *Ibis*, **138**, 47–63.

Gwinner, E. and Helm, B. (2003). Circannual and circadian contribution to the timing of avian migration. In *Avian Migration*, ed. P. Berthold, E. Gwinner, and E. Sonnenschein, pp. 81–95. Berlin: Springer-Verlag.

Hansson, B., Bensch, S. and Hasselquist, D. (2002). Predictors of natal dispersal in great reed warblers: results from small and large census areas. *J. Avian Biol.*, **33**, 311–314.

Hobson, K. A. (2005). Using stable isotopes to trace long-distance dispersal in birds and other taxa. *Divers. Distrib.*, **11**, 157–164.

Hobson, K. A., Wassenaar, L. I. and Bayne, E. (2004). Using isotopic variance to detect long-distance dispersal and philopatry in birds: an example with Ovenbirds and American Redstarts. *Condor*, **106**, 732–743.

Hüppop, O. and Winkel, W. (2006). Climate change and timing of spring migration in the long-distance migrant *Ficedula hypoleuca* in central Europe: the role of spatially different temperature changes along migration routes. *J. Ornithol.*, **147**, 326–343.

Jonzén, N., Lindén, A., Ergon, T. *et al.* (2006). Rapid advance of spring arrival dates in long-distance migratory birds. *Science*, **312**, 1959–1961.

Lack, D. (1966). *Population Studies of Birds*. Oxford: Oxford University Press.

Langin, K. M., Marra, P. P., Nemeth, Z. *et al.* (2009). Breeding latitude and timing of spring migration in songbirds crossing the Gulf of Mexico. *J. Avian Biol.*, **40**, 309–316.

Lehikoinen, E., Sparks, T. H. and Zalakevicius, M. (2004). Arrival and departure dates. *Adv. Ecol. Res.*, **35**, 1–31.

Lehikoinen, E. and Sparks, T. H. (2010). Changes in migration. In *Effects of Climate Change on Birds*, ed. A. P. Møller, W. Fiedler and P. Berthold, pp. 89–112. Oxford: Oxford University Press.

Lundberg, A. and Alatalo, R. V. (1992). *The Pied Flycatcher*. London: Poyser.

Marr, A. B., Keller, L. F. and Arcese, P. (2002). Heterosis and outbreeding depression in descendants of natural immigrants to an inbred population of song sparrows (*Melospiza melodia*). *Evolution*, **56**, 131–142.

Marra, P. P., Francis, C. M., Mulvihill, R. S. and Moore, F. R. (2005). The influence of climate on the timing and rate of spring bird migration. *Oecologia*, **142**, 307–315.

Martin, T. E. (1995). Avian life-history evolution in relation to nest sites, nest predation, and food. *Ecol. Monogr.*, **65**, 101–127.

McCleery, R. H. and Perrins, C. M. (1998). ... temperature and egg-laying trends. *Nature*, **391**, 30–31.

Merino, S. and Møller, A. P. (2010). Host-parasite interactions and climate change. In *Effects of Climate Change on Birds*, ed. A. P. Møller, W. Fiedler and P. Berthold, pp. 213–226. Oxford: Oxford University Press.

Møller, A. P. (1994). Phenotype-dependent arrival time and its consequences in a migratory bird. *Behav. Ecol. Sociobiol.*, **35**, 115–122.

Møller, A. P., Flensted-Jensen, E. and Mardal, W. (2006). Dispersal and climate change: a case study of the Arctic tern *Sterna paradisaea*. *Glob. Change Biol.*, **12**, 2005–2013.

Møller, A. P., Rubolini, D. and Lehikoinen, A. (2008). Populations of migratory bird species that did not show a phenological response to climate change are declining. *P. Natl. Acad. Sci. USA*, **105**, 16195–16200.

Newton, I. (2007). Weather-related mass-mortality events in migrants. *Ibis*, **149**, 453–467.

Norris, D. R., Marra, P. P., Kyser, T. K., Sherry, T. W. and Ratcliffe, L. M. (2004). Tropical winter habitat limits reproductive success on the temperate breeding grounds in a migratory bird. *Proc. R. Soc. B*, **271**, 59–64.

Overgaard, R., Gemmel, P. and Karlsson, M. (2007). Effects of weather conditions on mast year frequency in beech (*Fagus sylvatica* L.) in Sweden. *Forestry*, **80**, 553–563.

Parn, H., Jensen, H., Ringsby, T. H., and Saether, B. E. (2009). Sex-specific fitness correlates of dispersal in a house sparrow metapopulation. *J. Anim. Ecol.*, **78**, 1216–1225.

Pärt, T. (1990). Natal dispersal in the Collared Flycatcher: possible causes and reproductive consequences. *Ornis Scand.*, **21**, 83–88.

Perrins, C. M. (1970). The timing of birds' breeding seasons. *Ibis*, **112**, 242–255.

Pulido, F. (2007). Phenotypic changes in spring arrival: evolution, phenotypic plasticity, effects of weather and condition. *Climate Res.*, **35**, 5–23.

Pulido, F. and Berthold, P. (2004). Microevolutionary response to climate change. *Adv. Ecol. Res.*, **35**, 151–183.

Pulido, F., Berthold, P., Mohr, G. and Querner, U. (2001). Heritability of the timing of autumn migration in a natural bird population. *Proc. R. Soc. B*, **268**, 953–959.

Robinson, R. A., Baillie, S. R. and Crick, H. Q. P. (2007). Weather-dependent survival: implications of climate change for passerine population processes. *Ibis*, **149**, 357–364.

Root, T. L., Price, J. T., Hall, K. R. *et al.* (2003). Fingerprints of global warming on wild animals and plants. *Nature*, **421**, 57–60.

Rubolini, D., Møller, A. P., Rainio, K. and Lehikoinen, E. (2007). Assessing intraspecific consistency and geographic variability in temporal trends of spring migration phenology among European bird species. *Climate Res.*, **35**, 135–146.

Sandberg, R. and Moore, F. R. (1996). Fat stores and arrival on the breeding grounds: reproductive consequences for passerine migrants. *Oikos*, **77**, 577–581.

Sanz, J. J. (1997). Geographic variation in breeding parameters of the Pied Flycatcher *Ficedula hypoleuca*. *Ibis*, **139**, 107–114.

Sanz, J. J. (1998). Effect of habitat and latitude on nestling diet of Pied Flycatchers *Ficedula hypoleuca*. *Ardea*, **86**, 81–86.

Sanz, J. J., Potti, J., Moreno, J., Merino, S. and Frias, O. (2003). Climate change and fitness components of a migratory bird breeding in the Mediterranean region. *Glob. Change Biol.*, **9**, 461–472.

Schmidt, K. A. and Ostfeld, R. S. (2008). Numerical and behavioral effects within a pulse-driven system: Consequences for shared prey. *Ecology*, **89**, 635–646.

Schmidt, K. A., Rush, S. A. and Ostfeld, R. S. (2008). Wood thrush nest success and post-fledging survival across a temporal pulse of small mammal abundance in an oak forest. *J. Anim. Ecol.*, **77**, 830–837.

Seppanen, J. T. and Forsman, J. T. (2007). Interspecific social learning: novel preference can be acquired from a competing species. *Curr. Biol.*, **17**, 1248–1252.

Sheldon, B. C., Kruuk, L. E. B. and Merila, J. (2003). Natural selection and inheritance of breeding time and clutch size in the collared flycatcher. *Evolution*, **57**, 406–420.

Siikamäki, P. (1995). Habitat quality and reproductive traits in the pied flycatcher – an experiment. *Ecology*, **76**, 308–312.

Siikamäki, P. (1998). Limitation of reproductive success by food availability and breeding time in pied flycatchers. *Ecology*, **79**, 1789–1796.

Silverin, B., Massa, R. and Stokkan, K. A. (1993). Photoperiodic adaptation to breeding at different latitudes in Great Tits. *Gen. Comp. Endocr.*, **90**, 14–22.

Slagsvold, T. (1975). Competition between the great tit *Parus major* and the pied flycatcher *Ficedula hypoleuca* in the breeding season. *Ornis Scand.*, **6**, 179–190.

Slater, F. M. (1999). First-egg date fluctuations for the Pied Flycatcher *Ficedula hypoleuca* in the woodlands of mid-Wales in the twentieth century. *Ibis*, **141**, 497–499.

Smith, R. J. and Moore, F. R. (2005). Arrival timing and seasonal reproductive performance in a long-distance migratory landbird. *Behav. Ecol. Sociobiol.*, **57**, 231–239.

Spitzer, G. (1972). Jahreszeitliche Aspekte der Biologie der Bartmeise (*Panurus biarmicus*). *J. Ornithol.*, **113**, 241–275.

Studds, C. E., Kyser, T. K. and Marra, P. P. (2008). Natal dispersal driven by environmental conditions interacting across the annual cycle of a migratory songbird. *P. Natl. Acad. Sci. USA*, **105**, 2929–2933.

Thackeray, S. J., Sparks, T. H., Frederiksen, M. *et al.* (2010). Trophic level asynchrony in rates of phenological change for marine, freshwater and terrestrial environments. *Glob. Change Biol.*, **16**, 3304–3316.

Tilgar, V., Mand, R., Kilgas, P. and Magi, M. (2010). Long-term consequences of early ontogeny in free-living Great Tits *Parus major*. *J. Ornithol.*, **151**, 61–68.

Tinbergen, J. M. (2005). Biased estimates of fitness consequences of brood size manipulation through correlated effects on natal dispersal. *J. Anim. Ecol.*, **74**, 1112–1120.

van Noordwijk, A. J. (1984). Quantitative genetics in natural populations of birds illustrated with examples from the Great Tit, *Parus major*. In *Population Biology and Evolution*, ed. K. Woehrmann, and V. Loeschke, pp. 67–79. Heidelberg: Springer.

Verhulst, S. and Nilsson, J. A. (2008). The timing of birds' breeding seasons: a review of experiments that manipulated timing of breeding. *Phil. Trans. R. Soc. B*, **363**, 399–410.

Verhulst, S., Perrins, C. M. and Riddington, R. (1997). Natal dispersal of great tits in a patchy environment. *Ecology*, **78**, 864–872.

Visser, M. E., Adriaensen, F., van Balen, J. H. *et al.* (2003). Variable responses to large-scale climate change in European *Parus* populations. *Proc. R. Soc. B*, **270**, 367–372.

Visser, M. E. and Both, C. (2005). Shifts in phenology due to global climate change: the need for a yardstick. *Proc. R. Soc. B*, **272**, 2561–2560.

Visser, M. E., Both, C. and Lambrechts, M. M. (2004). Global climate change leads to mistimed avian reproduction. *Adv. Ecol. Res.*, **35**, 89–110.

Visser, M. E., Holleman, L. J. M. and Gienapp, P. (2006). Shifts in caterpillar biomass phenology due to climate change and its impact on the breeding biology of an insectivorous bird. *Oecologia*, **147**, 167–172.

Visser, M. E., van Noordwijk, A. J., Tinbergen, J. M. and Lessells, C. M. (1998). Warmer springs lead to mistimed reproduction in great tits (*Parus major*). *Proc. R. Soc. B*, **265**, 1867–1870.

Wesołowski, T. and Maziarz, M. (2009). Changes in breeding phenology and performance of Wood Warblers *Phylloscopus sibilatrix* in a primeval forest: a thirty-year perspective. *Acta Ornithol.*, **44**, 69–80.

Wesołowski, T., Rowiński, P. and Maziarz, M. (2009). Wood Warbler *Phylloscopus sibilatrix*: a nomadic insectivore in search of safe breeding grounds? *Bird Study*, **56**, 26–33.

Winkel, W. and Hudde, H. (1997). Long-term trends in reproductive traits of tits (*Parus major, P. caeruleus*) and Pied flycatchers *Ficedula hypoleuca*. *J. Avian Biol.*, **28**, 187–190.

CHAPTER EIGHTEEN

Australian birds in a changing landscape: 220 years of European colonisation

TARA G. MARTIN
CSIRO Ecosystem Sciences, Queensland
CARLA P. CATTERALL
Griffith University, Queensland
ADRIAN D. MANNING
The Australian National University, Canberra

and

JUDIT K. SZABO
University of Queensland

European colonisation of the Australian continent has caused immense changes in birds and their habitats during a timespan of just 220 years. A diverse and unique range of ecosystems and avifaunas is today in a state of flux as some species manage to exploit new and modified environments, while others fail to adapt, decline in abundance and become regionally uncommon or extinct (Barnard, 1925; Barnard, 1934; Blakers *et al.*, 1984; Saunders and Curry, 1990; Recher, 1999; Barrett *et al.*, 2003). In this chapter we consider the history of human occupation and scale of landscape change in Australia, the distinctively evolved life-history characteristics and habitat relationships of Australian birds, the type of contemporary landscape variation within Australia, and the nature of bird species and community responses to landscape change. This chapter is by no means an exhaustive review of the bird ecology literature in Australia, but rather provides an insight into the major landscape changes throughout Australia as a result of European colonisation, with a focus primarily on its impact on terrestrial birds. We examine potential reasons for differences and similarities in avifaunal responses to landscape change between Australia and Europe. We also highlight recent approaches to developing unifying conceptual frameworks for the complex range of species' responses to landscape change within Australia, and outline their broad relevance to guiding efforts to conserve and restore bird populations and their habitats in Europe and elsewhere.

Birds and Habitat: Relationships in Changing Landscapes, ed. Robert J. Fuller. Published by Cambridge University Press. © Cambridge University Press 2012.

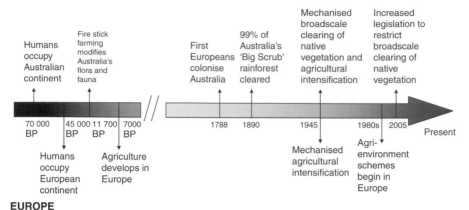

Figure 18.1 Selective time scale of human occupation and major landscape changes in Australia and Europe. Note that clearing of 'Big Scrub' rainforest is but one example of many cases of rapid extensive local land-clearing across the Australian continent.

History of habitat change and human occupation: Australia vs. Europe

The history of anthropogenic landscape change in Australia differs substantially from that of Europe (Fig. 18.1). Australia is estimated to have been occupied by humans for as long as 60 000–70 000 years (Briscoe and Smith, 2002). By the late Holocene the native vegetation of large areas had been transformed as a result of 'fire stick farming', a technique used by Aboriginal people to burn vegetation to facilitate hunting, food gathering and movement through the landscape (Archer *et al.*, 1991; Bowman, 2000). The practice of fire stick farming over thousands of years altered the composition of plants and animals and has been linked with megafaunal extinctions in the Pleistocene (Miller *et al.*, 2005). By the time European ships were regularly sighted along the horizon (*c.* 1700s), most Australian vegetation and fauna were well adapted to fire.

The first long-term European settlers arrived in 1788 and by the mid 1800s the Australian landscape was undergoing a new type of transformation. As settlement expanded during the 1800s, forests and woodlands were harvested for their timber and converted to agricultural areas or pasture for livestock (Hobbs and Hopkins, 1990). Large-scale mechanisation of farming practices followed World War II, resulting in an intensification of land clearing and agriculture involving fertilisation and cropping, sometimes accompanied by irrigation, across large parts of southern and eastern Australia (Fig. 18.2). In areas left uncleared, there has been extensive commercial grazing by introduced livestock, and the local extirpation of Aboriginal people has resulted in large changes to fire regimes (Woinarski and Catterall, 2004). These impacts,

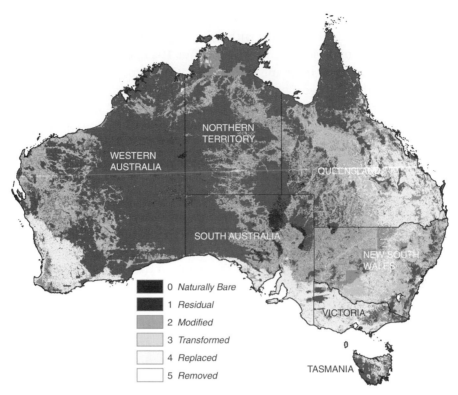

Figure 18.2 Human-induced vegetation change across Australia as depicted by the Vegetation Assets, States and Transitions (VAST) database V.2 (Thackway and Lesslie, 2008; Lesslie *et al.*, 2010), depicting six states of vegetation condition: 0 Naturally bare (e.g. bare mud, salt freshwater lakes), 1 Residual (e.g. ungrazed grassy woodlands, native grasslands, old growth forest), 2 Modified (e.g. low to moderately grazed grassy woodlands and grasslands), 3 Transformed (e.g. intensive native forestry, heavily grazed grassy woodlands and riparian vegetation), 4 Replaced (severe invasions of introduced weeds, cropping, sown pastures), 5 Removed (e.g. urban and industrial landscape).

together with an increasing rate of introduction and invasion by alien plant and animal species, have caused rapid and extensive changes to the quality and quantity of bird habitats (Saunders *et al.*, 1990; Recher, 1991; Kingsford, 2000; Maron and Lill, 2005; Martin and McIntyre, 2007; Paton *et al.*, 2009). On 'by far the oldest, most infertile, most nutrient-leached soils of any continent' (Diamond, 1998, p. 303) the desire to produce sufficient food and fibre to meet the needs of several times its own human population (Henzell, 2007) has had unintended consequences for Australian birds and their habitats.

By comparison, the earliest human occupation of Europe is estimated to have occurred 40 000–45 000 years ago (Anikovich *et al.*, 2007) and agriculture developed progressively over at least 7000 years (Edwards and Hirons, 1984). Mechanisation of agriculture along with a growing population led to increasing intensification of agricultural practices after 1945 (Attwood *et al.*, 2009). For example, today most remnant native vegetation across Great Britain has been lost or highly modified (Simmons, 2001), along with many woodland and forest-dependent species and today even 'farmland specialist' species adapted to long-established traditional farming practices are under threat (Newton, 2004; Wilson *et al.*, 2009).

The Australian terrestrial avifauna differs from that of Europe in its higher alpha- and beta-diversity and uniqueness, the result of a deep evolutionary history that spans roughly 60 million years (Sibley and Monroe, 1990; Christidis and Boles, 2008) on ice-free land, and in the much shorter timespan of direct anthropogenic habitat change resulting from agricultural, pastoral or urban land uses. The avifauna of northern Europe is less diverse, much more recently assembled (largely in the past 10 000 years since recent Pleistocene glaciation), is similar to that of northern Asia and America, and has largely developed in tandem with human agriculture. Consequently, while a substantial part of Europe's bird conservation effort has been oriented around sustaining a 'farmland-specialist avifauna' or at least a 'cultural-landscape avifauna', Australia's focus has been on avoiding a situation where avian specialists of pre-European habitats are lost, leaving only a depauperate 'newly-formed farmland avifauna'.

The distinctive nature of Australia's avifauna and habitats

Before considering how recent anthropogenic habitat change has affected the avifauna, it is helpful to consider the evolutionary history, pre-European diversity and ecological distinctiveness of Australian birds and their habitats. The Australian avifauna has a high level of endemism (Sibley and Ahlquist, 1990; Christidis and Boles, 2008) amongst its approximately 760 bird species. Australia separated from the Antarctic supercontinent Gondwana approximately 45 million years ago (Cracraft, 1972), broadly coinciding with the end of the dinosaur era, and began to drift northwards, isolated by surrounding ocean. Australia's distinctive avifauna includes a very diverse radiation of old endemic passerines, and a high diversity of parrots and pigeons (Sibley and Ahlquist, 1990; Geffen and Yom-Tov, 2000).

Rainforest was the dominant vegetation across the continent until around 20 million years ago, when the climate became more arid (Bowman, 2000), and the more open and fire-prone present-day native sclerophyll vegetation (characterised in particular by eucalypts and acacias) and its biota evolved and spread across much of the land surface. By this time, Australia had also moved sufficiently closer to Asia to receive new avian immigrants of northern origin, such as the genus *Corvus* and other passerines of the parvorder Passerida

(Sibley and Ahlquist, 1985; Sibley and Monroe, 1990). During the Pleistocene, while Europe experienced cycles of glaciation, Australian weather cycled between drier and moister periods.

By recent times, rainforest and its specialised avifauna had contracted to relatively small pockets near the eastern coast of the mainland and in Tasmania, moist eucalypt forests and heathlands were restricted to the east, southeast and southwest margins of the continent, and most of the continent supported different types of drought-adapted vegetation, including open eucalypt woodland, savanna, semi-arid grasslands, shrublands and desert. These major vegetation differences are associated with high turnover in bird species composition (Ford, 1989). Most Australian vegetation contains common tree and shrub species that are pollinated by birds and other vertebrates, and consequently nectarivores are prominent in the Australian avifauna (Ford, 1989). Frugivory is seen mostly in rainforest birds (although some frugivores are also important seed dispersers in drier ecosystems) and granivory is most prominent in the grassland avifauna of subcoastal and inland regions. Southern regions show warm–cool seasonality (mainly without snowfall), while a wet–dry seasonality predominates in the northern half of the continent. Across Australia, rains fall predominantly during winter in the south (Mediterranean climate) and summer (monsoon) in the north (Szabo *et al.*, 2010). Moreover the climate across most of Australia is characterised by extremely high between-year rainfall variability, largely driven by the Pacific El Niño–Southern Oscillation cycle (Allen *et al.*, 1996). Therefore, the avifauna has evolved in a context of irregularly occurring periods of drought and flood, and associated large spatio-temporal fluctuations in resource availability (Ford, 1989).

Rainfall influences birds through its effects on plant growth, flowering, fruiting and insect abundance (Bennett and Owens, 2002), with differing post-rainfall time lags for each (Nix, 1974). In a number of arid-zone birds, spatio-temporal variation in rainfall is associated with great fluctuations in both local abundance and spatial distribution. Such population irruptions have been reported for some aerial-feeding insectivores (Lord, 1956; Recher *et al.*, 1983), grass-feeding granivores (Wyndham, 1983; Zann *et al.*, 1995; Zann, 1996), rodent-feeding raptors (Hobbs, 1971; Matheson, 1978; Twigg and Kay, 1994) and nectar-feeding honeyeaters (Ford and Paton, 1985; Recher and Davies, 1997). These fluctuations are driven by both movement and breeding.

Large-scale population movements also occur in waterbirds such as ducks, cormorants and pelicans, as rain replenishes wetlands, ephemeral inland waterholes and lakes, providing rich food resources (Dorfman and Kingsford, 2001). The scale of movement varies, from 1 to over 100 km (local nomads such as honeyeaters and finches), to much longer, even continental-scale nomadism, seen in some ducks, parrots and pigeons (Chan, 2001).

Rainfall may even be the proximate trigger for breeding in some species (Zann *et al.*, 1995), although photoperiod still plays a role (Bentley *et al.*, 2000). In arid zone species that have a fixed breeding season, the amount of rainfall affects clutch size and breeding success (Davies, 1986; Maclean, 1996).

Across all habitats and regions, Australian birds display a wide range of different movement patterns: residency, migration, partial migration and nomadism (Rowley, 1975; Ford, 1989; Bennett and Owens, 1997). In regions that lack distinct seasonality, there are many resident, sedentary species (Rowley and Russell, 1997). While nomadism is prevalent throughout arid Australia, there is also a substantial sedentary bird community whose spatial distribution is more closely tied to vegetation type than particular resource pulses (Pavey and Nano, 2009). Australian bird species have relatively small clutch sizes and an extended fledging period, and are more likely than northern hemisphere birds to be cooperative breeders (Arnold and Owens, 1998; Geffen and Yom-Tov, 2000). The frequent occurrence of cooperative breeding in the parvorder Corvida suggests that it is an ancestral trait among Australian passerines (Russell, 1989; Cockburn, 1996). Cooperative breeders are generally sedentary, territorial and long-lived (Ford *et al.*, 1988). Especially in the east, latitudinal summer–winter migration patterns are also common (Chan, 2001; Griffioen and Clark, 2002). Partial migration, when some individuals of a species migrate, while others are sedentary, is typical for about a third of Australian landbirds (Chan, 2001). This has created differing patterns of avian seasonality: in the south, migrants generally appear in summer, whereas further north there is regular within-year turnover between summer immigrants, winter immigrants and passage migrants.

Hollow nesting is another prominent feature of Australian birds, with approximately 20% relying on hollows to nest, twice the proportion of European and North American bird fauna. Amongst hollow users are cockatoos, most parrots and owls, as well as many passerines (Saunders *et al.*, 1982; Ford *et al.*, 2001; Saunders *et al.*, 2003). Hollows generally form in the trunks and branches of mature trees and have become scarce in some regions as trees are cleared to make way for agricultural, pastoral and peri-urban development.

The diversity of Australian birds is a reflection of a unique and long evolutionary history and a high degree of natural heterogeneity across Australian ecosystems (Dwyer, 1972). Even superficially homogenous ecosystems contain internal heterogeneity, such as the strong differences in bird community composition that are found between riparian and upslope areas within eucalypt forests and woodlands (Bentley and Catterall, 1997; Mac Nally *et al.*, 2000; Palmer and Bennett, 2006). We now turn our discussion to understanding the human land-use changes that have been superimposed on this natural heterogeneity (Ford and Barrett, 1995).

Models of faunal response to anthropogenic landscape change

The general term 'habitat fragmentation' has been used to encompass a syndrome of changes that occur when the amount of any particular habitat in a landscape decreases, accompanied by an increase in the number of habitat patches, each of decreasing area and increasing isolation (Fahrig, 2003). Classical theories of habitat fragmentation view landscapes as binary mosaics, in which patches of one type of environment ('habitat') are surrounded by a matrix of a second type, which is unsuitable for use by the target species or species-group. Some Australian landscapes clearly fit this concept, especially cases where a substantial number of species are specialists of a habitat whose extent has been greatly reduced by either 'natural' or anthropogenic processes. Specialists of pre-European habitats include species that are confined to certain vegetation types whose recent spatial extent is limited, such as rainforest, heathland, wetland or grassland. Specialists of post-European habitat fragments are those which either avoid or cannot use the anthropogenic habitats of pasture grassland, cropland, tree plantation or urban development.

However, such fragmentation concepts alone do not adequately encompass the full range of anthropogenic habitat modification that has driven many recent avifaunal changes in some regions. Across much of Australia, habitats have been greatly altered, while still retaining many of their pre-European characteristics. For example, in the extensively cleared wheat–sheep zone of southern Australia, remnant original 'paddock' trees remain, while the understorey has been converted to sown exotic pasture or crops (Saunders and Ingram, 1987; Gibbons and Boak, 2002). In many grassy eucalypt woodlands of mid-northern Australia, the reverse is common, where the tree layer has been removed or thinned to promote the growth of native pasture for livestock, leaving a relatively intact native herbaceous layer (McIntyre and Martin, 2002; McIntyre et al., 2003). In savanna woodlands of the continent's far north, even more subtle habitat changes, associated with grazing and altered fire regimes in uncleared woodland, have been linked with substantial changes in the avifauna (Franklin, 1999). These types of vegetation modification create a form of spatial heterogeneity termed 'habitat variegation' (McIntyre and Hobbs, 1999); defined as 'landscapes dominated by original habitats that have been variously modified rather than extremely destroyed (p. 1283)'. In these landscapes the 'matrix', as defined in the classical fragmentation model, is either difficult to define spatially or can be used by so many species of the original habitat that the concept is severely limited in applicability (Manning et al., 2004a; Manning et al., 2006; Martin and McIntyre, 2007).

McIntyre and Hobbs (1999) proposed a 'landscape continuum' model to incorporate both the fragmentation and variegation viewpoints, based on the extent of landscape-scale habitat replacement (see Fig. 18.3) ranging

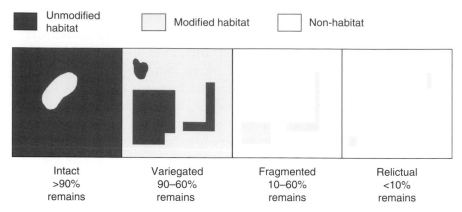

Figure 18.3 Landscape continuum model developed by McIntyre and Hobbs (1999) showing four states (intact, variegated, fragmented, relictual) of landscape alteration defined by the degree of habitat destruction and the degree of modification of remaining habitat.

from intact (>90% of habitat retained) to variegated (60–90%), then fragmented (10–60%) and finally relictual (<10% habitat retained). To illustrate this model's potential for representing bird–habitat relationships, Fig. 18.4 demonstrates how the occurrence of some typical woodland birds varies along the continuum from intact through to relictual landscapes.

Building on the landscape continuum model, Manning *et al.* (2004b) proposed the Continua-*Umwelt* landscape model that combines the individual perception and response of organisms to a landscape and different environmental, as well as spatial, continua. In addition, the concept also incorporates the trajectory of landscape change through time (Fig. 18.5). Similarly, Fischer *et al.* (2004) developed a landscape contour model to represent the suitability of habitat for individual species based on different environmental continua. These models emerging from research in Australian rural environments add conceptual complexity (there are as many landscapes as organisms) in order to better reflect reality. Landscape continua are also applicable to other regions of the world where ecosystems have been recently modified, without completely destroying native vegetation (e.g. many parts of the Americas and Eastern Europe). Examples of 'variegated' vegetation cover in areas that have been highly modified by humans for millennia (Manning *et al.*, 2004b) include shrubby 'ffridd' vegetation in Wales (Fuller *et al.*, 2006), wood-pastures in the UK (Peterken, 1996), dehesas in Spain (Díaz *et al.*, 1997) and isolated Scots pines *Pinus sylvestris* in Scotland (Brooker *et al.*, 2008).

In the following sections we review habitat use by Australian birds in intact-variegated and then fragmented-relictual landscapes. We then summarise recent findings about bird–habitat interactions across the Australian

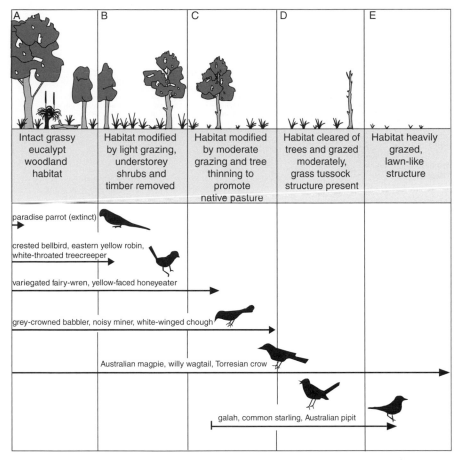

Figure 18.4 Landscape continua for birds in grassy eucalypt woodland. Grassy eucalypt woodlands are amongst the habitats most impacted by agriculture and development in Australia. Subsequently, their bird fauna has been severely impacted. We describe here the changes in a typical woodland bird species assemblage as grassy eucalypt woodland undergoes increasing modification from intact (inset A) to relictual landscapes (insets D–E) dominated by exotic pasture or herbaceous crops with <10% native vegetation. As the woodland is modified by grazing, clearing and thinning of native vegetation (insets B–D), bird species composition and abundance change as indicated by lines showing the range of habitats typically used by each species. The paradise parrot (*Psephotus pulcherrimus*) is an example of a species once dependent on intact woodland (inset A) that is now extinct. The eastern yellow robin (*Eopsaltria australis*) is amongst a group of woodland birds recorded in landscapes (A–B), but rarely C and not D and E, whereas the variegated fairy-wren (*Malurus lamberti*) and yellow-faced honeyeater (*Lichenostomus chrysops*) venture into C. The grey-crowned babbler and noisy miner (*Manorina melanocephala*) are amongst a group of species also found in landscapes moderately grazed by livestock and can benefit from some tree thinning (C). Several species, including Australian magpie (*Cracticus tibicen*) inhabit the entire continuum but at varying densities. The common starling *Sturnus vulgaris* (European introduction), and galah (*Eolophus roseicapillus*) profit from tree clearing and are found predominantly in C through E, along with grassland birds such as the Australian pipit (*Anthus novaeseelandiae*) (adapted from Martin and Green, 2002).

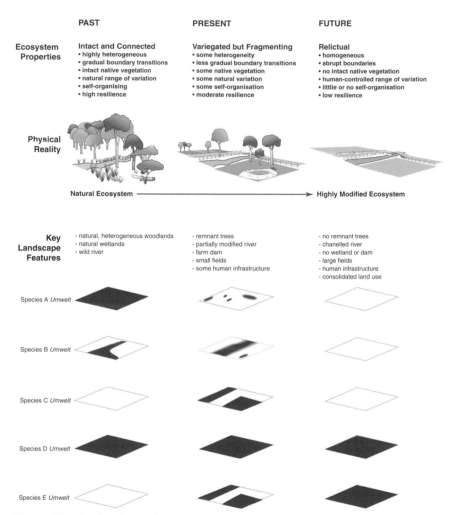

Figure 18.5 In the classic fragmentation model, a landscape is often represented as static (e.g. in the present), and is described from a human perspective (e.g. 'fragmented'). Parts of the landscape are seen as either habitat or non-habitat, and boundaries are abrupt. In contrast, the Continua–*Umwelt* landscape model (Manning *et al.*, 2004) takes into account changes in landscape and ecosystem properties through time, and different organisms' perceptions. In this illustration, the transition of physical reality from a natural ecosystem to a highly modified agricultural landscape through time is shown. This alternative approach encourages a consideration of the processes underpinning change. Different species will perceive and respond to this same landscape differently, and perception of habitat values, connectivity and boundary transitions will vary. The Continua–*Umwelt* landscape model reflects these differences, as illustrated here by five model species (A–E), where dark areas represent suitable habitat and white areas represent unsuitable habitat. Species A perceives all of the natural ecosystem as suitable habitat. In the fragmenting landscape, it perceives

continent and consider the implications of land-use change for the conservation of Australian birds. Nomenclature for bird species follows Christidis and
Boles (2008).

Bird responses to habitat change: intact to variegated landscapes

Variegated landscapes are widespread in Australia as a result of extensive
livestock grazing and pastoral practices across 70% of the continent
(Freudenberger and Landsberg, 2000; National Land and Water Audit, 2002).
In Fig. 18.2, variegated landscapes occur largely in regions mapped as residual,
modified and transformed. Impacts of livestock grazing on bird fauna can
result from complex interactions between the condition of the understorey
vegetation as a result of grazing intensity, altered fire management and the
thinning of the tree canopy to facilitate pasture growth (Martin and McIntyre,
2007). Livestock grazing and associated management have negative impacts
on particular suites of bird species (Saunders and Curry, 1990; Woinarski and
Ash, 2002; Maron and Lill, 2005; Martin and Possingham, 2005), especially
those dependent on the understorey for foraging and nesting (Martin and
Possingham, 2005). Livestock grazing and altered fire regimes are implicated
as causes of declines in granivorous birds across much of northern Australia
(Franklin, 1999; Franklin *et al.*, 2005).

Martin and McIntyre (2007) found that to some woodland bird species,
any form of commercial livestock grazing is detrimental, but extensively
managed, moderately grazed woodland areas can provide habitat for a rich
and abundant bird fauna including species that have declined elsewhere
in Australia. High grazing pressure on woodlands resulting in a short

---

Caption for Figure 18.5 (cont.)
habitat only associated with the remnant trees. In the relictual landscape, it perceives
no habitat. This species could be a woodland specialist. Species B perceives the wild
river and wetland as habitat in the natural ecosystem. In the fragmenting landscape, it
perceives habitat quality as reducing more gradually at river margins, and the farm
dam replaces some of the wetland habitat. In the relictual landscape, Species B does
not perceive any habitat. This species might be an aquatic or riparian organism.
Species C does not perceive any habitat in the natural ecosystem, but does consider
small fields as habitat in the fragmenting landscape. The relictual ecosystem provides
no habitat. This species represents one which depends on low-intensity agriculture,
but cannot persist in intensive agricultural landscapes. Species D perceives all
ecosystems as habitat, and this might represent an extreme habitat generalist. Species
E does not perceive the natural ecosystem as habitat, but begins to consider the small
fields in the fragmenting landscape as habitat. Finally it perceives all of the relictual
landscape as habitat. This species would represent an organism that is associated with
intensive agricultural practices and open landscapes.

lawn-like understorey structure, on the other hand, supported a depauperate bird assemblage dominated by common native and introduced birds that are increasing nationally (Barrett *et al.*, 2003). Woodlands that experience a low grazing pressure characterised by persistent native shrubs and native tussock-forming grasses contained richer and more abundant bird assemblages, suggesting that livestock exclusion will benefit most woodland bird species.

Across Australia's variegated landscapes it is difficult to know how closely present avifaunas resemble those of early pastoral times (Barnard, 1925; Barnard, 1934; Saunders and Curry, 1990; Woinarski and Catterall, 2004). However, it is likely that species most sensitive to livestock grazing, loss of large trees and their hollows, loss of vegetation on fertile lands and broadscale clearing elsewhere in Australia have already disappeared from these landscapes e.g. paradise parrot *Psephotus pulcherrimus*, crested bellbird *Oreoica gutturalis*. For other species, there may be a long time lag between livestock grazing, tree clearing and local bird extinction (Brooks *et al.*, 1999; Martin and McIntyre, 2007; Mac Nally, 2008).

The transition from variegated landscapes towards fragmented and relictual landscapes is driven by several factors. First, growing demand for livestock products and food stocks increases the pressure for extensive grazing operations to become more intensive, involving sowing of exotic pastures, fertilisation and irrigation (Krebs *et al.*, 1999; Food and Agriculture Organization, 2002; Martin and McIntyre, 2007). A second driver is the spread of pasture species beyond their original sown extent (Martin *et al.*, 2006a). Species such as buffel grass *Cenchrus ciliaris* and gamba grass *Andropogon gayanus*, selected for their ability to withstand fire and variable rainfall, were introduced throughout Australia's rangelands to improve pastures. Now large areas of high biodiversity value, including national parks and conservation reserves, are under threat of colonisation and dominance by these species (Grice, 2006). Once they have colonised, these grasses facilitate hot-burning fires which kill competitors such as trees, shrubs and seedlings, and further encourage the colonising grass (Smyth *et al.*, 2009). A third driver that threatens to transform variegated landscapes to fragmented and relictual landscapes is peri-urban encroachment, which is replacing both agricultural and pastoral land close to major urban centres (Greene and Stager, 2001). Peri-urbanisation has the potential to both intensify the use of these areas and force agriculture and grazing into less-fertile landscapes, which currently act as important refuges for many bird species. While some birds will be able to exploit these novel habitats, evidence suggests that most species of conservation concern will be negatively impacted by further intensification of grassy woodland landscapes (Catterall *et al.*, 1998; Martin and McIntyre, 2007).

Bird responses to habitat change: fragmented to relictual landscapes

Patterns of avian response to habitat loss and fragmentation

Detectable effects of habitat fragmentation on the Australian avifauna are both ancient and recent. Extensive rainforests 5–20 million years ago supported a diverse vertebrate fauna that is now largely extinct, due to subsequent climate-driven contraction and fragmentation of rainforest areas (Archer *et al.*, 1991). In some parts of eastern and northern Australia, relict islands of dense rainforest habitat now occur within the strikingly different habitat of open eucalypt forest. The smaller, more scattered rainforest patches that occur in drier regions support a narrower range of rainforest specialist bird species, and contain more eucalypt-associated species, than in the moister regions, where more extensive rainforest cover has been sustained over time (Howe *et al.*, 1981; Kikkawa *et al.*, 1981). The persistence of rainforest-associated bird species in small patches may also depend on the extent of habitat cover in the surrounding landscape. For example, some mobile frugivores occupy rainforest patches in the northern savannas only if the aggregate rainforest cover in other patches around them is more than 0.4% of the land area within a radius of 50 km (Price *et al.*, 1999). The contraction of ancient rainforests paved the way for the subsequent evolution of the distinctive eucalypt forest avifauna, and the resulting present-day avian diversity in landscapes that contain both vegetation types.

Most understanding of habitat fragmentation in Australia relates to the changes resulting from European settlement. Fragmented and relictual landscapes derived from human land use are concentrated in the moister or more fertile parts of the continent (the east, southeast and southwest, Fig. 18.2), where forests and woodland have been extensively cleared, resulting in a landscape matrix of crop production, livestock grazing and human settlement.

The consequences for avifauna of this habitat loss and fragmentation have been documented most comprehensively for the relictual eucalypt woodlands of southern Australia's wheat and sheep-growing regions found throughout Western Australia, South Australia and Victoria (Fig. 18.2) (Saunders and Curry, 1990; Saunders and Ingram, 1995). Targeted by early European settlers for their fertile soils, these landscapes have been dramatically modified (Beadle, 1981; Yates and Hobbs, 1997; Landsberg, 2000). For example, in southeastern Australia, 92% of box-gum grassy woodlands have been cleared, and of those remaining, less than 5% is considered to be in 'good' condition (Threatened Species Scientific Committee, 2006). Because of their high value for agriculture, temperate woodlands are also poorly represented in the formal reserve system (Department of Arts Heritage and the Environment,

2006). These regions now have many similarities with human-modified agricultural landscapes in Europe.

In the wheat–sheep belt of Western Australia (14 million ha), where 93% of native vegetation has been converted to agriculture in the past 120 years, there has been a decline in abundance and/or distribution in 49% of the 195 bird species of the region, whereas 17% of species increased in abundance and/or distribution (Saunders and Curry, 1990; Saunders and Ingram, 1995). These changes in bird abundance and distribution are attributed to clearing of native vegetation, provision of water (livestock troughs), new sources of food (crops), introductions of animal and plant species, livestock grazing or a combination of these factors, as opposed to fluctuations in climate (Saunders and Ingram, 1995).

In the Northern Plains of Victoria, where the median tree cover across replicate landscapes (mean size 277 km^2) was 3.7%, Bennett and Ford (1997) found substantial loss of bird species in landscapes entirely cleared of woodland. The rate of change of bird species richness relative to landscape tree cover was greatest in the final stages of habitat loss, leading the authors to conclude that a major decline in woodland species was underway.

Further examples of relictual landscapes are those formed by clearing of lowland rainforest in subtropical eastern Australia. For example, over 99% of a once-continuous 750 km^2 of rainforest was cleared from the 'Big Scrub' (northeastern New South Wales) in about 50 years prior to the early 1900s. Historical records reveal large declines in fruit-eating pigeons, which depended on these lowland forests for a winter food supply (Date *et al.*, 1996). Interestingly, in this case some recovery was evident by the early 2000s, in association with widespread re-growth dominated by camphor laurel *Cinnamomum camphora*, an exotic fruit-bearing tree (Neilan *et al.*, 2006). In other relictual rainforest landscapes, Howe *et al.*, (1981) and Warburton (1997) reported a range of species-specific abundance responses to decreasing remnant patch size, ranging from high area-sensitivity to a high tolerance of fragmentation.

Processes of avian response to habitat loss and fragmentation

Anthropogenic habitat fragmentation has been researched in a variety of landscapes, and area sensitivity of habitat specialists has been shown in a number of situations (Table 18.1). However, we know much more about the response patterns than we do about the various processes causing them. For example, there is ongoing debate over the role of local habitat vs. landscape-scale factors and the role of total habitat cover vs. its spatial configuration (Major *et al.*, 2001; Radford *et al.*, 2005; Hannah *et al.*, 2007; Ford *et al.*, 2009). It is clear that converting a large proportion of a landscape from one habitat to another will have equally large consequences for the landscape-scale bird

Table 18.1 *Mechanisms of bird species' response to habitat fragmentation in Australian case studies*

Mechanism	Type of bird	Examples of studies investigating the specific mechanism
Direct effects:		
Sedentary species undergo demographic stochastic population extinctions in small patches.	*Malurus, Climacteris*	Brooker and Brooker, 2003; Radford and Bennett, 2004
Local behavioural or population response following altered habitat structure in remnants.	Some hollow-nesters; understorey species (e.g. *Melanodryas, Climacteris*)	Martin and Possingham, 2005; Mac Nally and Horrocks, 2007; Ford *et al.*, 2009
Highly mobile species respond to landscape-scale resource loss, including wetlands.	Mobile nectarivores; mobile frugivores; wetland birds	Franklin *et al.*, 1989; Date *et al.*, 1996; Kingsford, 2000; Kingsford and Thomas, 2004
Some species select edge habitat and show elevated abundance at edges.	Some Artamids; noisy miner (*Manorina melanocephala*)	Grey *et al.*, 1997; Piper and Catterall, 2003, 2004; Clarke and Oldland, 2007
Indirect effects:		
Interspecific competition through aggression by 'advantaged' species.	*Manorina* species aggressively exclude small-bodied birds	Clarke and Schedvin, 1999; Mac Nally *et al.*, 2000; Major *et al.*, 2001; Piper and Catterall, 2003; Hannah *et al.*, 2007; Maron, 2007
Predation by 'advantaged' species.	Elevated nest predation in a range of small-bodied passerines	Berry, 2002; Piper and Catterall, 2004
Competition for hollows with range-expanding species	Large-bodied hollow nesters, e.g. Carnaby's black-cockatoo	Saunders and Ingram, 1987; Saunders, 1990

composition, with increases in species that use modified habitat and declines in those that depend on the remnant habitat (Fig. 18.4). However, further avifaunal responses to fragmentation occur within the remnant habitat patches, and these include both direct responses to the habitat change itself and indirect effects that arise from relationships between ecosystem components (Table 18.1).

Direct responses to habitat fragmentation may occur through either population or behavioural processes. At the population level there are well-developed general theoretical predictions that habitat specialists in small patches should suffer increased rates of demographically induced local extinction, and hence be frequently absent from small habitat patches (Mac Nally and Bennett, 1997). The conditions for this include that the species is sedentary, and is unable or unwilling to move frequently between patches. The detailed work needed to demonstrate this has been done for a handful of species (Table 18.1); many others are more mobile, nomadic or migratory, and hence their area sensitivity must be due to other causes.

On a simpler level, fragmentation may remove an important resource (such as nest hollows) that a species needs in the short term for survival or breeding, effectively rendering the habitat unsuitable, even though other resources remain present. Likewise, highly mobile species that track spatio-temporally variable resources (such as some nectarivores, frugivores and waterbirds; Table 18.1) are vulnerable to the combined behavioural and population effects of differential habitat loss in certain parts of an individual's annual or lifetime range, reducing the occupancy of suitable habitat elsewhere in the species' range (Ford and Paton, 1985; Kingsford and Thomas, 2004; Paton *et al.*, 2009).

An important direct behavioural response to habitat fragmentation is the differential occupancy of edge habitats at the interface between the remnant and adjacent ecosystems. This may also be linked with habitat-dependent population responses (through altered breeding success or survival at edges). Both positive and negative edge responses are possible. One bird species in particular, the noisy miner *Manorina melanocephala*, commonly shows elevated abundance in eucalypt forest fragments below 10–20 ha in size within agricultural and urban landscapes, because its density is higher within the first hundred metres (and sometimes more) of the forest edge than in the forest interior (Grey *et al.*, 1997; Piper and Catterall, 2003, 2004; Clarke and Oldland, 2007) (Table 18.1).

Bird species that respond positively to the novel habitat available at the interface between forest and agricultural or urban land edges also include nest predators, and evidence derived mainly from studies using artificial nests suggests that this is likely to result in lower productivity for a range of other bird species in forest fragments (Piper and Catterall, 2004). This phenomenon is at least superficially similar to the elevated edge-related nest predation reported in some studies from temperate north America and Europe (Chalfoun *et al.*, 2002), although the species (and to some extent the families) of predator and prey are different.

Species' responses to habitat change can have a cascading sequence of indirect effects on other bird species, as well as on other ecosystem components. For example, a reduced abundance and diversity of many small-bodied bird species has frequently been reported in eucalypt forest and woodland remnants, caused principally by an extremely high level of broad-spectrum interspecific aggression by noisy miners, which have responded positively to habitat fragmentation (Table 18.1). All three common species in the genus *Manorina* are known for their high levels of interspecific aggression, together with their capacity for increase in anthropogenically disturbed habitats, which leads to a near-exclusion of the small insectivore bird guild, whose members avoid sites occupied by *Manorina*. There have also been suggestions that this may lead to outbreaks of insect herbivores and tree dieback or even death in these areas, with the potential for positive feedback into cycles of ecosystem degradation (Clarke and Schedvin, 1999).

Another example of ecosystem-level feedbacks mediated by bird species' habitat use in fragmented landscapes arises from frugivore–plant interactions. The abundance of many large-gaped (and large-bodied) frugivores is reduced in small rainforest patches, and these larger frugivores are the dispersal agents of a significant proportion of plant species (Moran *et al.*, 2009). Frugivore declines may thus lead to reduced or altered tree regeneration, ultimately further affecting the habitat quality of these patches for the birds.

Other indirect effects of landscape modification in extremely modified relictual landscapes include those arising from competition for nest hollows. Having expanded their ranges in response to pastoral and agricultural development, species such as the galah *Eolophus roseicapillus* and introduced common myna *Sturnus tristis* and common starling *Sturnus vulgaris* now compete for the few remaining hollows in old trees in such landscapes. Along with the direct loss of habitat, competition for hollows with galahs is thought to have contributed to declines in Carnaby's black cockatoo *Calyptorhynchus latirostris* (Saunders and Ingram, 1987; Saunders, 1990).

Reflecting this diversity of ecological processes, Ford *et al.* (2001) listed a number of hypotheses to account for the decline and local extinction of eucalypt woodland birds in agricultural landscapes across southern Australia (Table 18.2). The authors grouped these effects under three headings: (1) habitat loss; (2) habitat fragmentation and (3) habitat degradation. Furthermore, they highlighted that the decline of birds in agricultural landscapes often results from the interaction of different threatening processes.

Conclusion: birds, habitats and their conservation in Australia

Ecological research can sometimes struggle to reach firm conclusions, because of the impracticality of conducting experiments that are large scale, long term, replicated and manipulative, and in which habitat factors are controlled and cause and effect can be teased apart. In observational studies comparing pre-existing habitats, it can be difficult to separate the role of confounded factors. For example, patch size may be correlated with variation

Table 18.2 *Hypotheses to account for decline in birds of temperate woodlands in southern Australia*

Theme	Hypotheses
Habitat loss	• Random extinctions due to sampling effects • Disproportionate loss of species habitats, affecting habitat specialists and mobile species
Habitat fragmentation	• Reduced dispersal due to patch isolation • Edge effects: increased nest predation from open-country species • Reduced food availability
Habitat degradation	• Increased competition from aggressive species • Reduced availability of nest sites due to loss of mature trees and shrubs • Increased nest predators • Increased predation on adults and juveniles, especially by exotic predators • Increased mortality from human activities and utilities • Increased level of nest parasitism • Increased disease and parasites • Reduced food abundance due to grazing, altered fire regime and habitat simplification

From Ford *et al.* (2001).

in the nature of local habitat due to selective land-clearing, or with variation in anthropogenic interventions such as fire frequency, extraction of timber or woody debris, and livestock grazing. Furthermore, these multiple effects may interact, often negatively (Martin *et al.*, 2006b; Hannah *et al.*, 2007; Martin and McIntyre, 2007).

The processes underlying avian responses to these habitat changes may vary according to specific combinations of within-fragment and matrix habitat types. For example, increased nest predator activity is evident at eucalypt forest/pasture edges, but not at rainforest/pasture edges (Hausmann *et al.*, 2005), and noisy miners show larger increases in abundance where eucalypt forest meets suburban areas compared with pasture areas, and no increase adjacent to pine plantations (Catterall *et al.*, 2002).

Nevertheless, there is a consistent pattern emerging with respect to the outcome of the interaction between the available bird species pool and the altered habitat configuration that comes with anthropogenic variegation and fragmentation: while species may respond positively or negatively to any given change, the observed number of negative responses typically exceeds the number of positive responses (Saunders, 1989; Saunders and Ingram, 1995; Woinarski and Catterall, 2004). In effect, anthropogenic habitat change is placing an ecological sieve on the avifauna, the consequences of which become more extreme as the vegetation changes from variegated through fragmented to relictual.

In both Australia and Europe these ecological sieves created by land-use intensification have allowed the most robust and generalist bird species to pass through while leaving those with life-history characteristics tied closely to intact vegetation most vulnerable. At a continental scale, Australian birds have not yet suffered the extinctions experienced by other Australian taxa, such as mammals (Short and Smith, 1994). One in four mammal species is extinct or threatened by changes brought about by European settlement (Recher and Lim, 1990). In contrast, only one mainland bird species, the paradise parrot, is considered extinct (Recher, 1999; Garnett *et al.*, 2010).

However, Recher (1999) warned that the full impact of European settlement on Australian birds is yet to be fully realised, and predicted a wave of bird extinctions to occur in Australia during the twenty-first century. Delayed extinctions (extinction debt) as a result of land-use decisions taken long ago are increasingly acknowledged as contributing to present-day population trends (Kuussaari *et al.*, 2009; Szabo *et al.*, 2011). Long-lived species such as parrots are particularly prone to extinction debt, persisting in a landscape even if they can no longer breed in the absence of nest hollows (Saunders *et al.*, 2003). Ford *et al.* (2009) reported on the progressive regional loss of hooded robins *Melanodryas cucullata* and brown treecreepers *Climacteris picumnus* despite most habitat loss occurring over 100 years ago. Declines of once-common bird species are familiar in Europe (Siriwardena *et al.*, 1998; Chamberlain *et al.*, 2000), and while Europe has a much longer history of agricultural development, the scale of land-use intensification following World War II is similar across both continents. Even under dedicated habitat restoration there is likely to be a long time-lag before the full benefits are realised (Mac Nally, 2008; Vesk *et al.*, 2008). This places great emphasis on protection of remaining habitat, wherever it occurs in the landscape.

Conceptual models of landscapes, together with a growing understanding of bird species' responses to landscape change and their life-history characteristics, are helping to define conservation strategies in Australia (Garnett *et al.*, 2010). The focus of conservation efforts is now on prioritising threat management actions to abate these threats, on and off reserves (Cowardine *et al.*, 2012).

However, potential future climate change places yet another filter on Australian birds. For example, environmental niche modelling has suggested that over 70% of bird species in northeastern Australia's wet tropics are vulnerable to climate change, including 26 critically endangered species (Shoo *et al.*, 2005). Habitat models for the golden bowerbird *Prionodura newtonia*, a high-altitude species, predict that a temperature increase of 2–3 °C would render 98% of its current habitat unsuitable (Hilbert *et al.*, 2004). Across eastern Australia, waterbirds have declined from an average of 1.1 million in 1983 to 0.2 million individuals in 2004 (Kingsford and Porter, 2006). This is due in part to changes in wetlands and rivers following vegetation clearing and water extraction for agriculture and pasture (Kingsford, 2000; Kingsford and Thomas, 2004; Paton *et al.*, 2009), but has also been influenced by drought conditions during much of that period; such droughts are also predicted to increase in severity and duration under climate change.

The interactions of fragmentation and climate change are expected to be greater than the effects of either in isolation (Peters, 1990; Erasmus *et al.*, 2002; Olsen, 2007). Birds can be expected to respond individualistically and ecological communities to disassemble and reassemble in new ways (Thuiller, 2004). Habitat corridors and ecological networks may help facilitate adaptive responses by birds to climate change (Bennett, 2004; Opdam and Wascher, 2004; Opdam *et al.*, 2006). However, their general usefulness will be limited by the individualistic and uncertain responses of different species (Lindenmayer and Fischer, 2006; Manning *et al.*, 2009). An alternative approach is to apply the conceptual framework of landscape continua, to manage a wider range of species-specific responses to both climate change and anthropogenic landscape change (Manning *et al.*, 2009). This approach suggests other conservation solutions, such as 're-variegating' fragmented landscapes with habitat elements such as scattered trees, and better integration of conservation and production in the same landscape (McIntyre *et al.*, 2002; Manning *et al.*, 2009).

This review of landscape change in Australia and its impact on bird species has revealed the following points: (1) continental-scale extinctions of birds are limited (so far); (2) most extinctions are at more local scales; (3) there are often long lag times, many species are continuing to decline, and even without further habitat loss and threatening processes it is likely that there will be further extinctions; (4) forest and woodland birds that remain common have still experienced a large reduction in population size due to loss of habitat area; (5) effects of landscape change are both direct and indirect; (6) many Australian birds are adapted to highly variable climate and resource conditions; (7) habitat variation is often continuous rather than binary, and hence suited to continuum-based rather than patch-matrix models and (8) there is an urgent need to understand the synergistic effects of climate change and landscape change.

To maintain Australia's diverse and distinctive bird fauna, a range of habitat management initiatives will be needed. These management actions include ending broadscale clearing of native vegetation, restoring sufficient native vegetation to highly cleared regions, reducing livestock grazing pressure, strategically controlling invasive species known to threaten native bird diversity, instigating appropriate fire regimes and implementing programmes to improve the quality of freshwater habitats and restore environmental flows (Saunders *et al.*, 1990; Recher, 1999; Kingsford and Thomas, 2004; Woinarski and Catterall, 2004; Martin and McIntyre, 2007).

Acknowledgements

Sincere thanks to Rob Fuller for inviting us to write this chapter and for providing critical feedback throughout the chapter's development. We are grateful to the Australian Research Council Futures Network for supporting a workshop where the ideas for this chapter were drafted. We thank Denis Saunders, Hugh Ford, Richard Fuller and Jean-Louis Martin for their insightful comments on this chapter. Thanks finally to Richard Thackway and Rob Lesslie for making their VAST map available to us.

References

Allen, R., Lindesay, J. and Parker, D. (1996). *El Niño – Southern Oscillation and Climatic Variability*. Collingwood: CSIRO publishing.

Anikovich, M. V., Sinitsyn, A. A., Hoffecker, J. F. *et al.* (2007). Early Upper Paleolithic in eastern Europe and implications for the dispersal of modern humans. *Science*, **315**, 223–226.

Archer, M., Hand, S. J. and Godthelp, H. (1991). *Riversleigh. The Story of Animals in Ancient Rainforests of Inland Australia*. Balgowlah: Reed Books.

Arnold, K. E. and Owens, I. P. F. (1998). Cooperative breeding in birds: a comparative test of the life-history hypothesis. *P. Roy. Soc. Lond. B*, **265**, 739–745.

Attwood, S. J., Park, S. E., Maron, M. et al. (2009). Declining birds in Australian agricultural landscapes may benefit from aspects of the European agri-environment model. *Biol. Conserv.*, **142**, 1981–1991.

Barnard, C. A. (1925). A review of the bird life on Coomooboolaroo Station, Duaringa district, Queensland, during the past fifty years. *Emu*, **24**, 252–265.

Barnard, H. G. (1934). Observations of the disappearance and probable cause of many of our native birds in central Queensland. *Queensland Nat.*, **9**, 3–7.

Barrett, G., Silcocks, A., Barry, S., Cunningham, R. and Poulter, R. (2003). *The New Atlas of Australian Birds*. Hawthorn East: Royal Australian Ornithologists Union.

Beadle, N. C. W. (1981). *The Vegetation of Australia*. Cambridge: Cambridge University Press.

Bennett, A. F. and Ford, L. A. (1997). Land use, habitat change and the distribution of birds in fragmented rural environments: a landscape perspective from the northern plains, Victoria, Australia. *Pacific Conserv. Biol.*, **3**, 244–261.

Bennett, G. (2004). *Integrating Biodiversity Conservation and Sustainable Use. Lessons Learned from Ecological Networks*. Gland: World Conservation Union (IUCN).

Bennett, P. M., and Owens, I. P. F. (1997). Variation in extinction risk among birds: chance or evolutionary predisposition? *P. Roy. Soc. Lond. B*, **264**, 401–408.

Bennett, P. M., and Owens, I. P. F. (2002). *Evolutionary Ecology of Birds: Life-Histories, Mating Systems, and Extinction*. Oxford: Oxford University Press.

Bentley, G. E., Spar, B. D., MacDougall-Shackleton, S. A., Hahn, T. P. and Ball, G. F. (2000). Photoperiodic Regulation of the Reproductive Axis in Male Zebra Finches, *Taeniopygia guttata*. *Gen. Comp. Endocr.*, **117**, 449–455.

Bentley, J. M. and Catterall, C. P. (1997). The use of bushland, corridors, and linear remnants by birds in southeastern Queensland, Australia. *Conserv. Biol.*, **11**, 1173–1189.

Berry, L. (2002). Predation rates of artificial nests in the edge and interior of a southern Victorian forest. *Wildlife Res.*, **29**, 341–345.

Blakers, M. S., Davies, J. J. F. and Reilly, P. N. (1984). *The Atlas of Australian birds*. Melbourne: Melbourne University Press.

Bowman, D. M. J. S. (2000). *Australian Rainforests. Islands of Green in a Land of Fire*. Cambridge: Cambridge University Press.

Briscoe, G. and Smith, L. (2002). *The Aboriginal Population Revisited: 70,000 Years to the Present*. Aboriginal History Monograph No. 10. Canberra: ANU.

Brooker, L. and Brooker, M. (2003). Local distribution, metapopulation viability and conservation of the Blue-breasted Fairy-wren in fragmented habitat in the Western Australian wheatbelt. *Emu*, **103**, 185–198.

Brooker, R. W., Osler, G. H. R. and Gollisch, J. (2008). Association of vegetation and soil mite assemblages with isolated Scots pine trees on a Scottish wet heath. *Landscape Ecol.*, **23**, 861–871.

Brooks, T. M., Pimm, S. L. and Oyugi, J. O. (1999). Time lag between deforestation and bird extinction in tropical forest fragments. *Conserv. Biol.*, **13**, 5, 1140–1150.

Carwardine, J., O'Connor, T., Legge, S. *et al.* (2012). Prioritizing threat management for biodiversity conservation. *Conserv. Lett.*, **5**, 196–204.

Catterall, C. P., Kingston, M. B., Park, K. and Sewell, S. (1998). Deforestation, urbanisation and seasonality: interacting effects on a regional bird assemblage. *Biol. Conserv.*, **84**, 65–81.

Catterall, C. P., Piper, S. D. and Goodall, K. (2002). Noisy miner irruptions associated with land use by humans in south east Queensland: causes, effects and management implications. In *Landscape Health in Queensland*, ed. A. Franks, J. Playford and A. Shapcott, pp 117–127. Brisbane: Royal Society of Queensland.

Chalfoun, A. D., Thompson, F. R. and Ratnaswamy, M. J. (2002). Nest predators and fragmentation: a review and meta-analysis. *Conserv. Biol.*, **16**, 306–318.

Chamberlain, D. E., Fuller, R. J., Bunce, R. G. H., Duckworth, J. C. and Shrubb, M. (2000). Changes in the abundance of farmland birds in relation to the timing of agricultural intensification in England and Wales. *J. Appl. Ecol.*, **37**, 771–788.

Chan, K. (2001). Partial migration in Australian landbirds: a review. *Emu*, **101**, 281–292.

Christidis, L. and Boles, W. E. (2008). *Systematics and Taxonomy of Australian Birds*. Collingwood: CSIRO Publishing.

Clarke, M. F. and Oldland, J. M. (2007). Penetration of remnant edges by noisy miners (*Manorina melanocephala*) and implications for habitat restoration. *Wildlife Res.*, **34**, 253–261.

Clarke, M. F. and Schedvin, N. (1999). Removal of bell miners *Manorina melanophrys* from *Eucalyptus radiata* forest and its effect on avian diversity, psyllids and tree health. *Biol. Conserv.*, **88**, 111–120.

Cockburn, A. (1996). Why do so many Australian birds cooperate: social evolution in the Corvida? In *Frontiers of Population Ecology*, ed. R. B. Floyd, A. W. Sheppard and P. J. De Barro, pp. 451–472. Melbourne: CSIRO Publishing.

Cracraft, J. (1972). Continental drift and Australian avian biogeography. *Emu*, **72**, 171–174.

Date, E. M., Recher, H. F., Ford, H. A. and Stewart, D. A. (1996). The conservation and ecology of rainforest pigeons in northeastern New South Wales. *Pacific Conserv. Biol.*, **2**, 299–308.

Davies, S. J. J. F. (1986). A biology of the desert fringe. Presidential address – 1984. *J. Roy. Soc. West. Aust.*, **68** (2), 37–50.

Department of Arts Heritage and the Environment. (2006). *EPBC Policy Statement 3.5 – White Box – Yellow Box – Blakely's Red Gum Grassy Woodlands and Derived Native Grasslands listing*.

Diamond, J. (1998). *Guns, Germs and Steel: A Short History of Everybody for the Last 13,000 Years*. London: Vintage.

Díaz, M., Campos, P. and Pulido, F. J. (1997). The Spanish dehesa: a diversity in land use and wildlife. In *Farming and Birds in Europe: The Common Agricultural Policy and its Implications for Bird Conservation*, ed. D. J. Pain and M. W. Pienkowski, pp.178–209. London: Academic Press.

Dorfman, E. J., and Kingsford, R. T. (2001). Scale-dependent patterns of abundance and habitat use by cormorants in arid Australia and the importance of nomadism. *J. Arid Environ.*, **49**, 677–694.

Dwyer, P. (1972). Feature, patch and refuge area: some influences on diversity of bird species. *Emu*, **72**, 149–156.

Edwards, K. J., and Hirons, K. R. (1984). Cereal pollen grains in pre-elm decline deposits: implications for the earliest agriculture in Britain and Ireland. *J. Archaeol. Sci.*, **11**, 71–80.

Erasmus, B. F. N., Van Jaarsveld, A. S., Chown, S. L., Kshatriya, M. and Wessels, K. J. (2002). Vulnerability of South African animal taxa to climate change. *Glob. Change Biol.*, **8**, 679–693.

Fahrig, L. (2003). Effects of habitat fragmentation on biodiversity. *Annu. Rev. Ecol. Evol. Syst.*, **34**, 487–515.

Fischer, J., Lindenmayer, D. B. and Fazey, I. (2004). Appreciating ecological complexity: habitat contours as a conceptual landscape model. *Conserv. Biol.*, **18**, 1245–1253.

Food and Agriculture Organization (2002). *World Agriculture: Towards 2015/2030: Summary Report*. Rome: Food and Agriculture Organization of the United Nations.

Ford, H. A. (1989). *Ecology of birds – An Australian Perspective*. Chipping Norton, Australia: Surrey Beatty and Sons.

Ford, H. A. and Barrett, G. W. (1995). The role of birds and their conservation in agricultural systems. In *People and Nature Conservation: Perspectives on Private Land Use and Endangered Species Recovery*, ed. A. F. Bennett, G. N. Backhouse and T. W. Clark, pp.128–134. Mosman: Royal Zoological Society of NSW.

Ford, H. A., Barrett, G. W., Saunders, D. A. and Recher, H. F. (2001). Why have birds in the woodlands of Southern Australia declined? *Biol. Conserv.*, **97**, 71–88.

Ford, H. A., Bell, H., Nias, R. and Noske, R. (1988). The relationship between ecology and the incidence of cooperative breeding in Australian birds. *Behav. Ecol. Sociobiol.*, **22**, 239–249.

Ford, H. A., and Paton, D. C. (1985). Habitat selection in Australian Honeyeaters, with special reference to nectar productivity. In *Habitat Selection in Birds*, ed. M. L. Cody, pp.367–388. London: Academic Press.

Ford, H. A., Walters, J. R., Cooper, C. B., Debus, S. J. S. and Doerr, V. A. J. (2009). Extinction debt or habitat change? – Ongoing losses of woodland birds in north-eastern New South Wales, Australia. *Biol. Conserv.*, **142**, 3182–3190.

Franklin, D. C. (1999). Evidence of disarray amongst granivorous bird assemblages in the savannas of northern Australia, a region of sparse human settlement. *Biol. Conserv.*, **90**, 53–68.

Franklin, D. C., Menkhorst, P. W. and Robinson, J. (1989). Ecology of the Regent Honeyeater *Xanthomyza phrygia*. *Emu*, **89**, 140–154.

Franklin, D. C., Whitehead, P. J., Pardon, G. *et al.* (2005). Geographic patterns and correlates of decline of granivorous birds in northern Australia. *Wildlife Res.*, **32**, 399–408.

Freudenberger, D. and Landsberg, J. (2000). Management of stock watering points and grazing to maintain landscape function and biological diversity in rangelands. In *Management for Sustainable Ecosystems*, ed.

P. Hale, A. Petrie, D. Molony and P. Sattler, pp. 71–77. Brisbane: Centre for Conservation Biology, The University of Queensland.

Fuller, R. J., Atkinson, P. W., Garnett, M. C. *et al.* (2006). Breeding bird communities in the upland margins (ffridd) of Wales in the mid-1980s. *Bird Study*, **53**, 177–186.

Garnett, S. T., Szabo, J. K. and Gutson, G. (2010). *The Action Plan for Australian Birds 2010*. Canberra: CSIRO Publishing.

Geffen, E. and Yom-Tov, Y. (2000). Old endemics and new invaders: alternative strategies of passerines for living in the Australian environment. *Behav. Ecol. Sociobiol.*, **47**, 250–257.

Gibbons, P. and Boak, M. (2002). The value of paddock trees for regional conservation in an agricultural landscape. *Ecol. Manage. Restor.*, **3**, 205–210.

Greene, R. P. and Stager, J. (2001). Rangeland to cropland conversions as replacement land for prime farmland lost to urban development. *Soc. Sci. J.*, **38**, 543–555.

Grey, M. J., Clarke, M. F. and Loyn, R. H. (1997). Initial changes in the avian community of remnant eucalypt woodlands following a reduction in the abundance of Noisy Miners, *Manorina melanocephala*. *Wildlife Res.*, **24**, 631–648.

Grice, A. C. (2006). The impacts of invasive plant species on the biodiversity of Australian rangelands. *Rangeland J.*, **28**, 27–35.

Griffioen, P. A. and Clark, M. F. (2002). Large-scale bird-movement patterns evident in eastern Australian atlas data. *Emu*, **102**, 99–125.

Hannah, D., Woinarski, J. C. Z., Catterall, C. P. *et al.* (2007). Impacts of clearing, fragmentation and disturbance on the bird fauna of Eucalypt savanna woodlands in central Queensland, Australia. *Austral Ecol.*, **32**, 261–276.

Hausmann, F., Catterall, C. P. and Piper, S. D. (2005). Effects of edge habitat and nest characteristics on depredation of artificial nests in fragmented Australian tropical rainforest. *Biodivers. Conserv.*, **14**, 2331–2345.

Henzell, T. (2007). *Australian Agriculture: Its History and Challenges*. Collingwood: CSIRO Publishing.

Hilbert, D. W., Bradford, M., Parker, T. and Westcott, D. A. (2004). Golden bowerbird (*Prionodura newtonia*) habitat in past, present and future climates: predicted extinction of a vertebrate in tropical highlands due to global warming. *Biol. Conserv.*, **116**, 367–377.

Hobbs, J. N. (1971). A plague of mice at Warren. *Bird Watcher*, **4**, 43–46.

Hobbs, R. J. and Hopkins, A. J. M. (1990). From frontiers to fragments: European impact on Australia's vegetation. In *Australian Ecosystems: 200 Years of Utilization Degradation and Reconstruction*, ed. D. A. Saunders, A. J. M. Hopkins and R. A. How, pp. 93–114. Chipping Norton, Australia: Surrey Beatty and Sons.

Howe, R. W., Howe, T. D. and Ford, H. A. (1981). Bird distributions on small rainforest remnants in New South Wales. *Aust. Wildlife Res.*, **8**, 637–651.

Kikkawa, J., Webb, L. J., Dale, M. B. *et al.* (1981). Gradients and boundaries of monsoon forests in Australia. In *Ecological Gradients and Boundaries*, ed. M. J. Littlejohn and P. Y. Ladiges, pp. 39–52. Proc. Ecol. Soc. Australia, Vol. 11.

Kingsford, R. T. (2000). Ecological impacts of dams, water diversions and river management on floodplain wetlands in Australia. *Austral. Ecol.*, **25**, 109–127.

Kingsford, R. T. and Porter, J. L. (2006). *Waterbirds and Wetlands across Eastern Australia*. Canberra: Technical report for the Department of the Environment and Heritage. http://www.environment.gov.au/soe/2006/publications/technical/waterbirds/pubs/waterbirds.pdf. Accessed 27 September 2010.

Kingsford, R. T. and Thomas, R. F. (2004). Destruction of wetlands and waterbird populations by dams and irrigation on the Murrumbidgee River in arid Australia. *Environ. Manage.*, **34**, 383–396.

Krebs, J. R., Wilson, J. D., Bradbury, R. B. and Siriwardena, G. M. (1999). The second Silent Spring? *Nature*, **400**, 611–612.

Kuussaari, M., Bommarco, R., Heikkinen, R. K. *et al.* (2009). Extinction debt: a challenge for biodiversity conservation. *Trends Ecol. Evol.*, **24**, 10, 565–571.

Landsberg, J. (2000). Status of temperate woodlands in the Australian Capital Territory. In *Temperate Eucalypt Woodlands in Australia: Biology, Conservation, Management and Restoration*, ed. R. J. Hobbs and C. J. Yates, pp. 32–44. Chipping Norton, Australia: Surrey Beatty and Sons.

Lesslie, R., Thackway, R. and Smith, J. (2010). *A National-level Vegetation Assets, States and Transitions (VAST) Dataset for Australia (version 2)*. Canberra: Bureau of Rural Sciences.

Lindenmayer, D. B. and Fischer, J. (2006). *Habitat Fragmentation and Landscape Change: An Ecological and Conservation Synthesis*. Washington D.C.: Island Press.

Lord, E. A. R. (1956). The birds of the Murphy's Creek district, southern Queensland. *Emu*, **56**, 100–128.

Maclean, G. L. (1996). *Ecophysiology of Desert Birds*. Berlin: Springer.

Mac Nally, R. (2008). The lag dæmon: hysteresis in rebuilding landscapes and implications for biodiversity futures. *J. Environ. Manage.*, **88**, 1202–1211.

Mac Nally, R. and Bennett, A. F. (1997). Species-specific predictions of the impact of habitat fragmentation: local extinction of birds in the box-ironbark forests of central Victoria, Australia. *Biol. Conserv.*, **82**, 147–155.

Mac Nally, R., Bennett, A. F. and Horrocks, G. (2000). Forecasting the impacts of habitat fragmentation. Evaluation of species-specific predictions of the impact of habitat fragmentation on birds in the box-ironbark forests of central Victoria, Australia. *Biol. Conserv.*, **95**, 7–29.

Mac Nally, R. and Horrocks, G. (2007). Inducing whole-assemblage change by experimental manipulation of habitat structure. *J. Anim. Ecol.*, **76**, 643–650.

Major, R. E., Christie, F. J. and Gowing, G. (2001). Influence of remnant and landscape attributes on Australian woodland bird communities. *Biol. Conserv.*, **102**, 47–66.

Manning, A. D., Fischer, J., Felton, A. *et al.* (2009). Landscape fluidity – a unifying perspective for understanding and adapting to global change. *J. Biogeog.*, **36**, 193–199.

Manning, A. D., Lindenmayer, D. B. and Barry, S. C. (2004a). The conservation implications of bird reproduction in the agricultural 'matrix': a case study of the vulnerable superb parrot of south-eastern Australia. *Biol. Conserv.*, **120**, 363–374.

Manning, A. D., Lindenmayer, D. B., Barry, S. and Nix, H. A. (2006). Multi-scale site and landscape effects on the vulnerable superb parrot of south-eastern Australia during the breeding season. *Landscape Ecol.*, **21**, 1119–1133.

Manning, A. D., Lindenmayer, D. B. and Nix, H. A. (2004b). Continua and Umwelt: novel perspectives on viewing landscapes. *Oikos*, **104**, 621–628.

Maron, M. (2007). Threshold effect of eucalypt density on an aggressive avian competitor. *Biol. Conserv.*, **136**, 100–107.

Maron, M. and Lill, A. (2005). The influence of livestock grazing and weed invasion on habitat use by birds in grassy woodland remnants. *Biol. Conserv.*, **124**, 439–450.

Martin, T. G., Campbell, S. and Grounds, S. (2006a). Weeds of Australian rangelands. *Rangeland J.*, **28**, 3–26.

Martin, T. G., and Green, J. G. (2002). Wildlife and core conservation areas. In *Managing and Conserving Grassy Woodland*, ed. S. McIntyre, J. G. McIvor and K. M. Heard, pp. 111–142. Melbourne: CSIRO Publishing.

Martin, T. G. and McIntyre, S. (2007). Impacts of livestock grazing and tree clearing on birds of woodland and riparian habitats. *Conserv. Biol.*, **21**, 504–514.

Martin, T. G., McIntyre, S., Catterall, C. P. and Possingham, H. P. (2006b). Is landscape context important for riparian conservation? Birds in grassy woodland. *Biol. Conserv.*, **127**, 201–214.

Martin, T. G. and Possingham, H. P. (2005). Predicting the impact of livestock grazing on birds using foraging height data. *J. Appl. Ecol.*, **42**, 400–408.

Matheson, W. E. (1978). A further irruption of native hens in 1975. *South Aust. Ornithol.*, **27**, 270–273.

McIntyre, S., Heard, K. M. and Martin, T. G. (2002). How grassland plants are distributed over five human-created habitats typical of eucalypt woodlands in a variegated landscape. *Pacific Conserv. Biol.*, **7**, 274–289.

McIntyre, S., Heard, K. M. and Martin, T. G. (2003). The relative importance of cattle grazing in subtropical grasslands: does it reduce or enhance plant biodiversity? *J. Appl. Ecol.*, **40**, 445–457.

McIntyre, S. and Hobbs, R. (1999). A framework for conceptualizing human effects on landscapes and its relevance to management and research models. *Conserv. Biol.*, **13**, 1282–1292.

McIntyre, S. and Martin, T. G. (2002). Managing intensive and extensive land uses to conserve grassland plants in sub-tropical eucalypt woodlands. *Biol. Conserv.*, **107**, 241–252.

Miller, G. H., Fogel, M. L., Magee, J. W. *et al.* (2005). Ecosystem collapse in Pleistocene Australia and a human role in megafaunal extinction. *Science*, **309**, 287–290.

Moran, C., Catterall, C. P. and Kanowski, J. (2009). Reduced dispersal of native plant species as a consequence of the reduced abundance of frugivore species in fragmented rainforest. *Biol. Conserv.*, **142**, 541–552.

National Land and Water Audit (2002). *Australians and Natural Resources Management 2002.* National Land and Water Resources Audit, Commonwealth Australia.

Neilan, W., Catterall, C. P., Kanowski, J. and McKenna, S. (2006). Do frugivorous birds assist rainforest succession in weed dominated oldfield regrowth of subtropical Australia? *Biol. Conserv.*, **129**, 393–407.

Newton, I. (2004). The recent declines of farmland bird populations in Britain: an appraisal of causal factors and conservation actions. *Ibis*, **146**, 579–600.

Nix, H. A. (1974). *Environmental Control of Breeding, Post-breeding Dispersal and Migration of Birds in the Australian Region.* pp. 272–305. 16th Int. Ornithol. Congr. Canberra: Australia.

Olsen, P. (2007). The State of Australia's Birds. *Wingspan*, **14** (suppl.).

Opdam, P., Steingrover, E. and van Rooij, S. (2006). Ecological networks: a spatial concept for multi-actor planning of sustainable landscapes. *Landscape Urban Plan.*, **75**, 322–332.

Opdam, P. and Wascher, D. (2004). Climate change meets habitat fragmentation: linking landscape and biogeographical scale levels in research and conservation. *Biol. Conserv.*, **117**, 285–297.

Palmer, G. C. and Bennett, A. F. (2006). Riparian zones provide for distinct bird assemblages in forest mosaics of south-east Australia. *Biol. Conserv.*, **130**, 447–457.

Paton, D. C., Rogers, D. J., Hill, B. M., Bailey, C. P. and Ziembicki, M. (2009). Temporal changes to spatially stratified waterbird communities of the Coorong, South Australia: implications for the management of heterogenous wetlands. *Anim. Conserv.*, **12**, 408–417.

Pavey, C. R. and Nano, C. E. M. (2009). Bird assemblages of arid Australia: Vegetation patterns have a greater effect than disturbance and resource pulses. *J. Arid Environ.*, **73**, 634–642.

Peterken, G. F. (1996). *Natural Woodland: Ecology and Conservation in Northern Temperate Regions.* Cambridge: Cambridge University Press.

Peters, R. L. (1990). Effects of global warming on forests. *For. Ecol. Manage.*, **35**, 13–33.

Piper, S. D. and Catterall, C. P. (2003). A particular case and a general pattern: hyperaggressive behaviour by one species may mediate avifaunal decreases in fragmented Australian forests. *Oikos*, **101**, 602–614.

Piper, S. D. and Catterall, C. P. (2004). Effects of edge type and nest height on predation of artificial nests within subtropical Australian eucalypt forests. *For. Ecol. Manage.*, **203**, 361–372.

Price, O. F., Woinarski, J. C. Z. and Robinson, D. (1999). Very large area requirements for frugivorous birds in monsoon rainforests of the Northern Territory, Australia. *Biol. Conserv.*, **91**, 169–180.

Radford, J. Q. and Bennett, A. F. (2004). Thresholds in landscape parameters: occurrence of the white-browed treecreeper *Climacteris affinis* in Victoria, Australia. *Biol. Conserv.*, **117**, 375–391.

Radford, J. Q., Bennett, A. F. and Cheers, G. J. (2005). Landscape-level thresholds of habitat cover for woodland birds. *Biol. Conserv.*, **124**, 317–337.

Recher, H. F. (1991). The conservation and management of eucalypt forests birds: resource requirements for nesting and foraging. In *Conservation of Australia's Forest Fauna*, ed. D. Lunney, pp. 25–34. Mosman: Royal Zoological Society of NSW.

Recher, H. F. (1999). The state of Australia's avifauna: a personal opinion and prediction for the new millennium. *Aust. Zool.*, **31**, 11–27.

Recher, H. F. and Davies, W. E. (1997). Foraging ecology of a mulga bird community. *Wildlife Res.*, **24**, 27–43.

Recher, H. F., Gowing, G., Kavanagh, R., Shields, J. and Rohan-Jones, W. (1983). Birds, resources and time in a tablelands forest. *Proc. Ecol. Soc. Aust.*, **12**, 101–123.

Recher, H. F. and Lim, L. (1990). A review of current ideas of the extinction, conservation and management of Australia's terrestrial vertebrate fauna. *Proc. Ecol. Soc. Aust.*, **16**, 287–301.

Rowley, I. (1975). *Bird life*. Sydney: Collins.

Rowley, I. and Russell, E. (1997). *Fairy-wrens and Grasswrens: Maluridae*. Oxford: Oxford University Press

Russell, E. M. (1989). Co-operative breeding – a Gondwanan perspective. *Emu*, **89**, 61–62.

Saunders, D. A. (1989). Changes in the avifauna of a region, district and remnant as a result of fragmentation of native vegetation: the wheatbelt of Western Australia. A case study. *Biol. Conserv.*, **50**, 99–135.

Saunders, D. A. (1990). Problems of survival in an extensively cultivated landscape: the case of Carnaby's cockatoo *Calyptorhynchus funereus latirostris*. *Biol. Conserv.*, **54**, 277–290.

Saunders, D. A. and Curry, P. J. (1990). The impact of agricultural and pastoral industry on birds in the southern half of Western Australia: past, present and future. *Proc. Ecol. Soc. Aust.*, **16**, 303–321.

Saunders, D. A., Hopkins, A. J. M. and How, R. A. (1990). *Australian Ecosystems: 200 Years of Utilisation, Degradation and Reconstruction*. Chipping Norton, Australia: Surrey Beatty and Sons.

Saunders, D. A. and Ingram, J. (1995). *Birds of Southwestern Australia. An Atlas of Changes in Distribution and Abundance of the Wheatbelt Fauna*. Chipping Norton, Australia: Surrey Beatty and Sons.

Saunders, D. A. and Ingram, J. A. (1987). Factors affecting the survival of breeding populations of Carnaby's Cockatoo *Calyptorhynchus funereus latirostris* in remnants of native vegetation. In *Nature Conservation: The Role of Remnants of Native Vegetation*, ed. D. A. Saunders, G. W. Arnold, A. A. Burbidge and A. J. M. Hopkins, pp. 249–258. Chipping Norton, Australia: Surrey Beatty and Sons.

Saunders, D. A., Smith, G. T., Ingram, J. A. and Forrester, R. I. (2003). Changes in a remnant of salmon gum *Eucalyptus salmonophloia* and York gum *E. loxophleba* woodland, 1978 to 1997. Implications for woodland conservation in the wheat–sheep regions of Australia. *Biol. Conserv.*, **110**, 245–256.

Saunders, D. A., Smith, G. T. and Rowley, I. (1982). The availability and dimensions of tree hollows that provide nest sites for cockatoos (Psittaciformes) in Western Australia. *Aust. Wildlife Res.*, **9**, 541–556.

Shoo, L. P., Williams, S. E. and Hero, J.-M. (2005). Climate warming and the rainforest birds of the Australian Wet Tropics: using abundance data as a sensitive predictor of change in total population size. *Biol. Conserv.*, **125**, 335–343.

Short, J. and Smith, A. (1994). Mammal decline and recovery in Australia. *J. Mammal.*, **75**, 288–297.

Sibley, C. G. and Ahlquist, J. E. (1985). The phylogeny and classification of the Australo-Papuan passerine birds. *Emu*, **85**, 1–14.

Sibley, C. G. and Ahlquist, J. E. (1990). *Phylogeny and Classification of Birds: A Study in Molecular Evolution*. New Haven and London: Yale University Press.

Sibley, C. G. and Monroe, B. L. (1990). *Distribution and Taxonomy of Birds of the World*. New Haven and London: Yale University Press.

Simmons, I. G. (2001). *An Environmental History of Great Britain: From 10,000 Years Ago to the Present*. Edinburgh: Edinburgh University Press.

Siriwardena, G. M., Baillie, S. R., Buckland, S. T. et al. (1998). Trends in the abundance of farmland birds: a quantitative comparison of smoothed Common Birds Census indices. *J. Appl. Ecol.*, **35**, 24–43.

Smyth, A. K., Friedel, M. and O'Malley, C. (2009). The influence of buffel grass (*Cenchrus ciliaris*) on biodiversity in an arid Australian landscape. *Rangeland J.*, **31**, 307–320.

Szabo, J. K., Baxter, P. W. J., Vesk, P. A. and Possingham, H. P. (2011). Paying the extinction debt: declining woodland birds in the Mount Lofty Ranges, South Australia. *Emu*, **111**, 59–70.

Szabo, J. K., Fedriani, E. M., Segovia, M. M., Astheimer, L. B. and Hooper, M. J. (2010). Dynamics and spatio-temporal variability of environmental factors in eastern Australia using Functional Principal Component Analysis. *J. Biol. Syst.*, **18**, 1–23.

Thackway, R. and Lesslie, R. (2008). Describing and mapping human-induced vegetation change in the Australian landscape. *Environ. Manage.*, **42**, 572–590.

Threatened Species Scientific Committee (2006). *Commonwealth Listing Advice on White

Box-Yellow Box-Blakely's Red Gum Grassy Woodland and Derived Native Grassland*. Canberra.

Thuiller, W. (2004). Patterns and uncertainties of species' range shifts under climate change. *Glob. Change Biol.*, **10**, 2020–2027.

Twigg, L. E. and Kay, B. J. (1994). Changes in the relative abundance of raptors and house mice in western New South Wales. *Corella*, **18**, 83–86.

Vesk, P. A., Nolan, R., Thomson, J. R., Dorrough, J. W. and Mac Nally, R. (2008). Time lags in provision of habitat resources through revegetation. *Biol. Conserv.*, **141**, 174–186.

Warburton, N. H. (1997). Structure and conservation of forest avifauna in isolated rainforest remnants in tropical Australia. In *Tropical Forest Remnants. Ecology, Management and Conservation of Fragmented Communities*, ed. W. F. Laurance and R. O. Bierregaard, pp. 190–206. Chicago: University of Chicago Press.

Wilson, J. D., Evans, A. D. and Grice, P. V. (2009). *Bird Conservation and Agriculture*. Cambridge: Cambridge University Press

Woinarski, J. C. Z. and Ash, A. J. (2002). Responses of vertebrates to pastoralism, military land use and landscape position in an Australian tropical savanna. *Austral. Ecol.*, **27**, 311–323.

Woinarski, J. C. Z. and Catterall, C. P. (2004). Historical changes in the bird fauna at Coomooboolaroo, northeastern Australia, from the early years of pastoral settlement (1873) to 1999. *Biol. Conserv.*, **116**, 379–401.

Wyndham, E. (1983). Movements and breeding seasons of the budgerigar. *Emu*, **82** (Suppl.), 276–282.

Yates, C. J. and Hobbs, R. J. (1997). Temperate eucalypt woodlands: a review of their status, processes threatening their persistence and techniques for restoration. *Aust. J. Bot.*, **45**, 949–973.

Zann, R. A. (1996). *The Zebra Finch: A Synthesis of Field and Laboratory Studies*. Oxford: Oxford University Press.

Zann, R. A., Morton, S. R., Jones, K. R. and Burley, N. T. (1995). The timing of breeding by Zebra Finches in relation to rainfall in central Australia. *Emu*, **95**, 208–222.

CHAPTER NINETEEN

Birds in cultural landscapes: actual and perceived differences between northeastern North America and western Europe

JEAN-LOUIS MARTIN

CEFE/CNRS, Montpellier

PIERRE DRAPEAU

Université du Québec à Montréal

LENORE FAHRIG

Carleton University

KATHRYN FREEMARK LINDSAY

Environment Canada

DAVID ANTHONY KIRK

Aquila Conservation & Environment Consulting

ADAM C. SMITH

Carleton University

and

MARC-ANDRÉ VILLARD

Université de Moncton

This chapter presents an intercontinental comparison of studies on bird–habitat relationships in three types of cultural landscapes: those created by forestry (managed forests), agriculture (farmed land and remnant native habitats in a matrix of farmed land) and urbanisation. The geographical emphasis is on temperate and boreal regions of eastern Canada (hereafter referred to as 'North America') and western Europe/Fennoscandia. We seek out differences and similarities in patterns and discuss responses of birds to processes of landscape change. We consider the influence of human perception of landscapes on the development of research ideas and the extent to which there has been intercontinental exchange and application of ideas and research findings.

One of the most striking differences in the history of habitats in North America and Europe often put forward is the timing and rate of land clearing. The clearing of a predominantly forested landscape has often been described as one of the major

Birds and Habitat: Relationships in Changing Landscapes, ed. Robert J. Fuller. Published by Cambridge University Press. © Cambridge University Press 2012.

tasks European settlers faced arriving in North America (Whitney, 1994), whereas in Europe land clearing had started around 6000 years ago (Williams, 2003).

However, the common picture of eastern North America as a vast forested wilderness before European colonisation is coming into question. Aboriginal people probably managed the landscape quite extensively through permanent or shifting agriculture and the use of fire to clear land for cultivation, to create parklands favourable to game and to open forest understorey to facilitate travel (Williams, 2003, 2008). These managed landscapes disappeared with the annihilation of over 90% of aboriginal populations starting in the 1500s, mainly due to diseases transmitted by Europeans. In southern Ontario, for instance, the extent of forested lands probably reached a low just before these epidemics (Pyne, 1982; Williams, 1989). Forests subsequently re-grew and the area covered by forest peaked just before the beginning of large-scale land cultivation by European farmers and the advent of extensive logging. Similar historical patterns are described elsewhere in North America e.g. Wisconsin (Waller and Rooney, 2008). In Europe, forests were still widespread in the middle ages and plummeted to a minimum in the seventeenth century (Cantor, 1994; Williams, 2003), at a time when land conversion by European industrialists and settlers was only about to start in North America.

On both continents the pace and intensity of land-use change increased over the past 150 years (Williams, 2008), but with much geographical variation. Canada and Fennoscandia, for instance, retained most of their forests until the

(A)   (B)

Figure 19.1 Farmed cultural landscapes of the sixteenth century in North America (A) and Europe (B). Watercolour drawing (left) *Indian Village of Secoton* by John White (created 1585–1586) (Licensed by the Trustees of the British Museum. © Copyright the British Museum) and (right) oil painting *The Harvesters* by Pieter Bruegel in 1565 (Metropolitan Museum of Art, located in New York City).

nineteenth century, though in both regions, forestry operations have intensified over the past century. In contrast, Scotland and southwestern France saw afforestation over the same period through plantations of exotic or native conifers (Angelstam *et al.*, 2004) and, in recent decades, on both continents, natural forest has re-grown over large areas where farming has become economically marginal such as in Mediterranean France (Debussche and Lepart, 1992) and Italy (Farina, 1997), and in the temperate forest zone of the USA (Foster *et al.*, 1998).

In this chapter, we explore three questions that are important in assessing whether and how research findings about bird–habitat relationships can be extrapolated from one continent to another:

1. What are the key differences and similarities in the origins, attributes and habitat relationships of birds in human-modified landscapes in North America and Europe?
2. Are differences explained by actual intercontinental differences in the history, management and nature of these cultural landscapes?
3. Alternatively, are apparent differences due to intercontinental differences in human perceptions and research approaches?

Review method

For each of the landscape types considered – landscapes managed for forestry, farmed landscapes, urban landscapes – we searched the ISI Web of Science for all studies that included any avian-related term. We removed all empirical studies that were not conducted in Europe or North America. We separated the remaining studies into three groups (European, North American and intercontinental) based on either the continent(s) where the field work was conducted (if an empirical study) or the countries in the authors' addresses (if a more theoretical study). This search resulted in a few hundred papers for each landscape type. To those we added relevant studies of which we were aware but were not, for different reasons, picked up by the search. Our objective was not a complete review of this literature. Rather, we first searched for general conclusions in the most cited papers, those with at least 30 citations, and we then re-visited the rest of the literature to complement or correct these conclusions. Many of the papers cited in this chapter should be regarded as examples of the phenomena or issues under discussion.

Birds in managed boreal forests

In both eastern North America and western Europe, managed forest landscapes are mainly located in the boreal region; we therefore focus this section on birds in boreal forests. The keywords 'bird* AND boreal forest*' yielded 258 references; 250 (97%) were from North America (USA: 18; Canada: 122) or Europe (110). Of the 52 studies cited at least 30 times, 31 were conducted in North America, 17 in

Europe, and 4 on both continents. The most cited studies were 12–16 years old, irrespective of the continent where the work was conducted.

Differences and similarities between continents

Boreal forest avifaunas evolved in environments affected by large-scale climatic fluctuations during the Quaternary which did not translate into similar forest conditions in North America and Europe (Mönkkönen and Welsh, 1994). Contacts between latitudinal forest zones in North America were more continuous, allowing relatively easy movement of species from boreal forests to temperate or tropical forests, whereas this was not the case in northern Europe (Huntley, 1993).

Overall, the North American avifauna of the boreal forest is taxonomically more diverse than that of Europe (Niemi *et al.*, 1998). The proportion of species that are long-distance migrants (wintering in the tropics) is larger in North America than in Europe (Mönkkönen and Welsh, 1994). However, long-distance migrants represent a significantly greater proportion of breeding birds in early- than late-successional stages in both continents (Imbeau *et al.*, 2001). Hence, long-distance migrants in boreal forests are less likely to be sensitive to landscape-scale changes induced by timber harvesting, which increases the availability of early- and young-seral stages. The proportions of short-distance migrants (wintering in temperate ecosystems) are similar and Europe harbours proportionately more species of permanent residents than North America

(A)   (B)

Figure 19.2 Managed boreal forests in North America (Yukon Territory, Canada (A)) and Europe (Southern Finland (B)). Extensive intercontinental collaboration has taken place between researchers attempting to minimise the impacts of boreal forest management on birds and other wildlife. Northern European forests have a relatively long history of intensive management and deadwood quantities tend to be lower than in North America. Furthermore, forest re-growth is more often achieved by natural regeneration in North America than in Europe. These differences in management have implications for habitat quality for several bird species. © J.-L. Martin.

(Niemi *et al.*, 1998). Residents or short-distance migrants are the most taxonomi-cally related group of species (creepers, kinglets, nuthatches, woodpeckers) on the two continents (Mönkkönen and Welsh, 1994).

Since the last glaciation, boreal forests have responded to many natural disturbances, including fire, insect outbreaks and storms. Fire has the most widespread influence in structuring the regional amount and distribution of forest cover types. In the eastern boreal forest of North America, reconstruc-tion of natural fire history through dendroecological and paleoecological records shows that forests older than the current timber harvesting rotation age (> 100 years) were historically dominant (Bergeron *et al.*, 2006; Cyr *at al.*, 2009). This high proportion of old forest in unharvested forest landscapes of eastern Canada contrasts with a common perception that large-scale fire dis-turbances lead to relatively small proportions of late-seral forests (Niemi *et al.*, 1998). In Sweden, Engelmark (1984) also observed that fire frequency was low in spruce forests. Historical forest inventory records in northern Finland before industrial timber harvesting suggest that the forest was also dominated by stands older than 150 years (Kouki *et al.*, 2001).

Contrary to other environments, boreal forests host few bird species that colonised these forest landscapes following the development of extensive forest management. On both continents native species remain dominant in managed forest landscapes. Compared with naturally disturbed landscapes, however, the bird communities in these modified forests contain higher proportions of habitat generalists and early successional species and a lower proportion of late-seral species (Drapeau *et al.*, 2000). Late-seral species include a high proportion of resident species that share habitat-selection traits, such as a requirement for large-diameter trees or decayed wood that are used as nesting and foraging substrates (Imbeau *et al.*, 2001). These species are strongly affected by the net reduction in the overall amount of deadwood that results from loss of late-seral forests (Fridman and Walheim, 2000; Vaillancourt *et al.*, 2008; Drapeau *et al.*, 2009a). Residents as a group have low densities (Schmiegelow and Mönkkönnen, 2002), but constitute a relatively high proportion of the bird assemblage in late-seral forests compared with other stages (Imbeau *et al.*, 2001). North American residents are more evenly distributed among abundance ranks in the community than their European counterparts that mainly occupy the rarer categories (Schmiegelow and Mönkkönnen, 2002).

On both continents, the question of 'how much late-seral forest is enough' is a key issue for maintaining forest specialists, especially residents that form the most vulnerable species group in these landscapes. Schmiegelow and Mönkkönnen (2002) showed that in both Finland and Canada, resident species had a higher probability of being absent when the amount of late-seral forest was low. Recent developments in the detection of ecological thresholds

(Guénette and Villard, 2005; Drapeau *et al.*, 2009b; Villard and Jonsson, 2009) hold promise for setting conservation targets for these sensitive species.

Influence of forest management practices and history

Management of the boreal forest for timber production has a shorter history in North America than in northern Europe. Nonetheless, large-scale clear-cutting on both continents has massively increased the proportion of early-seral forest (Edenius and Elmberg, 1996; Gauthier *et al.*, 1996; Bergeron *et al.*, 2002). In northern Europe there have been regional declines in birds specialising on older forests and increases in species associated with early-seral stages (Helle and Järvinen, 1986). Even-aged management has profoundly altered the older forest cover types, which are habitats of concern for boreal birds in both continents (Imbeau *et al.*, 2001; Schmiegelow and Mönkkönen, 2002). There are, however, two important differences between boreal management systems of North America and northern Europe: the higher severity of the disturbance created by timber harvesting and the extensive fire suppression in Nordic countries of Europe. In Fennoscandia, intensive silviculture and forest plantations have been widely developed in the last 50 years and 75% of all clear-cuts were planted (Esseen *et al.*, 1997). In the Canadian boreal forest, extensive use of clear-cutting in the last 40 years has been mainly followed by natural regeneration of stands and less than 25% of clear-cuts were planted (Haddon, 1997). Plantations have a simplified tree species composition and structure that result in less diversified bird communities than in naturally regenerated stands (Edenius and Elmberg, 1996).

Forest mosaics of the Canadian boreal are still shaped by large-scale wildfires (Bergeron *et al.*, 2006), whereas in northern Europe, natural fire regimes now occur only in parts of Russia (Esseen *et al.*, 1997). Birds that are associated with burned sites and standing deadwood, such as the black-backed woodpecker *Picoides arcticus*, are the first to benefit from post-fire conditions (Hoyt and Hannon, 2002; Nappi and Drapeau, 2009). Recent increase in salvage logging in wildfires throughout Canada (Nappi *et al.*, 2004; Schmiegelow *et al.*, 2006) may reduce habitat quality for such species. In northern Europe, fire suppression combined with planting reduced early post-fire habitats and inhibited deciduous tree growth (Esseen *et al.*, 1997), affecting resident birds of deciduous stands (Enoksson *et al.*, 1995).

The more severe landscape-scale transformation of the forest cover by intensive silvicultural practices in Nordic European countries likely explains the greater population declines of resident species in Europe than in North America. For instance, the highly threatened status of the white-backed woodpecker *Dendrocopos leucotos* (Virkkala *et al.*, 1993) is linked to the extirpation of deciduous and mixed-wood forest cover through a regulated age structure dominated by conifer stands (Esseen *et al.*, 1997; Carlson, 2000; Mikusiński *et al.*, 2001). Although there are concerns about reduction of older mixed-wood stands and its consequences for bird assemblages in the southern portion of the Canadian boreal forest at stand (Hobson and Bayne, 1999) and landscape scales (Drapeau *et al.*, 2000), bird species that show strong affinities with mixed-wood forests are not currently as severely threatened as some European residents.

The drastic reduction in deadwood availability resulting from intensive forestry and its effects on deadwood associates in Northern Europe (Angelstam and Mikusinski, 1994) is not currently evident in North America. For example, in eastern Canada snag densities of large trees (> 20 cm) in remnant habitats within managed landscapes were similar to or higher than those in unharvested late-seral forests (Mascarúa-Lopez *et al.*, 2006; Vaillancourt *et al.*, 2008). However, remnant forests in cutover areas had fewer of the largest (> 30 cm diameter at breast height (DBH)) dead trees than adjacent unharvested late-seral forest (Vaillancourt *et al.*, 2008). The loss of these largest trees raises concerns for cavity nesters in managed landscapes of eastern Canada (Imbeau *et al.*, 2001). Studies are needed to determine whether these species are likely to show similar population declines to those in Northern Europe. The Fennoscandian experience could be taken as a warning of the likely effects of landscape changes on boreal birds of the eastern Canadian boreal forest if management there is not altered to allow more large dead trees (Imbeau *et al.*, 2001).

The shorter history of forest management in North America may further explain bird community differences between the two continents. The proportion of remaining unharvested natural forest is much higher in the Canadian boreal forest (> 40%) than in Fennoscandia (< 5%) (Imbeau *et al.*, 2001). Effects of loss of late-seral forests on birds in North American managed forests may be dampened by these remaining large blocks of unmanaged forest and this may, in turn, explain the low power of landscape pattern to account for bird community patterns in these recently managed forests (Schmiegelow *et al.*, 1997; Drapeau *et al.*, 2000). In contrast, Kouki and Vaananen (2000) found that species richness and individual abundance of residents of late-seral forests in Finland's natural forest reserves declined significantly with the distance from the continuous forest in Russian Karelia.

Influence of cultural differences

North America lacks Northern Europe's long history of monitoring bird populations in boreal forest; the North American Breeding Bird Survey does not cover the boreal forest sufficiently to allow a sound assessment of population trends. Hence, a broad perspective of regional-scale changes in boreal bird populations has yet to be developed in North America. In contrast, the longer surveys of population trends in boreal Europe allow analyses of changes and the mechanisms involved (Helle and Järvinen, 1986; Haila and Järvinen, 1990).

Nevertheless, in the last 20 years avian research in the boreal forest on both continents has focused on similar issues, conceptual frameworks, methodologies and study designs (Schmiegelow and Mönkkönen, 2002). The response of boreal birds to habitat loss and habitat fragmentation following timber harvesting has been a main focus. In their review, Schmiegelow and Mönkkönnen (2002) concluded that loss of late-seral forests is the main driver of avian responses to timber harvesting in both regions (but see Kouki and Vaananen, 2000). The fact that habitat fragmentation (biotic edge effects, area effects or isolation effects) seems less influential in managed boreal forests than in temperate forests converted for agriculture (see below) may be attributed to several inter-related factors. First, boreal ecosystems have evolved in a context where natural disturbances generate large-scale fragmentation of forest, so species may be more tolerant than in other ecosystems (Niemi *et al.*, 1998; Schmiegelow and Mönkönnen, 2002). A possible indication of this is the persistence of sensitive residents in old-growth refuges in otherwise intensively managed Fennoscandian landscapes (Virkkala, 1991; Kouki and Vaananen, 2000). Second, landscapes managed for timber production remain forested and are not converted into fundamentally different environments (e.g. agriculture) that may attract a greater diversity of predators (Bayne and Hobson, 1997; Kurki *et al.*, 2000). The matrix that results from timber harvesting is thus not as inhospitable to boreal birds as it may be for temperate forest birds in landscapes transformed for agriculture (Brotons *et al.*, 2003). Nonetheless, as discussed above, the loss of late-seral stages clearly has negative effects on several boreal bird species on both continents.

The development of forest management strategies that tackle loss of key habitats in boreal forest is urgently needed. Approaches founded on the principle of narrowing the gap between currently managed landscapes and the diverse forest conditions generated by natural disturbance regimes are promising (Franklin, 1993; Haila *et al.*, 1994; Bergeron *et al.*, 2002). However, these should be used alongside approaches targeted on species of concern (Lindenmayer *et al.*, 2007; Drapeau *et al.*, 2009b), including identification of potential ecological thresholds (Betts and Villard, 2009).

Intercontinental co-operation within the scientific community working in the boreal forest has become quite extensive in the last 15 years and increased considerably our understanding of this ecosystem (see Korpilahti and Kuuluvainen, 2002; Angelstam *et al.*, 2004). In parallel, environmental certification of managed forests and international biodiversity agreements have encouraged forest-management approaches incorporating values additional to timber production. This situation, coupled with similarities in responses of boreal birds to habitat alteration, is likely to facilitate further transfer of concepts and findings between continents.

Forest birds in farmed landscapes

The keywords 'bird* AND forest fragment* AND agric*' yielded 301 references; 272 were from North America (USA: 122; Canada: 60) or Europe (90). Of the 58 studies cited at least 30 times, 36 were conducted in North America, 16 in Europe and 6 on both continents. The most cited studies were 10–15 years old, irrespective of the continent of origin.

Differences and similarities between continents

The fragmented forests examined here mainly occupy the temperate zone, where human activity has left virtually no old-growth forest. There are broad biogeographical differences between the temperate forest avifaunas of North America and Europe. While 45% and 67% of resident species have a holarctic distribution in North America and Europe, respectively, migratory species of these continents do not share a single genus (Mönkkönen and Welsh, 1994). Migratory species dominate the temperate forest breeding avifauna of North America (Holmes and Sherry, 2001) and this is also the case in central Europe (Wesołowski and Tomiałojć, 1997). However, in central Europe, many of these birds are short-distance, rather than tropical, migrants (Wesołowski and Tomiałojć, 1997). Most of these short-distance migrants are residents in western Europe, so the contribution of residents to forest breeding assemblages varies across Europe (R.J. Fuller pers. comm.). Neotropical and Paleotropical migrant avifaunas differ taxonomically and in habitat associations. Most Neotropical migrants are associated with mid- to late-seral forest, whereas most Paleotropical migrants are mainly associated with early-seral stages and, therefore, are not sensitive (as a group) to the loss/fragmentation of late-seral forests (Mönkkönen *et al.*, 1992; Böhning-Gaese and Oberrath, 2003; Chapter 1). Neotropical migrants seem especially sensitive to forest landscape change following agricultural expansion (Rodewald and Yahner, 2001). There are few equivalent European studies, possibly because deforestation occurred long ago. Few, if any, non-native species have colonised fragmented forest landscapes on either continent.

On both continents, forest fragments have been subjected to disturbance by domestic herbivores, firewood cutting and wild animals that benefit from surrounding agricultural habitats. The last include nest predators that reduce the reproductive success of forest birds and are different from the nest predators of managed forests (Andrén, 1992; Kurki *et al.*, 2000). In North America, the brood parasitic brown-headed cowbird *Molothrus ater*, historically associated with bison *Bos bison* herds of the Great Plains, has a significant negative effect on the reproduction of hosts in eastern forests where it expanded following forest removal for agriculture (Hoover and Brittingham, 1993). More generally, the nature of matrix habitat matters for the persistence of forest birds in fragments (Brotons *et al.*, 2003; Dunford and Freemark, 2004).

(A)   (B)

Figure 19.3 Temperate forest fragments in farmed landscapes in North America
(Tennessee, USA (A)) and Europe (South western France (B)). Studies of the birds in these
fragments have taken rather different trajectories on the two continents and there
has been very little intercontinental collaboration. In Europe these woodland patches
tend to be seen as an integral part of cultural landscapes, whereas in North America
they are largely perceived as a legacy of forest fragmentation. © S. Blangy and G. Balent.

Andrén (1994) reported a tendency for fragmentation effects to be more prominent in landscapes with less than *c.* 20–30% forest cover. This sparked a debate on
both continents on the existence of a 'fragmentation threshold', a phenomenon
later simulated through modelling (Fahrig, 1997; Flather and Bevers, 2002). In
North America, this encouraged further empirical tests of the relative influence
of habitat amount/loss vs. configuration/fragmentation on species response to
landscape change (McGarigal and McComb, 1995; Trzcinski *et al.*, 1999; Villard
et al., 1999). In Europe, Mönkkönen and Reunanen (1999) pointed out that the
fragmentation threshold suggested by Andrén (1994) coincided with a shift from
studies conducted in managed forest landscapes (higher overall forest cover) to
ones in island archipelagos or in forests fragmented by agriculture.

Within forest landscapes fragmented by agriculture, teasing apart the relative
influence of habitat amount, configuration and their interaction remains con-
tentious and statistically challenging (Koper *et al.*, 2007; Chapter 4). Some North
American studies suggested a stronger influence of forest cover (McGarigal and
McComb, 1995; Trzcinski *et al.*, 1999), whereas others have emphasised species-
specific responses to cover or configuration (Villard *et al.*, 1999).

Influence of management practices, history and culture

In North America, considerable attention has been devoted to the effects of
forest fragmentation on nest predation (Robinson *et al.*, 1995; Tewksbury *et al.*,
1998; Burke and Nol, 2000; Flaspohler *et al.*, 2001; Burke *et al.*, 2004; Driscoll
and Donovan, 2004). European researchers have given much less attention to

this issue, except in Fennoscandia (Andrén and Angelstam, 1988; Andrén, 1992; Chapter 4). In Europe, proportionally greater attention has been given to fragmentation effects on populations and individuals, including alteration of dispersal patterns (Lens and Dhondt, 1994; Matthysen and Currie, 1996), physiological stress and brood sex ratio (Suorsa *et al.*, 2003, 2004), or survival rate (Robles *et al.*, 2007). The effects of management practices and browsing impacts within European forest fragments, and consequences for avian habitat quality, has been a recent focus of much work (Chapter 14). While European researchers have mainly examined dispersal patterns through individually banded populations or band recoveries (Paradis *et al.*, 1998), North American researchers have investigated fragmentation effects on movements using indirect approaches such as gap-crossing experiments (Desrochers and Hannon, 1997), translocations (Bélisle *et al.*, 2001; Gobeil and Villard, 2002) and radio-telemetry (Norris and Stutchbury, 2001).

In North America, studies tended to be shorter, to cover larger areas, and to focus more on open-nesting species (Robinson *et al.*, 1995; Burke and Nol, 2000; Flaspohler *et al.*, 2001; Weldon and Haddad, 2005) than European studies. In Europe, long-term population studies using nest-boxes or the monitoring of colonies located in buildings are common (Kuitunen and Mäkinen, 1993; Huhta *et al.*, 2004; Tufto *et al.*, 2005; but see Robles *et al.*, 2008). The extensive use of nest-boxes in European forests may have allowed very high breeding densities (Wesołowski, 2007), low predation rates (Kuitunen and Alecknonis, 1992), or high nestling ectoparasitism (Wesołowski and Stańska, 2001) relative to levels in old-growth forests. Surprisingly, this potential source of bias received little attention when interpreting data on species occurrence and relative abundance in European studies of birds in forest fragments.

Most forest patches in agricultural landscapes of North America are remnants of native forests or naturally regenerated stands, whereas in many agricultural regions of Europe, forest patches were planted. Such patches are usually structurally very different from remnants. Nonetheless, a planted fragment is subject to similar effects (e.g. edge, isolation) as a more 'natural' fragment; Villard and Taylor (1994) showed that the colonisation of planted 'fragments' could, to some extent, reflect the relative tolerance of individual bird species to forest fragmentation.

Perhaps as a result of their different historical landscape trajectories, differences in landscape perception are apparent among researchers on the two continents. For example, the recent origin of forest fragments in North America may explain why 'fragmentation' is more often adopted as a theoretical framework in studies there than in Europe. North Americans take a more forest-focused perspective, whereas Europeans seem to put a greater emphasis on landscape complementation/supplementation, i.e. the use by forest breeding birds of other habitat types to supplement or complement their resources (Dunning *et al.*, 1992; Rolstad *et al.*, 2000; Barbero *et al.*, 2008). Such studies are less common in North America (Leonard *et al.*, 2008; Wilson and Watts, 2008). Part of the explanation could be that the North American forest avifauna includes a smaller proportion of generalist species, those most likely to exhibit landscape supplementation. The higher prevalence of generalists in Europe may reflect local extirpation of certain guilds by long-term anthropogenic effects, in addition to biogeographic differences between the continents (Mönkkönen and Welsh, 1994; see also Chapter 6). Interestingly, we found no intercontinental comparisons of forest birds in farmed landscapes, suggesting that the two research communities are working rather independently.

Finally, with the retreat of agriculture on marginal farmland and urban sprawl in many regions on both continents, the major threat to birds of temperate forest fragments has shifted from agriculture to urbanisation (Hedblom and Söderström, 2008).

Farmland birds in farmed landscapes

The key words 'bird* AND agriculture*', 'bird* AND grassland*', or 'bird* AND farmland*' yielded 578 references: 208 were from North America (175 USA; 33 Canada); 359 were from Europe of which 194 were from the UK alone. Of the papers cited 30 or more times, 26 were from North America and 63 from Europe. Of the 10 most cited American papers, 8 were older than 13 years, while 8 of the 10 most cited European papers were published in the past 10 years at the time of the survey. We found no intercontinental studies.

Differences and similarities between continents

In North America, agricultural landscapes are typically composed of a matrix of remnant native or semi-natural habitats such as grasslands, forests, wetlands and wooded fencerows, as well as land managed for agricultural production such as row crops, forage crops, orchards, summer fallow, pasture and rangeland. Historically, the grasslands of the Great Plains in the United States and southern Canada were dynamic landscapes maintained by grazing and fire (Samson and Knopf, 1996). With the loss of large herbivores, notably bison, and fire suppression, invasion of woody plants has become a significant threat to indigenous biodiversity in some of these grasslands (Grant *et al.*, 2004; Johnson, 2005). In the Great Plains, some farming practices have become surrogates for natural disturbance and create/maintain habitats that are no longer present (e.g. cattle and mowing for bison and fire; managed grasslands for native prairie). Row crops, in contrast, are generally impoverished from an avian perspective (Rodenhouse *et al.*, 1995; Best *et al.*, 1995). While some grassland species do nest in managed agricultural landscapes, their occupancy rates and reproductive output there are not as high as they

(A)   (B)

Figure 19.4 Farmland landscapes in North America (Outaouais, Québec, Canada (A)) and Europe (central England (B)). In Europe the conservation of birds that are adapted to living in long-established open agricultural landscapes is a high priority. In North America the perspective is strikingly different in that the negative effects of agriculture on 'natural habitats' are generally emphasised. Hence, the reference landscapes are very different on the two continents. © J.-L. Martin and G. Siriwardena.

would be in extensive native prairie grassland (Best, 1986; Rodenhouse *et al.*, 1995; Davis *et al.*, 1999).

The greatest perceived threat to grassland birds in the North American prairies and Great Plains is the loss of native grasslands to agriculture, urbanisation and industrial development. In contrast, in parts of eastern North America, the greatest threat is from abandonment of farmland and subsequent vegetation succession, together with conversion of pasture to row crops as a result of changes in market forces. For these open-habitat bird species, farming facilitated range expansion and population increases (Peterjohn, 2003) at the beginning of the twentieth century (Askins, 1999) (e.g. bobolinks *Dolichonyx oryzivorus*, barn swallows *Hirundo rustica*, eastern meadowlark *Sturnella magna*), some gaining pest status (red-winged blackbird *Agelaius phoeniceus* and brood parasitic cowbirds *Molothrus* spp.).

In much of Europe, semi-natural habitats that remain in farmed landscapes usually have a history of regular management and are far removed from a natural state, whereas comparable habitat fragments in North America can be more similar to their native state in plant species composition. A high proportion of European landbirds depend in some way on farmland for their persistence. For example, 173 species of 'high conservation priority' are associated with agriculture and grassland – more than with any other broad habitat type (Tucker and Evans, 1997). Trends in 36 of these species are used to produce a common farmland bird indicator (www.ebcc.info). Sixteen of these species are long-distance migrants. Many of them have exhibited continent-wide declines and continue to be at risk from intensification or farm abandonment.

Few North American authors refer to 'farmland birds' per se; species are typically defined by their native habitat association such as grasslands, forests, shrublands or wetlands. Nevertheless, in southern Ontario, Kirk *et al.* (2001) reported 109 bird species using crop fields or apple orchards; 14% were resident (of which 3% were non-native), 50% were Neotropical migrants and 36% were short-distance migrants. Almost a quarter (23), mostly grassland species, showed significant declines at the end of the twentieth century, according to the North American Breeding Bird Survey (Downes and Collins, 2008). If North American researchers developed a list of specialist farmland birds, it would likely look very similar to the European list in terms of the types of species included, except that migrant species would predominate in North America (e.g. killdeer *Charadrius vociferus* vs. lapwing *Vanellus vanellus*; vesper sparrow *Pooecetes gramineus* vs. corn bunting *Emberiza calandra*).

Influence of history and culture on research approaches

It seems that historical context is responsible for intercontinental differences in research perspectives on birds in farmed landscapes. Broadly speaking, in North America research has focused on short-term, synecological studies that explore landscape and ecological theory through a hypothesis-testing paradigm. Most North American applied ecological studies of birds in farmland are relatively recent (since the 1970s). As approximately 70% of Canadian and Northern USA species are migratory, most of these studies focused on the breeding season and to a lesser extent spring and fall migration.

North American studies of birds in farmland tend to focus on birds in remnant native habitats rather than in the farmed fields (Robinson *et al.*, 1995; Herkert *et al.*, 2003). The effects of agriculture have been examined through: (1) the loss and fragmentation of native habitats (see 'Forest birds in farmed landscapes' above); (2) the mechanisms involved in adverse effects (e.g. edge effects/area sensitivity, meso-carnivore release/predation, cowbird parasitism) and only to a lesser extent, (3) the effects of management practices (mowing, tillage, pesticide use) and intensification (increased specialisation, larger fields, chemical use) on birds in remnant habitats (Davis *et al.*, 1999; Shutler *et al.*, 2000; Martin and Forsyth, 2003; Davis, 2004) and in wider farmed landscapes (Jobin *et al.*, 1998; Boutin *et al.*, 1999; Freemark and Kirk, 2001; Kirk *et al.*, 2001; Murphy, 2003). 'How much habitat is enough?' has become the prevailing question in relation to management of native habitats within the farmed matrix, an approach that originated within the paradigm of island biogeography theory. However, this is rarely based on modelling of habitat-specific densities to determine how much habitat would be needed to maintain certain population sizes. Some Canadian studies suggest that farming practices have a secondary influence on bird species composition and abundance compared with habitat composition, but this effect is stronger in eastern North America than in the prairies (Freemark and Kirk, 2001). Studies on the effects of field management on bird species' presence or abundance in North America have looked at effects of hay mowing, tillage, burning and pesticides (Frawley and Best, 1991; Freemark and Boutin, 1995; Martin and Forsyth, 2003; Mineau *et al.*, 2005).

In contrast to North America, European research has focused on empirical, long-term (sometimes back to the 1950s) autecological studies with in-depth analysis of population demographics, trends and causal factors contributing to changes in farmland bird populations (see review by Wilson *et al.*, 2009). These studies cover both the breeding season and winter (a much higher proportion of farmland birds in western Europe are resident than observed in North America). Results from the breeding season have shown that for many declining species, changes in agricultural practices have reduced food availability and the number of nesting attempts that birds can achieve during a breeding season (see also Chapter 7). However, for many granivorous species the key pressures operate in winter through a drastic reduction in seed availability, a consequence of more intensive herbicide use, lower availability of winter stubble and decreased local habitat heterogeneity in the landscape (Newton, 2004; Wilson *et al.*, 2009; Chapter 7).

In Europe, habitat selection research on farmland birds has drawn less on concepts stemming from island biogeography and more from concepts of landscape complementation and supplementation (as with forest fragments). Many European papers focus intensively and directly on habitat selection of birds in farmed areas and on causal mechanisms explaining distribution and abundance. They also examine the efficacy of changes in management practices (e.g. shift in autumn to spring tillage – Aebischer *et al.*, 2000), mitigation measures (e.g. field margin management – Vickery *et al.*, 2009) or agri-environment schemes (e.g. EU Bird Directive – Donald *et al.*, 2007). In Europe, there has been an especially strong focus on arable systems, but increasingly there has been concern about loss and intensified use of semi-natural grassland (Vickery *et al.*, 2001; Billeter *et al.*, 2007).

Interestingly, several European studies consider how the presence of semi-natural habitats affects the distribution and abundance of birds *within* the farmed component of the landscape (examples in Wilson *et al.*, 2009 and in Chapter 7). We suggest that the effects of habitat mosaics (interspersion of natural, semi-natural and productive patches) on landscape quality for birds needs more emphasis on both continents.

In summary, the main difference across continents is that in North America, the research emphasis is on comparing the species in farmland to the species that would have been there without farmland; the benchmark is non-farmland. In contrast, in Europe the research emphasis has been on the type of farming practice and the heterogeneity and interspersion of crops and semi-natural field-edge habitats necessary to maintain a suite of farmland specialist species. So, in Europe, the benchmark is 'traditional' farmland and its characteristic species.

Influence of history and culture on conservation

In North America farming is perceived as inimical to wildlife and agricultural landscapes as being unable to protect it (Peterjohn, 2003). Much land was converted to agriculture after the Homesteading Act (1862). Homesteaders had a frontier mentality that nature was limitless; witness the killing of thousands of Eskimo curlews *Numenius borealis* on their spring migration through the Great Plains – a bird now almost certainly extinct (COSEWIC, 2009). Thus in North America today, declining grassland birds as a group are considered a conservation issue, but more general range reductions and declines in other 'farmland' birds are not, though this is changing with the recognition that other open-country birds are also declining (see below).

In the UK and other parts of western Europe, the land tenure system arose out of the feudally derived system of the Middle Ages. Landed gentry owned the land, with tenant farmers renting individual smallholdings and having a vested interest in preserving uncropped areas to favour game (O'Connor and Shrubb, 1986). Such traditional agriculture (small fields, hedgerows, minimal or no pesticide use) is widely regarded as beneficial to wildlife, many species of which have a long history of co-dependence on human land use (see also Chapter 6). In Europe, declines in these farmland birds is recognised by governments as a conservation crisis.

Over the past decades in eastern North America widespread declines of grassland and shrubland species have been observed (Brennan and Kuvlesky, 2005; Askins *et al.*, 2007a; Sauer *et al.*, 2008). Many bird species now at risk are ones associated with successional habitats (shrubland, grasslands, old fields, woody pastures) that have been lost either because of intensification of farming practices or land abandonment (Askins, 1993; Vickery *et al.*, 2005; Askins *et al.*, 2007a, 2007b). Land abandonment has become a concern in parts of Europe too, where the reduction of traditional grazing systems has generated large shifts in bird communities (Sirami *et al.*, 2008).

North American avian conservation initiatives began with the North American Waterfowl Management Program (NAWMP), which remains the most well-funded bird conservation program in North America, a reflection of the traditional emphasis on game birds (Cooke, 2003). While declines in Neotropical migrant forest birds precipitated the formation of Partners in Flight (PIF), only recently has avian conservation in North America embraced other groups, such as grassland birds, under the umbrella organisation of the North American Bird Conservation Initiative (NABCI). But, despite the population declines over the last 40 years of many grassland and shrubland species, birds have not been considered an important indicator of biodiversity in farm-land by North American decision-makers. There are no North American agri-environment schemes specifically designed to benefit birds and other wildlife. In the absence of conservation policies for biodiversity on farmland, ancillary benefits for biodiversity have come from, for example, programmes targeting soil erosion reduction (Best *et al.*, 1997; Sutter *et al.*, 2000; McMaster *et al.*, 2001).

In contrast, European farmland birds have become the focus of large-scale management and mitigation measures through agri-environment schemes providing incentives to landholders (Donald *et al.*, 2007; Chapter 7). Population trends of species such as the skylark *Alauda arvensis* and grey partridge *Perdix perdix* are indices against which land management policies are assessed. The high profile of this group of species is illustrated by the result of a general web search (via Google) that used 'farmland birds' and 'Europe' as keywords. It yielded over 450 directly relevant hits, which included a high proportion of links to press releases and information pamphlets for the general public or for policy-makers.

Birds in urban landscapes

From the 359 papers that we compiled through the database search and our own knowledge, we identified four intercontinental papers and about 110 from each continent that described empirical studies of bird responses to urbanisation. Of the 27 studies that have been cited more than 30 times, 18 are North American, six are European and three are intercontinental. Eleven of the highly cited North American studies and four of the highly cited European studies were published within the last 10 years.

Differences and similarities between continents

Overall, the urban bird literature suggests that birds respond similarly to urbanisation in North America and in Europe and that much of what has been learned on one continent can be applied on the other. There are similarities in the resources and habitat patterns that are important predictors of bird distributions in urban areas. The amount of vegetated area in an urban landscape, and the fine-scale structure of the vegetation, are important drivers of species diversity (Clergeau *et al.*, 1998; Turner *et al.*, 2004), community composition (Jokimäki *et al.*, 1996; Blair, 1996) and individual species distribution and abundance (Germaine *et al.*, 1998; Wilkinson 2006). Similarly, the distribution of food resources, particularly supplemental feeding and the availability of human refuse, has been strongly linked to species distributions (Hunt, 1972; Brittingham and Temple, 1992; Schmidt and Bock, 2005). The nature of the predator communities (Jokimäki and Huta, 2000; Thorington and Bowman, 2003) is often mentioned, although it is not clear whether predation generally increases or decreases with urbanisation (Martin and Clobert, 1996; Gering and

Blair, 1999; Chiron and Juliard, 2007; Sims *et al.*, 2008). Finally, the disturbance created by high levels of human activity (Fernandez-Juricic and Telleria, 2000; Schlesinger *et al.*, 2008) and increased mortality from collisions with human structures (Verheijen, 1981; Boal and Mannan, 1999; Klem, 2004) are also implicated in urbanisation effects in both North America and Europe.

Similar species traits are associated with strong positive or negative responses to urbanisation in North America and Europe (Johnston, 2001; Clergeau *et al.*, 2006; Bonier *et al.*, 2007; Croci *et al.*, 2008). Species that are positively affected by urbanisation are generally those with broad distributions and environmental tolerances, that are highly social and behaviourally adaptive, that nest in cavities and that are omnivorous or granivorous. In contrast, species that are insectivorous or that nest on the ground are generally negatively affected by urbanisation.

At the community level, North American, European and intercontinental studies have found comparable responses to increasing urbanisation (Clergeau *et al.*, 1998, 2001; Turner *et al.*, 2004). In both continents there is a general increase in bird density and/or biomass, a decrease in evenness, an overall decrease in species richness from rural areas to the urban core (Lancaster and Rees, 1979; Melles *et al.*, 2003) and a general homogenising effect, where bird communities in the urban cores of distant cities are more similar than are the bird communities in the surrounding non-urban areas (Blair, 2004; Clergeau *et al.*, 2006). However, studies on both continents have at times found conflicting patterns in community metrics along an urbanisation gradient, so these generalisations are not absolute (Marzluff, 2001; Caula *et al.*, 2008).

(A)   (B)

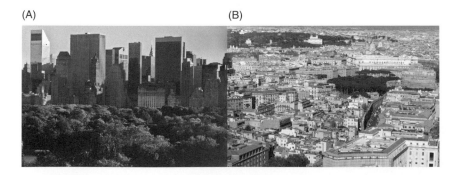

Figure 19.5 Urban landscapes in North America (New York City, USA (A)) and Europe (Rome, Italy (B)). Despite similarities in the ways that birds respond to urbanisation in Europe and North America, so far there has been little collaboration or convergence in research. In North America, urban areas are generally considered to have negative impacts on biodiversity and there are strong concerns about negative effects on 'natural habitats'. In Europe there has been more work on the adaptation of species to urban environments and it is increasingly recognised that urban areas can have conservation value. © J.-L. Martin

The most striking difference in findings between the continents is the increase in the proportion of non-native species with urbanisation in North America. This is not surprising considering that the dominant non-native species in North American cities are three highly successful synanthropic species from Europe (rock dove/feral pigeon *Columba livia*, European starling *Sturnus vulgaris* and house sparrow *Passer domesticus*). European cities have some non-native species that have successfully established populations (many belonging to the *Psittacidae*, Murgui and Valentín, 2003), yet these species still have limited distributions and do not dominate the urban bird community as do the non-native species in North American cities.

Some North American studies suggest that migratory species are more negatively affected by urban development than residents (Friesen *et al.*, 1995). Although at least one review suggested that this difference is general (Chase and Walsh, 2006), we found little evidence to support a migratory effect in Europe. In the single European study that showed a differential response, the patterns were different from those found in North America: turnover and local extinction rates were higher and more related to urbanisation for migratory than for resident species, but species richness or abundance were not different (Husté and Boulinier, 2007). Another European study that compared migratory and resident species did not find strong differences (Jokimäki and Suhonen, 1998), and qualitatively suggested migratory birds may even be more common than residents in urban and suburban areas. A potential explanation for the apparent lack of a migratory effect in Europe is that very few studies have tested for it. Among the empirical studies in this review that include migration-related terms in the abstract, there are 28 from North America and nine from Europe (of which only two actually tested for an effect).

Perhaps the most interesting difference between the continents has more to do with the types of questions asked. In North America, there is a greater focus on the impacts of urbanisation: the limited energy (primary productivity) or food in urban systems (Shochat *et al.*, 2006); the changes to food webs and species interactions (Anderies *et al.*, 2007) and the degradation of relatively natural areas, where urbanisation is perceived as an ecological crisis (McKinney, 2002). In Europe, there is a stronger focus on evolutionary and behavioural adaptations to urban habitats (Slabbekoorn and den Boer-Visser, 2006; Møller, 2008); of the 21 papers that deal directly with the evolution of birds to urban environments, four had only North American authors, 16 had only European authors and the remaining study had authors from both continents. European studies also focus on common synanthropic species as the subject of study (Partecke and Gwinner, 2007), and parks and natural areas within an urban context (Fernandez-Juric and Jokimäki, 2001), whereas North American studies focus on the effect of urbanisation on non-urban species.

Of course, these continental differences are far from absolute and related research threads in the two continents do exist. Indeed, urban ecology has generated complementary and collaborative research streams between the continents, as well as a great deal of diversity within each continent. The differences between continents suggest that there is still much to be gained through further intercontinental collaborations. The recent surges in studies on energy and food-web dynamics in North America (Shochat *et al.*, 2006) and on adaptations to urban environments in Europe (Slabbekoorn *et al.*, 2007) may have great potential for comparative work across the Atlantic.

Influence of variation in nature of urban habitats

Urban and suburban microhabitats are strikingly similar worldwide (Pickett *et al.*, 2001). The similarities in species traits, community-level responses and mechanisms that we have outlined suggest that there are common patterns and processes in urbanisation and that much avian research is applicable across the Atlantic. Considering the strong homogenisation effects that seem to dominate in urban environments, this may be more true in urban landscapes than managed forests or agriculture (McKinney, 2002; Clergeau *et al.*, 2006).

Although urban areas themselves are very similar, latitudinal, climatic and regional factors, and the effects of surrounding land use, the amount of remaining natural area, and the degree of contrast between the urban structure and the natural landcover are also important (Marzluff, 2001; Clergeau *et al.*, 2006). Therefore much of our understanding of urban effects on birds seems to apply across the Atlantic but contrasts within continents – arid vs. temperate systems (Shochat *et al.*, 2006; Bock *et al.*, 2008) and high vs. low development intensity in the surrounding landscape matrix (Melles *et al.*, 2003; Palomino and Carrascal, 2007) – will continue to be important factors.

The rate of urbanisation has been generally higher in North America than in Europe (Richardson and Bae, 2005), which may have reduced the potential for species to adapt in North America (Martin and Clobert, 1996; Clergeau *et al.*, 2004), suggesting that North American species should be more adversely impacted by urbanisation. However, rates of urban sprawl in Europe have recently increased (Richardson and Bae, 2005), suggesting that European researchers may benefit from some North American studies (Friesen *et al.*, 1995). Increased urbanisation rates in Europe may present both an opportunity for researchers and a challenge for urban bird conservation (Shaw *et al.*, 2008).

Influence of history and culture

Some of the differences between urban bird communities in North America and Europe are likely due to the idiosyncrasies of history. The important role of non-native species in North American studies is primarily due to the introduction of European species that were pre-adapted to urban conditions.

Rock doves were first introduced to North America in the early 1600s (Schorger, 1952), leaving little time for any native species to occupy a vacant urban niche. House sparrows and European starlings were also introduced when urban areas were still relatively new and rare features in North America (Robbins, 1973; Cabe, 1993).

Although the historical extent of exposure to urbanisation may explain the success of some European species in North America, the rates at which urban landscapes continue to change and the relatively recent adaptations of many species to urban conditions suggest that short-term effects are at least as important as historical effects. Some North American species have been associated with urban areas for hundreds of years (e.g. chimney swifts *Chaetura pelagica*, barn swallows, many gull species), others have colonised cities more recently (e.g. merlins *Falco columbarius*, Sohdi and Oliphant, 1992). Some European species have also shown relatively recent, abrupt adaptations to urban environments (see Chapter 3) while long-term synanthropic species are showing steep population declines (De Laet and Summers-Smith, 2007).

Preferences for different research questions in North America and Europe likely result from different perceptions of the reference landscape. North American researchers tend to use a 'pristine' landscape as the reference, while Europeans tend to assume some level of human activity. This explains why, in North America, species that are negatively affected by urbanisation are most often the research focus while synanthropic species receive less attention and questions about the evolutionary or behavioural adaptations to urban habitats are rarely asked. Urbanisation is perceived as a process that degrades or destroys a pristine landscape, and the urban bird community as a depauperate group dominated by low-quality species.

In Europe the behavioural and evolutionary adaptations of species to urban habitats is a more active field of study. Synanthropic species are more likely to be studied and questions about the design and management of urban parks are asked more frequently. These patterns reflect a perception of urban areas as a complex part of the landscape which, if managed well, can support a valuable and diverse bird community.

These different tendencies in research focus can have important consequences. For example, the chimney swift and the European swift *Apus apus* are similar in that both nest in human structures, reach peak densities in the urban core, are synanthropic to a similar degree, and have been declining by approximately 3–4% annually since 1994 (Sauer *et al.*, 2008; Baillie *et al.*, 2010). A simple literature search within the ISI Web of Science produces nine hits on the North American chimney swift; the only one published since 1997 is a rarity-sighting from Spain. This compares with 76 hits on the European swift, with 41 published since 1997. The dearth of research on this declining North American 'city bird' reflects a North American bias against synanthropic species.

Conclusions: lessons and implications for conservation
Differences and similarities across continents

For birds of managed boreal forests there is a well-identified species pool with species, ecology and research trends showing much in common across continents. There is also a common concern and research emphasis on the negative effects of the current reduction in late-seral stages in these forests. The longer history of forestry intensification in Europe and the resulting knowledge on forest birds' response to levels of habitat alteration should act as a warning for bird conservation in North American managed forests.

By contrast, research on use of forest fragments by birds in agricultural landscapes has taken rather different routes on the two continents. This is partly a result of phylogenetic differences in bird communities, with migrants dominating late-seral stages in North America and early-seral stages in Europe. North American researchers essentially perceive forest fragments as the result of habitat destruction by agriculture, and consequently focus on negative effects of the agricultural matrix on native forest bird communities persisting in fragments, with emphasis on Neotropical migrants. Initially at least, many of these studies adopted the island metaphor, while European studies did less so, instead perceiving patches of forest as components of the cultural landscape, and focusing on understanding how bird populations function in their landscape context.

For farmland birds, the research emphasis, both in North America and Europe, is on causes of species losses relative to a reference. But in North America the reference landscape is 'natural' (non-farmed) land, whereas in Europe the reference landscape is 'traditional' farmland. This difference is likely due to differences in time since conversion to farmland and the historical rate of conversion. This has led to an emphasis on farmland-associated species in European studies, and on forest-, wetland- and grassland-associated species in North American studies. It has also resulted in a recognised suite of farmland species in Europe, but not in North America. Thus, while Europe sees farmland as 'nature' and the challenge as finding ways to change farming in a favourable way, North America continues to see farmland more as conflicting with nature and the challenge is to find ways to minimise adverse effects of agriculture in the landscape. The latter attitude tends to forget that, in North America, farmland is extensively used by some native bird species, and does not encourage the development of practices favourable to bird diversity in farmland.

There is a recognised suite of urban species in North America and Europe. Overall, birds respond similarly to urbanisation in North America and Europe and much of what has been learned in one continent can be applied in the other. North American researchers have tended to ignore the urban-adapted species and focused on impacts of urbanisation on other species, whereas

European research is focused on adaptation to urban landscapes. Time since urban development does not seem to be an important determinant of the urban bird community; some bird populations have adapted or adjusted quickly to urbanisation in the few hundred years that urban areas have existed in North America. The effects on urban bird communities of the surrounding land use, the amount of remaining natural area and the degree of contrast between the urban structure and the natural land cover deserve further investigation on both continents. There is great potential for inter-continental collaborations that embrace both the European focus on the conservation value of urban areas, and the North American focus on the detrimental effects of unchecked urban development.

From the perceived to the actual: a necessary shift for conservation?

Although the biological processes involved are often probably identical, marked differences in research emphasis are evident between the two con-tinents. These seem mainly to result from divergent reference points: human-dominated 'traditional' landscapes in Europe vs. 'natural' landscapes in North America. The assumption in North America of a 'non-cultural' benchmark (the pre-colonial period), in which humans had little effect on wild bird populations, is accompanied by the corollary that human-modified land-scapes are less desirable than the 'pre-settlement' landscape (Hulse *et al.*, 2000; Santelmann *et al.*, 2008).

This attitude faces major challenges. The historical data on the reference situation is rather limited, but seems likely to have been much less 'natural' (unaffected by humans) than commonly assumed. The notion of an 'empty frontier' ignores the influence of populous Aboriginal societies that shaped landscapes and faunas through fire, agriculture and forest management to favour certain trees and animals. It likely refers only to the short period that followed the decimation of these societies by disease introduced by early European explorers (Mann, 2005).

In Europe, the trajectories of land transformation by humans have been documented for over 2000 years and cultural landscapes have become an intri-cate part of the perception of the natural world by Europeans. Culturally modi-fied 'traditional' landscapes are often perceived positively in Europe and are often considered more desirable than forested 'natural' landscapes that result from land abandonment. This is probably the reason that many European studies focus on understanding and preserving the biological diversity found in cultural landscapes at a time when they are subject to profound changes.

The intercontinental differences in research questions and conclusions are smallest in the cultural landscapes that have been least subject to recent human interference (the boreal forest) and largest in the cultural landscapes most subject to transformation in recent history. While farmland and urban landscapes have a high degree of similarity in structure between continents, the questions asked in them are different on the two continents. Those differences have led to different conclusions in the farmed landscapes, but have not

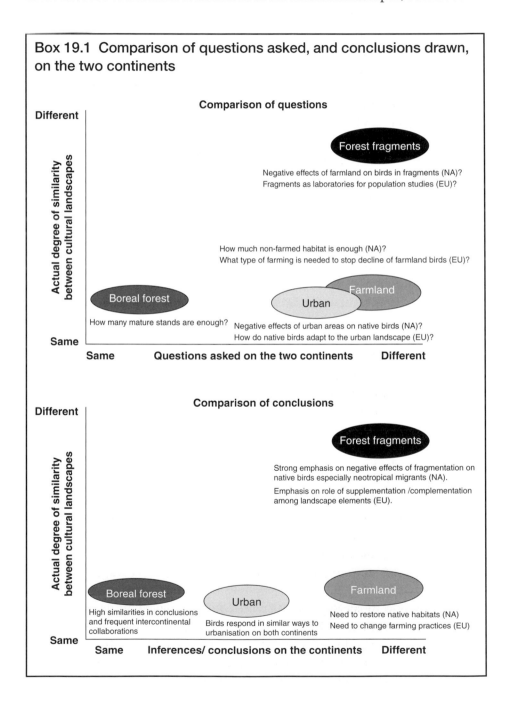

Box 19.1 Comparison of questions asked, and conclusions drawn, on the two continents

prevented some convergence in conclusions in studies on birds in urban landscapes (Box 19.1).

Appreciation of how different perspectives on similar situations can influence our conclusions could help revitalise the approach to studying birds in cultural landscapes, by facilitating a shift in focus from 'what was there' to 'what could be there' under appropriate landscape management. Indeed, the return to either reference state – a 'pre-settlement' mythological ideal world in North America or the past land-use practices in Europe – is unrealistic.

The challenge on both continents is rather to look at current patterns of bird habitat selection in cultural landscapes, and those predicted in response to climate change, and to use the knowledge gained to shape future cultural landscapes in which opportunities are maximised for wild species to prosper alongside production for human consumption. European research could elicit the emergence of a new biodiversity management paradigm in North America that would give increased emphasis to the ecological potential of cultural landscapes. For example, the importance of multi-scaled habitat heterogeneity for biodiversity within agricultural landscapes is strongly recognised in Europe (see Chapter 7). Conversely, European researchers and land managers could draw from the North American experience a renewed interest in the value of 'benign neglect' as a conservation approach that would, for example, take advantage of changes in agricultural regulation of subsidies to abandon some farmland to natural succession or active forest restoration. Interestingly, a lot of current conservation schemes developing in Europe aim at creating habitat networks (see Boitani *et al.*, 2007), a restoration process often misleadingly propounded as fragmentation in reverse, and there is also growing interest in the value of natural disturbance as an integral process in landscape-scale conservation (Hodder *et al.*, 2009). The development of an intercontinental common vision on the ecology of cultural landscapes, enriched by the diversity of backgrounds and situations found on the two continents, would be an extraordinary context for ensuring a more sustainable future for biodiversity.

Acknowledgements

We are grateful to Rob Fuller for suggesting we should take up the challenge of bringing this 'intercontinental' chapter together. We thank Sue Hannon, K. Martin and A. Desrochers for their insights during early discussions of this contribution. J.L.M. would like to thank Tony Gaston at the National Wildlife Research Centre (Environment Canada) on the campus of Carleton University for hosting him in such a stimulating working environment during his secondment in Ottawa, and his home institution (CEFE/CNRS) for letting him go! Weekly discussions fostered by the Geomatics and Landscape Ecology Research Lab at Carleton University played a critical role in the emergence of a more integrated intercontinental perception.

References

Aebischer, N. J., Green, R. E. and Evans, A. D. (2000). From science to recovery: four cases of how research has been translated into conservation action in the UK. In *Ecology and Conservation of Lowland Farmland Birds*, ed. N. J. Aebischer, A. D. Evans, P. V. Grice, and J. A. Vickery, pp. 43–54. Tring: BOU.

Anderies, J. M., Katti, M. and Shochat, E. (2007). Living in the city: Resource availability, predation, and bird population dynamics in urban areas. *J. Theor. Biol.*, **247**, 36–49.

Andrén, H. (1992). Corvid density and nest predation in relation to forest fragmentation: a landscape perspective. *Ecology*, **73**, 794–804.

Andrén, H. (1994). Effects of habitat fragmentation on birds and mammals in landscapes with different proportions of suitable habitat: a review. *Oikos*, **71**, 355–366.

Andrén, H. and Angelstam, P. (1988). Elevated predation rates as an edge effect in habitat islands. *Ecology*, **69**, 544–547.

Angelstam, P., Boutin, S., Schmiegelow, F. *et al.* (2004). Targets for boreal forest biodiversity conservation – a rationale for macroecological research and adaptive management. *Ecol. Bull.*, **51**, 487–509.

Angelstam, P. and Mikusiński, G. (1994). Woodpecker assemblages in natural and managed boreal and hemiboreal forest: a review. *Ann. Zool. Fenn.*, **31**, 157–172.

Askins, R. A. (1993). Population trends in grassland, shrubland, and forest birds in eastern North America. *Curr. Ornithol.*, **11**, 1–34.

Askins, R. A. (1999). History of grassland birds in eastern North America. *Stud. Avian Biol.*, **19**, 60–71.

Askins, R. A., Chavez-Ramirez, F., Dale, B. C. *et al.* (2007b). Conservation of grassland birds in North America: understanding ecological processes in different regions. *Ornithol. Monogr.*, **64**, 1–46.

Askins, R. A., Zuckerberg, B. and Novak, L. (2007a). Do the size and landscape context of forest openings influence the abundance and breeding success of shrubland songbirds in southern New England? *For. Ecol. Manage.*, **250**, 137–147.

Baillie, S. R., Marchant, J. H., Leech, D. I. *et al.* (2010). *Breeding Birds in the Wider Countryside: Their Conservation Status 2009.* (http://www.bto.org/birdtrends).

Barbero, L., Couzi, L., Bretagnolle, V., Nezan, J. and Vétillard, F. (2008). Multi-scale habitat selection and foraging ecology of the Eurasian hoopoe (*Upupa epops*) in pine plantations. *Biodivers. Conserv.*, **17**, 1073–1087.

Bayne, E. M. and Hobson. K. A. (1997). Comparing the effects of landscape fragmentation by forestry and agriculture on predation of artificial nests. *Conserv. Biol.*, **11**, 1418–1429.

Bélisle, M., Desrochers, A. and Fortin, M.-J. (2001). Influence of forest cover on the movements of forest birds: a homing experiment. *Ecology*, **82**, 1893–1904.

Bergeron, Y., Cyr, D., Drever, R. *et al.* (2006). Past, current and future fire frequency in Québec's commercial forests: implications for the cumulative effects of harvesting and fire on age-class structure and natural disturbance-based management. *Can. J. For. Res.*, **36**, 2737–2744.

Bergeron, Y., Gauthier, S., Leduc, A. and Harvey, B. (2002). Natural fire regime: a guide for sustainable management of the Canadian boreal forest. *Silva Fenn.*, **36**, 81–95.

Best, L. B. (1986). Conservation tillage: ecological traps for nesting birds? *Wildlife Soc. Bull.*, **14**, 308–317.

Best, L. B., Freemark, K. E., Dinsmore, J. J. and Camp, M. (1995). A review and synthesis of habitat use by breeding birds in agricultural landscapes of Iowa. *Am. Midl. Nat.*, **134**, 1–29.

Best, L. B., Campa III, K. E., Kemp, R. J. *et al.* (1997). Bird abundance and nesting in CRP fields and cropland in the Midwest: a regional approach. *Wildlife Soc. Bull.*, **25**, 864–877.

Betts, M. G. and Villard, M.-A. (2009). Landscape thresholds in species occurrence as quantitative targets in forest management: generality in space and time? In *Setting Conservation Targets in Managed Forest Landscapes*, ed. M.-A. Villard and B.-G. Jonsson, pp. 185–206. Cambridge: Cambridge University Press.

Billeter, R., Liira, J., Bailey, D. *et al.* (2007). Indicators for biodiversity in agricultural landscapes: a pan-European study. *J. Appl. Ecol.*, **45**, 141–150.

Blair, R. B. (1996). Land use and avian species diversity along an urban gradient. *Ecol. Appl.*, **6**, 506–519.

Blair, R. B. (2004). The effects of urban sprawl on birds at multiple levels of biological organization. *Ecol. Society*, **9**, 21.

Boal, C. W. and Mannan, R. W. (1999). Comparative breeding ecology of Cooper's hawks in urban and exurban areas of southeastern Arizona. *J. Wildlife Manage.*, **63**, 77–84.

Bock, C. E., Jones, Z. F. and Bock, J. H. (2008). The oasis effect: response of birds to exurban development in a southwestern savanna. *Ecol. Appl.*, **18**, 1093–1106.

Böhning-Gaese, K. and Oberrath, R. (2003). Macroecology of habitat choice in long-distance migratory birds. *Oecologia*, **137**, 413–420.

Boitani, L., Falcucci, A., Maiorano, L. and Rondinini, C. (2007). Ecological networks as conceptual frameworks or operational tools in conservation. *Conserv. Biol.*, **21**, 1414–1422.

Bonier, F., Martin, P. R. and Wingfield, J. C. (2007). Urban birds have broader environmental tolerance. *Biol. Lett.*, **3**, 670–673.

Boutin, C., Freemark, K. E. and Kirk, D. A. (1999). Farmland birds in southern Ontario: field use, activity patterns and vulnerability to pesticide use. *Agr. Ecosyst. Environ.*, **72**, 239–254.

Brennan, L. A. and Kuvlesky, W. P. (2005). North American grassland birds: an unfolding conservation crisis. *J. Wildlife Manage.*, **69**, 1–13.

Brittingham, M. C. and Temple, S. A. (1992). Use of winter bird feeders by Black-capped Chickadees. *J. Wildlife Manage.*, **56**, 7.

Brotons, L., Mönkkönen, M. and Martin, J. L. (2003). Are fragments islands? Landscape context and density-area relationships in boreal forest birds. *Am. Nat.*, **162**, 343–357.

Burke, D. M., Elliott, K., Moore, L. *et al.* (2004). Patterns of nest predation on artificial and natural nests in forests. *Conserv. Biol.*, **18**, 381–388.

Burke, D. M. and Nol, E. (2000). Landscape and fragment size effects on reproductive success of forest-breeding birds in Ontario. *Ecol. Appl.*, **10**, 1749–1761.

Cabe, P. R. (1993). European Starling (*Sturnus vulgaris*). In *The Birds of North America Online*, ed. A. Poole. Cornell Lab of Ornithology: http://bna.birds.cornell.edu/bna/species/048

Cantor, N. F. (1994). *The Civilization of the Middle Ages.* New York: Harper Perennial.

Carlson, A. (2000). The effect of habitat loss on a deciduous forest specialist species: the White-backed Woodpecker (*Dendrocopos leucotos*). *For. Ecol. Manage.*, **131**, 215–221.

Caula, S., Marty, P. and Martin, J. L. (2008). Seasonal variation in species composition of an urban bird community in Mediterranean France. *Landscape Urban Plan.*, **87**, 1–9.

Chase J. F. and Walsh, J. J. (2006). Urban effects on native avifauna: a review. *Landscape Urban Plan.*, **74**, 46–69.

Chiron, F. and Julliard, R. (2007). Responses of songbirds to magpie reduction in an urban habitat. *J. Wildlife Manage.*, **71**, 2624–2631.

Clergeau, P., Croci, S. and Jokimäki, J. (2004). How useful are urban island ecosystems for defining invader patterns? *Environ. Conserv.*, **31**, 181–184.

Clergeau, P., Croci, S., Jokimäki, J., Kaisanlahti-Jokimäki, M. L. and Dinetti, M. (2006). Avifauna homogenisation by urbanisation: analysis at different European latitudes. *Biol. Conserv.*, **127**, 336–344.

Clergeau, P., Jokimäki, J. and Savard, J. P. L. (2001). Are urban bird communities influenced by the bird diversity of adjacent landscapes? *J. Appl. Ecol.*, **38**, 1122–1134.

Clergeau, P., Savard, J. P. L., Mennechez, G. and Falardeau, G. (1998). Bird abundance and diversity along an urban-rural gradient: A comparative study between two cities on different continents. *Condor*, **100**, 413–425.

Cooke, F. (2003). Ornithology and bird conservation in North America – a Canadian perspective. *Bird Study*, **50**, 211–222.

COSEWIC (2009). COSEWIC assessment and status report on the Eskimo Curlew *Numenius borealis* in Canada. Committee on the Status of Endangered Wildlife in Canada. Ottawa. vii + 32 pp. (www.sararegistry.gc.ca/status/status_e. cfm).

Croci, S., Butet, A. and Clergeau, P. (2008). Does urbanization filter birds on the basis of their biological traits? *Condor*, **110**, 223–240.

Cyr, D., Gauthier, S., Bergeron, Y. and Carcaillet, C. (2009). Forest management is driving the eastern North American boreal forest outside its natural range of variability. *Front. Ecol. Environ.*, **7**, 519–524.

Davis, S. K. (2004). Area sensitivity in grassland passerines: effects of patch size, patch shape, and vegetation structure on bird abundance and occurrence in southern Saskatchewan. *Auk*, **121**, 1130–1145.

Davis, S. K., Duncan, D. C. and Skeel, M. (1999). Distribution and habitat associations of three endemic grassland songbirds in southern Saskatchewan. *Wilson Bull.*, **111**, 389–396.

De Laet, J. and Summers-Smith, J. D. (2007). The status of the urban house sparrow *Passer domesticus* in north-western Europe: a review. *J. Ornithol.*, **148**, S275–S278.

Debussche, M. and Lepart, J. (1992). Establishment of woody plants in Mediterranean old fields: opportunity in space and time. *Landscape Ecol.*, **6**, 133–145.

Desrochers, A. and Hannon, S. J. (1997). Gap crossing decisions by forest songbirds during the post-fledging period. *Conserv. Biol.*, **11**, 1204–1210.

Donald, P. F., Sanderson, F. J., Burfield, I. J. *et al.* (2007). International conservation policy delivers benefits for birds in Europe. *Science*, **317**, 810–813.

Downes, C. M. and Collins, B. T. (2008). *Canadian Bird Trends* Web site Version 2.2. Gatineau: Canadian Wildlife Service, Environment Canada.

Drapeau, P., Leduc, A. and Bergeron, Y. (2009b). Bridging ecosystem and multiple species approaches for setting conservation targets in managed boreal landscapes. In *Setting Conservation Targets in Managed Forest Landscapes*, ed. M.-A. Villard and B.-G. Jonsson, pp. 129–160. Cambridge: Cambridge University Press.

Drapeau, P., Leduc, A., Giroux, J.-F. *et al.* (2000). Landscape scale disturbances and changes in bird communities of boreal mixed-wood forests. *Ecol. Monogr.*, **70**, 423–444.

Drapeau, P., Nappi, A., Imbeau, L. and Saint-Germain, M. (2009a). Standing deadwood for keystone bird species in the eastern boreal forest: managing for snag dynamics. *Forest. Chron.*, **85**, 227–234.

Driscoll, M. L. and Donovan, T. M. (2004). Landscape context moderates edge effects: nesting success of Wood Thrushes in central New York. *Conserv. Biol.*, **18**, 1330–1338.

Dunford, W. and Freemark, K. E. (2004). Matrix matters: effects of surrounding land uses on forest birds near Ottawa, Canada. *Landscape Ecol.*, **20**, 497–511.

Dunning, J. B., Danielson, B. J. and Pulliam, H. R. (1992). Ecological processes that affect populations in complex landscapes. *Oikos*, **65**, 169–175.

Edenius, L. and Elmberg, J. (1996). Landscape level effects of modern forestry on bird communities in North Swedish boreal forests. *Landscape Ecol.*, **11**, 325–338.

Engelmark, O. (1984). Forest fires in the Muddus National Park (northern Sweden) during the past 600 years. *Can. J. Bot.*, **62**, 893–898.

Enoksson, B., Anglestam, P. and Larsson, K. (1995). Deciduous forest and resident birds: the problem of fragmentation within coniferous forest landscape. *Landscape Ecol.*, **10**, 267–275.

Esseen, P.-A., Ehnström, B., Ericson, L. and Sjöberg, K. (1997). Boreal forests. *Ecol. Bull.*, **46**, 16–47.

Fahrig, L. (1997). Relative effects of habitat loss and fragmentation on species extinction. *J. Wildlife Manage.*, **61**, 603–610.

Farina, A. (1997). Landscape structure and breeding bird distribution in a sub-Mediterranean agro-ecosystem. *Landscape Ecol.*, **12**, 365–378.

Fernandez-Juricic, E. and Jokimäki, J. (2001). A habitat island approach to conserving birds in urban landscapes: case studies from southern and northern Europe. *Biodivers. Conserv.*, **10**, 2023–2043.

Fernandez-Juricic, E. and Telleria, J. L. (2000). Effects of human disturbance on spatial and temporal feeding patterns of Blackbird *Turdus merula* in urban parks in Madrid, Spain. *Bird Study*, **47**, 13–21.

Flaspohler, D. J., Temple, S. A. and Rosenfield, R. N. (2001). Species-specific edge effects on nest success and breeding bird density in a forested landscape. *Ecol. Appl.*, **11**, 32–46.

Flather, C. H. and Bevers, M. (2002). Patchy reaction-diffusion and population abundance: the relative importance of habitat amount and arrangement. *Am. Nat.*, **159**, 40–56.

Foster, D. R., Motzkin, G. and Slater, B. (1998). Land-use history as long-term broad-scale disturbance: regional forest dynamics in central New England. *Ecosystems*, **1**, 96–119.

Franklin, J. F. (1993). Preserving biodiversity: Species, ecosystems or landscapes? *Ecol. Appl.*, **3**, 202–205.

Frawley, B. J. and Best, L. B. (1991). Effects of mowing on breeding bird abundance and species composition in alfalfa fields. *Wildlife Soc. Bull.*, **19**, 135–142.

Freemark, K. E. and Boutin, C. (1995). Impacts of agricultural herbicide use on terrestrial wildlife in temperate landscapes: a review with special reference to North America. *Agr. Ecosyst. Environ.*, **52**, 67–91.

Freemark, K. E. and Kirk, D. A. (2001). Birds breeding on organic and nonorganic farms in Ontario: partitioning effects of habitat and practices on species composition and abundance. *Biol. Conserv.*, **101**, 337–350.

Fridman, J. and Walheim, M. (2000). Amount, structure, and dynamics of dead wood on managed forestland in Sweden. *For. Ecol. Manage.*, **131**, 23–36.

Friesen, L. E., Eagles, P. F. J. and MacKay, R. J. (1995). Effects of residential development on forest dwelling neotropical migrant songbirds. *Conserv. Biol.*, **9**, 1408–1414.

Gauthier, S., Leduc, A. and Bergeron. Y. (1996). Forest dynamics modelling under a natural fire cycle: a tool to define natural mosaic diversity in forest management. *Environ. Monit. Assess.*, **39**, 417–434.

Gering, J. C. and Blair, R. B. (1999). Predation on artificial bird nests along an urban gradient: predatory risk or relaxation in urban environments? *Ecography*, **22**, 532–541.

Germaine, S. S., Rosenstock, S. S., Schweinsburg, R. E. and Richardson, W. S. (1998). Relationships among breeding birds, habitat, and residential development in Greater Tucson, Arizona. *Ecol. Appl.*, **8**, 680–691.

Gobeil, J.-F. and Villard, M.-A. (2002). Permeability of three boreal forest landscape types to bird movements as determined from experimental translocations. *Oikos*, **98**, 447–458.

Grant, T. A., Madden, E. M. and Berkey, G. B. (2004). Tree and shrub invasion in northern mixed-grass prairie: implications for breeding grassland birds. *Wildlife Soc. Bull.*, **32**, 807–818.

Guénette, J.-S. and Villard. M.-A. (2005). Thresholds in forest bird response to habitat alteration as quantitative targets for conservation. *Conserv. Biol.*, **19**, 1168–1180.

Haddon, B. (1997). The status of forest regeneration in Canada. *Forest Chron.*, **73**, 586–589.

Haila, Y. and Järvinen. O. (1990). Northern conifer forests and their bird species assemblages. In *Biogeography and Ecology of Forest Bird Communities*, ed. A. Keast,

pp.61–85. The Hague: SPB Academic
Publishing.

Haila, Y., Hanski, I. K., Niemelä, J. *et al*. (1994).
Forestry and the boreal fauna: matching
management with natural forest dynamics.
Ann. Zool. Fenn., **31**, 187–202.

Hedblom, M. and Söderström, B. (2008).
Woodlands across Swedish urban gradients:
status, structure, and management
implications. *Landscape Urban Plan*., **84**, 62–73.

Helle, P. and Järvinen, O. (1986). Population trends
of North Finnish land birds in relation to
their habitat selection and changes in forest
structure. *Oikos*, **46**, 107–115.

Herkert, J. R., Reining, D. L., Weidenfeld, D. A.
et al. (2003). Effects of prairie fragmentation
on the nest success of breeding birds in the
midcontinental United States. *Conserv. Biol*.,
17, 587–594.

Hobson, K. A. and Bayne, E. (1999). Breeding bird
communities in boreal forests of western
Canada: consequences of "unmixing" the
mixedwoods. *Condor*, **102**, 759–769.

Hodder, K. H., Buckland, P. C., Kirby, K. J. and
Bullock, J. M. (2009). Can the pre-Neolithic
provide suitable models for re-wilding the
landscape of Britain? *Brit. Wildlife*, **20**
(suppl.), 4–15.

Holmes, R. T. and Sherry, T. W. (2001). Thirty-
year bird population trends in an
unfragmented temperate deciduous forest:
importance of habitat change. *Auk*, **118**,
589–610.

Hoover, J. P. and Brittingham, M. C. (1993).
Regional variation in cowbird parasitism of
wood thrushes. *Wilson Bull*., **105**, 228–238.

Hoyt, J. S. and Hannon, S. J. (2002). Habitat
associations of Black-backed and Three-toed
Woodpeckers in the boreal forest of Alberta.
Can. J. For. Res., **32**, 1881–1888.

Huhta, E., Aho, T., Jantti, A. *et al*. (2004). Forest
fragmentation increases nest predation in
the Eurasian Treecreeper. *Conserv. Biol*., **18**,
148–155.

Hulse, D. W., Eilers, J., Freemark, K., Hummon, C.
and White D. (2000). Planning alternative
future landscapes in Oregon: evaluating

effects on water quality and biodiversity.
Landscape J., **19**, 1–19.

Hunt, G. L. (1972). Influence of food distribution
and human disturbance on the reproductive
success of Herring Gulls. *Ecology*, **53**, 10.

Huntley, B. (1993). Species-richness in north-
temperate zone forests. *J. Biogeogr*., **20**,
163–180.

Husté, A. and Boulinier, T. (2007). Determinants
of local extinction and turnover rates in
urban bird communities. *Ecol. Appl*., **17**,
168–180.

Imbeau, L., Mönkkönen, M. and Desrochers, A.
(2001). Long-term effects of forestry on birds
of the eastern Canadian boreal forests: a
comparison with Fennoscandia. *Conserv.
Biol*., **15**, 1151–1162.

Jobin, B., DesGranges J.-L. and Boutin C. (1998).
Farmland habitat use by breeding birds in
southern Québec. *Can. Field Nat*., **112**,
611–618.

Johnson, D. H. (2005). Grassland bird use of
Conservation Reserve Program fields in the
Great Plains. In *Fish and Wildlife Benefits of
Farm Bill Conservation Programs: 2000–2005
Update*, ed. J. B. Haufler, pp.17–32. The
Wildlife Society Technical Review 05–02.

Johnston, R. F. (2001). Synanthropic birds of
North America. In *Avian Ecology and
Conservation in an Urbanizing World*, ed. J. M.
Marzluff, R. Bowman and R. Donnelly,
pp. 49–67. Norwell, MA: Kluwer Academic
Publishers.

Jokimäki, J. and Huhta, E. (2000). Artificial nest
predation and abundance of birds along an
urban gradient. *Condor*, **102**, 838–847.

Jokimäki, J. and Suhonen, J. (1998). Distribution
and habitat selection of wintering birds in
urban environments. *Landscape Urban Plan*.,
39, 253–263.

Jokimäki, J., Suhonen, J., Inki, K. and Jokinen, S.
(1996). Biogeographical comparison of
winter bird assemblages in urban
environments in Finland. *J. Biogeogr*., **23**,
379–386.

Kirk, D. A., Boutin, C. and Freemark K. E. (2001). A
multivariate analysis of bird species

composition and abundance between crop types and seasons in southern Ontario. Canada. *Ecoscience*, **8**, 173–184.

Klem, D., Keck, D. C., Marty, K. L. *et al.* (2004). Effects of window angling, feeder placement, and scavengers on avian mortality at plate glass. *Wilson Bull.*, **116**, 69–73.

Koper, N., Schmiegelow, F. K. A. and Merrill, E. H. (2007). Residuals cannot distinguish between ecological effects of habitat amount and fragmentation: implications for the debate. *Landscape Ecol.*, **22**, 811–820.

Korpilahti, E. and Kuuluvainen, T. (2002). Disturbance dynamics in boreal forests: defining the ecological basis of restoration and management of biodiversity. *Silva Fenn.*, **36**, 1–447.

Kouki, J., Löfman, S., Martikainen, P., Rouvinen, S. and Uotila, A. (2001). Forest fragmentation in Fennoscandia: linking habitat requirements of wood-associated threatened species to landscape and habitat changes. *Scand. J. Forest Res.*, **S3**, 27–37.

Kouki, J. and Väänänen, A. (2000). Impoverishment of resident old-growth forest bird assemblages along an isolation gradient of protected areas in eastern Finland. *Ornis Fennica*, **77**, 145–154.

Kuitunen, M. and Aleknonis, A. (1992). Nest predation and breeding success in common treecreepers nesting in boxes and natural cavities. *Ornis Fennica*, **69**, 7–12.

Kuitunen, M. and Mäkinen, M. (1993). An experiment on nest site choice of the common treecreeper in fragmented boreal forest. *Ornis Fennica*, **70**, 163–167.

Kurki, S., Nikula, A., Helle, P. and Linden. H. (2000). Landscape fragmentation and forest composition effects on grouse breeding success in boreal forests. *Ecology*, **81**, 1985–1997.

Lancaster, R. K. and Rees, W. E. (1979). Bird communities and the structure of urban habitats. *Can. J. Zool.*, **57**, 2358–2368.

Lens, L. and Dhondt, A. A. (1994). Effect of habitat fragmentation on the timing of Crested Tit *Parus cristatus* dispersal. *Ibis*, **136**, 147–152.

Leonard, T. D., Taylor, P. D. and Warkentin, I. G. (2008). Landscape structure and spatial scale affect space use by songbirds in naturally patchy and harvested boreal forests. *Condor*, **110**, 467–481.

Lindenmayer, D. B., Fischer, J., Felton, A. *et al.* (2007). The complementarity of single-species and ecosystem-oriented research in conservation research. *Conserv. Biol.*, **116**, 1220–1226.

Mann, C. C. (2005). *1491: New Revelations of the Americas Before Columbus.* New York: Knopf.

Martin, P. A. and Forsyth D. J. (2003). Occurrence and productivity of songbirds in prairie farmland under nonorganic versus minimum tillage regimes. *Agr. Ecosyst. Environ.*, **96**, 107–117.

Martin, T. E. and Clobert, J. (1996). Nest predation and avian life-history evolution in Europe versus North America: a possible role of humans? *Am. Nat.*, **147**, 1028–1046.

Marzluff, J. M. (2001). Worldwide urbanization and its effects on birds. In *Avian Ecology and Conservation in an Urbanizing World*, ed. J. M. Marzluff, R. Bowman and R. Donnelly, pp. 20–47. Norwell, MA: Kluwer Academic Publishers.

Mascarúa-López, L., Harper, K. and Drapeau, P. (2006). Edge influence on forest structure in large forest remnants, cutblock separators and riparian buffers in managed black spruce forests. *Ecoscience*, **13**, 226–233.

Matthysen, E. and Currie, D. (1996). Habitat fragmentation reduces disperser success in juvenile nuthatches *Sitta europaea*: evidence from patterns of territory establishment. *Ecography*, **19**, 67–72.

McGarigal, K. J. and McComb, W. C. (1995). Relationships between landscape structure and breeding birds in the Oregon Coast Range. *Ecol. Monogr.*, **65**, 235–260.

McKinney, M. L. (2002). Urbanization, biodiversity, and conservation. *BioScience*, **52**, 883–890.

McMaster, G. D., Devries, J. H. and Davis, S. K. (2001). Grassland birds nesting in haylands of southern Saskatchewan: landscape influences and conservation priorities. *J. Wildlife Manage.*, **69**, 211–221.

Melles, S., Glenn, S. and Martin, K. (2003). Urban bird diversity and landscape complexity: Species-environment associations along a multiscale habitat gradient. *Conserv. Ecol.*, **7**, 22.

Mikusiński, G., Gromadski, M. and Chylarecki, P. (2001). Woodpeckers as indicators of forest bird diversity. *Conserv. Biol.*, **15**, 208–217.

Mineau, P., Downes C. M., Kirk D. A., Bayne, E. and Csizy, M. (2005). Patterns of bird species abundance in relation to granular insecticide use in the Canadian prairies. *EcoScience*, **12**, 267–278.

Møller, A. P. (2008). Flight distance of urban birds, predation, and selection for urban life. *Behav. Ecol. Sociobiol.*, **63**, 63–75.

Mönkkönen, M. and Reunanen, P. (1999). On critical thresholds in landscape connectivity – a management perspective. *Oikos*, **84**, 302–305.

Mönkkönen, M. and Welsh, D. A. (1994). A biogeographical hypothesis on the effects of human caused landscape changes on the forest bird communities of Europe and North America. *Ann. Zool. Fenn.*, **31**, 61–70.

Mönkkönen, M., Helle, P. and Welsh, D. A. (1992). Perspectives on Palearctic and Nearctic bird migration: comparisons and overview of life-history and ecology of migrant passerines. *Ibis*, **134**, S7–S13.

Murgui, E. and Valentín, A. (2003). Relationships between the characteristics of the urban landscape and the introduced bird community in the city of Valencia (Spain). *Ardeola*, **50**, 201–214.

Murphy, M. T. (2003). Avian population trends within the evolving agricultural landscape of eastern and central United States. *Auk*, **120**, 20–34.

Nappi, A. and Drapeau P. (2009). Reproductive success of the black-backed woodpecker (*Picoides arcticus*) in burned boreal forests: are burns source habitats? *Biol. Conserv.*, **142**, 1381–1391.

Nappi, A., Drapeau, P. and Savard. J.-P. L. (2004). Salvage logging after wildfire in the boreal forest: is it becoming a hot issue for wildlife? *Forest. Chron.*, **80**, 67–74.

Newton, I. (2004). The recent declines of farmland bird populations in Britain: an appraisal of causal factors and conservation actions. *Ibis*, **146**, 579–600.

Niemi, G., Hanowski, J. Helle, P. *et al.* (1998). Ecological sustainability of birds in boreal forests. *Conserv. Ecol.*, **2**, 1–17.

Norris, D. R. and Stutchbury, B. J. (2001). Extraterritorial movements of a forest songbird in a fragmented landscape. *Conserv. Biol.*, **15**, 729–736.

O'Connor, R. J. and Shrubb, M. (1986). *Farming and Birds*. Cambridge: Cambridge University Press.

Palomino, D. and Carrascal, L. M. (2007). Threshold distances to nearby cities and roads influence the bird community of a mosaic landscape. *Biol. Conserv.*, **140**, 100–109.

Paradis, E., Baillie, S. R., Sutherland, W. J. and Gregory, R. D. (1998). Patterns of natal and breeding dispersal in birds. *J. Anim. Ecol.*, **67**, 518–536.

Partecke, J. and Gwinner, E. (2007). Increased sedentariness in European Blackbirds following urbanization: a consequence of local adaptation? *Ecology*, **88**, 882–890.

Peterjohn, B. G. (2003). Agricultural landscapes: can they support healthy bird populations as well as farm products. *Auk*, **120**, 14–19.

Pickett, S. T. A., Cadenasso, M. L., Grove, J. M. *et al.* (2001). Urban ecological systems: Linking terrestrial ecological, physical, and socioeconomic components of metropolitan areas. *Ann. Rev. Ecol. Syst.*, **32**, 127–157.

Pyne, S. J. (1982). *Fire in America: a Cultural History of Wildland and Rural Fire*. Princeton: Princeton University Press.

Richardson, H. W. and Bae, C. (2005). *Globalization and Urban Development*. Heidelberg: Springer-Verlag.

Robbins, C. S. (1973). Introduction, spread, and present abundance of the House Sparrow in North America. *Ornithol. Monogr.*, **14**, 3–9.

Robinson, S. K., Thompson, F. R., Donovan, T. M., Whitehead, D. R. and Faaborg, J. (1995). Regional forest fragmentation and the nesting success of migratory birds. *Science*, **267**, 1987–1990.

Robles, H., Ciudad, C., Vera, R. and Baglione, V. (2007). No effect of habitat fragmentation on post-fledging, first-year, and adult survival in the middle spotted woodpecker. *Ecography*, **30**, 685–694.

Robles, H., Ciudad, C., Vera, R., Olea, P. P. and Matthysen, E. (2008). Demographic responses of Middle Spotted Woodpeckers (*Dendrocopos medius*) to habitat fragmentation. *Auk*, **125**, 131–139.

Rodenhouse, N. L., Best, L. B., O'Connor, R. J. and Bollinger, E. K. (1995). Effects of agricultural practices and farmland structures. In *Ecology and Management of Neotropical Migratory Birds: A Synthesis and Review of Critical Issues*, ed. T. E. Martin and D. M. Finch, pp. 269–293. New York: Oxford University Press.

Rodewald, A. D. and Yahner, R. H. (2001). Influence of landscape composition on avian community structure and associated mechanisms. *Ecology*, **82**, 3493–3504.

Rolstad, J., Loken, B. and Rolstad, E. (2000). Habitat selection as a hierarchical spatial process: the green woodpecker at the northern edge of its distribution range. *Oecologia*, **124**, 116–129.

Santelmann, M. V., White, D., Freemark Lindsay, K. *et al.* (2008). An integrated assessment of alternative futures for Iowa watersheds. In *From the Corn Belt to the Gulf: Societal and Ecological Implications of Alternative Agricultural Futures*, ed. J. I. Nassauer, M. V. Santelmann and D. Scavia, pp. 162–174. Washington, DC: Resources for the Future Press.

Samson, F. and Knopf, F. (1996). *Prairie Conservation: Preserving North America's Most Endangered Ecosystem*. Washington, DC: Island Press.

Sauer, J. R., Hines, J. E. and Fallon, J. (2008). *The North American Breeding Bird Survey, Results and Analysis 1966–2007*. Version 5.15.2008. Laurel, MD: USGS Patuxent Wildlife Research Center.

Schlesinger, M. D., Manley, P. N. and Holyoak, M. (2008). Distinguishing stressors acting on land bird communities in an urbanizing environment. *Ecology*, **89**, 2302–2314.

Schmidt, E. and Bock, C. E. (2005). Habitat associations and population trends of two hawks in an urbanizing grassland region in Colorado. *Landscape Ecol.*, **20**, 469–478.

Schmiegelow, F. K. A., Machtans, C. S. and Hannon. S. J. (1997). Are boreal birds resilient to forest fragmentation? An experimental study of short-term community responses. *Ecology*, **78**, 1914–1932.

Schmiegelow, F. K. A., Stepnisky, D. P., Stambaugh, C. A. and Koivula, M. (2006). Reconciling salvage logging of boreal forests with a natural-disturbance management model. *Conserv. Biol.*, **20**, 971–983.

Schmiegelow, F. K. A. and Mönkönnen, M. (2002). Habitat loss and fragmentation in dynamic landscapes: avian perspectives from the boreal forest. *Ecol. Appl.*, **12**, 375–389.

Schorger, A. W. (1952). Introduction of the domestic pigeon. *Auk*, **69**, 462–463.

Shaw, L. M., Chamberlain, D. and Evans, M. (2008). The House Sparrow *Passer domesticus* in urban areas: reviewing a possible link between post-decline distribution and human socioeconomic status. *J. Ornithol.*, **149**, 293–299.

Shochat, E., Warren, P. S., Faeth, S. H., McIntyre, N. E. and Hope, D. (2006). From patterns to emerging processes in mechanistic urban ecology. *Trends Ecol. Evol.*, **21**, 186–191.

Shutler, D., Mullie, A. and Clark R. G. (2000). Bird assemblages of prairie uplands and wetlands in relation to farming practices in Saskatchewan. *Conserv. Biol.*, **14**, 1441–1451.

Sims, V., Evans, K. L., Newson, S. E., Tratalos, J. A. and Gaston, K. J. (2008). Avian assemblage structure and domestic cat densities in urban environments. *Divers. Distrib*., **14**, 387–399.

Sirami, C., Brotons, L., Burfield, I., Fonderflick, J. and Martin, J.-L. (2008). Is land abandonment having an impact on biodiversity? A meta-analytical approach to bird distribution changes in the north-western Mediterranean. *Biol. Conserv*., **141**, 450–459.

Slabbekoorn, H. and den Boer-Visser, A. (2006). Cities change the songs of birds. *Curr. Biol*., **16**, 2326–2331.

Slabbekoorn, H., Yeh, P. and Hunt, K. (2007). Sound transmission and song divergence: A comparison of urban and forest acoustics. *Condor*, **109**, 67–78.

Sohdi, N. and Oliphant, N. (1992). Hunting ranges and habitat use and selection of urban-breeding Merlins. *Condor*, **94**, 743–749.

Suorsa, P., Helle, H., Koivunen, V. *et al*. (2004). Effects of forest patch size on physiological stress and immunocompetence in an area-sensitive passerine, the Eurasian treecreeper (*Certhia familiaris*): an experiment. *Proc. R. Soc. B*, **271**, 435–440.

Suorsa, P., Huhta, E., Nikula, A. *et al*. (2003). Forest management is associated with physiological stress in an old–growth forest passerine. *Proc. R. Soc. B*, **270**, 963–969.

Sutter, G. C., Davis, S. K. and Duncan, D. C. (2000). Grassland songbird abundance along roads and trails in southern Saskatchewan. *J. Field Ornithol*., **71**, 110–116.

Tewksbury, J. J., Hejl, S. J. and Martin, T. E. (1998). Breeding productivity does not decline with increasing fragmentation in a Western Landscape. *Ecology*, **79**, 2890–2903.

Thorington, K. K. and Bowman, R. (2003). Predation rate on artificial nests increases with human housing density in suburban habitats. *Ecography*, **26**, 188–196.

Trzcinski, M. K., Fahrig, L. and Merriam, G. (1999). Independent effects of forest cover and fragmentation on the distribution of forest breeding birds. *Ecol. Appl*., **9**, 586–593.

Tucker, G. M. and Evans, M. I. (1997). *Habitats for Birds in Europe*. Cambridge: BirdLife International.

Tufto, J., Ringsby, T. H., Dhondt, A. A., Adriaensen, F. and Matthysen, E. (2005). A parametric model for estimation of dispersal patterns applied to five passerine spatially structured populations. *Am. Nat*., **165**, E13–E26.

Turner, W. R., Nakamura, T. and Dinetti, M. (2004). Global urbanization and the separation of humans from nature. *BioScience*, **54**, 585–590.

Vaillancourt, M.-A., Drapeau, P., Gauthier, S. and Robert, M. (2008). Availability of standing trees for large cavity-nesting birds in the eastern boreal forest of Québec. *For. Ecol. Manage*., **255**, 2272–2285.

Verheijen, F. J. (1981). Bird kills at tall lighted structures in the USA in the period 1935–1973 and kills at a Dutch lighthouse in the period 1924–1928 show similar lunar periodicity. *Ardea*, **69**, 199–203.

Vickery, J. A., Feber, R. E. and Fuller, R. J. (2009). Arable field margins managed for biodiversity conservation: a review of food resource provision for farmland birds. *Agr. Ecosyst. Environ*., **133**, 1–13.

Vickery, J. A., Tallowin, J. R., Feber, R. E. *et al*. (2001). The management of lowland neutral grasslands in Britain: effects of agricultural practices on birds and their food resources. *J. Appl. Ecol*., **38**, 647–664.

Vickery, P. D., Jones, A. L, Zuckerberg, B., Shriver, W. G. and Weik, A. (2005). Influence of fire and other anthropogenic practices on grassland and shrubland birds in New England. *Stud. Avian Biol*., **30**, 139–146.

Villard, M.-A. and Jonsson, B.-G. (2009). *Setting Conservation Targets in Managed Forest Landscapes*. Cambridge: Cambridge University Press.

Villard, M.-A. and Taylor, P. D. (1994). Tolerance to habitat fragmentation influences the colonization of new habitat by forest birds. *Oecologia*, **98**, 393–401.

Villard, M.-A., Trzcinski, M. K. and Merriam, G. (1999). Fragmentation effects on forest birds: relative influence of woodland cover and configuration on landscape occupancy. *Conserv. Biol.*, **13**, 774–783.

Virkkala, R. (1991). Population trends of forest birds in a Finnish Lapland landscape of large habitat blocks: consequences of stochastic environmental variations or regional habitat alteration? *Biol. Conserv.*, **56**, 223–240.

Virkkala, R., Alanko, T., Laine, T. and Tiainen. J. (1993). Population contraction of the White-backed Woodpecker (*Dendrocopos leucotos*) in Finland as a consequence of habitat alteration. *Biol. Conserv.*, **66**, 47–53.

Waller, D. and Rooney, T. P. (ed.) (2008). *The Vanishing Present: Wisconsin's Changing Lands, Waters and Wildlife*. Chicago: Chicago University Press.

Weldon, A. J. and Haddad, N. M. (2005). The effects of patch shape on indigo buntings: evidence for an ecological trap. *Ecology*, **86**, 1422–1431.

Wesołowski, T. (2007). Lessons from long-term hole-nester studies in a primaeval forest. *J. Ornithol.*, **148**, S395–S405.

Wesołowski, T. and Stańska, M. (2001). High ectoparasite loads in hole-nesting birds: a nestbox bias? *J. Avian Biol.*, **32**, 281–285.

Wesołowski, T. and Tomialojc, L. (1997). Breeding bird dynamics in a primaeval temperate forest: long-term trends in Białowieza National Park (Poland). *Ecography*, **20**, 432–453.

Whitney, G. G. (1994). *From Coastal Wilderness to Fruited Plain: A History of Environmental Change in Temperate North America from 1500 to the Present*. Cambridge: Cambridge University Press.

Wilkinson, N. (2006). Factors influencing the small-scale distribution of House Sparrows *Passer domesticus* in a suburban environment. *Bird Study*, **53**, 39–46.

Williams, M. (1989). *Americans and their Forests*. Cambridge: Cambridge University Press.

Williams, M. (2003). *Deforesting the Earth: from Prehistory to Global Crisis*. Chicago: University of Chicago Press.

Williams, M. (2008). A new look at global forest histories of land clearing. *Annu. Rev. Environ. Resour.*, **33**, 345–367.

Wilson, J. D., Evans, A. D. and Grice, P. V. (2009). *Bird Conservation and Agriculture*. Cambridge: Cambridge University Press.

Wilson, M. D. and Watts, B. D. (2008). Landscape configuration effects on distribution and abundance of whip-poor-wills. *Wilson J. Ornithol.*, **120**, 778–783.

CHAPTER TWENTY

Birds and their changing habitat: thoughts on research and conservation strategies

ROBERT J. FULLER
British Trust for Ornithology

The chapters in this book show that relationships of birds with habitat take many different forms, both across and within species; they are affected by numerous processes and are frequently difficult to predict with accuracy. This concluding chapter draws out some general themes and considers implications for conservation strategies at a time when environmental trends appear to be moving towards greater volatility, disturbance and uncertainty.

Habitat is not a fixed trait

Most species clearly have limits to their potential habitat, though in the case of some generalists, such as the blackbird *Turdus merula* and the great tit *Parus major* in western Europe, these limits are set very wide indeed. Nonetheless, within these limits, there are many reasons why patterns of habitat occupancy may differ in space and time. There is always the possibility that what appears different to the human eye represents no real difference to the bird – the essential requirements may be met in very different contexts. Evidence comes from the rapid colonisation by open country and woodland species of 'novel habitats' provided by lowland conifer plantations in the twentieth century (Fuller and Ausden, 2008). Equally, evidence now exists of more fundamental plasticity and flexibility in the ways that many birds select and use habitat.

Habitat is not an immutable and clearly defined characteristic of many species (Box 20.1). It is essential, however, not to overstate or exaggerate this observation. Some species are so strongly adapted to particular habitat conditions that even rather small changes in habitat quality can lead to population declines. For example, the responses of several wetland species to management specifically aimed at meeting their critical requirements indicates that these species were declining due to habitat changes to which they could not adapt (Gilbert and Smith, Chapter 10; Ausden and Bolton, Chapter 11). At a continental scale, the transformation of the Australian avifauna since European colonisation demonstrates that habitat loss and deterioration can have massive negative effects on bird populations (Martin

---

Box 20.1 Variation in habitat occupancy within species

Spatial variation

1. A species may be *locally* absent from apparently suitable habitat or *locally* restricted to just a part of the known habitat spectrum occupied by the species within a particular region. This can arise due to diverse processes, some involving interactions between species, others causing aggregations (and consequently absence elsewhere) and various other behavioural mechanisms (Fuller, Chapter 2). Ecologists typically try to explain what a species needs and then predict where it should occur; sometimes a more illuminating approach may be to ask why many potential patches remain unoccupied.
2. At larger spatial scales it is evident that a species may occupy very different habitats in different parts of its geographical range (Wesołowski and Fuller, Chapter 3). This phenomenon is not confined to particular taxonomic or ecological groups – absence of habitat differences may be the exception rather than the norm. The potential mechanisms are numerous and overlap with those explaining habitat differences at smaller spatial scales.

Temporal variation

3. A species may expand the range of habitat types it occupies. There are many striking examples in Europe and some are ongoing, in particular the responses of species to urban environments (Wesołowski and Fuller, Chapter 3).
4. Habitat switches may occur, with a decrease in part of the habitat spectrum, possibly accompanied by an increase in another part. Both (Chapter 17) gives the example of pied flycatchers *Ficedula hypoleuca* decreasing in broadleaved, but not coniferous or mixed forest in response to the mismatching between food availability and timing of breeding.

---

et al., Chapter 18). Similarly, boreal forest bird assemblages are highly sensitive to loss of old forest and industrial exploitation that reduces the abundance of large trees and decaying wood (Martin *et al.*, Chapter 19). European farmland bird populations have declined as modernisation of agricultural production has reduced habitat complexity and availability at all scales (Vickery and Arlettaz, Chapter 7).

Notions of specialisation are relevant to assessing flexibility and, therefore, how susceptible a species might be to environmental change. But placing a species on the specialist–generalist continuum (though often a simple dichot-omous classification is used) is not straightforward. The term 'generalist' can be applied both to species that are able to exploit a wide range of contrasting opportunities or resources, and to species with more precise needs that happen to be widely available. In cultural landscapes, even species that have exacting requirements may find these in contrasting landscape/habitat con-texts, with the consequence that most classifications of species by habitat type are ecologically simplistic (Hinsley and Gillings, Chapter 6). Perceptions of specialism are strongly dependent on context (Devictor et al., 2010) and a species can appear to be more of a specialist in some parts of its range than others (Wesołowski and Fuller, Chapter 3). There are situations, however, where identifying specialists appears to work, as in alpine birds (Thompson et al., Chapter 9). Species tend to respond in continuous, rather than binary, ways to landscapes such that they are rarely confined to sharply defined locations on any ecological gradient (Fischer and Lindenmayer, 2006). Determining where species occur along gradients – for example in altitude, vegetation type, soil wetness – can help quantify how species respond to variation within landscapes including the transitions that characterise many cultural landscapes (Fuller, Chapter 5).

Developing better ways of defining species in terms of critical resource and habitat needs may help to identify the circumstances under which a species may be capable of adjusting or adapting to environmental change. Behavioural flexibility also needs to be accounted for, but is less easy to assess than ecological flexibility. The discussion by Both (Chapter 17) indicates how difficult predictions about adaptability to climate change will be. Urbanisation provides one of the best available test-beds we have for assessing flexibility and adaptability, both through comparisons of traits in conspecific rural and urban populations (Evans, 2010) and of the traits of species that do and do not colonise urban areas.

Context and the limits to generalisation

Defining the habitat needs and associations of any species depends on a variety of contexts (Box 20.2). Findings about habitat relationships need to be applied with extreme caution outside the context in which they were established. Wesołowski and Fuller (Chapter 3) make this point for birds within different regions of Europe. Many of the principles of landscape ecol-ogy have been based on work conducted in North America and Australia; the quantity of European work lags far behind. How much of the available evi-dence on, for example, scale and landscape processes, is relevant to historic cultural landscapes of the kinds found in western Europe? Indeed, contempo-rary use of the term 'fragmentation' can seem inappropriate in most European landscapes where the critical thresholds of habitat loss have long

---

Box 20.2 Some key contexts that can result in different perceptions of habitat selection within individual species of birds

Historical processes: The history of landscape change may be an important determinant of relationships with habitat. Historic habitat loss may result in filtered subsets of species adapted to different habitat conditions (Wesołowski and Fuller, Chapter 3; Dolman, Chapter 4; Martin *et al.*, Chapter 18; Martin *et al.*, Chapter 19).

Region: Within the same biogeographical region, species frequently show large regional differences in habitat use (Wesołowski and Fuller, Chapter 3).

Scale: Perceived associations with habitat are strongly scale-dependent (Fuller, Chapter 1; Dolman, Chapter 4; Gill, Chapter 12; Naef-Daenzer, Chapter 16).

Landscape structure: Composition and configuration of landscapes affect how individuals distribute themselves across habitat patches and edges, and how they obtain resources (Dolman, Chapter 4; Fuller, Chapter 5; Hinsley and Gillings, Chapter 6).

Population size: Intraspecific competition is likely to be a major determinant of distribution across habitat types through, for example, buffer effects (Fuller, Chapters 1 and 2; Wesołowski and Fuller, Chapter 3; Dolman, Chapter 4; Gill, Chapter 12).

Predation risk: The presence of predators may have a large influence on fine-scale patterns of habitat and may even exclude individuals from otherwise suitable habitat. Spatial variation in types and numbers of predators may therefore generate different patterns of habitat association (Fuller, Chapter 2; Piersma, Chapter 15).

Season: Many species show seasonal contrasts in habitat use. Carry-over effects from one season may affect habitat occupancy in another season (Fuller, Chapter 2; Gill, Chapter 12; Piersma, Chapter 15).

Body condition and nutrition: Individuals may vary in their use of habitats depending on nutritional demand (Piersma, Chapter 15).

---

since been passed. Species may have adapted to these historically fragmented landscapes and indeed may be filtered subsets of those present under primeval conditions (Dolman, Chapter 4).

Is it justifiable to take principles largely founded on work in other continents as a basis for habitat creation and landscape restructuring in Europe? The mechanisms that affect population persistence vary with landscape context (Dolman, Chapter 4). In landscapes experiencing relatively recent habitat loss and fragmentation, processes such as species–area relationships, filtering and core–edge relationships will be critically important, whereas in ancient cultural landscapes factors such as habitat quality and habitat heterogeneity may be more relevant. Research in the former types of landscapes may not, therefore, have focused on questions that are critical to habitat restoration in cultural landscapes. There is clearly a need for substantially more attention to be paid to the mechanisms that determine species distributions and individual fitness in European landscapes. Comparison of North American and European research perspectives is revealing (Martin *et al.*, Chapter 19). Differences in the emphasis of research conducted on the two continents and in the conclusions drawn were greatest in farmland landscapes i.e. those subjected to the greatest level of transformation.

The importance of developing conservation approaches that are context-specific was recognised in several chapters. In the real world of conservation management and environmental policy, generalised approaches will always be adopted at some level simply because detailed knowledge is lacking. Ideally we need to know when such general approaches are ineffectual or even damaging. Contemporary research and publishing agendas in ecology are, however, widely driven by the demand for generality. There are instances where we should acknowledge the limits to generality; this applies to many of the processes affecting habitat distributions in birds and other organisms.

Approaches to studying habitat relationships

Multi-scale approaches to the habitat responses of birds are now the norm. More recently, cross-season linkages have emerged as potentially powerful influences on habitat selection and demography in migrant birds. Different segments of populations may utilise distinct breeding, stopover and wintering habitats varying in productivity and survival (Gill, Chapter 12). Research on the ecology of migrant birds is increasingly focusing on such seasonal interactions. The importance of social dimensions in habitat selection has also grown rapidly (Fuller, Chapter 2). This raises the challenge of how social factors can be built into traditional resource-based or vegetation-based models of habitat selection. Social interactions, principally intraspecific competition, form a major component of behaviour-based models used to predict local-scale population changes (Gill, Chapter 12). However, we are probably some way from being able to incorporate information derived from conspecifics and heterospecifics into resource-based models, though this is being explored with shorebirds (Piersma, Chapter 15).

It could be argued that there are considerable benefits from developing better understanding of the cues that birds use to identify their habitat. On the one hand, distribution models might be improved if better account were taken of the actual cues used by birds to identify habitat. Manipulating cues could become part of the conservation manager's tool box; this might extend to the manipulation of conspecific attraction (Ahlering and Faaborg, 2006). There are, however, risks with such techniques. Birds could be attracted to poor-quality habitat; they need to be applied only in situations where key resource needs of the species can be met and where ecological traps are unlikely to develop. The importance of understanding the causal mechanisms underlying habitat selection is stressed by both Dolman (Chapter 4) and Naef-Daenzer (Chapter 16). As habitat recognition markers, cues have functional importance and ideally should be considered alongside other functional aspects of habitat including foraging, predator avoidance, roosting and nesting.

Developing functional approaches to measuring landscape complexity is a high priority for biodiversity studies (Fahrig *et al.*, 2011). Functional approaches are starting to be advocated as a basis for conservation management; these are based on maintaining the diverse habitat features that species require, at the scales on which they use them, rather than managing habitat types according to general prescriptions designed to achieve what is perceived to be 'good habitat condition' (Dolman *et al.*, 2011). These approaches are novel and could represent a major advance; they also link closely with concepts of multi-scale habitat heterogeneity (see below). However, even for birds, there is probably much to learn about how individual species actually use the patch types that constitute many terrestrial cultural landscapes. This contrasts with intertidal environments where the exploitation of resources is far better documented (Gill, Chapter 12; Burton, Chapter 13; Piersma, Chapter 15). It is surprising how few descriptive studies of terrestrial landscapes, at least in Europe, have taken a holistic functional perspective on avian habitat use. Often the emphasis is on one part of a species' habitat spectrum rather than its full breadth of habitat use.

Especially in cultural landscapes it appears that many species exploit a diversity of patch types, often for complementary resources (Dolman, Chapter 4; Grant and Pearce-Higgins, Chapter 8; Burton, Chapter 13). There are also reasons for thinking that specialisation, and tight dependence on particular habitat types, may be reduced in these highly patchy mosaic landscapes (Hinsley and Gillings, Chapter 6). Exploration of how individuals utilise all the landscape elements at their disposal and, importantly, how this changes seasonally, could form the basis of more realistic distribution models. The ultimate goal is to understand dispersal processes and the spatial demography of populations occupying patchy landscapes. Developing more realistic models of species distribution across habitat types and gaining some understanding of spatially referenced seasonal and longer-term dynamics would be a good start.

Do avian habitat relationships have wider relevance?
It could seem parochial to devote an entire book to the responses of birds to habitat. Does this vast body of knowledge (of which this book covers a rather

small part) have any significance beyond the birds themselves? This topic deserves close attention given the large scale of resources devoted to bird research and conservation relative to that afforded most other groups of species. It is undeniable that bird-focused research has been massively influential in many aspects of ecological and behavioural thinking. Bird research has opened up new perspectives on how species and individuals interact with their environments. But many unanswered questions remain. What do birds tell us about the habitat relationships of other organisms, about how biodiversity responds to change and about the most appropriate conservation strategies for wider nature?

Although the cultural values of birds are indisputable, it is frequently stated that birds have little relevance in the context of regulating, supporting and provisioning ecosystem services. Is it really as simple as that? Birds influence ecosystem function through seed dispersal (Herrera, 1984), grazing (Vera, 2009) and modification of invertebrate communities (Bridgeland et al., 2010). As conspicuous and familiar elements of nature, birds have particular benefits to human well-being (e.g. Collar et al., 2007; Fuller et al., 2007). In-depth investigation is needed of the services that birds provide humans, ranging well beyond the cultural.

These are challenging subjects with which ornithologists have hardly started to engage. One of the main difficulties is the vast divergence of scale on which resources are used by different species groups. Taking invertebrates as a focus, the spatial requirements and mobility of even relatively sedentary birds are frequently several orders of magnitude larger than most invertebrates. Birds may respond to landscape configuration in rather different ways to less mobile organisms. This probably underlies the findings of Gilbert-Norton et al. (2010) that so-called 'corridors' linking habitat fragments are used less by birds than by invertebrates, non-avian vertebrates and plants. Haddad and Tewksbury (2006) also found that corridor effects were most frequent in small taxa with short generation times. Birds rarely show the tight dependence on specific plants or vegetation microstructures exhibited by many invertebrates. Nonetheless, some bird species may have considerable value as indicators of specific clearly defined habitat conditions upon which large numbers of non-avian species depend. This was part of the rationale of the bittern Botaurus stellaris habitat restoration project in Britain (Gilbert and Smith, Chapter 10). Birds may also have particular value in understanding how species at the limits of ecological tolerance, in extreme environments, respond to environmental change (Thompson et al., Chapter 9; Naef-Daenzer, Chapter 16). It may be possible to identify suites of bird species occupying different niches that may reflect high levels of diversity across other animal groups.

The notion that certain higher taxa can be used as surrogates for other groups, perhaps ones that are less readily sampled, is appealing and potentially extremely useful (Prendergast and Eversham, 1997). Studies of relationships in community organisation amongst different species groups appear to be mainly, possibly only, ones of spatial variation in species richness. The evidence is that correlations between different taxa are weak, though generally positive and scale-dependent (Wolters *et al.*, 2006; Rodrigues and Brooks, 2007). New approaches are needed for assessing multi-taxa patterns of community composition and structure at different spatial scales and in the context of particular habitat types.

Strategies for an uncertain future

Cultural landscapes in western Europe have always been in a state of flux but the pace and extent of change increased hugely during the last century with large impacts on bird populations (Fuller and Ausden, 2008; Hinsley and Gillings, Chapter 6). Evidence is mounting that bird assemblages in Europe have become increasingly homogeneous and that this trend may be associated with changes in both habitat and climate (Devictor *et al.*, 2008; Davey *et al.*, 2012). The coming decades will see no abatement: the demands of food security, water management, urbanisation and energy generation will intensify. Forestry will probably expand and need to meet multiple functions. The changing climate will interact in uncertain ways with all these pressures on land and the full consequences for avian habitat quality are impossible to predict (Mustin *et al.*, 2007).

Habitat connectivity, extent and quality

Conservation strategies for habitat creation are hotly contested, but there is general agreement that restoration and increasing extent of semi-natural habitat in cultural landscapes is a high priority to buffer wildlife against the large changes ahead. In many parts of Europe ambitious plans exist, and in some cases are well advanced, for new areas and networks of semi-natural habitat to provide opportunities and space for nature (e.g. Boitani *et al.*, 2007). The most frequent design recommendation for landscape schemes aimed at climate change adaptation is that connectivity between habitat patches should be enhanced (Heller and Zavaleta, 2009). However, the importance of connectivity relative to other approaches is controversial (e.g. Doerr *et al.*, 2011; Hodgson *et al.*, 2009, 2011). The concern frequently expressed is that benefits derived from enhanced connectivity are difficult to measure, hard to distinguish from other components of landscape structure and that evidence of benefits is equivocal. More specifically, the debate pivots around whether it is a better investment of conservation resources to create larger areas of high-quality habitat than to enhance connectivity. There is also the possibility that under some circumstances 'new connecting habitats' could replace existing habitats of conservation value.

Dolman (Chapter 4) points out that whilst connectivity may enhance move-ment of some birds through terrestrial landscapes, there is little evidence of demographic benefits. He also argues that in the absence of a clear under-standing of the mechanisms that affect populations at landscape scales, it is not possible to define optimum strategies. This may be true, but the world cannot wait. Several of the chapters in this book offer messages pertinent to the planning of future reserves, habitat networks or nature restoration areas (Box 20.3). These points would seem to have relevance to wider nature. The value of connectivity should certainly not be dismissed, but its effectiveness may vary with taxa, scale and landscape context. There is, however, strong and more consistent evidence of the gains from maintaining and developing large areas of high-quality habitat that will support persistent populations that can act as population sources. This broadly aligns with the views of Hodgson *et al.* (2009, 2011). An influential review of priorities for improving English landscapes for nature (Lawton *et al.*, 2010) concludes that 're-building nature' needs a multi-faceted approach that increases the quality, size and connections between existing wildlife sites, coupled with new habitat crea-tion and improvements to the wider environment. Population persistence and maintenance of biodiversity cannot be achieved solely through a narrow focus on landscape connectivity (Taylor *et al.*, 2006). Habitat creation or restoration should not be regarded as the reversal of long processes of land-scape transformation – the starting points in biological communities and landscape contexts are totally different. Nonetheless, in the shift from near-natural to highly managed cultural landscapes, the evidence overwhelmingly points to habitat loss having had a far greater negative impact on biodiversity than fragmentation, which is the reduction of habitat into smaller parcels when controlling for habitat loss (Fahrig, 2003).

The above discussion addressed connectivity within terrestrial landscapes. Stopover sites for migrating birds represent another aspect of connectivity. These can provide essential, but often widely spaced, links between breeding and wintering areas. Habitat connectivity on an intercontinental or flyway scale is crucial for maintaining populations of many wetland birds. The ongoing massive losses of intertidal habitat used by refuelling shorebirds on the Chinese Yellow Sea coast have troubling implications (Piersma, Chapter 15).

Habitat heterogeneity and complementarity

Exactly what constitutes high-quality habitat is species-specific. Managing for habitat heterogeneity should, therefore, logically be an integral part of con-servation strategies (Box 20.3). This has been advocated as a pragmatic basis for conservation management in British forests where functional heterogeneity for birds can potentially be achieved through the adoption of different man-agement systems and tree species mixtures (Fuller *et al.*, Chapter 14; Hewson

---

Box 20.3 Considerations for conservation strategies in cultural landscapes

Habitat extent: Large areas of near-natural and semi-natural habitat are likely to support larger and more viable populations, provide source populations, have lower extinction rates, have higher habitat heterogeneity and be more buffered from external influences than small areas. There is strong evidence that habitat extent is a critical factor in many landscape-scale mechanisms affecting population persistence and community diversity (Dolman, Chapter 4). In wetlands, effective control of water regimes and provision of suitable conditions for species with diverse requirements is only feasible on large sites (Gilbert and Smith, Chapter 10).

Habitat heterogeneity: Species have different ecological requirements and some species require different habitat elements for providing complementary resources. This diversity of needs can only be met by managing for habitat heterogeneity at different scales. Strategies that maintain high alpha, beta and gamma diversity are required. The implication is that different types and levels of heterogeneity are desirable in different locations. It needs to be recognised that not all species benefit from high habitat heterogeneity and that complementarity of habitat types and structures is important. See Vickery and Arlettaz (Chapter 7), Grant and Pearce-Higgins (Chapter 8) and Fuller *et al.* (Chapter 14) for discussions of how heterogeneity affects bird communities in agricultural, upland and woodland environments, respectively.

Patch quality and management: All species require particular resources and will not colonise and persist if these are absent. In cultural landscapes, habitat management has a major role in determining both the provision of resources and habitat heterogeneity. Although much recent attention has been given to aspects of 'landscape design' (configuration and connectivity), the quality of the constituent habitat patches ultimately determines whether individual species can meet their needs.

Ecological transitions: Many species are probably well adapted to coping with different kinds of ecological transitions in ancient cultural landscapes (Fuller, Chapter 5). Edges and early successional vegetation contribute greatly to habitat heterogeneity. Complex shrubland structures, associated with varied successional stages, offer niches that are scarce in heavily managed landscapes and can provide opportunities for species to shift habitats in response to changing climate.

et al., 2011). Young-growth woodland, especially shrubland vegetation, should form an integral element of this spectrum of habitat conditions, given the number of species that are strongly associated with these early successional structures (Fuller, Chapter 5). Emphasising just the later successional stages will exclude a substantial portion of forest biodiversity. This seems especially important in ancient cultural landscapes where young-growth will have been a major element of landscapes over very long periods of time.

Exactly how species and assemblages will respond to climate change super-imposed on future land uses and landscape patterns is unknown. Maintaining high levels of habitat heterogeneity will increase the probability that species will be able to adapt through expanding or shifting their realised niches. There is already evidence of recent habitat shifts in butterflies (Davies *et al.*, 2006) and birds (Both, Chapter 17) and much evidence of past habitat shifts in birds (Wesołowski and Fuller, Chapter 4). Maintaining a diversity of comple-mentary structures across different types of successional gradients, and at different spatial scales, would provide some level of insurance that opportu-nities were available for species to shift their realised niches and for new assemblages to develop. The implication of complementarity is that different approaches to conservation policy and management would be needed in different places and possibly at different times (Vickery and Arlettaz, Chapter 7; Fuller *et al.*, Chapter 14).

In countries such as Britain, where substantial areas of land are under some form of conservation protection or management, it should be possible to achieve a measure of strategic planning for habitat heterogeneity. So far this has been most successful for wetlands and, whilst impressive management is taking place within protected areas, not surprisingly, the extension of these concepts to the landscape scale is far less advanced (Ausden and Fuller, 2009; Gilbert and Smith, Chapter 10; Ausden and Bolton, Chapter 11).

Integrating wetland and terrestrial systems is highly desirable (Lindenmayer *et al.*, 2008). Not only is there potential for enhancing habitat quality for some organisms through resource subsidies (Fuller, Chapter 2), but there may be considerable ecosystem service gains through better water management. Thinking about how best to deliver gradients in water regimes and in other ecological dimensions could form a useful framework for opti-mising habitat heterogeneity. Gradients can be difficult to accommodate in cultural landscapes, but there would be benefits in moving away from a binary patch-based approach wherever possible, both in research and con-servation approaches (Manning *et al.*, 2004; Fischer and Lindenmayer, 2006).

A fresh view?

Recently some fresh outlooks and concepts have emerged that are relevant to multi-scale conservation in future landscapes (Manning *et al.*, 2004, 2009;

Lindenmayer *et al.*, 2008). These approaches acknowledge the environmental gradients and complexity upon which biodiversity depends and that conservation strategies should ideally aim to maintain; they also acknowledge the value of natural change in ecosystems and landscapes. Some of these ideas may also fit well with improving delivery of ecosystem services, for example through water regulation, soil protection and carbon storage. However, the extent to which natural processes can form the foundation for conservation management in cultural landscapes is currently very limited, largely due to the severe competing pressures on land and the huge spatial scale required for these processes to follow natural trajectories. Naturalistic grazing and non-intervention systems may be possible under some circumstances (Ausden and Fuller, 2009; Hodder and Bullock, 2009) but multi-scale habitat heterogeneity is only likely to be achieved through interventions of varying intensity. There are, however, serious risks in operating within frameworks delimited by conservation targets and traditional ways of doing things (Hodgson *et al.*, 2009). This outlook will tend to reduce opportunities for adaptive management in response to environmental change.

Can a middle way be found that learns from wider experience of research and conservation practice in different types of landscapes? This view is well articulated by Martin *et al.* (Chapter 19). They suggest that in North America there would be some advantage in integrating European concepts of habitat heterogeneity into agricultural landscapes, whereas in Europe much could be learnt from the North American emphasis on natural habitat. 'Benign neglect' could well be a valuable addition to the European conservation philosophy.

Acknowledgements

I thank Helen Baker, Paul Dolman, Jenny Gill and Rob Robinson for comments on an early version of this chapter.

References

Ahlering, M. A. and Faaborg, J. (2006). Avian habitat management meets conspecific attraction: if you build it, will they come? *Auk*, **123**, 301–312.

Ausden, M. and Fuller, R. J. (2009). Birds and habitat change in Britain. Part 2: past and future conservation responses. *Brit. Birds*, **102**, 52–71.

Boitani, L., Falcucci, A., Maiorano, L. and Rondinini, C. (2007). Ecological networks as conceptual frameworks or operational tools in conservation. *Conserv. Biol.*, **21**, 1414–1422.

Bridgeland, W. T., Beier, P., Kolb, T. and Whitham, T. G. (2010). A conditional trophic cascade: birds benefit faster growing trees with strong links between predators and plants. *Ecology*, **91**, 73–84.

Collar, N. J., Long, A. J., Robles Gil, P. and Rojo, J. (2007). *Birds and People: Bonds in a Timeless Journey*. Mexico City: CEMEX-Agrupación Sierra Madre-BirdLife International.

Davey, C. M., Chamberlain, D. E., Newson, S. E., Noble, D. G. and Johnston, A. (2012). Rise of the generalists: evidence for climate driven homogenization in avian communities. *Global Ecol. Biogeogr.*, **21**, 568–578.

Davies, Z. G., Wilson, R. J., Coles, S. and Thomas, C. D. (2006). Changing habitat associations of a thermally constrained species, the silver-spotted skipper butterfly, in response to climate warming. *J. Anim. Ecol.*, **75**, 247–256.

Devictor, V., Clavel, J., Julliard, R. *et al.* (2010). Defining and measuring ecological specialization. *J. Appl. Ecol.*, **47**, 15–25.

Devictor, V., Julliard, R., Clavel, J. *et al.* (2008). Functional biotic homogenization of bird communities in disturbed landscapes. *Global Ecol. Biogeogr.*, **17**, 252–261.

Doerr, V. A. J., Barrett, T. and Doerr, E. D. (2011). Connectivity, dispersal behaviour and conservation under climate change: a response to Hodgson *et al. J. Appl. Ecol.*, **48**, 143–147.

Dolman, P., Mossman, H., Panter, C. *et al.* (2011). The importance of Breckland for biodiversity. *Brit. Wildlife*, **22**, 229–239.

Evans, K. L. (2010). Individual species and urbanisation. In *Urban Ecology*, ed. K. J. Gaston, pp. 53–87. Cambridge: Cambridge University Press.

Fahrig, L. (2003). Effects of habitat fragmentation on biodiversity. *Annu. Rev. Ecol. Syst.*, **34**, 487–515.

Fahrig, L., Baudry, J., Brotons, L. *et al.* (2011). Functional landscape heterogeneity and animal biodiversity in agricultural landscapes. *Ecol. Lett.*, **14**, 101–112.

Fischer, J. and Lindenmayer, D. B. (2006). Beyond fragmentation: the continuum model for fauna research and conservation in human-modified landscapes. *Oikos*, **112**, 473–480.

Fuller, R. A., Irvine, K. N., Devine-Wright, P., Warren, P. H. and Gaston, K. J. (2007). Psychological benefits of greenspace increase with biodiversity. *Biol. Lett.*, **3**, 390–394.

Fuller, R. J. and Ausden, M. (2008). Birds and habitat change in Britain. Part 1: a review of losses and gains in the twentieth century. *Brit. Birds*, **101**, 644–675.

Gilbert-Norton, L., Wilson, R., Stevens, J. R. and Beard, K. H. (2010). A meta-analytic review of corridor effectiveness. *Conserv. Biol.*, **24**, 660–668.

Haddad, N. M. and Tewksbury, J. J. (2006). Impacts of corridors on populations and communities. In *Connectivity Conservation*, ed. K. R. Crooks and M. Sanjayan, pp. 390–417. Cambridge: Cambridge University Press.

Heller, N. E. and Zavaleta, E. S. (2009). Biodiversity management in the face of climate change: a review of 22 years of recommendations. *Biol. Conserv.*, **142**, 14–32.

Herrera, C. M. (1984). A study of avian frugivores, bird-dispersed plants, and their interaction in Mediterranean scrublands. *Ecol. Monogr.*, **54**, 1–23.

Hewson, C. M., Austin, G. E., Gough, S. J. and Fuller, R. J. (2011). Species-specific responses of woodland birds to stand-level habitat characteristics: the dual importance of forest structure and floristics. *For. Ecol. Manage.*, **261**, 1224–1240.

Hodder, K. H. and Bullock, J. M. (2009). Really wild? Naturalistic grazing in modern landscapes. *Brit. Wildlife*, **20** (suppl.), 37–43.

Hodgson, J. A., Moilanen, A., Wintle, B. A. and Thomas, C. D. (2011). Habitat area, quality and connectivity: striking the balance for efficient conservation. *J. Appl. Ecol.*, **48**, 148–152.

Hodgson, J. A., Thomas, C. D., Wintle, B. A. and Moilanen, A. (2009). Climate change, connectivity and conservation decision making: back to basics. *J. Appl. Ecol.*, **46**, 964–969.

Lawton, J. H., Brotherton, P. N. M., Brown, V. K. *et al.* (2010). *Making Space for Nature: a Review of England's Wildlife Sites and Ecological Network*. Report to Defra.

Lindenmayer, D., Hobbs, R. J., Montague-Drake, R. *et al.* (2008). A checklist for ecological management of landscapes for conservation. *Ecol. Lett.*, **11**, 78–91.

Manning, A. D., Lindenmayer, D. B. and Nix, H. A. (2004). Continua and Umwelt: novel perspectives on viewing landscapes. *Oikos*, **104**, 621–628.

Manning, A. D., Fischer, J., Felton, A. et al. (2009). Landscape fluidity – a unifying perspective for understanding and adapting to global change. *J. Biogeogr.*, **36**, 193–199.

Mustin, K., Sutherland, W. J. and Gill, J. A. (2007). The complexity of predicting climate-induced ecological impacts. *Climate Res.*, **35**, 165–175.

Prendergast, J. R. and Eversham, B. C. (1997). Species richness covariance in higher taxa: empirical tests of the biodiversity indicator concept. *Ecography*, **20**, 210–216.

Rodrigues, A. S. L. and Brooks, T. M. (2007). Shortcuts for biodiversity conservation planning: the effectiveness of surrogates. *Annu. Rev. Ecol. Evol. Syst.*, **38**, 713–737.

Taylor, P. D., Fahrig, L. and With, K. A. (2006). Landscape connectivity: a return to the basics. In *Connectivity Conservation*, ed. K. R. Crooks and M. Sanjayan, pp. 29–43. Cambridge: Cambridge University Press.

Vera, F. W. M. (2009). Large-scale nature development – the Oostvaardersplassen. *Brit. Wildlife*, **20** (suppl.), 28–36.

Wolters, V., Bengtsson, J. and Zaitsev, A. S. (2006). Relationships among the species richness of different taxa. *Ecology*, **87**, 1886–1895.

Species index
(bird names only)

Subject index